GENDER AND WAR

GENDER AND WAR

International and Transitional Justice Perspectives

Edited by
Solange Mouthaan
Olga Jurasz

intersentia
Cambridge – Antwerp – Chicago

Intersentia Ltd
Sheraton House | Castle Park
Cambridge | CB3 0AX | United Kingdom
Tel.: +44 1223 370 170 | Fax: +44 1223 370 169
Email: mail@intersentia.co.uk
www.intersentia.com | www.intersentia.co.uk

Distribution for the UK and Ireland:
NBN International
Airport Business Centre, 10 Thornbury Road
Plymouth, PL6 7PP
United Kingdom
Tel.: +44 1752 202 301 | Fax: +44 1752 202 331
Email: orders@nbninternational.com

Distribution for Europe and all other countries:
Intersentia Publishing nv
Groenstraat 31
2640 Mortsel
Belgium
Tel.: +32 3 680 15 50 | Fax: +32 3 658 71 21
Email: mail@intersentia.be

Distribution for the USA and Canada:
Independent Publishers Group
Order Department
814 North Franklin Street
Chicago, IL 60610
USA
Tel.: +1 800 888 4741 (toll free) | Fax: +1 312 337 5985
Email: orders@ipgbook.com

Gender and War. International and Transitional Justice Perspectives

ISBN 978-1-78068-686-8
D/2019/7849/3
NUR 828

GPRC Guaranteed Peer Reviewed Content

British Library Cataloguing in Publication Data. A catalogue record for this book is available from the British Library.

CONTENTS

LIST OF CASES

EUROPEAN COURT OF HUMAN RIGHTS

EXTRAORDINARY CHAMBERS IN THE COURTS OF CAMBODIA

INTER-AMERICAN COURT OF HUMAN RIGHTS

INTERNATIONAL CRIMINAL COURT

INTERNATIONAL CRIMINAL TRIBUNAL FOR THE FORMER YUGOSLAVIA

INTERNATIONAL CRIMINAL TRIBUNAL FOR RWANDA

INTERNATIONAL MILITARY TRIBUNALS

PERMANENT COURT OF INTERNATIONAL JUSTICE

SPECIAL COURT FOR SIERRA LEONE

UN HUMAN RIGHTS COMMITTEE

BOSNIA AND HERZEGOVINA

SOUTH AFRICA

LIST OF ABBREVIATIONS

AFRC	Armed Forces Revolutionary Council
BIRN	Balkans Investigative Reporting Network
BiH	Bosnia and Herzegovina
CAAFAG	children associated with armed groups and armed forces
CDF	Civil Defence Forces
CRSV	conflict-related sexual violence
CEDAW	Convention on the Elimination of all forms of Discrimination Against Women
CRC	Convention on the Rights of the Child
DRC	Democratic Republic of Congo
DDR	disarmament, demobilisation and reintegration
EULEX	European Union's rule-of-law mission
ECHR	European Convention on Human Rights
ECtHR	European Court of Human Rights
ECCC	Extraordinary Chambers in the Courts of Cambodia
FYR	Former Yugoslav Republic
ICC	International Criminal Court
ICL	international criminal law
ICTR	International Criminal Tribunal for Rwanda
ICTY	International Criminal Tribunal for the Former Yugoslavia
IHRL	international human rights law
IHL	international humanitarian law
ILC	International Law Commission
KLA	Kosovo Liberation Army
MICT	Mechanism for International Criminal Tribunals
MRND	National Republican Movement for Democracy and Development
NGOs	non-governmental organisations
OHR	Office of the High Representative
OTP	Office of the Prosecutor
OSCE	Organization for Security and Co-operation in Europe
PCIJ	Permanent Court of International Justice
PTSD	post-traumatic stress disorder
PSVC	Prevent Sexual Violence in Conflict
RUF	Revolutionary United Front

SGBV or SGV	sexual and gender-based violence
SSA	Smallest Space Analysis
SFRY Code	Socialist Federal Republic of Yugoslavia Criminal Code
SCSL	Special Court for Sierra Leone
Special WC Department	Special Department for War Crimes
SPRK	Special Prosecution Office of the Republic of Kosovo
Syria	Syrian Arab Republic
TFV	Trust Fund for Victims
TRC	Truth and Reconciliation Commission
UNMIK	UN Interim Administration Mission in Kosovo
UN	United Nations
UNSC	United Nations Security Council
WCS-BiH	War Crimes Section within the State Court of Bosnia and Herzegovina
WPS	Women, Peace and Security

LIST OF CONTRIBUTORS

Alison Bisset
Associate Professor in International Human Rights Law at the University of Reading, UK. She researches in the field of transitional justice, with a particular focus on the work of truth commissions.

Louise Chappell
Director of the Australian Human Rights Institute; Professor in the Law Faculty at the University of New South Wales, Sydney, Australia. Her research focuses on gender justice and institutions, including the International Criminal Court.

Anne-Marie de Brouwer
Co-founder and team member of IMPACT: Center against Human Trafficking and Sexual Violence in Conflict; Chair of the Mukomeze Foundation; Research Fellow with the International Victimology Institute Tilburg (INTERVICT) at Tilburg University, The Netherlands.

Priya Gopalan
International Criminal Law, Human Rights and Gender Justice Practitioner; Former Prosecutor and Appeals Counsel at the Office of the Prosecutor of the UN International Tribunal for the Former Yugoslavia (ICTY). Former Legal Advisor, UN International Impartial and Independent Mechanism on Syria.

Rosemary Grey
Postdoctoral Fellow in the Sydney Law School and Sydney Southeast Asia Centre, University of Sydney, Australia. Her research focuses on the gender dimensions of international criminal law and international human rights law, with a particular focus on the International Criminal Court (ICC) and Extraordinary Chambers in the Courts of Cambodia (ECCC).

Olga Jurasz
Senior Lecturer in the Law School at the Open University, UK. She works in the fields of international law, human rights, gender-based violence as well as gender, and post-conflict reconstruction.

Sheri A. Labenski
Teaching Fellow in the School of Law at the University of Warwick, UK. Her research interests include female perpetrators, international criminal law, and feminist approaches to international law.

Chanté Lasco
Jurisprudence Collections Coordinator, Gender and International Criminal Law Project, American University Washington College of Law, USA; Project Coordinator of the 'Strengthening Victims' Access to Justice in Bosnia and Herzegovina' Project.

Solange Mouthaan
Associate Professor at the University of Warwick, UK. Her research interests focus on the gendered experiences of children affected by armed conflict and the restrictive interpretation of international criminal law in this area.

Valerie Oosterveld
Associate Professor at the University of Western Ontario, Canada. She researches and publishes in the field of gender-sensitive international criminal justice.

Laetitia Ruiz
Phd Researcher at the International Victimology Institute Tilburg (INTERVICT), The Netherlands. She is currently working in a secondary school in Bogota, Colombia, while she finishes her PhD.

Alette Smeulers
Professor of Criminal Law and Criminology of International Crimes at the University of Groningen, The Netherlands. In her research she takes an interdisciplinary approach and focuses on the international crimes of genocide, crimes against humanity and war crimes, as well as terrorism, the causes of these crimes, the perpetrators thereof and international criminal justice.

Susana SáCouto
Professorial Lecturer-in-Residence and Director, War Crimes Research Office, American University Washington College of Law, United States of America.

Olivera Simić
Senior Lecturer at the Law School of Griffith University, Australia. She works in the fields of international law, transitional justice and gender-based violence.

Lauren Vogel
Independent Research Consultant and Data Analyst, formerly Postdoctoral Research Fellow on the Prosecution Project at Griffith University, Australia. Her research interests include women and political violence, legal history, and research methods and analysis.

Valorie K. Vojdik
Waller Lansden Distinguished Professor of Law at the University of Tennessee College of Law, USA. Her research focuses on gender, feminist theory, and masculinities theory. Her work includes research on violence against women and men within social institutions including the military, and as conceptualised in US constitutional and international law

INTRODUCTION

Olga JURASZ and Solange MOUTHAAN

Gender is an important factor shaping the reality and lived experiences of men and women in armed conflicts. 'New wars' in which violence is directed predominantly towards civilians, have a significant gender dimension.[1] In particular, the use of sexual violence in modern armed conflicts evidences the strategic nature of gendered violence which is commonly deployed to achieve not only political control but also to terrorise or expel members of the opposing group – be it ethnic, religious or national. Furthermore, as the experience of the past three decades of new wars demonstrates, gender retains its significance in the aftermath of conflict, during the time of transition from 'conflict' to 'peace'. Although it is increasingly difficult to draw a defining line between phases of modern conflict, it can be observed that transitional justice processes are highly gendered and often lead to exacerbation of gender-based violence and a return to unequal gender relations existing prior to the conflict. Frequently, the 'post-war' political reality and the new legal order do not prioritise the need to address the structural discrimination and inequalities nor the gendered consequences of conflict. This often leads to the creation of a 'post-war' economy where continued violence and gendered abuse are common features, for example in cases of human trafficking from 'post-conflict' states. Despite the pervasiveness of gendered violence in new wars and in transitional contexts, international law has been crucial in bringing about meaningful change. This book aims to analyse the progress made in relation to addressing gendered impacts of new wars through the lens of the international criminal justice system and transitional justice processes. While these two perspectives represent merely a particular section of the international legal regime, they are representative of the major changes that have taken place in these fields in recent years.

1 The term 'new wars' has been coined by Mary Kaldor and is used to describe a new type of organised violence which developed especially in Africa and Eastern Europe in the late 20th century and where the main violence is directed against civilians rather than battles between opposing military forces (as in 'old wars'). M. KALDOR, *Old and New Wars*, Polity Press 2012.

Traditionally, international law has given little recognition to the gendered effects of war and focused largely on prohibiting conflict-related sexual violence (CRSV) through international humanitarian law treaties in the aftermath of World War II. Despite this, international law's narrative of experiences of that conflict documented through trial judgments of the International Military Tribunal at Nuremberg and the International Military Tribunal for the Far East does not reflect the gendered nature of violence nor its mass scale and the impact it had on the victims. Accordingly, the accountability and redress for rapes, forced prostitution, forced sterilisations and other forms of gender-based abuse has not been a feature of what one could refer to today as 'transitional justice' in the aftermath of World War II.

However, 50 years after the Nuremberg and Tokyo judgments, international law's silence concerning gender-based violence in conflict was challenged by ground-breaking decisions of the International Criminal Tribunal for the Former Yugoslavia (ICTY) (*Furundžija, Kunarac*) and the International Criminal Tribunal for Rwanda (ICTR) (*Akayesu*), which saw the first ever prosecutions of rape and other forms of CRSV as war crimes, crimes against humanity and genocide. This historical shift in international law was further strengthened by the adoption of the Rome Statute of the International Criminal Court (ICC), which contains the most comprehensive provisions concerning gender-based crimes to date.

By criminalising and prosecuting CRSV, international law acknowledges the seriousness of such crimes and the effects on survivors of such crimes. Additionally, important initiatives have emerged, such as the publication of the Best Practices Manual on the Prosecution of Sexual Violence crimes by the International Criminal Tribunal of Rwanda (2014) and the UK government-led initiative to Prevent Sexual Violence in Conflict. Prosecutions of CRSV also opened new areas which could be developed and explored from a gender perspective, such as victim participation and the issue of reparations. However, although there are many reasons to be pessimistic about the progress towards achieving gender justice, that important steps in the direction of understanding some of the gendered dimensions of armed conflict and its consequences are being made. Critically, it is crucial not to become complacent and to persist in questioning the appropriateness of the gender legacies of international law that continue to influence responses. Equally, it is also important to understand CRSV *vis-à-vis* women in the broadest possible sense even if that process may unveil uncomfortable truths.

CRSV has received much scholarly attention continuing to question assumptions and probe novel ways in which to provide meaningful outcomes and responses for its victims. Anne-Marie de Brouwer has effectively explored the adequacy of prosecution of sexual violence by international criminal tribunals while highlighting that further steps need to be taken in order to take into account the realities and seriousness of the crimes, as well as the needs of and respect for the victims.[2] Louise Chappell similarly argues that despite articulating principles of gender justice, the ICC has a poor record in prosecuting sexual violence due to continuing legacies and silences in international criminal law.[3]

However, other voices also narrating experiences of CRSV have emerged: men, boys and girls. Importantly, contemporary understandings of armed conflict show us that women's roles in armed conflict go beyond that of passive actors, such as perpetrators of crimes, including CRSV. These different voices and narratives have been the overarching theme of this edited collection.

But this brings with it the issue of whether the law and the international criminal justice system, as well as transitional justice processes, have the capacity and adequate tools to deal with this appropriately. Furthermore, questions remain about the political will of states, as well as other international actors, to challenge assumptions about CRSV, effectively prosecute its perpetrators, and provide adequate and timely remedies to the victims.

The project to put together an edited collection exploring the varied gendered experiences of armed conflict has been in the back of our minds for a while. We are extremely pleased to have brought it to fruition. Along the way, we have met some exceptional people driven by a similar desire: to understand, explore and improve the gendered experiences of armed conflict.

We first met in 2012 at a conference which Olga Jurasz organised with Ryszard Piotrowicz and Anel Marais at Aberystwyth University entitled 'Women in War and at War'. The title of the conference was intriguing, as it purposefully opened the door for a variety of narratives around the experiences of armed conflict by women. The conference gathered together a selection of individuals with a common interest in understanding the positions and experiences of women in armed conflict. It was an eye-opener because of the varied and thought-provoking research around women and armed conflict presented. It also alerted us to the nascent UK government-led initiative to Prevent Sexual Violence in Conflict. Olga Jurasz explained her rationale for organising the conference: to create a welcoming place for discussion of gender and conflict and to be surrounded by kin rather than to be perceived as 'the other'. The conference has now become an established biennial occurrence and has since been hosted by the University of Warwick (2014) and the Open University (2016). Most importantly, it has allowed for the creation of a vibrant (and still growing) network of over 200 academics, lawyers and members of civil society who share interest in multidisciplinary explorations of the relationship between gender and conflict.

---

2 A-M.L.M. de Brouwer, *Supranational Criminal Prosecution of Sexual Violence – The ICC and the Practice of the ICTY and ICTR*, Intersentia 2005; A-M.L.M. de Brouwer et al., *Sexual Violence as an International Crime: Interdisciplinary Approaches*, Intersentia 2013.

3 L. Chappell, *The Politics of Gender Justice at the International Criminal Court: Legacies and Legitimacy*, OUP 2016.

The conference unlocked several doors to dependable spaces to discuss our research as feminist scholars or as scholars who deal with some of the lesser discussed experiences of war. Our networks grew not in the least thanks to Troy Lavers and Loveday Hodson who organise the *Feminism and International Law Interest Group* of the European Society of International Law and who lead the *Feminist International Judgments Project*. Dawn Sedman's kind invitation to join a roundtable at Oxford Brookes University exploring CRSV with Zainab Hawa Bangura (the Special Representative of Secretary-General on Sexual Violence in Conflict) led to the creation of a Research Network on Sexual Violence in Armed Conflict. This in turn enabled us to present our research at roundtables, such as the Oxfam Roundtable on Gender, Conflict and Masculinities (2013) in Kenya and at the Annual Conference of the American Society of International Law Conference in 2014.

A number of scholars whose research contributed to discussions at these events centred around the gendered experiences of armed conflict while frequently highlighting various different modes of participation or experiences of modern conflicts beyond those limited to women. These debates continuously reaffirmed the need to analyse gender and modern conflicts from a variety of perspectives and multidisciplinary angles. It became our objective to reflect that variety of views in the edited collection which includes contributors from different backgrounds: academics in law, criminology, international relations, politics and psychology, as well as legal practitioners.

This book centres on international and transitional justice response to some of the gendered experiences of armed conflict. It purports to broaden understandings of armed conflict and CRSV, as well as to interrogate the approaches to remedying harms arising from CRSV in post-conflict situations. Contemporary experiences of armed conflicts challenge the traditional understandings of how the wars are waged and their power dynamics, as well as experiences of victims. They further confirm that both victims and perpetrators are multi-dimensional and highlight the difficulty of addressing these complex narratives in conflict prevention, conflict and post-conflict scenarios. We conclude that so much still needs to be achieved and that too often gender stereotypes blur justice responses. In order to reflect these complexities and the contemporary debates about gendered experiences of armed conflicts, as well as the shortcomings of the avenues deployed thus far by the justice processes to deal with these broader narratives, the edited collection is divided into four parts: gendered experiences of armed conflict (Part 1), women's involvement in armed conflict (Part 2), gender in international criminal justice (Part 3), and transitional justice mechanisms (Part 4).

Part 1 centres on women's involvement in armed conflict. Although most perpetrators are men, women are also perpetrators of international crimes, including crimes involving sexual violence. However, international criminal law has developed narratives dominated by sexual violence against women and the brutality of violence perpetrated by men. First, Lauren Vogel disproves prevailing assumptions that women's active participation in contemporary or revolutionary motivated conflict is minor, one-dimensional and defined and circumscribed to that of victim and peacemaker. Instead, her empirical and quantitative research using population level trends establishes that women's involvement is varied and can be arranged into four categories: active, caring, ideological and support. Lauren Vogel's theoretical framework emphasises the importance of context, and the necessity to look beyond the personal to understand women's involvement in armed conflict, which should include their potential for violence and support for extremism. Only then will women's involvement be properly addressed and acknowledged in post-conflict responses, thus opening up a broader variety of spaces for women's participation in post-conflict political peace and security processes. The chapter sets the tone for the following chapters in questioning the overly simplistic assumption that a victim and a perpetrator cannot coexist within the same person. The two chapters that follow focus on women who commit international crimes and are subsequently prosecuted. Sheri Labenski discusses two examples of women perpetrators of international crimes who have been tried by the ad hoc international criminal tribunals: Biljana Plavšić (ICTY) and Pauline Nyiramasuhuko (ICTR). Far from dismissing the importance of existing sexual violence jurisprudence, Sheri argues that examining female perpetrators not only helps to identify gaps in international criminal law or feminist scholarship but also nuances women's involvement in conflict as well as in the commission of international crimes. She argues that international criminal courts should question assumptions and ask the appropriate questions which disrupt gender binaries and stereotypes. Thus, rather than reproducing the same gendered outcomes as the conflict, courts have the opportunity to contribute to developing a more accurate understanding of armed conflicts. Alette Smeulers and Olivera Simič provide a potent discussion of the role of women in the Bosnian and Herzegovina war. They analyse the roles of a selection of women accused of committing war crimes before the Bosnian State Court and what might have driven them to carry out such acts: viciousness, revenge, mistaken identity. They demonstrate that ordinary women in extraordinary circumstances can be just as cruel as men. What may explain the imbalance between women and men committing war crimes is the underrepresentation of women in militarised units and in positions of leadership.

Part 2 investigates some of the gendered experiences of armed conflict from the perspective of male victims of CRSV and children, in order to add to the rich literature on women's experiences of armed conflict. It invites a multi-dimensional understanding of each of the possible actors. Valorie Vojdik focuses on CRSV against men. Thus far, international law's responses have ignored sexual violence against men and boys and consequently international criminal prosecutions lack a theoretical framework when confronted with such crimes. As a result, international prosecutions are wide-ranging in the extent and manner in which these crimes are addressed. Through the lens of masculinities theory, she explores the gendered nature, purpose and harms suffered by men who are victims of CRSV and suggests this as a way forward. A recognition that there is an inter-relationship between CRSV against women and against men is a necessary step towards fighting impunity. Similarly, Solange Mouthaan continuing the focus on children, warns against an overly simplistic narrative that ignores the gendered experiences of children in armed conflict. There is a risk that girls will find themselves at the margins of legal protections if the dominant narratives focus on either boys or women. In a sense, the common thread of the chapters in Part 1 and 2 is to invite law and policy makers not to assume, flout or oversimplify.

Part 3 focuses on the prosecution of gender-based crimes by international tribunals and questions whether these have been able to effectively embrace the diverse gendered experiences of armed conflict into their judgments. Valerie Oosterveld examines the case law of the Special Court for Sierra Leone to analyse the gendered impacts of various forms of enslavement, revealing the gendered consequences on the war economy in Sierra Leone. Lessons learnt, in particular a more nuanced contextualisation of such crimes which addresses the gender of the affected civilians and resulting gender violence experienced, should provide a more complete understanding of the armed conflicts. Anne-Marie de Brouwer and Laetitia Ruiz return to two marginalised categories at the peripheries of conflict narratives, namely men and boys who have suffered, and women and girls who have committed, CRSV. They provide a useful analysis of the way international criminal tribunals such as the ICTY, the ICTR, the Extraordinary Chambers in the Courts of Cambodia, the Special Courts for Sierra Leone and the ICC have engaged with such crimes. The authors highlight that these are often understood unhelpfully through the limited lens of binary gendered stereotypes. They argue that traditional understandings of masculinity and femininity wrongly influence the legal characterisation and sentencing of crimes committed, thus resulting in injustice. Instead, each instance should be merited on the facts of the case. Louise Chappell and Rosemary Grey, through quantitative and qualitative analysis, map the track record of the ICC in prosecuting gender-based crimes. Despite hard-won gender justice provisions included in the Rome Statute and a commitment by the Office of the Prosecutor to integrating gender perspective into all stages of ICC's work, progress towards achieving gender justice is still incomplete. They argue that one of the main difficulties for the ICC has been to challenge existing gender-biased norms of international criminal law. Continuing the theme of gender justice at the ICC, Olga Jurasz explores the concept of gender-sensitive and transformative reparations at the ICC. She questions the meaningfulness and long-term viability of the ICC reparations regime, not in the least because of its practical as well as conceptual shortcomings in delivering gender-inclusive reparations. In assessing the early practice of the ICC in awarding reparations, she argues that (a) ICC reparations must be understood as complimentary to the efforts of states, which bear the primary responsibility for redressing gendered harms, and (b) the design and award of reparations must address the gendered nature of the harms and structural inequalities. Part 3 demonstrates that gender is now firmly embedded international criminal law institutions and procedures, yet further progress is needed, in particular recognising a more nuanced approach to the gendered consequences of armed conflict.

The final Part looks at transitional justice processes and whether these address the gendered experiences more appropriately. First, Alison Bisset returns to the issue of children affected by armed conflict and explores their lack of involvement in transitional justice processes. The chapter usefully places children at the centre of each of the key mechanisms of transitional justice, as they are most affected by the outcomes. Yet, despite the UN Committee on the Rights of the Child 2009 recommendation, they remain underrepresented in transitional justice schemes due to general political indifference to children's issues and being conceived as a homogenous group with identical needs. She points out that due to such misperceptions children are not perceived as gendered in transitional justice responses. Priya Gopalan supplements Olga's chapter by examining gender justice and transformative reparations in post-conflict Kosovo as a tool to directly impact victims of CRSV. A transformative reparation regime must correct the underlying structural inequalities which shape the lives of women and girls in Kosovo Albanian Society. She recommends a cohesive transitional justice strategy that delivers both judicial and non-judicial remedies including transformative, gender-sensitive reparations. She argues that such a reparation regime does not necessarily have to be to the detriment of the needs of individual victims as long as the reparations programme offers an array of remedies and is context-specific. Finally, Susanna SáCouto and Chanté Lasco offer an account of prosecutions for CRSV in Bosnia and Herzegovina before the special war crimes section of the State Court of Bosnia and Herzegovina. They investigate evidentiary, legal and political difficulties and challenges faced by the justice system actors in the prosecution of CRSV which has resulted in a substantial backlog. They argue for continued support and engagement by the international community of accountability efforts. The authors hope that lessons learnt from the Bosnian experience will inform future national justice mechanisms in other post-conflict contexts. Particularly useful here is the set of recommendations made by the authors.

In the concluding chapter of this volume, we share our thoughts on the future opportunities and avenues for international and transitional justice processes to evolve in order to better facilitate diverse and gendered experiences of modern conflicts. We hope that perspectives presented in this book will provide food for thought to a wide and multidisciplinary community of students, scholars, practitioners and activists whose continuing work and commitment to furthering gender justice makes a difference, however small or large, to survivors of conflict-related gendered harms.

PART I

WOMEN'S INVOLVEMENT IN ARMED CONFLICT

HOW AND WHY WOMEN PARTICIPATE IN ARMED CONFLICT

A Population-Level Quantitative Model

Lauren VOGEL

1. INTRODUCTION

Women have participated in conflict and violence throughout history and across multiple contexts. However, prevailing concepts of conflict generally depict women as victims and men as aggressors. Hence, women's active participation has typically been perceived as minor, with highly visible instances (e.g. female suicide bombers) viewed as abnormal and isolated deviations from the norm. There remains a lack of understanding regarding exactly how women participate beyond these one-dimensional depictions of victim and peacemaker, despite a recent increase in scholarly and policy interest in women's involvement in political and revolutionary conflict.[1] Furthermore, female involvement is typically attributed to personal and emotional factors with little consideration given to the possible influence of broader structural factors. As such, the research described in this chapter was undertaken with the aim to develop

[1] K. JACQUES AND P.J. TAYLOR, 'Female Terrorism: A Review' (2009) 21 *Terrorism and Political Violence* 499.

a theoretical framework based on population-level trends in how women participate in contemporary politically or revolutionarily motivated conflict and what contextual factors influence variation in their involvement.

The conceptual rationale for such a framework lies in the recognition that there is currently no overarching theory of either women's or men's involvement in extremist conflict.[2] There is a lack of large-scale empirical research exploring women's involvement,[3] meaning that how and why women participate in conflict at the population level – rather than at the individual or case level – is not well understood or conceptualised. As such, extrapolations regarding women in conflict take place in the absence of a comprehensive theoretical foundation built on verifiable research findings, potentially leading to context-specific conceptualisations, gendered explanations for female involvement, and isolated and fragmented research. Given the general absence of population-level research there is a need to build a theoretical model from the ground up that incorporates both past research and original empirical findings from large-scale research.

Building on the logic of this rationale, this chapter outlines the theoretical framework in the following three sections. First, previous research that systematically established exactly how a large representative sample of women were involved in conflict will be outlined in section 2, including the primary roles that women were found to hold. The primary focus of this chapter, however, will be on the section 3, describing current research that builds upon and incorporates this previous research by quantitatively examining the contextual factors that impacted upon women's varied involvement. The focus will be on describing the macro and meso variables that were found to consistently influence variation in women's roles in conflict. The research outlined in this chapter contributed to building the theoretical framework (summarised in section 4), capturing not only the methods of female involvement but also the factors that predict their involvement in differing capacities and contexts.

2. CRITICAL BACKGROUND ISSUES

2.1. GROWING GLOBAL RECOGNITION OF EMERGING TRENDS IN CONTEMPORARY CONFLICT

By the turn of the millennium, the number of countries involved in conflict was greater than at any other time during the previous five decades.[4] In the first

2 P.W. Eager, *From Freedom Fighters to Terrorists: Women and Political Violence*, Ashgate Publishing Ltd 2008, p. 23.

3 Jacques and Taylor, above n. 1.

4 C.O.N. Moser, 'The Gendered Continuum of Violence and Conflict: An Operational Framework' in C.O.N. Moser and F.C. Clark (eds.), *Victims, Perpetrators or Actors: Gender, Armed Conflict and Political Violence*, Zed Books 2001, p. 32.

15 years of the millennium such global conflict has only appeared to increase. ISIS in Syria, the mass refugee emergency, and the Ukraine crisis – to name a few topical examples – attest to this contemporary global disorder. Women are increasingly salient on both ends of the peace and security spectrum; three women were awarded the Nobel Peace Prize in 2011 while simultaneously women have become increasingly visible as suicide bombers in Eastern Europe, the Middle East and South Asia. Indeed, contemporary estimates of the prevalence of female involvement in political and revolutionary conflict are high and suggest that women's involvement will only continue to increase.[5] Such estimates suggest that women comprise anywhere between 10 to 30 per cent of all armed groups worldwide,[6] and between 30 to 40 per cent of combatants in ethno-separatist struggles.[7] Women are also increasingly prominent in martyrdom operations – a phenomenon at the forefront of modern conflict. In the Russia/Chechnya conflict, for instance, 43 per cent of suicide bombers were female, with women additionally involved in some manner in the execution of 81 per cent of all martyrdom operations in the region.[8] Zedalis reports that between 1985 and 2008 there were 600 killed and 800 wounded by 49 female suicide bombers,[9] while Bloom reports that up to 2007 there had been 220 female suicide bombers.[10]

These figures clearly indicate that women's involvement in modern conflict is significant; yet they only represent visible women and violent roles. There are a range of activities that are necessary for conflict to continue and for operations to be successfully executed, including such activities as smuggling/couriering weapons and ammunition, community support tasks and intelligence gathering. Women often perform activities such as these in conflict,[11] although they are

---

5 K.J. Cunningham, 'Countering Female Terrorism' (2007) 30 *Studies in Conflict & Terrorism* 113; D. Zedalis, 'Beyond the Bombings: Analysing Female Suicide Bombers' in C.D. Ness (ed.), *Female Terrorism and Militancy: Agency, Utility and Organisation*, Routledge 2008, p. 51; L. Sjoberg, 'Conclusion: The Study of Women, Gender, and Terrorism' in L. Sjoberg and C. Gentry (eds.), *Women, Gender, and Terrorism*, The University of Georgia Press 2011, p. 228.

6 T. Bouta, G. Frerks and I. Bannon, *Gender, Conflict and Development*, The World Bank 2005, p. 9.

7 C.D. Ness, 'The Rise in Female Violence' [2007] *Daedalus* 84, 85.

8 A. Speckhard and K. Akhmedova, 'Black Widows: The Chechen Female Suicide Terrorists' in Y. Schweitzer (ed.), *Female Suicide Bombers: Dying for Equality*, Jaffe Center for Strategic Studies, Tel Aviv University 2006, p. 63.

9 Zedalis, above n. 5, p. 49.

10 M. Bloom, 'Female Suicide Bombers: A Global Trend' [2007] *Daedalus* 94, 2.

11 F. Ni Aoláin, D.F. Haynes and N. Cahn, *On the Frontlines: Gender, War and the Post-Conflict Process*, Oxford University Press 2011, p. 6; R. Kim Cragin and S.A. Daly, *Women as Terrorists: Mothers, Recruiters, and Martyrs*, ABC-CLIO 2009; K. von Knop, 'The Multi-Faceted Roles of Women Inside al-Qaeda' (2008) 6 *Journal of National Defense Studies* 139.

usually not considered soldiering activities when performed by a woman.[12] Indeed the fact that women 'only' perform support tasks has been used as a basis to exclude them from disarmament, demobilisation and reintegration (DDR) programs, despite the inclusion of men who have acted in these positions.[13] Aoláin, Haynes and Cahn note that women 'often create the social and economic networks that support and enable violence to continue'.[14] In recognition of some of these issues the World Bank published a report in which it was recommended that the definition of combatant be expanded to include support activities,[15] although it is unclear exactly what these support activities would entail.

Despite this growing recognition in specific research and policy niches, women's involvement in conflict – beyond victim and peacemaker – is rarely acknowledged in either mainstream research or policy. The picture of women as the disproportionate victims of male-instigated violence – raped, widowed and displaced – is both familiar and enduring.[16] Indeed, the majority of official resolutions and declarations related to the incorporation of women into peace and security processes are rooted in this very premise; that women are the primary victims of conflict and the occasionally effective but unofficial peacemakers.[17] Unfortunately, including women in political peace and security processes because they are victims or inherent peacemakers limits their contribution to that of a stereotypical and often token presence.[18] Seldom is the argument made that women should be included in political peace and security processes because they are active participants in war and conflict. In contrast to male militants who are included in conflict resolutions, peace negotiations and DDR programs because they are believed to have 'fought' for their place.[19] Problematically, this means that women's voices are consistently overlooked and women who have participated in the conflict are often denied access to skills

---

12 M. MacKenzie, 'Securitization and Desecuritization: Female Soldiers and the Reconstruction of Women in Post-Conflict Sierra Leone' (2009) 18 *Security Studies* 241; S. McKay, 'Girls as "Weapons of Terror" in Northern Uganda and Sierra Leonean Rebel Fighting Forces' in C.D. Ness (ed.), *Female Terrorism and Militancy: Agency, Utility, and Organisation*, Routledge 2008.

13 MacKenzie, above n 12.

14 Aoláin, Haynes and Cahn, above n. 11, p. 6.

15 Bouta, Frerks and Bannon, above n. 6, p. 22.

16 M. Utas, 'West-African Warscapes: Victimcy, Girlfriending, Soldiering: Tactic Agency in a Young Woman's Social Navigation of the Liberian War Zone' (2005) 78 *Anthropological Quarterly* 403, 404.

17 H. Charlesworth, 'Are Women Peaceful? Reflections on the Role of Women in Peace-Building' (2008) 16 *Feminist Legal Studies* 347.

18 ibid.; D. Pankhurst, 'The "Sex War" and Other Wars: Toward a Feminist Approach to Peace Building' (2003) 13 *Development in Practice* 154; K. Lockett, 'The Mechanisms of Exclusion: Women in Conflict' (2008) 16 *Feminist Legal Studies*; J. West, 'Feminist IR and the Case of the "Black Widows": Reproducing Gendered Divisions' (2004–2005) 5 *Innovations: A Journal of Politics* 1.

19 S. Parashar, 'Gender, Jihad, and Jingoism: Women as Perpetrators, Planners, and Patrons of Militancy in Kashmir' (2011) 34 *Studies in Conflict & Terrorism* 295.

training, education, rehabilitation and monetary resources,[20] and can remain active supporters of continued violence.[21] The continued involvement of women in support and community networks can make sustainable peace difficult to achieve.

2.2. CONSIDERATIONS IN DEVELOPING A FRAMEWORK

The development of any theoretical framework faces considerable challenges. Different analytical and theoretical conceptualisations exist both across and within disciplines.[22] Research on women in conflict tends to take place in isolation, with the majority of research carried out by feminist or specialised scholars. Feminist scholarship tends to focus on the experiences of individual women and has been critical of the empiricist paradigm.[23] In contrast, the empiricist paradigm tends to aim for larger sample sizes and many observations in order to draw inferences about trends in the population of interest.[24] Both approaches, however, are useful when examining women's participation; feminist scholarship for drawing attention to women and the complexities of their experiences, and the empiricist standpoint for advocating a focus on population trends in developing generalisable theoretical conceptualisations. Indeed, Sjoberg acknowledges that mixed methods approaches are frequently required in order to answer research questions related to women within the field of international relations and security studies.[25] Such an approach is relatively common in psychology, for instance, where it is important to understand population trends in mental health, such as the prevalence, incidence, indicators of disorder and course, and risk and resilience factors. However, in-depth exploration of individuals' mental health gives an empathic insight, lending context and highlighting the complexity of experience. Thus, the present research attempts to incorporate the empirical findings, theoretical propositions, and analytical approaches from feminist scholarship on women in conflict and what might be considered more conventional political violence and terrorism scholarship.

However, the research presented in this chapter is unapologetically empirical and quantitative, focused on developing a theoretically sound but operationally useful framework for understanding female involvement in political and revolutionary conflict that is at once holistic and adequately nuanced. Any

---

20 McKay, above n. 12, p. 177.

21 S. Dharmapuri, 'Just Add Women and Stir' (2011) 41 *Parameters* 56, 62.

22 Moser, above n. 4, p. 33.

23 S. Reinharz, *Feminist Methods in Social Research*, Oxford University Press 1992.

24 'Empiricism' in W.A. Darity (Jr.) (ed.), *International Encyclopedia of the Social Sciences*, vol. 2, 2nd edn, Macmillan Reference USA 2008.

25 L. Sjoberg, 'Feminist Interrogations of Terrorism/Terrorism Studies' (2009) 23 *International Relations* 69.

theoretical framework should be broad enough to account for population trends but flexible enough to also account for individual case-by-case complexity. Such a framework should be parsimonious, operationally useful, theoretically sound, based on verifiable empirical research, and validated through appropriate testing. Developing the framework consisted of: first, testing how women's involvement could be conceptualised accurately; and, second, examining what (if any) factors influenced variation in this involvement. The general research process involved systematically documenting the individual participation characteristics of a representative sample of women involved in conflict, statistically developing a model that accurately represented these activities in the form of conceptual roles, and finally examining how this model varied according to contextual factors (i.e. systematically building the framework from the ground up and testing the components at each stage).

While any theoretical framework should be broad and representative in nature, it must also have constraints. This research began with an interest in terrorism where this evolved into a broader conceptualisation of terrorism as a strategy utilised by individuals, groups or movements rather than an end in and of itself.[26] However, this research was not focused on specific acts of violence (of which terrorism is a form) but on the activities that are required to maintain a proscribed movement/organisation that may utilise terrorism as a strategy. Thus, the sample is comprised of women who were non-state actors involved in a movement or group committed to generally proscribed violence in the furtherance of political or revolutionary objectives.[27] The temporal scope was 1960 to the present, selected as it encompasses the third (1960s–1980s) and fourth waves (1979–present) of modern terrorism,[28] and allowed the quantitative examination of two distinct historical periods in modern conflict.

2.3. WOMEN'S ROLES IN POLITICAL AND REVOLUTIONARY CONFLICT

Can women's involvement in conflict be categorised according to a set of defined roles? Indeed, is their participation substantial enough to warrant such a categorisation? As noted, traditionally women are understood to be victims of conflict or, more recently, effective but usually unofficial peacemakers.[29]

---

26 D.C. Rapoport, *The Four Waves of Rebel Terror and September 11*, Anthropoetics 2002; L. Weinberg, A. Pedahzur and S. Hirsch-Hoefler, 'The Challenges of Conceptualising Terrorism' (2004) 16 *Terrorism and Political Violence* 777.

27 L. Sjoberg and C. Gentry, *Mothers, Monsters and Whores: Women's Violence in Global Politics*, Zed Books 2007, p. 11.

28 D.C. Rapoport, 'The Four Waves of Modern Terrorism' in A.K. Cronin and J.M. Ludes (eds.), *Attacking Terrorism: Elements of a Grand Strategy*, Georgetown University Press 2004.

29 Charlesworth, above n. 17.

Women's involvement that contravenes these traditional understandings (e.g. female combatants or suicide bombers) is generally treated with fascination and as abnormal in both research and policy. Such women are, on the whole, studied and understood in an individualised manner with a focus on high visibility women perpetrating high impact attacks.[30] As such, there is a relatively large amount of scholarly information available in the form of case studies of how specific women have participated in political and revolutionary conflict, but little information regarding how women participate *en masse* beyond these specific instances. Women's *en masse* involvement is consistently portrayed in research and policy as relatively minor, occurring on a small scale, and primarily taking the form of unimportant auxiliary support activities.[31]

Unfortunately, research that examines exactly how women participate in political and revolutionary conflict is rare. Of all publications related to female terrorism since 1983, just 11 per cent had women's roles as the primary focus.[32] The lack of original population-level research regarding how women participate in conflict can perpetuate stereotypes regarding women in conflict, over-inflate the perceived prevalence of certain types of participation, and obscure the many women who participate in political and revolutionary conflict and the myriad ways in which they do so. Aoláin, Haynes and Cahn argue that 'the quantification of and rationale for women's political violence is grossly under-researched' and that 'a nuanced focus on women as benefactors or perpetrators of systematic violence ultimately helps us better address the cause of violence and prevent its recurrence'.[33] The lack of large-scale empirical research means that we are unable to examine or establish population-level trends in female involvement across contexts. Thus, it is impossible to determine with reliability the means, extent and prevalence of women's involvement in political and revolutionary conflict. Not only does this limit our scholarly understanding of women's involvement, but also it also consistently undermines the credibility – or even plausibility – of women's involvement in conflict beyond being a victim or occasional peacemaker.

While the majority of research in the area has focused on specific cases of female involvement in conflict or on specific activities performed by women (usually suicide bombing), in practice women perform a variety of activities. Che Guevara, in his infamous handbook on guerrilla warfare, addressed the role of women in guerrilla conflict specifically, claiming that 'the part that the woman

30 K. Stanski, 'Terrorism, Gender, and Ideology: A Case Study of Women who Join the Revolutionary Armed Forces of Colombia (FARC)' in J.J.F. Forest (ed.), *The Making of a Terrorist: Recruitment, Training, and Root Causes*, Praeger Security International 2006, p. 136.

31 K.J. Cunningham, 'Cross-Regional Trends in Female Terrorism' (2003) 26 *Studies in Conflict & Terrorism* 171; MacKenzie, above n. 12.

32 Jacques and Taylor, above n. 1, p. 503.

33 Aoláin, Haynes and Cahn, above n. 11, p. 42.

can play in the development of a revolutionary process is of extraordinary importance'.[34] He subsequently listed a spectrum of activities that women could perform, including fighting, passing messages, traditional domestic tasks, teaching revolutionary theory in schools and within the guerrilla group, providing medical aid, and participating in war industry manufacture. Similarly, the data available on the women and girls who have gone through DDR programs or who have accessed conflict-related services provided by the United Nations or non-governmental organisations indicates that women around the world are involved in conflict in a number of ways, from fighting to leadership to practical and emotional support of combatants.[35]

However, while several speculative models of female roles in conflict had previously been proposed,[36] no research had systematically documented the range of activities reportedly performed by women in political and revolutionary conflict. Thus, previous empirical research conducted by Vogel, Kebbell and Porter quantitatively examined how a sample of 482 women were involved in contemporary political and revolutionary conflict from 1960 to the present.[37] This was the first study to examine the specific activities performed by a large sample of women representative of a range of regional, temporal and organisational contexts, as well as types of involvement. This study found that women performed, with varying degrees of frequency, 41 distinct activities in political and revolutionary conflict (see Table 1 where all 41 activities are included). Not only did this study clearly demonstrate that women are involved a wide variety of ways in conflict, but it also proposed – based on the statistical co-occurrence of these activities in the sample – that these 41 activities coalesced in such a way as to indicate the existence of four conceptual roles. As can be seen in Figure 1, Smallest Space Analysis (SSA)[38] indicated the existence of an

---

34 C. Guevara, *Guerilla Warfare: A Method (the authorised translation)* (J.P. Morray tr., University of Nebraska Press 1961/1985, p. 132.

35 O. Bennett, J. Bexley and K. Warnock (eds.), *Arms to Fight, Arms to Protect: Women Speak Out About Conflict*, Panos 1995; Bouta, Frerks and Bannon, above n. 6; Y.E. Keairns, *The Voices of Girl Child Soldiers: Sri Lanka*, Qaker United Nations Office 2003; Y.E. Keairns, *The Voices of Girl Child Soldiers: Colombia*, Quaker United Nations Office 2003; Y.E. Keairns, *The Voices of Girl Child Soldiers: Philippines*, Quaker United Nations Office 2003; D. Mazurana and K. Carlson, *From Combat to Community: Women and Girls of Sierra Leone*, Women Waging Peace, Hunt Alternatives Fund 2004; S. McKay and D. Mazurana, *Where are the Girls? Girls in Fighting Forces in Northern Uganda, Sierra Leone, and Mozambique: Their Lives During and After War*, Rights and Democracy 2004; I. Specht, *Red Shoes: Experiences of Girl-Combatants in Liberia*, International Labour Office 2006.

36 Cragin and Daly, above n. 11; S. Mahan and P.L. Griset, *Terrorism in Perspective*, Sage Publications 2008.

37 L.K. Vogel, L. Porter and M.R. Kebbell, 'The Roles of Women in Contemporary Political and Revolutionary Conflict: A Thematic Model' (2013) 37 *Studies in Conflict & Terrorism* 91.

38 R. Guttman and C.W. Greenbaum, 'Facet Theory: Its Development and Current Status' (1998) 3 *European Psychologist* 13; S. Shye, D. Elizur and M. Hoffman, *Introduction to Facet Theory: Content Design and Intrinsic Data Analysis in Behavioral Research*, Sage Publications 1994.

underlying behavioural structure, proposed to consist of the four conceptual roles labelled caring, support, ideological and active. Each of these conceptual roles represents a specific set of activities that were found to most commonly co-occur in the sample (the closer together two activities are in Figure 1, the more likely they are to co-occur in the sample or, in other words, two activities that are close to each other are significantly more likely to be performed by the same woman in the sample).

Figure 1. Two-dimensional SSA of women's participation in contemporary political and revolutionary conflict in 482 cases of involvement

Notes: Coefficient of alienation = .19 in 40 iterations. Note that whilst the positioning of the variables is based on statistical associations (where distance equates to strength of association), the partitioning of the plot is a conceptual proposition.

Table 1 replicates the information in Figure 1 but includes the relative frequency of each activity within each conceptual role, as well as some expanded definitions of certain activities. The active role represents activities that commonly constitute combatant status in conflict, including fighting, various violent acts and leadership positions. It also included some activities that are conventionally considered non-combatant (particularly for women[39]) such as administration, provision of resources, logistical responsibilities and recruiting resources. The results from this study suggest, however, that these conventionally non-combatant activities occur in the context of active violent participation. The ideological role consists of activities related to ideological production and propagation to a wider audience, including recruitment, actively encouraging others to join, fundraising and production of propaganda. It also included suicide bombing, indicating that suicide operations for women most commonly occurred in the context of other ideological activities performed for the group/movement. The caring role is indicative of those activities most conventionally considered feminine in nature, thus representing the reproduction of the private sphere in an extremist organisation. Finally, the support role represents activities related to the operational capacity of the group, including gathering intelligence, smuggling resources and performing skilled work such as bomb construction.

The model specifically refutes dominant one-dimensional scripts of female victimhood and/or peacemaking in conflict scenarios, as well as the notion that women's involvement in support networks in contemporary conflict is minor or on a small scale. Only one role in this model is related to fighting or leadership activities; the remaining three roles related to wider practical and ideological support for conflict, violence and extremist thought. Thus, it can be seen how women are vital to the maintenance of extremism and extremist networks[40] through ideological production, practical support, community liaison and political activities. This model clearly demonstrates exactly how women actively contribute to the long-term survival of the extremist group/movement and conflict itself.

Importantly, in terms of the criteria discussed at the beginning of the chapter regarding any theoretical framework, this empirically based model of roles is parsimonious while allowing for the complexity of women's experiences in conflict situations. The model is comprised of the various activities systematically documented in original sources without extrapolating about methods of recruitment or motivation for performing the activity or role. This is important when considering that women in conflict are often portrayed as one-dimensional, for example as either a victim or a combatant. In reality, the lines demarcating victim from perpetrator in conflict are often blurred.[41] Abduction or experiences of violence can be catalysts for initial mobilisation and, even while perpetrating

---

39 MacKenzie, above n. 12.

40 Aoláin, Haynes and Cahn, above n. 11; 6; Cragin and Daly, above n. 11; K. von Knop, 'The Female Jihad: Al Qaeda's Women' (2007) 30 *Studies in Conflict & Terrorism* 397; von Knop, above n. 11.

41 A. Berko and E. Erez, 'Martyrs or Murderers? Victims or Victimisers? The Voices of Would-Be Palestinian Female Suicide Bombers' in C.D. Ness (ed.), *Female Terrorism and Militancy: Agency, Utility, and Organisation*, Routledge 2008; McKay, above n. 12.

or supporting violence, a woman may experience continued brutality within an extremist group that both entrenches violent behaviour and/or extremist beliefs, as well as further isolates her from society.[42] The model allows for such complexity as it includes a range of activities commonly considered indicative of being a combatant (e.g. fighting, kidnapping) or a victim (e.g. sex partner, marriage by family members to another group member for strategic purposes) and clearly illustrates that such activities frequently co-occur (e.g. sex partner commonly co-occurred with practical activities undertaken in guerrilla camps).

Table 1. The activities within each conceptual role and their relative frequencies

Caring Role	**%**	**Support Role**	**%**
Sex partner – forced or consensual	44.7	Courier	32.3
Perform household chores	42.9	Intelligence gatherer	29.2
Nursing duties	19.7	Smuggler	21.9
Lookout	17.1	Decoy	16.7
Married by family to another participant for strategic/tactical purposes	7.9	Perform skilled work (e.g. bomb construction, mechanic)	10.4
Camp manager	7.9	Lure	8.3
		Spy	6.3
Active Role	**%**	**Ideological Role**	**%**
Fighter	34.9	Suicide bomber	23.8
Marriage/partnership with another member of own accord	22.5	Propaganda – distribution or production	23.2
Responsible for planting/detonating IEDs	18.2	Political/government official	17.8
Participate in murder	16.3	Hostage	15.1
Provide resources	15.6	Encourage radicalisation of male relatives	13.5
Overall leader	13.7	Facilitate recruitment of others (non-family)	9.2
Warrior (battalion/cell) leader	13.4	Indoctrinate children	8.1
Recruit resources forcefully (e.g. robbery)	9.1	Messenger	6.5
Participate in kidnapping	8.8	Trainer	6.5
Responsible for operational logistics	8.1	Fundraiser	5.4
Recruit resources legitimately (e.g. purchase)	5.9	Hijacker	2.7
Strategic leadership	5.9		

(continued)

42 M. Denov and R. Maclure, 'Turnings and Epiphanies: Militarisation, Life Histories, and the Making and Unmaking of Two Child Soldiers in Sierra Leone' (2007) 10 *Journal of Youth Studies* 243; Utas, above n. 16.

Table 1 *continued*

Active Role	%	Ideological Role	%
Participate or organise jailbreak	4.9		
Ideological leader/inspiration	4.6		
Founder of group/movement	4.2		
Motivational leader/speaker for group/ movement	3.9		
Administrative support	3.6		

3. CONTEXTUAL FACTORS THAT INFLUENCE WOMEN'S ROLES IN CONFLICT

> Women who lack the characteristics and traits that society considers appropriate – gentleness, passivity, non-violent personalities, seductiveness, physically attractive faces and figures – may seek success in some non-feminine realm, by displaying aggression, unadorned faces and bodies, toughness, or other masculine qualities.[43]
>
> These women are victims of the conflict, victims of their attackers, and victims of the situation in which they find themselves. We cannot help but sympathise with women in this situation.[44]

These statements were made almost 30 years apart and yet these quotes illustrate the lack of theoretical progression in understanding the range of factors that influence female involvement in political and revolutionary conflict.[45] As noted, female belligerents are usually studied in an individualised manner with a focus on high visibility, high impact women and operations.[46] As these women are viewed as abnormal, research has almost exclusively focused on finding explanations for their behaviour; resulting in a plethora of gendered explanations for female involvement.[47] This is not a critique of the case study approach, which is a valid methodology to employ. It is a critique of a commonly analytical approach in the area, that generalises from a case study to the normative population with little evidential base for doing so, for example portraying all female involvement in political violence as stemming from a small set of individual factors garnered

43 D.E. Georges-Abeyie, 'Women as Terrorists' in L.Z. Freedman and Y. Alexander (eds.), *Perspectives on Terrorism*, Scholarly Resources 1983, p. 62.

44 M. Bloom, *Bombshell: Women and Terrorism*, University of Pennsylvania Press 2011, p. 237.

45 Jacques and Taylor, above n. 1.

46 C. Brunner, 'Occidentalism Meets the Female Suicide Bomber: A Critical Reflection on Recent Terrorism Debates: A Review Essay' (2007) 32 *Signs* 957, 958; Stanski, above n. 30, p. 136.

47 Sjoberg and Gentry, above n. 27.

from a selective sample of politically violent women.[48] Relying solely on speculative case studies to generate theory limits our understanding of women in conflict as the influence of broader structural influences is usually difficult to garner from individuals.[49]

Bloom's model of influences on female suicide bombers – based on a series of selective case studies – exemplifies the limitations of focusing solely on personal factors in conceptualising women's involvement in conflict.[50] This model proposes that all women commit violent attacks due to the 'four R's plus one': revenge for the death of a family member; redemption for past sins; because they have been influenced or coerced as a result of a relationship with a man; to gain respect from their communities'; or because they have been raped. This set of factors – proposed as a general theory of female terrorism across contexts and conflicts – contains no mention of genuine political or ideological belief, little systematic consideration of structural factors beyond the individual that may influence their involvement, and no method of participation aside from violent operational activity. Problematically, a gendered approach such as this implicitly denies female participants in conflict the ability to act with agency,[51] displaces responsibility for their actions onto their communities and/or the men in their lives, and refutes their credibility as a terrorist or combatant by denying any political, ideological or religious motivations.[52]

Focusing solely on personal factors in understanding women's involvement neglects the range of factors that play a role in conflict and violence, including the community, socio-political, national and historical context.[53] Scholars in the more traditional terrorism and political violence arena are beginning to utilise a range of a range of factors to understand (male) involvement,[54] recognising that context is vital in understanding the involvement of individuals in conflict.[55] On the individual level, such an approach aligns with notions of relational autonomy,

---

48 See also L. O'Rourke, 'What's Special About Female Suicide Terrorism?' (2009) 18 *Security Studies* 681, p. 701.

49 J.S. Viterna, 'Pulled, Pushed, and Persuaded: Explaining Women's Mobilisation into the Salvadoran Guerrilla Army' (2006) 112 *American Journal of Sociology* 1, 2.

50 Bloom, above n. 44.

51 Sjoberg and Gentry, above n. 27; West, above n. 18.

52 Vogel, Porter and Kebbell, above n. 37, p. 93.

53 Moser, above n. 4, p. 39.

54 M. Crenshaw, 'The Psychology of Terrorism: An Agenda for the 21st Century' (2000) 21 *Political Psychology* 405; D. della Porta, 'On Individual Motivations in Underground Political Organisation' in J. Horgan and K. Braddock (eds.), *Terrorism Studies: A Reader*, Routledge 2012; A.W. Kruglanski and S. Fishman, 'Psychological Factors in Terrorism and Counterterrorism: Individual, Group, and Organisational Levels of Analysis' (2009) 3 *Social Issues and Policy Review* 1; G. LaFree and G. Ackerman, 'The Empirical Study of Terrorism: Social and Legal Research' (2009) 5 *The Annual Review of Law and Social Science* 347; J. Victoroff, 'The Mind of the Terrorist: A Review and Critique of Psychological Approaches' (2005) 49 *Journal of Conflict Resolution* 3.

55 Crenshaw, above n. 54, p. 418; Viterna, above n. 49.

where choices 'are not independent of the gendered social and political contexts of ... local and global worlds'[56] and tactic agency, where agency 'is something you maintain in relation to a social field inhabited with other actors ... dependent on specific social situations'.[57] Individuals experience varying levels of freedom and constraint within their environments and, thus, can follow very different pathways to mobilisation and, once involved, can perform a number of activities aside from those that are purely soldiering or operational. In this sense, searching for one explanatory factor limits scholarly understanding of the revolutionary process as a whole.[58] In particular, emphasising solely the personal factors that influence women's involvement obscures the reality of their participation, including population-level trends in the activities that women perform across multiple conflicts, their broader theoretical roles in conflict, and how specific mobilisation factors as well as broader contextual factors may influence how and why they are involved.

As such, a theoretical framework incorporating multiple levels of analysis – depicted in Figure 2 – more accurately reflects the reality of involvement in conflict.[59] The basic proposition inherent within this approach is that involvement in political and revolutionary conflict cannot be understood by reference to a single factor (or level of analysis), but rather that involvement (and specifically the activities and roles undertaken) is influenced by, and varies according to, a variety of macro, meso and micro level factors. It does not discount the influence of personal factors or circumstances on involvement, but situates the individual within their context and its inherent complexities and inter-relationships. Particular aspects of this approach have been utilised in previous research in the area of gender in conflict,[60] and also in the mainstream area of terrorism and political violence research.[61] In this approach, the macro level includes structural and historical characteristics, the meso level includes organisational/network and community characteristics, and the micro level includes individual causes and interpersonal relationships. This approach recognises that conflict itself, as well as individuals' decision-making within conflict, is complex, context-specific and multi-layered, and that factors at each level play mutually reinforcing roles.[62] Thus, it facilitates an understanding of involvement in conflict both on a case-by-case basis and according to population-level trends across contexts.

---

56 Sjoberg and Gentry, above n. 27.

57 Utas, above n. 16, p. 407.

58 Viterna, above n. 49, p. 2.

59 E.D. Mason, 'Women's Participation in Central American Revolutions: A Theoretical Perspective' (1992) 25 *Comparative Political Studies* 63; LaFree and Ackerman, above n. 54.

60 K.M. Blee, 'Women and Organised Racial Terrorism in the United States' in C.D. Ness (ed.), *Female Terrorism and Militancy: Agency, Utility, and Organisation*, vol. 28, Routledge 2008; Cunningham, above n. 31; Eager, above n. 2; Mason, above n. 59; Moser, above n. 4.

61 Kruglanski and Fishman, above n. 54; LaFree and Ackerman, above n. 54.

62 Moser, above n. 4, p. 39.

Figure 2. Conceptual framework for understanding influential factors on women's involvement in political and revolutionary conflict, incorporating multiple levels of analysis

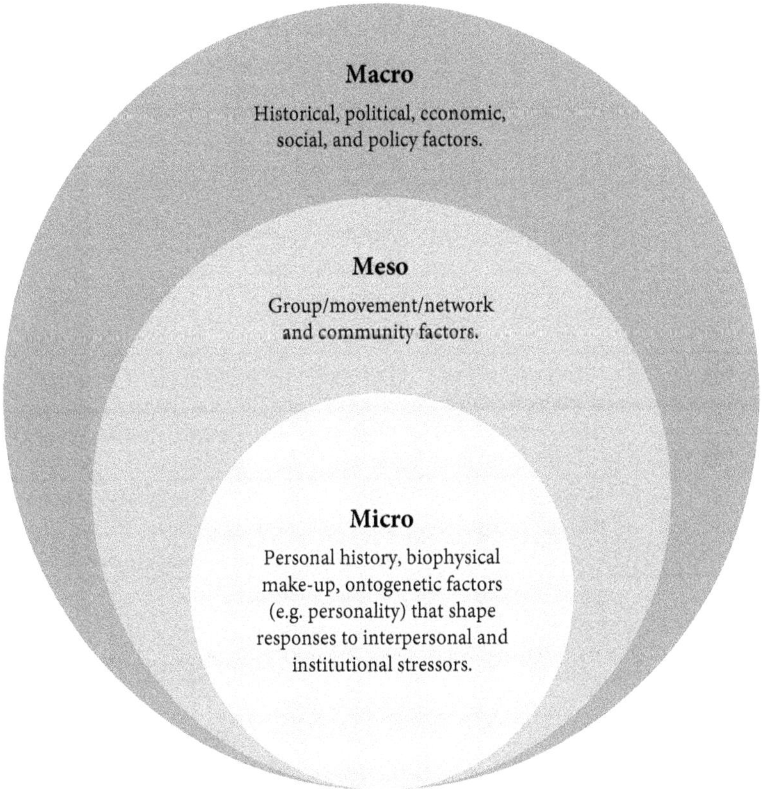

Quantifying women's extremist activities according to the four conceptual roles of active, caring, ideological, and support allows a systematic comparison of the influence of specific macro and meso factors on female involvement in conflict. Such an analysis allows us to test if, and how, contextual factors beyond the personal influence female involvement in conflict. Thus, building upon the research of Vogel, Kebbell and Porter[63] and utilising the same sample, variation in the four roles according to two macro and three meso factors were quantitatively examined (see Table 2). This chapter focuses only on the macro and meso level as neglected foci in research on women in political and revolutionary conflict. Other unpublished but forthcoming research has collected original data regarding micro level influences on female involvement in conflict.

63 VOGEL, PORTER AND KEBBELL, above n. 37.

Table 2. Macro and meso variables included in the study

Level of analysis	Variable	Categories
Macro level	Wave of terrorism[64]	New Left third wave: conflict occurring between the 1960s and 1980s
		Religious fourth wave: conflict occurring from 1979 to the present
	World region[65]	Europe
		Middle East
		South Asia
		Northern America
		Latin America
		Eastern Europe
		Africa
Meso level	Ideological basis of group/movement[66]	Left-wing: liberal, radical and/or reforming ideology
		Right-wing: conservative and/or reactionary ideology
	Religious orientation of group/movement[67]	Religious: some form of religious commitment to a particular religious agenda
		Secular: no religious commitment or platform
	Agenda of group/ movement	Nationalist/separatist
		Communist/socialist
		Nationalist/separatist & communist/socialist
		Islamist
		Islamist and nationalist/separatist
		Christian/racist
		Non-specific revolutionary

Notes: Mann-Whitney U tests or Kruskal Wallis tests were employed in order to examine group differences across the four roles. In each set of analyses one of the variables in Table 2 was the independent variable and the four roles of active, caring, ideological and support were the dependent variables. Each analysis tested whether the four roles varied significantly according to the categories included within each of the macro and meso variables. Where there were more than two categories in an independent variable (i.e. world region, group agenda) follow up pairwise comparisons were conducted using a Bonferroni adjustment for multiple comparisons. In these instances a more conservative overall alpha level was also employed in recognition of the presence of heterogeneity of variance.[68]

64 Rapoport, above n. 26.

65 Cunningham, above n. 31.

66 ibid; Jacques and Taylor, above n. 1.

67 C.D. Ness, 'In the Name of the Cause: Women's Work in Secular and Religious Terrorism' in C.D. Ness, *Female Terrorism and Militancy: Agency, Utility, and Organisation*, Routledge 2005.

68 B.G. Tabachnick and L.S. Fidell, *Using Multivariate Statistics* 5th ed., Pearson Education 2007, p. 86.

3.1. INFLUENTIAL MACRO FACTORS ON WOMEN'S INVOLVEMENT IN CONFLICT

The macro level is related to the broad historical, political, economic, social and policy factors that influence female involvement in contemporary political and revolutionary conflict. The factors examined in this research were 'wave of terrorism' and 'world region'. Wave of terrorism encompasses a historical or temporal element to female involvement, based on the notion of terrorism evolving in specific and identifiable waves across modern history.[69] The two waves relevant to this research, as noted in Table 2, were the third wave (1960s–1980s) and fourth wave (1979–present). Rapoport[70] suggests that women participated to a greater extent in terrorism in wave three, while other scholars[71] suggest that women's involvement is increasing in contemporary times (wave four) and predict that it will continue to increase into the future. The findings from the present study indicate that it is not necessarily a question of prevalence but of method of involvement. It was found that women participated to a greater extent in the active role[72] in wave three, and in the ideological[73] and caring[74] roles in wave four (the support role did not vary significantly across the waves of terrorism[75]). As women participated to a greater extent in combat and leadership positions in wave three they were more visible; however, in wave four women are participating to a greater extent in the more subversive or hidden caring and ideological roles. This trend means that women are not necessarily participating less in contemporary political and revolutionary conflict, but are doing so in less visible capacities, consistent with the arguments put forth by other scholars.[76]

World region – the second macro factor examined – encompasses the cultural, social, political and economic contexts found in different parts of the world. The seminal comparative regional research of Cunningham[77] demonstrated the importance of considering this broader context in female involvement in

---

69 Rapoport, above n. 26; Rapoport, above n. 28; K. Rasler and W.R. Thompson, 'Looking for Waves of Terrorism' (2009) 21 *Terrorism and Political Violence* 28; L. Weinberg and W. Eubank, 'An End to the Fourth Wave of Terrorism?' (2010) 33 *Studies in Conflict & Terrorism* 594.

70 Rapoport, above n. 28.

71 Cunningham, above n. 31; Sjoberg, above n. 5; Zedalis, above n. 5.

72 $U = 19{,}717.50$, $z = -6.14$, $p < .001$.

73 $U = 35{,}115.50$, $z = 4.63$, $p < .001$.

74 $U = 32{,}158.50$, $z = 3.23$, $p = .001$.

75 $U = 28{,}358.50$, $z = -1.32$, $p = .525$.

76 Cunningham, above n. 31; von Knop, 'The Female Jihad: Al Qaeda's Women', above n. 40; von Knop, 'The Multi-Faceted Roles of Women Inside al-Qaeda', above n. 11.

77 Cunningham, above n. 31.

political and revolutionary conflict. Similarly, other research has demonstrated that specific aspects of a country's context may be important in female involvement. Dalton and Asal,[78] for example, found that a high level of economic development and lower level of women's social rights predicted the deployment of women in a violent operational capacity. Qualitative work has also examined the potential influence of particular regional factors on women's involvement in conflict, including historical female involvement in revolutions in Europe, South Asia and Latin America;[79] the long-term divisive effects of colonisation policies on contemporary conflicts in South Asia and Africa;[80] the pervasive effect of militarised societies in Africa;[81] and the impact of dependent development displacement and poverty on female mobilisation in guerrilla groups in Latin America.[82] Although the present study did not include this level of detail (i.e. it did not examine specific factors within regions), it did demonstrate consistent patterns in female involvement according to world region (see Figure 3).[83]

Fairly similar patterns in female involvement were found across Europe, Latin and Northern America, and Africa, as seen in Figure 3 – although it should be noted that female involvement in the caring role was more prominent in Africa and (to a degree) Latin America, while female involvement in the active role was more prominent in Europe, Latin America and Northern America. Cunningham noted some similarities, observationally, between Northern American and Europe, particularly with regards to the liberal social and cultural context.[84] Both regions experienced similar manifestations of extremism as it evolved from 1960 to the present (i.e. an outbreak of New Left extremism in the 1960s with high profile examples of women in the active role and similar experiences with regards to religion extremism from the 1980s, including high impact attacks and a decrease in the visibility of female involvement in extremism). A high prevalence of women in the active role in Europe and Northern America

---

78 A. Dalton and V. Asal, 'Is it Ideology or Desperation: Why do Organizations Deploy Women in Violent Terrorist Attacks?' (2011) 34 *Studies in Conflict & Terrorism* 802.

79 M. Alison, *Women and Political Violence: Female Combatants in Ethno-National Conflict*, Routledge 2009; L.M. Lobao, 'Women in Revolutionary Movements: Changing Patterns of Latin American Guerrilla Struggle' (1990) 15 *Dialectical Anthropology* 211.

80 E.M. Alison, '"In the War Front We Never Think That We are Women": Women, Gender, and the Liberation Tigers of Tamil Eelam' in L. Sjoberg and C. Gentry (eds.), *Women, Gender, and Terrorism*, University of Georgia Press 2011.

81 M. Turshen, 'Women's War Stories' in M. Turshen and C. Twagiramariya (eds.), *What Women do in Wartime: Gender and Conflict in Africa*, Zed Books Ltd 1998; D. Volman, 'The Militarisation of Africa' in M. Turshen and C. Twagiramariya (eds.), *What Women do in Wartime: Gender and Conflict in Africa*, Zed Books Ltd 1998.

82 Mason, above n. 59.

83 Caring role, $\chi^2(6, N = 482) = 99.55, p < .001$; ideological role, $\chi^2(6, N = 482) = 113.12, p < .001$; active role, $\chi^2(6, N = 482) = 95.34, p < .001$; support role, $\chi^2(6, N = 482) = 26.77, p < .001$.

84 Cunningham, above n. 31, p. 176.

Figure 3. Variation on the four female roles in conflict according to world region

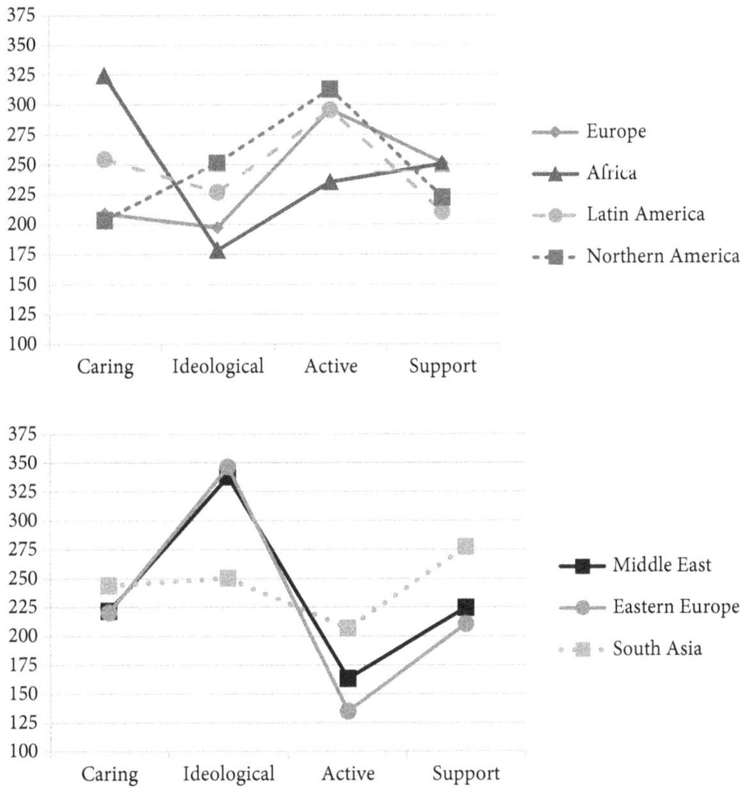

Notes: Findings depicted according to similarity in patterns of female involvement. The numbers represent mean ranks, as employed by the Kruskal Wallis test – higher numbers represent greater involvement.

also concurs with Dalton and Asal,[85] who found that a high level of economic development predicted women's involvement in violent operations, in relation to the active role.

Similarly, women in Latin America were highly involved in the active role in conflict. Weinberg and Eubank[86] found that Europe and Latin America were two of the three regional centres of third wave terrorism, which may have resulted in similarities in female involvement. Cunningham also noted the presence of generalised poverty and a 'youth bulge' in Latin America[87] – where younger people are more likely to be involved in militancy.[88] Similarly,

85 Dalton and Asal, above n. 78, p. 810.
86 Weinberg and Eubank, above n. 69, p. 596.
87 Cunningham, above n. 31, p. 179.
88 LaFree and Ackerman, above n. 54.

Mason examined the unique effect of poverty on female mobilisation to guerrilla groups in Central America; proposing that dependent development led to family abandonment by male breadwinners and, consequentially, an increase in female-headed households and urban migration.[89] These women, as part of the new urban poor, became increasingly politicised as they protested their socio-economic plight. As such, they attracted increasingly brutal government reprisals, which in turn encouraged them to join guerrilla organisations that offered solidarity and valued their activist skills.[90]

In contrast to both Europe and Northern America, however, women in Latin America were often involved in the caring role (although not as frequently as women in Africa). This may reflect the different cultural and social contexts between Northern America/Europe and Latin America. In contrast to the relatively liberal culture of Northern America and Europe, a patriarchal culture of 'machismo' – where women are assigned a subservient role in looking after the home and family – still prevails in Latin America.[91] Thus, while women often participate in the active role in Latin American conflict – possibly due to limited social rights, poverty and a prevalence of young people – women may still be bound by traditional gender norms in a way that may not apply to Western countries.

Africa – a region that perhaps more than any other features the divisive effects of colonisation and militarisation – exhibited the highest prevalence of women in the caring role. Bearing in mind that that the caring role encompassed sexual relationships, camp maintenance, nursing and household-type chores, such a finding is consistent with the literature that has noted the high frequency of forced recruitment of women to African guerrilla groups and their subsequent sexual servitude and participation in other camp-related activities.[92] Women in Africa were involved in the active role, but not to the extent that Latin American, Northern American and European women were.

The Middle East and Eastern Europe exhibited almost identical patterns in female involvement in conflict. South Asia exhibited comparable trends in female involvement; however, to an extent that was less extreme. In both the Middle East and Eastern Europe, women were involved significantly more often in the ideological role and the least often in the active role. Other scholarship has observed the relatively hidden nature of women's involvement in these

---

89 Mason, above n. 59.

90 ibid.

91 Cunningham, above n. 31, p. 179.

92 M.E. Baaz and M. Stern, 'Making Sense of Violence: Voices of Soldiers in the Congo (DRC)' (2008) 46 *Journal of Modern African Studies* 57; McKay and Mazurana, above n. 35; Specht, above n. 35.

regions, attributed to Islamist ideology and its strict gender role demarcations.[93] Despite the presence of secular nationalist/separatist movements in these regions, it appears that women's involvement is still dictated by the cultural and religious context of their countries.[94] This finding confirms, however, that women do participate in a range of ways in these regions, as the ideological role included a variety of activities, such as propaganda, recruitment and political participation.

Compared to other world regions, women in South Asia were found most often in the support role, where this role included activities such as spying, intelligence gathering, couriering, smuggling and deflecting attention during operations, consistent with the work of Parashar.[95] Similar to the Middle East and Eastern Europe, women were also found fairly often in the ideological role; perhaps reflecting the frequency with which women in this region participate in suicide attacks, and the infusion of some conflicts in this region with Islamist ideology.[96] However, this finding may also reflect the involvement of women in other types of ideologically based activities. Some research has found that women in this region are vital to the commission of the ideological activities that sustain extremist movements and provide legitimacy for their existence.[97]

3.2. INFLUENTIAL MESO FACTORS ON WOMEN'S INVOLVEMENT IN CONFLICT

The meso level encompasses factors related to organisations, systems, networks and institutions. In this research it was operationalised as factors related to the extremist group or movement, including the religious and ideological orientation and specific agenda or aims, as outlined in Table 2. As might be expected, groups/movements that were either left-wing or secular in nature exhibited a higher prevalence of women in the active role compared to right-wing

93 K.J. Cunningham, 'The Evolving Participation of Women in Palestine, Chechnya, and the Global jihadi Movement' in C.D. Ness (ed.), *Female Terrorism and Militancy: Agency, Utility, and Organisation*, Routledge 2008; F. Qazi, 'The Mujahidaat: Tracing the Early Female Warriors of Islam' in L. Sjoberg and C. Gentry (eds.), *Women, Gender, and Terrorism*, University of Georgia Press 2011; von Knop, 'The Female Jihad: Al Qaeda's Women', above n. 40; von Knop, 'The Multi-Faceted Roles of Women Inside al-Qaeda', above n. 11.

94 Cunningham, ibid.

95 S. Parashar, 'Aatish-e-Chinar: In Kashmir, Where Women Keep Resistance Alive' in L. Sjoberg and C. Gentry (eds.), *Women, Gender, and Terrorism*, University of Georgia Press 2011.

96 Parashar, ibid.

97 Alison, above n. 79; Eager, above n. 2; C.C. Fair, *Urban Battle Fields of South Asia: Lessons Learned from Sri Lanka, India, and Pakistan*, RAND 2004; Parashar, above n. 19; Parashar, above n. 95.

or religious movements.[98] In contrast, right-wing and religious groups/movements exhibited a higher prevalence of women in the ideological role.[99] These results indicate, again, that it is not necessarily a question of prevalence but of nature of involvement (i.e. women participate in more prominent/visible positions in secular and left-wing movements, in contrast to religious or right-wing movements where women participate in more covert ways). Interestingly, women participated to equal extents in both the caring and support roles across left-wing, secular, right-wing and religious movements,[100] indicating that women are generally involved in these activities regardless of the ideological and religious orientation endorsed by their particular group/movement.

In terms of the specific agenda or aims of the group/movement, results indicated that there were fairly distinct patterns in female involvement (see Figure 4).[101] Available scholarship examining women's involvement according to this type of factor is primarily related to Christian-based movements, Islamism and nationalist/separatist groups. The results of the present research indicate that women in Christian-based or racist movements were involved most often in the active and caring roles. This finding clarifies the scholarship in the area that portrays women in these groups as subordinates of men and as participating primarily in support functions.[102] Research by Blee indicates that women's involvement in the White supremacist movement is not clear-cut and has fluctuated over time[103] – indeed the results from the present study indicate that female involvement in Christian-based groups was quite dissimilar to female involvement in other groups/movements with a religious agenda. In fact, their involvement was more akin to women in communist/socialist groups or movements. Blee proposed that variation in women's involvement in White supremacy was influenced by fluctuations in the movement's definition of the enemy and the type of violence employed.[104] While this study did not contain Blee's level of specificity, the findings do confirm the unusual breadth of activities that women in these Christian-based movements have played.[105]

---

98 Active role: group ideology (left-wing vs. right-wing), $U = 12{,}326.50$, $z = -5.50$, $p < .001$; group religious orientation (secular vs. religious), $U = 15{,}356$, $z = -4.78$, $p < .001$.

99 Ideological role: group ideology, $U = 23{,}722.50$, $z = 6.20$, $p < .001$; group religious orientation, $U = 27{,}047.50$, $z = 5.66$, $p < .001$.

100 Caring role: group ideology, $U = 18{,}673.00$, $z = 1.31$, $p = .189$; group religious orientation, $U = 21{,}286$, $z = .38$, $p = .701$). Support role: group ideology, $U = 17{,}273.00$, $z = -.92$, $p = .355$; group religious orientation, $U = 19{,}880.50$, $z = -1.32$, $p = .187$.

101 Caring role: $\chi^2(6, N = 427) = 84.82$, $p < .001$. Ideological role, $\chi^2(6, N = 427) = 65.11$, $p < .001$. Active role, $\chi^2(6, N = 427) = 100.86$, $p < .001$. Support role, $\chi^2(6, N = 427) = 10.62$, $p = .101$.

102 Eager, above n. 2, p. 71; M. Gonzalez-Perez, *Women and Terrorism: Female Activity in Domestic and International Terror Groups*, Routledge 2008, p. 53; L. Weinberg and W. Eubank, 'Italian Women Terrorists' (1987) 9 *Terrorism: An International Journal* 241.

103 Blee, above n. 60.

104 ibid.

105 See also Cunningham, above n. 31.

Figure 4. Variation on the four female roles in conflict according to group/movement agenda

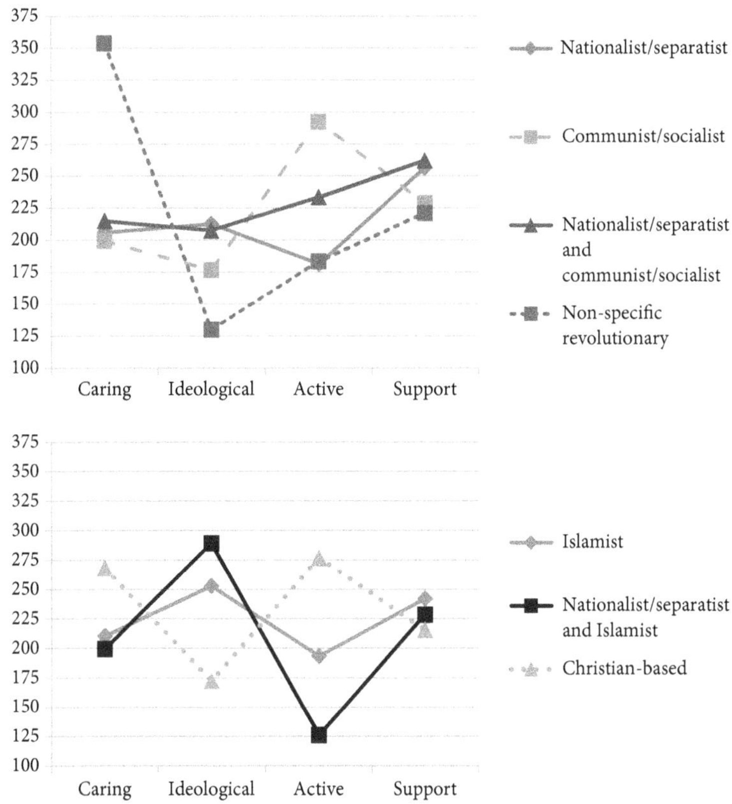

Notes: Findings depicted according to similarity in group/movement ideological basis and religious orientation. The numbers represent mean ranks, as employed by the Kruskal Wallis test – higher numbers represent greater involvement.

Perhaps surprisingly – particularly given the findings regarding other religiously based groups – women affiliated with Christian-based groups/movements were involved least often in the ideological role.

Women in the Islamist movement – including Islamist movements with a nationalist/separatist agenda – were found most often in the ideological role. Similar to the research of von Knop,[106] Cook,[107] and Parashar,[108] this finding highlights the involvement of women in Islamist-based movements in more

---

106 von Knop, 'The Female Jihad: Al Qaeda's Women', above n. 40; von Knop, 'The Multi-Faceted Roles of Women Inside al-Qaeda', above n. 11.

107 D. Cook, 'Women Fighting in Jihad?' in C.D. Ness (ed.), *Female Terrorism and Militancy: Agency, Utility, and Organisation*, Routledge 2008.

108 Parashar, above n. 19; Parashar, above n. 95.

covert and subversive ways. Although the literature in regards to the specific sanctioned role of women in jihad is by no means uniform or conclusive, in general terms the notion is interpreted according to gender. Jihad is connected to public fighting for men but to private suffering for women.[109] Traditionally, a woman obtained the honour associated with jihad through her male relatives and her own religiously appropriate behaviour, while men obtained honour through martyrdom.[110] However, women are undeniably participating in the conventional male jihad by perpetrating suicide attacks. Significantly, the locations in which these suicide bombings originated are Palestine and Chechnya – both of which are conflicts with secular nationalist roots that have fused over time with Islamism.[111] They are also conflicts that have persisted in specific locales for some time, leading to significant operational constraints that may have influenced the increasing use of women in suicide operations.[112] As argued by Cunningham, 'while the use of Islam in this context is a potent symbolic and ideological tool, it is more instrumental and ideological than truly religious'.[113] The results of this study in combination with this scholarship suggests that women primarily participate in the Islamist movement in ideological activities, rather than in prominent and high profile activities – with suicide bombing being an exception rather than a norm of participation for women in Islamism.

The findings regarding nationalist/separatist groups fail to elucidate the contradictions found in the literature with regards to female involvement. Usually it is posited that these groups offer an enhanced space for women, as their basic goal is freedom from state constraints.[114] Thus, groups such as the LTTE in Sri Lanka and the IRA in Northern Ireland have traditionally incorporated women in prominent and visible positions.[115] However, the involvement of women in nationalist/separatist movements is by no means universal; for example, women have been noted to participate to a far lesser degree in the ETA in the Basque region of Spain.[116] There is a significant argument in the scholarship that the way in which a nationalist movement is constructed will inevitably determine the role and representation of women within that movement; for example, liberatory or anti-state movements may be more likely to feature women in combat positions as they are challenging the status quo, while conservative groups may offer less

109 Cook, above n. 107.

110 ibid.; C.D. Ness, 'In the Name of the Cause: Women's Work in Secular and Religious Terrorism' in *Female Terrorism and Militancy: Agency, Utility, and Organisation*, Routledge 2005.

111 Cook, above n. 107; Cunningham, above n. 93.

112 Cunningham, above n. 31; Cunningham, above n. 93; Dalton and Asal, above n. 78.

113 Cunningham, above n. 93, p. 86.

114 Jacques and Taylor, above n. 1.

115 Alison, above n. 79; Eager, above n. 2.

116 Jacques and Taylor, above n. 1.

visible space for women.[117] The findings from this study indicate that women affiliated with nationalist/separatist movements are involved least often in the active role, most often in the support role, and reasonably frequently in the caring and ideological role; however, not with a frequency that was significantly different to any other group. Thus, groups/movements with nationalist or separatist goals did not display exceptional patterns of female involvement (in terms of significant differences from other groups); however, groups that had nationalist/separatist goals in combination with other aims did display some interesting patterns of female involvement.

Groups or movements that endorsed nationalist/separatist goals in combination with an Islamist ideology evidenced the lowest frequency of women in the active role and the highest frequency of women in the ideological role (as already noted). Thus, it may be that these particular nationalist/separatist movements have taken on the strict gender norms found in the broader Islamist movement. In contrast, nationalist/socialist movements that also endorsed a communist or socialist ideology evidenced significantly more women in the active role than Islamist groups with nationalist/separatist goals. Given that women who were affiliated with pure communist/socialist movements exhibited the highest frequency of women in the active role (significantly higher than any other group), the results of this study may indicate that it is the communist/socialist element that is important in determining women's active militant involvement at the meso level. This finding concurs with both observations regarding third wave terrorism[118] and the findings from this study regarding the prevalence of female involvement in the New Left wave of terrorism. Elements of the communist/socialist ideology may be conducive to female involvement; for example, the emphasis on protracted struggle involving mass mobilisation,[119] and the prominence of the civil rights movement and general activism during periods when the communist/socialist ideology was prevalent.[120] As a final point, non-specific revolutionary groups featured women most often in the caring role, where the majority of these groups were found in Africa.

Overall, across the macro and meso variables that were quantitatively examined, the active role and ideological role evidenced the most variability, indicating that female involvement in these roles was associated to a greater extent with specific contexts (i.e. female involvement in the active and ideological roles is more context-specific). In contrast, the caring role evidenced minimal variation and the support role the least variation, indicating that women were involved in these two roles fairly consistently across historical, regional and

117 Alison, above n. 79; N. Yuval-Davis, 'Gender and Mation' in R. Wilford and R.L. Miller (eds.), *Women, Ethnicity and Nationalism: The Politics of Transition*, Routledge 1998.

118 Eager, above n. 2; C.A. Russell and B.H. Miller, 'Profile of a Terrorist' (1977) 1 *Terrorism* 17.

119 Lobao, above n. 79.

120 Cunningham, above n. 31; Eager, above n. 2; Rapoport, above n. 28.

organisational context (i.e. female involvement in the caring and support roles was less dependent on context). By way of summary, the macro and meso factors significantly associated with greater female involvement in each of the four roles are depicted in Table 3.

Table 3. Categories within each of the macro and meso variables associated with increased female involvement in each of the four roles

Level of analysis/variable	Active role	Ideological role	Caring role	Support role
Macro				
Wave of terrorism				
New Left third wave	✓			
Religious fourth wave		✓	✓	
World region				
Europe	✓			
Northern America	✓			
Latin America	✓		~	
Africa	~		✓	
Middle East		✓		
Eastern Europe		✓		
South Asia		~		✓
Meso				
Ideological basis				
Left-wing	✓			
Right-wing		✓		
Religious orientation				
Religious		✓		
Secular	✓			
Agenda				
Nationalist/separatist				
Nationalist/separatist & communist/socialist				
Communist/socialist	✓			
Non-specific revolutionary			✓	
Islamist and nationalist/separatist		✓		
Islamist		✓		
Christian/racist	✓		✓	

Key:

✓ Strong and significant association
~ Moderate association

4. TOWARDS AN INTEGRATED THEORETICAL FRAMEWORK OF FEMALE INVOLVEMENT IN CONFLICT

It is clear that macro and meso factors are important considerations in women's participation in a range of ways in contemporary conflict scenarios. Drawing together the original quantitative research outlined in this chapter and past research, a theoretical framework is conceptualised as illustrated in Figure 5. This framework incorporates the specific activities performed by women in contemporary political and revolutionary conflicts and how these activities are related so as to form conceptual roles,[121] as well as the previously unpublished findings regarding the variation in conceptual roles according various macro and meso factors (as outlined in the preceding section). The basic theoretical proposition of this framework is that the macro, meso and micro levels interact to influence the specific activities and, thus, roles that women have in contemporary political and revolutionary conflict. Context – encompassing a variety of factors as indicated by the levels of analysis – is crucial in determining and understanding conflict itself and individuals' varied involvement within it. Utilising or searching for one explanatory factor limits both theoretical and practical understandings of the revolutionary process. In particular, this theoretical proposition clearly demonstrates the importance of looking beyond the personal when conceptualising female involvement in conflict.

The first part of the framework comprises multiple levels of analysis, including the macro, meso and micro levels. These factors, solely and in interaction, influence the type of female involvement (active, caring, ideological, support) presented in the second part of the framework. It is proposed, specifically, that the three levels influence the type of activities that women perform in contemporary political and revolutionary conflict where these activities are indicative of the broader conceptual roles of women in the conflict. The specific activities included in each of the quadrants of the lower part of Figure 5 are those that were found to consistently associate within the sample of female participants in conflict.[122] The specific macro and meso variables included as examples in the framework are those that were found to significantly influence variation in the aforementioned conceptual roles. Based on these findings, it should be noted that the three levels potentially exert greater influence on the active and ideological roles than on the caring and support roles (where these two roles are performed fairly consistently by women across contexts). It is also suggested that the relationship between contextual factors and roles is reciprocal.

---

121 Vogel, Porter and Kebbell, above n. 37.

122 ibid.

Figure 5. Theoretical framework for conceptualising and researching the roles of women in contemporary political and revolutionary conflict.

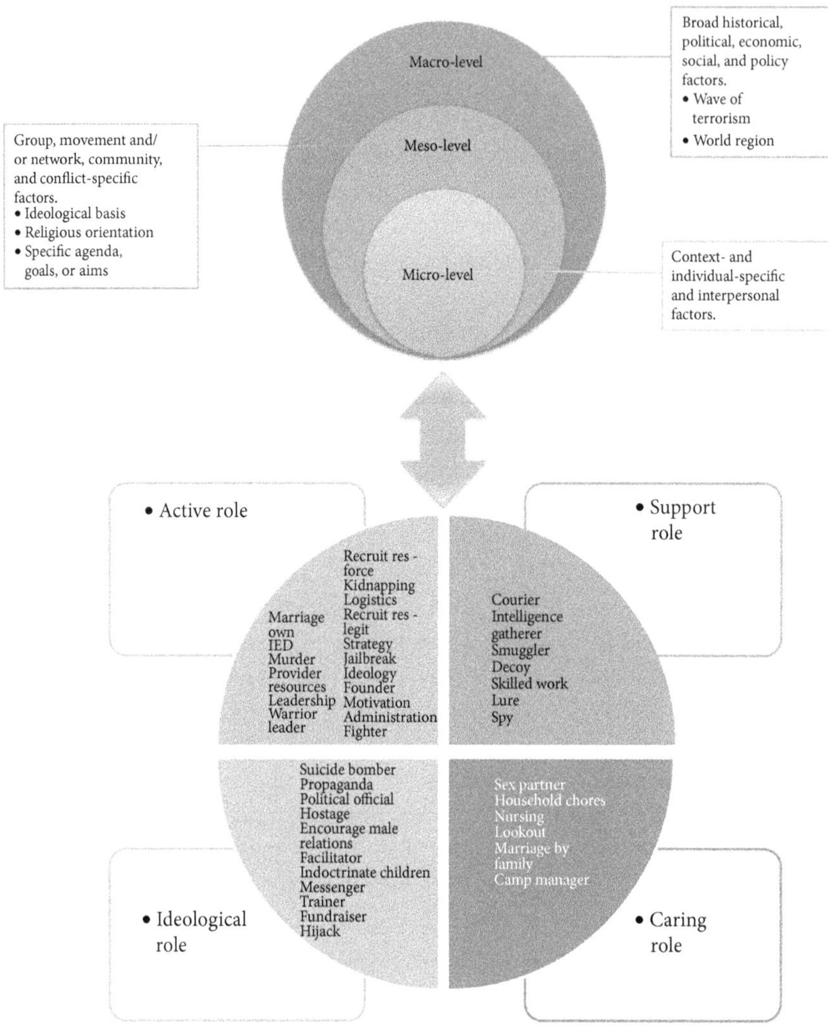

While this is an initial theoretical framework that requires further exploration and validation, it has important implications for theory and research. At the theoretical level, this framework belies the current narrative of women in conflict that portrays their involvement as stemming from victimhood, and thus their clear participation as being either minor or abnormal in nature. This framework supports the argument that the predominant notions of female involvement in conflict need to expand to include their violence and support for extremism.[123] At the methodological/research level, this framework illustrates

[123] See also Aoláin, Haynes and Cahn, above n. 11; Bouta, Frerks and Bannon, above n. 6.

the utility and potential of empirical and quantitative research in disrupting this dominant narrative or script. This framework provides an evidence base for conceptualising women's involvement in political and revolutionary conflict on a case-by-case basis as well at the population level. It provides a systematic operational framework for both studying and theorising female involvement in conflict. For example, in forthcoming research this framework was utilised in a systematic empirical case study of the conflict in Northern Ireland colloquially known as the Troubles, where female involvement in the four roles was examined through an interaction of the macro, meso and micro levels. In this example, the theoretical framework was vital in conceptualising female involvement, as well as in systematising the collection and analysis of primary and secondary data. The multiple levels and roles were parsimonious while flexible enough to identify determinants of mobilisation and involvement without reducing the analysis to a single cause.[124] Overall, the theoretical framework is an important contribution to an empirically based theoretical foundation that can support systematic research into female involvement in political and revolution conflict.

124 See also Moser, above n. 4, p. 40.

FEMALE PERPETRATORS IN THE FORMER YUGOSLAV REPUBLIC AND RWANDA

Disrupting Common Understandings

Sheri A. Labenski

1. INTRODUCTION

Female perpetrators do not feature prominently in the mainstream narratives surrounding the armed conflicts in the Former Yugoslav Republic (FYR) and Rwanda. Women's involvement in both of these conflicts has been primarily relegated to that of victims of sexual violence.[1] This particular understanding of women's roles in armed conflict was perpetuated and reaffirmed through Western feminist interventions into international criminal law in the 1990s,

[1] See D. Buss, 'Expert Witnesses and International War Crimes Trials: Making Sense of Large-Scale Violence in Rwanda' in D. Zarkov and M. Glasius (eds.), *Narrative of Justice In and Out of the Courtroom Former Yugoslavia and Beyond*, Springer International Publishing 2014; K. Askin, 'Gender Crimes Jurisprudence in the ICTR: Positive Developments' (2005) 3 *Journal of International Criminal Justice* 1007; D. Buss, 'The Curious Visibility of Wartime Rape: Gender and Ethnicity in International Criminal Law' (2007) 25 *Windsor Yearbook of Access to Justice* 3.

which focused on sexual violence against women, and was made visible through the work of the International Criminal Tribunal for the Former Yugoslavia (ICTY) and the International Criminal Tribunal for Rwanda (ICTR). The lack of attention afforded by the international media to the range of women's activities in armed conflict further contributed to this limited account. However, women were documented to have been involved in the hostilities in the FYR and Rwanda.[2] Women were accused of murder, torture and sexual violence.[3] They participated in crimes against humanity, war crimes and genocide.[4] Some women were in positions of leadership which granted them the ability to use their status to affect great harm. Other women, who were not in particular positions of power, still significantly contributed to the violence of war.[5] Despite this information, the existence of women who actively took part in the hostilities is not evident in the mainstream narratives around the conflicts or in the jurisprudence of the Tribunals: Biljana Plavšić was the only woman tried by the ICTY[6] and Pauline Nyiramasuhuko was the only woman brought before the ICTR.[7] Women were also understood to have contributed to the violence of each armed conflict, evidenced by their prosecutions locally;[8] however, knowledge regarding the participation of female perpetrators has not influenced mainstream understandings of women in armed conflict.

The reason it is beneficial to engage with the experiences of female perpetrators in the conflicts in the FYR and Rwanda is twofold. First, the existence of female perpetrators leads to questions about the system of international criminal law (ICL). The focus on these particular conflicts' narratives has predominantly developed around sexual violence against women and the loss of life or brutality of the violence perpetrated by men. However, in order for ICL to be its most

---

2 See K. Engle, 'Judging Sex in War' (2008) 106 *Michigan Law Review* 941; N. Hogg, 'I Never Poured Blood: Women Accused of Genocide in Rwanda', LLM dissertation, McGill University 2001.

3 International examples include: Biljana Plavšić, ICTY; Pauline Nyiramasuhuko, ICTR; Ieng Thirith and Im Cheam, ECCC; and Simone Gbagbo, ICC. Some other cases include: K. Richburg, 'Rwandan Nuns Jailed in Genocide' *Washington Post*, New York 2001; E. Martinez, 'Kentucky Woman Indicted for Bosnian War Crimes' *CBS News*, New York 2011; 'Dutch Yvonne Basebya Jailed for Rwanda Crimes' *BBC News*, London 2013 <http://www.bbc.co.uk/news/world-africa-21632819> accessed 28.09.2015; A. Cerkez, 'US Extradites War Crimes Suspect to Bosnia' *NBC News*, New York 2011; K. Seguegila, 'Women Lied About Role in Rwanda Genocide, U.S. Jury Says' *CNN News* 2013; 'Bosnia Arrests "Female Monster" – Wife of Warlord "Serb Adolf"' *Mirror*, London 2011 <http://www.mirror.co.uk/news/uk-news/bosnia-arrests-female-monster---98517> accessed 28.09.2015; BBC News – Rwanda Jails Journalist Valerie Bemeriki for Genocide' *BBC News*, London 2009 <http://news.bbc.co.uk/1/hi/8412014.stm> accessed 28.09.2015.

4 ibid.

5 Hogg, above n. 2, pp. 67–71.

6 See section 4 'Biljana Plavšić as a Female Perpetrator'.

7 See section 6 'Pauline Nyiramasuhuko as a Female Perpetrator'.

8 For further discussion, see Smeulers and Simić in this volume.

effective, it must acknowledge the wider range of women's and men's experiences in armed conflict. What currently occurs in ICL is a continual reproduction of binaries and stereotypes around men's and women's roles, which prevent the overall growth of the legal system. When a female perpetrator becomes visible in ICL, she is often spoken about and referred to with shock and condemnation, based on the fact she is a woman and should know better. Studying female perpetrators disrupts these presumptions, as it is only when the larger range of human experience in armed conflict is recognised that ICL can make long lasting gains.

Second, looking at female perpetrators can highlight the ways in which gender is understood, from both an international legal perspective and a feminist perspective. The lack of confrontation by Western feminists with female perpetrators seems to signal a naiveté or uncomfortableness with issues that involve women who perpetrate violence. By focusing on women as victims, which has been the primary aim of the Western feminist interventions in both the ICTY and ICTR, discussions become too centred on the harms committed against women. Due to this, women are limited to strict gender roles. If women who commit violence and engage in hostilities are recognised, then it is usually in relation to the sexual violence they sustained. This was the case in the FYR, where many feminists assumed that women only took up arms because they were mentally impaired by the sexual violence they experienced.[9] By avoiding a discussion around the varying roles women inhabit, gender norms continue to remain rigid and incapable of dealing with the aftermath of armed conflict. Improving the lives of women or a community and ushering in justice cannot occur if the understanding of the hostilities remains tied to actions that rest along narrow gender lines: men fight and women suffer without recourse. The dialogue that incorporates women as perpetrators sits alongside the understanding that sexual violence does occur in armed conflict and often in greater proportion against women than against men. However, if feminists only include women in legal initiatives when they are recognised as victims, then the entirety of the project to aid women, rebuild a community or bring justice is suspect. Additionally, feminist interventions cannot operate without also acknowledging that much of the success of Western intervention is reliant upon the work of Third World women, on whose behalf Western feminists have tended to speak. Looking at female perpetrators exposes the differences in feminist goals, evident in what 'women issues' get elevated to the international plane.

The aim of this chapter is not to understand the way women involved in armed conflict see their own actions or to suggest specific ways prosecutors or investigators should approach the aftermath of armed conflict. Instead, this chapter identifies and critiques the ways in which conflicts are seen and

9 K. Engle, 'Feminism and Its (Dis)Contents: Criminalizing Wartime Rape in Bosnia and Herzegovina' (2005) 99 *American Journal of International Law* 788, 795.

appropriated, by feminists, advocates, academics and the media. The chapter critiques the way these groups situate themselves within surrounding debates and simultaneously decide what aspects of a crisis retain value and deserve primacy. Female perpetrators must be recognised as part of a mainstream conflict narrative, from the perspective of the international response to a crisis. By approaching armed conflict from the viewpoint of female perpetrators, feminists and international law practitioners and scholars alike can 'hold a mirror up to themselves' in order to better discern future conflicts and identify the gaps in the work done thus far. In an effort to prevent the Global North from speaking on behalf of the Global South, this work situates itself as a critique of the way women in armed conflict have been spoken about in international law and in Western feminist dialogues. Through the continued use of gender as a way to highlight female perpetrators in the media, and the use of gender to encourage protection of women, as well as gender being utilised to understand female perpetrators from a feminist perspective, gender becomes ultimately unhelpful when used as the only mode of analysis. Much like ICL cannot be solely responsible for repairing all of the harms done during armed conflict, neither can gender be thought of as the only way to understand women in conflict situations.

Addressing the two benefits of engaging with female perpetrators listed above will be carried out as follows. In the second section, examples of female perpetrators will be sifted through, citing the common narratives present when women engage in hostilities. This will identify tendencies to rest on stereotypical gendered assumptions of 'women's character' and role in war, in both ICL and feminist discourses. This section will also develop more fully the reasons why female perpetrators are a relevant topic of study. The third section will examine the ICTY, Western feminist interventions into ICL and the media, which can be argued to be the beginning of victim feminism. The case of Biljana Plavšić will be detailed in the fourth section. The fifth section will highlight the media representation of the Rwandan genocide, and move to a critique of Western feminist interventions and its perception of race in and around the ICTR.

Pauline Nyiramasuhuko's case will be examined in section six. Analysing the only two female perpetrators indicted by the Tribunals will demonstrate nuances in the responses to female perpetrators, as well as the larger issues present when engaging in a solely gender based analysis. The final section will synthesise the information from the Tribunals, providing links to international criminal law's development. The last section will also examine why many feminists are reluctant to properly address female perpetrators. This chapter will demonstrate that ICL projects fail to realise the benefits from studying female perpetrators due to the Western feminist focus on sexual violence against women, which has avoided addressing the areas of women's experiences that confront stereotypical assumptions. This work continues a dialogue that acknowledges the necessity of critically engaging with the female perpetrator from both a gendered and a legal perspective, while recognising the breadth of women's participation in armed conflict.

2. COMMON NARRATIVES

When detailing the actions of female perpetrators, common or stereotypical notions of women often tend to interplay within understandings of armed conflict and violence. There are three general narratives that appear in ICL, mainstream feminist interventions and armed conflict history that support a limited perspective of both female perpetrators and women, which include notions that women are: predominantly peaceful and non-violent, victims of sexual violence, or do not hold levels of leadership that would necessitate their inclusion in ICL proceedings. Each of the three narratives will be described while highlighting the assumptions they imply. The relevancy of studying female perpetrators from both ICL and feminist perspective will also be discussed. Positioning these two conversations in the same section is especially helpful, in order to simultaneously question the motives behind feminist interventions and the aims of ICL.

2.1. JUSTIFYING ACTS OF VIOLENCE

One of the narratives that affect the way female perpetrators are understood details women in general as non-violent, inherently peaceful and on the side of the 'good'.[10] The work of Sjoberg and Gentry details the characteristics that women are assumed to inhabit and how the realities of women's lives and women's actions, which can include violence, confronts these ideas in a manner that begs for justification.[11] Headlines centre on women's 'femaleness' and often imply traditionally female roles. A reason is needed when women step outside of the strict binaries set to encompass acceptable behaviour. Even though feminists understand that women are capable of a violence, they still imply that women should work for 'good' once in traditional male careers and spaces.[12] Examples of women committing acts of violence are often reported in the media with links to gender; an article on Rasema Handanovic, found to have committed acts of torture and abuse in the FYR, read, 'The US single mother who was actually a war criminal'.[13] The article's headline disassociates the ability of being a mother with

---

10 See L. Sjoberg and C.E. Gentry, *Mothers, Monsters, Whores*, Zed Books 2007.

11 ibid.

12 See B. Ehrenreich, 'Feminism's Assumptions Upended' (2007) 24 *South Central Review* 170.

13 A. Oliver, 'The US Single Mother Who Was Actually a War Criminal: Killer Becomes First Woman to Be Convicted of Bosnian War Crimes' *Mail Online* 2012.

the ability to commit war crimes; being a mother is about caring and nurturing and cannot exist within someone who also commits crimes. Her criminal behaviour prevents her from fully claiming her title as a mother.

When women are tried before international courts and tribunals their actions are related to their gender in ways men's actions are not. Sjoberg and Gentry point to gender norms as a way of punishing women for denying their gendered role.[14] Female perpetrators who are brought before either local or international courts are shamed within the media. When Pauline Nyiramasuhuko was on trial in the ICTR, the media commented on her dress and appearance as contradicting the violence that she had perpetrated.[15] Nyiramasuhuko was cited as looking like a 'dear aunt' during courtroom proceedings.[16] The fact that her son was also on trial was often referred to, and this reiterated her role as a mother and her ability to steer her son towards committing crimes.[17] Being tried as women, then, is another sort of punishment; women who are tried are shamed because they are women and because their gender would dictate that they should not have been involved in actions that would lead to criminal proceedings. Reports of male perpetrators do not typically include commentary on their crime as a violation of their masculinity or role as a father – if anything, war crimes would solidify evidence of their gendered identity.[18] War and violence has continued to reinforce and often mirror traditional displays of masculinity, albeit toxic, which makes it unnecessary to cite male acts of violence in relation to their gender. Violence committed by men in armed conflict is then expected and allowed. Criminal acts become masculine by definition, which leads to an assumption that men are the default perpetrators and cannot be involved in the promotion of peace.

These assumptions need to be analysed further, as there is a recognised link that the international media has with the ideals in a given society. The media's inferences also point to an idea that is based within a Western notion of gender. Defining 'the West' is not particularly straightforward, but in this case it is referring to a predominately white, Christian mindset evident within states in the global north. The way women are described in the Western media relies upon stereotypical notions of peace and non-violence, within a larger Western conception of women and men. The work around female perpetrators needs to also accept that there exists great nuance in the way female perpetrators are seen across the societies they inhabit. Scenes of women carrying machine guns engaging in violent combat is not necessarily shocking to those who have grown up with stories of female fighters, possibly in the Global South, and therefore

14 Sjoberg and Gentry, above n. 10, p. 15.

15 D. Harman, 'A Woman on Trial for Rwanda's Massacre', *The Christian Science Monitor*, 2003 <http://www.csmonitor.com/2003/0307/p09s01-woaf.html> accessed 27.09.2015.

16 ibid.

17 ibid.

18 Engle, above n. 1, pp. 956–57.

women who then commit crimes in these roles may not seem out of place. The idea is to be mindful of the spaces in which female perpetrators are situated when analysing individual reactions in relation to ICL.

2.2. JUSTIFYING THE PRESENCE OF WOMEN IN INTERNATIONAL CRIMINAL LAW

Another common critique against the work around female perpetrators is that women do not commit the same level of violent crime as men. Focusing on the lack of prosecution of female perpetrators in ICL is making an issue about something that is not a denial of women's participation. This narrative does not necessarily assume women are less capable of violence than men in a given society, but rather that women do not typically commit violent crimes with the same occurrence as men and are therefore tried with less frequency. Further, it can be argued that this is not a denial of agency, but based on facts and figures. The problem with this argument is that it dismisses the existence of female perpetrators and seems to support the assumed stereotype of peacefulness and non-violence. What this narrative also assumes is that the binaries that exist in ICL are valid, with no need to be challenged. In ICL there is an assumption of what gender means, irrespective or culture, race, religion or ethnicity. What is also overlooked are the deeply embedded biases that limit the types of questions that are asked by prosecutors and judges, and the ways in which a given conflict is understood from the 'outside'. This work is not suggesting that women commit a greater number of violent acts during armed conflict than men or that the level of violent crime committed by men and women is equal. It is not being suggested that, given the opportunity, women would commit more violent crimes. However, women do commit crimes and it is possible that many such crimes go unnoticed due to the perception that women remain the victims during armed conflict.

Charlesworth discusses the roles of men and women in crisis situations and argues that women are only recognised as being a part of the crisis when they are violated, and when that violation is seen as harming their social group.[19] Charlesworth writes that men are the main focus, as they were in the ICTY and ICTR, acting in various ways, while women enter only as an afterthought. Women are on the other side of the binary, and are predominately focused upon when they are victims of sexual violence. Charlesworth rightly states that while men are often seen as perpetrators, they are also simultaneously viewed as the 'saviour' who solves the crisis, 'saving' women in the process.[20] This only leaves

19 See H. Charlesworth, 'International Law: A Discipline of Crisis' (2002) 65 *Modern Law Review* 389.

20 ibid.

room for women on the margins, to be included when men deem it appropriate. While this view is especially limiting for women, it captures the view from mainstream conflict narratives.[21]

ICL's main goals are to end the impunity of leaders and punish violations of *jus cogens* norms and, like the domestic law, both realms operate on a basis of wrong and right and the finality of their judgments. ICL must not only follow the general principles of criminal law, but also reconcile itself as a part of the international system, dealing with the critiques on the lack of enforcement, state consent and legitimacy. ICL incorporates different societies, cultures and legal systems while predominately entering into a situation post conflict, accommodating extreme levels of violence and longstanding feuds. The characteristics that make ICL a unique form of criminal law also limit how much nuance it can contain in its judgments. While ICL's unique characteristics can be a reason for its limiting gender binaries, ICL's goals and measures of effectiveness are the main issue for its reliance on binaries. By reimagining what ICL's end goals should be it may be possible to gain a better understanding of the roles and relationships that exist within an armed conflict.

The international criminal legal system, instead of focusing on punishing leaders for violations of *jus cogens*, should also recognise its part in history telling as well as contributing towards repairing a community. ICL is already implicated in both activities, but because these are not sufficiently focused on during proceedings it misses the opportunity to develop. The critique to this argument might underscore that ICL is not designed to complete all of these goals. It cannot punish leaders, while telling an accurate history, bringing charges against people from each side of a conflict, and rebuilding the relationships within a given society. However, whether or not ICL's goals include providing a more nuanced view of gender within a conflict, ICL is already implicated in this practice. ICL's role as an international project, and the normative value placed upon it by the international community, are very much a part of shaping the way gender, race, culture and ethnicity are understood by the mainstream post conflict. The background provided in each court case judgment, the media focus, the way in which prosecutors pick cases and conduct trials, the witnesses who are chosen to tell their stories, and the way in which the public responds to all of these actions, situate ICL as an authority when trying to decipher the nuances of an armed conflict. While ICL is only one part of the justice process and work needs to be done post conflict at a local level, ICL must acknowledge that it carries responsibility internationally and, therefore, must address the issues that occur within its framework. Female perpetrators offer a way into this discussion. ICL can question how the stories of those outside the main conflict

---

21 C. Coulter, 'Female Fighters in the Sierra Leone War: Challenging the Assumptions?' (2008) 88 *Feminist Review* 54, 55. Coulter notes that 10–30 per cent of all fighters in the Sierra Leone War were women.

narratives can be included, and what can be learned about the conflict, as well as identifying the biases of those who work within the legal system.

2.3. FOCUS ON SEXUAL VIOLENCE

By critiquing the international community's focus on crisis, Charlesworth highlights the binaries in the broader area of IL. Moving to ICL specifically, Charlesworth's analysis lends itself to unpacking the Western feminist interventions into crisis found in the ICTY and ICTR, which especially focused on women as victims of sexual violence, and subsequently reinforced a male and female binary. This push to identify and punish various forms of sexual violence was an important step, but it did not come without negative after effects. Western feminists involved in this dialogue continued a narrative that unintentionally limited the roles women were able to inhabit. Charlesworth continues her discussion by identifying the sets of contrast that exist within international law. Binaries of, 'objective/subjective, legal/political, logic/emotion, order/anarchy, mind/body, culture/nature, action/passivity, public/private, protector/protected', are listed as distinctions having both male and female characteristics.[22] Charlesworth argues that international law primarily values the first (male) characteristic.[23] Through the focus on sexual violence in the ICTY, the binaries of man and woman, perpetrator and victim are seen as synonymous. Without highlighting the different roles of women in the conflict, examples of female perpetrators like Plavšić and Nyiramasuhuko are seen as anecdotal.

Another problem with the rhetoric of victim feminism and highlighting the sexual violence in the conflict, besides that it ignores the other roles women inhabit, it also identifies rape as special to a particular armed conflict. Engle states that when female activists, journalists, and scholars were trying to ascertain stories of rape after the conflict in the FYR, they employed the assumption that all women were victims of rape.[24] Engle further stated that the ICTY, at the urging of Western feminists, has limited women's stories and denied sexual, political and military agency.[25] Many feminists in and around the ICTY tended to portray Bosnian Muslim women as victims and continued to deny women's participation.[26] Journalists and feminists were frequently frustrated with women's lack of cooperation as they tried to elicit stories of sexual violence, which made many interpret women's silence as evidence of sexual violence.[27]

---

22 Charlesworth, above n. 19, p. 390.
23 ibid.
24 Engle, above n. 9, pp. 795 and 803.
25 ibid, p. 807.
26 ibid.
27 ibid, p. 795.

Serbian men were then seen as the 'typical' sexual perpetrator.[28] Feminists further limited women's participation by suggesting that if a woman took up arms after she was subjected to sexual violence, then she must have only done so due to the rape she had experienced.[29]

MacKinnon was an advocate of ICL's work on aiding women who have been victimised by sexual violence. She advocated for a stricter reading of crimes that dealt with violence against women.[30] Engle has stated that advocates carried large assumptions about the ethnic differences between Serbs, Croats and Bosnian Muslims.[31] Many of the advocates in the ICTY wanted rape to be seen as genocide and believed that rapes by Serbian men of Croatian and Bosnian Muslim women constituted genocide. As the conflict continued and Croatia became more of an aggressor, these same advocates shifted their definition of 'rape as genocide' to only the rape of Bosnian Muslims. The work done around the Tribunal concerning women in conflict reinforces the idea that women are victims,[32] generally acknowledged to be in continual need of protection.[33]

Women involved in the armed conflict as combatants were seen as reactionary, limiting the possibility that women can support the ideals of either side of a conflict and become motivated to take up arms. Sexual violence in armed conflict is seen as an attack on women as a group because they are women, and while that has been the case in certain instances, it also misses the way sexual violence can be used against both women and men because of their ethnicity or class. Studying cases of female perpetrators and incidents of female violence is not to suggest that these are somehow equal to or similar to the crimes men commit in every instance. It is important to recognise these women's actions in order to better understand violence and the nature of armed conflict. The following sections demonstrate the wide array of factors that influence the ways in which female perpetrators are understood.

3. THE FORMER YUGOSLAV REPUBLIC

Interventions into the ICTY were largely focused upon the push to recognise sexual violence in armed conflict, as well as to encourage protection for women

---

28 ibid, pp. 785 and 786.

29 ibid, pp. 795 and 796.

30 See C. MacKinnon, 'The ICTR'S Legacy on Sexual Violence' (2008) 14 *New England Journal of International and Comparative Law* 101.

31 Engle, above n. 9, p. 794.

32 See R. Kapur, *Erotic Justice: Law and the New Politics of Postcolonialsim*, Glass House Press 2005, p. 120.

33 Notable cases: *The Prosecutor vs Tadić, The Prosecutor v. Mučić et al. Prosecutor v. Kunarac, Prosecutor v. Krstić*. Icty.org, 'ICTY – TPIY: Crimes of Sexual Violence' <http://www.icty.org/sid/10312> accessed 27.09.2015; Engle, above n. 9, p. 952.

in international law. This section will look at Western feminist engagement with the ICTY as well as the development of ICL. In doing so it will highlight the way binaries such as male/female and perpetrator/victim were solidified in and around the tribunal.

The role of feminists, lobbyists and non-governmental organisations (NGOs) was paramount in the successful prosecution of sexual violence crimes in the ICTY.[34] Feminists, especially within NGOs, credited themselves with the development of law.[35] However, Engle stated that many assumed that all women were powerless, victims, incapable of defending themselves, taking sides and participating in war.[36] Revenge was seen as a product of the sexual violence that women experienced. If women wanted to join the army or expressed vengeance, they were seen as exceptional or pathological.[37] Journalist Alexandra Stiglmayer equated the desire for revenge with atypical behaviour.[38] She stated that most women who were raped were broken and unable to think about revenge; therefore, those who did so were not normal.[39] If revenge is considered to be pathological, potential mothers who were victims of rape are believed to be suicidal, and rape is assumed to leave women 'broken', then there are few options for women to express themselves within the parameters of armed conflict without their actions being explained by a type of trauma. However, focusing on sexual violence against women in armed conflicts in the FYR and Rwanda highlighted the experiences of women which had not received primacy until this point in ICL. The Nuremberg trials did not prosecute sexual violence as such, and the Tokyo trials overlooked the enslavement of comfort women,[40] but both the ICTY and ICTR contributed by increasing the attention to sexual violence and developing jurisprudence. In order to bring the issues facing women in armed conflict to the attention of ICL, feminists needed to continually stress the importance of defining sexual violence terms, identify criminal acts within the conflict, and underscore the harm felt by women who experience sexual violence. Western feminist interventions also had to contend with violence against women due to their gender in societies where women did not, in their estimation, hold positions of power or agency. Considering all of these factors, it is not difficult to understand why there were continual efforts by feminists to highlight these issues.

---

34 See J. Halley et al., 'From the International to the Local in Feminist Legal Response to Rape, Prostitution / Sex Work and Sex Trafficking: Four Studies in Contemporary Governance Feminism' (2007) 29 *Harvard Journal of Law and Gender* 335.

35 ibid.

36 Engle, above n. 9, p. 795.

37 ibid.

38 ibid, pp. 795 and 796.

39 ibid.

40 *Crimes of Sexual Violence*, available at <http://www.icty.org/en/in-focus/crimes-sexual-violence>.

However, continually reaffirming women's role as victims of violence again establishes that women are connected to a specific view of femininity. Criminal courts should be disrupting these binaries and encouraging the understanding of the nuances of women's and men's roles. This would do more to promote women as active participants in conflict and prevent assumptions that women remain helpless during times of violence. Males were considered the aggressors: strong, powerful and a forceful representative of the nation.[41] As a result, men who were victims of sexual violence remain outside the mainstream understanding of sexual violence in the conflict of the FYR.[42] By framing the Tribunal along the same gender lines as the conflict, ICL runs the risk of reproducing similar gendered outcomes. If women are argued to be disadvantaged during armed conflict, which produces distinct understandings of masculinity and femininity, then creating a tribunal that also predominately focuses on women as victims and men as perpetrators, reaffirms the gender binaries from the conflict and does not allow the possibility that human experience during the conflict may be nuanced and varied.

The way Western feminists have shaped the understanding of sexual violence and gender can be directly linked to the media representation of the conflict. Zarkov discusses the Western feminist response to the conflict, stating that in the summer of 1992 the international media began focusing on the sexual violence in the FYR.[43] Zarkov highlights the shift in Western feminist engagement from a discussion of war to an emphasis on war rapes and a limited understanding of ethnicity.[44] The classification of sexual violence as a result of ethnic identities was problematic; instead, there should have been more effort to ascertain the way in which a certain identity may become elevated and seen as desirable in a given society.[45] The former approach does not question the structures of the conflict, but rather upholds and perpetuates their existence. Zarkov states that female survivors of rape and rape camps have also been a part of the efforts to deal with the aftermath of rape, as well as other conflict-related issues.[46]

41 A. Jones, 'Gender and Genocide' (2002) 4 *Journal of Genocide Research* 65, 66–69.

42 The case of *Prosecutor v. Mučić et al.* is an example where sexual violence against men is noted. The account of Mučić's actions included a description of him forcing two male detainees to engage in fellatio with each other. *See Prosecutor v. Mučić et al.* (Judgment), IT-96-21-T, ICTY, 16 November 1998; *Prosecutor v. Tadić* (Judgment), IT-94-1, ICTY, 26 January 2000; *Prosecutor v. Češić* (Judgment), IT-95-10/1, ICTY, 11 March 2004; *Prosecutor v. Todorović* (Judgment), IT-95-9/1, ICTY, 31 July 2001; *Prosecutor v. Simić* (Judgment), IT-95-9/2, ICTY, 17 October 2002. See A.-M. de Brouwer, *Supranational Criminal Prosecution of Sexual Violence*, Intersentia 2005.

43 D. Zarkov, 'Ontologies of International Humanitarian and Criminal Law: "Locals" and "Internationals' Internationals" in Discourses and Practices of Justice', *Narratives of Justice In and Out of the Courtroom Former Yugoslavia and Beyond*, Springer 2014, p. 7.

44 ibid, p. 8.

45 ibid.

46 ibid, p. 7.

Yet, the international media and Western feminists have depicted these women as helpless and silent,[47] and while sexual violence came to the forefront of international feminist study, the work of local feminists was not recognised.[48]

Before the conflict began, Benderly noted that Yugoslav feminism was directly opposed to nationalism and expressed solidarity among the different territories.[49] After it was clear that the conflict would continue, many local feminists began working to end the conflict; they established anti-war groups, groups for women refugees, centres for those affected by violence, and telephone lines for support.[50] Feminists on all sides had difficulty in defining the perpetrators and the victims during the conflict. Some groups did acknowledge that their own ethnic forces were also involved in acts of sexual violence;[51] others focused their work on all women harmed by the conflict and established links with other states as well.[52]

Through the combination of both local and international presumptions about women's personal experiences within the armed conflict, the narrative around women's roles was restricted to that of passive victims. Zarkov comments on this point as well, stating that feminists, local and international, assumed that women were powerless and that men were active players.[53] Women who were capable of perpetrating or permitting violence and men who were powerless were not acknowledged.[54] From this perspective it is possible to see why female perpetrators have remained on the fringes of the armed conflict's narrative.

4. BILJANA PLAVŠIĆ AS A FEMALE PERPETRATOR

The statistics on the work of the ICTY included only one case involving a female perpetrator, Biljana Plavšić. Plavšić was the Serbian representative to the collective Presidency of Bosnia and Herzegovina, a member of the collective and expanded Presidencies of the Bosnian Serb Republic, and had de facto control and authority over members of the Bosnian Serb armed forces.[55]

---

47 ibid.

48 See D. Zarkov, 'Feminism and the Disintegration of Yugoslavia: On the Politics of Gender and Ethnicity' (2003) 24 *Social Development Issues* 1.

49 ibid, p. 2.

50 ibid.

51 ibid., p. 8, 'Croatian anti-nationalist feminists, for example, were the first to explicitly accuse Croatian forces of raping Serb and Muslim women, and to condemn national and international demonization of Serb men and the Serb nation'.

52 ibid., 'Serbian anti-nationalist feminists also directed their activities towards all women, regardless of their ethnic background. They were among the few to establish links with Albanian women from Kosovo, for example'.

53 ibid., p. 13.

54 ibid.

55 *Case Information Sheet Biljana Plavšić* (1st edn., The International Criminal Tribunal for the Former Yugoslavia) <http://www.icty.org/x/cases/plavsic/cis/en/cis_plavsic_en.pdf> accessed 25.09.2015.

The charges included genocide and murder. Plavšić pleaded guilty to crimes against humanity.[56] The Trial Chamber gave weight to Plavšić's guilty plea as well as the statement she made in court, signifying her remorse.[57] She was eventually sentenced to 11 years' imprisonment, but only served two-thirds of her sentence.[58]

What is particularly interesting about Plavšić's case is her admission of guilt in front of the ICTY, which helped to reduce the charges against her as well as her sentence. What was not within the purview of the court was the redaction of her confession, published while in prison.[59] Plavšić was the only high ranking officer to admit guilt, yet this seems to have only been an attempt to lower her sentence. The reason Plavšić's case is useful is because her behaviour and attitude while serving her sentence cast aside preconceived notions of how women are presumed to feel and act, especially after committing a crime, yet the way her actions were framed in the media reaffirms her role as a woman.

The connection between remorse and gender seems to presume that women will be more likely to feel guilty after committing a crime.[60] Therefore, when Plavšić retracted her statements in prison and instead displayed that she had not benefited from any rehabilitation, she contrasted herself to stereotypical gender roles. However, Plavšić's case does not offer an alternative understanding of women's roles in conflict or the ways in which gender influences armed conflict. This work suggests that Plavšić's situation was read and interpreted along strict gender lines and did more to reaffirm stereotypical notions of gender. Plavšić was seen as an aberration of the way women should act, while at the same time she still maintained her femininity. The crimes Plavšić committed were highlighted in the media, describing her as the 'Iron Lady' or 'female Mengele', along with stories of her sexual relationships or ability to encourage displays of violence.[61] Both are characteristics that reference her feminine sexual appeal and her nurturing mothering side. When Plavšić was serving her sentence, her good behaviour was praised, as was her cooking and baking – signs she that she was readjusting to 'proper' womanly life.[62] Plavšić never seemed to slip outside designated female roles, and even when her actions were less than desirable they were still set within feminine or gendered language.

---

56 Trial Chamber of ICTY, Sentencing Judgment, Biljana Plavšić (IT-00-39 & 40/1) 27 February 2003, Section 2.

57 Trial Chamber of ICTY, Judgment Summary, Biljana Plavšić (IT-00-39 & 40/1) 27 February 2003.

58 ibid.

59 Biljana Plavšić, Svedočim [I Testify], 2005, (Banjaluka: Trioprint).

60 See K.E. Niedermeier, I.A. Horowitz and N.L. Kerr, Exceptions to the Rule: The Effects of Remorse, Status, and Gender on Decision Making (2001) 31 *Journal of Applied Social Psychology* 604.

61 Sjoberg and Gentry, above n. 10, p. 156.

62 J. Subotić, 'The Cruelty of False Remorse: Biljana Plavšić at The Hague' (2012) 36 *Southeastern Europe* 39, 49.

It is not strange that Plavšić's actions were framed from a gender biased lens or that her actions do more to support the 'female identity' than to disrupt it. This work is arguing that to suggest female perpetrators somehow *actually* break the idea of what it means to be women would be false. Women have always committed violence and disruption. Maybe that is why when highlighting the ways specific women buck ideas of gender, it is actually doing more to support limited notions regarding women's abilities. Every action 'outside' strict gender binaries can be explained back through femininity. If Plavšić is encouraging genocide, then she is like a mother encouraging children. If Plavšić is corrupt and viscous, then she is somehow enthralled in an influential sexual relationship and also a female monster. Every 'wrong' action can be attributed back to a traditional female role. Even when Plavšić is in prison serving a sentence for international crimes, she is still described as being on good behaviour by baking in her leisure time. Considering the limited amount that has been learned from analysing Plavšić's case along gender lines, it may be more useful to use ethnicity, race, or in this case a mix of ethnicity and nationalism, to understand Plavšić's actions as a female perpetrator. If the goal is to offer a full narrative of an armed conflict, then gender cannot be utilised as the only tool, as it seems to reaffirm a strict reading of women's actions in conflict.

The fact that only one female was tried in the ICTY would suggest that women's involvement as perpetrators did not become a part of the narrative that surrounded the conflict, established through Tribunal proceedings.[63] Of the prosecuted persons in local judiciaries, women have been among those indicted, charged and sentenced, with more frequency than in the ICTY.[64] Identifying that women were charged with crimes in the FYR and other conflicts not only draws attention to their existence, but also allows a deeper discussion into the way other identities interact. It is beneficial to give evidence of female perpetrators, but beyond this little else can be gained from mere identification. Work needs to be done to unpack the nuances of female perpetrators and the way their actions are framed. Plavšić's case displayed a different story from the mainstream account of women's experiences during the conflict in the FYR, but also unearthed the way gender is interpreted and reaffirmed though both media and biased analysis. While it is useful to dissect the ways in which gender is used to understand Plavšić's actions, it may be more beneficial to step away from a gender analysis. The following section on Rwanda and Pauline Nyiramasuhuko will build upon the work in this section in order to demonstrate how focusing on gender only or women as victims misses potential opportunities for new understandings. This underscores the benefit of using ethnicity and race to critique the actions of female perpetrators in Rwanda.

---

63 This is referring to an international perspective gained through the ICTY. Local courts have produced more examples of women engaging in acts of violence.

64 See Smeulers and Simić, in this volume.

5. RWANDA

The response to the Rwandan genocide by Western feminists, the international media and the ICTR, shaped and gave meaning to the way women and their actions were viewed during the conflict. Rwanda offers a unique opportunity to see the way ethnicity and gender are interwoven into the way the conflict was interpreted and how this interpretation links to Rwanda's past. While this work will not attempt to discuss the colonial history of Rwanda, it will demonstrate how limited understandings of race, ethnicity and gender influenced the narrative of the genocide and thereby limited the way women were presumed to take part. The desire to include sexual violence in ICTR cases by Western feminists and an uncertainty on the part of international law, in general, to give issues affecting women primacy in an international legal context are highlighted. The international media's portrayal of the sexual violence against women during the Rwandan genocide affirmed assumptions around brutality and savagery, which further influenced the perception of the conflict. This section will give an overview of the Western feminist response to the Rwandan genocide, and also identify the major issues preventing the recognition of female perpetrators by mainstream narratives.

Misinterpretation of the armed conflict in Rwanda influenced the stories and headlines of news reports.[65] However, despite the shift from disinterest to intense scrutiny of victims,[66] international audiences knew little about Rwanda's colonial past. Reports centred on descriptions of excessive violence and brutality, which distanced Rwanda from 'civilised' viewers, as well as shaping the way people involved in the Rwandan genocide were seen and understood. The international media has continually overlooked Africa and when they do report it is done with limited attention or rather specific attention to certain topics, as was the case with the Rwandan genocide,[67] especially surrounding the ICTR.

The Tribunal also contributed to further misunderstandings by remaining focused on a very narrow jurisdiction.[68] The ICTR and global interest ignored the ongoing conflict that surrounded Rwanda's colonial past, as well as its decolonialisation, and focused only on the 100 days of the genocide. By reinforcing the genocide as a singular 100-day period, it projects notions of brutality and chaos onto Rwanda specifically and Africa generally. Spivak's work elaborates how colonialism in India can be seen as justifiable by the British,

---

65 See G. Caplan, *'Rwanda: Walking the Road to Genocide'* in A. Thompson (ed.), *The Media and the Rwanda Genocide*, Pluto Press 2007.

66 See A. Thompson, 'Introduction' in A. Thompson (ed.), *The Media and the Rwandan Genocide*, Pluto Press 2007.

67 See S. Carruthers, 'Tribalism and Tribulation: Media Construction of "African Savagery" and "Western Humanitarianism"' in S. Allan and B. Zelizer (eds.), *Reporting War: Journalism in Wartime*, Routledge 2004.

68 International Criminal Tribunal for Rwanda (ICTR) Statute.

due to the presence of barbaric practices,[69] which then equates colonialism with an expulsion of the barbaric and harmful. The presence of 'Western' mediated justice after the Rwandan genocide reproduces this similar colonial aspect.[70] If the genocide, with what is described as extreme violence and a high death toll, is a standalone event, then it is unpredictable. This unpredictability encourages a perception that another wave of violence might break out without any pretext, thus maintaining the concept that the genocide is a part of Africa's barbaric climate and further relegates this to an 'African issue'.

Western feminists along with NGOs urged the indictments in the ICTR to include rape and other sexual violence crimes as they did in the ICTY.[71] The ICTR made significant advances in jurisprudence relating to genocide and crimes against humanity in the *Akayesu* case,[72] and many other cases that have contributed to sexual violence jurisprudence.[73] Considering how common sexual violence was during the armed conflict, many feminists and advocates felt that the jurisprudence and prosecution of sexual violence, outside of the *Akayesu* case, was far from adequate.[74] However, Askin noted that judges would often discuss crimes of sexual violence in the judgments of cases that did not include crimes of a sexual nature in the original indictment.[75] MacKinnon encouraged the prosecution of rape even when murder charges were present, due to the frequency of focusing on murder and dropping 'lesser' sexual violence charges.[76] Her work showcased that the ICTR found it difficult to charge men with inciting rape, as they would be charged with acts that other men committed on behalf of their superiors.[77]

This brief review of the work of feminists in the ICTR displays the overarching focus on securing sexual violence jurisprudence. While it is evident that sexual

---

69 See S. Morton, 'Subalternity and Aesthetic Education in the Thought of Gayatri Chakravorty Spivak' (2011) 17 *Parallax* 70; *Sati* referring to traditional Indian widow sacrifice.

70 Critiques around the ICTR, i.e. proximity to the conflict, handling of witnesses, lack of political will. See Makau Mutua's work on the topic, M.W. Mutua, 'A Critique of Rights in Transitional Justice: The African Experience' in G. Ore Aguilar and F. Gomez Isa (eds.), *Rethinking Transitions: Equality and Social Justice in Societies Emerging from Conflict*, Intersentia 2011, pp. 31–45, Buffalo Legal Studies Research Paper No. 2012-032.

71 See J. Halley, 'Rape at Rome: Feminist Interventions in the Criminalization of Sex-Related Violence in Positive International Criminal Law' (2008) 30 *Michigan Journal of International Law* 1.

72 'The Cases – United Nations International Criminal Tribunal for Rwanda' <http://www.unictr.org/Cases/StatusofCases/tabid/204/Default.aspx> accessed 24.09.2015.

73 See *Prosecutor v. Semanza*, Judgment, Appeals Chamber (ICTR-97-20, 20 May 2005); *Prosecutor v. Gacumbitsi*, Judgment, Appeals Chamber (ICTR-01-64, 7 July 2006); *Prosecutor v. Nahimana et al.*, Judgment, Appeals Chamber (ICTR-99-52, 28 November 2007). This work is not dismissing the importance of prosecuting sexual violence crimes and the need to include definitions of sexual violence in international law.

74 Askin, above n. 1, pp. 1007–08.

75 ibid., p. 1013.

76 MacKinnon, above n. 30, p. 104.

77 ibid.

violence was a large part of the genocide, by limiting women's roles in conflict to victims of sexual violence, the ways colonialism, race, ethnicity and gender interplay within the ICTR cannot be adequately addressed. From the lack of initial indictments with sexual violence charges and the seeming lack of will, the ICTR came at a time where there was an increased awareness of sexual violence in armed conflict by Western feminists, coupled with a lack of effort from the international legal community to push women's issues.[78] Bedont and Martinez cite the publicity surrounding the 'mass rapes' in both Yugoslavia and Rwanda as the driving force in the creation of the ICTY and ICTR.[79] While this was a large part of the Tribunals' creation, the concern the international community had over the sexual violence, or mass rapes, did not extend into the interworking of international law at the time, which still remains a product of a patriarchal creation. However, by publicising the violence women endured in both conflicts, the predominant narrative of women's experience was one of sexual violence, at the cost of all other forms of women's participation.

Concepts of race and ethnicity in the ICTR and within the genocide itself entered debates by influencing the perception of the violence, but not as a tool of analysis. The international media effectively 'othered' those involved in the armed conflict and referred to 'ethnic issues', but did not recognise the extent to which this influenced the actions of those involved in the violence. One's ethnicity, although an extremist manifestation, was often the main mode of identification. Therefore, instead of focusing on sexual violence, as something done to women because they are women, there needed to be more work done around the way Hutu and Tutsi extremist ethnicities and military extremism influenced the perception of vulnerability during the conflict. This would have allowed for a reading of the conflict that incorporated both men and women as victims of sexual violence, and both women and men as perpetrators of violence. By limiting the narrative to women as victims, Western feminists centred upon gender as a mode of analysis and thereby ignored the other factors that influenced the conflict. This leads to missed opportunities to gain valuable insights into the ways in which gender intersects with other identities and power structures.

6. PAULINE NYIRAMASUHUKO AS A FEMALE PERPETRATOR

Pauline Nyiramasuhuko was the Minister of Family and Women's Development in the Interim Government of Rwanda at the time up to her indictment

78 This is referencing the current UN Women Peace and Security agenda.

79 B. Bedont and K. Hall Martinez, 'Ending Impunity for Gender Crimes under the International Criminal Court' (1999) 6 *The Brown Journal of World Affairs* 65.

in the ICTR.[80] She was a member of the National Republican Movement for Democracy and Development (MRND) and a political figure in Butare prefecture.[81] Nyiramasuhuko, tried in conjunction with her son Arséne Shalom Ntahobali,[82] used a roadblock, set up near her home, to identify, abduct and kill Tutsis.[83] Nyiramasuhuko encouraged the killing of Tutsis on multiple occasions, and engaged in crimes of a sexual nature by inciting rape.[84]

Nyiramasuhuko was charged with crimes against humanity and genocide, and eventually sentenced to life in prison, which was later reduced to 47 years. Nyiramasuhuko was the first woman to be tried by an international court and was the first woman ever to be indicted and convicted for rape as a crime against humanity.[85] Nyiramasuhuko was considered by Prime Minister Kambanda as one of the 'inner circle' responsible for organising the genocide,[86] and was the main instigator of the genocide in Butare.[87] News reports, writers, scholars, victims, Nyiramasuhuko herself and her family all had a difficult time connecting her actions with her being a woman and a mother, and reports often commented on her contradicting appearance and dress.[88] Writers and scholars expressed shock or pointed to sexist notions in order to explain Nyiramasuhuko's actions.[89] Victims and Nyiramasuhuko's family all signalled to motherhood, as either something that made her crimes worse or as a defence.[90] Nyiramasuhuko said she had no power, no capability and was therefore not guilty.[91] Nyiramasuhuko also cited sexism as the reason she was being prosecuted, because she was an educated woman.[92] Sperling has noted that either Nyiramasuhuko chose to use gender as a means of casting doubt onto her actions, or she believed that women truly did not have the capacity to commit acts that would require a substantial amount of power.[93] Nyiramasuhuko's case is not the only time women were involved in the Rwandan genocide.

---

80 Trial Chamber II of ICTR, Amended Indictment, *Nyiramasuhuko et al.* (ICTR-97-21-I, 1 March 2001) para 4.2.

81 ibid.

82 Ibid para 4.3.

83 Ibid para 6.27.

84 Ibid para 6.30-1, 6.37, 6.53 and 6.56.

85 P. Nyiramasuhuko, 'The Hague Justice Portal' <http://www.haguejusticeportal.net/index.php?id=10482> accessed 24.09.2015.

86 C. Sperling, 'Mother of Atrocities: Pauline Nyirmasuhuko's Role in the Rwandan Genocide' (2005) 33 *Fordham Urban Law Journal* 637, 637.

87 ibid.

88 D. Moshenberg, *The Rwandan Glass Ceiling*, (June 2011), available at <http://africasacountry.com/2011/06/29/when-does-being-a-rwandan-woman-matter/>.

89 Sperling, above n. 86, pp. 651–2.

90 See M. Drumbl, '"She Makes Me Ashamed to Be a Woman": The Genocide Conviction of Pauline Nyiramasuhuko' (2013) 34 *Michigan Journal of International Law* 559.

91 Sperling, above n. 86, pp. 650–1.

92 ibid.

93 ibid., pp. 650–53.

Hogg states that of 'Category 1' genocide suspects, 47 are women.[94] This list includes those in leadership roles in the government, political parties, the military and religious organisations, as well as planners, organisers, instigators and direct perpetrators of genocide and crimes against humanity.[95] Examples of female defendants have been unearthed in the work of Adler, Loyle and Globerman, as well as Hogg's research in Rwanda.[96] Even though many of the participants in their studies are without names, it is evident that the number of women accused of genocide or genocide-related crimes is far higher than the ICTR would suggest. Hogg reported in 2010 that around 2,000 women were still awaiting trial in Rwanda for crimes related to the genocide.[97] What has also been a common occurrence is for those women involved to deny their crimes using gender as a defence. Hogg has also stated that women who were awaiting trial were actively denying their involvement due to the fact they were women.[98] If women are claiming that their gender equals a lack of power even while perpetrating violence, then it is possible that women do not see their gender as their primary mode of identity or associate the ability to participate in the genocide as a form of agency. Analysing Nyiramasuhuko's actions based on gender, highlighting her ability to break through gender ideals of typical 'female' behaviour, only provide part of the context. She only used her gender to deny allegations, or as a facade when holding a ministerial position. Nyiramasuhuko's actions were more closely related to her extremist Hutu ethnicity. Her place as a Hutu in Rwandan society mattered much more, and her ability to perpetrate acts resulted from her ethnicity and position and had little to do with her being a woman. It is possible then that feminists, news outlets and the ICTR did not ask the right questions. Extremist ethnicity, which was a main focus of the conflict itself, needed to become the central tool of analysis. Secondary to this, both feminists and ICL needed to be aware of the different understandings and definitions of terms. Rwandan women have disagreed with the perspective of Western feminists, that women who committed crimes in the Rwandan genocide had power, establishing that definitions of power are not absolute. What it means to be a woman in Rwandan society, and, indeed, an educated woman, may be very different from the perspective of the West.

---

94 N. Hogg, 'Women's Participation in the Rwandan Genocide: Mothers or Monsters' (2010) 92 *International Review of the Red Cross* 69, 90.

95 ibid.

96 See R.N. Adler, C.E. Loyle and J. Globerman, 'A Calamity in the Neighbourhood: Women's Participation in the Rwandan Genocide' (2007) 2 *Genocide Studies and Prevention: An International Journal* 209; also see Hogg's work (above n. 2).

97 Hogg, above n. 94, p. 70.

98 ibid., pp. 89 and 90.

7. CONCLUSION: COMBINING INTERNATIONAL CRIMINAL LAW AND FEMINIST INTERVENTION

After shifting through the situations in the FYR and Rwanda, it is clear that understanding the nuances in armed conflict is essential in order to identify the complexities surrounding female perpetrators. This discussion has shown that while gender roles may influence the way in which women commit genocide, war crimes or crimes against humanity, it does not prevent women from being active participants during armed conflict. When the realities of a situation like the conflict in the FYR and the Rwandan genocide are ignored, namely the perpetration of crimes by women, then the history of the conflict is altered. Incorporating women into peace processes after a conflict, addressing post conflict justice, or providing services to women who engaged in hostilities cannot be achieved by reproducing the idea that women were not involved in perpetrating crimes. This limited mindset reinforces narrow notions of gender, race and ethnicity and prevents reconciliation.

One of the ways in which ICL can utilise the work on female perpetrators is by recognising the international versus local dichotomy. Zarkov discusses the difference between the 'local' and 'international' identity in the FYR. She suggests that although the acts that are associated with the conflict matter, the location of these acts is just as important.[99] The location of the armed conflict justifies the classification of 'local' men as sexual perpetrators and women as victims.[100] 'International' women and men are then signified as non-violent, non-rapists.[101] By using these signifiers to separate the 'local' and 'international', sexual violence in the conflict becomes tied to the 'local'.[102] Sexual violence is then considered to be unique to armed conflict and unique to the 'local', where the treatment of women is harmful. This binary elevates the position of the international and dismisses/essentialises the realities of the domestic. Discussing the international and local also relates to the way the Rwandan genocide was interpreted. The focus of the ICTR on a limited time frame, as well as the genocide's extremely high death toll, encourages the perception of Rwanda and then the whole of Africa as a barbaric, violent society.

The local and international dichotomy links to the Western feminist intervention in both the FYR and Rwanda. Kapur notes that '(t)hus, culture is invoked primarily to explain the different ways in which women experience violence – in the process often reinforcing essentialist understandings of culture

---

99 Zarkov, above n. 43, pp. 10–1.
100 ibid.
101 ibid.
102 ibid.

and representing particular cultures as brutal and barbaric'.[103] In this case the female perpetrator's connection and active engagement with violence is related to a barbaric culture. The brutal nature of both conflicts, especially Rwanda, is tied to the culture of the state. Mohanty's scholarship counters the work done by the Western 'white middle class' feminist, as they have often been criticised for universalising their own experiences and projecting this onto the international community as a whole, as well as universalising 'Third World' women.[104] By projecting Western ideas on to women involved in armed conflict not only is there a presumption that women need to be saved, but that women who have perpetrated crimes have done so due to other uncontrollable factors at play, which deny their agency.

Kapur also discusses the interplay between Western feminism and postcolonial feminism, and cites the international women's rights movement as strengthening female victimisation rhetoric through a focus on violence against women.[105] Kapur notes that the discussion of 'metanarratives' around women as victims has equated all women with the same experience of sexual violence and objectification.[106] This was seen with the Western feminist work in the ICTY, which promoted a singular narrative about women as rape victims, as well as the international/local binary, where all women are victims and local men perpetrators. Kapur has critiqued MacKinnon's work for essentialising women and gender, assuming gender is the basis of women's oppression and that women must 'prioritise issues of sexuality and sexual violence'.[107]

Engaging in discussions around female perpetrators often brings up questions about the larger aims of this work. The critique of sexual violence jurisprudence does not dismiss its importance or suggest that fewer cases of sexual violence should be prosecuted. Drawing out the actions of female perpetrators does not necessarily advocate a push to put more females on trial. However, looking at the instances of female perpetrators not only illuminates the gaps in ICL and feminist intervention, but also highlights what questions are asked about a conflict. Gender binaries and the acts traditionally associated with gendered roles were reinforced in and around the Tribunals. It has also been argued that the gender binaries permeate feminist intervention as well.

On one level, this chapter recognises the nuances of women's humanness instead of adding to the stereotypes around women and men. By limiting the view of women's roles in conflict to victims of sexual violence, the ways in

103 See R. Kapur, 'The Tragedy of the Victimization Rhetoric: Resurrecting The "Native" Subject in International/Post-Colonial Feminist Legal Politics' (2002) 1 *Harvard Human Rights Journal* 10.

104 C. Talpade Mohanty, *Feminism Without Borders*, Duke University Press 2003 17–43.

105 Kapur, above n. 103, p. 5.

106 ibid., p. 10.

107 ibid., p. 9.

which ethnicity, race and gender interplay within the ICTY and ICTR cannot be adequately addressed. On a local scale, the importance of acknowledging female perpetrators in the ICTY and ICTR contributes positively to post conflict justice aims. ICL is aided by introducing further complexity into the legal system through local justice processes. Internationally, the benefit of confirming that women in fact commit crimes during armed conflict pushes towards a realisation of women as human beings.

FEMALE WAR CRIME PERPETRATORS IN BOSNIA AND HERZEGOVINA

Alette Smeulers and Olivera Simić

People who know her would never believe this.[1]

1. INTRODUCTION

Most of the literature on women and warfare, or women and genocide, analyses women's role from a victim-centred perspective. Although research has shown that most perpetrators are men, women too have been involved in the perpetration of war crimes.[2] Yet research and literature on the role of women as war criminals

---

1 H. Jung, 'Family, Friends Weep as Magistrate Refuses to Release Beaverton Woman Accused for Bosnian War Crimes' *The Oregonian*, 15.04.2011 <http://www.oregonlive.com/beaverton/index.ssf/2011/04/family_friends_weep_as_magistate_refuses_to_release_beaverton_woman_accused_of_bosnian_warm_crimes.html> accessed 07.08.2015.

2 See among others A. Smeulers, 'Female Perpetrators: Ordinary or Extra-ordinary Women' (2015) 15 *International Criminal Law Review* 205–51. It also shows in the convictions of Biljana Plavšić, vice president under Karadžić of the Republika Srpska by the ICTY and Pauline Nyiramasuhuko, the former national Minister of Family and Women's Affairs in Rwanda, sentenced to life in prison by the ICTR in 2011 for her role in instigating the Rwandan genocide, the first and only woman to be tried by the ICTR; Ieng Thiery, who had

and enablers of genocide remain staggeringly meagre, especially compared with the weight of research preoccupied with women as victims of violence rather than its agent. The existing scholarship on women perpetrators or active supporters of violent regimes is largely focused on the role of women in Nazi Germany[3] or, more recently, women who committed acts of genocide in Rwanda.[4] However, as the evidence suggests, women, in much larger numbers than usually presumed, can become active agents of genocide and torture – and their role and motivations therefore demand greater attention. Sjoberg and Gentry propose that women today are continuously being idolised as pristine and pure objects incapable of mass murder and genocidal behaviour.[5] They argue that convicted female perpetrators, instead of becoming a representation of female capabilities in the perpetration of genocide, tend to be stripped of agency, with the severity of their actions reduced to pure happenstance, or the result of male manipulation or previous abuse. Alternatively, these women are characterised as mentally disturbed, or wicked, with a deviant sexual appetite. Sjoberg and Gentry call this the mother/monster/whore narrative.[6] In short their argument is that, female perpetrators are generally not perceived as being real women.

Although Bosnia and Herzegovina (BiH) became notorious for war crimes committed primarily against women, this chapter will explore the role of women in BiH as perpetrators during the armed conflict of the 1990s, in order

---

been charged by the ECCC for her role during the genocidal Khmer Rouge regime lead by Pol Pot in Cambodia 1975–1979; and Simone Gbagbo, wife of the former president of Cote D'Ivoire, the first and only indicted woman before the International Criminal Court (ICC) for crimes against humanity, including murder and rape. M. Drumbl, '"She Makes Me Ashamed to Be a Woman": The Genocide Conviction of Pauline Nyiramasuhuko, 2011' (2013) 34 *Melbourne Journal of International Law* 559; N. Hogg and M. Drumbl, 'Women as Perpetrators: Agency and Authority in Genocidal Rwanda' in A. Randall (ed.), *Genocide and Gender in the Twentieth Century: A Comparative Study*, Bloomsbury 2015.

3 See, e.g., C. Koonz, *Mothers in the Fatherland: Women, the Family and Nazi Politics*, St Martin's Press 1987; K. Passmore (ed.), *Women, Gender and Fascism in Europe: 1919–45*, Manchester University Press 2003; K. Kompisch, *Täterinnen: Frauen im Nationalsozialismus*, Böhlau Verlag, Cologne 2008, pp. 204; W. Lower, *Hitlers Furiën*, Spectrum 2013.

4 L. Sharlach, 'Gender and Genocide in Rwanda: Women as Agents and Objects of Genocide' (1999) 1 *Journal of Genocide Research* 387–99; R.N. Adler, C.E. Loyle and J. Globerman, 'A Calamity in the Neighbourhood: Women's Participation in the Rwandan Genocide' (2007) 2 *Genocide Studies and Prevention* 209–34; African Rights, *Rwanda, Not So Innocent: When Women Become Killers*, African Rights 1995.

5 L. Sjoberg and C.E. Gentry, *Mothers, Monsters, Whores: Women's Violence in Global Politics*, Zed Books 2007.

6 'The mother narrative describes women's violence as a need to belong, a need to nurture, and a way of taking care of and being loyal to men: motherhood gone awry. The monster narrative eliminates rational behaviour, ideological motivation, and culpability from women engaged in political violence. Instead, they describe violent women as insane, in denial of their femininity, no longer women or human. The whore narrative blames violence on the evils of female sexuality at its most intense or its most vulnerable', Sjoberg and Gentry, above n. 5, p. 13.

to get a better insight in the agency of women who commit such crimes. Apart from Biljana Plavšić, the former co-President of the Bosnian Serb leadership whose case has received international publicity (as the first and only woman tried before the International Criminal Tribunal for the former Yugoslavia (ICTY)), so far there has been little scholarly interest in female perpetrators of war crimes. Yet, over the past few years, several women have been charged with committing war crimes before the Bosnian domestic courts. This chapter will draw on cases of women accused of war crimes in BiH whose stories have become public, such as Monika Karan-Ilić and Rasema Handanović. The chapter will explore the crimes for which these women were prosecuted, the ways they were portrayed by the press, and the arguments women used in their defence. It will also assess the extent to which these women fit the mother/monster/whore narrative as described above. Are these women indeed disturbed sadists, or were they entirely controlled and manipulated by powerful men in their environment, or are these women just ordinary women in extraordinary circumstances, not much different from their male counterparts?

The following section (section 2) will explore the role of women in the BiH war. The role of women who have been accused of committing war crimes will then be described (section 3) and analysed (section 4). Section 5 concludes the chapter. The core of the chapter is based on extensive research of the literature on female perpetrators and a systematic analysis of the cases of female perpetrators mentioned in the English version of the daily newsletter *Balkan Transitional Justice* issued by the Balkan Investigative Reporting Network (BIRN), which is an authoritative news agency bringing the latest stories from the Balkans on war crimes and other transitional justice related topics. The research also relied on the BIRN Justice reports which has a number of useful databases on people, cases, cities, courts and topics related to the prosecution of war crimes. This database was searched for female perpetrators by reading through the file reports.

In addition, two senior journalists with BIRN based in Sarajevo were interviewed. Both journalists have been following and reporting on war crime trials for the past decade and are valuable source of insider perspectives on court cases, including cases against female perpetrators. The aim of the interviews was to gain better insight in the cases written about in the reports and to ask some additional questions. The interviews were conducted by the second author, Olivera Simić, during a field trip to BiH in June 2015. Due to the sensitivity of the topic, both journalists wished to remain anonymous and will therefore be referred to in this text as X and Y.

2. FEMALE COMBATANTS IN THE BiH WAR

War generally affects the entire population: men and women. Yet within the portrayal of war, men are usually portrayed as the aggressors and perpetrators, and women as their helpless victims. The stories of women in BiH who were victims of mass rape set a precedent in legal history. Due to the international attention surrounding the widespread and systematic reports of rape in BiH, rape was prosecuted as a war crime before the ICTY for the first time.[7] Due to the large-scale sexual violence and the extraordinary attention[8] focused on this violence, both internationally and domestically, Bosnian women have become stereotyped as rape victims.[9] This preoccupation with the rape of women[10] reinforces the identification of 'the rape victim' that frames females as (uniquely) vulnerable and 'rapable'.[11]

Although women suffered from grave violations of human rights, in particular sexual abuse, this portrayal is not adequate and neglects both the suffering and victimisation of men, as well as the active role played by (some) women. It also neglects other roles of women as activists, peace builders[12] and civil resistants,[13] and also as bystanders or supporters of their husbands and sons,[14] or political elites,[15] in a war effort. The most prominent players within an armed conflict are the political leaders of the warring parties. Biljana Plavšić was one of the very few women within the political leadership of one of the main warring parties in the Yugoslavian conflict.[16] Her story will not be considered

7 *The Prosecutor v. Tadic* (Judgment) ICTY IT-94-1-T (7 May 1997). Tadic was convicted for, among other things, sexual violence which was qualified as a war crime and a crime against humanity.

8 I. Skjelsbæk, 'Victim and Survivor: Narrated Social Identities of Women Who Experienced Rape During the War in Bosnia Herzegovina' (2006) 16 *Feminism & Psychology* 373–403.

9 See O. Simić, 'Challenging Bosnian Women's Identity as Rape Victims, as Unending Victims: The "Other" Sex in Times of War' (2012) 13(4) *Journal of International Women's Studies* 129–42.

10 E. Helms, *Innocence and Victimhood: Gender, Nation, and Women's Activism in Postwar Bosnia-Herzegovina*, University of Wisconsin Press 2013, p. 64.

11 D. Žarkov, 'War Rapes in Bosnia: On Masculinity, Femininity and Power of the Rape Victim Identity' (1997) 39(2) *Tijdschrift voor Criminologie* 140–51.

12 Z. Šiljak, *Shining Humanity: Life Stories of Women Peacebuilders in Bosnia and Herzegovina*, Cambridge Scholars Publishing 2014.

13 See C. Mann, *Kucne Amazonke: Amazons of the Home, The Resistance of Women During the Siege of Sarajevo*, Svjetlost 2006.

14 See D. Žarkov, *The Body of War: Media, Ethnicity, and Gender in the Break-up of Yugoslavia*, Duke University Press 2007.

15 90 per cent of women of what became Nazi Germany voted for Hitler as chancellor in 1933: C. Mann, 'Women in War' (*Speech at AAUW Educational Foundation Symposium 2002*, 16.11.2002) <http://www.femaid.org/women_war.pdf> accessed 7.08.2015. Lilly and Irvine argue that more women than men in 1994 in both Serbia and Croatia supported the nationalist ruling parties: C.S. Lilly and J.A. Irvine, 'Negotiating Interests: Women and Nationalism in Serbia and Croatia, 1990–1997' (2002) 16 *East European Politics and Societies* 109–44.

16 In 1992, when the Serbian Republic of Bosnia Herzegovina became independent under the name of Republika Srpska, and Radovan Karadžić became its first president, Plavšić became one of the two acting vice presidents. She was tried at the ICTY: *Prosecutor v. Biljana Plavšić*, ICTY 27 February 2003, Case no: IT-00-39&40/1-S.

here as her role has been commented on in Valerie Vojdik's chapter in this book and elsewhere.[17]

Most hands-on perpetrators were members of militarised units such as the regular armies, or police forces, or one of the many paramilitary forces that operated during the war. Although most members of these militarised groups were men, women too were drafted into the groups.[18] Women operated in units alongside men, but there were also several all-female units. Some of these units were implicated in war crimes, and this included all parties to the conflict: Serbs, Croats and Bosnians.[19]

There is no official data available on the total number of combatants in the BiH war 1992–1995. According to unofficial data received from the representative of the government institution in Republika Srpska, there were 430,000 participants in the armed conflict in total: around 120,000 in the Army of BiH, 50,000 Croatian Armed Forces and 95,000 in the Serb Army.[20] Out of these 95,000, according to data from the Ministry of Labour, War Veterans and Disabled Persons' Protection Republika Srpska, there were 7,068 or 7,44% women 'participants' in war. Out of this number, 3,303 were Serb women, 3,756 were not identified according to their ethnicity, there was one Slovene, two Croats, five Bosniaks and one 'undeclared' woman.[21] It has been calculated that 5,360 women were recruited and deployed to various duties in the Army of BiH.[22] The fact that women were in combat is not so surprising, since the former Yugoslavia has a history of female mobilisation in war, in particular the Second World War.[23] It thus seems logical that many women were involved in this war as well.

However, it is unknown how many women were actual combatants and fighters in the 1990s conflict, and how many merely provided support as cooks

17 See, e.g., Smeulers, above n. 2; J. Subotić, 'The Cruelty of False Remorse: Biljana Plavšić at The Hague' (2012) 36 *Southeastern Europe* 39–59; N.A. Combs, 'International Decisions: Prosecutor v Plavšić' (2003) 97 *American Journal of International Law* 292–937; P. Chifflet and G. Boas, 'Sentencing Coherence in International Criminal Law: The Cases of Biljana Plavšić and Miroslav Bralo' (2012) 23 *Criminal Law Forum* 135–59.

18 See F. Wilmer, *The Social Construction of Man, the State and War: Identity, Conflict and Violence in the Former Yugoslavia*, Routledge 2002, p. 215.

19 J.P. Kaufman and K.P. Williams, *Women, the State, and War: A Comparative Perspective on Citizenship and Nationalism*, Lexington Books 2007, p. 92.

20 Statement by senior representative of the government (Personal email correspondence with Simić 19.09.2015). The representative wanted to remain anonymous.

21 Statements by Ministry official representatives (Personal email correspondence with Simić 25.02.2015).

22 A. Omanić *et al.*, 'Participation of Women in War in Bosnia and Herzegovina from 1992 to 1995' (2009) 21 *Materia Socio Medica* 175–78. Only 13 received the 'Zlatni Ljiljan' (Golden Lily) medal as war heroes: A. Aganović and Z. Delić, 'The Nineties: The War and Post War period in Bosnia and Herzegovina' <https://www.gwi-boell.de/sites/default/files/uploads/2015/03/part_iv_the_ninties.pdf> accessed 09.08.2018.

23 See J. Batinić, *Women and Yugoslav Partisans: A History of World War II Resistance*, Cambridge University Press 2015.

or nurses, or served in other support service roles. In many countries women who serve in the army are given supporting roles away from the battlefield but this is slowly and gradually changing, especially in countries which are engaged in war as women become more and more involved in the actual fighting. To many outsiders, seeing a woman on the battlefield is, however, still a curiosity. While conscription was legally prescribed for males over 18 years, women were not legally obliged to serve in the military or be drafted into war. There has been scant research into women combatants in BiH or their motives for joining the army. According to Hadžiahmić and Dautbegović, women who voluntarily joined the Bosnian Army had a variety of motives, including feelings of personal and moral responsibility to protect their community from attack, to protect their lives, to join their husbands or for the love for their homeland.[24] Some other women joined after their sons were either killed or drafted.[25]

During the war, women who had trained as nurses were drafted into the army, and were sent to the front lines where a number of them died. Other women were not compelled to join the army by draft, although they were readily accepted as volunteers, and were also publically invited to join the ranks.[26] However, women were formally drafted into the civilian protection sector, and were expected to take care of their local communities and undertake humanitarian work. There is scant information on the experiences of any of these women. No official data was maintained, and only a few scattered references or stories about them can be found within local media or grassroots articles.[27] Today in BiH, there are no organisations or local associations that focus on former combatants who are female. Many women who participated in war feel forgotten and not valued for their contributions.[28] Women soldiers have been marginalised and their needs seem to have been neglected by institutions, the community and non-governmental organisations (NGOs).[29]

---

24 L. Hadžiahmić, 'Women-Combatants in Defense of Sarajevo: Agents or Victims' (2011) 6(19) *Western Balkans Security Observer* 36–45; S. Dautbegović-Bošnjaković, 'Zaboravljena Dimenzija Ratu u BiH – Vojnikinje' in D. Arsenijević and T. Flessenkamper, *Kojeg Je Roda Sigurnost?*, Sarajevski Otvoreni Centar 2013, pp. 79–98.

25 Halida Bojadži joined to the Army of BiH after her two sons aged 13 and 15 were killed at the beginning of the war. Halida spent the entire war in ranks serving as a cook and laundress. See A. Omanić *et al*, 'Participation of Women in the 1992–1995 War in Bosnia and Herzegovina' (2010) 8 *Acta Medico-Historica Adriatica* 135–44, 138.

26 Hadžiahmić, above n. 24.

27 See O. Simić, *Surviving Peace*, Spinifex 2014.

28 A. Omanić et al, 'Participation of women in the 1992–1995 war in Bosnia and Herzegovina', <https://hrcak.srce.hr/file/93064>, accessed 13 July 2017.

29 There is no women's NGO which either gathers or works with former women combatants in order to promote their rights and specific needs: A. Aganović and Z. Delić, 'The War and Post-War Period in Bosnia and Herzegovina: This Was Not Our War' in J. Čaušević (ed.), *Women Documented: Women and Public Life in Bosnia and Herzegovina in the 20th Century*, Sarajevski Otvoreni Centar 2014, p. 121.

According to Dautbegović, female ex-combatants often live in extremely poor socio-economic conditions, on the edge of survival and forgotten.[30] Dautbegović recently observed that while these women joined the war with enthusiasm and patriotism, all of her interviewees communicated that they would never again fight in a war as they did in the early 1990s, because they now feel disappointed, neglected, betrayed and forgotten by the state.[31] While women combatants were praised at the beginning of the war for their bravery and commitment, as soon as the war ended, they were forced to go back to their traditional gender roles and re-occupy their full-time positions as housewives and mothers.[32] As one of the female ex-combatants stated, once they were demobilised after the war 'they continued their lives right there where they were in 1992' before they joined the army.[33]

Around 30 women combatants within the Army of BiH established the Association of Women-Combatants from the Sarajevo area in October 1994, while war was still raging, with the aim of voicing some of their concerns and needs. However these women did not receive support from the top leadership of the army, nor from the government, so they ceased operation in 1998 with some 200 women registered.[34]

Due to the lack of interest in female combatants, only a handful of their experiences have been documented so far. The data that is available concerns women in the Army of BiH, but not in Republika Srpska.[35] Despite the lack of information, it is a well-known fact that women participated in the regular fighting alongside men and thus could easily have become involved in the crimes committed by their group. Apart from Plavšić, who was a high-ranking political leader and the only woman to have been prosecuted by the ICTY, not one of the lower-ranking women was indicted and prosecuted by the ICTY. Next to the 160 men, the percentage of females prosecuted on the international level is thus less than 1 per cent. The percentage of women charged nationally is also low but slightly higher than on the international level: between 4–6 per cent.

---

30 S. Dautbegović, 'Socio-Ekonomski Položaj ena Boraca u Proslom Ratu u Bosni I Hercegovini' ('Socio-Economic Situation of Women Combatants in Post-War Bosnia and Herzegovina'), unpublished MA thesis, University of Sarajevo 2011.

31 M. Šoštarić, 'War Victims and Gender-Sensitive Truth, Justice, Reparations and Non-Recurrence in Bosnia and Herzegovina' *Impunity Watch Research Report 2012*, p. 23 <http://www.impunitywatch.org/docs/Gender_Research_Report_BiH_English.pdf> accessed 09.08.2015.

32 Dautbegović-Bošnjaković, above n. 24, p. 90.

33 ibid., p. 91.

34 Hadžiahmić, above n. 24, p. 43.

35 There is only one monograph published in the Bosnian language that is concerned with women war criminals: A. Krupić, *Žene Ratni Zločinci*, Dobra Knjiga 2010. The book discusses only Serb women war criminals.

According to some reports at least 30 women were indicted at the domestic level,[36] compared to over 500 men.[37] Out of 68 people prosecuted before the Court of BiH, only three were women, as noted by one of the journalists interviewed.

> There are other women under investigation and women tend to be mentioned in connection with other crimes and cases. So, it is now well established that we are not talking about one or two women but more ... It is not something that should be ignored and at the moment we have four cases before the Court of BiH.[38]

These figures show most perpetrators were men but that women were also involved.

3. FEMALE WAR CRIMINALS

The following subsections will analyse a few cases in which female perpetrators were indicted. In the first subsection (section 3.1), four women who have been convicted for particularly vicious, brutal and cruel crimes will be discussed. The second subsection (section 3.2) will focus on two women who were involved in crimes that were seemingly perpetrated to avenge earlier crimes. The third subsection (section 3.3) will focus on a number of women who were accused of terrible crimes but who have persistently maintained their innocence, insisting they are victims of mistaken identity. The eight cases discussed are the publically known cases which have been documented in the newsletters issued by BIRN and the database compiled by BIRN. It is not entirely clear whether these are indeed all the cases tried so far, or only a few of them, nor do we know how these cases were selected by BIRN. However, on reading the stories these cases seem to be fairly representative of the roles played by female perpetrators, taken the fairly consistent stories which follow from them.

3.1. VICIOUS CRIMES – VICIOUS WOMEN?

In 2011, Albina Terzić, nicknamed Nina, was the first woman charged with war crimes by the Court of BiH.[39] She was a member of the Military Police of the

36 Ž. Kovačević, 'BiH: I Žene Činile Ratne Zločine u BiH' (2011) *Slobodna Evropa* <http://www.slobodnaevropa.org/content/bih_i_zene_su_cinile_ratne_zlocine/9504408.html> accessed 11.08.2015.

37 See Balkan Transitional Justice, 07.10.2015.

38 Interview with BIRN journalist.

39 For an overview of articles on the case, see 'Case: Terzic Albina' *BIRN Justice Reports* <http://www.justice-report.com/en/cases/terzic-albina-news-analysis-and-opinion> accessed 11.08.2015. The information in this section relating to this case is drawn from these

Croat Defence Council (HVO) and was charged with crimes against Bosnian Serb civilians illegally detained in the northern Bosnian town of Odžak in 1992. Terzić was alleged to have committed the crimes when she was in her early twenties. She was accused of sexual violence, including forcing detainees into having sexual intercourse. Terzić pleaded not guilty. According to witness testimony, she allegedly made the prisoners sing, laughed while prisoners were beaten up, threatened to make her dog attack them and 'bite their genitals off', and forced one prisoner to rape another. On 19 October 2012, she was found guilty by the Court of BiH and sentenced to five years' imprisonment. She was acquitted of forcing a prisoner to have intercourse with a mentally ill female prisoner.[40] The court concluded that they had no doubt that the events took place, but could not prove beyond reasonable doubt what the role of Terzić had been.

The Office of the Prosecutor noted in a statement on its website that it considered the sentence 'inadequate and too lenient'. It argued that: '[the court had] not properly weighed the circumstances which affect the gravity of the sentence' and therefore appealed the decision.[41]

Despite the fact that the court on appeal found that: 'she beat prisoners, set dogs on them, and tortured, abused and humiliated them in various other ways', her sentence was reduced to three years' imprisonment on appeal.[42] Mitigating circumstances that were taken into account were that she was young, had no criminal record and also concluded, remarkably, that her 'acts were not that severe'.[43]

Monika Karan-Ilić (born Simonović) is probably the most famous female perpetrator in Bosnia Herzegovina.[44] She was not a member of a militarised unit, but was the sister of the camp commander Konstantin Simonović at Brčko, who had been sentenced to six years' imprisonment by local courts before

articles. See full judgment: Predmet Tužilaštva Bosne i Hercegovine protiv Albine Terzić, No S1 1K005665 13 Krž 2, Judgment, 5 July 2013.

40 'Albina Terzic Sentenced to Five Years in Prison' *BIRN Justice Reports*, 19.10.2012 <http://www.justice-report.com/en/articles/albina-terzic-sentenced-to-five-years-in-prison> accessed 11.08.2015.

41 See 'News' *Office of the Prosecutor in BiH* (verdict rendered on Albina Terzec appealed, 4 January 2013) <http://www.tuzilastvobih.gov.ba/index.php?id=1683&jezik=e> accessed 12.08.2015.

42 S. Ucanbarlic, 'Female Bosnian War Criminal's Sentence Cut' *BIRN Justice Reports*, 26.09.2013 <http://www.justice-report.com/en/articles/female-bosnian-war-criminal-s-sentence-cut> accessed 11.08.2015.

43 A. Jahić, 'Iznesene Žalbe Na Presudu Albini Terzić' *BIRN Justice Reports*, 05.7.2013 <http://www.justice-report.com/bh/sadr%C5%BEaj-%C4%8Dlanci/iznesene-%C5%BEalbe-na-presudu-albini-terzi%C4%87> accessed 11.08.2015.

44 For an overview of articles on the case, see 'Case: Karan-Ilić Monika' *BIRN Justice Reports* <http://www.justice-report.com/en/cases/karan-ilic-monika-news-analysis-and-opinion> accessed 28.08.2015.

Monika herself was indicted. Her infamy was not due to her brother, however, but because she was the girlfriend of Goran Jelisić, who was sentenced by the ICTY to 40 years' imprisonment.[45] In both the testimonies and judgment at the ICTY she was mentioned as having participated in the abuse committed by Jelisić.[46] It was alleged that she spurred him on to commit further crimes and that Jelisić was eager to impress her with his violent and aggressive behaviour.[47]

Monika Karan-Ilić was arrested in December 2011 under suspicion that she had committed war crimes against Bosniaks and Croats in the Luka prison camp in Brčko. She was charged with torture, inhumane treatment, and both physical and mental abuse of prisoners from May to July 1992. She faced trial before the elementary court of Brčko.

Monika Karan-Illić was only 16 years old when she was involved in the atrocities. One of the inmates of Luka prison testified at her trial, stating:

> She did things no one would have at that age. She was a little girl with only a woman's name. She was not a woman, she was a monster. There aren't many people like that. Was she born like that or was she taught, or did she do all that unknowingly?[48]

According to witnesses, she cursed prisoners, spurred her boyfriend to hit them, stole from them, and cut some prisoners with a knife and ordered others to lick the blood off the knife. One witness testified that she poured a liquid over his wounds after he had been beaten up the day before, leaving him in excruciating pain.[49] Karan-Ilić without doubt committed terrible crimes, and in the media she was portrayed as a female monster.[50] She is the female war criminal who has arguably received the most attention by the media due to her age, relationship with Jelisić, and the nature of the acts she committed. 'Woman monster' was the usual headline in the media at the time of her trial. According to journalist X during his interview, this 'was too dark and I think too sensational and too satanistic'.[51]

---

45 *Prosecutor v. Goran Jelisić*, ICTY IT-95-10-A (5 July 2001).

46 See *Prosecutor v. Goran Jelisić* (Judgment) ICTY IT-95-10-T (14 December 1999).

47 The Trial Chamber notes that the presence of a woman at Goran Jelisić's side also seems to have encouraged him to commit certain murders in order to impress the young woman. See *Prosecutor v. Goran Jelisić*, above n. 46, s 105, fn. 163.

48 See Justice Report, 'Monika Simonović Arrested on War Crimes Charges' *Balkan Transitional Justice Reports*, 22.12.2011 <http://www.balkaninsight.com/en/article/local-judiciary-in-brcko-interrogation-of-monika-simonovic-s-soon> accessed 05.08.2015.

49 See 'Local Justice – Brčko: Pouring Acid Over Wounds' *BIRN Justice Reports*, 04.09.2012 <http://www.justice-report.com/en/articles/local-justice-brcko-pouring-acid-over-wounds> accessed 05.08.2015.

50 See Cerkez, 'Bosnia Police Detain Female War Crime Suspect' *USA Today*, 21.12.2011 <http://usatoday30.usatoday.com/news/world/story/2011-12-21/bosnia-woman-war-crimes/52138606/1> accessed 05.08.2015.

51 Interview with X in Sarajevo (June 2015).

At the trial, Karan-Ilić pled not guilty, and blamed her behaviour on Jelisić. Witnesses testified that Monika had been abused and mistreated by him and that he had threatened her. Her father also seemed to blame Jelisić and testified: 'I still cannot believe that Monika committed the things charged upon her, because she had never demonstrated animosity towards any persons of different ethnicity before the war'.[52] During the closing statements of the trial Monika stated that she suffered under Jelisić's tyranny: 'I am Jelisić's war trophy, a sexual object with a damaged mind, a victim, a Croat mother's child who was forced to come to the Luka camp with him two or three times'.[53] Despite her plea of being a victim rather than a perpetrator, Monika Karan-Ilić was sentenced to four years by the court. The Appeals Chamber found that two charges, one related to sexual abuse and one in which she allegedly had burned a prisoner with cigarette butts, had not been proven and reduced the sentence to two-and-a-half years.

Two other women, Bora Kuburić and Radmila Banjac, who were members of the women's front of the Bosnian Serb Army's Petrovac Brigade, were accused of torturing and humiliating a wounded Bosniak nurse, who was a member of the Bosnian Army, in 1992.[54] Initially the two accused entered into negotiations for a plea bargain, but they finally decided not to proceed with this and instead pled not guilty. The commander of the unit, Rada Tomić, was described by one of the witnesses at trial as a 'notorious and dangerous woman'[55] who had ordered the victim to strip naked and crawl on the floor before she was sexually abused with branches.

Đukić, who eventually shot the nurse, testified at the trial and described the torment the victim had to go through: 'They forced her to eat animal faeces, to sing Serbian songs, and to dig her own grave. She was totally naked. Bora Kuburić cut her ear, so she started bleeding heavily, while Radmila cut her hair off'.[56] Radmila Banjac, claimed that she was not responsible and that this was a case of mistaken identity, while Kuburić admitted that she had cut off the victim's ear but stated that she was ordered to do so:

> Rada was a dangerous woman and we were all afraid of her. When the prisoner was handed to us, we were ordered to beat her. There were many of us. I hit her with a

---

52 See M.A., 'Local Justice – Ilić: Upset and Scared' *BIRN Justice Reports*, 16.10.2012 <http://www.justice-report.com/en/articles/local-justice-ilic-upset-and-scared> accessed 28.08.2015.

53 M. Arnautovic, 'Bosnia Woman Accused of Jail Torture Awaits Verdict' *BIRN Justice Reports*, 14.05.2013 <http://www.justice-report.com/en/articles/bosnia-woman-accused-of-jail-torture-awaits-verdict> accessed 11.08.2015.

54 For an overview of the articles on their trial, see 'Case: Kuburić and Banjac' *BIRN Justice Reports* <http://www.justice-report.com/en/cases/kuburic-and-banjac-news-analysis-and-opinion> accessed 28.08.2015.

55 D. Duraković, 'Witnesses Describe Torture and Murder of Bosniak Army Nurse in Veliki Radic' *BIRN Justice Reports*, 17.02.2015 <http://www.justice-report.com/en/articles/witnesses-describe-torture-and-murder-of-bosniak-army-nurse-in-veliki-radic> accessed 28.08.2015.

56 ibid.

> stick and cut her ear. As soon as I could, I ran to the school. I later heard that Đukić killed her.[57]

The judges however did not accept the defendants' defence and found both of them guilty. The cruel and humiliating nature of the crimes was considered an aggravating circumstance, but their young age and the fact that they both had families were considered mitigating circumstances. Other mitigating circumstances that were taken into account were that Kuburić had confessed and showed remorse and that Banjac suffered from bad health. Both women were sentenced to four years' imprisonment on 25 February 2015 by the court in Bihać.

3.2. THE AVENGERS

> … anything she done, it was army related. I don't think she's guilty of anything but being a human being.[58]

Probably the best documented case concerning a female perpetrator in former Yugoslavia was that against Rasema Handanović.[59] On 30 April 2012, she was the first female soldier convicted of war crimes in BiH. She was a member of a special unit of the Bosnian Army, and was charged with participation in an attack on a village and the execution-style killings of captured civilians on 16 April 1993. Handanović, who was known during the war as 'Zolja' (meaning wasp), was about 21 years old at the time of the killings. According to the verdict, the attack was well prepared and well planned. Nihad Bojadžić who was the commanding officer and had ordered the attack, told his subordinates, including Handanović, 'that there must be no survivors in the village.' During the killing, 22 people, 18 civilians and 4 prisoners of war, who had surrendered, were killed.

Before Handanović could be tried in Bosnia, she had to be extradited from the United States (US) as she had moved there and had gained US citizenship

---

57 D. Duraković, 'Verdict for Torture and Murder of Bosniak Army Nurse Expected on Thursday' *BIRN Justice Reports*, 24.02.2015 <http://www.justice-report.com/en/articles/verdict-for-torture-and-murder-of-bosnian-army-nurse-expected-on-thursday> accessed 28.08.2015.

58 Comments from the family with whom Hadanović was living in the USA on news that she was arrested for war crimes in BiH. See M. Gay, 'Dark Past in Balkan War Intrudes on New Life' *The New York Times*, 03.04.2011 <http://www.nytimes.com/2011/04/04/us/04hide.html?_r=0> accessed 16.08.2015.

59 For an overview of articles on the case, see 'Case: Handanović Rasema' *BIRN Justice Reports*, 28.12.2011 <http://www.justice-report.com/en/cases/handanovic-rasema-news-analysis-and-opinion> accessed 16.08.2015.

in 2002.[60] In the US, she had lived peacefully as a single mother with her 11-year-old son until BiH requested her extradition in 2011. According to media reports, she 'screamed and wailed about her handcuffs' during the first extradition hearing, but was more composed during the second hearing, while the magistrate qualified her as 'truly a danger to the community, both here in the United States and abroad in Bosnia'.[61] During the extradition hearing it was stated that she had been suffering from a post-traumatic stress disorder and had been under medical treatment since 2009, but the US district attorney dismissed this defence, stating that she had brought the suffering upon herself by harming others (rather than by others hurting her).[62] Extradition was granted and effected in December 2011.

At the beginning of the trial, she pleaded guilty, declaring: 'I committed a crime, but at the time I did not know that it was a crime'.[63] She also expressed remorse:

> Once more, I would like to express my deep regrets for everything I did ... I am sorry for having attended the execution. I convey my deepest condolences to those whom I harmed. I committed a crime and I want to complete this and serve my sentence as soon as possible.[64]

She pleaded guilty to the killing of six people, but denied involvement in the shooting of an older couple, who she claimed were shot by Edin Džeko, one of the other members of the unit.[65] At her trial she also shed some light on her reasons and motivations for becoming an active participant in the war. She explained that before joining the war she was gang-raped by Serb soldiers while her 'partner and several family members were killed', and that it was this event that 'turned me into a war criminal'.[66]

60 For the extradition request, see *In the Matter of the Extradition of Rasema Handanovic*, Case No 11-MC-9097, 829 F Supp 2d 979 (D Or, 2011) <http://media.oregonlive.com/beaverton_news/other/Memo%20of%20Law%20Detenton.pdf> accessed 16.08.2015.

61 Jung, above n. 1.

62 ibid.

63 'First Woman Convicted of Bosnia War Crimes' *Herald Sun*, 01.05.2012 <http://www.heraldsun.com.au/news/law-order/first-woman-convicted-of-bosnia-war-crimes/story-fnat7jnn-1226343394096> accessed 20.08.2015.

64 See G. Mezzofiore, 'Bosnian Muslim Rasema Handanovic: Gang Rape Turned Me into War Criminal' *International Business Times*, 30.04.2012 <http://www.ibtimes.co.uk/bosnia-rasema-handanovic-croats-conflicts-war-crimes-335119> accessed 20.08.2015.

65 A. Jahić, 'Someone Opened Fire from a Group' *BIRN Justice Reports*, 21.01.2014 <http://www.justice-report.com/en/articles/someone-opened-fire-from-a-group> accessed 20.08.2015.

66 A. Salter, 'First Female Soldier Convicted of War Crimes in Bosnia' *International Business Times*, 30.04.2012 <http://www.ibtimes.co.uk/first-female-soldier-convicted-of-war-crimes-in-bosnia-333> accessed 21.08.2015; 'First Woman Convicted of Bosnia War Crimes', above n. 63.

On 30 April 2012, Handanović was convicted of war crimes in BiH and sentenced to five-and-a-half years before the War Chambers in Sarajevo.[67] The judges noted that her sentence had taken into account that she was still young when she had committed the crimes, that she had no prior convictions, and that she had survived traumatic experiences of rape and the loss of her family members. They had also considered Handanović's serious and prolonged mental illness and that she is a single mother.[68] Finally, it was taken into account that she had shown remorse and openness, and was prepared to testify against her co-perpetrators. Her sentence was thus well below the 10-year minimum sentence prescribed for the kinds of crimes with which she had been charged.[69] As part of her plea agreement, Handanović agreed to testify in the trials of the other members of her unit. Although they tried to discredit her testimony,[70] four other members, including the commander of the unit, were sentenced to prison sentences between 10 and 15 years.[71]

Local and international media reported on the case of Handanović. In the US, most media reports were dominated by the disbelief voiced by her friends that she could have been involved in such terrible crimes: 'People who know her would never believe this' and 'How is it that the hands of a woman who only knew how to love, hug and care for people could possibly pull the trigger on an automatic rifle and kill innocent Croats and Serbs?'.[72] Other reports focused on the fact that after the conviction of Plavšić by the ICTY, Handanović was the first woman to be tried and convicted for international crimes by a Bosnian court. The media also highlighted her victimisation prior to her crimes. Although the media reports did not draw a flattering picture of her, she was not portrayed as

---

67 *Prosecutor's Office of Bosnia and Herzegovina v. Rasema Handanovic* (First Instance Verdict) S1 1 K 009162 12 Kro (30.04.2012) <http://www.sudbih.gov.ba/files/docs/presude/2012/9162_1K_HR_prvostupanjska_30_04_2012_ENG.pdf> accessed 21.08.2015.

68 Interview with journalists in Sarajevo. Rasema requested that the court not reveal the location of her parents or child.

69 One of her co-perpetrators, Edin Džeko, was sentenced to 13 years' imprisonment: *Prosecutor's Office of Bosnia and Herzegovina v. Edin Džeko* (Second Instance Verdict) S1 1 K 010294 14 Krž6 (4 December 2014) <http://www.sudbih.gov.ba/predmet/2981/show> accessed 21.08.2017.

70 A. Jahić, 'Rasema Handanovic as Political Refugee' *BIRN Justice Reports*, 07.07.2014 <http://www.justice-report.com/en/articles/rasema-handanovic-as-political-refugee> accessed 17.08.2015.

71 See A. Jahić, 'Pronouncement of Verdict for Trusina Crimes Postponed until September' *BIRN Justice Reports*, 10.07.2015 <http://www.justice-report.com/en/articles/pronouncement-of-verdict-for-trusina-crimes-postponed-until-september> accessed 22.08.2015; Justice Report, 'Three Bosniak Soldiers Convicted of Trusina Massacre' *Balkan Transitional Justice Reports*, 01.09.2015 <http://www.balkaninsight.com/en/article/bosnian-court-hands-down-37-years-for-trusina-massacre-09-01-2015> accessed 22.08.2015.

72 ibid. See also the neighbours who commented in disbelief: A. Oliver, 'The US Single Mother Who Was Actually a War Criminal: Killer Becomes First Woman to be Convicted of Bosnian War Crime' *Daily Mail*, 01.05.2012 <http://www.dailymail.co.uk/news/article-2137411/Rasema-Handanovic-guilty-war-crimes-Bosnia.html> accessed 21.08.2015.

a monster. In July 2014 new charges were issued against her, this time relating to the abuse of a victim in May 1993, but so far no additional prosecution has followed.[73]

Another woman, Azra Bašić, was also arrested in 2011 in the US and extradited in 2016. She had been a guard at a detention centre. She was accused of horrible atrocities which seem to show a vicious and sadistic nature: 'slitting the throat of a prisoner and making other prisoners drink his blood; carving symbols into prisoners' foreheads; making prisoners drink gasoline; setting fire to prisoners' hands and faces'.[74] In other news reports, it was stated that she made prisoners kneel on broken glass.[75] Despite the horrible nature of the allegations, she, like Handanović, had lived a peaceful life in the US after the war. She lived with an American family and had told them about her wartime experiences:

> the first man she killed, it made her sick. She came face to face with him. And she had to kill him or be killed. She said it made her sick at her stomach, and then she said, after that it all went down pretty easy – after you kill your first.[76]

She told them how she once witnessed a gang rape and then later recognised one of the perpetrators who was about to be shot. She asked her fellow soldiers not to shoot him and to hand him over to her; then according to her friends she told them that 'she cut his penis off, and she said, "now, you so-and-so, you'll never rape anyone again"'.[77]

These reported confidences seem to indicate that Azra Bašić was motivated by a desire to set the record straight. According to her friends, she is a 'fundamentally good person whom the horrors of war had forced to make impossible moral choices.'[78] For four years she has been fighting extradition, but on 10 July 2015, federal judges ruled that she could be extradited.[79] Her defence attorney appealed the decision but in April 2016 the appeals court upheld the decision of the court allowing the extradition of Azra Bašić.[80] Her trial started

---

73 See Justice Report, 'Bosniak Soldiers Charged With War Time Abuse' *Balkan Transitional Justice Reports*, 18.07.2014 <http://www.balkaninsight.com/en/article/bosniak-soldiers-charged-with-wartime-abuse> accessed 07.09.2015.

74 See 'Profile of Azra Basic TRIAL: Track Impunity Always' <http://www.trial-ch.org/en/resources/trial-watch/trial-watch/profiles/profile/1089/action/show/controller/Profile.html> accessed 06.09.2015.

75 See KY, Louisville, 'Judge: Croatian Woman Can be Extradited on War Crimes Charges' *Chicago Tribune*, 10.07.2015 <http://www.chicagotribune.com/news/nationworld/ct-azra-basic-war-crime-charges-20150710-story.html> accessed 21.08.2015.

76 See Gay, above n. 58.

77 ibid.

78 ibid.

79 ibid.

80 See B. Estep, 'Kentucky women accused of war crimes can be extradited to Bosnia, court says' *Lexington Herald Leader*, 20.04.2016, available at <http://www.kentucky.com/news/state/article72889177.html> accessed 13.05.2016.

in January 2017. She 'was found guilty of killing a kneeling detainee by stabbing him in the neck. Alone, or with other military personnel, she had also tortured a dozen other detainees with kicks and punches and baseball bat strikes, he said. She inscribed crosses with a knife on their backs and foreheads', according to the judges and was sentenced to 14 years imprisonment.[81]

3.3. ABUSIVE BEHAVIOUR AND MISTAKEN IDENTITY

Some women have been accused of war crimes, but have denied guilt, claiming mistaken identity. One of them is Indira Kamerić.[82] She has been accused of being a former member of the 101st Bosanski Brod Brigade, and in that capacity, participating in torture and sexual abuse against Serb and Bosniak civilians and prisoners of war on police premises in Bosanski Brod from April to October 1992.[83] She was indicted in November 2013 and pleaded not guilty. During the trial, a witness accused her of being present and slapping the witness while she had been sexually abused. Some witnesses considered her to be the ringleader, but a number of witnesses did not recognise her in court. Kamerić tried to convince the court that this was a case of mistaken identity. One witness testified that there was another woman called Indira at the police premises, but she was not Kamerić; in the meantime, the defendant herself claimed that she had never been a member of the Bosanski Brod Brigade and had never been present at the police premises. According to journalist X, who followed her trial, she stated that she had been a clerk in the municipality of Bosanski Broad and in charge of delivering humanitarian aid.

Kamerić stated that she only learned about the crimes committed at the police premises when investigations against her started: 'I was shocked and went into hospital. I saw nothing for 72 hours and I got diabetes. My suffering has lasted eight years and my family has been under heavy scrutiny, by both the media and the public. I am suffering for my sons.'[84] On 15 April 2015, she was found guilty of the physical and mental torture and inhumane treatment of the detained prisoners, and was sentenced to three years' imprisonment.[85] She was

81 *Prosecutor v Azra Basic*, S1 1 K 018557 18 Krz – Bašić Azra, Judgment, 27.12.2017, available at <http://www.sudbih.gov.ba/predmet/3622/show> accessed 07.08.2018.

82 For an overview of articles on the case, see 'Case: Kamerić Indira' *BIRN Justice Reports* <http://www.justice-report.com/en/cases/kameric-indira-news-analysis-and-opinion> accessed 12.08.2015.

83 A. Jahić, 'Indira Kamerić's Trial Nears End' *BIRN Justice Reports*, 15.01.2015 <http://www.justice-report.com/en/articles/indira-kameric-s-trial-nears-end> accessed 12.08.2015.

84 See D. Dzidic, 'Female Bosnian Croat Denies Abusing Prisoners' *BIRN Justice Reports*, 06.11.2014 <http://www.justice-report.com/en/articles/female-bosnian-croat-denies-abusing-prisoners> accessed 15.08.2015.

85 See the Information Justice Report, 'Bosnia convicts Kameric for wartime crimes against Serbs' *BIRN*, 17.04.2015.

acquitted of assisting in several rapes. The sentence was low, because according to the judge: 'She was young, she showed respect towards the victims, and the crimes were not severe'.[86] The fact that the court stated that the crimes were not severe is remarkable as it also concluded that the crimes 'resulted in great suffering' of the victims, as the prosecutor noted in his appeal.[87] The court of appeal followed the judgment in first instance in relation to the question of guilt but increased the sentence to four years as the court in first instance had not sufficiently taken the severity of the crimes into account.[88]

Similarly, Marina Grubišić-Fejzić, a member of Croatian armed forces, was indicted before the Court of BiH for the forced removal of Serb civilians from Herzegovina between May and August 1992, and their subsequent physical and sexual abuse at the Dretelj prison camp. Grubišić-Fejzić was indicted and tried together with four co-perpetrators in the so-called 'Zelenika *et al.*' case.[89] They all pleaded not guilty.

Witnesses testified about the inhumane circumstances, mistreatment and sexual abuse in which Grubišić-Fejzić allegedly participated. They accused Marina of having abused and beaten prisoners, hit men in their sexual organs,[90] and forced prisoners to have oral sex with each other.[91] Other women were present too. As one witness testified: 'I did not want to watch, but prisoners had to do things to each other which are not for talking about. There were women present, who giggled and commented'.[92] Another witness, Bojanić, stated:

> One time they brought a bitch and told us to lick her under the tail and lick her sexual organ. They asked me to do this, but I do not know who else. The dog was brought by

86 A. Sorguc, 'Bosnia Convicts Kameric of Wartime Crimes Against Serbs' *BIRN Justice Reports*, 17.04.2015 <http://www.justice-report.com/en/articles/bosnia-convicts-kameric-of-wartime-crimes-against-serbs> accessed 19.08.2015.

87 See 'Appeals presented to Indira Kameric verdict' *BIRN Justice Report*, 15.12.2015.

88 'Appeals chamber increases Indira Kameric prison sentence' *BIRN Justice Report*, 11.02.2016.

89 For an overview of articles on the case, see 'Case: Zelenika et al' *BIRN Justice Reports* <http://www.justice-report.com/en/cases/zelenika-et-al-news-analysis-and-opinion> accessed 19.08.2015, and the overview on the official court website: 'Cases in Trial or On Appeal Against Verdict: Zelenika Ivan et al' *Court of Bosnia and Herzegovina* <http://www.sudbih.gov.ba/?opcija=predmeti&id=698&jezik=e> accessed 13.09.2015. See also Profile of Marina Grubišić-Fejzić *TRIAL: Track Impunity Always* <http://www.trial-ch.org/en/resources/trial-watch/trial-watch/profiles/profile/4345/action/show/controller/Profile.html> accessed 19.08.2015.

90 Justice Report, 'Bosnian Serbs "Constantly Beaten" at Dretelj Jail Camp' *Balkan Transitional Justice Reports*, Sarajevo 06.03.2013 <http://www.balkaninsight.com/en/article/prisoners-looked-like-wraiths-in-dretelj-camp> accessed 02.09.2015.

91 'Zelenika et al: Murder in Dretelj Camp' *BIRN Justice Reports*, 05.12.2012 <http://www.justice-report.com/en/articles/zelenika-et-al-murder-in-dretelj-camp> accessed 02.09.2015.

92 D. Dzidic, 'Witness Recalls Beatings and Abuse in Dretelj' *BIRN Justice Reports*, 20.08.2013 <http://www.balkaninsight.com/en/article/provocations-beatings-and-abuse-in-dretelj> accessed 01.09.2015.

> a woman, a member of the Croatian Defence Army, about twenty-five years old, she was dark with bad teeth, she asked us to do this.[93]

At the trial, Grubišić-Fejzić stated that she had never abused anyone and that there were a few other female guards, some called Marina, and that it must have been a case of mistaken identity.[94] In court she said: 'I plead to this honourable council to acquit me on all counts, because I'm not guilty'.[95] According to journalist X:

> She never denied that crimes had taken place and she apologised to each victim who testified but never admitted that she had committed any of the crimes ... She was just a soldier coming to work, a bystander ... She was in the army to earn a living since she was coming from a poor family. Her sister was also with HOS [Croatian Defence Forces] in Dretelj, but her sister is not under indictment.[96]

One witness confirmed that Grubišić-Fejzić was never involved in any of the abuse. He stated that there were four Marinas at the detention camp and that one of the other Marinas had a very bad reputation: 'I saw when Marina from Osijek stabbed a knife in a man's head. I heard that she cut one [man's] genitals, that she tortured prisoners, that she loved to hit them. I just know that she was not a good person'.[97] But this was not the Marina who was now on trial. Thus, the defence maintained that Grubišić-Fejzić was just a soldier defending her country and was never involved in any abuse.[98]

The trial verdict was pronounced on 14 April 2015 and Grubišić-Fejzić was found guilty and sentenced to five years' imprisonment for abusing prisoners and forcing them to have sex with each other.[99] Her sentence was lower than the

---

93 See D. Erjavec, 'Dretelj Prisoners Forced to Lick the Dog' *BIRN Justice Reports*, 05.11.2013 <http://www.justice-report.com/en/articles/dretelj-prisoners-forced-to-lick-the-dog> accessed 01.09.2015.

94 S. Ucanbarlic, 'Female Bosnian Croat Fighter Denies Abusing Prisoners' *BIRN Justice Reports*, 25.03.2014 <http://www.justice-report.com/en/articles/female-bosnian-croat-fighter-denies-abusing-prisoners> accessed 28.08.2015.

95 A. Jahić, 'Grubišić-Fejzić Gives Closing Statement, Verdict for Zelenika et al Expected in April' *BIRN Justice Reports*, 10.03.2015 <http://www.justice-report.com/en/articles/grubisic-fejzic-gives-closing-statement-verdict-for-zelenika-et-al-expected-in-april> accessed 05.08.2015.

96 Interview with X, a journalist who followed her trial for three-and-a-half years and on many occasions also had a chance to talk to her outside a courtroom.

97 S. Ucanbarlic, 'Female Bosnian Croat Fighter "Never Abused Prisoners"' *BIRN Justice Reports*, 18.03.2014 <http://www.justice-report.com/en/articles/female-bosnian-croat-fighter-never-abused-prisoners> accessed 29.08.2015.

98 ibid.

99 For an overview of the case, see the official court website: 'Cases in Trial or On Appeal Against Verdict: Zelenika Ivan et al', above n. 88. The deputy commander of the barracks was sentenced to 34 years because an earlier sentence of 34 years was taken into account, two confederates were sentenced to 6 and 7 years while one defendant was acquitted.

sentences of the others because, according to the court, she was 'an emotionally immature person' and was now married to someone from a different ethnicity.[100] It is not clear why the latter fact was relevant, since her husband was a Bosniak and she was accused of torturing Serbs, not Bosniaks. Among other mitigating circumstances that were stated was that she is the mother of a bright, successful young daughter.[101] Grubišić-Fejzić now lives in Ilidža, Sarajevo, and has converted to Islam.[102]

The main point of argument during these two trials was whether the two women who stood trial were actually the women who committed the atrocities. In the opinion of the present authors, it is impossible to tell whether these were indeed cases of mistaken identity, but the evidence that women (whether the women who stood trial or other women) were involved in terrible atrocities seems overwhelming.[103]

4. ANALYSIS OF THE CASE STUDIES

In this section the case studies will be analysed, but before going into them, what is currently known about the perpetrators of mass violence in general (section 4.1) and female perpetrators in Bosnia (section 4.2) will be briefly explained. The discussion will then focus on the trial and sentence (section 4.3), as well as the portrayal (section 4.4) of female perpetrators.

4.1. PERPETRATORS OF MASS ATROCITIES

Confronted with terrible crimes, people naturally tend to distance themselves from the crimes and the perpetrators thereof. After the terrible atrocities committed by the Nazis during World War II in Auschwitz and other concentration and death camps, it was believed that the people who commit mass atrocities must be cruel and sadistic psychopaths with a violent past and criminal record. In research on perpetrators of mass atrocities, many

---

100 S. Ucanbarlic, 'Bosnia Convicts Four of Dretelj Jail Camp Abuses' *BIRN Justice Reports*, 14.04.2015 <http://www.justice-report.com/en/articles/bosnia-convicts-four-of-dretelj-jail-camp-abuses> accessed 29.08.2015.

101 Interview with BIRN journalist on file with the authors.

102 ibid.

103 It is likely that due to stereotyped gender perceptions, victims and bystanders may very well remember that women were involved in the abuse rather than merely males, but that these witnesses then only remember the most striking characteristic of the female perpetrators, namely their sex, rather than any other personal and distinguishable features (which may then explain the claim that cases involving female perpetrators can more easily lead to cases of mistaken identities).

scholars at the time tried to find proof for what Waller dubbed the 'Mad-Nazi theory',[104] but within scholarly literature it is now a common understanding that most perpetrators who commit mass atrocities are ordinary people within extraordinary circumstances.[105] Although perpetrators may have different motives, most of them are very ordinary people who within very particular political, ideological and institutional circumstances commit so-called 'crimes of obedience'. A crime of obedience can be defined as 'an act performed in response to orders from an authority that is considered illegal or immoral by the international community'.[106] Human beings are social beings and very much affected by the social context in which they operate and have a general tendency to conform to their situation and obey others.[107] The consequence is that people who live in a dictatorial and genocidal regime, or in a country at war which has become very polarised, may get caught up in a continuum of destructiveness in which they gradually transform into perpetrators.[108]

Most hands-on perpetrators are members of militarised units, which are generally characterised by a hierarchical structure in which discipline, obedience and conformity are important values; which have a monopoly on the use of arms and have the task to defend the country against their 'dangerous' fellow human beings, whom they start to see as enemies. Within such a context the use of violence and the killing of fellow human beings ('the enemy') is considered necessary and legitimised. Recruits fighting within a war are pressured to conform and obey and to do what is asked of them, while the line between the legitimate and illegitimate use of violence is sometimes very thin. This is very well illustrated by Browning who noted that many perpetrators of the unit he studied joined the execution of Jews because 'they did not want to be considered a coward'.[109] Research has furthermore shown that the first time a recruit

---

104 J. Waller, *Becoming Evil: How Ordinary People Commit Genocide and Mass Killing*, 2nd ed., Oxford University Press 2007, 63.

105 See the work of H. Arendt, *Eichmann in Jerusalem – A Report on the Banality of Evil*, Penguin Books USA 1964; R. Hilberg, *Perpetrators, Victims, Bystanders – the Jewish Catastrophe*, Harper Perennial 1992; Ch.R. Browning, *Ordinary Men – Reserve Police Battalion 101 and the Final Solution in Poland*, Aaron Asher Books 1992; P.G. Zimbardo, *The Lucifer Effect – Understanding How Good People Turn Evil*, Random House 2007; and Waller, above n. 103.

106 H.C. Kelman and V.L. Hamilton, *Crimes of Obedience*, New Haven: Yale University Press 1989.

107 See also psychological experiments such as by Asch, Milgam and Zimbardo: S. Asch, 'Opinions and Social Pressure' (1995) 193(5) *Scientific American* 31; S. Milgram, *Obedience to authority*, Harper and Row 1974; P.G. Zimbardo, C. Haney, W. Curtis Banks and D. Jaffe, 'The Psychology of Imprisonment: Privation, Power, and Pathology' in R. Zick (ed.), *Doing unto Others*, Englewood Cliffs 1974, pp. 61–73.

108 See E. Staub, *The Roots of Evil – the Origins of Genocide and Other Group Violence*, Cambridge University Press 1989 on continuum of destructiveness, and A. Smeulers, 'What Transforms Ordinary People into Gross Human Rights Violations?' in S. Carey and S. Poe (eds.), *Understanding Human Rights Violations: New Systematic Studies*, Ashgate Publishing Ltd 2004, 239–56 on the transformation process.

109 See Browning, above n. 105.

commits a crime he usually feels very bad about what he has done, but in order to soothe his conscience he starts to rationalise and justify his behaviour.[110] These rationalisations and justifications pave the way for further crimes and ultimately perpetrators start to believe in their own excuses. Perpetrators seldom see themselves as criminals but rather as people who are protecting their country or trying to create a better world. They all seem to believe that they are doing the right thing.[111]

Perpetrators, however, differ in the role, rank, motive and the extent to which they have the power to control the situation, and several typologies have been developed in literature to acknowledge this.[112] Overall, however, it can be stated that the three main driving forces for people to commit mass atrocities are ideology, greed and fear.[113]

Remarkably enough within scientific literature – until very recently – little attention has been paid to female perpetrators. As most perpetrators are indeed men, female perpetrators have often been ignored or considered atypical. As mentioned earlier, women involved in mass atrocities are generally still considered not to be 'real' women and are portrayed are shown as mentally disturbed, sexually deviated or lacking any agency (just like men were after WWII). It was following the genocide in Rwanda in 1994, which showed the world that alongside men, many women were also involved, that the interest in female perpetrators started to emerge. African Rights published a report entitled 'Not So Innocent' which focuses on the role of women in the genocide, and since then several other studies have been published which seem to show that women can be just as cruel as men and that in fact they are not so very different from their male counterparts.[114] This, however, is a message which is not yet generally accepted, and more research and case studies are needed to get a better insight in the role of women as active participants in the war and perpetrators of mass atrocities.

4.2. FEMALE PERPETRATORS IN BOSNIA

The eight cases discussed above (section 3) illustrate that women can be just as cruel as men, as the crimes for which these women have been indicted

---

110 See Smeulers, above n. 108.

111 See, e.g., A. Smeulers and L. Hoex, 'Studying the Micro-dynamics of the Rwandan Genocide' (2010) 50(3) *British Journal of Criminology* 435–54.

112 See R.D. Crelinsten, 'In Their Own Words: The World of the Torturer' in R.D. Crelinsten and A.P. Schmid (eds.), *The Politics of Pain – Torturers and Their Masters*, Leiden: COMT 1993; M. Mann, *The Dark Side of Democracy – Explaining Ethnic Cleansing*, Cambridge University Press 2005; A. Smeulers, 'Perpetrators of International Crimes: Towards a Typology' in A. Smeulers and R. Haveman (eds.), *Supranational Criminology: Towards a Criminology of International Crimes*, Intersentia 2008, pp. 233–66.

113 ibid.

114 African Rights, above n. 4, and see for an overview Smeulers, above n. 2.

and convicted are horrendous. These women were mainly indicted for abuse, inhumane treatment and torture. The aim of these crimes was clearly to humiliate and make the (mostly male) victims suffer. All defendants, with the exception of Rasema Handanović who was indicted for the killing of six people, were indicted for sexual abuse and (sexual) mistreatment of fellow countrymen who had been captured and imprisoned. The war in BiH was known for the widespread and systematic use of sexual violence as a means to terrorise the population. The findings on which this chapter is based seem to indicate that women, just like men, were involved in this type of violence – a discovery which on the one hand counters intuitive expectations, but which on the other hand is confirmed by research from other conflicts in which sexual violence has been used, such as in Rwanda, Sierra Leone, the Democratic Republic of Congo, and the War on Terror.[115]

So far, the present authors are not aware of any literature specifically related to the involvement of women in sexual violence in the war in BiH, yet the data seem to clearly indicate that this is a topic which warrants further investigation. The preliminary conclusion is that most sexual violence is committed by men, but that the involvement of women in sexual violence in BiH is probably much larger than initially expected. It is notable to mention that while Rasema was not accused of sexual mistreatment, she was a victim of gang rape, which allegedly motivated her to join the army and seek revenge. She stated that it was the suffering from these crimes that made her take up arms and turned her into a war criminal.

Unfortunately, little personal information on the female perpetrators prosecuted so far is available, and the authors had to rely mainly on the reports written by BIRN, but what is clear is that just like most male perpetrators all these women (with the exception of 16-year-old Monika Karan-Ilić, Jelisić's girlfriend), were members of militarised units. The fact that they operated within a military unit and probably committed their crimes under direction, is nothing out of the ordinary. As already stated earlier most international crimes are so-called 'crimes of obedience': crimes committed by subordinates, on orders of

---

115 See African Rights, above n. 4, on the involvement of women in sexual violence during the Rwanda genocide; D.K. Cohen, 'Female Combatants and the Perpetration of Violence: Wartime Rape in the Sierra Leone Civil War' (2013) 65 WP 383–415 on the involvement of women in wartime rape in Sierra Leone; the quantitative study by L. Lawry, K. Johnson and J. Asher, 'Evidence-Based Documentation of Gender-Based Violence' in A.-M. de Brouwer, C. Ku, R. Römkens and L. van den Herik (eds.), *Sexual Violence as an International Crime: Interdisciplinary Approaches*, Intersentia 2013, p. 300, in which the authors conclude that 17 per cent of the survivors of wartime sexual violence name a woman as perpetrator; and K.A. Huskey, 'The Sex Interrogators of Guantánamo' in T. McKelvey (ed.), *One of the Guys: Women as Aggressors and Torturers*, Seal Press 2007, on the role of women in sexual violence in the war on terror.

their superiors, giving the subordinates the impression that the orders issued are legal, and the acts legitimised and justified, rather than (international) crimes.[116]

The context in which these women operated is thus no different from the context in which men operate. The only difference might be the expectations related to the behaviour of men and women, which can be influenced and affected by prescribed gender roles. The effect might be that most women in the military have subordinate roles. The case study of these eight women shows that at least some women were, however, directly involved in abuse, torture, sexual violence and killing. Most would have occupied subordinate positions, but at least one, Rada Tomić, who has not yet been arrested, was clearly in a position of leadership. This however is the exception rather than the rule. Most women were subordinates, and in one case (Kuburić and Banjac), it became clear that the main reason for participating in the atrocities may have been because they were afraid of their (female) commander.

Other typical characteristics of the crimes committed which follow from the cases is that the crimes were committed together with others in an apparently permissive environment, and that although the violence seems to have been ordered or otherwise condoned by the superiors, personal motives such as revenge, hatred, contempt and sadism could also play a role.

However, just like most male perpetrators, it does not seem that any of the women discussed had been involved in crimes either before or after the war. In all cases, it appears that their crimes were only committed in and related to the ongoing war in BiH, in which many other terrible crimes were committed, and were thus very much context related.

4.3. TRIAL AND SENTENCING

All of the women who have been tried so far were found guilty. According to one of our interviewees, during the trials the women were not treated any different from the male indictees by the judges. The only case in which there seemed to be a stereotypical portrayal of a female perpetrator as described by Sjoberg and Gentry, is the case of Monika Karan-Ilić, Jelisić's girlfriend. She was clearly portrayed by the prosecutor and his witnesses as a vicious woman who 'looked like a little girl but was in fact a monster'.[117] Monika Karan-Ilić, however, countered these allegations – also by a stereotypical defence – and alleged that

---

116 The concept of 'crimes of obedience' was developed by Kelman and Hamilton in their book: H.C. Kelman and V. Lee Hamilton, *Crimes of Obedience*, Yale University Press 1989.

117 See Justice Report, 'Monika Simonović Arrested on War Crimes Charges' *Balkan Transitional Justice Reports*, 22.12.2011 <http://www.balkaninsight.com/en/article/local-judiciary-in-brcko-interrogation-of-monika-simonovic-s-soon> accessed 05.08.2015.

she in fact was a victim too, suffering from Goran Jelisić's tyranny. She claimed that he had forced her to do what she did, a line of defence that was not accepted by the judges. The other cases seemed to focus on the crimes or the question as to whether the women on trial were the same women who were responsible for the terrible atrocities described by the witnesses.

Rasema Handanović was the only defendant to plead guilty, but nevertheless received a sentence of five-and-a-half years, which might be due to the fact that she was the only one convicted for killing people. Azra Bašić received the longest sentence: 14 years. All others pleaded not guilty and received sentences of between three and five years. So far, three women have appealed their sentence(s): in two cases (Terzić and Karan-Ilić), their sentences were reduced to two-and-a-half years and three years respectively, and in one case the sentence was increased by one year (Kamerić). In four cases (Terzić, Karan-Ilić, Kubric, Banjac), the relatively young age of the defendants was taken into account, and in one case the defendant was considered to be emotionally immature (Grubišić-Fejzić). In two cases (Kubric and Banjac), the fact that the defendant had family, and in one case (Grubišić-Fejzić) the fact that the defendant had married someone from another ethnicity, were referred to as mitigating circumstances. Only two women showed remorse (Kuburić and Handanović).

In 2011, Balkan Transitional Justice published an article entitled: 'Bosnian war's wicked women get off lightly' complaining about the fact that many victims say that some women 'appear to have been far more cruel than their male abusers', but that the courts seem 'reluctant to act'.[118] It has to be acknowledged though that at that time not one of the women mentioned above had yet stood trial. In that sense progress has been made but it still seems that overall the sentences given (between two-and-a-half and five years) seem rather lenient given the crimes of which these women were accused until the recent sentencing of Azra Bašić to 14 years. However, Barbora Hola, an expert in sentencing, has calculated that on average the sentences of the courts for men and women accused of war crimes in the courts at the constitutive level (Republika Srpska, Federation and Brčko) are between 4 and 7.6 years and, thus, not very high either.[119] The average sentences of the women discussed in this chapter are, however, with the exception of Bašić, still quite a bit lower than the average sentences given to the men convicted of war crimes. In two cases in which female perpetrators were tried the judges concluded – while explaining the sentence – that the crimes were not severe. This was remarkable when taking the descriptions by the witnesses into account, and in particular in relation to

---

118 M. Husejnovic, 'Bosnian War's Wicked Women Get Off Lightly' *Balkan Transitional Justice*, 07.02.2011.

119 Summary statistics provided by Barbora Hola based on an original database collected during her field work in Bosnia in 2015 and 2016 for the purposes of the research project 'Vertical (In)consistency of International Sentencing', on file with author.

Kamerić this was contradicted by their own conclusion earlier on in the verdict that the crimes led to great suffering. In cases related to men this is, according to Hola, only acknowledged as a mitigating circumstance if there were no serious consequences for the victims.

The other mitigating circumstances mentioned are fairly similar to the ones mentioned in cases against male perpetrators: young age and lack of a criminal record. Overall, however, the sentences seem to be fairly lenient and certainly more lenient than the sentences for men. In order to corroborate this intuitive feeling, however, it would be necessary to conduct a full statistical analysis and carefully compare the cases in which male and female perpetrators were indicted. As the present authors were not in a position to undertake such an analysis, it can merely be stated that these women, with the exception of Rasema Handanović and Azra Bašić, received prison sentences that were in the low range given the gravity of their crimes. It is, however, unclear to what extent this was influenced by their sex.

4.4. THE PORTRAYAL OF FEMALE PERPETRATORS IN BOSNIA

BIRN was often the only media house in BiH to follow the trials of the women from beginning to end. Other media houses attended the beginning of the trial and then returned only to hear the verdict, probably because they lacked sufficient interest. The trials were open to the public except when a protected witness had been called to testify. The accused could also request exclusion of public because of the protection of their 'intimate life'.[120]

In the BIRN reports, however, none of the accused women were portrayed as monsters, despite the horrendous nature of their crimes. It seems that there is no obvious gender perspective related to the portrayal of female perpetrators, at least not in the news agency BIRN which issues the Justice Reports studied by the authors. This might be due to the fact that those, including journalists, who have seen and experienced the war in BiH themselves, are not surprised that women were involved in the atrocities alongside men, and that most of these women, just like most men, were still ordinary people within extraordinary circumstances, despite the horrendous nature of their crimes.

However, other (international) media did sometimes refer to the prosecuted women as monsters.[121] According to the journalist interview, the perception in Bosnian society is that these crimes are an 'anomaly' and that the crimes 'were less natural' and consequently more 'monstrous' than the crimes committed

---

120 Interview with BIRN journalist.

121 See, for instance, Cerkez, 'Bosnia Police Detain Female War Crime Suspect' *USA Today*, 21.12.2011 <http://usatoday30.usatoday.com/news/world/story/2011-12-21/bosnia-woman-war-crimes/52138606/1> accessed 05.08.2015.

by men.[122] 'The focus of our [society's] attention are victims of wartime sexual violence', reported journalist Y, 'rarely anyone is interested in this topic', referring to the fact that the authors of this chapter were the first researchers to interview BIRN journalists about female perpetrators. Journalist Y told us that no other scholars had expressed an interest in writing or researching about women accused of war crimes, and as far as he was aware, no civil society organisation had demonstrated an interest in this topic either.

5. CONCLUSION

These case studies show that it would be a misrepresentation of the facts to stereotype the roles of men and women as aggressors and victims respectively. The cases studied above confirm, in support of the conclusions of research from other conflict situations, that women are capable of terrible atrocities, and that men too can be victimised, not only women.[123] It is true that many more men have been involved in violent wartime crimes than women, for the simple reason that women are still underrepresented in militarised units. Because women are underrepresented in total numbers, they are also underrepresented in positions of leadership, but the few reports studied by the authors show that there have been female superiors with the reputation of being dangerous and cruel, like Rada Tomić.

The case of Biljana Plavšić, which has not been discussed in detail in this chapter, illustrates that a woman who has forged a political career and gained a powerful position can be a ruthless politician, deeply involved in the war and crimes committed therein. While Plavšić was welcomed back from The Hague as a hero,[124] the lower-ranked women discussed in this chapter were never described as such. They were simply not of interest even to the members of their own ethnic group. They, as with many low-ranked men who were prosecuted for war crimes, have not been discussed in positive terms. The leaders, 'the big fish', have received attention and support from their people, but not the 'ordinary' perpetrators.[125]

This case study of women in BiH thus seems to confirm the overall conclusions in relation to women involved in international crimes; that women do not differ that much from men. From the cases discussed, it is sometimes hard to tell why these women became involved, or what really motivated them, but it seems probable that just like men they were driven by ideology, greed or

122 Interview with BIRN journalist.

123 Almost all victims of the women discussed in the cases above are men.

124 See O. Simić, 'Bringing "Justice" Home: Bosnians, War Criminals and the Interaction Between the Cosmopolitan and the Local' (2011) 12 *German Law Journal* 1388–1407.

125 Interview with BIRN journalist.

fear, and were caught up in the social dynamics of war in which they came to see certain groups of their fellow countrymen as the enemy.[126]

The women studied are certainly not monsters. Their crimes are indeed sometimes monstrous, but so are the crimes of their male counterparts, and this does not mean that they are monsters. Just like their male counterparts, most of them committed their crimes during a war and with other members of their militarised unit in an environment which seemed to condone the crimes. The women will probably have felt some pressure from their environment to obey orders, conform to the group and join the abuse, but nothing in the reports read by the authors suggests that these women generally lacked agency. As little information was available on these women apart from the case reports written by BIRN, it is hard to say whether there might be some minor differences between male perpetrators and female perpetrators, as suggested in some literature, and further research would be needed in order to investigate this. This chapter, however, does support the conclusion that women can be involved in mass atrocities just like men, and that they can be just as cruel as their male counterparts.

---

126 There are also examples of women who were among the strongest opponents of the Serbo-Croatian conflict. See WILMER, above n. 18, p. 215.

PART II

MEN AND CHILDREN'S EXPERIENCES OF ARMED CONFLICT

TOWARDS A GENDER ANALYSIS OF SEXUAL VIOLENCE AGAINST MEN AND BOYS IN CONFLICT

Incorporating Masculinities Theory into Feminist Theories of Sexual Violence Against Women

Valorie K. Vojdik

1. INTRODUCTION

Although international law has recognised the use of sexual violence against women and girls during conflict, the International Criminal Court and international tribunals have largely failed to recognise or adequately theorise rape or sexual violence against men and boys, ignoring or denying its gendered nature.[1] The Rome Statute of the International Criminal Court (ICC) defines rape and sexual violence in gender-neutral terms, permitting prosecution for the sexual violation of males.[2] Yet in *Prosecutor v. Muthaura, Kenyatta & Ali Kenyatta*, the Pre-Trial Chamber of the ICC found that the forced circumcision and penile amputation of Luo men in Kenya did not constitute sexual violence

1 S. Sivakumaran, 'Sexual Violence Against Men in Armed Conflict' (2007) 18 *European Journal of International Law* 253, 253–55.

2 ibid.

within the meaning of the Rome Statute.[3] The *Kenyatta* decision exemplifies the failure of the ICC and international tribunals to adequately conceptualise the gendered nature of sexual violence against men and its relationship to sexual violence against women and girls.

Like sexual violence against women, sexual violence against men deserves similar condemnation by the international community. For such crimes against men to be punished, however, prosecutors and courts need to understand how sexual violence against men serves a gendered purpose and results in gendered harms that merit vindication. While feminist and human rights activists and theorists have worked diligently to educate courts and prosecutors about sexual violence against women and girls, there has been little attention focused on the nature and harm of sexual violence against men and boys. In 2014, the ICC's Office of the Prosecutor (OTP) issued a Policy Paper on Sexual and Gender-Related Crimes ('Policy Paper' or 'OTP Policy Paper') that announced its adoption of a 'gender analysis' to better contextualise and prosecute crimes of sexual violence against both men and women.[4] The Policy Paper, however, failed to offer a nuanced analysis of sexual violence against men and boys.

Masculinities theory is a useful tool to build upon feminist theories of sexual violence to help explain to courts the relationship between gender, power and sexual violence against men during war.[5] As Miranda Alison observes, feminist theories of wartime rape of women and girls have tended to explain sexual violence as a manifestation of unequal gender relations between men and women, ignoring male victims.[6] Masculinities theory helps illuminate the meaning and role of sexual violence against men and boys during conflict, allowing prosecutors and courts to recognise its function as a gendered means of domination and genocide. Masculinities theory focuses on the social construction of men within particular societies and the process by which particular groups of men achieve and maintain power. Like feminist anti-essentialism, masculinities theory recognises that different groups of men occupy different positions of power within a particular society, resulting in not one, but multiple masculinities within a particular social location. Masculinities also intersect with race, ethnicity, class, sexual orientation and other forms of

---

3 *Prosecutor v. Muthaura, Kenyatta & Ali* (Decision on the Prosecutor's Application for Summonses to Appear) ICC-01/09–02/11 (8 March 2011), para. 27.

4 ICC Office of the Prosecutor, 'Policy Paper on Sexual and Gender-Based Crimes' (2014) <https://www.icc-cpi.int/iccdocs/otp/otp-Policy-Paper-on-Sexual-and-Gender-Based-Crimes--June-2014.pdf> accessed 19.07.2018 ('Policy Paper' or 'OTP Policy Paper').

5 V.K. Vojdik, 'Sexual Violence Against Men in War: A Masculinities Approach' (2014) 14 *Nevada Law Journal* 923. Miranda Alison similarly argues that analysis of 'wartime sexual violence' needs to examine 'local hegemonic and subordinate masculinities' and their relationship to 'ethno-national identity, militarism, violence, and constructions of femininity'. M. Alison, 'Wartime Sexual Violence: Women's Human Rights and Questions of Masculinity' (2007) 33 *Review of International Studies* 75, 89–90.

6 Alison, ibid.

identity to create, enforce and reproduce relations of power on multiple levels: between men as individuals; between men as groups; between men and women; and within larger social institutions, including the military and the nation-state.[7]

Masculinities theory can help explain to courts that sexual violence against men in conflict is not an isolated aberration, but a gendered means of domination. As Sandesh Sivakumaran observes, wartime sexual violence against men is about masculine domination and power, just as it is for women.[8] Both function as an actual and symbolic means of masculinised dominance between competing ethnic, national and other collectives. Like the rape of women, the rape and sexual violation of men constructs and enforces actual and symbolic gendered power on multiple levels, empowering the perpetrator while feminising and conquering the victim.[9] At the same time, it terrorises, weakens and destroys the collective to which the victim belongs.[10] Building on feminist theories of gender violence, masculinities theory reveals that sexual violence against men and women are inter-related: both function to construct and enforce masculinised domination of particular groups during war. By focusing on the gendered nature of sexual violence against men, prosecutors and human rights advocates can help persuade the ICC and other tribunals to characterise and punish such crimes as rape and sexual violence.

2. THE PREVALENCE OF SEXUAL VIOLENCE AGAINST MEN IN WAR

Despite its invisibility, sexual violence against men in war has occurred throughout history and across cultures. In ancient times, Persian armies cut off the penises of enemy soldiers and displayed them on plates to celebrate their military domination over competing groups of men.[11] Reports of rape and sexual violation of male civilians, detainees and combatants have recently surfaced in dozens of conflicts including in Syria, Sudan, Congo, Afghanistan, the former Yugoslavia, Kurdistan, El Salvador, Sierra Leone, East Timor, Sri Lanka, Iraq and Rwanda.[12]

---

7 Vojdik, above n. 5, p. 926.

8 Sivakumaran, above n. 1, p. 267.

9 ibid.

10 See D. Žarkov, 'The Body of the Other Man: Sexual Violence and the Construction of Masculinity, Sexuality and Ethnicity in Croatian Media' in C.O.N. Moser and F.C. Clark (eds.), *Victims, Perpetrators or Actors? Gender, Armed Conflict and Political Violence*, Zed Books 2001, pp. 69, 78, '[W]hen the male body is ethnic and male at the same time, the castration of a single man' represents the castration of the entire ethnic group.

11 J.S. Goldstein, *War and Gender*, Cambridge University Press 2001, pp. 357, 359, 363.

12 Sivakumaran, above n. 1, pp. 264–65. See also M.A. Onyango and K. Hampanda, 'Social Constructions of Masculinity and Male Survivors of Wartime Sexual Violence: An Analytical

The UN Secretary-General reported in 2009 that '[w]hile women and girls are particular targets and are the majority of the victims of sexual violence, the case law of the International Criminal Tribunal for the Former Yugoslavia (ICTY) and the Special Court for Sierra Leone (SCSL) also bears testimony to the use of sexual violence against men'.[13] ICTY judgments, for example, document incidents in several cases in which perpetrators engaged in multiple forms of sexual violence against men, including forcing male detainees to commit fellatio on their brothers or other male detainees, ramming a police truncheon and other objects into the anus of detainees, and forcing detainees to bite off the testicles of another detainee.[14]

Like violence against women, sexual violence against men is a broad category of abuse, both physical and mental.[15] It includes rape, including anal or oral penetration with the penis or other objects, including sticks, truncheons and other instruments.[16] It also encompasses castration, which can result in sterilisation and infertility; genital violence, such as blunt force trauma to the penis or scrotum; and forced circumcision.[17] It also includes forced incest, where men or boys are forced to have sex with family members (brothers, fathers, daughters, sisters, or other relatives) or non-relatives (male or female detainees or members of their community). Sometimes the sexual violence is not physical but involves humiliation or the violation of sexual or social norms, such as forced nudity, where men are forced to strip naked, often in public; forced masturbation; and other forms of sexual humiliation.[18]

Much of the abuse occurs in detention, where it is often characterised as torture rather than sexual violence or rape. During the armed conflict in the former Yugoslavia, more than 50 per cent of male detainees experienced sexual torture, including 80 per cent of men at a concentration camp in Sarajevo.[19] In El Salvador, 76 per cent of male political detainees experienced sexual torture and 21 per cent of Sri Lankan men treated at a London treatment centre for torture reported sexual abuse during detention.[20] The forms of violence in

Review' (2011) 23 *International Journal of Sexual Health* 237, 237–39; H.M. Zawati, 'Impunity or Immunity: Wartime Male Rape and Sexual Torture as a Crime Against Humanity' (2007) 17 *Torture* 27, 34–35.

13 U.N., Report of the Secretary-General Pursuant to Security Council Resolution 1820 (2009) (U.N. Doc. S/2009/362 (15 July 2009), para. 6.

14 *Prosecutor v. Duško Tadić* (Opinion and Judgment) IT-94-1-T (7 May 1997), para. 206; *Prosecutor v. Delalić* (Judgment) IT-96-21-T (16 November 1998), paras. 24, 26; *Prosecutor v. Sikirica et al.* (Second Amended Indictment), IT-95-8-PT, 3 January 2001, para. 46; *Prosecutor v. Simić et al.*

15 See D.A. Lewis, 'Unrecognised Victims: Sexual Violence Against Men in Conflict Settings Under International Law' (2009) 27 *Wisconsin International Law Journal* 1, 3.

16 Onyango and Hampanda, above n. 12, pp. 23, pp. 237–40.

17 ibid.

18 ibid.

19 ibid., pp. 238–39.

20 W. Storr, 'The Rape of Men: The Darkest Secret of War', *Observer* 16 July 2011, p. 36.

detention have included rape, forced rape and incest, and multiple forms of genital violence, such as circumcision, castration, electric shocks to the scrotum, amputation of the penis, and other forms of sexual mutilation.[21] In Abu Ghraib, United States military troops sexually abused Iraqi male detainees, forcing them to strip naked and masturbate in front of others, photographing their naked bodies in sexually explicit positions, and sodomising at least one detainee with a light.[22] More recently, reports of sexual abuse have surfaced in Syria, where government forces have raped boys and male detainees and beat men's genitals.[23]

Sexual violence against male civilians is also well-documented. Armed military groups frequently abduct and forcibly conscript men and boys for use as child soldiers; some are raped and held as sexual slaves. In the Eastern territories of Congo, 20.3 per cent of men reported being held as sexual slaves by opposition forces.[24] Other times, military troops sexually violate male civilians along with female civilians in raids against communities and villages, castrating or killing men, often forcing them to rape family members or community women in public, while also raping and mutilating women. Male civilians are often forced by enemy troops to commit incest, often considered one of the biggest social taboos in society.[25] In Bosnia, fathers and sons were forced to rape each other and men were forced to rape their female relatives.[26] Alternatively, men have been forced to witness the rape or sexual violation of their family members, which is a psychological form of abuse.[27]

The mental and physical consequences of rape and other forms of sexual violence against men are severe, including loss of sexual function, infertility, anxiety and depression.[28] Male victims suffer great social stigma and shame,

---

21 See, e.g., M. Gerecke, 'Explaining Sexual Violence in Conflict Situations: Preliminary Findings from Bosnia and Herzegovina, Rwanda and Sierra Leone' in L. Sjoberg and S. Via (eds.), *Gender, War, and Militarism: Feminist Perspectives* (Praeger Security International 2010), observing that while early feminists assumed a connection between sex and gender, later feminist work claimed that gender is a performed identity and, therefore, they expect that sexual violence may be targeted towards both women and men.

22 'Taguba Report on Treatment of Abu Ghraib Prisoners in Iraq' *FindLaw* <http:news.findlaw.com/hdocs/docs/iraq/tagubarpt.html> accessed 19.07.2018; S. Hersch, 'Torture at Abu Ghraib' *The New Yorker*, 10.05.2004 <http://www.newyorker.com/magazine/2004/05/10/torture-at-abu-ghraib> accessed 19.07.2018.

23 Human Rights Watch, *Syria: Sexual Assault in Detention*, Human Rights Watch, 15.06.2012 <http://www.hrw.org/news/2012/06/15/syria-sexual-assault-detention> accessed 19.07.2018.

24 Onyango and Hampanda, above n. 12, p. 239.

25 R.C. Carpenter, 'Recognizing Gender-Based Violence Against Civilian Men and Boys in Conflict Situations' (2006) 37 *Security Dialogue* 83, 95, 'In Sierra Leone, "[t]he rebels have forced civilians to commit incest, one of the biggest taboos in any society"'.

26 ibid.

27 See, e.g., E.J. Wood, '*Variation in Sexual Violence During War*' (2006) 34 *Politics & Society* 307, 314 (citing *Final Report of Truth & Reconciliation Commission of Sierra Leone*, vol. 3B, ch. 3, paras. 292–96 (2005).

28 P. Oosterhoff *et al.*, 'Sexual Torture of Men in Croatia and Other Conflict Situations: An Open Secret' (2004) 12 *Reproductive Health Matters* 68, 74.

fearing social ostracism if they seek medical treatment. In (most) cultures that assign men the role of protector of the family and community, the inability to protect women or children from sexual violence causes men humiliation and emotional trauma. In many countries, homosexuality is a crime, which deters men and boys from reporting these crimes for fear they will be presumed to be homosexual and in violation of the law.[29] In these places, a victim of rape by another man can be found guilty of engaging in homosexuality, a crime punished by the law.[30] Victims also fear police, who are perceived as homophobic.[31] For these reasons, sexual violence against men is vastly underreported and largely invisible.[32]

In other nations, the law does not recognise rape of men as a crime. Traditionally, many legal systems defined rape as unlawful sexual intercourse by a man with a woman who is not his wife, involving vaginal penetration by a penis, and did not criminalise rape of males.[33] This reluctance to acknowledge rape of men as a crime persists. The South African Constitutional Court in 2007, for example, extended the common-law definition of rape in *Masiya v. Director of Public Prosecutions* to include the anal rape of women, but not the anal rape of men.[34] The Court explained that rape is a form of 'manifesting male supremacy over females' and that the criminalisation of rape focuses on protecting women, who are its systemic target.[35] While South Africa subsequently amended its laws to define rape in gender-neutral terms, other nations have yet to do so, perpetuating the invisibility of the crime and its male victims.[36]

3. MARGINALISED AND IGNORED UNDER INTERNATIONAL LAW

While the international community has focused much attention on sexual violation of women and girls in war, it has largely ignored and failed to theorise sexual violence against men and boys. During the 1990s, feminists

29 See, e.g., G. Mezey and M. King, 'The Effects of Sexual Assault on Men: A Survey of Twenty-two Victims' in M.E. Odem and J. Clay-Warner (eds.), *Confronting Rape and Sexual Assault*, Rowman and Littlefield 1998, pp. 83, 88. See also E. Dugan, 'More Than 70 Countries Make Being Gay a Crime' *Independent*, 01.08.2010 <http://www.independent.co.uk/news/world/politics/more-than-70-countries-make-being-gay-a-crime-2040850.html> accessed 07.08.2016.

30 Sivakumaran, above n. 1, p. 256.

31 ibid.

32 ibid., pp. 254–55.

33 UN World Health Organization, *Sexual Health, Human Rights and the Law*, United Nations World Health Organization 2015, p. 36.

34 *Masiya v. Director of Public Prosecutions* 2007 (8) BCLR 827 (CC).

35 ibid., para. 37.

36 UN World Health Organisation, above n. 33.

and human rights advocates succeeded in persuading international tribunals to reconceptualise rape of women from a crime of 'honour' to a means of war and crime against humanity.[37] The Women's Caucus for Gender Justice, for example, theorised wartime rape of women as male violence against women.[38] Many feminist theorists have explained the rape of women's bodies as a means of genocide, a sexualised attack on an individual woman because of both her gender and her ethnicity or membership in another collective.[39] With some notable exceptions, however, these accounts have ignored or failed to conceptualise sexual violence against male bodies.[40]

In contrast to violence against women, wartime rape and sexual violence against men and boys have been largely absent or marginalised in international criminal jurisprudence.[41] With rare exceptions, prosecutors and courts have not recognised or conceptualised such acts as sexual violence but rather as 'torture' or outrages upon personal dignity, particularly where the violence is directed at male detainees and prisoners of war.[42] In *Prosecutor v. Duško Tadić*, for example, the ICTY documented an incident where male detainees were forced to perform

---

37 See Alison, above n. 5, p. 82; K. Engle, 'Feminism and Its (Dis)contents: Criminalizing Wartime Rape in Bosnia and Herzegovina' (2005) 99 *American Journal of International Law* 778, 786–87.

38 See Gerecke, above n. 21, p. 13, observing that while early feminists assumed a connection between sex and gender, later feminist work claimed that gender is a performed identity and therefore expects that sexual violence may target both women and men.

39 See, e.g., D.E. Buss, 'Rethinking 'Rape as a Weapon of War' (2009) 17 *Feminist Legal Studies* 145, 148–49. In conflicts such as the 1971 Bengali war or the conflict in Yugoslavia, 'rape narratives were deployed in different ways to construct shifting conceptions of national self-identity' (2009) 17 *Feminist Legal Studies* 154. See also J. Nagel, 'Ethnicity and Sexuality' (2000) 26 *Annual Review of Sociology* 107, 107, 109, discussing constructivist theories of sexuality, ethnicity, and nationalism; S.L. Russell-Brown, 'Rape as an Act of Genocide' (2003) 21 *Berkeley Journal of International Law* 350, 351, noting the intersectionality of genocidal rape, and arguing for the acknowledgement 'that genocidal rape is in fact a crime that implicates both gender and ethnicity and to understand that *certain* women are being raped by *certain* men for *particular* reasons'; C.S. Snyder *et al.*, 'On the Battleground of Women's Bodies: Mass Rape in Bosnia-Herzegovina' (2006) 21 *Affilia: Journal of Women and Social Work* 184, 193.

40 But see Buss, ibid., pp. 159–60; Alison, above n. 5, pp. 75, 90, arguing that 'sexual violence against men and boys is no less a gendered issue than sexual violence against women and girls'. For an overview of the case law of the ICTR, ICTY, SCSL and ICC, see de Brouwer and Ruiz, in this volume.

41 See V. Oosterveld, 'Atrocity Crimes Litigation Year-in-Review (2010): A Gender Perspective' (2011) 9 *Northwestern Journal of International Human Rights* 325, 326, 331; R. Grey and L.J. Shepherd, '"Stop Rape Now?": Masculinity, Responsibility, and Conflict-Related Sexual Violence' (2012) 16 *Men & Masculinities* 115, 116 (gender-based violence against men has been marginalised in international criminal jurisprudence); Sivakumaran, above n. 1, p. 261.

42 See Sivakumaran, above n. 1, p. 256. See also R.P. Petchesky, 'Rights of the Body and Perversions of War: Sexual Rights and Wrongs Ten Years Past Beijing' (2005) 184 *International Social Science Journal* 301, 312.

oral sex upon another detainee, and then were forced to bite off his testicles.[43] The prosecutor characterised and charged these acts as torture or inhuman treatment, as well as a grave breach of the Geneva Conventions, war crime and crime against humanity. The prosecutor did not, however, charge it as a crime of rape.

In *Prosecutor v. Delalić*, the ICTY convicted three defendants for the acts of subordinates, including placing burning fuse cords around the genitals of male detainees and forcing two detainees, who were brothers, to perform oral sex on each other.[44] The defendants were convicted for grave breaches of the Geneva Conventions and of violations of the laws or customs of war for crimes including murder, torture, inhuman treatment and unlawful confinement.[45] The Trial Chamber noted that the act of forcing two brothers to commit fellatio on each other could constitute rape if it had been pleaded 'in the appropriate manner', but the prosecutor had not done so.[46] Similarly, in *Prosecutor v. Simić et al.*, witnesses at the trial testified that the defendants rammed a police truncheon into the anus of a detainee and forced male prisoners to perform oral sex on each other and on a police chief, sometimes in front of other prisoners.[47] The defendants were not charged with rape but with crimes against humanity and grave breach of the Geneva Convention.[48]

There have been some exceptions, however, where the ICTY prosecutor charged defendants with rape for sexual assaults upon male detainees. For example, in *Prosecutor v. Sikirica et al.*, the prosecutor charged defendants with crimes against humanity for committing rape by forcing a male detainee to commit fellatio on another prisoner and for inserting an object into his anus.[49]

The reluctance to charge acts of forced fellatio and anal rape of men as crimes of sexual assault and/or rape contrasts markedly with the willingness of prosecutors to charge defendants with crimes of rape against female detainees. As Solange Mouthaan argues, the failure to charge defendants with committing rape or sexual assault disguises the gendered meaning of these crimes and the specific harms suffered by male victims.[50] It also perpetuates the erroneous belief that sexual violence in war is a crime against women, not men.

The Rome Statute, which took effect in 2002, is the first international document that explicitly includes various forms of sexual and gender-based

---

43 *Prosecutor v. Tadić* (Opinion and Judgment) IT-94-1-T, para. 206.
44 *Prosecutor v. Delalić* (Judgment) IT-96-21-T, paras. 24, 26.
45 ibid., para. 1066.
46 ibid., para. 1066.
47 *Prosecutor v. Simić* (Trial Judgment) IT-95-9-T, para. 728.
48 ibid., para. 1.
49 *Prosecutor v. Sikirica et al.* (Second Amended Indictment) IT-95-8-PT, para. 46.
50 S. Mouthaan, 'Sexual violence against men and international law: criminalising the unmentionable' (2013) *International Criminal Law Review* 665–95.

violence as crimes against humanity and war crimes.[51] The Statute applies to both international and non-international armed conflicts. Written in gender-neutral terms, it is broad enough to encompass the various forms of sexual violence against men. The Statute specifically enumerates rape, sexual slavery, enforced prostitution, forced pregnancy, enforced sterilisation and 'any other form of sexual violence of comparable gravity' as underlying acts of crimes of war and crimes against humanity in both international and national armed conflicts.[52] Sexual violence is defined broadly to encompass the commission of 'an act of a sexual nature' committed 'by force, or by threat of force or coercion, such as that caused by fear of violence, duress, detention, psychological oppression or abuse of power ... or by taking advantage of a coercive environment or such person's ... incapacity to give genuine consent'.[53]

Since the adoption of the Rome Statute, the United Nations has begun to recognise the prevalence of sexual violence against men during war. UN Security Resolution 1325, adopted in 2000, addressed sexual violence in war specifically as a gender-based crime against women and girls; Security Resolution 1820, adopted in 2008, emphasised the need to protect women and girls from sexual violence, ignoring men and boy victims.[54] It was not until 2009 that the UN Secretary-General recognised that men are also victims of sexual violence during conflict, observing that 'the case-law of the International Criminal Tribunal for the Former Yugoslavia (ICTY) and the Special Court for Sierra Leone (SCSL) also bears testimony to the use of sexual violence against men'.[55] UN Security Resolution 1888, adopted that same year, uses gender-neutral language that includes both male and female civilian victims of wartime violence.[56] In 2013, the UN Security Council explicitly recognised men and boys as victims of sexual violence during war in Security Resolution 2106. The resolution notes that 'sexual violence in armed conflict and post-conflict situations disproportionately affects women and girls, as well as groups that are particularly vulnerable or may be specifically targeted, *while also affecting men and boys* and those secondarily traumatized as forced witnesses of sexual violence against family members ...' (emphasis added).[57]

Given the relatively recent acknowledgement that men are also victims of sexual violence during war, it is not surprising that international criminal law has failed to adequately theorise the nature of the harm or vindicate the wrong.[58] There have been some positive developments, however, that suggest that courts

---

51 See Policy Paper, above n. 4, p. 5.

52 Rome Statute, art. 7(1)(g)-1–5, art. 8(2)(b)(xxii)-1–5; Article 8(b)(xxii); 8(e)(iv).

53 Elements of Crimes, Rome Statute of the International Criminal Court, art. 7(1)(g)(6).

54 UNSCR 1325, U.N. Doc. S/RES/1325 para. 10, 11 (31 October 2000).

55 S.G. Report, above n. 13.

56 See S.C. Res. 1888, U.N. Doc. S/RES/1888 para. 3 (30 September 2009).

57 UN S.C. Res. 2106, U.N. Doc. S/RES/2106 (24 June 2013).

58 See Sivakumaran, above n. 1, p. 256. See also Petchesky, above n. 42, p. 312.

and prosecutors are willing to focus attention on male victims. In 2010, the Trial Chamber for the Special Court for Sierra Leone (SCSL) in *Prosecutor v. Sesay et al.* convicted members of the Revolutionary United Front (RUF) for crimes including sexual violence against men and boys.[59] The violence occurred when the RUF captured a group of civilians and then committed grave acts of sexual violence against both men and women, including slitting the sexual organs of male captives, forcing the men and women to have sex with each other, forcing nudity of male captives, as well forcibly recruiting boys as child soldiers.[60] The prosecution situated the sexualised violence against the male victims within the context of an attack on the entire community that included the use of sexualised force against force against both men and women. By including charges of sexual violence and forced recruiting of men and boys, the prosecutor also illustrated the sex-specific ways in which men and boys are targeted because of their sex and gender.

While the ICC has recognised that the rape of men constitutes a crime under the Rome Statute, it has shown reluctance to recognise other forms of sexual violence against men. In 2016, the ICC convicted John-Pierre Bemba Gombo of crimes against humanity and war crimes for, *inter alia*, raping both men and women during the conflict in the Central Republic of Africa in 2002 and 2003. Specifically, Bemba was convicted of the crime of rape against two male civilians after male troops under his command penetrated the anuses of the male civilians with their penises.[61] The court emphasised that, according to the Elements of Crimes, 'the concept of "invasion" is intended to be broad enough to be gender-neutral' and includes same-sex penetration, and both male and/or female perpetrators and victims.[62] In *Kenyatta*, however, the ICC failed to recognise other forms of sexual violence against men as gendered crimes by refusing to categorise the forced circumcision of men as a crime of 'sexual violence' within the meaning of the Rome Statute.[63]

In *Kenyatta*, the Pre-Trial Chamber of the ICC in 2010 authorised the investigation into crimes against humanity committed in Kenya during post-election violence in 2007.[64] The Prosecutor applied to the Pre-Trial Chamber for Summons to Appear for high-ranking Kenyans accused of various crimes

---

59 *Prosecutor v. Sesay* (Judgment) SCSL-04-15-T (2 March 2009), para. 1067, 1207–08, 1616; see also V. Oosterveld, above n. 41, pp. 326, 334.

60 ibid.

61 *Prosecutor v. Jean-Pierre Bembo Gomba* (Judgment) ICC-01/05-01/08 (21 March 2016), para. 494.

62 ibid., para. 100.

63 *Prosecutor v. Kenyatta et al.*, (Decision on the Confirmation of Charges Pursuant to Article 61(7)(a) and (b) of the Rome Statute) ICC-01/09-02/11-382-Red, 23 January 2012, para. 266 ('*Kenyatta* Confirmation of Charges'); see also Grey and Chappell, in this volume.

64 *Situation in the Republic of Kenya* (Decision Pursuant to Article 15 of the Rome Statute) ICC-01/09, (31 March 2010); see also Oosterveld, above n. 41, p. 331.

against humanity, including the forced circumcision and penile amputation of men who belonged to the Luo tribe, whose male members are not circumcised.[65] Like the RUF attack in *Sesay*, the attack against the Luo people in the Rift Valley targeted both men and women and involved not only gang rape of women and mutilation, but also murder, including by beheading, and destruction of property and businesses. The Prosecutor alleged numerous incidents in which the perpetrators, sometimes in groups of up to 50 men, forcibly circumcised and, in some cases, amputated the penises of Luo men, using broken bottles and other weapons, resulting in some cases in the amputation of the men's penises.[66] Some men who resisted were beheaded.[67] In one incident, perpetrators cut off the testicles of a young Luo man and put them in his hand, then cut off his penis and put it in his mouth.[68]

The Prosecutor originally charged the acts of forced circumcision as 'other inhumane acts causing serious injury', but later sought to reclassify the acts as a form of 'sexual violence'.[69] The Pre-Trial Chamber rejected the request, holding that forced circumcision is not an act of a sexual nature.[70] At the hearing to confirm the charges, the Prosecutor argued the forced circumcisions were 'not just attacks on men's sexual organs but were intended as attacks on men's identities as men in their society and were designed to destroy their masculinity'.[71] The Prosecutor also argued that the forced circumcisions were punishment for post-election violence, alleging that the perpetrators had threatened to circumcise Luo men if they engaged in post-election violence. The Prosecutor referred to these threats as reflecting 'ethnic hatred, some already colored in sexually violent terms'. Unfortunately, the Prosecutor relied on conclusory assertions and did not offer any detailed explanation of why or how the forced circumcisions 'destroyed [the Luo men's] masculinity', or how the ethnicity of the Luo men was related to the actual or symbolic meaning of their forced circumcision.

Ignoring the Prosecutor's attempt to explain the gendered impact of the crime on the victims' masculinity and gender identity, the Pre-Trial Chamber II held that 'not every act of violence which targets parts of the body associated with sexuality should be considered an act of sexual violence'.[72] Whether an act is of sexual nature, the Chamber held, is a 'question of fact'. This language

65 *Prosecutor v. Francis Kirimi Muthaura, Uhuru Muigai Kenyatta and Mohammed Hussein Ali* (Transcript) ICC-01/09-02/11-T-5-Red-ENG CT WT 22-09-2011 1/108 NB PT (22 September 2011) at 89, lines 12-15 (International Criminal Court, Pre-Trial Chamber II) ('*Kenyatta* September 2011 Transcript').

66 ibid., pp. 88–90.

67 ibid., p. 90.

68 ibid., p. 63.

69 *Situation in the Republic of Kenya*, ICC-01/09-19, paras. 166–71; *Kenyatta* Confirmation of Charges, ICC-01/09-02/11-382-Red, para. 254–255.

70 *Kenyatta* Confirmation of Charges, ICC-01/09-02/11-382-Red, para. 264.

71 ibid.

72 ibid., para. 265.

appears to suggest that the forced mutilation of male genitals is not per se sexual in nature. The court did not offer any explanation of the meaning of 'sexual nature' or suggest what facts might be relevant to such a finding. It concluded, without explanation, that the evidence in *Kenyatta* did not support 'the sexual nature of the acts', explaining that 'it appears from the evidence that the acts were motivated by ethnic prejudice and intended to demonstrate cultural superiority of one tribe over the other'.[73] The Pre-Trial Chamber II instead found that forced circumcisions and penile amputation were serious physical injuries that constituted other inhumane acts under the Statute.[74]

The *Kenyatta* decision reveals a fundamental gap in the understanding of the ICC and other courts regarding the gendered nature of sexual violence against men and boys in war. The Pre-Trial Chamber fails to explain why the intentional assault of a sexual organ is not per se 'sexual in nature' and punishable as sexual violence. The perpetrators did not merely 'target' the penis, they forcibly and deliberately cut off the foreskin and sometimes the entire penis, permanently removing some or all of the sexual organ which, in some cases, resulted in forced sterilisation. The Chamber's treatment of the forced circumcision of Luo men contrasts markedly with the treatment of sexual violence against female victims by other tribunals.

In cases involving female victims, courts have interpreted sexual violence broadly to encompass mutilation of sexual organs and acts other than rape. In *Prosecutor v. Jean-Paul Akayesu*, for example, the ICTR defined sexual violence broadly in a case involving female victims, holding that '[s]exual violence is not limited to physical invasion of the human body and may include acts which do not involve penetration or even physical contact'.[75] In *Akayesu*, the ICTR considered the acts of undressing of a female student and forcing her to do gymnastics naked in a public courtyard to constitute sexual violence.[76] In cases involving amputation of women's breasts or mutilation of female genitals, other courts have not hesitated to treat the conduct as sexual in nature. Indeed, the UN Rapporteur on Systematic Rape, Sexual Slavery, and Slavery-like Practices in 1998 defined sexual violence as 'any violence, physical or psychological, carried out through sexual means or by targeting sexuality', including physical or psychological attacks against a person's sexual characteristics, such as mutilating genitals or slicing off a woman's breasts.[77] Had the perpetrators in *Kenyatta* cut

---

73 ibid., para. 266.

74 ibid., para. 270.

75 *Prosecutor v. Akayesu* (Judgment) ICTR-96-4-T (2 September 1998), paras. 688, 731, 732.

76 ibid.

77 UNCHR Sub-Commission on the Prevention of Discrimination and Protection of Minorities, 'Systematic rape, sexual slavery and slavery-like practices pursued during armed conflict: Final report submitted by Gay J. McDougall, *Special Rapporteur*', UN Doc E/CN.4/Sub.2/1998/13, 22 June 1998, paras. 21–22 ('Report of the Special Rapporteur on Systematic Rape').

off a portion of a woman's breast or genitals, the court most certainly would have concluded the act was sexual in nature. The mutilation and amputation of the penises of Luo men encompasses the same type of harm. The Pre-Trial Chamber failed to offer any explanation why it treated the intentional physical attack on men's sexual organs differently than physical attacks on women's sexual organs.

In cases involving female victims, courts also have recognised that rape and other forms of sexual violence can also constitute genocide, an attempt to destroy an ethnic group. In *Akayesu*, the ICTR found that rape of Tutsi women constituted both sexual violence and genocide. In that case, the male perpetrators specifically targeted Tutsi women for rape and sexual violence, targeting them because of their sex as well as their ethnicity, and using rape as a weapon to destroy their community. The court concluded that 'the sexualized representation of ethnic identity supports a finding that Tutsi women were subjected to sexual violence because they were Tutsi women'.[78]

While the *Kenyatta* case did not allege genocide, the perpetrators similarly targeted their victims based upon both their gender and ethnic identity. The perpetrators similarly incorporated sexualised representations of the ethnic identity of Luo men, threatening to circumcise Luo men as punishment for post-election violence. Unlike the perpetrators, Luo men are not circumcised; an intact foreskin is both a sexualised and gendered marker of Luo men as men and as members of the Luo tribe. The forced circumcision of Luo men thus constituted the use of sexual violence to dominate and subordinate a particular ethnic group by destroying an important marker of the victims' ethnic and gender identity and violently forcing conformance to the perpetrators' ethnic identity. Had the perpetrators in *Kenyatta* removed the clitoris of female members of an ethnic group that do not engage in female genital cutting, the Pre-Trial Chamber would almost certainly have held that the physical attack on the female's sexual organs constituted both sexual violence and genocide. The fact that the women would have been targeted because of their ethnic identity would not have erased the act of sexual violence against them.

4. MISSED OPPORTUNITY: THE ICC'S OFFICE OF THE PROSECUTOR'S 2014 POLICY PAPER

As the *Kenyatta* decision demonstrates, human rights advocates must work to ensure that courts understand, and take seriously, the gendered meaning and harms of sexual violence against men and boys in conflict. In 2014, the ICC's Office of the Prosecutor published a Policy Paper on Sexual and Gender-Based Crimes acknowledging the challenges in investigating and prosecuting crimes of

78 *Akayesu* Judgment, at paras. 688, 731, 732.

sexual and gender-based violence.[79] The OTP Policy Paper recognises that 'sexual and gender-based crimes against both females and males are often widespread, and/or used systematically as a tool of war or repression'.[80] Recognising that 'gender-based crimes are among the gravest under the Statute', the OTP affirmed its commitment to ending impunity for such violence, reiterating its commitment to integrating a gender perspective and analysis in all of its work. Unfortunately, the Policy Paper fails to address specifically the gendered nature and consequences of sexual violence against men and boys, missing an important opportunity to educate the international courts and community.

On the positive side, the OTP's Policy Paper represents a commitment to contextualising sexual violence during war through the lens of gender to help insure that perpetrators are held accountable for sexual violence. For male victims, like female victims, this is an essential first step in recognising acts of sexual violence as sexual and gendered crimes. The Policy Paper, for example, recognises the serious physical and mental harm caused by sexual violence and the social stigma and harm to communities, and affirms that sexual violence may be part of the pattern of destruction of a particular group that constitutes genocide. It also explains that '[o]ther crimes such as torture, mutilation, persecution, inhuman acts, and outrages upon personal dignity, may also have a sexual and/or gender element'.[81]Recognising the need 'to reflect the severity and multifaceted character' of such crimes, the Office states that it will bring cumulative charges for sexual and gender-based crimes, charging them as crimes per se as well as other forms of violence, such as torture.[82] This is an important departure from the reasoning in *Bemba*, in which the ICC Pre-Trial Chamber II refused to confirm cumulative charges for sexual crimes.[83] Similarly, the Office will also charge acts of sexual and gender-based crimes as different categories of crimes (war crimes, crimes against humanity and/or genocide) to more fully describe 'the nature, manner of commission, intent, impact, and context' of the crimes.[84] The Policy Paper also explicitly embraces an intersectional approach that examines the use of sexual violence to 'diminish gender, ethnic, racial,

---

79 OTP Policy Paper, above n. 4.

80 ibid., p. 30.

81 ibid.

82 ibid., p. 6, para. 7.

83 In the *Bemba* case, the Prosecution charged the perpetrators with rape or other forms of sexual violence, as well as the crime of outrages upon personal dignity through acts of rape or other forms of sexual violence. The Pre-Trial Chamber II declined to confirm the charge of outrages upon personal dignity on the grounds, inter alia, that most of the facts reflected the constitutive elements of force or coercion in the crime of rape, the count of outrages upon personal dignity is subsumed by the count of rape, and rape was 'the most appropriate legal characterisation of the conduct presented'. *Prosecutor v. Jean-Pierre Bemba Gombo* (Decision Pursuant to Article 61(7)(a) and (b) of the Rome Statute on the Charges of the Prosecutor Against Jean-Pierre Bemba Gombo) ICC-01/05-01/08-424 (15 June 2009), paras. 307–13.

84 OTP Policy Paper, above n. 4, para. 8.

and other identities'.[85] The use of cumulative charges and intersectional focus can help courts and prosecutors recognise and understand the meaning and consequences of sexual violence against men.

The ICC Policy Paper also sets forth a broad definition of sexual crimes that is helpful in many respects for male victims. In discussing the crime of 'other acts of sexual violence', the Policy Paper explicitly recognised that a 'sexual act' is not limited to physical violence and 'may even not involve any physical contact', and offers forced nudity as an example.[86] The Policy Paper emphasises that sexual crimes 'cover both physical and non-physical acts directed at a person's sexual characteristics'.[87] In a footnote, the Paper indicates its disagreement with the *Kenyatta* decision, affirming that it 'will continue to present acts of genital mutilation or deliberate injuries to the genitalia as sexual crimes'.[88] The Office's recognition that sexual acts are not required to be physical is helpful in prosecuting all forms of sexual violence against men during conflict. The forced nudity and masturbation at Abu Ghraib, for example, constituted non-physical acts that were directed at the male detainees' sexual characteristics and, as affirmed by the Policy Paper, thus meet the definition of a crime of sexual violence.

The Policy Paper's discussion of physical and non-physical sexual violence, however, is arguably limited in two important respects. First, the Paper defines 'sex' as referring 'to the biological and physiological characteristics that define men and women'.[89] Consequently, a court might interpret 'acts directed at a person's sexual characteristics' narrowly to refer to violence directed at biological or physical characteristics and not acts directed at one's gender. Violence that targets men or women for failing to conform to social norms of gender, including norms of heterosexuality or masculinity, might not fall within the Office's definition. Such a narrow reading, however, would be inconsistent with the Office's stated intent to apply a gender analysis to crimes that take into account the social roles of men and women.

Second, the Policy Paper's discussion of sexual violence incorporates some, but not all, of the definition of sexual violence in the 1998 Report of the Special Rapporteur on Sexual Slavery. The Special Rapporteur defined sexual violence to cover both physical and psychological attacks carried out by sexual means or by targeting sexuality.[90] It specifically defined sexual violence to include both (a) physical or psychological attacks 'carried out through sexual means or by targeting sexuality', such as 'mutilating a person's genitals',[91]

---

85 ibid., para. 20.
86 ibid., para. 17.
87 ibid.
88 ibid., para. 17, fn 14.
89 ibid., p. 3.
90 Report of the Special Rapporteur on Systematic Rape, above n. 77, para. 21.
91 ibid.

and (b) 'situations where two persons are forced to have sex with each other or harm one another in a sexual manner'.[92] This definition is broader and specifically recognises genital mutilation as sexual violence. It also recognises other forms of sexual violence against men, such as forced sex or forced incest, that may not constitute acts 'directed at a person's sexual characteristics' within the meaning of the Policy Paper.

While the OTP states that it will seek to enhance a 'gender perspective and analysis' in its work, its Policy Paper fails to specifically address the dynamics of sexual violence against men. Instead, its analysis focuses primarily on gender inequalities between men and women, missing an opportunity to specifically address male-on-male sexual violence. The Policy Paper defines 'gender' in accordance with Article 7(3) of the Rome Statute, referring to 'the two sexes, male and female, within the context of society',[93] which 'acknowledges the social construction of gender and the accompanying roles, behaviours, activities, and attributes assigned to women and men, and girls and boys'.[94] As described in the Paper, the Office of the Prosecutor will consider 'whether, and in what ways, crimes, including sexual and gender-based crimes, are related to gender norms and inequalities'.[95] While the language is admittedly vague, the Policy Paper explained that the analysis requires 'an examination of the underlying differences and inequalities between women and men, and girls and boys, and the power relationships and other dynamics which determine and shape gender roles in a society, and give rise to assumptions and stereotypes'.[96] The Policy Paper states that 'gender analysis' as rooted in an examination of the differences between men and women, i.e. 'the roles of females and males; the different patterns of involvement, behaviour, and activities that they have in economic, social, and legal systems; the constraints they face relative to one another; and available opportunities'.[97] Similarly, it describes 'gender perspective' as requiring 'an understanding of differences in status, power, roles, and needs between males and females, and the impact of gender on people's opportunities and interactions'.[98]

The Office's proposed gender analysis fails to address the specifics of sexual violence against men or offer guidance on how to explain the dynamics of men raping other men during war. Instead, it echoes familiar feminist theories that explain wartime rape of women as rooted in patriarchy and the social and economic inequality of women. These sex-specific explanations of wartime sexual violence are inadequate to explain the nature and impact of violence

92 ibid., para. 22.
93 ibid., p. 3.
94 OTP Policy Paper, above n. 4, para. 15.
95 ibid., para. 20.
96 ibid.
97 ibid., p. 13, fn. 17.
98 ibid., p. 3.

against men and boys. Focusing on the inequalities between men and women is simply not enough. A gender analysis that seeks to theorise and understand sexual violence against male victims must look more closely at gender relations between different groups of men within particular social locations to understand the social meaning and impact of this form of violence against men.

5. USING MASCULINITIES THEORY TO EXPLAIN SEXUAL VIOLENCE AGAINST MEN

Masculinities theory provides critical insights that allow us to see how sexual violence against both men *and* women functions as a gendered means to empower particular groups of men in specific spaces during conflict. As the present author has previously argued elsewhere, sexual violence against men and women can be understood as a masculinised practice deployed against both men and women, within particular social systems of gender that privilege and empower heterosexualised masculinity.[99]

A fundamental insight of masculinities theory is that masculinity is not a fixed category of identity, but rather a social practice.[100] R.W. Connell explains that masculinity is 'simultaneously a place in gender relations, the practices through which men and women engage that place in gender, and the effects of these practices in bodily experience, personality and culture'.[101] Masculinities theory recognises that not all men share the same position in society but rather, that different groups of men occupy different positions of power within a particular society. One's position as a man in any particular society intersects with race, ethnicity, class, sexual orientation and other forms of subordination. Thus, masculinities theorists speak of multiple masculinities, some of which are hegemonic and powerful while others are marginalised and subordinated. Masculinities create, enforce and reproduce relations of power between men as individuals; between men as groups; between men and women; and within larger social institutions such as the military, the workplace and the nation-state.[102]

In most societies, hegemonic masculinities typically construct men as powerful, sexually aggressive and heterosexual, defined in opposition to those men who are constructed as effeminate or homosexual, and in opposition to women.[103] As a social practice, masculinity is constructed 'in front of and for

99 This section incorporates sections from a previous publication by the present author which discussed a masculinities approach to sexual violence against men in war. See Vojdik, above n. 5, pp. 940–49.

100 R.W. Connell, *Masculinities*, 1st edn., Polity Press 1995, p. 68; Vojdik, above n. 5, p. 926.

101 Connell, ibid.

102 Vojdik, above n. 5, p. 926.

103 V.K. Vojdik, 'Gender Outlaws: Challenging Masculinity in Traditionally Male Institutions' (2002) 17 *Berkeley Journal of Gender, Law & Justice* 68, 91.

other men and against femininity'.[104] Within groups of men, rites of institution are used to continually test the masculinity of individual men while simultaneously reinforcing the solidarity of the group.[105] French sociologist Pierre Bourdieu explains that 'manliness must be validated by other men, in its reality as actual or potential violence, and certified by recognition of membership of the group of "real men"'.[106]

During wartime, sexualised violence against both men and women is a critical means of creating and enforcing masculine power.[107] As Joshua Goldstein argues in *War and Gender*, war and gender are reciprocal: warriors are constructed as male and masculine, and masculinity is constructed through war.[108] Through a myriad of social and institutional practices, military institutions tend to construct warriors as masculine and dominant, enforcing a violent form of masculinity. In the United States military, for example, various rituals compel soldiers to 'prove their social identity as men through both the symbolic and actual enactment of a hypermasculinity' that denigrates women, as well as men.[109] Examples include drill chants using anti-women and homophobic and hazing rituals that involve genital violence against men.[110]

Goldstein explains that militaries typically sexualise and 'feminise' the enemy, using sexually violent language to describe military domination of the enemy.[111] Militaries throughout history, he explains, have symbolically feminised the enemy as a means to construct themselves as masculine and dominant and to motivate troops to fight. Military and political leaders often refer to the symbolic castration or rape of the male enemy. Former U.S. President Lyndon Johnson, Goldstein observes, referred to the defeat of Vietnamese soldiers during the Tet Offensive as castration: 'I didn't just screw Ho Chi Minh. I cut his pecker off'![112] During the Gulf War, a cartoon depicted Saddam Hussein bowing down in prayer, an enormous U.S. missile positioned to penetrate his anus.[113]

---

104 P. Bourdieu, *Masculine Domination*, Richard Nice trans., Stanford Press 2001, p. 53.

105 ibid., p. 52.

106 ibid.

107 Vojdik, above n. 5, p. 941.

108 Goldstein, above n. 11, pp. 265–66.

109 See, e.g., M.W. Segal, 'Military Culture and Military Families' in M.F. Katzenstein and J. Reppy (eds.), *Beyond Zero Tolerance: Discrimination in Military Culture*, Rowman and Littlefield 1999.

110 V.K. Vojdik, 'Beyond Stereotyping in Equal Protection Doctrine: Reframing the Exclusion of Women from Combat' (2005) 57 *Alabama Law Review* 303, 342, analysing social practices that construct militaries as masculine; C. Linhares de Albuquerque and E. Paes-Machado, 'The Hazing Machine: The Shaping of Brazilian Military Police Recruits' (2004) 14 *Policing & Society* 175, 184, documenting use of anti-women and homophobic language, forced cross-dressing and other acts of humiliation that reflect masculine norms in Brazilian training of military police.

111 Goldstein, above n. 11, p. 358.

112 ibid.

113 C. Cohn, 'Wars, Wimps, and Women' in M. Cooke and A. Woollacott (eds.), *Gendering War Talk*, Princeton 1993, p. 237.

It is not surprising, then, that military groups often engage in sexual violence against both men, women and homosexuals (actual or perceived) as a form of masculinised domination, both within the military organisation itself and against the enemy during conflict.[114] Recent surveys in the United States and Australia, for example, have documented intra-military sexual abuse and assault of male troops by their peers or superiors.[115] Members of military groups sometimes use sexual violence and rape to punish men who refuse to join a militia or participate in killing.[116] In Rwanda, for example, Hutu male combatants sexually assaulted other Hutu men to humiliate and shame those who refused to join in the killing.[117] During conflict, male combatants similarly use rape as a weapon against enemy women to prove their manhood and toughness to other members of the armed group while constructing and enforcing the cohesion of the military unit.[118] Female soldiers are also socialised to exhibit militarised aggressiveness, which has led to them participating as perpetrators of sexual violence against men and women in recent conflicts.[119]

Using the lens of masculinity theory, sexual violence against male combatants and civilians thus can be seen as a gendered tool of war – a social practice that intersects with gender, ethnicity and national identities, deployed as a means to subordinate the male victim and his enemy group.[120] This occurs in several ways.

First, sexual violence against men, like violence against women, is a gendered means of domination which symbolically feminises the enemy while constructing the military perpetrators as masculine.[121] As Sivakumaran argues,

---

114 See Goldstein, above n. 11, p. 283. See also Wood, above n. 27, p. 326, 'One result of such practices is that soldiers then represent domination of the enemy in a gendered way, leading to the use of specifically *sexual* violence against enemy women and, occasionally, against enemy men who are dominated through male rape and castration'.

115 US Dep't of Veterans Affairs, 'Military Sexual Trauma' (2013) <http://www.mentalhealth.va.gov/docs/mst_general_factsheet.pdf> accessed 12.11.2016; R. Evans, 'Hazing in the ADF: a Culture of Denial?' (2013) 10 *Australian Army Journal* 113.

116 Vojdik, above n. 5, p. 949.

117 Buss, above n. 39, p. 159, discussing research revealing sexual assault of Hutu men by other Hutus; sexual assault used to humiliate and shame men who would not join killing.

118 See A. Maedl, 'Rape as Weapon of War in the Eastern DRC? The Victims' Perspective' (2011) 33 *Human Rights Quarterly* 128, 141, describing the ways in which gang rapes by armed groups improve group bonding and cohesion. See also Wood, above n. 27, p. 327; Goldstein, above n. 11, p. 365.

119 In Sierra Leone, women were participants in one out of four gang rapes along with men, and had a reputation for encouraging excessive violence. D.K. Cohen, 'Female Combatants and the Perpetration of Violence: Wartime Rape in the Sierra Leone Civil War' (2013) 65 *World Politics* 383, 383–85, 399. In the Democratic Republic of Congo, a 2010 population survey found that 41 per cent of female sexual violence victims and 10 per cent of male victims reported having been victimised by female perpetrators. ibid., p 385.

120 Vojdik, above n. 5, pp. 944–45.

121 See, e.g., Vojdik, above n. 5, p. 945; Onyango and Hampanda, above n. 12, p. 41, 'Socially constructed notions of gender and sexuality can also provide motivation for perpetrators to commit sexual violence against men in armed conflict settings. For example, leaders often tell soldiers that to be a real man is to assert a militaristic, masculine dominance and emasculate

the rape of men during war is not about sexual desire, but rather masculine domination.[122] Sexual violence against men by combatants, he and others argue, serves a similarly gendered function as rape of women: it symbolically masculinises the perpetrator as dominant and aggressive, while symbolically constructing the enemy men, who are violated, as stereotypically feminine, weak and powerless.[123] The experience of rape as victimisation conflicts with the social construction of masculinity, which typically requires men to be strong, dominant and heterosexual. When men are raped, they symbolically lose their gendered identity as men.[124] As Miranda Alison explains, the sexual violation of men repositions them as powerless victims, challenging social definitions of masculinity.[125] Male victims are stigmatised as weak and effeminate because they have been unable to protect themselves, their families and their community from enemy aggression.[126]

The sexual violation of men can thus be seen as an attack upon the male victim's masculine gender identity.[127] Accounts by male victims of wartime rape have described the gendered nature of the harm; many explain that they have lost their social identity as men in their communities, where they are stigmatised, ostracised and rejected. One male survivor of rape in the Eastern DRC explained that being raped stripped him of his identity as a man, effectively transforming him into a woman. He had not told his wife about the rape, because 'two wives cannot live in the same house'.[128] Another male survivor from Uganda, taken by rebels into the forest and gang raped 11 times one night, refused to tell his brother because he feared his brother would say, 'Now, my brother is not a man'.[129] A male survivor from the Congo, who was abducted and kept as a sexual slave by opposing forces who raped him repeatedly, explained that members of his village derided him for losing his masculinity, calling him 'a bush wife' and ostracising him from his community.[130]

---

other men. Sexual violence against the perceived enemy, either male or female, is one way of expressing this notion of masculinity'.

122 See Sivakumaran, above n. 1, p. 276.

123 See ibid.; Vojdik, above n. 5, p. 945.

124 ibid., pp. 265–66.

125 See Alison, above n. 5, p. 81.

126 See Oosterhoff *et al.*, above n. 28, p. 70. See also A. DelZotto and A. Jones, 'Male-on-Male Sexual Violence in Wartime: Human Rights' Last Taboo?' (March 2002) (unpublished manuscript) <http://adamjones.freeservers.com/malerape.htm> accessed 19.07.2018.

127 See, e.g., Onyango and Hampanda, above n. 12, p. 241, '[M]en who become helpless and are overpowered by other males may be judged to have failed in their masculine duty. Therefore, compared with female survivors, males become more stigmatised, ashamed with their situation, and less likely to report the incident or seek help'.

128 M. Chistian, O. Safari, P. Ramazani, G. Burnham and N. Glass, 'Sexual and Gender Based Violence against Men in the Democratic Republic of Congo: Effects on Survivors, Their Families and the Community' (2011) 27 *Medicine, Conflict and Survival* 227, 235.

129 Storr, above n. 20, based upon interviews of Makerere University's Refugee Law Project and interviews with male victims of rape in Uganda.

130 See Sivakumaran, above n. 1, p. 266.

Because of the taboo against homosexuality in many societies, the shame and stigma are arguably even greater for men than women. In such societies, men who are victims of male rape are not recognised as victims but branded as homosexual. This stigma, arguably heightened during wartime, encourages men to remain silent and not report sexual violence.[131] The silence and shame around male victims of rape helps explain the courts' reluctance to recognise the sexualised and gendered harm suffered by male victims.

Second, sexual violence against male bodies also functions as a gendered means to attack the larger ethnic, racial, religious or political collective to which the individual man belongs.[132] As feminist advocates have long argued, women are raped not solely because they are women, but because they are also members of particular collective.[133] Because women are embodied symbols of their community, the rape of an individual woman during armed conflict symbolically feminises and subordinates her group while constructing the perpetrators' group as masculine and dominant.[134] The same dynamic occurs when male members of a community are raped or sexually violated during war. Male bodies also symbolically embody the collective. As Dubravka Žarkov argues, the phallus represents the virility of the collective; sexual violence that targets the penis thus represents the attempted destruction or subordination of the larger collective.[135] Genital violence, including castration and forced circumcision, also constitutes sexualised forms of violence that seek to destroy the larger collective, either symbolically or actually, as in cases when the violence results in the forced sterilisation of men. Like the rape of women, the sexual violation of men represents the destruction and subordination of the ethnic or racial group to which he belongs.[136]

Third, sexual violence against men, like mass or gang rape of women in wartime, is an effective weapon to terrorise and displace the enemy population.[137] As numerous experts have reported, sexual violence against women, particularly when committed in public, has been deployed to create fear and terror among entire communities and thereby empower the perpetrators.[138] Public genital

---

131 Onyango and Hampanda, above n. 12, p. 241; Mezey and King, above n. 29, p. 87; see, e.g., K.O. Dunivin, 'Military Culture: Change and Continuity' (1994) 20 *Armed Forces & Society* 531, 533–35.

132 Engle, above n. 37, pp. 788, 791; Carpenter, above n. 25, p. 96; Vojdik, above n. 5, p. 947.

133 See, e.g., Buss, above n. 39, pp. 148–49, discussing feminist theories of sexual violence against women as embodiment of national collective or ethnic group.

134 See, e.g., Alison, above n. 5, pp. 80–81.

135 See Žarkov, above n. 10, p. 78, '[W]hen the male body is ethnic and male at the same time, the castration of a single man' represents the castration of the entire ethnic group.

136 ibid. See also Alison, above n. 5 p. 86, explaining that the castration and forced rape and sexual performance by male prisoners 'illustrates how male to male sexual violence is both gendered and ethnicised, acting to feminise victims and their homosexualised ethno-nationality whilst masculinising perpetrators and their heterosexualised ethno-nationality'.

137 Vojdik, above n. 5, pp. 948–49.

138 DelZotto and Jones, above n. 126.

and sexual violence against men serves similar purposes. As in *Sesay*, military groups enter villages or communities and unleash a reign of terror of sexual violence against both men and women, along with the amputation of limbs of men and boys and murder.[139] Males have been forced to have sexual intercourse with other family members, both male and female.[140] The public rape, torture or killing of men sends a powerful message to the community that their men cannot protect themselves, let along protect the community, instilling a sense of powerlessness and deep fear in the entire community.

Incorporating these insights from masculinities theory can help international courts and prosecutors recognise and understand the gendered nature and harm of sexual violence against men and boys in conflict. Wartime sexual violence against both men and women is inter-related; both empower certain groups of men while subordinating both female and male victims, terrorising the entire community.

6. KENYATTA REVISITED

To vindicate the gendered harms that male victims suffer, the Office of the Prosecutor and human rights advocates need to broaden their gender analysis to theorise sexual violence against men and boys. The ICC and international tribunals need to understand that the rape of men boys during conflict, like that of women, functions as a gendered means of domination. Incorporating insights from masculinities theory can help both prosecutors and courts recognise and understand the gendered nature of such violence and the harms inflicted upon its male victims.

Seen through the lens of masculinities theory, the forcible circumcision and penile amputation of Luo men in the *Kenyatta* case indisputably constitutes sexual violence. The forcible circumcision and penile amputation of Luo men did not merely result in serious bodily injury, as the Pre-Trial Chamber found. It also constituted a physical attack on their genitals and thus their sexual characteristics. The forcible circumcision of Luo men, who are not traditionally circumcised, was gendered in meaning and harm. It symbolically attacked their sexual identity as males as well as their masculine gender identity. The act itself enacted the ritualistic and public sexual domination of the Luo men by the perpetrators, symbolically feminising the Luo men, who were powerless to protect themselves from sexual assault. The sexual attacks on the Luo men did not occur in a vacuum, but as part of a reign of terror that included the rape

139 See, e.g, *Prosecutor v. Sesay* (Judgment) SCSL-04-15-T para. 1600, describing acts of sexual violence directed at both men and women of particular village.

140 See DelZotto and Jones, above n. 126.

and mutilation of women and other men, murder and destruction of property. As such, it functioned to terrorise the entire Luo community.

7. CONCLUSION

Now that the international community has recognised that men and boys may also be victims of sexual violence, it is imperative that the ICC, prosecutors, and human rights advocates develop a gender analysis that adequately theorises and explains the gendered nature of such violence. Sexual violence, whether against men or women, inflicts serious and gendered harm upon its victims and perpetuates masculinised domination of enemy communities. Recognising that wartime sexual violence against men and women is inter-related is a critical first step that will help the ICC and other tribunals enforce the Rome Statute and eliminate impunity for sexual violence that has been hidden for far too long.

CHILDREN AND ARMED CONFLICT

Pitfalls of a 'One Size Fits All' Approach

Solange Mouthaan

The impact of armed conflict on children is everyone's responsibility. And it must be everyone's concern.[1]

1. INTRODUCTION

With her words, more than 20 years ago, Graça Machel urged the United Nations' General Assembly to devote attention to the plight of children in armed conflict. Her report highlighted the devastating effects of armed conflict on children's day-to-day lives and communities.[2] It proved to be a real eye-opener for the World and thus, under the helm of the Security Council, the United Nations (UN) established a system to afford children better protections.

1 G. Machel, First Special Representative on Children in Armed Conflict, *Impact of Armed Conflict on Children*, 1996, UNGA, A/51/306, p. 4.

2 Ibid., section 24.

We have come a long way since this influential report. Children affected by armed conflict occupy an important place within the UN's peace and security agenda. They are also the recipients of international legal protections. However, when exploring the effects on children of the conflict in the Syrian Arab Republic (Syria), it is difficult to discern meaningful progress on the ground. Children still suffer unduly from the consequences of armed conflict, particularly in areas under siege, thus it may be questioned whether existing legal protections are effective and sufficiently child-centred in their approaches.[3] In addition, the Syrian conflict demonstrates how specific concerns of girls may be silenced by the broader framework of childhood or womanhood, thus positioning girls at the peripheries of legal protections.[4]

First, girls are children. There are many common ways in which children suffer from the consequences of armed conflict, such as death, injury and poverty. Each of these harms are detrimental to children's well-being. However, international law takes a gender-neutral approach by which children are identified as a homogenous category, but in which the boy-child's experiences have become the dominant norm. This stance fails to recognise that children are also identifiable by other categories, such as religion, ethnicity or indeed gender, as influenced by their contextual background in existence before and during armed conflict.[5] The UN's approach to children in conflict has been to identify six grave violations on a case-by-case basis, against which children should be protected. These are killing and maiming of children; recruitment or use of children as soldiers; sexual violence against children; attacks against schools or hospitals; denial of humanitarian access for children; and abduction of children.[6] Thus many areas in which gender inequality impacts girls, such as gendered economic, health and educational harms, are not adequately addressed. A case-by-case approach challenges specific harms, but fails to acknowledge the broader context and cause of gender inequality and discrimination. So far, the specific effects of armed conflict experienced by girls or boys remain largely underexplored. An understanding of gendered effects on children of armed conflict would foster more effective responses both during and after the conflict ends.

Second, girls are also women, albeit women 'in the making'. Even though all women have been girls and the situation in which women find themselves have

---

3 Reports that children are trapped in building under attack in Aleppo, see *The Guardian*, 13.12.2016, available at <https://www.theguardian.com/world/2016/dec/13/red-cross-urgent-plea-to-save-civilians-aleppo-syria>.

4 The author acknowledges that the suffering of sexual violence by boys should be further explored and the Syrian conflict could provide an illustration of this, but this does not form part of the remit of this chapter.

5 In addition, there are other equally important contextual factors, such as race, class, place.

6 Child Recruitment, UN Security Council Resolution 1379 (2001); killing and maiming of children and/or sexual violence against children, UN Security Council Resolution 1882 (2009); attacks on schools and hospitals, UN Security Council Resolution 1998 (2011); abductions.

a direct bearing on that of girls, girlhood is different to womanhood. Age is an important marker of experience that should not be overlooked. There has been a steady growing interest in preventing conflict-related sexual violence against women since the mid-1990s. Several recent initiatives highlight that children and men may also suffer such harms and advocate the need to address this as well.[7] In this respect, a shift towards engaging with a more complete understanding of victims of conflict-related sexual violence can be observed. However, those initiatives that are women-focused tend to target 'women and girls' in the same breath. Yet here the experiences of the adult woman dominate the discourse while erasing those of girls.

Hence, rather than being viewed as an autonomous individual, the girl-child finds herself at the margins of many vulnerable groupings, increasing the risk that her experiences and needs will be overlooked, thus perpetuating inequality. This chapter highlights the importance of recognising difference while also advocating a more child-centred approach in its legal protections of children affected by armed conflict: one that acknowledges the intersections between childhood and other characteristics such as age and gender, while also providing agency to children in determining how their needs are addressed. The first part will demonstrate that the working model adopted by the UN to address the needs of children affected by armed conflict, albeit promising, favours a gender-neutral approach in its understanding of children. The second part will turn its gaze towards Syria and explore some of the differential effects of Syria's armed conflict on girls and boys due to, in part, gendered underpinnings. In a final part, the examples of child recruitment and early marriage will emphasise some of the unintended consequences of a gender-neutral and non-distinct approach for girls. Thus, this demonstrates that our understandings of the consequences of armed conflict cannot be simplified without the risk of overlooking girls and supporting gender inequality.

2. THE UN AND CHILDREN AFFECTED BY ARMED CONFLICT

This section will focus on the UN's work to protect children in armed conflict either directly or via its responses to conflict-related sexual violence which find their basis in international law. It demonstrates that despite a potentially effective action-oriented approach the impact of the UN's efforts remains minimal and international law meaningless due to political interference, lack of enforcement mechanisms and the understanding that children are a homogenous category of individuals regardless of gender or age difference.

7 *Prosecutor v. Bemba*, ICC-01/05-01/08.

2.1. CHILDREN, ARMED CONFLICT AND INTERNATIONAL LAW

International law offers the legal basis for the protection of children against the adverse effects of armed conflict. On the one hand, children's human rights law addresses some of the harms that children suffer during armed conflict within the remit of the Convention on the Rights of the Child (CRC) and the Optional Protocol to the Convention on the Rights of the Child on the Involvement of Children in Armed Conflict.[8] The brutality of modern day armed conflict is not easily reconcilable with the principle of best interest of children which guides the CRC.[9]

The CRC recognises that all children, defined as all human beings under the age of 18 years, belong to a specific category to which States need to offer protection, while at the same time bestowing rights to enable children to reach their full potential. Hence, children should be protected from all forms of violence, including sexual violence and sexual exploitation.[10] Places that children are likely to use, such as schools and hospitals, should be protected from direct attacks.[11]

On the other hand, in international humanitarian law the protection of children is not a priority. By their age, children should enjoy special protection under the Geneva Conventions. All parties to a conflict should be obliged to prioritise the welfare of children during hostilities. This is specified in Resolution 1261 in which the UN Security Council:

> calls upon parties to armed conflicts to undertake feasible measures during armed conflicts to minimise the harm suffered by children, such as 'days of tranquillity', to allow the delivery of necessary services, and further calls upon all parties to armed conflicts to promote, implement and respect such measures.[12]

Nevertheless, the four Geneva Conventions are scant in their interest in protecting children.[13] The two 1977 Additional Protocols offer slightly increased

---

8 UN Convention on the Rights of the Child [hereinafter CRC], U.N.T.S. 3, entered into force 2 September 1990. Syria ratified the CRC in 1990. The Optional Protocol I to the CRC on the Involvement of Children in Armed Conflict (2000). Syria ratified the Optional Protocol in 2003.

9 The Optional Protocol on the Involvement of Children in Armed Conflict (2000) and the Optional Protocol on the sale of children, child prostitution and child pornography (2000).

10 CRC, Arts. 19 and 34.

11 The Optional Protocol I on the Involvement of Children in Armed Conflict (2000).

12 UN Security Resolution 1261 (1999) U.N. Doc S/Res/1261, §8.

13 Among relevant provisions which mention children under 15 are the possibility to establish hospitals or safety zones (Article 14, Fourth Geneva Convention); to conclude local agreements for the removal from besieged and encircled areas (Article 17, Fourth Geneva Convention); to permit the free passage of all consignments of essential foodstuffs, clothing

protections. Additional Protocol I declares that children shall be the object of special respect and be protected from any form of indecent assault and should receive all the necessary care and aid in times of armed conflict. Schools and hospitals are protected civilian objects.

Whereas the overall approach of children's human rights is very much centred around the needs of the child and potential for empowerment, that of international humanitarian law broadly relies on the protection afforded to civilians in general. Children are perceived as incidental to the aims and objectives of international humanitarian law. However, children's human rights provisions provide a different but complementary perspective on the effects of armed conflict on children. A reinterpretation of existing provisions from a children's human right perspective may contribute to the reduction of suffering of children. Yet, for the moment, legal protections remain inadequate. Notably, international humanitarian law and children's human rights provisions emphasise the protection offered to children from recruitment and use by armed groups.[14] Markedly absent is a recognition of the specificity of sexual violence against children. These two issues will be discussed in further detail in section 4. For now, the focus will be on the way in which the UN protects children from armed conflict and conflict-related sexual violence.

2.2. THE UN'S ACTION-ORIENTED APPROACH TO PROTECT CHILDREN IN ARMED CONFLICT

Recent figures estimate around 230 million children live in territories affected by armed conflict.[15] The UN has recognised the plight of children in armed conflict by establishing a Special Representative of the Secretary General for Children and Armed Conflict.[16] In addition, the Security Council embedded the protection of children in armed conflict in its maintenance of international peace and security agenda.[17] While it could have remained at the stage of expression of principles, the UN has adopted an action-oriented working method and an innovative monitoring system to tackle violations of children's rights during armed conflict.

The UN Security Council provides the overall impetus for action based on regular annual reports by the UN's Secretary General to raise awareness and inform on progress in situations on the agenda of the UN Security Council. In turn, these reports give rise to several actions.

and tonics (Article 23, Fourth Geneva Convention); to ensure that children orphaned or separated from their families as a result of war are not left to their own resources (Article 24, Fourth Geneva Convention).

14 A theme discussed by Alison Bisset in of this volume.

15 UNICEF, *Children and Emergencies in 2014 – Facts and Figures*, New York: UNICEF 2014.

16 UN General Assembly Resolution (1997), A/RES/51/77.

17 UN Security Council Resolutions 1314 (2000) S/RES/1314 & 2225 (2015) S/RES/2225.

First, these reports provide the basis for the UN Security Council to identify grave violations against children on a needs basis. So far, among the broad ranging harms suffered, including the loss of life, safety, security, education, health, nutrition and specific gendered concerns, six grave violations which are sufficiently founded in international law have been recognised.

Second, the UN Secretary General's reports contain Annexes 'naming and shaming' all parties that commit one or more grave violations against children in contravention of international law.[18] This strategy is intended to have a stigmatic and deterrent effect on potential offenders. The 2012 report led to parties involved in the Syrian conflict to be named and shamed.[19] The Syrian Government Forces have been named and shamed for more than five years and are thus considered persistent perpetrators of the grave violations of killing and maiming children, committing rape and other forms of sexual violence and engaging in attacks on schools and hospitals.

Third, the UN Security Council established a Working Group on Children and Armed Conflict to respond to the experiences of children on the ground with practical steps.[20] It may recommend appropriate action to parties to a conflict, governments and the UN, such as a national action place, a UN Security Council resolution or presidential statement.[21]

The overall aim of the UN's approach is to persuade identified parties to seek removal from the 'naming and shaming' list. Each party must demonstrate they have adopted and executed a purposefully designed national action plan to respond to their specific situation in order to end and prevent violations.[22] For instance, if government forces have been identified as recruiting and using children to actively participate in armed conflict, the negotiated action plan may call upon the authorities to criminalise the recruitment and use of children; to adopt age-verification mechanisms; and to ensure children's reintegration in civilian life. The UN Secretary General will remove those parties from the list based on positive reports received from the UN Monitoring and Reporting Mechanism.[23]

---

18 In 2016 in the Syrian Arab Republic, the lists identifies Ahrar al-Sham al-Islami, Free Syria Army (FSA), Islamic State of Iraq and the Levant, Nusrah Front and People's Protection Units (YPG) as parties who recruit and use children; Ahrar al-Sham al-Islami, Free Syria Army (FSA), Government forces, including the National Defence Forces and the Shabbiha, Islamic State of Iraq and the Levant, Nusrah Front and People's Protection Units (YPG) as parties who kill and maim children; and Government forces, including the National Defence Forces and the Shabbiha, Islamic State of Iraq and the Levant as parties who commit rape and other forms of sexual violence and engage in attacks on schools and/or hospitals. See Report on Children in Armed Conflict of the Secretary General, A/70/836-S/2016/360, 20 April 2016.

19 Report of the Secretary General on Children and Armed Conflict (2012) A/66/782-S/2012/261.

20 UN Security Council Resolution 1612 S/RES/1612 (2005).

21 Ibid., preamble and §8.

22 UN Security Council Resolution 1539, 5(a), S/RES/1539 (2004).

23 UN Security Council Resolution 1612 (n. 20). For instance, Chad was delisted from the Secretary General's report in 2014.

Thus, the UN Secretary General, his or her special representative and the UN Security Council work in tandem to identify and implement an action-oriented approach to improve the well-being of children living through conflict. For example, in 2016 the UN Secretary General presented its conclusions on the Syrian armed conflict's impact on Syrian children and found that all six grave violations were committed by all sides to the conflict. It details how, in one incident in Syria, Da'esh abducted approximately 150 young boys on their way home after school exams in Aleppo. They were released from captivity after a few months, during which they were physically abused, indoctrinated and made to observe violent practices.[24] As a result, the UN Working Group strongly condemned the abduction and subsequent treatment of children by parties to the conflict.[25] Subsequently, the UN Security Council adopted resolution 2225 which added the abduction of children as a trigger to list parties to conflict in the annexes of the annual report of the Secretary General on children and armed conflict.[26] To enhance effectiveness, actions are coordinated with relevant non-governmental organisations and other relevant UN organisations such as UNESCO, ILO, UNHCR and the WHO.

The UN Security Council provides a platform to induce action by States. The dialogue between the UN's Secretary General and the Security Council to explore meaningful protections for children in each of the armed conflicts under scrutiny shows promise, but there are challenges.

2.3. CHALLENGES

This working method has been hailed as a success by UN institutions and UN Member States. It demonstrates that provided there is a clearly identified common goal, different entities can work together effectively. It has also been adopted as a model to combat conflict-related sexual violence with similar monitoring, analysis and reporting mechanisms and targeted sanctions.[27] The overall results, however, remain insufficient.

To begin with, the process of naming and shaming countries has a symbolic value, but is also prone to politicisation. Indeed, recently Saudi Arabia, placed on the list for its deliberate attacks on schools, exerted pressure to have its name removed from the 2016 Annex to avoid international scrutiny. It successfully

24 Report of the Secretary General on Children and Armed Conflict in the Syrian Arab Republic, 27 January 2014, S/2014/31.

25 Conclusions on Syria of the UNSC Working Group on Children and Armed Conflict, 26 November 2014, S/AC.51/2014/4.

26 UN Security Council Resolution 2225, S/RES/225 (2015) listing abduction of children as a trigger for listing.

27 For targeted sanctions in the DRC, see UNSC Resolution 1533 S/RES/1539 (2004).

threatened to withhold funding for children. Secretary General Ban Ki Moon justified the removal out of concern for the protection of Yemeni children, thus ignoring that the protection of children may be best facilitated by the determination of a national action plan for States to work towards removal from the list under close monitoring. This, while demonstrating that States perceive such listing as damaging their reputation, equally puts into question the credibility of the UN's integrity and commitment to protect children affected by armed conflict.[28] Ideally, if what we seek to demonstrate is a commitment to the protection of children, international politics should not be able to trump even symbolic accountability for one of the identified grave violations against children. In reality, financial and other pressures are powerful tools to induce compromise over the heads of children. Ultimately, pressures by or lack of cooperation from States can deprive children of vital interventions.

Additionally, an adequate targeted measures and sanctions regime would strengthen further the action-oriented approach towards influencing perpetrators to end grave violations against children in situations of armed conflict. In other words, a comprehensive targeted measures and sanctions regime that can be put into place swiftly and which considers the variety of violations and perpetrators to ensure a reasonable chance of success. This would thus clearly signal international disapproval of violations against children. Indeed, the UN Security Council includes the possibility to resort to targeted sanctions in its resolutions. It has suggested the possibility of a *quid pro quo* approach to using targeted measures or sanctions,[29] such as a ban on the export or supply of small arms, resources or other military equipment, and assistance, travel bans and asset freezes, or indeed commencing accountability procedures,[30] to induce compliance of identified reluctant parties. Unfortunately, to date the UN Security Council has made limited use of such measures and so it is difficult to assess their effectiveness. An important first step would be to include conflict-related violations of children's rights on the agendas of the different sanction committees. The UN Security Council risks facing difficult political challenges to agreement on an adequate sanction regime against the appropriate perpetrators of violations against children. Moreover, such measures and sanctions must minimise devastating humanitarian consequences. Nonetheless, this may prove an effective tool to target different sets of perpetrators with appropriate measures from the early stages of conflicts.

---

28 Amnesty International, 07.06.2016, 'UN: Shameful pandering to Saudi Arabia over children killed in Yemen conflict, available at <https://www.amnesty.org/en/latest/news/2016/06/un-shameful-pandering-to-saudi-arabia-over-children-killed-in-yemen-conflict/> accessed 14.07.2016.

29 UN Security Council Resolution 1998 (n. 6); UN Security Council Resolution 1539, 2 April 2004.

30 UN Security Council Resolution 2068, 3.

Most importantly for UN responses to be effective, the author believes that, while it is imperative to explore the specific vulnerabilities faced by children, it is equally important to recognise that the general category of children necessarily includes variations arising from differences due to, among other factors, gender or age. During armed conflict boys and girls share many similar experiences. However, the way these are experienced is shaped by their gender roles, the traditions in which gender relations pan out, the pressure and expectation of society that their members (adult or children) should behave in line with socially and politically constructed notions of masculinity and femininity and the ensuing social and cultural differences. Boys and girls have distinctive symbolic values, responsibilities and roles in their families and communities. They are vulnerable and targeted differently. The effects of physical and mental injury have different social impacts.

If social gender constructs are established during childhood, understanding social and gendered patterns of armed conflict becomes an essential step. If in times of peace women and girls are bound by traditional patterns of kinship, legalised discrimination and social subordination, how is this performed in times of armed conflict? If traditional patterns shift, how is this experienced by children, girls and boys?

If this is indeed the case, this is an important element of differentiation to take into consideration in our legal, humanitarian and transitional justice responses to protecting children. Furthermore, gender is often only considered when it comes to understanding the impacts of conflict, and not when analysing what drives conflicts or motivates conflict-fuelling behaviours. For instance, what are the gendered realities in Syria? Has the armed conflict altered these or indeed exacerbated the consequences for some children, and if so, to what extent and why?

3. THE SYRIAN ARMED CONFLICT AND A LOST GENERATION OF CHILDREN

The conflict in Syria will provide an illustration of a range of conflict-related harms suffered by children. The author seeks to draw attention more specifically to selected gendered consequences for children.

3.1. THE EFFECTS OF THE SYRIAN ARMED CONFLICT ON CHILDREN

Since March 2011, Syria has been in the grips of a brutal armed conflict. While the initial conflict may have started as a by-product of the 2011 Arab Spring uprisings and a desire to topple President Assad's regime, presently it is also fuelled by sectarian fighting, particularly with the more recent participation of Da'esh. This protracted and complex armed conflict questions the effectiveness for children of international humanitarian laws and the UN's work.

Civilians, including children, are the primary victims. Populated areas are no longer protected from indiscriminate attack, explosive weapons or from the use of terror tactics directly targeted at civilians.[31]

> Syrians live in a world where decisions about whether to go to the mosque for prayers, to go to the market for food and to send their children to school have become decisions about life and death.[32]

Children are simply caught in the middle of the Syrian armed conflict. According to Zerrougui 'the lives of millions of children have been disrupted by this war',[33] with an estimated 5,500,000 children affected by the conflict,[34] and an estimated 1,000,000 children having left Syria.[35]

Children are a particularly vulnerable category of civilians without any actual physical, economic, political or military capabilities. Their experiences of armed conflict are complex, varied and distinct from that of adults. Yet, they are at direct risk of being killed, physically injured and mentally damaged. The indirect consequences of armed conflict are also non-negligible. Children experience extreme violence in the form of torture or sexual violence, abductions displacement and witnessing the suffering endured by members of their families and communities.

In addition, children's healthy development is hampered. Children become more vulnerable because of deteriorating economic, social and living conditions. They are more likely to be poor, malnourished and in poor health, out of school and experience a lack of livelihood options.[36] Attacks against supposedly safe spaces, such as schools, hospitals and other community hubs fragment family, cultural and social networks and result in a loss of security and lack of structure

---

31 Report of the Independent International Commission of Inquiry on Syria, 2016, A/HRC/33/55.

32 Oral Update of the Independent International Commission of Inquiry on the Syrian Arab Republic to the Human Rights Council, 16 June 2014, A/HRC/26/CRP.2.

33 L. Zerrougui, Special Representative of the Secretary General on Children and Armed Conflict, *The Fourth Year of the Conflict*, 13.03.2015, available at <https://childrenandarmedconflict.un.org/syria-statement-by-leila-zerrougui/> accessed 26.02.2016.

34 War Child, 'Double Catastrophe – Voices from a War on Childhood', 2013, available at <https://reliefweb.int/sites/reliefweb.int/files/resources/War%20Child%20Syria%20Appeal%20Report.pdf>.

35 S. Tremblay, 'One Million Children from Syria Forced to Flee their Country: The Story of Ibrahim and Yusuf', available at <https://childrenandarmedconflict.un.org/one-million-children/> accessed 10.06.2016.

36 *Machel Study 10-Year Strategic Review Children and Conflict in a Changing World*, 2009, UNICEF, p. 18.

in daily life.[37] The hardship caused by sieges is particularly alarming, increasing the risk of death through malnutrition. The Syrian Centre for Policy Research reported that two-thirds of the Syrian population lived in extreme poverty, thus unable to access basic food and non-food items.[38] Preventable diseases such as polio and cholera have returned.[39] In addition, access to water is all too often disrupted or used as a war tactic.[40]

Consequently, children's needs and rights are trampled on without effective deterrent. Since 2012, numerous UN Security Council resolutions have called for an end to the conflict, particularly to protect civilians but without tangible success.[41] The following section will explore two specific grave violations against Syrian children to highlight the gendered implications and different outcomes in terms of vulnerability, livelihoods, protection and access to services: conflict-related casualties and education.

3.2. GRAVE VIOLATIONS AGAINST CHILDREN IN SYRIA AND GENDER

Syrian children experience each of the six grave violations identified by the UN Security Council. However, a gendered lens under which to understand how children are affected by these grave violations is lacking: how gender influences their experiences and levels of vulnerability.

Prior to the armed conflict and particularly since the ratification of the Convention on the Elimination of all forms of Discrimination Against Women (CEDAW),[42] many efforts to achieve greater gender equality, particularly in the public sphere, were made.[43] Syria's Constitution upholds justice and equality for all its citizens.[44] Nonetheless, many practices and laws endorse discriminatory

---

37 Oral Update of the Independent International Commission of Inquiry on the Syrian Arab Republic to the Human Rights Council, 16 June 2014, A/HRC/26/CRP.2, §27.

38 Syrian Centre for Policy Research, 'Syria: Alienation and Violence Report Impact of Syria Crisis 2014', 2014.

39 Save the Children, 'A Devastating Toll – The Impact of Three Years of War on the Health of Syria's Children', 2014.

40 Report of the Secretary General on Children in Armed Conflict to the Security Council, A/70/836-S/2016/360, 20 April 2016, §162.

41 Among others, Resolution 2042, UNDoc. S/RES/2042 (2012); 2254 UNDoc. S/RES/2254 (2015); 2268, UNDoc S/RES/2268 (2016).

42 UN General Assembly resolution 34/180, 18 December 1979, entered into force 3 September 1981, United Nations, Treaty Series, vol. 1249, p. 13. Syria acceded to CEDAW in 2003 with reservations.

43 UNICEF, *MENA Gender Equality Profile on Syria – Status of Girls and Women in the Middle East and North Africa; Women's Human Rights and Gender Equality, 2010*, National Situation Analysis Report on Syria 2011.

44 Articles 25–27 and 45, Syria's Permanent Constitution, 13 March 1973.

provisions against women and encourage impunity for gender-based violence. The Personal Status Law and the Penal Code contain provisions that discriminate against women and girls. This is the case for the protection from rape, spousal rape, child marriage, honour killings or gender-based violence.

Legal discriminations and stereotypes of traditional roles for women and men in the family and in society have persisted with noticeable differences between rural and urban areas. Inherited traditions place women in an inferior position to men. Within a patriarchal familial structure, the male head of households decides on issues of education, marriage of children and finances. Women perform all the household chores, if necessary in conjunction with a paid job. If before the armed conflict Syrian girls were marginalised, the armed conflict has increased girls' family and social responsibilities, mobility restrictions and exposure to gender-based violence.

Children's experiences will be, at least in part, influenced by their gender. For example, there is little data available that documents conflict-related casualties, which both differentiates between direct and indirect deaths and between genders, let alone data related to children and their gender. It is therefore difficult to provide an accurate gender analysis. A recent study suggests that in areas held by non-state armed groups, children were more likely than women and men or combatants to die from injuries caused by explosive weapons.[45] Among children, boys are killed or injured by explosive weapons in greater numbers. For security reasons, boys are allowed a greater freedom of movement than girls. Boys are more likely to be allowed to play outside, attend school or work, and are thus more at risk from explosive weapons. Boys are also more likely to be recruited to actively participate in hostilities. Thus boys, like men, tend to suffer more from direct consequences of armed conflict; whereas girls and women die at higher rates from the indirect consequences of armed conflict, such as food shortages, poor sanitation and hygiene, limited healthcare and increased displacement.

Syria's education system has been seriously disrupted by random bombings, displacement or exploitation by contending powers to promote their specific views and ideals, thus undermining children's well-being and future opportunities.[46] Children are kept at home. Girls are affected in greater numbers, because armed conflict encourages a return to optional and mixed gender education, traditional gender roles and inequalities. Young girls experience forced physical

---

[45] D. Guha-Sapir, 'Civilian Deaths from Weapons Used in the Syrian Conflict' (2015) BMJ 351:h4736.

[46] 6,500 schools have been destroyed or are inaccessible. Report of the Secretary General on Children in Armed Conflict to the Security Council, A/70/836-S/2016/360, 20 April 2016, §157. Syrian Centre for Policy Research, 'Syria: Alienation and Violence Report Impact of Syria Crisis 2014' (2014), p. 50; N. Benotman and N. Malik, 'The Children of Islamic State', March 2016; K. Couvee, 'Children living under ISIS "forced to participate in public executions and play with decapitated heads"', *Independent*, 06.03.2016.

confinement to 'protect' them, because they are more vulnerable to sexual and verbal harassment.[47] Many young boys, but also girls, need to work and support the household. Girls take on greater household obligations. This disrupts the power dynamics within families, particularly if income generation is first and foremost seen as the father's role, and this may indirectly increase domestic violence.

Furthermore, extremist Islamist groups have recruited and trained children militarily through free, but compulsory, schooling campaigns.[48] Some armed groups are, however, opposed to secular and girls' education. More resources are devoted to educating boys, albeit in a military school environment. In November 2015, Da'esh regulated on compulsory education for boys from grade 1 to 12 and girls from grade 1 to 4.[49]

Non-school attendance decreases children's well-being and increases the threat of other harms. Girls are at greater risk of early marriage to alleviate the economic burden or to protect the girl's and family's reputation. Boys risk child labour or child recruitment into military groups to boost family income.

Education plays a strategic role in recovery from armed conflict, development and security. Before the start of the conflict, Syria had a well-developed free educational system based on gender parity. Nearly all Syrian children were attending school. Providing girls with an education reduced early marriages and childbirth-related deaths, and increased financial growth. Four years into the conflict, enrolment rates had dropped below 50 per cent and progress in children's education reversed.[50] The situation does not improve for refugee children.[51] The lack of education will have economic, financial and social development implications for Syria's recovery from armed conflict. The return to gender inequality will further limit the full potential and development of girls, thus pushing back transformative change tackling gender discrimination.

The examples of conflict-related casualties and lack of education demonstrate the importance of acknowledging gendered consequences if only to identify

---

47 Report of the Secretary General to the Security Council, S/2015/203, 23 March 2015.

48 In December 2015, Da'esh imposed compulsory education for all boys from grades 1 to 12, and for all girls grades 1 to 4, Report of the Special Representative to the Secretary General for Children in Armed Conflict, 20 April 2016, A/70/836-S/2016/360. In addition, see Human Rights Watch, June 2014, '"Maybe We Live and Maybe We Die" – Recruitment and Use of Children by Armed Groups in Syria', available at <https://www.hrw.org/report/2014/06/22/maybe-we-live-and-maybe-we-die/recruitment-and-use-children-armed-groups-syria> accessed 13.05.2016.

49 UNICEF 'No Place for Children' 2015.

50 UNESCO, Syria country profile, available at <http://www.uis.unesco.org/DataCentre/Pages/country-profile.aspx?code=SYR&regioncode=40525> accessed 22.07.2016; see also Save the Children, 'The Cost of War – Calculating the Impact of the Collapse of Syria's Education System on the Country's Future' 2015, available at <http://static.guim.co.uk/ni/1427711553264/Save-the-Children-Cost-of-W.pdf> accessed 22.07.2016.

51 Ibid., Save the Children.

appropriate required actions and measures. This far, a common thread in international law provisions and the UN's approach is to understand children as a homogenous group.[52] International law adopts gender-neutral language not to prioritise one gender over another. But if then language itself necessitates a positive effort (the 'he or she' approach) or more detrimentally leaves gender neutrality behind by enabling the dominance of one gender over another, it become meaningless. Rarely does international law acknowledge the gendered experiences of children, thus questioning whether law in fact perpetuates gender inequality instead of embracing its transformative power for change. A similar linguistic weakness is also visible in the UN's responses to conflict-related sexual violence, because it prioritises (adult) women as main recipients. The language used in resolutions such as 1325 (2000) and 2106 (2013), while recognising that these harms befall women, girls, boys and men, expressly invites measures aimed primarily at adult women.[53] This is particularly the case for the inclusion of women in peace processes. These dominant narratives have the unintended consequences of subsuming the experiences of girls within those of boys or adult women and ignoring the differential experience related to gender or age. This will now be examined against the backdrop of the Syrian armed conflict.

4. GIRLS AT THE PERIPHERIES OF LEGAL PROTECTIONS

All children are affected by armed conflict, yet legal protections focus predominantly on child soldiers and the experiences of boys.[54] Issues that specifically affect girls are left unacknowledged, suggesting male-gender dominance of children's protections from the consequences of armed conflict. This section will explore the unintended consequences of international law adopting a narrative in which children are unsituated, ageless and unspecified people, and the role the UN might fulfil to enhance legal protections of the girl-child.

4.1. RECRUITMENT AND USE OF CHILDREN

Thus far, international law has developed a restrictive understanding of who should be protected against the child soldiering experience, but this leaves the girl-child on the margin and at risk of being overlooked.

52 A similar conclusion is discussed by Alison Bisset in of this volume.

53 UN Security Council Resolution S/RES/1325 (2000); S/RES/1820 (2008); S/RES/1888 (2009); S/Res 1960 (2010) and S/RES/2106 (2013).

54 D.M. Rosen, *Child Soldiers in the Western Imagination – From Patriots to Victims*, New York: Rutgers University Press 2015, p. 140.

The recruitment and use of children to actively participate in armed conflict by groups on all sides of the conflict has become part and parcel of the Syrian conflict.

Data reveals that numerous groups involved in the Syrian conflict recruit boys and some also recruit girls.[55] A significant proportion of these children are under the age of 15.[56] The diversity of armed groups recruiting children, all with their own specific set of goals and motives, such as overthrowing a government or creating a different state backed by a regime of terror, complicates the matter.[57] Children may be abducted into armed groups. Children may be actively encouraged to join the armed conflict by offering them gifts or even a salary as an economic incentive for children and parents to support children joining.[58] In addition, indoctrination can play an important part in recruitment processes, particularly through militarisation of schools.

Compared to the other five grave violations, the recruitment and use of child soldiers is the most developed area of international law. The UN's early work focused exclusively on this issue as a grave violation.[59] The prohibition is aimed at those who recruit and use children to actively participate in armed conflict. State armed forces are discouraged and armed groups are never permitted to recruit or use children in hostilities.[60]

The Additional Protocols to the four Geneva Conventions were the first instruments to emphasise that recruitment is particularly inhumane and that there exists a duty of care towards children under the age of 15 years so that they do not take direct part in hostilities. The CRC and the Optional Protocol on the Involvement of Children Armed Conflict confirm that children have the right to be protected from this practice.[61] The CRC's Optional Protocol amends the CRC's minimum age of recruitment of persons into armed forces from 15 to 18 years of age.[62] It was hoped that this change would stem the growing numbers of

---

55 Children under the age of 18 join and fight with the Kurdish armed group YPG and YPJ, its female branch.

56 Report of the Secretary General on Children in Armed Conflict, 20 April 2016, A/70/836-S/2016/360: 56 per cent of the verified cases are children under the age of 15.

57 Armed groups included ISIL, the Free Syrian Army and affiliated groups, Liwa' al Tawhid, popular committees, Kurdish People's Protection Units, Ahrar al-Sham, the Nusrah Front and the Army of Islam, Popular Committee of Tallkalakh.

58 UNICEF and Save the Children, 'Small Hands, Heavy Burden' 2016: children are offered salaries of US$400/month.

59 Child Recruitment, UN Security Council Resolution 1379, S/RES/1379 (2001).

60 Article 4 Optional Protocol to the Convention on the Rights of the Child on the Involvement of Children in Armed Conflict; Article 77(1)(2) & (3) Additional Protocol I (1977); and Article 4(3)(c) Additional Protocol II (1977).

61 CRC, Art. 38 and Art. 1, Optional Protocol to the Convention on the Rights of the Child on the Involvement of Children in Armed Conflict, G.A. Res. 54/263, U.N. Doc. /RES/54/263, 25 May 2000.

62 Article 1, Optional Protocol to the Convention on the Rights of the Child on the Involvement of Children in Armed Conflict.

child soldiers, and also recognise the inappropriateness of 15 years as the cut-off point for the prohibition of recruitment and use of children by armed forces.

Furthermore, the Cape Town Principles and Paris Principles were adopted in 1997 and 2007 respectively.[63] These are non-binding documents concerned with children affected by armed conflict. They are useful in that they can guide the interpretation and application of relevant international law provisions. The Paris Principles provide a comprehensive and inclusive definition of child recruitment and suggests children should be referred to as 'children associated with an armed force or group'. Indeed, it encourages a better understanding of the effects of armed conflict on children beyond direct or active participation as child soldiers in hostilities. The definition is as follows:

> 'A child associated with an armed force or armed group' refers to any person below 18 years of age who is or who has been recruited or used by an armed force or armed group in any capacity, including but not limited to children, boys and girls, used as fighters, cooks, porters, messengers, spies or for sexual purposes. It does not only refer to a child who is taking or has taken a direct part in hostilities.[64]

Combined with a child-centred rights approach, the current legal protections can be invaluable. First, child recruitment is understood broadly to include not only children recruited, trained and used as combatants, but also children recruited in any capacity. These children's involvement with an armed group or force means that they are in danger and experience extreme violence. Such an understanding of the adverse effects of children's involvement with armed forces or groups will ensure that children recruited as cooks, porters or for sexual purposes receive the highest protection possible and will be able to be recognised as victims.

Second, all recruitment of children should be prohibited based on the child's right to survival, good development and freedom from violence.[65] The recruitment of children by a brutal armed group violates international humanitarian law and human rights law, as they suffer forms of violence due to maltreatment and exploitation, including sexual abuse. Thus, from a children's human rights perspective all recruitment of children is prohibited, particularly since it contravenes the child's right to survival and good development and freedom from violence.

The Rome Statute recognised the practice as a war crime[66] and confirmed this in its case law, thus echoing the jurisprudence of the Special Court of Sierra

63 Cape Town Principles and Paris Principles.

64 Paris Principles, principle 2.1.

65 CRC, Arts. 6 and 19.

66 Rome Statute of the International Criminal Court (1998), UNDoc. A/CONF.183/9, Art. 8(2)(e)(vii) and Art. 7(1)(g), and Art. 8(2)(e)(vi).

Leone (SCSL).[67] However, the International Criminal Court (ICC) in its first judgment failed to promote a more holistic, including gendered, understanding of the war crime as promoted by the Paris Principles. Rather than view the experience of recruitment into an armed group as being against the best interests of children, the ICC judges focused on one of the three separate criminal acts that may constitute the crime, namely 'use to participate actively in hostilities' and adopted a restricted interpretation thereof.[68] The majority opinion, however, understood this not to be limited to the 'immediate scene of the hostilities' and to include a child's support role to combatants that 'exposes him or her to real danger as a potential target'.[69] Nonetheless, this excludes children who are harmed by the armed group that recruited them, including harms that are more likely to affect girls. Young Syrian children are recruited and used by armed groups in combat roles to kill, including as executioners, snipers and suicide or victim bombers.[70] However, their roles are not limited to fighting. Many start out in support functions to perform common duties such as porters, often carrying heavy loads, including supplies and ammunition, or helping to evacuate injured soldiers.[71] Some children act as guards, lookouts, messengers, cooks, attend to the wounded or record events for propaganda purposes.[72] Such support tasks also entail great risk to life, but may not expose them to real danger as a potential target. More importantly, it excludes girls who carry out primarily domestic and sexual roles and become the wives of fighters. For instance, the recruitment message presented by Da'esh is shaped by a religious and gendered lens. At its core are men as masculine fighters, husbands and providers, and women as feminine wives, mothers and protected. If men are to perform their roles successfully, young girls are needed to join, whether voluntarily or not, to become wives for the unmarried fighters to clean, cook and look after the children. According to Da'esh's statements, from the age of nine girls can legitimately be married, thus creating a group of girls entangled in an armed group yet outside the protections of child recruitment. A further unintended consequence is that reparations are closely tied to the crime of conviction.[73] Thus, girls who endure domestic and sexual abuse at the hands of their own commanders will be excluded.

It is a delicate line to walk. On the one hand the aim is to protect recruited children from the use as active participants in armed conflict, because that is

---

67 See *Prosecutor v. Lubanga*, ICC-01/04-01/06; *Prosecutor v. Ntaganda*, ICC-01/04-02/06; and *Prosecutor v. Ongwen*, ICC-02/04-01/15.

68 For an in-depth discussion of the *Lubanga* case, see Grey and Chappell, in this volume.

69 *Prosecutor v. Lubanga*, section 628.

70 UNICEF, 'No Place for Children' 2015.

71 Report of the Special Representative to the Secretary General for Children in Armed Conflict, 18 April 2013.

72 Report of the Secretary General to the UN Security Council, 5 June 2015, A/69/926-S/2015/409 (re-issued 4 August 2015).

73 For a more in-depth discussion of this, see Jurasz, in this volume.

when they are most vulnerable to real danger from the enemy. On the other hand, the aim should also be to ensure that those children who are recruited into an armed group and are victims of other war crimes will not be excluded from protection because they are deemed to have actively participated in armed conflict. In the *Ntaganda* case, the ICC addressed the latter for the war crime of rape by determining that the prohibition of rape had attained the status of *jus cogens* and the commission of the crime is thus prohibited always and against all persons.[74]

However, not all war crimes have achieved the status of *jus cogens*, but this also leaves unaddressed the harms and violence that is the experience of recruitment into armed groups and which should in fact also be the focus of the prohibition: the protection of children from the horrendous experience of being part of an armed group, thus primarily focusing on crimes committed against children by members of their own group and enemy groups. Within the broader context of duty of care towards children, no violence against children in all settings is justifiable. Article 19 of the CRC establishes the human rights imperative to protect children from 'all forms of violence, injury or abuse, neglect or negligent treatment, maltreatment or exploitation, including sexual abuse, while in the care of parent(s), legal guardian(s) or any other person who has the care of the child'. Consequently, within the recruitment into an armed group, children are protected from a variety of harms, including sexual abuse. Rather than seek prosecution for a separate crime, sexual violence including rape could be prosecuted as part of the crime to recruit child soldiers, thus recognising a more gendered understanding of the overall experience and giving a voice to children who suffered such harms. The broad definition of 'caregivers' applies to any person who is entrusted with the protection and well-being of the child.[75] This could cover the commanders of armed groups.

Moreover, article 32 of the CRC provides children with an indirect protection by asserting the right of children to be protected from economic exploitation, but more importantly from performing any work that is likely to be hazardous or will interfere harmfully with the education, health or physical, mental, spiritual, moral and social development of the child. The tasks that child soldiers are required to carry out are more than likely to be hazardous and require them to be in close contact with extreme violence. And although it is important not to equate sexual violence and girl-child soldiers, the gendered nature of the crime is an important component.[76] Some tasks performed by children as part of the experience have a gendered connotation, such as porters and body guards, cooks

---

[74] *Prosecutor v. Ntaganda*, ICC-01/04-02/06, 4 January 2017, §§47 and 51–53.

[75] Committee on the Rights of the Child, General Comment 13: The Right of the Child to Freedom from all Forms of Violence (2011), CRC/c/GC/13.

[76] See also Grey and Chappell in this volume.

and cleaners; but despite these being a direct consequence of recruitment, these are not deemed of sufficient importance to be worthy of protection.

Understanding the child soldier's experience requires a comprehensive examination of the political, social, economic and cultural context, but also a gender analysis to ensure more successful prosecutions while being aware of any detrimental effects to the children, families and communities. Importantly, neither of these were carried out in the *Lubanga* trial and this may set an unhelpful precedent in future cases.

4.2. SEXUAL VIOLENCE AGAINST CHILDREN

Conflict-related sexual violence or exploitation of children is a prominent feature of many armed conflicts including the Syrian conflict. Rape and other forms of sexual violence against children are human rights violations,[77] and may amount to grave breaches of international humanitarian law.[78] If committed as part of a widespread or systematic attack against a civilian population, sexual violence can constitute war crimes and crimes against humanity or may be a constitutive act of genocide under the Rome Statute of the International Criminal Court.[79] The SCSL, the International Criminal Tribunal for the former Yugoslavia, the International Criminal Tribunal for Rwanda and the ICC have convicted individuals of forced marriage, rape, torture and enslavement.[80] In addition, a number of treaties prohibit the sexual abuse and exploitation of children.[81] Under Security Council Resolution 1882 (2009), the Council designated sexual violence committed against children as a critical priority and called on parties to armed conflict to prepare and implement action plans to address this violation.

---

77 The CRC, Arts. 34, 35 and 37; CRC's Optional Protocol on Trafficking and Exploitation, Art. 3; African Charter on the Rights and Welfare of the Child (1990), Art. 27.

78 Art. 27(2) Geneva Convention IV; Arts. 75(2), 76(1) and 77(1) Additional Protocol I (hereinafter AP I) of 12 August 1949 Relating to the Protection of Victims of International Armed Conflict; Art. 4(2)(e), 1125 *UNTS* 3; Additional Protocol II (hereinafter AP II) of 12 August 1949 Relating to the Protection of Victims of non-International Armed Conflicts, 1977, 1125 *UNTS* 609 – which specifically adds 'rape' to the list of forms of indecent assault. See also: Customary Rule 93 in: ICRC, p. 323. Child-specific provisions: Art. 77 AP I; Art. 4(3) AP II.

79 ICC Statute, Arts. 7(1)(c), 7(1)(g), 8(2)(b), 8(2)(c) and 8(2)(e).

80 *Prosecutor v. Tamba, Brima, Camara & Kanu* SCSL (2007); *Prosecutor v. Akayesu*, ICTR (1998); *Prosecutor v. Musema*, ICTR (2000); *Prosecutor v. Furundžija* (1998), *Prosecutor v. Kunarac*, ICTY (2000); *Prosecutor v. Bemba*, ICC 2016, ICC-01/05-01/08 which heard testimony on rapes of girls as young as 10 years old.

81 In particular, the Convention against Torture (1984), Art. 1; the Convention for the Suppression of the Traffic in Persons and of the Exploitation of the Prostitution of Others (1949), Art. 1; and the Vienna Declaration of the World Conference on Human Rights (1993), Part 5.

Sexual violence is also a trigger for inclusion on the list of the Secretary General of parties to conflict which commit grave violations against children in armed conflict.

In the Syrian conflict, sexual violence against children occurs in a variety of circumstances including because of abductions, detention and forced displacements and as we have seen recruitment and use of children. It takes many forms, such as forced or early marriage,[82] sexual slavery,[83] rape and sexual harassment. Syrian teenage girls are a frequent target of rape and other forms of sexual violence. For instance, in 2014 Da'esh issued a document justifying the sexual slavery in Syria of Yezidi girls abducted in Iraq.[84] Zawati goes as far as to suggest that rape has been used as a weapon of 'sectarian cleansing'.[85] At the very least, such acts are a potent means of communication between the different fighting factions to 'dishonour' the family, community and young girls.[86] Young women and girls have been abducted at checkpoints and later returned to their families, intentionally exposing them as rape victims in order to subject them to shame and rejection.[87] Moreover, to protect the girls, their movements are restricted by their families and girls are confined at home.

Patriarchal attitudes in the family and community reinforce the lower status of girls and the way girls are intrinsically linked to honour. The bodies of teenage girls are first and foremost representative of the honour of their families, communities, religion and cultures. Consequently, sexual violation of the girls' bodies is perceived to stain the entire familial or communal group, not just that of the individual girls, thereby decisions that are not in the best interest of the girls may be taken. For instance, according to Yezidi customs, marriage

---

82 For instance, the abduction of Yezidi girls to be sold in markets across Ar-Raqqa to be used sex slaves, in Report of the Secretary General to the Security Council, S/2015/203, 23 March 2015.

83 Ibid.

84 Dabiq, Issue 4: 'Unlike the Jews and Christians, there was no room for jizyah (non-Muslim residents) payment. Also, their women could be enslaved ... After capture, the Yazidi women and children were then divided according to the Sharī'ah among the fighters of the Islamic State who participated in the Sinjar operations, after one fifth of the slaves were transferred to the Islamic State's authority to be divided as khums [fifth] ... Before Shaytān [Satan] reveals his doubts to the weak-minded and weak hearted, one should remember that enslaving the families of the kuffār [infidels] and taking their women as concubines is a firmly established aspect of the Sharī'ah ...', available at: Amnesty International Report, 'Escape from Hell' 2014 <https://www.amnesty.org.uk/files/escape_from_hell_-_torture_and_sexual_slavery_in_islamic_state_captivity_in_iraq_-_english_2.pdf> accessed 11.11.2016.

85 H.M. Zawati, *Sectarian War in Syria Introduced New Gender-Based Crimes* (16 February 2016). Huffington Post, February 2016. Available at SSRN <http://ssrn.com/abstract=2733359>.

86 International Rescue Committee, *Syrian Women & Girls: Fleeing Death, Facing Ongoing Threats and Humiliation – A Gender-based Violence Rapid Assessment*, 2012.

87 Office of the Special Representative of the Secretary General for Children in Armed Conflict, Press Release Based on the Report of the Secretary General to the Security Council, para. 149, A/68/878–S/2014/339 (15 May 2014) <https://childrenandarmedconflict.un.org/countries/syria/>.

with members of other faiths and sexual relations outside of marriage are not accepted. Such practices are shameful for the whole family. Syrian girls are more vulnerable to honour killings.[88] Defending the chastity of female family members is an important social obligation for males. Thus, the effectiveness of conflict-related sexual violence has altered the gendered role assigned to girls in which their bodies, from the expression of family and community honour, become the space over which to claim dominance by the various exploitative actors.

Conflict-related sexual violence also takes other forms that are not necessarily addressed by international law or within the grave violation identified by the UN, such as early marriage or survival sex. Yet these are harms to which girls are particularly vulnerable.

Early marriage is not a new issue for Syria. It is related to traditions, culture, family norms and a way to prevent sexual intercourse before marriage. Patriarchy places the decision of their daughters' marriage with fathers, thus it is rarely the girls' decision. According to Syria's personal status law, the legal age for marriage for girls is 17 and for boys it is 18. However, religious leaders have competence to authorise exceptions to allow couples to live together and have children. In this case, the minimum age is 15 for boys and 13 for girls. Such marriages are informal until both partners turn 18 and formally register the marriage. The informality of the arrangement puts girls at greater risk of losing rights in case of divorce or dispute with their partner.

The occurrence of early marriages has increased significantly and the average age of girl brides has decreased notably since the start of the conflict, in particular among the Syrian refugee population. Rather than a cultural tradition, early marriage has become a necessity to counter conflict-related insecurity. It is a means for families to protect their girls by ensuring they are under the protection of their husband or as a coping strategy against economic and financial pressures.[89] Dowry money becomes a welcome relief from economic hardships suffered by families, particularly single mothers. In some cases, the girls are married off to cover up the 'dishonour' suffered by the family, thereby only extending the girls' suffering.

In most cases, rather than offering girls protection and access to improved economic means, early marriage leads to the loss of childhood, educational opportunities, poverty and early forced sexual activity and the resulting mental and health risks, such as maternity-related deaths or birth complications. As a result, the girls are in a more vulnerable position.

In addition, particularly among the displaced population, survival sex performed by girls in exchange for money, resources, services and assets has

---

88 US Department of State, Syria 2013 Human Rights Report.

89 International Rescue Committee, *Syrian Women & Girls: Fleeing Death, facing ongoing Threats and Humiliation – A Gender-based Violence Rapid Assessment*, 2012.

become an accepted occurrence. Such commoditisation is not uncommon in conflict zones or among displaced populations. However, it does signify that dire economic needs alter gender roles, in which girls' sexuality is offered to exploitative men.

However, there are too few specific provisions that deal with armed conflict-related sexual violence against children. Thus conflict-related sexual violence against children becomes a subset of the general framework of tackling sexual violence against women. Most notable is the absence from the CRC of provisions related to child or early marriage. Instead it may be dealt with as contrary to the best interest of the child. CEDAW consider early marriage a form of violence against women and girls.[90] This is further supported by General Recommendation 24 on the elimination of discriminatory practices related to marriage. Legal protections are insufficient or even lacking in the case of survival sex. Thus, the gender-neutral approach adopted to children and their rights and protections has meant that early marriage has not been identified as a signifier of gender inequality and against the best interest of the child. This puts a low value on girls who are defined by their possible economic gain.

4.3. THE UN AS A ROLE MODEL

International law and the UN still perceives of children as a homogenous group without distinctive gendered needs. However, a slow change can be observed.

The six grave violations are perceived to be committed on children without distinction as to how these might be experienced by the different genders or indeed age groups. A gender-neutral narrative in which the specific experiences, roles and vulnerabilities of boys and girls affected by armed conflict are not explored is meaningless and makes children primarily bystanders of their own fate. It ignores the role of gender bias, different social contexts and underlying gendered effects induced and/or deepened by armed conflict. It perpetuates gender-based differences and risks disadvantaging girls more acutely through unequal treatment and increased vulnerability. It also carries the risk of girls becoming invisible, because it promotes a dominant narrative around boys. Indeed, the information related to sexual violence as one of the six grave violations against children provided by the Office of the Special Representative of the Secretary General for Children and Armed Conflict speaks volumes.[91] The tone adopted in the four short paragraphs ensures a gender-balanced understanding of sexual violence suffered by boys and girls. However, whereas

[90] CEDAW, Article 16.1 establishes an equal right for men and women to enter marriage with their free and full consent. Article 16.2 deems a marriage of a child to have no legal effect.

[91] Office of the Special Representative of the Secretary General for Children and Armed Conflict website, available at: <https://childrenandarmedconflict.un.org/six-grave-violations/>.

previously the emphasis may have primarily been on girls as the recipients of such violence, the current information presents a narrative in which sexual violence against boys is disproportionately emphasised. If Syria's government armed groups commit conflict-related crimes of sexual violence against its children, how can we gather data that provides an accurate picture that effectively takes account of cultural and gender norms to identify girls' and boys' experiences and gendered impact?

In a narrative dominated by the experiences of boys, the girl-child who seeks protection must demonstrate that her plight is as distressing as that of the boy-child. If, to boot, the girl-child is also drowned out by the adult woman for some of the harms, such as conflict-related sexual violence, then this is twice as unfair. Thus, what is lacking is an analysis of the broader ways in which gender, age and conflict interact vis-à-vis children, such as the different roles that girls and boys, including sexual and gender minorities, play as conflict actors.

A tentative shift can be observed at the ICC level. For instance, one of the strategic goals of the ICC's Office of the Prosecutor is to 'pay particular attention to crimes against children'.[92] It has been proactive in identifying best practices for children affected by armed conflict.[93] It also acknowledges that children are differently affected by crimes depending on their identity, including gender.[94] In addition, it recognises the commission of gender-based crimes against children and defines these as crimes committed against boys or girls because of their sex and/or socially constructed roles, and are not always manifested as a form of sexual violence.[95] This is a valuable step forward in understanding the gendered experiences of armed conflict.

The UN Monitoring and Reporting Mechanisms equally has good practice in place. When gathering information to assist in developing an understanding of the specific experiences of children, it is guided, among other principles, by the specific needs of boys and girls. It also encourages the disaggregation of relevant information on children's rights violations per sex.

Similar principles should guide the work carried out by other UN institutions who have a stake in protecting children in armed conflict. Indeed, the UN Working Group on Children in Armed Conflict could provide the impetus for meaningful further action in the form of resolutions and declarations.

International law provides a solid basis for the UN to complement relevant treaty and customary law provisions by 'soft law' instruments which could prove to be invaluable. Several important instruments have already been adopted.

---

92 ICC-OTP, Strategic Plan, June 2012–2015, p. 27, reaffirmed in the Strategic Plan 2016–2018, 19.

93 OTP's Policy Paper on Children, November 2016.

94 Ibid., para. 18.

95 Ibid., para. 19 refers to the OTP's Policy Paper on Sexual and Gender-Based Crimes, 2014, para. 16.

In 1974, the UN General Assembly adopted the Declaration on the Protection of Women and Children in Emergency and Armed Conflict.[96] This non-binding declaration highlighted the specific harms and need for protection of this vulnerable group. The declaration actively promotes gender equality, the elimination of all forms of discrimination and all forms of violence for girls. In particular, gender perspectives will be applied in all policies and programmes.[97]

In 2004, UNGA resolution on the Rights of the Child calls for more diversity within the concept of children, particularly addressing the needs of the girl-child, children with disabilities, refugee and internally displaced children, child workers etc.

The UN Security Council has adopted a considerable number of resolutions around the theme of children affected by armed conflict. The first resolution adopted after the Machel Report condemned the violation of children's rights in armed conflict.[98] Since then UN Security Council resolutions on children have regularly been agreed to, such as UN Security Council Resolution 1314 (2000) which urged all UN Member States to sign and ratify the Optional Protocol on Children involved in Armed Conflict to the CRC. The UN Security Council has also highlighted specific harms suffered by children, such as abductions or the military use of schools.[99]

None of these resolutions are binding, but reflect some issues on which there is international agreement and consensus on the obligations of the States and other international actors in relation to children's rights. The recommendations they contain may be implemented by States and other international actors working with children. Each resolution contributes to developing an understanding of the effects of armed conflict on children. They provide an indication of what the law should aim to achieve and thus an effective marker of how the law should be interpreted.

This goes hand in hand with a stronger connectivity between human rights, children's rights and international humanitarian law. Human rights and children's rights provide the lens through which to view the UN Security Council resolutions. They connect human rights and international humanitarian violations relating to children to the maintenance of international peace and security agenda by reaffirming pre-existing obligations, crystallising these as part of the Peace and Security agenda and inducing compliance. So even though UN Security Council resolutions may not be legal acts, they may induce legal effects. They have a *de facto* normative power as they present material evidence of the attitude of

96 UNGA Resolution 3318 (XXIX).

97 Report of the Ad Hoc Committee of the Whole of the twenty seventh special session of the General Assembly, 2002, A/S-27/19/Rev.1.

98 UN Security Council Resolution 1261, S/RES/1261 (1999).

99 UN Security Council Resolution 2225, S/RES/2225 (2015) and UN Security Council Resolution 2143, S/RES/1243 (2014).

States towards particular rules, the presence or absence of consensus. They help interpretation and are evidence of State practice.

They are of a recurring nature and steadily increase the level of obligation. The normative power is increased with each resolution.

These resolutions have an expressive value, but there is still limited interaction between CRC and UN resolutions and declarations on children and armed conflict.

Future resolutions should include a gendered perspective as this can only be beneficial to induce transformative change. Gender could be mainstreamed as a guiding principle alongside the best interest of the child. In terms of future prosecutions, this establishes a clearer link between the mandates and policies of the ICC's Office of the Prosecutor on crimes against children and conflict-related gender-based crimes.[100] Instead they are still perceived as two separate strategic goals, even though one can inform and complement the other to support gender equality as a mainstreamed norm even among younger human beings.

5. CONCLUSION

Greater emphasis on the intersection between children and gender deepens understandings of children's experiences of armed conflict, particularly if such understandings are adequately placed within the broader context of pre-conflict gendered realities. In this manner, the UN's action plans will meet children's needs in a more meaningful manner, but also induce adequate post-conflict change to gender inequalities.

Not to attempt to understand these gendered and age-related experiences does not bode well for a future peaceful Syria, which would short-change its children, particularly its girls. Indeed, any response should consider a gender analysis of the roles, experiences and perspectives of boys and girls, but should not be to the detriment of analysis of the attitudes and behaviours of boys and girls. In addition, when relevant it is important to recognise gender, but also age, as markers of difference.

---

100 ICC Statute, Art. 54(1)(b).

PART III

GENDERED EXPERIENCES OF INTERNATIONAL CRIMINAL JUSTICE

GENDER, ENSLAVEMENT AND WAR ECONOMIES IN SIERRA LEONE

A Case Study from the Special Court for Sierra Leone

Valerie OOSTERVELD*

1. INTRODUCTION

Enslavement of civilians played a central role in sustaining the war economy during Sierra Leone's 1991–2002 armed conflict.[1] In particular, two warring parties – the Revolutionary United Front (RUF) and the Armed Forces Revolutionary Council (AFRC) – used various kinds of enslavement to further

* The author wishes to thank the Social Sciences and Humanities Research Council of Canada and the Canadian Partnership for International Justice for funding support, to make this chapter possible. Any errors are the author's own.

1 SIERRA LEONE TRUTH AND RECONCILIATION COMMISSION, *Witness to Truth: Report of the Sierra Leone Truth and Reconciliation Commission*, Graphic Packaging 2004, vol. 3(A), ch. 4, paras. 54–60.

their war effort, including forced diamond mining, forced food procurement, forced carrying of loads, forced domestic labour and sexual slavery. Certain types of enslavement were highly gendered, as were the roles played by that enslavement in advancing the financial and organisational sustainability of the RUF and AFRC as fighting forces. For example, men were often targeted for forced portering of heavy loads and forced diamond mining.[2] These forms of enslavement were crucial to the continuity of the two groups, which generated tradable commodities such as diamonds, food and looted valuables through forced labour. The RUF and AFRC also used forced labour of women and girls to create social units to undertake domestic duties, such as cooking and laundry, to keeping their forces fed and clothed.[3] Finally, they also instituted sexual slavery as a form of extreme control over female (and, by extension, male) civilians and a reward for their forces.[4]

The Special Court for Sierra Leone was created to prosecute those bearing the greatest responsibility for crimes committed during the 1996–2002 period of the decade-long civil war.[5] Given the prevalence of enslavement during the war, it is not surprising that the Special Court examined various forms of forced labour in some depth. It did so in cases involving former RUF and AFRC leaders, as well as the former President of Liberia, Charles Taylor.[6] But did the Court's analysis recognise the gendered nature of the enslavement and thus the gendered nature of the war economy? This chapter analyses this question through an examination of the Special Court's Trial Chamber judgments in the RUF, AFRC and *Taylor* cases. It also considers why the linkage between gender, enslavement and the war economy is an important consideration in international criminal law.

The chapter begins by providing background on the Special Court for Sierra Leone in addressing serious international crimes committed during the war. It then discusses enslavement as charged in the AFRC, RUF and *Taylor* cases. This section sets out the Special Court's legal definitions of enslavement and sexual slavery, and turns to an exploration of the Court's factual findings on the various forms of enslavement identified by the Prosecutor – forced diamond mining; forced food procurement; forced portering; and forced domestic labour,

2 See sections 3.2.1 and 3.2.3 below.

3 See section 3.2.4 below.

4 *Prosecutor v. Sesay, Kallon and Gbao* (Judgment) SCSL-04-15-T (2 March 2009) paras. 1347–50 ('RUF Trial Judgment').

5 Agreement Between the United Nations and the Government of Sierra Leone on the Establishment of a Special Court for Sierra Leone, Annex – Statute of the Special Court for Sierra Leone (adopted 16 January 2002, entered into force 12 April 2002) 2178 UNTS 138, art. 1(1) ('SCSL Agreement').

6 RUF Trial Judgment, above n. 4; *Prosecutor v. Brima, Kamara and Kanu* (Judgment) SCSL-04-16-T (20 June 2007) ('AFRC Trial Judgment'); *Prosecutor v. Taylor* (Judgment) SCSL-03-01-T (18 May 2012) ('*Taylor* Trial Judgment').

sexual slavery and forced marriage – especially as they reveal the gendered underpinnings of the war economy. This chapter ends with a discussion of the lessons that may be drawn from the Special Court's consideration of enslavement and gender within the larger picture of the economics of war – lessons that may be useful in investigations and prosecutions involving other situations involving gendered war economies, such as in ISIS-held areas of northern Iraq and Syria.[7]

2. THE SPECIAL COURT FOR SIERRA LEONE

The Special Court for Sierra Leone was created in 2002 as a result of an agreement between the United Nations and the Government of Sierra Leone.[8] The Court was mandated to try those bearing the greatest responsibility for crimes against humanity, war crimes and certain violations of Sierra Leone law committed during the 1996–2002 phase of the civil war.[9]

The Special Court's Prosecutor indicted a number of individuals, whose cases were clustered according to the armed group to which they belonged. One case, which resulted in the Special Court's first trial judgment, involved the prosecution of Alex Tamba Brima, Brima Bazzy Kamara and Santigie Borbor Kanu of the AFRC.[10] The AFRC was formed as a result of a 1997 coup by members of the Sierra Leone Army, who overthrew the elected government of President Kabbah and invited the RUF to form a junta.[11] Brima was a high-ranking member of the AFRC's Supreme Council and Principal Liaison Officer in the AFRC government.[12] He was responsible for overseeing AFRC-controlled diamond mining activities and, at times, served as an overall commander.[13] Kamara was also a member of the Supreme Council and a Principal Liaison Officer in the AFRC government.[14] He was responsible for supervising the Agriculture,

---

7 UNSC, 'The Eighth Annual Report of the Secretary-General on Conflict-related Sexual Violence' (2017) UN Doc S/2017/249, para. 39.

8 SCSL Agreement, above n. 5.

9 ibid., arts. 1–5. The 1996–2002 time period was the result of political compromise within the UN Security Council and has been the subject of criticism for excluding serious crimes committed in rural areas during the five years prior to this time period: A. Smith, 'The Expectations and Role of International and National Civil Society and the SCSL' in C. Jalloh (ed.), *The Sierra Leone Special Court and Its Legacy: The Impact for Africa and International Criminal Law*, Cambridge University Press 2014, pp. 46, 48.

10 *Prosecutor v. Brima, Kamara and Kanu* (Sentencing Judgment) SCSL-04-16-T (19 July 2007) Disposition; *Prosecutor v. Brima, Kamara and Kanu* (Judgment) SCSL-04-16-A (22 February 2008) 105–106 ('AFRC Appeals Judgment').

11 AFRC Trial Judgment, above n. 6, para. 164.

12 ibid., para. 322.

13 ibid., paras. 332, 378, 420.

14 ibid., paras. 434–35.

Forestry, Fisheries, Energy and Power, Lotto and Income Tax Ministries.[15] Kanu was a senior commander in the AFRC, with overall or deputy command of forces in Kono, Port Loko, Koinadugu and Bombali Districts, including of the forces that invaded Sierra Leone's capital, Freetown, in 1999.[16] Kanu planned and took part in the coup, and served on the Supreme Council.[17] He also was a senior commander and Chief of Staff in the AFRC fighting forces.[18] He was in charge of abducted civilians, including girls and women assigned as forced wives.[19] All three AFRC accused were convicted of numerous acts, including enslavement, and sentenced to 45–50 years of imprisonment.[20]

The second completed trial involved members of the Civil Defence Forces (CDF) militia, a rural security force aimed at supporting the elected government of Sierra Leone in its fight against the AFRC and RUF.[21] Sam Hinga Norman, the former National Coordinator of the CDF, died after the completion of trial but before the issuance of the judgment.[22] Moinina Fofana was the CDF's Director of War and Allieu Kondewa was the High Priest of the CDF.[23] As these individuals were not charged with enslavement, this chapter will not discuss the CDF case.

The third case brought to judgment involved three members of the RUF: Issa Sesay, Morris Kallon and Augustine Gbao. Each of the accused was charged with – among other crimes – enslavement as a crime against humanity in respect of forced labour in a number of districts in Sierra Leone between 1997–2000.[24] Sesay was a senior officer and commander in the RUF, including Battle Field Commander.[25] Kallon was also a senior officer and commander in the RUF, serving as Deputy Area Commander, Battle Group Commander and, subsequently, Battle Field Commander.[26] Within the RUF, Gbao served as Commander of the RUF Internal Defence Unit, senior RUF Commander in charge of Kailahun Town, Overall Security Commander, and joint Commander of AFRC/RUF Forces in the Makeni Area at different points in time.[27] All three RUF accused were convicted of numerous charges, including enslavement, and sentenced to 25–52 years of imprisonment.[28]

---

15 ibid., para. 436.
16 ibid., paras. 461, 468, 474, 500.
17 ibid., paras. 507–09.
18 ibid., paras. 526, 532, 535.
19 ibid., paras. 523–26. Forced marriage is discussed in section 3.2.4 below.
20 AFRC Appeals Judgment, above n. 10, para. 106.
21 *Prosecutor v. Fofana and Kondewa* (Judgment) SCSL-04-14-T (2 August 2007) para. 2.
22 ibid., para. 4. The trial proceedings were therefore terminated: ibid., para. 5.
23 ibid., para 1.
24 *Prosecutor v. Sesay, Kallon and Gbao* (Corrected Amended Consolidated Indictment) SCSL-04-15-PT (2 August 2006) paras. 69–76 and Count 13 (RUF Indictment).
25 ibid., paras. 21–23.
26 ibid., paras. 24–28.
27 ibid., paras. 30–33.
28 *Prosecutor v. Sesay, Kallon and Gbao* (Judgment) SCSL-04-15-A (26 October 2009) 480 ('RUF Appeals Judgment').

The final case decided by the Special Court for Sierra Leone involved Charles Taylor, the former President of Liberia. He was charged under a number of modes of responsibility – joint criminal enterprise, aiding and abetting, planning, instigating, ordering and superior responsibility – for his involvement in crimes perpetrated by the RUF and AFRC, as well as others.[29] Taylor was charged with, *inter alia*, enslavement as a crime against humanity and cruel treatment as a war crime related to forced diamond mining. The enslavement charges related, in part, to forced alluvial diamond mining in Kenema, Kono and Kailahun Districts of Sierra Leone between 1997–2002.[30] Taylor was convicted and sentenced to 50 years of imprisonment.[31]

3. THE SPECIAL COURT'S CONSIDERATION OF ENSLAVEMENT

The Prosecutor of the Special Court for Sierra Leone brought a charge of the crime against humanity of enslavement in three out of four cases.[32] In doing so, the prosecution identified several different types of enslavement, including forced diamond mining, forced farming and other forms of food procurement, forced carrying of loads, forced domestic labour, sexual slavery and forced marriage.[33] The Special Court became the first international criminal tribunal to examine enslavement related to conflict-related mining, as well as the first to consider and convict individuals for the crime against humanity of sexual slavery and forced marriage as an inhumane act.[34]

This section will examine the Special Court's legal definition of enslavement, followed by a description – through the lens of gender – of the Court's factual findings on four different types of enslavement: forced mining; forced food procurement; forced portering; and forced domestic labour, sexual slavery and forced marriage.

---

29 *Taylor* Trial Judgment, above n. 6, paras 13–14.

30 *Prosecutor v. Taylor* (Prosecutor's Second Amended Indictment) SCSL-03-01-PT (29 May 2007) paras. 23–27 ('*Taylor* Indictment').

31 *Prosecutor v. Taylor* (Judgment) SCSL-03-01(26 September 2013), para. 305.

32 There were no charges of enslavement in *Prosecutor v. Fofana and Kondewa*.

33 See, for example the analysis in the *Taylor* trial judgment of Count Ten (Enslavement): *Taylor* Trial Judgment, above n. 6, paras. 572–740. Forced marriage was charged under the crime against humanity of other inhumane acts; however, as the Court considered evidence of sexual slavery and forced domestic labour in evaluating this charge, this chapter will consider forced marriage under the theme of enslavement and the war economy.

34 Special Court for Sierra Leone Office of the Prosecutor Press Release, 'Special Court Prosecutor Hails RUF Convictions' (Special Court for Sierra Leone, 25 February 2009) <http://www.rscsl.org/Documents/Press/OTP/prosecutor-022509.pdf> accessed 14.04.2018; Special Court for Sierra Leone Office of the Prosecutor Press Release, 'Prosecutor Hollis hails the historic conviction of Charles Taylor' (Special Court for Sierra Leone, 26 April 2012) <http://www.rscsl.org/Documents/Press/OTP/prosecutor-042612.pdf> accessed 14.04.2018.

3.1. THE SPECIAL COURT'S LEGAL DEFINITIONS OF ENSLAVEMENT

Enslavement was defined by the Trial Chamber in both the AFRC and *Taylor* trial judgments as follows:

1. The perpetrator exercised any or all of the powers attaching to the right of ownership over one or more persons, such as by purchasing, selling, lending or bartering such a person or persons, or by imposing on them a similar deprivation of liberty.
2. The perpetrator exercised these powers intentionally.[35]

The RUF trial judgment adopted a very similar definition, but added that the accused may also have acted in the reasonable knowledge that the act of enslavement was likely to occur,[36] a point which was disputed by the *Taylor* Trial Chamber.[37] Sexual slavery was defined in a similar manner, with the additional element that 'The Accused cause such a person or persons to engage in one or more acts of a sexual nature'.[38] All three judgments based their approach on the definition of enslavement found in the International Criminal Court's Elements of Crime document,[39] which, in turn, was based in part on the 1926 Slavery Convention and the 1956 Supplementary Convention on the Abolition of Slavery.[40]

Building on the jurisprudence of the International Criminal Tribunal for the Former Yugoslavia's *Kunarac* case on enslavement, the Special Court identified indicia of enslavement as 'control of someone's movement, control of physical environment, psychological control, measures taken to prevent or deter escape, force, threat of force or coercion, duration, assertion of exclusivity, subjection to cruel treatment and abuse, control of sexuality and forced labour'.[41] The Special

---

35 *Taylor* Trial Judgment, above n. 6; AFRC Trial Judgment, above n. 6, para. 749.

36 RUF Trial Judgment, above n. 4, para. 197.

37 *Taylor* Trial Judgment, above n. 6, para. 450.

38 RUF Trial Judgment, above n. 4, para. 158; AFRC Trial Judgment, above n. 6, para. 708; *Taylor* Trial Judgment, above n. 6, para. 418.

39 Elements of Crimes of the International Criminal Court (2000) ICC-ASP/1/3 at 108, UN Doc. PCNICC/2000/1/Add.2 (2000) art. 7(1)(c).

40 Slavery Convention (adopted 25 September 1926, entered into force 9 March 1927) 60 LNTS 253, art. 1(1); 1956 Supplementary Convention on the Abolition of Slavery, the Slave Trade, and Institutions and Practices Similar to Slavery (adopted 7 September 1956, entered into force 30 April 1957) 226 UNTS 3, art. 6(1); as cited in AFRC Trial Judgment, above n. 6, para. 742 and n. 1435. See also R.S. Lee *et al.*, *The International Criminal Court: Elements of Crimes and Rules of Procedure and Evidence*, Transnational Publishers 2001, pp. 84–86.

41 AFRC Trial Judgment, above n. 6, para. 745; RUF Trial Judgment, above n. 4, para. 199; *Taylor* Trial Judgment, above n. 6, para. 447; citing *Prosecutor v. Kunarac et al.* (Judgment) ICTY-96-23-T and ICTY-96-23/1-T (22 February 2001), para. 543; cited with approval by

Court's Trial Chambers confirmed that lack of consent of the victim is not an element to be proven by the prosecution, although it may be relevant from an evidentiary perspective.[42] In addition, they indicated that there is no specific duration required for the relationship between the accused and the victim, but that the duration may be relevant in determining the quality of the relationship.[43] The AFRC trial judgment noted that 'a person may be enslaved for a short period of time provided that[,] in that time[,] the perpetrator intentionally exercises a degree of control over the person sufficient to constitute the *actus reus* of the crime'.[44]

Given that many of the enslavement charges related to forced labour, the Trial Chambers considered whether 'the relevant persons had no choice as to whether they would work', a determination which requires objective evidence of the situation.[45] Objective indicators include 'threats or use of violence by the perpetrators and lack of compensation'.[46] The Trial Chambers also recognised that enslavement is a continuing crime.[47] This is due to its prolonged nature over time and location, 'especially in the context of the Sierra Leone conflict where the perpetrators were often on the move between villages and Districts for a significant period of time'.[48] The Trial Chamber additionally recognised that enslaved civilians were 'used to perform a multiplicity of critical tasks for the troops'.[49] The framework within which the enslavement took place was systematic, continuous, organised and large-scale, requiring 'a substantial degree of planning and preparation'.[50] For example, the rebels kept records of the women and girls who were sexually enslaved and the AFRC had a position within the brigade with designated responsibility for abducted civilians.[51] The result was that the RUF and AFRC furthered their ultimate goal of securing, among other things, economic control over Sierra Leone.[52]

Note that, while forced marriage was recognised as a form of forced labour, it was charged separately under the crime against humanity of 'other inhumane

---

Prosecutor v. Kunarac et al. (Judgment) ICTY-96-23-A & ICTY-96-23/1-A (12 June 2002), para. 119.

42 AFRC Trial Judgment, above n. 6, para. 746; RUF Trial Judgment, above n. 4, para. 200; *Taylor* Trial Judgment, above n. 6, para. 447.

43 RUF Trial Judgment, above n. 4, para. 200; *Taylor* Trial Judgment, above n. 6, para. 447.

44 AFRC Trial Judgment, above n. 6, para. 1282.

45 *Taylor* Trial Judgment, above n. 6, para. 448; RUF Trial Judgment, above n. 4, para. 202; both referring to *Prosecutor v. Krnojelac* (Judgment) ICTY-97-25-A (17 September 2003) paras. 194–95.

46 AFRC Trial Judgment, above n. 6, para. 1283.

47 ibid., para. 39. See also *Taylor* Trial Judgment, above n. 6, paras. 119, 1018.

48 AFRC Trial Judgment, above n. 6, para. 40.

49 ibid., para. 1821.

50 ibid., paras. 1824, 1826.

51 ibid., para. 1824.

52 RUF Trial Judgment, above n. 4, para. 2159.

acts' in the AFRC and RUF cases.[53] The AFRC Appeals Chamber defined forced marriage as 'a perpetrator compelling a person by force or threat of force, through the words or conduct of the perpetrator or those associated with him, into a forced conjugal association with another person resulting in great suffering, or serious physical or mental injury on the part of the victim'.[54] This was endorsed in the RUF appeals judgment.[55] The *Taylor* trial judgment, in *dicta*, took a different approach, characterising the acts as 'a conjugal form of enslavement'.[56] This conjugal enslavement included sexual slavery, forced domestic labour such as cooking and cleaning, forced pregnancy and forced childrearing.[57]

In sum, the Special Court's legal findings on enslavement both confirmed previous international criminal law understandings on enslavement and pushed the application of that law into new territories, as explained in the following subsection.

3.2. THE SPECIAL COURT'S FACTUAL FINDINGS ON ENSLAVEMENT THROUGH A GENDER LENS

3.2.1. Forced Diamond Mining

In the AFRC, RUF and *Taylor* cases, the accused were charged with forcing civilians in Kenema, Kono and Kailahun Districts to mine for alluvial diamonds.[58] As the Trial Chamber notes, 'alluvial diamond mining in Kono [as well as elsewhere] was the major source of income for the AFRC/RUF regime'.[59] Diamonds, therefore, were a 'vital source of revenue for the AFRC/RUF'.[60] This was because the regime 'was experiencing difficulties generating revenue from taxes as the private sector was non-operational, there was widespread civil disobedience and the international embargo against Sierra Leone reduced trade'.[61] The AFRC/RUF's Supreme Council therefore created an internal structure to enforce and supervise mining in Sierra Leone's diamond districts under their control.[62] The revenue from forced diamond mining was used for

53 For example, RUF Indictment, above n. 24, para. 60 (Count 8).
54 AFRC Appeals Judgment, above n. 10, para. 195.
55 RUF Appeals Judgment, above n. 28, para. 735.
56 *Taylor* Trial Judgment, above n. 6, para. 427.
57 ibid.
58 *Prosecutor v. Brima, Kamara and Kanu* (Further Amended Consolidated Indictment) SCSL-04-16-PT (18 February 2005) paras. 66–73; RUF Indictment, above n. 24, paras 69–76; *Taylor* Indictment, above n. 30, paras. 23–27.
59 RUF Trial Judgment, above n. 4, para. 1088.
60 ibid., para. 1485.
61 ibid., para. 1088.
62 ibid.

the salaries of members of the Council, procurement of arms and ammunition and logistics support for the fighters, and basics such as food and medicine.[63]

Key witnesses described how, throughout the periods of AFRC/RUF control of the diamond mining area, the mining was organised and strategic, with forced civilian labour and coerced assistance at its core. Additionally, the Trial Chamber found that 'the conditions worked at the mines cumulatively created an atmosphere of terror in which genuine consent was not possible'.[64] This combination of strategic organisation and control through terror was accomplished through a system reliant on captured civilians' intent on survival, child soldiers and fear.

In order to create an enslaved workforce and identify mine locations, the AFRC/RUF created committees 'made up of predominantly elderly civilians who had been captured', with the mandate to 'assist the fighters in obtaining civilian labour, to identify potential mining sites and to help assess the diamonds found'.[65] The AFRC/RUF troops would conduct house-to-house searches, or village raids, to capture at gunpoint 150–500 civilians per day.[66] While many of the witnesses referred to male civilians (both men and boys) being forced to mine, the judgments also reveal that some women and girls were also forced to mine.[67] However, young men seemed to be preferred.[68] This preference largely reflected a continuation of the gendered division of mining prior to the armed conflict.

The captured civilians were stripped naked or left only with their underpants (to prevent escape), tied together with their shirts, ropes or chains, and marched to the mining work.[69] Those who tried to hide or escape these raids were detained, stripped and left naked.[70] The wives of the captured male civilians were often left behind to do other work for the rebels.[71]

---

63 ibid., paras. 1088 and 1240.

64 *Taylor* Trial Judgment, above n. 6, para. 1657.

65 RUF Trial Judgment, above n. 4, para. 1090.

66 AFRC Trial Judgment, above n. 6, para. 1326 (one witness indicated that 240 civilians were forced to mine each day by the RUF in Kono District); *Taylor* Trial Judgment, above n. 6, paras. 1627, 1629, 1639, 1720; RUF Trial Judgment, above n. 4, paras. 1246 (approximately 200 civilians were forced to mine in each major pit), 1247 (up to 300 civilians per day), 1249 (400 civilians forced to mine in Kono), 1256 (more than 500 civilians), and 1257 (200 civilians).

67 RUF Trial Judgment, above n. 4, para. 1089. See also Susan McKay and Dyan Mazurana, *Where are the Girls? Girls in Fighting Forces in Northern Uganda, Sierra Leone, and Mozambique: Their Lives During and After War* (Rights & Democracy, 2004) noting at pp. 91–93 that some girls were labourers in diamond mines.

68 For example, RUF Trial Judgment, above n. 4, para. 1258.

69 AFRC Trial Judgment, above n. 6., para. 1297; *Taylor* Trial Judgment, above n. 6, paras. 1627, 1639, 1742; RUF Trial Judgment, above n. 4, paras 1094, 1252.

70 RUF Trial Judgment, above n. 4, para. 1093.

71 *Taylor* Trial Judgment, above n. 6, para. 1639 (reference to wives of captured civilians).

Once at the mining site, the miners 'were not allowed to move freely in the mining sites and had to obtain passes for any movement'.[72] They were forced at gunpoint to mine from sunrise to sunset, though not usually at night.[73] If they refused, would be flogged or shot dead.[74] The miners were kept in difficult conditions for long periods of time (e.g. in muddy water, washing the gravel) and were fed either nothing or very little, such as one plantain or some garri per day.[75] They were not provided with compensation, clothing (with most mining in their underwear only), medical care or housing.[76] They were often bitten by mosquitoes and ants, but were not given any medication to protect against disease, and consequently some died.[77] Some were forced to erect their own shacks so they could live near the mine.[78] Some of these civilians had nowhere else to live, as the RUF had burned their houses down.[79] As a result of this treatment, the miners were haggard.[80] Captured civilians were sometimes moved from mine to mine, as the war front moved and the rebels gained and lost control of land.[81] When civilians did not find diamonds, the rebels would punish them, accusing them of being wizards or witches and flogging, stabbing or restraining the older civilians in cells.[82]

Child soldiers were sometimes left to guard the mines.[83] These children had been brutalised and brainwashed. They were often addicted to drugs and were effective mining guards, as they would kill civilians whom they suspected of mining for themselves rather than for the 'government'.[84] In addition, they would sometimes shoot at the miners as a result of internal RUF disagreements unrelated to the behaviour of the miners.[85]

The AFRC/RUF initially designated certain days of the week – sometimes Monday to Thursday – as 'government' days, during which the civilians were

72 RUF Trial Judgment, above n. 4, para. 1094.

73 *Taylor* Trial Judgment, above n. 6, para. 1742; RUF Trial Judgment, above n. 4, paras. 1095, 1247, 1251.

74 *Taylor* Trial Judgment, above n. 6, paras. 1621, 1725, 1742.

75 RUF Trial Judgment, above n. 4, para. 1433; *Taylor* Trial Judgment, above n. 6., paras. 1617–18, 1620, 1642, 1742; RUF Trial Judgment, above n. 5, para. 1094; AFRC Trial Judgment, above n. 6, para. 1292. While there was evidence that the miners were not given food, there were other situations in which some food was provided: AFRC Trial Judgment, above n. 6, para. 1296; *Taylor* Trial Judgment, above n. 6, paras. 1642, 1742; RUF Trial Judgment, above n. 4, paras. 1251, 1256.

76 *Taylor* Trial Judgment, above n. 6, paras. 1617–18, 1620, 1642, 1742; RUF Trial Judgment, above n. 4, paras. 1248, 1251, 1258; AFRC Trial Judgment, above n. 6, para. 1292.

77 RUF Trial Judgment, above n. 4, para. 1251.

78 ibid., para. 1248.

79 ibid.

80 ibid., para. 1094.

81 For example, AFRC Trial Judgment, above n. 6, para. 1327.

82 RUF Trial Judgment, above n. 4, para. 1253.

83 ibid., para. 1251.

84 *Taylor* Trial Judgment, above n. 6., para. 1641.

85 RUF Trial Judgment, above n. 4, paras. 1084–87.

forced to work from sunrise to sunset in the mines and were not provided with any compensation or housing.[86] The civilians were forced to hand over any diamonds to the AFRC/RUF fighters supervising the mining, and these fighters were armed with an array of weapons, such as rocket-propelled grenades and AK-47s.[87] Civilians who tried to keep the diamonds they mined on 'government days' were flogged almost to death, or were killed as an example to other civilians.[88] When released from the mining, the civilians would go to surrounding villages to find food.[89] This system was also referred to as the 'one-pile' system, 'meaning that the RUF confiscated the entirety of the diamonds extracted'.[90]

As the RUF Trial Chamber noted, the AFRC/RUF's 'government' system was markedly different from the civilian mining that had occurred prior to the conflict.[91] In peacetime, mining sites were operated by civilians as private enterprises. The civilian bosses who owned the mining sites were responsible for negotiating remuneration with the workers and providing them with food and medical assistance. Workers generally handed diamonds to their bosses in return for a share of the profits from the sale of the diamonds.[92]

Prior to 1999, forced mining was largely done by hand using shovels, pickaxes, sieves and pans.[93] After 1999, and more so after 2000, mining became mechanised, with the use of diggers and mechanical washers, to wash the gravel to reveal the stones.[94] The system also changed to the 'two pile system', in which the gravel was divided into two shares, one for the RUF and one for the miners.[95] This meant that some personal mining re-emerged, as had been the case in peacetime, and, in theory, 'civilians were allowed to keep the diamonds for resale'.[96] However, the RUF set up checkpoints around the mines, at which the RUF would 'take the diamonds found on civilians or force the sale of the diamonds to the RUF at prices fixed by the RUF agents'.[97] Additionally, if 'something attractive' was in a labourer's pile, it would be confiscated by the RUF.[98] In some places, the 'two pile system' was implemented through designation of non-'government days', though the AFRC/RUF would still be present at the mines, and would take the larger

86 AFRC Trial Judgment, above n. 6, para. 1292; *Taylor* Trial Judgment, above n. 6, paras. 1617–18, 1620; RUF Trial Judgment, above n. 4, para. 1248.
87 AFRC Trial Judgment, above n. 6, para. 1293; *Taylor* Trial Judgment, above n. 6, para. 1621.
88 AFRC Trial Judgment, above n. 6, para. 1293; RUF Trial Judgment, above n. 4, para. 1095.
89 RUF Trial Judgment, above n. 4, para. 1248.
90 ibid., para. 1250.
91 ibid., para. 1093.
92 ibid.
93 ibid., para. 1250.
94 ibid., paras. 1250, 1255.
95 ibid., para. 380.
96 ibid., para. 1250.
97 ibid; *Taylor* Trial Judgment, above n. 6, para. 1742.
98 *Taylor* Trial Judgment, above n. 6, para. 1727.

diamonds found by civilians and force them to wash the gravel.[99] The Court heard evidence that the 'two pile' system did not benefit civilians in reality.[100]

Within the RUF-controlled mines, of which there were over 30, the civilians were put in groups of nine, called 'gangs', each with a leader.[101] They were provided with shovels, diggers and, sometimes, boots.[102] The miners were told to hand over any diamonds to the gang leader, who would then give it to the RUF Operation Commander.[103] The Operation Commander and the Deputy Commander would collect and weigh the diamonds, 'before reporting and passing them to the Overall Mining Commander and his team of diamond evaluators and clerks'.[104] The Overall Mining Commander was in charge of deploying the civilians to the mine sites, detailed bookkeeping and registering diamonds in Diamond Production Records according to area of providence.[105] The Records provided evidence of 8,000 pieces of diamonds extracted from Kono and Kailahun District between 30 October 1998 and 31 July 1999, and of 2,134 pieces of diamonds extracted in Kono between 2 February 1999 and 11 January 2000.[106] The Overall Mining Commander and Minister for Mines collected the diamonds, weighed and packaged them in sealed parcels and delivered them to one of the accused, Sesay, in his capacity as Battlefield Commander.[107] Sesay then conveyed them to the Chief of Defence Staff, and the diamonds would be bartered or sold for arms, ammunition, medicine and food.[108]

While the rebels' centralised scheme provided significant economic benefit to the AFRC/RUF, there was also corruption within the system, with some AFRC/RUF commanders operating mining sites for their personal profit.[109] In these situations, AFRC/RUF commanders forced both civilians and bodyguards to mine and hand over any diamonds from the mines directly to the commanders.[110]

In sum, enslavement of largely male, but including some female, civilians for the purposes of forced diamond mining was a key element of the wartime economy for the AFRC/RUF. Without the mass civilian labour used to extract diamonds, which were then used to pay for weapons, food and other wartime provisions, it is unlikely that the rebels would have been able to sustain their war effort over a decade.

---

99 AFRC Trial Judgment, above n. 6, para. 1293; *Taylor* Trial Judgment, above n. 6, paras. 1622, 1632.
100 *Taylor* Trial Judgment, above n. 6, paras. 1730, 1736.
101 RUF Trial Judgment, above n. 4, paras. 1243, 1246.
102 ibid., para. 1244.
103 ibid., para. 1243.
104 ibid.
105 ibid., para. 1244.
106 ibid.
107 ibid., para. 1245.
108 ibid.
109 ibid., paras. 1092, 1259.
110 ibid.

3.2.2. *Forced Farming, Forced Food-Finding Missions and Forced Fishing*

As with the forced mining, the rebels – particularly the RUF – put into a place a 'widespread and systematic' program of slavery to supply food for the fighters.[111] This was done in a number of ways: through forced farming, harvesting in the wild, and fishing, as well as through forced food-finding missions in which food was stolen from the civilian population.

The forced farming system was extensive. The RUF established so-called 'government' farms in order to supply its fighters.[112] The logistics of the forced farming were managed by the RUF's Army Agricultural Unit.[113] Captured civilians were screened by a branch of the RUF tasked with addressing civilian-military issues, with some allocated to the Unit for forced farming to cultivate food.[114] Some districts had farms with anywhere from 100–500 forced labourers.[115] The civilians were forced to work at gunpoint.[116] They had no choice as to when, where and how they worked.[117] Civilians who refused to farm were beaten.[118]

As with the other forms of forced labour, the working conditions on the RUF farms were difficult.[119] Many civilians walked many miles to and from the farms each day, while some were forced to live at the farms for extended periods or in 'zoo bushes', semi-permanent communities with civilians and fighters living in the bush to evade attack.[120] Those forced to farm were expected to undertake various hard labour tasks such as 'brushing roads, weeding, cutting trees, cultivating crops and carrying the crops to trading posts' or to RUF commanders for distribution.[121] They were not permitted to have personal crops, and did not receive any pay, accommodation or food supply.[122] All of the food produced by the farm was designated exclusively for the RUF commanders.[123] Since the forced labourers were not fed, many resorted to scavenging wild crops such as bananas and bush yams to survive.[124] Some of the civilians were injured, suffered from starvation or died as a result of their mistreatment.[125]

---

111 ibid., para. 2158.
112 ibid., para. 1417.
113 ibid.
114 ibid., para. 1414.
115 ibid., paras. 1417, 1422 (300 labourers for two large 'government' farms).
116 ibid., paras. 1422–23.
117 ibid., paras. 1418–19.
118 ibid., para. 1420.
119 ibid., para. 1418.
120 ibid., paras 1415, 1418, 1425, 2367.
121 ibid., para. 1418.
122 ibid., paras. 1418, 1424.
123 ibid., para. 1424.
124 ibid., para. 1420.
125 ibid., para. 1418.

The rebels also forced civilians to cultivate rice farms, harvest the rice, pound the rice and hand it over to the rebels.[126] If civilians refused to work, they were beaten or killed.[127] The RUF fighters checked the rice on the farms, and if any of it was missing, they would beat the civilians.[128] In certain parts of the country, this forced rice cultivation and harvesting was central to the war economy, as rice was the main source of food.[129] Others were forced to harvest palm fruits and process the palm oil for the AFRC/RUF fighters.[130] All food grown and gathered by the civilians was referred to as 'government property' and was given to the rebels.[131]

As with internal corruption within the forced diamond mining system, civilians were also forced to labour at gunpoint on the private farms of the RUF commanders, often suffering maltreatment and beatings.[132] The food produced on these farms was for the exclusive enjoyment of the specific commanders who controlled the farms.[133] For example, civilians were forced to farm and harvest rice, and also build a rice storage barn on a farm controlled by the accused Sesay.[134]

In addition to the RUF farms, the RUF created a forced subscription system: each town occupied by the RUF was forced to provide a certain amount of farm produce to the RUF.[135] This included contributions of rice, cocoa, palm oil, coffee and meat, as well as other food.[136] While some of this food was used for RUF consumption, cocoa, coffee and palm oil were sold to buy ammunition.[137] For example, from 1997–1999 in Talia, up to 150 civilians would 'subscribe' to harvest and deliver 300 bags of cocoa per year to the RUF.[138] Apart from forced farming and the forced subscription system, the RUF also 'simply confiscated from civilians'.[139]

Some civilians were forced to fish and hand over anything caught to the rebels.[140] For example, in Talia, women were forced to fish for the RUF.[141]

---

126 AFRC Trial Judgment, above n. 6, paras. 1348, 1349, 1368–69.
127 ibid., para. 1349.
128 RUF Trial Judgment, above n. 4, para. 1423.
129 AFRC Trial Judgment, above n. 6, para. 1821.
130 RUF Trial Judgment, above n. 4, para. 1230.
131 ibid., para. 1235.
132 ibid., paras. 1425, 1480.
133 ibid., para. 1425.
134 ibid., para. 1426.
135 ibid., para. 1427.
136 ibid.
137 ibid.
138 ibid., para. 1428.
139 ibid., para. 1479.
140 ibid., para. 1230.
141 ibid., para. 1428.

Those who did not catch fish were beaten.[142] In the same region, women were also forced to hunt as a means of providing food to the RUF.[143]

Apart from forced farming, forced fishing and forced food 'subscription', witnesses also described being forced to search for food and fetch water for the rebels, sometimes through food-finding missions.[144] These missions could last as long as a week and included looting food from other civilians.[145] If they refused to find food, the civilians risked being killed by the rebels.[146]

Forced trading sometime accompanied the forced farming, subscription or seizure of food. For example, those who were near the border with Guinea were forced to trade farm products such as cocoa, coffee and palm oil at border trading sites once a week, in exchange for rice, salt, Maggi (stock cubes) and clothes.[147] The money earned in these transactions was given to the RUF.[148]

The enslaved civilians were sometimes kept in camps surrounded by checkpoints, and were not permitted to move alone outside the camps.[149] Their lives were so prescribed that they could not even urinate without an escort.[150] The camp leaders assembled the civilians on a daily basis and informed them of the rules, 'the first of which was that escape was prohibited'.[151] Civilians who attempted to escape were beaten, given extra work or executed.[152] Conditions in these camps were difficult, with frequent shortages of food and medicine.[153]

The rebels targeted both women and men, including older civilians, for enslavement related to food procurement.[154] This is not surprising, as women, men and children all farmed – albeit often with differing, gender-specific tasks – in pre-war Sierra Leone.[155] Indeed, civilians living in rural Sierra Leone produced 70 per cent of the nation's food, with women constituting 80 per cent of that labour force.[156] Within the forms of enslavement, the Special Court's judgments reveal both gender-neutral targeting (insofar as both women and

142 ibid.
143 ibid., para. 1479.
144 ibid., paras. 1218, 1233, 1237; AFRC Trial Judgment, above n. 6, paras. 1346, 1360, 1387.
145 RUF Trial Judgment, above n. 4, para. 1235.
146 ibid.
147 ibid., paras. 1430–31.
148 ibid., para. 1431.
149 ibid., paras. 1218, 1233.
150 ibid., para. 1234.
151 ibid., paras. 1222, 1231.
152 ibid., paras. 1218, 1231.
153 ibid., para. 1220.
154 ibid., para. 1423.
155 J. Beoku-Betts, 'Agricultural Development in Sierra Leone: Implications for Rural Women in the Aftermath of the Women's Decade' (1990) 37(1) *Africa Today* 19 at pp. 21, 23, 24, 27, 29.
156 Ministry of Social Welfare, Gender and Children's Affairs, *National Policy on the Advancement of Women* (Government of Sierra Leone, 2000) 7, cited in Human Rights Watch, *We'll Kill You if You Cry: Sexual Violence in the Sierra Leone Conflict*, Human Rights Watch 2003, n. 84.

men were forced to carry out food procurement labour)[157] and gender-specific targeting, for example, in the example noted above of women forced to fish in Talia.

Forced farming and other means of food procurement by civilian women, men and children were absolutely crucial features of Sierra Leone's war economy: without these forms of enslavement, the rebels would not have been able to survive and carry out their modes of control and exploitation.

3.2.3. *Forced Carrying of Loads*

Several accused were convicted by the Special Court for Sierra Leone for the crime against humanity of enslaving civilians, including by forcing them to carry loads.[158] Both male and female civilians, including children, were captured and forced to carry loads at gunpoint, often on their heads, from place to place, in order to supply the fighters.[159] These loads included pillaged goods, the possessions of rebels moving from one encampment to another, arms, ammunition, medicine and food (such as rice, beans and ground nuts).[160] For example, some civilians were forced to carry beds, baling machines, communications equipment, radio batteries, logged wood, corrugated iron, doors from houses and bombs.[161] The forced portering of arms and ammunition ensured that the RUF could move weapons supplies procured in Liberia to RUF headquarters in Sierra Leone and out to RUF-held areas.[162] It also ensured the movement of valuable loads, such as coffee and cocoa, to RUF headquarters and the return supply of staples such as salt, Maggi and cigarettes for the troops.[163]

Civilians who were unable to carry their loads were executed rather than released, and their loads were transferred to the heads of other civilians.[164] Children who did not walk very fast were beaten.[165] Sometimes these groups of forced labourers were as large as 500 captured civilians.[166] The rebels sought

157 RUF Trial Judgment, above n. 4, para. 1423.

158 AFRC Trial Judgment, above n. 6, paras. 569, 571–72; RUF Trial Judgment, above n. 4, paras. 679, 683, 686.

159 AFRC Trial Judgment, above n. 6, paras. 1315, 1316, 1317, 1342, 1343, 1344, 1348, 1356, 1369, 1451.

160 ibid., paras 1324, 1326, 1338, 1343, 1345, 1359, 1379; RUF Trial Judgment, above n. 4, para. 1218.

161 AFRC Trial Judgment, above n. 6, paras. 1330, 1340, 1370 (the iron was sold in Liberia and the doors in Guinea), 1383; RUF Trial Judgment, above n. 4, para. 1217.

162 RUF Trial Judgment, above n. 4, para. 1221.

163 ibid., para. 1237.

164 AFRC Trial Judgment, above n. 6, para. 1326; RUF Trial Judgment, above n. 4, paras. 1216, 1221: 'This was also done in order to prevent them from reporting the abductions and location of the rebels': para 1216.

165 AFRC Trial Judgment, above n. 6, para. 1348.

166 ibid., para. 1326.

out strong civilians for forced portering,[167] which is why they often targeted males.[168] For example, the RUF Trial Chamber noted that, in Kono, '[s]trong men were used to carry food for the troops'.[169] However, they would also use a wide range of captured civilians, both female and male, from children to adult, when necessary. Some were children as young as 8 years old.[170] Sometimes the captured civilians were guarded by armed boys.[171]

Forced construction was also touched upon in the judgments of the Special Court for Sierra Leone. For example, the AFRC trial judgment discusses the case of a male civilian captured by the RUF and former members of the Sierra Leone Army who was forced to build over 20 huts and guard posts along a strategically important road for RUF fighters.[172] Another witness described how civilians were forced by the RUF to construct roads for vehicles.[173]

The forced carrying of loads and forced road construction contributed to the rebels' war economy because it created a human and vehicular supply chain for a variety of provisions. As noted earlier, although the selection of forced porters was sometimes highly gendered, with the RUF seeking out strong men to carry heavy loads, at other times, particularly when mass movement was occurring within the war front or substantial looting had occurred, all types of civilians were pressed into service and used to porter goods. There is not enough detail on the forced road and other construction to make gender-related conclusions.

3.2.4. *Forced Domestic Labour, Sexual Slavery and Forced Marriage*

A highly gendered type of enslavement within the Sierra Leonean war economy related to forced domestic labour, sexual slavery and forced marriage: three separate but also, at times, intertwined forms of servitude. Girls and women were abducted or captured and often assigned tasks that were considered 'female' in nature in order to support the political and socio-economic structures of the AFRC and RUF. In this sense, these captured girls and women were fundamental to the ability of the rebels to focus on the waging of war. This section will focus on the so-called 'bush wife' or forced marriage system as it encapsulates both forced domestic labour and sexual slavery under the heading of a single form of harm. However, it is important to note that forced domestic labour and sexual slavery also existed outside of the forced marriage framework,

167 ibid., para. 1355.
168 AFRC Trial Judgment, above n. 6, para. 1357.
169 RUF Trial Judgment, above n. 4, para. 1215.
170 AFRC Trial Judgment, above n. 6, paras. 1331, 1338.
171 ibid., para. 1384.
172 ibid., para. 1341.
173 ibid., para. 1371.

particularly when the victims were very young or were not assigned to a particular fighter.[174]

The AFRC, RUF and *Taylor* trial judgments provide significant detail on the 'bush wife' system implemented during the Sierra Leone civil war. This was important, as this form of servitude had never before been examined by an international criminal tribunal. The judgments explained how abducted or coerced girls and women (some as young as 10 years old)[175] were forcibly assigned to AFRC and RUF commanders and soldiers regardless of whether they were already legally married,[176] and this assignment was registered.[177] The RUF Trial Chamber found that 'the use of the term 'wife' by the rebels was deliberate and strategic, with the aim of enslaving and psychologically manipulating the women and with the purpose of treating them like possessions'.[178] The term 'wife' was used although no marriage had occurred under law.[179] As with the forced diamond mining, the bush wife system was systematic in its operation and documentation – for example, with paperwork to document the dispersion of the captured girls and women as property, and mechanisms to punish girls and women who refused to do as they were told by their 'husbands'.[180]

These 'wives' were expected to submit to rape on demand by their 'husbands' and maintain an exclusive sexual relationship.[181] They were required to cook, clean, carry their 'husband's' possessions when he had to move, bear and rear any resulting children, and otherwise do whatever their 'husband' instructed.[182] Some RUF 'husbands' has multiple 'bush wives'.[183] The 'husbands' knew that they held power over their 'wives' and that the victims were not consenting to their 'bush wife' status.[184] The rebels created systems of punishment for 'bush wives' who did not do what they were told by their 'husbands', including being lashed and locked in a box.[185] The lives of these 'bush wives' were often filled with extreme violence. The deliberate and concerted campaign to rape women constitutes 'an extension of the battlefield to the women's bodies, a degrading treatment that inflicts physical, mental and sexual suffering to the victims and

174 For example, after the invasion of Freetown, the retreating RUF forces intentionally abducted girls and women and forced many of them to do domestic chores: RUF Trial Judgment, above n. 4., paras. 1589–91.
175 RUF Trial Judgment, above n. 4, para. 1553.
176 ibid., para. 1412.
177 AFRC Trial Judgment, above n. 6, paras. 1128–29.
178 RUF Trial Judgment, above n. 4, para. 1466.
179 AFRC Trial Judgment, above n. 6, para. 701.
180 ibid., paras. 1115–33.
181 RUF Trial Judgment, above n. 4, paras. 460, 1154–55, 1211–13, 1293, 1295, 1413, 1469, 1472.
182 ibid., paras. 152, 164, 460, 1154–55, 1211–13, 1293, 1295, 1413, 1469, 1472; AFRC Trial Judgment, above n. 6, p. 711, paras 13–18 (Sebutinde Concurring Opinion).
183 RUF Trial Judgment, above n. 4, para. 1411.
184 ibid., para. 1293.
185 AFRC Trial Judgment, above n. 6, para. 1138.

their communities'.[186] The status of 'bush wife' led to a number of physical, psychological and sociological harms, including injuries caused by rape and beatings, and 'a lasting social stigma which hampers [the victim's] recovery and reintegration into society'.[187]

Forced marriage was the subject of intense discussion by the Trial and Appeals Chambers of the Special Court for Sierra Leone for several legal reasons.[188] However, the contribution of forced marriage (and, separately, forced domestic labour and sexual slavery) to Sierra Leone's war economy was not as clearly articulated as the contribution of, for example, forced diamond mining. This may be because the work captured by these labels – for example, cooking, cleaning and childrearing – resembles the types of work often overlooked and undervalued in economic valuations as occurring in the 'private' sphere. Additionally, the sexual violence present in forced marriage is challenging to articulate as part of a war economy but certainly should be considered as such. Sexual slavery was present in the forced marriages for specific reasons, including an overarching 'calculated and concerted pattern … to use sexual violence as a weapon of terror' to assert physical and psychological control of the female (and, by extension, male) civilian population,[189] and as a 'reward' or incentive for troops not otherwise receiving pay.[190]

---

186 RUF Trial Judgment, above n. 4, para. 1602.

187 ibid., para. 1296.

188 The Trial and Appeals Chambers grappled with a number of conceptual legal issues, outlined in V. Oosterveld, 'Forced Marriage and the Special Court for Sierra Leone: Legal Advances and Conceptual Difficulties' (2011) 2 *Journal of International Humanitarian Legal Studies* 127.

189 RUF Trial Judgment, above n. 4, para. 1347. Note that the AFRC and RUF Trial Chambers came to differing conclusions on this. The AFRC Trial Judgment, above n. 6, para. 1454 found that the 'primary purpose behind commission of abductions and forced labour was not to spread terror among the civilian population, but rather was primarily utilitarian or military in nature'. The AFRC Trial Chamber came to the same conclusion with respect to sexual slavery, ibid., para. 1459: 'the primary purpose behind commission of sexual slavery was not to spread terror among the civilian population, but rather was committed by the AFRC troops to take advantage of the spoils of war, by treating women as property and using them to satisfy their sexual desires and to fulfil other conjugal needs'. Even if subjection to forced labour indeed did spread terror among the civilian population, this was rather a 'side-effect' and did not satisfy the specific intent required for this crime: ibid., para. 1453. The Appeals Chamber declined to overturn these findings because the accused had already been convicted of the war crime of committing acts of terror for other acts and therefore adding the enslavement crimes was 'an unnecessary exercise': AFRC Appeals Judgment, above n. 10, para. 172. In contrast, the RUF Trial Judgment found that the consistent pattern of sexual violence, such as sexual slavery and forced marriage, demonstrated the requisite intent to terrorise the civilian population, and therefore constituted acts of terrorism: RUF Trial Judgment, above n. 4, paras. 1346–52, 1493. On other types of enslavement, the RUF Trial Judgment found that the prosecution had failed to prove, in relation to forced farming, that the accused acted with the specific intent to terrorise the civilian population: RUF Trial Judgment, above n. 4, para. 1494. However, forced diamond mining was an act of terror: ibid., para. 2051.

190 AFRC Trial Chamber, above n. 6, para. 1459.

In sum, the AFRC and RUF put into place organised systems of enslavement to provide 'female' domestic work, such as cooking and cleaning, to support the roles of male commanders and fighters. They also simultaneously created a system of sexual slavery to allow for sanctioned rape as a means of control of the civilian population, and as a reward for male commanders and fighters.[191]

4. LESSONS FROM THE COURT'S CONSIDERATION OF ENSLAVEMENT, GENDER AND WAR ECONOMIES

The depth of analysis by the Special Court for Sierra Leone of the role of gender in war economies grew from case to case, with the most sophisticated consideration found in the RUF and *Taylor* trial judgments. That said, the type of analysis was still somewhat rudimentary and there are lessons that can be learned from the Special Court's approach.

The first lesson is that future courts could and should be more explicit about the gender of the affected or targeted populations in order to 'surface' the gendered impacts of various crimes, including enslavement.[192] While the above examination of various forms of enslavement highlighted the gender of the civilians involved in forced diamond mining, food procurement and portering, the Special Court often only referred to the affected population generically as 'civilians'. The gender of these civilians was revealed through an examination of the pronouns used in the description of evidence, or by referring to the transcripts. Thus, it only became clear through this textual analysis that although men were largely the targets of forced diamond mining, they were not the sole targets. The exception to this approach related to evidence and analysis of forced marriage, sexual slavery and forced domestic labour: the judgments clearly highlighted the impact of these violations on girls and women. A more explicit articulation of the gender of the victims would provide a sharper picture of modes of victimisation and therefore inform the Court's analysis of harm caused to victims – and categories of victims – by the perpetrators.

The second lesson is that even a basic articulation of the link between gender and the war economy provides important gender-sensitive contextualisation of how particular fighting forces integrated themselves into a geographic area

---

191 Note that not all males assigned 'bush wives' likely accepted such 'wives' willingly. Aijazi and Baines highlight that most men assigned forced 'wives' by the Lord's Resistance Army in the Ugandan conflict had no choice about who would be their wife: O. Aijazi and E. Baines, 'Relationality, Culpability and Consent in Wartime: Men's Experiences of Forced Marriages' (2017) 11(3) *International Journal of Transitional Justice* 463, 476–77.

192 This term is taken from R. Copelon, 'Surfacing Gender: Re-engraving Crimes Against Women in Humanitarian Law' (1994) 5(2) *Hastings Women's Law Journal* 243.

at particular points in time through massive social disruption.[193] For example, the explanations of forced diamond mining and forced marriage provided in the AFRC, RUF and *Taylor* judgments demonstrated that this integration was oftentimes carried out along highly gendered lines: for example, forcing men to work in the mines left many women and girls in vulnerable situations, and they were abducted into forced marriages.

A third, related, lesson is that gendered violence used to secure the functioning of war economies is part of a continuum of gendered social, political and economic violence in conflict.[194] Gendered violence is often committed in tandem with other types of atrocities. Additionally, there is often an overlap between war economies and economies of criminality.[195] Thus, attention to the place of gendered international crimes in the creation and perpetuation of war economies helps to more fully explain the overarching context of the armed conflict. At present, explanations of conflicts tend to overlook how gendered ideologies or inequalities are intrinsic to the 'sustenance and legitimization' of the violence.[196]

Some may question why an international criminal tribunal should situate crimes such as the crime against humanity of enslavement within the context of a war economy. The answer to that question may be clear for violations such as forced diamond mining, in which an economic analysis reveals how diamonds fuelled, for example, weapons supplies for the RUF. However, the same reasoning applies to other types of enslavement, which were also necessary or beneficial to the supply of food and other goods, and the supply of free domestic and sexual services to the fighting forces.

The Special Court for Sierra Leone's judgments set a positive precedent in the implicit and explicit prosecutorial and judicial recognition of the links

---

193 Such contextualisation is fundamental to a thorough understanding of the interconnections between crimes in a conflict: L. Baig, M. Jarvis, E. Martin Selgado and G. Pinzauti, 'Contextualizing Sexual Violence – Selection of Crimes' in S. Brammertz and M. Jarvis, *Prosecuting Conflict-Related Sexual Violence at the ICTY*, OUP 2016, pp. 172, 173.

194 F. Ní Aoláin, D.F. Haynes and N. Cahn, *On the Frontlines: Gender, War and the Post-Conflict Process*, Oxford University Press 2011, p. 36.

195 ibid., p. 35. The authors note at p. 35 that this examination can expose how 'women's labour operates to sustain and support ongoing hostilities within and between states'. This crime-conflict overlap allows for various forms of resource exploitation and money-laundering, providing 'incentive to foster more conflict in order to spirit away and hide more resources', at p. 249.

196 Dubravka Zarkov notes that "there is still no substantial feminist scholarship of war economies": D. Zarkov, 'From Women and War to Gender and Conflict? Feminist Trajectories' in F. Ní Aoláin, D.F. Haynes, N. Cahn and N. Valji, *The Oxford Handbook of Gender and Conflict*, Oxford University Press 2017, pp. 17, 29. Thus, she calls for more analysis of, *inter alia*, how women and men 'become modes of both economic production and social reproduction' and 'how racialized and sexualized gendered ideologies and practices, hierarchies and inequalities become necessary for the sustenance and legitimization of the violence world order', at p. 29. This chapter posits that there is a role for international courts to contribute to this analysis.

between, and harms stemming from,[197] the confluence of enslavement, war economies and gender. But the Court's efforts represent only a start for international criminal law. Further and more nuanced contextualisation of crimes such as enslavement within the larger picture of war economies, and the role gender plays within both these crimes and these economies, will more clearly identify and explain the role of the accused and the experiences of the victims.

197 Ní Aoláin, Haynes and Cahn, above n. 194, pp. 35–36: '[W]omen are deeply affected by violent disorder in complex and multifaceted ways' and an understanding of their forced contributions to the war economy would assist in a deeper understanding of the harms they have experienced.

MALE VICTIMS AND FEMALE PERPETRATORS OF SEXUAL VIOLENCE IN CONFLICT

Anne-Marie de Brouwer and Laetitia Ruiz

1. INTRODUCTION

For a long time, sexual violence in conflict has been seen and largely prosecuted as crimes committed by men against women. Only recently, the international community is becoming aware of the brutality of sexual violence perpetrated against men in conflict situations, and that the number of these atrocities is much higher than has always previously been assumed. Similarly, like men, women and girls are capable – and indeed have done so – of committing atrocious forms of conflict-related sexual violence against men, boys, women and girls alike.

According to Rosalind Petchesky, 'acts of sexual violence against men, women … are named and experienced differently, which is what it means to say they are gendered'.[1] Building on this insight, this chapter deals with the two often marginalised categories of conflict situations with regards to sexual violence, namely male victims and female perpetrators. It first explores the lack of awareness and knowledge surrounding both male victims and female perpetrators of sexual violence and the underlying reasons for such violence. It then discusses how gender norms regarding sexual violence impact on all aspects of the international justice process. In the case of male victims of sexual violence, attention is drawn to the tendency to erase the sexual nature of the crime by using a more general label, such as torture. It will be argued that this state of affairs derives from gender norms, which make male victimisation, and especially male sexual victimisation, inconsistent with ideals of masculinity. In the case of female perpetrators of conflict-related sexual violence, it will be argued that the existence of female perpetrators of sexual violence in conflict is at odds with ideals of femininity. Attention will, *inter alia*, be drawn to the tendency of these women to deny their ability – as women – to commit sexual violence. The chapter ends with some concluding remarks on the ways forward in understanding and prosecuting male sexual victimisation and sexual violence perpetrated by women.

2. SEXUAL VIOLENCE COMMITTED AGAINST MEN IN CONFLICT SITUATIONS

2.1. MALE SEXUAL VICTIMISATION IN CONFLICT

Whereas the sexual victimisation of men is commonly understood to comprise only of 'the penetration of the anus using the penis',[2] sexual violence against men can take several forms which include – but are in no way limited to – enforced nudity, enforced masturbation, enforced sterilisation, beatings, mutilation or other forms of trauma to the genitals, castration, rape, forced marriage and

---

1 R. Petchesky, 'Rights of the Body and Perversions of War: Sexual Rights and Wrongs Ten Years Past Beijing' (2005) 57 *International Social Science Journal* 301–18, 302.

2 Office of the United Nations Special Representative of the Secretary-General on Sexual Violence in Conflict, *Report of Workshop on Sexual Violence against Men and Boys in Conflict Situations* (25–26 July 2013) 11 <http://ifls.osgoode.yorku.ca/wp-content/uploads/2014/01/Report-of-Workshop-on-Sexual-Violence-against-Men-and-Boys-Final.pdf> accessed 11.09.2016.

sexual slavery.[3] It has been found that male sexual victimisation can occur at the hands of both men and women.[4]

In spite of notable exceptions such as the Abu Ghraib Prison scandal[5] and the 2014 US Senate Select Committee on Intelligence report on the CIA's interrogation program,[6] male victims of sexual violence have largely remained invisible in, or at least placed at the periphery of, conflict narratives. This can be observed with, for instance, the explicit reference, for the first time in 2013, to male victims of sexual violence in a UN Security Council resolution on women, peace and security.[7]

This absence is quite remarkable considering that the sexual victimisation of men has a long history, which testifies to it being a common feature of armed conflict in a wide range of societies.[8] Castration and rape of enemy soldiers were widespread in ancient cultures, from ancient Persia to ancient Greece and Mesoamerica, in order to show the defeated's loss of manhood.[9] This loss of manhood included the impossibility for the victim to be a ruler or a warrior

---

3 This list, which does not pretend to be exhaustive, is drawn from S. Sivakumaran, 'Sexual Violence Against Men and Boys in Armed Conflicts' (2007) 18 *European Journal of International Law* 253, and C. Carpenter, 'Recognizing Gender-Based Violence Against Civilian Men and Boys in Conflict Situations' (2006) 37 *Security Dialogue* 83–103. A more detailed list is provided in ibid., 11.

4 Based on available information, men are generally the perpetrators of sexual violence. However, some cases have shown that women can take on this role. For instance, a male detainee in the former Yugoslavia reported that 'They would undress a man, line the rest of us up and make us perform oral sex on him, another prisoner. There were two Ustasa women, sisters, who liked to force us to do this: Marina and Gordana Grubisić. They would make fifty or sixty of us do this.' Helsinki Watch, *War Crimes in Bosnia-Herzegovina, Volume II*, Human Rights Watch 1993, p. 339. See also K. Johnson *et al.*, 'Association of Sexual Violence and Human Rights Violations With Physical and Mental Health in Territories of the Eastern Republic of the Congo' (2010) 304 *Journal of the American Medical Association* 553–62, 558; D.K. Cohen, 'Female Combatants and the Perpetration of Violence: Wartime Rape in the Sierra Leone Civil War' (2013) 65(3) *World Politics* 383–415.

5 See specifically the Taguba Report, 'AR 15-6 Investigation of the 800th Military Police Brigade' (May 2004) <https://www.thetorturedatabase.org/files/foia_subsite/9._article_15-6_investigation_of_the_800th_military_police_brigade.pdf> accessed 11.09.2016.

6 United States Senate Select Committee on Intelligence, *Committee Study of the Central Intelligence Agency's Detention and Interrogation Program* (released 9 December 2014) <http://www.intelligence.senate.gov/sites/default/files/documents/CRPT-113srpt288.pdf> accessed 11.09.2016.

7 UN Security Council Resolution 2106 (2013), UN Doc. S/Res/2106, 6984th meeting, 24 June 2013.

8 See for instance, J.S Goldstein, *War and Gender. How Gender Shapes the War System and Vice Versa*, Cambridge University Press 2001, p. 359; S. Sivakumaran, 'Lost in Translation: UN Responses to Sexual Violence Against Men and Boys in Situations of Armed Conflict' (2010) 82 *International Review of the Red Cross* 259–77, 264; I.H. Jones, 'Cultural and Historical Aspects of Male Sexual Assault' in G.C. Mezey and M.B. King (eds.), *Male Victims of Sexual Assault*, 2nd edn, Oxford University Press 2000, pp. 113–25, 118.

9 Goldstein, above n. 8, pp. 357–58.

any longer.[10] Male sexual victimisation has not spared contemporary conflict situations, with sexual violence against men being reported in virtually all of them, spreading across all continents and cultures, from Colombia[11] to Sri Lanka,[12] South Africa and the Balkans.[13] Sexual violence against men has similarly been reported in some of the most recent conflicts, such as Libya[14] and Syria,[15] as evidenced by the numerous incidents reported by the respective Commissions of Inquiry over the past few years.

As is commonly the case with the examination of sexual violence in general, prevalence rates are extremely difficult to establish. The sexual victimisation of men is no exception. Only two population-based surveys on sexual violence directed at men in time of conflict have been conducted to date. The first

---

10 H.M. Zawati, 'Impunity or Immunity: Wartime Male Rape and Sexual Torture as a Crime Against Humanity' (2007) 17(1) *Torture* 27–47, 33–34.

11 A. Moloney, 'Stigma Silences Colombia's Male War Rape Victims' *Thomson Reuters Foundation* (9 September 2014) <http://www.trust.org/item/20140909071808-pvsjc> accessed 11.09.2016.

12 M. Peel *et al.*, 'The Sexual Abuse of Men in Detention in Sri Lanka' (2000) 355 *The Lancet* 2069–70, 2069.

13 For lists of, and references to, contemporary conflicts with reported sexual violence against men, see for instance UNOCHA, 'Use of Sexual Violence in Armed Conflict: Identifying Gaps in Research to Inform More Effective Interventions. Discussion Paper 2 – The Nature, Scope and Motivation for Sexual Violence Against Men and Boys in Armed Conflict' (2008) Research Paper, 1; Sivakumaran, above n. 3, pp. 257–58.

14 UN Human Rights Council, *Report of the International Commission of Inquiry to investigate all alleged violations of international human rights law in the Libyan Arab Jamahiriya* (A/HRC/17/44, 1 June 2011), para. 124; UN Human Rights Council, *Report of the International Commission of Inquiry on Libya* (A/HRC/19/68, 2 March 2012), paras. 343–44, 504, 506, 514, 525–26, 528–30, 532–33.

15 UN Human Rights Council, *Report of the Independent International Commission of Inquiry on the Syrian Arab Republic* (A/HRC/S-17/2/Add.1 23 November 2011), para. 66; UN Human Rights Council, *Report of the Independent International Commission of Inquiry on the Syrian Arab Republic* (A/HRC/21/50, 16 August 2012), paras. 77–79, 96, 100; UN Human Rights Council, *Report of the Independent International Commission of Inquiry on the Syrian Arab Republic* (A/HRC/21/50, 16 August 2012, Annex VIII), para. 8; UN Human Rights Council, *Report of the Independent International Commission of Inquiry on the Syrian Arab Republic* (A/HRC/21/50, 16 August 2012, Annex IX), para. 20; UN Human Rights Council, *Report of the Independent International Commission of Inquiry on the Syrian Arab Republic* (A/HRC/22/59, 5 February 2013), para. 107; UN Human Rights Council, *Report of the Independent International Commission of Inquiry on the Syrian Arab Republic* (A/HRC/22/59, 5 February 2013, Annex VIII), paras. 16, 18–19, 25; UN Human Rights Council, *Report of the Independent International Commission of Inquiry on the Syrian Arab Republic* (A/HRC/22/59, 5 February 2013, Annex IX), paras. 11–13, 17; UN Human Rights Council, *Report of the Independent International Commission of Inquiry on the Syrian Arab Republic* (A/HRC/23/58, 18 July 2013), paras. 82, 92; UN Human Rights Council, *Report of the Independent International Commission of Inquiry on the Syrian Arab Republic* (A/HRC/25/65, 12 February 2014), paras. 65, 67–68; UN Human Rights Council, *Report of the Independent International Commission of Inquiry on the Syrian Arab Republic* (A/HRC/28/69, 5 February 2015), paras. 136, 145, 175; UN Human Rights Council, *Report of the Independent International Commission of Inquiry on the Syrian Arab Republic* (A/HRC/30/48, 13 August 2015), paras. 94–95.

one found that, out of the 549 former combatant respondents (367 men and 182 women) 32.6 per cent of male former combatants and 42.3 per cent of female former combatants in Liberia experienced forms of sexual violence during the conflict.[16] The second study aimed at establishing the incidence of sexual violence in the Eastern part of the Democratic Republic of Congo (DRC), for which 998 persons responded (405 men and 593 women). In this part of the DRC, which was particularly affected by the conflict, 23.6 per cent of men said they had experienced sexual violence in their life, the majority of whom reported that the violence was conflict-related, while this was the case for 39.7 per cent of women.[17] While both studies find a higher proportion of female victims of conflict-related sexual violence when compared to men, they do not support the widely held view that sexual violence affects women disproportionately.

The rest, and vast majority, of data gathered concerning sexual violence directed at men in conflict situations is mostly anecdotal and cannot provide a comprehensive picture of the prevalence of this specific form of violence. However, it gives credence to the affirmation that the lack of visibility of male sexual victimisation cannot be attributed to a lack of victims.[18] For instance, in 1992, 4,000 former detainees in the Sarajevo Canton (where the now infamous Omarska and Keraterm prison camps were located) reported being raped during the conflict in the former Yugoslavia.[19] Prison camps proved to be a fertile ground for male sexual victimisation.[20] The Final Report of the United Nations Commission of Experts Established Pursuant to Security Council Resolution 780,[21] has contributed more testimonies of male sexual victimisation to the narrative of the conflict in the former Yugoslavia,[22] among them castration,

16 K. Johnson *et al.*, 'Association of Combatant Status and Sexual Violence with Health and Mental Health Outcomes in Postconflict Liberia' (2008) 300 *Journal of the American Medical Association* 676–90, 683.

17 Johnson, above n. 4, p. 558.

18 S. Sivakumaran 'Prosecuting Sexual Violence Against Men and Boys' in A.-M. de Brouwer *et al.* (eds.), *Sexual Violence as an International Crime: Interdisciplinary Approaches*, Intersentia 2013, pp. 79–97, 80.

19 Ž. Mudrovčić, 'Sexual and Gender-Based Violence in Post-Conflict Regions: The Bosnia and Herzegovina Case' in UNFPA, *The Impact of Conflict on Women and Girls – A UNFPA Strategy for Gender Mainstreaming in Areas of Conflict and Reconstruction*, UNFPA 2002, pp. 60–76, 64, <http://www.unfpa.org/webdav/site/global/shared/documents/publications/2002/impact_conflict_women.pdf> accessed 11.09.2016.

20 M. Loncar *et al.*, 'Mental Health Consequences in Men Exposed to Sexual Abuse during the War in Croatia and Bosnia'(2009) 24 *Journal of Interpersonal Violence* 191–203, 193.

21 The work of the Commission of Experts formed the basis for the decision to establish the ICTY and the Commission of Experts later provided information and evidence to the Prosecutor of the ICTY. See ICTY website, 'The Tribunal – Establishment' (UN ICTY) <http://www.icty.org/en/about/tribunal/establishment> accessed 11.09.2016. See also UN, *Final Report of the United Nations Commission of Experts Established Pursuant to Security Council Resolution 780 (1992)* (1994, UN Doc. S/1994/674) 2.

22 See for instance UN, *Final Report of the United Nations Commission of Experts Established Pursuant to Security Council Resolution 780 (1992)* (1994, UN Doc. S/1994/674, Annex IX, 'Rape and Sexual Assault', 11), para. 20.

forced nudity and trauma to the genitals.[23] The available information regarding the sexual victimisation of men over the course of the Yugoslav conflict has been judged by some commentators to show that 'men were also subjected to widespread systematic sexual violence'.[24]

In the case of Syria, the UN-mandated Commission of Inquiry has reported that men have suffered from a wide range of sexual violence acts, mainly while in detention.[25] Of particular significance in the Commission of Inquiry's work is the emphasis on the systematic use of sexual violence directed against men and therefore its role as an integral part – rather than an exceptional or disconnected feature – of the conflict.[26] From February 2013 onwards, the Commission found that the sexual violence perpetrated against men was even part of a widespread and systematic attack against a civilian population, thereby constituting not only a crime against humanity, but also war crimes,[27] used to terrorise, humiliate and punish victims.[28] Of course, men are not always subjected to widespread and systematic sexual violence[29] – just as it has been established in the case of sexual violence against women[30] – but it is important to note that it can be the case, especially within the context of the current hegemonic discourse of the rape of women used as a weapon of war.[31]

What this (very) brief overview of the scope and prevalence of sexual violence against men during armed conflict intends to show is that the absence of, or peripheral, discussions and debates about male sexual victimisation should not be understood as a sign of its non-existence. Rather, the relative

---

23 UN, above n. 21, p. 56, para. 236, p. 57, para. 242 and p. 59, para. 247. See also E.S. Carlson, 'The Hidden Prevalence of Male Sexual Assault During War: Observations on Blunt Trauma to the Male Genitals' (2006) 46 *British Journal of Criminology* 16–25, 19.

24 D. Žarkov, 'The Body of the Other Man: Sexual Violence and the Construction of Masculinity, Sexuality and Ethnicity in Croatian Media' in C.O.N. Moser and F.C. Clark (eds.), *Victims, Perpetrators or Actors? Gender, Armed Conflict and Political Violence*, Zed Books 2001, pp. 69–82, 72.

25 The Commission of Inquiry has distinguished two patterns of sexual violence: women tend to be targeted in house raids by the military and security forces while men (and women) are targeted for sexual violence when in detention settings. See A/HRC/22/59, above n. 15, para. 106. However, the Commission reported a few cases of men subjected to sexual violence during house raids. See A/HRC/21/50, above n. 15, para. 7; A/HRC/28/69, above n. 15, para. 181.

26 A/HRC/S-17/2/Add.1, above n. 15, para. 66; A/HRC/25/65, above n. 15, para. 65; A/HRC/30/48, above n. 15, paras. 94–95.

27 A/HRC/22/59 Annex IX, above n. 15, para. 19; A/HRC/25/65, above n. 15, para. 69.

28 UN Human Rights Council, *Report of the independent international commission of inquiry on the Syrian Arab Republic* (A/HRC/24/46, 16 August 2013), para. 95; A/HRC/22/59 Annex IX, above n. 15, para. 5; A/HRC/28/69, above n. 15, para. 174.

29 Sivakumaran, above n. 8, p. 80.

30 E.J. Wood, 'Variation in Sexual Violence During War' (2006) 34 *Politics and Society* 307–42.

31 This view – that women are always the subjects of sexual violence and that sexual violence is always used as a weapon of war – has been criticised by several academics. See for instance D.E. Buss, 'Rethinking "'Rape as a Weapon of War'"' (2009) 17 *Feminist Legal Studies* 145–63.

invisibility of male sexual victimisation has been attributed to the gender norms that define masculinity, earlier alluded to, in ancient Greece and ancient Rome. In this regard, several scholars – Sandesh Sivakumaran and Dubravka Žarkov in particular – have offered in-depth insights into the meaning of male sexual victimisation, which constitute the object of study of the following section.

2.2. MALE SEXUAL VICTIMISATION AND MASCULINITY

Masculinity[32] is commonly constructed around two concepts, namely power and heterosexuality. Looking first at power, the UN Special Rapporteur on Violence Against Women depicts this central tenet of masculinity as 'the ability to exert power over others, especially through the use of force'.[33] Stemming from the ability to exert power, expectations of strength, toughness, independence, aggressiveness, the protection of oneself and other, and dominance are also constitutive of masculinity.[34] The exercise of power also encompasses a strong sexual component: not any kind of sexual component, but exclusively a heterosexual one.

It has been argued that 'constructions of masculinity are … closely connected to heterosexuality'.[35] In turn, heterosexuality has been viewed as 'a matter of feminine submission to aggressive masculinity'[36] in which men are seen as the initiators of sexual relations.[37] This understanding of heterosexuality is presented as heteronormativity, namely the dominant societal conceptualisation of sexual relations as taking place between men and women according to a hierarchy of

---

32 Masculinity can take a variety of forms according to specific cultures and it would be more accurate to speak of 'masculinities' as within each gender system there exist several masculinities, mainly shaped by the power relationships that link them together. Nevertheless, it is argued here that some common traits can be identified, especially in the case of norms regulating sexual violence, thereby allowing for a certain degree of generalisation. See for instance R.W. Connell et al., 'Introduction' in M.S. Kimmel et al. (eds.), *Handbook of Studies on Men & Masculinities*, Sage 2004, pp. 1–12, 1–3. See also C.S. Mibenge (2013), *Sex and International Tribunals: The Erasure of Gender from the War Narrative*, University of Pennsylvania Press 2013, p. 11. A theme of masculinity in the context of male sexual victimisation is also discussed by Valorie Vojdik in this volume.

33 R. Coomaraswamy, *Preliminary Report of the United Nations Special Rapporteur on Violence against Women, Its Causes and Consequences* (UN Doc. E.CN.4/1995/42, 22 November 1994), para. 64.

34 J.A. Turchik and K.M. Edwards, 'Myths About Male Rape: A Literature Review' (2012) 13 *Psychology of Men and Masculinity* 211–26, 213; See also Žarkov, above n. 24, p. 77 and D. Žarkov, 'War Rapes in Bosnia: On Masculinity, Femininity and Power of the Rape Victim Identity' (1997) 39 *Tijdschrift voor Criminologie* 140–51, 143.

35 Turchik and Edwards, above n. 34, p. 213. See also S. Sivakumaran, 'Male/Male Rape and the "Taint" of Homosexuality' (2005) 27 *Human Rights Quarterly* 1274–1306, 1289.

36 D.J. West, 'Homophobia: Covert and Overt' in Mezey and King, above n. 8, pp. 20–21.

37 G.C. Mezey and M.B. King, 'Preface to the First Edition' in Mezey and King, above n. 8, p. ix.

power that privileges men.[38] Therefore, in a sexual violence scenario, the man is cast as the perpetrator while the victim is inevitably female.[39]

Male sexual violence subverts this logic and the gender norms that define masculinity. Indeed, the infliction of male sexual victimisation is considered as an act of power, aggression and dominance. It is contended that the aim of such violence is to humiliate and degrade the victim[40] by forcing the victim to deviate from the heteronormative masculine standard. This subversion leads to a loss of the victim's masculine identity or, at least, to the victim being 'less' masculine,[41] or not a 'proper'[42] man. In Uganda, a victim refuses to tell his brother that he was gang-raped 11 times in one night by rebel fighters because he 'fear[s] he will say: "Now my brother is not a man."'[43] Another one, who was raped explains that '[rape] 'is not normal for us men'.[44] Yet another victim recounts that the rape is 'painful … to the extent that you feel you no longer want to be the head of the family'.[45] Similar accounts also come from victims in the DRC. In the study conducted by Christian *et al.*, both victims and service providers interviewed stated that sexual violence was 'a strategy to humiliate men by emasculating them'.[46] The Commission of Inquiry on Libya reported victims 'feeling less of a man' or 'no longer being a man' following sexual violence endured while in detention.[47]

In a binary thinking of gender, the victimised male finds himself lowered to the position of a woman, since he is not a man anymore. For instance, a former prisoner in the Iraqi prison of Abu Ghraib explains that '[US soldiers] wanted us to feel as though we were women', 'the way that women feel, and this is the worst insult, to feel like a woman'.[48]

---

38 A. Jones, 'Straight as a Rule: Heteronormativity, Gendercide, and the Noncombatant Male' (2006) 8 *Men and Masculinities* 451–69, 451.

39 Sivakumaran, above n. 3, p. 270.

40 For instance, see L. Stemple, 'Male Rape and Human Rights' (2009) 60 *Hastings Law Journal* 605–47, 614–15; Goldstein, above n. 8, p. 363; Carlson, above n. 23; Peel, above n. 12, p. 2070; Sivakumaran, above n. 3, p. 267; Zawati, above n. 10, p. 33.

41 Sivakumaran, above n. 3, p. 270.

42 Žarkov, above n. 24, p. 77.

43 W. Storr, 'The Rape of Men: The Darkest Secret of War' (2011) 16 July *Observer* 36.

44 Refugee Law Project, 'They Slept with Me' (Documentary, 10 December 2011, at 04:19) <https://www.youtube.com/watch?v=6dxaFqezrXg> accessed 11 September 2016.

45 ibid., at 06:50.

46 M. Christian *et al.*, 'Sexual and Gender Based Violence against Men in the Democratic Republic of Congo: Effects on Survivors, Their Families and the Community' (2011) 27(4) *Medicine, Conflict and Survival* 227–246, 235.

47 UN Human Rights Council, *Report of the International Commission of Inquiry on Libya* (A/HRC/19/68, Annex I, 8 March 2012), para. 533.

48 S. Faramarzi, *Former Iraqi Prisoner Turns Against His American Jailors for Humiliating Him as Allegations of US Torture Are Investigated* (Associated Press, 2004), quoting Dhia al-Shweiri in C. MacKinnon, 'Women's September 11th: Rethinking the International Law of Conflict' in *Are Women Human? And Other International Dialogues*, Bleknap Press of Harvard University Press 2006, pp. 259–78, 273.

Through sexual violence, male victims are not only 'feminised' but also 'homosexualised' in cases of rape according to Sivakumaran.[49] He argues that the homosexualisation of the victim occurs because of the heteronormative standard which defines masculinity and femininity. In this respect, while the perpetrator retains his heterosexual identity (when it is a man), the victim is ascribed a homosexual identity because he allowed for his body to be penetrated. Žarkov comes to a similar conclusion after analysing articles published in Croatian media during the conflict in the former Yugoslavia. According to her, the media systematically questioned the masculinity and heterosexuality of Muslim men who had been sexually mutilated.[50] Her analysis provides additional insights into the treatment of male sexual victimisation. She argues, for instance, that the media fell silent about sexual violence against men in prison camps but did mention types of violence that are more in conformity with masculine gender norms.[51]

She goes on to argue, in the same vein as Sivakumaran,[52] that the emasculation operated on the victim through feminisation and homosexualisation is further extended to the group to which the victim belongs, because notions of masculinity are deeply embedded in ethnic and state identity.[53]

Whereas victimhood and weakness are the attributes of femaleness and power that of maleness, the phrase 'male victim' – and even more so 'male sexual victim' – is a contradiction in terms. This 'impossibility' of the 'male sexual violence victim' explains the low rate of reporting on the part of the victims who feel ashamed and fear stigmatisation within their own community.[54] In some cases, even if victims want to report their experience, they may lack the words to express it,[55] not consider it as sexual violence,[56] or fear prosecution in countries where homosexual relations are criminalised.[57] This construction of men as implausible sexual violence victims also partly explains the hitherto

49 Sivakumaran, above n. 35.

50 Žarkov, above n. 24, p. 77.

51 ibid.

52 Sivakumaran, above n. 3, pp. 257–68.

53 Žarkov, above n. 24, p. 78; see also D.A. Lewis, 'Unrecognized Victims: Sexual Violence Against Men in Conflict Settings Under International Law' (2009) 27 *Wisconsin International Law Journal* 1–50, 16.

54 See for instance Johnson, above n. 16, p. 688; Sivakumaran, above n. 35, p. 1288; Carlson, above n. 23, pp. 22–23; and Peel, above n. 12, p. 2069.

55 See for instance Sivakumaran, above n. 3, pp. 255–56; S. Mouthaan, 'Sexual Violence Against Men and International Law – Criminalising the Unmentionable' (2013) 13 *International Criminal Law Review* 665–695, 667; Peel, above n. 12, p. 2069.

56 Carlson, above n. 23.

57 For an overview of countries that criminalise same-sex relations, see A. Carroll and L.P. Itaborahy, *State-Sponsored Homophobia: A World Survey of Law: Criminalization, Protection and Recognition of Same-Sex Love*, ILGA 2015 <http://old.ilga.org/Statehomophobia/ILGA_State_Sponsored_Homophobia_2015.pdf> accessed 11.09.2016.

limited academic interest for this subject,[58] and the scarce amount of available information gathered by practitioners. Indeed, about the latter, some argue that practitioners are not always aware that men can be victims of sexual violence and usually lack the necessary training to recognise the signs of this specific type of violence.[59]

The problems associated with the ability to conceptualise male victims of sexual violence, which it is argued here, have permeated the international justice process in several ways. The following analysis focuses on how gender norms of masculinity may influence the application of the law rather than the nature of the law itself.[60] As such, attention will be drawn to investigating, charging and labelling practices and its consequences for possible convictions.

3. GENDER AND THE INTERNATIONAL PROSECUTION OF SEXUAL VIOLENCE AGAINST MEN IN CONFLICT SITUATIONS

In this section, prosecutions which have taken or are taking place before the International Criminal Tribunals for the Former Yugoslavia and Rwanda (respectively the ICTY and ICTR), the Special Court for Sierra Leone (SCSL) and the International Criminal Court (ICC) are examined.[61] Regarding the ICTY,

58 Žarkov, above n. 34, p. 145.

59 See for instance P. Oosterhoff *et al.*, 'Sexual Torture of Men in Croatia and Other Conflict Situations: An Open Secret' (2004) 12 *Reproductive Health Matters* 68–77, 68; E.A.P. Gorris, 'Invisible Victims? Where Are Male Victims of Conflict-Related Sexual Violence in International Law and Policy?' (2015) 22(4) *European Journal of Women's Studies* 412–27. The ideas of feminisation and homosexualisation have permeated the nascent literature on sexual violence. However, it has recently been argued that these ideas rely on problematic, mysogynistic and homophobic assumptions that portray being a woman or a homosexual male as degrading. Rather, some scholars argue that male victims experience a "displacement from gendered personhood" (P. Schulz, 'Displacement from Gendered Personhood: Sexual Violence and Masculinities in Northern Uganda' (2018) 94(5) *International Affairs* 1101–1119). This analytical framework aims at circumventing the misogyny, homophobia and essentialist assumptions upon which the ideas of feminisation and homosexualisation rely. It argues that the victimisation is multi-layered, may evolve over time and can be mitigated. The testimonies of victims used to support the idea of a 'displacement from gendered personhood' nevertheless convey a deep sense of loss of masculinity on the part of victims because of (i) victimisation itself and (ii) the sexual nature of the victimisation.

60 For analyses of the gendered nature of the international law, see for instance Stemple, above n. 40 and Sivakumaran, above n. 8, pp. 79–97.

61 Acts of sexual violence against men have also been brought before the Extraordinary Chambers in the Courts of Cambodia, specifically allegations of forced marriage, where both men and women were forced into marriages. See S. Studzinsky, 'Victims of Sexual and Gender-Based Crimes Before the Extraordinary Chambers in the Courts of Cambodia: Challenges of Rights to Participation and Protection' in de Brouwer, above n. 18, pp. 173–86.

focus is drawn specifically to rape because, in contrast to the other tribunals, rape was the only form of sexual violence included in the Tribunal's Statute.[62]

3.1. INTERNATIONAL CRIMINAL TRIBUNAL FOR THE FORMER YUGOSLAVIA

First and foremost, the ICTY is the only international criminal tribunal to have given significant visibility to sexual violence against men in conflict situations. This fact alone has been applauded for providing a certain degree of visibility to the occurrence of this type of victimisation during conflict.[63] What is even more laudable is that acts of male sexual violence have been charged in a high number of cases, which is, according to Kirsten Campbell, 'in clear contrast to the general lack of visibility of male sexual assault in the Yugoslavian conflict; both in terms of media coverage and in comparison to the institutional and legal focus upon sexual violence against women'.[64] In 2007, Campbell identified 17 cases charged by the prosecution that include allegations of sexual violence crimes, of which seven considered sexual violence acts committed against men.[65]

The very first case before the ICTY could have been a trailblazer in the prosecution of sexual violence crimes. The Second Amended Indictment against Duško Tadić, a former camp guard in Bosnia and Herzegovina, contained groundbreaking language, stating, 'Both female and male prisoners were beaten, tortured, raped, sexually assaulted, and humiliated'.[66] However, for 'forc[ing] two … prisoners, "G" and "H", to commit oral sexual acts',[67] Tadić was charged with torture or inhuman treatment, wilfully causing great suffering or serious injury to body or health, cruel treatment and inhumane acts.[68] Concurrently, the Prosecutor charged Duško Tadić with inhuman treatment, cruel treatment and rape for 'forcible sexual intercourse with "F", a female detainee at Omarska camp.[69] Uncertainty about which acts exactly constituted rape at the time may explain this disparity.[70] Yet, it can also be argued that characterising forced

---

62 ICTY Statute, Article 5(g).

63 K. Campbell, 'The Gender of Transitional Justice: Law, Sexual Violence and the International Criminal Tribunal for the Former Yugoslavia' (2007) 1 *International Journal of Transitional Justice* 411–32, 423.

64 ibid.

65 ibid., p. 422.

66 *Prosecutor v. Duško Tadić*, Second Amended Indictment, Case No. IT-94-1-I, 14 December 1995, para. 2.6.

67 ibid., para. 6.

68 ibid., counts 8–11.

69 ibid., counts 2–4.

70 While forced fellatio squarely fits within the current definition of rape as defined in the ICC's Elements of Crimes, it is noteworthy to remember that when the Second Amended Indictment in the *Tadić* case was issued (1995), a definition of rape did not exist in international criminal

fellatio as a more general category of crime may have appeared closer to the masculinity-abiding conception of men's experience of conflict.

The failure to call rape 'rape' became a pattern in subsequent cases before the ICTY. The *Čelebići Camp* case is a good example of this tendency to shy away from explicitly mentioning the sexual nature of the crime committed in the labelling practice of the Office of the Prosecutor. For 'forcing persons to commit fellatio with each other', the accused were charged with inhuman treatment and cruel treatment without mention of the word 'rape' anywhere.[71] The Trial Chamber noticed the inconsistency in the labelling practice and made it known in its judgment: 'The Trial Chamber notes that the aforementioned act [forced fellatio] could constitute rape for which liability could have been found if pleaded in the appropriate manner.'[72]

This remark did not catalyse a revision of indictments containing charges for acts constituting rape to re-label them as rape. Forced fellatio and the insertion of objects in the anus were routinely charged as torture, inhuman acts, cruel treatment or persecution rather than rape, as in the cases of *Milošević*,[73] *Martić*[74] and *Simić*.[75] Similarly, Naletilić and Martinović were found guilty of cruel treatment and wilfully causing great suffering or serious injury to body or health for a wide array of abuses perpetrated against Nenad Harmandžić.[76] These acts included rape but they were never charged as such.[77]

On the other hand, rape charges as a crime against humanity were filed against Češić for forcing two brothers to perform fellatio on each other.[78] While this indictment appears to make leaps and bounds in the prosecution of sexual violence against men, a closer look calls for a mitigation of enthusiasm. Indeed,

---

law. The first definition of rape only emerged in 1998 with the landmark ICTR *Akayesu* judgment. Jarvis and Vigneswaran noted the influence of uncertainty regarding the specific elements of sexual violence on the prosecution of these crimes before the ICTY. M. Jarvis and K. Vigneswaran, 'Challenges to Successful outcomes in Sexual Violence Cases' in S. Brammertz and M. Jarvis (eds.), *Prosecuting Conflict-Related Sexual Violence at the ICTY*, Oxford University Press 2016, pp. 33–72, 34.

71 *Prosecutor v. Mucić et al.*, Indictment, Case No. IT-96-21, 19 March 1996, counts 44 and 45.

72 *Prosecutor v. Mucić et al.*, Trial Chamber Judgment, Case No. IT-96-21, 16 November 1998, para. 1066.

73 *Prosecutor v. Slobodan Milošević*, Decision on Motion for Judgment of Acquittal, Case No. IT-02-54-T, 16 June 2004.

74 *Prosecutor v. Milan Martić*, Amended Indictment, Case No. IT-95-11, 9 December 2005, counts 1 and 6–9.

75 *Prosecutor v. Blagoje Simić et al.*, Trial Judgment, Case No. IT-95-9-T, 17 October 2003, paras. 728 and 772.

76 *Prosecutor v. Mladen Naletilić and Vinko Martinović*, Trial Judgment, Case No. IT-98-34, 31 March 2003, para. 496.

77 ibid., para. 464. Paragraph 464 indicates that a soldier 'took out his penis, forced it into Nenad Harmandžić's mouth and asked him whether he liked it'.

78 *Prosecutor v. Ranko Češić*, Third Amended Indictment, Case No. IT-95-10/1, 26 November 2002, count 8. The same acts were also charged as humiliating and degrading treatment as a violation of the laws and customs of war (count 7).

while count 8 charges forced fellatio under Article 5(g) of the ICTY Statute, the indictment specifies that 'rape [under Article 5(g)] includes other forms of sexual assault'. The heading for these counts furthermore reads 'sexual assault', not rape. As a result, these charges were legally characterised as sexual assault rather than rape, thereby using more general terminology that includes sexual acts other than rape.

The same practice was followed in the *Todorović* case for the same crime.[79] Todorović was charged with rape – understood to include other forms of sexual assaults – and persecution as crimes against humanity for forcing six prisoners to perform fellatio on each other.[80] Todorović entered into a plea agreement with the Prosecution, which saw him convicted of the crime of persecution while all other counts were withdrawn, including that of sexual assaults.[81] Todorović agreed that the acts of sexual assaults were true in the plea agreement but he was only found guilty of the crime of persecution.[82] Therefore, even though Todorović admitted that the sexual assaults occurred, they were not prosecuted as such. Češić also entered into a plea agreement with the Prosecution but, unlike Todorović, pled guilty to all counts of the indictment, therefore to forced fellatio as sexual assault.[83]

While the plea agreements differ, both cases applied Article 5(g) of the ICTY Statute to acts which by all accounts constitute rape but did not actually bring rape charges, rather charges of sexual assault. By charging sexual assault, the Prosecutor demonstrated an understanding of the sexual nature of the crimes while at the same time indicating ambivalence towards considering these acts as what they really are: rape.

The trends described hitherto apply to other forms of sexual violence against men before the ICTY. In the *Stakić* case, a group of men was divided in two. According to the Trial Chamber, 'Half of the group was naked from the waist-down and standing, and half the group was kneeling. According to Witness B: "They were positioned in such a way as if engaged in intercourse."'[84] This specific incident was prosecuted under paragraph 49 of the indictment, under the rubric of causing serious bodily or mental harm. In spite of the eventual prosecution of sexual violence against men, this paragraph proposes a dichotomous vision of men and women's experiences in camps: men were beaten and tortured while women were raped and sexually assaulted.[85] In other cases, the sexual nature of

---

79 *Prosecutor v. Todorović*, Second Amended Indictment, Case No. IT-95-9/1, 19 November 1998, counts 16–24.

80 ibid., counts 16, 19, 22 (sexual violence) and 1 (persecution).

81 *Prosecutor v. Todorović*, Sentencing Judgment, Case No. IT-95-9/1, 31 July 2001, para. 8.

82 ibid., paras. 9 and 17.

83 *Prosecutor v. Ranko Češić*, Sentencing Judgment, Case No. IT-95-10/1, 11 March 2004, paras. 4, 13–14, 33, 35–36.

84 *Prosecutor v. Milomir Stakić*, Trial Judgment, Case No. IT-97-24, 22 March 2006, para. 241.

85 *Prosecutor v. Milomir Stakić*, Fourth Amended Indictment, Case No. IT-97-24, 10 April 2002, para. 49.

the acts was recognised, even though it could not be prosecuted under limited statutory provisions. For instance, Milan Simić was charged with the crimes of torture, inhumane acts and cruel treatment for kicking four prisoners in the genitals and forcibly pulling down the trousers and threatening to cut off the penis of another detainee.[86] In relation to these acts, the Trial Chamber explained, in the Sentencing Judgment, that the 'sexual, violent, and humiliating, nature of the acts are therefore considered in aggravation'.[87] The Tribunal therefore sometimes found a way to highlight the limitations of the ICTY Statute with respect to sexual violence crimes and to name sexual violence for what it is, sexual violence.

Taken as a whole, the vast majority of these legal findings nevertheless characterise these acts of sexual violence as torture, inhuman treatment or humiliating and degrading acts – labels which do not entirely reflect the sexual character of the acts.[88] Charges of rape and sexual assault would have better reflected the nature of the crimes inflicted on victims. In this regard, Campbell concludes that 'men appear to testify to conflict and women testify to rape'.[89] She further adds, 'women are visible victims of sexual violence, while men remain the invisible victims. … The sexually assaulted man … appears more problematic than the heterosexual rape of a woman, and for this reason is not made visible'.[90] The prosecution of sexual violence against men in the former Yugoslavia thereby seems to entrench the traditional gender roles during conflict and confirm the impossibility to conceive of male victims of sexual violence.

This hypothesis is further strengthened by the analysis conducted by the Prosecuting Sexual Violence Working Group established in 2009 within the ICTY's Office of the Prosecutor (OTP) and set out in a recently published book.[91] Jarvis and Vigneswaran argue that within the OTP, misconceptions about sexual violence against men, such as the readiness to acknowledge the violent nature of the acts but not their sexual component, can have influenced the mischaracterisation of the crimes which elides its sexual nature.[92] Establishing a direct correlation between misconceptions and mischaracterisation is too simplistic as many other factors, such as statutory limitations and prosecutorial discretion play an important role. Yet, Jarvis and Vigneswaran contend that prosecutorial discretion has, more often than not, magnified the choices made based on misconceptions rather than being impervious to them.[93]

86 *Prosecutor v. Milan Simić*, Fourth Amended Indictment, Case No. IT-95-9/2, 9 January 2002, paras. 24–27.
87 *Prosecutor v. Milan Simić*, Sentencing Judgment, Case No. IT-95-9/2, 17 October 2002, para. 63.
88 For an in-depth discussion, see Campbell, above n. 63.
89 ibid., p. 425.
90 ibid., p. 427.
91 Brammertz and Jarvis, above n. 70.
92 Jarvis and Vigneswaran, above n. 70, pp. 41–42.
93 ibid., p. 45.

On the other hand, Patricia Viseur Sellers has advanced the argument that mislabelling can help the prosecution of male sexual victimisation. She argues,

> Charging provisions such as torture, persecution, inhumane acts etc., unlike rape are not dependant [sic] upon the establishment of coercive circumstances or lack of the victim's consent. Characterizing male sexual assault acts under crimes such as torture on inhumane acts, spare and possibly privilege male victim/survivors over women.[94]

Indeed, circumventing the issue of consent can privilege men in this instance. Yet, it does not exclude the possibility that masculine gender norms play a role in how specific acts are legally characterised.

3.2. INTERNATIONAL CRIMINAL TRIBUNAL FOR RWANDA

Similarly constrained as the ICTY, the ICTR was mandated to prosecute only a few forms of sexual violence, namely rape as a crime against humanity and rape and enforced prostitution as violations of Article 3 common to the Geneva Conventions and of Additional Protocol II.[95] The jurisprudence of the ICTR is extremely limited regarding male sexual victimisation. It records only two instances of male sexual victimisation. The first instance occurred spontaneously during the *Bagosora* trial when two witnesses testified to seeing the 'mutilated genitals of men' at civilian roadblocks.[96] This reference to male sexual victimisation was only included as factual findings, meaning that it is included in the record of the ICTR but no legal consequences were attached to it. Over the course of the *Bagosora* trial, other witnesses testified to male sexual violence. General Dallaire stated that 'men … were mutilated also, their genitals and the like'.[97] However, the Trial Chamber only acknowledged sexual violence against women and omitted Dallaire's reference to male sexual violence later on without explaining its decision to do so.[98]

The second recorded instance of male sexual victimisation provides an interesting example of how the ICTR has approached this issue. Niyitegeka was charged with the decapitation and castration of a Tutsi man, Kabanda,

---

94 P.V. Sellers, 'The Prosecution of Sexual Violence in Conflict: The Importance of Human Rights as Means of Interpretation' (2008) <http://www2.ohchr.org/english/issues/women/docs/Paper_Prosecution_of_Sexual_Violence.pdf> accessed 11.09.2016.

95 ICTR Statute, Articles 3(g) and 4(e), respectively.

96 *Prosecutor v. Bagosora et al.*, Trial Judgment, Case No. ICTR-98-41-T, 18 December 2008, para. 1908.

97 Testimony of General Dallaire in the *Bagosora* case as reproduced in Mibenge, above n. 32, p. 80.

98 *Prosecutor v. Bagosora et al.*, Trial Chamber Decision on motions for judgment of acquittal, Case No. ICTR-98-41-T, 2 February 2005, note 63.

as a crime against humanity, under the category of other inhumane acts.[99] In its discussion, the Trial Chamber considered the act of castration as an aggravating circumstance when deciding on sentencing.[100] The exact same crime was brought up in *Muhimana*. Mikaeli Muhimana was accused of having participated in the mutilation of Kabanda but, in spite of several testimonies pointing to Muhimana's involvement,[101] the Trial Chamber ignored the sexual violence acts and it therefore remained a factual finding.[102] The Trial Chamber only considered the act of decapitation.[103] The *Niyitegeka* case is therefore the only ICTR case to include charges of sexual violence against men.

This observation shows two aspects of the Tribunal's attitude towards male sexual victimisation. The first one, as analysed by Sivakumaran, is that the ICTR has mostly ignored male sexual victimisation, and when it has acknowledged it, it has refused to attach legal consequences to it.[104] The second one is that there seems to have been no willingness on the part of the ICTR to investigate male sexual victimisation at all, even though testimonies have shown that a significant number of men were victims of sexual violence during the conflict.[105] Chisebe Mibenge concludes that the exclusion of male sexual violence from the ICTR's jurisprudence is a product of gender norms that makes it impossible for men to be the victims of a sexual attack or to be sexually humiliated.[106] She argues, as a corollary of the gender norms established earlier, that 'gender prescribed ideas of a man's body, which cannot or should not be sexually victimised, unlike the weak, sexually desirable, and vulnerable body of a Tutsi woman',[107] has led to the erasure of male sexual victimisation from the ICTR's jurisprudence.

3.3. SPECIAL COURT FOR SIERRA LEONE

The jurisprudence of the SCSL calls for a nuanced analysis. Unlike the ICTR, the SCSL's Statute allowed the Court to prosecute several types of sexual violence as crimes in their own right rather than as an expanded understanding of a previously existing non-sexual violence crime. The Statute mandated the SCSL

---

99 *Prosecutor v. Niyitegeka*, Trial Judgment, Case No. ICTR-96-14-T, 16 May 2003, para. 303.
100 ibid., paras. 417 and 499.
101 *Prosecutor v. Muhimana*, Trial Judgment, Case No. ICTR-95-1B, 28 April 2005, paras. 441–44.
102 ibid., paras. 448–50.
103 ibid., para. 429.
104 Sivakumaran, above n. 8, p. 274.
105 See for instance, S.M. Khan, *The Shallow Graves of Rwanda*, I.B. Tauris Publishers 2000, p. 16; Buss, above n. 31, p. 159; U. Kaitesi, *Genocidal Gender and Sexual Violence: The Legacy of the ICTR, Rwanda's ordinary courts and gacaca courts*, Intersentia 2013, pp. 175–179; Mibenge, above n. 32, pp. 80–82.
106 Mibenge, above n. 32, pp. 81–82.
107 ibid., p. 80.

to prosecute rape, sexual slavery, enforced prostitution, forced pregnancy, any other form of sexual violence and of mutilation, and any form of indecent assault.[108] Tellingly, for the purposes of the present discussion, the SCSL Statute also allowed the prosecution of individuals for the violation of crimes under Sierra Leonean law which, with regards to acts of sexual violence, were restricted to abuses directed against girls.[109] This limitation to girls as victims of sexual violence already indicates a bias with respect to the possibility of boys as sexual violence victims. Yet, boys were victims of sexual violence during the conflict, and so were men.[110]

In spite of the wide array of statutory provisions regarding sexual violence crimes, the SCSL did not prosecute any instances of male sexual victimisation under specific sexual violence crimes because the SCSL Prosecutor did not bring any charges to that effect. In the *RUF* case, the Prosecutor restricted its pleadings on sexual violence in the Indictment to crimes committed against 'women and girls', thereby excluding male victims of sexual violence,[111] and only filed charges for these acts of sexual violence against men under the rubric of outrages upon personal dignity, a broader category of crimes. Yet, the Trial Chamber heard evidence of forced rape between male and female civilians,[112] castration[113] and forced nudity.[114] The Trial Chamber adopted a progressive understanding of sexual violence by explicitly naming forced rape 'enforced rape',[115] possibly implying that both the man and the woman in this specific situation were victims of rape, and stated that RUF 'fighters employed perverse methods of sexual violence against women and men of all ages'.[116]

In spite of the progressive stance taken in the *RUF* case regarding male sexual violence, the Prosecutor again limited charges of sexual violence to women and girls in the *AFRC* and *Taylor* cases. The original indictment in the *Taylor* case did contain unspecific allegations of sexual violence against men,[117] which were then

---

108 Rape and enforced prostitution fall within the scope of crimes against humanity and violations of Article 3 common to the Geneva Conventions and of Additional Protocol II according to Articles 2(g) and 3(e) of the SCSL Statute. Sexual slavery, forced pregnancy and any other form of sexual violence fall within the scope crimes against humanity under Article 2(g). Lastly, mutilation and any form of indecent assault fall within the scope of Article 3(a) and (e) respectively.

109 SCSL Statute, Article 5(a).

110 Human Rights Watch, *"We'll Kill You if You Cry": Sexual Violence in the Sierra Leone Conflict*, Human Rights Watch 2003, p. 42; Cohen, above n. 4, p. 385.

111 *Prosecutor v. Sesay et al.*, Trial Judgment, Case No. SCSL-04-15-T, 2 March 2009, para. 1303 (internal citation omitted).

112 ibid., paras. 1208, 1307 and 1303 (internal citation omitted).

113 ibid., paras. 1208 and 1307.

114 ibid., paras. 1067 and 1207.

115 ibid., para. 1302.

116 ibid., para. 1347.

117 *Prosecutor v. Charles Taylor*, Indictment, Case No. SCSL-03-91-T, 7 March 2003, para. 30.

removed in the Second Amended Indictment.[118] The *AFRC* Further Amended Consolidated Indictment alleges sexual violence against men,[119] but then limits charges of sexual violence to women and girls.[120] The reasons behind these changes are not indicated in the final indictments. In light of these changes, the Trial Chambers in both cases were unable to reach legal findings regarding sexual violence against men.[121]

Male sexual victimisation was therefore not completely excluded from the SCSL prosecutorial strategy but it was hidden behind a broader, more generic, category of crime or not charged. SCSL jurisprudence indicates unwillingness on the part of the Prosecutor to prosecute sexual violence against men as such.

3.4. INTERNATIONAL CRIMINAL COURT

Similar to the Statute of the SCSL, the Rome Statute offers the ICC the opportunity to prosecute a wide array of forms of sexual violence as crimes against humanity and war crimes.[122] In addition, rape and other forms of sexual violence can also be prosecuted as genocide, as can be found in the ICC's Elements of Crimes.[123]

The situation in the DRC, however, did not constitute a promising start to the work of the ICC regarding sexual violence against men. Indeed, the case against Lubanga[124] did not include any reference to sexual violence (against women or men as a matter of fact), even though evidence suggests that persons close to Lubanga committed sexual violence against men and women.[125] Sexual violence was at the core of the debate about amending the *Lubanga* charges. This request

---

118 *Prosecutor v. Charles Taylor*, Second Amended Indictment, Case No. SCSL-03-91-T, 29 May 2007, para. 14.

119 *Prosecutor v. Alex Tamba Brima et al.*, Further Amended Consolidated Indictment, Case No. SCSL-04-16-PT, 18 February 2005, para. 39.

120 ibid., para. 51.

121 *Prosecutor v. Charles Taylor*, Trial Judgment, Case No. SCSL-03-91-T, 18 May 2012, paras. 124–134; *Prosecutor v. Alex Tamba Brima et al.*, Judgment, Case No. SCSL-04-16-T, 20 June 2007, paras. 968–69.

122 Rome Statute, Articles 7(1)(g), 8(2)(b)(xxii) and 8(2)(e)(vi).

123 ICC Elements of Crimes, Article 6(b)-1, footnote 3. Footnote 3 indicates that causing serious bodily or mental harm 'may include, but is not restricted to, acts of torture, rape, sexual violence or inhuman or degrading treatment'. This footnote, just like the rest of the Elements of Crimes, 'shall assist the Court in the interpretation and application of article 6, 7 and 8'. See Rome Statute, Article 9(1).

124 The ICC Prosecutor charged Thomas Dyilo Lubanga with enlisting and conscripting children under the age of 15 years and using them to participate actively in hostilities. *Prosecutor v. Lubanga*, Decision on the Confirmation of Charges, Case No. ICC-01/04-01/06, 29 January 2007, p. 156.

125 K. Glassborow, 'Call for Lubanga Charges to Cover Rape' (12.05.2008) available at: <https://iwpr.net/global-voices/call-lubanga-charges-cover-rape> accessed 11.09.2016; Sivakumaran, above n. 8, p. 96.

was denied.[126] Throughout the trial, emphasis was particularly put on sexual violence against girls.[127] The only reference to sexual violence committed against boys in the main body of the judgment was in a footnote.[128] Judge Odio Benito nevertheless included sexual violence directed against boys and discussed the plight of 'victims' rather than that of girl victims of sexual violence in her dissenting opinion.[129]

The *Bemba* case provided more hope as to the inclusion of sexual violence against men in the charges from the start. Bemba was charged with the rape of men, women and children.[130] The Pre-Trial Chamber confirmed these charges and explicitly stated that 'civilian women and *men* were raped'.[131] The language used by the Court here indicates significant progress in labelling the crime of rape. Rather than avoid the word 'rape', the Pre-Trial Chamber reports that 'Witness 23 [a man] was ordered to lie down in the position of a horse and was raped'.[132] Even more significantly, Witness 23 testified during the trial – the first time in the history of international criminal justice that a male rape victim provided his testimony to support a rape charge, as opposed to a more generic charge such as torture or inhuman acts. In his testimony, Witness 23 shed light, based on his experience, on the highly gendered nature of male sexual victimisation, recounting: '... somebody like me, a man lying with me, that's why I consider myself to be dead because a man cannot sleep with another man. With what they did to me, I knew I was dead.'[133]

The Prosecutor also presented expert testimony about the specific harms of sexual violence against men in the Central African Republic.[134] In particular,

---

126 *Prosecutor v. Lubanga*, Appeals Judgment, Case No. ICC-01/04-01/06, 8 December 2009, 3.

127 See for instance the Prosecution's argument that 'girls who were recruited were even in a worse situation than boys, as they were used as sex slaves and were subject to systematic sexual abuse'. See *Prosecutor v. Lubanga*, Transcript Office of the Prosecutors Closing Statements, Case No. ICC-01/04-01/06, 25 August 2011, p. 53, lines 15–17.

128 *Prosecutor v. Lubanga*, Judgment, Case No. ICC-01/04-01/06, 14 March 2012, footnote 1811. Footnote 1811 reads 'Ms Coomaraswamy suggested that the use for sexual exploitation of boys and girls by armed forced or groups constitutes an "essential support function"'.

129 *Prosecutor v. Lubanga*, Separate and Dissenting Opinion of Judge Odio Benito, Case No. ICC-01/04-01/06, 14 March 2012, para. 16. Para. 16 contains the following: 'By failing to deliberately include within the legal concept of "use to participate actively in hostilities" the sexual violence and other ill-treatment suffered by girls and boys, the Majority of the Chamber is making this critical aspect of the crime invisible. Invisibility of sexual violence in the legal concept leads to discrimination against the victims of enlistment'.

130 *Prosecutor v. Jean-Pierre Bemba*, Public Redacted Version of the Amended Document Containing the Charges, Case No. ICC-01/05-01/08, 30 March 2009, para. 39.

131 *Prosecutor v. Jean-Pierre Bemba*, Decision pursuant to Article 61(7)(a) and (b) of the Rome Statute on the Charges of the Prosecutor Against Jean-Pierre Bemba Gombo, Case No. ICC-01/05-01/08, 15 June 2009, para. 286 (emphasis added).

132 ibid., para. 171.

133 *Prosecutor v. Jean-Pierre Bemba Gombo*, Trial Transcript, Case No. ICC-01/05-01/08-T-50-Red-ENG, 21 January 2011, p. 32.

134 The Prosecution called on two experts to testify about the motivations and effects of sexual violence against men. See *Prosecutor v. Jean-Pierre Bemba Gombo*, Trial Transcript, Case

the idea that rape is used as a means of humiliating a man was put forward.[135] On 21 March 2016, Bemba was convicted, again for the first time in the history of international criminal justice, specifically of rape as a war crime and a crime against humanity, for the rape of two men, Witness 23 and Witness 69.[136] This ground-breaking decision was, however, reversed on 8 June 2018, when the Appeals Chamber acquitted Bemba of all charges.[137] The *Bemba* case, despite its ending, stands in stark contrast to the conduct of the investigation and trial of the *Lubanga* case.

This inconsistency in labelling and understanding male sexual victimisation has continued. One of the Kenya cases is illustrative in this regard. In the *Muthaura and Kenyatta* case, the suspects were charged with rape and other forms of sexual violence in the case of forced circumcision and sexual mutilation of men.[138] However, the Pre-Trial Chamber confirmed the charge of rape but declined to confirm that of other forms of sexual violence.[139] The Judges argued that 'not every act which targets part of the body commonly associated with sexuality should be considered an act of sexual violence'.[140] Problematically, the Pre-Trial Chamber did not justify its decision more than what is written in the previous sentence, nor did it provide any examples of what constitutes and does not constitute sexual violence, thereby effectively leaving the Prosecutor in the dark regarding the acts it should seek to charge as sexual violence. In turn, this uncertainty may lead the Prosecutor to refrain from charging 'other forms of sexual violence' in the future for fear of the charges not being confirmed. Even though the legal characterisation of sexual circumcision as a form of sexual violence was unsuccessful, the Pre-Trial Chamber's decision indicates progress, on the part of the Office of the Prosecutor, in framing sexual violence against men as a gendered crime. It recalls the Prosecutor's submission: '... these weren't just attacks on men's sexual organs as such but were intended as attacks on men's identities as men within their society and were designed to destroy their masculinity'.[141]

No. ICC-01/05-01/08-T-100-ENG, 13 April 2011, p. 38, lines 3–17 [Bemba Transcript, 13 April 2011]; *Prosecutor v. Jean-Pierre Bemba Gombo*, Trial Transcript, Case No. ICC-01/05-01/08-T-38-ENG, 29 November 2010, p. 25, lines 5–19.

135 Case No. ICC-01/05-01/08-T-100-ENG (134) p. 11, lines 15–25.

136 *Prosecutor v. Jean-Pierre Bemba Gombo*, Judgment pursuant to Article 74 of the Statute, Case No. ICC-01/05-01/08, 21 March 2016, para. 633.

137 *Prosecutor v. Jean-Pierre Bemba Gombo*, Judgment on the appeal of Mr Jean-Pierre Bemba Gombo against Trial Chamber III's 'Judgment pursuant to Article 74 of the Statute', Case No. ICC-01/05-01/08, 8 June 2018.

138 *Prosecutor v. Francis Kirimi Muthaura and Uhuru Muigai Kenyatta*, Decision on the Confirmation of Charges Pursuant to Article 61(7)(a) and (b) of the Rome Statute, Case No. ICC-01/09-02/11, 23 January 2012, para. 254.

139 ibid., para. 154.

140 ibid., para. 265.

141 ibid., para. 264.

The Pre-Trial Chamber's decision was strongly criticised by commentators, along with the Prosecutor's strategy which was deemed to be lacking in linking the political and sexual nature of the crimes. Specifically, it was argued that the Prosecutor failed to place the acts of forced circumcision within the broader context of force and coercive environment and to explain its political meaning, in addition to its ethnic and cultural significance.[142]

Until the current Prosecutor, Fatou Bensouda, was elected in December 2011 (she took office in June 2012), sexual violence against men was only charged or attempted to be charged in these three cases. Based on these cases, the ICC shows a mixed attitude towards sexual violence against men. It appears to oscillate between, on one hand, a lack of investigation and unwillingness to tackle the sexual nature of some of the crimes, and on the other hand, a progressive approach to legal characterisation and to the intricacies of masculinity and its links to sexuality.

Giving teeth to her campaign promise that more attention would be devoted to sexual violence should she be elected, Fatou Bensouda filed new charges against Bosco Ntaganda; more particularly, charges of sexual violence which included charges of sexual violence against men which were confirmed in 2014.[143] Originally, he was not charged with any sexual violence crimes in 2006.[144] These new charges were confirmed in 2014. They allege rape as a crime against humanity and as a war crime for forcing male prisoners to rape female detainees and for the rape of three men by Ntaganda's soldiers.[145] Other unspecific charges of rape and sexual violence against 'civilians' and 'child soldiers' have been confirmed, thereby allowing for the inclusion of more sexual violence crimes against men and boys to be prosecuted, should the evidence allow it.

In addition to bringing more charges of sexual violence (including violence perpetrated against women), Bensouda has also pushed for the elaboration of the ICC's Policy Paper on Sexual and Gender Based Crimes.[146] The policy is promising in its language and the result of extensive consultation with civil society organisations. It promises a systematic inclusion of gender and sexual violence crimes in OTP's activities. Importantly, it discusses men and boys as similarly potential victims of sexual violence (and other gender-based crimes) as women and girls, a welcome commitment in light of the historical and, as shown earlier, jurisprudential, invisibility of male victims of conflict-related sexual violence. It commits, for instance, to include men in future indictments

---

142 Women's Initiative for Gender Justice, 'Gender Report Card on the International Criminal Court 2011', Women's Initiative for Gender Justice 2011, pp. 180–81.

143 *Prosecutor v. Bosco Ntaganda*, Decision Pursuant to Article 61(7)(a) and (b) of the Rome Statute, Case No. ICC-01/04-02/06, 9 June 2014.

144 *Prosecutor v. Bosco Ntaganda*, Warrant of Arrest, Case No. ICC-01/04-02/06, 22 August 2006.

145 Case No. ICC-01/04-02/06, above n. 142, paras. 50–52.

146 Office of the Prosecutor of the ICC, 'Policy Paper on Sexual and Gender-Based Crimes', June 2014.

and strategies,[147] and to account for the gendered meaning of crimes.[148] As the policy was only issued in June 2014, it is difficult to assess its impact today. Only future prosecutions can show the ICC's commitment to implement a genuine and comprehensive policy regarding sexual violence crimes perpetrated against all victims. The amendment of charges against Bosco Ntaganda, and the decision on the confirmation of charges on which it is based, suggests a promising start.[149]

4. SEXUAL VIOLENCE COMMITTED BY WOMEN IN CONFLICT SITUATIONS

4.1. FEMALE PERPETRATORS OF SEXUAL VIOLENCE IN CONFLICT

Like men and boys, women and girls are capable of committing atrocious forms of conflict-related sexual violence against men, boys, women and girls alike. Although sexual violence in conflict was long considered to be committed by men and boys only, in several studies women and girls have been identified as either the physical perpetrators of conflict-related sexual violence, the co-perpetrators by helping others to inflict sexual violence on the victims, or the ones ordering sexual violence.

Conflicts where women and girls have been reported to have committed sexual violence include countries such as Sierra Leone, DRC, Iraq, Rwanda, Liberia, Haiti, Ivory Coast, Sudan, Armenia, Poland, Germany and the former Yugoslavia. In the DRC prevalence study cited earlier (involving 593 women and 405 men), the researchers reported that 'by simply asking respondents to report the sex of the perpetrator, we found that 41.1% of the female survivors reported the perpetrator as female, and 10% of the male survivors reported the perpetrator as female', and 17 per cent of the survivors of sexual violence perpetrated by the militia group Mai-Mai named females as the perpetrators.[150] In Liberia, one-third of combatants are female and female fighters were implicated in the rape of women, including rape with objects such as guns, and in sexual violence

---

147 ibid., paras. 16, 20, 27–28.

148 ibid., para. 20.

149 *Prosecutor v. Bosco Ntaganda*, Decision Pursuant to Article 61(7)(a) and (b) of the Rome Statute, Case No. ICC-01/04-02/06, 9 June 2014, paras. 50, 52.

150 L. Lawry *et al.*, 'Evidence Based Documentation of Gender-based Violence' in A.-M. de Brouwer *et al.* (eds.), *Sexual Violence as an International Crime: Interdisciplinary Approaches*, Intersentia 2013, p. 258. See also, K. Johnson *et al.*, 'Association of Sexual Violence and Human Rights Violations with Physical and Mental Health in Territories of the Eastern Democratic Republic of the Congo' (2010) 304 *Journal of the American Medical Association* 538.

against men, such as cutting off their genitals.[151] In Rwanda, cases are known in which women aided and abetted perpetrators of sexual violence crimes by delivering women to the rapists to be raped or by holding them to the ground for others to rape them.[152] A notorious woman, who was convicted by the ICTR for crimes against humanity for, *inter alia*, ordering the rape of Tutsi women is Pauline Nyiramasuhuko, the then Minister of Family and Women's Development; a case that will be discussed in more detail below. Rwandan women have, furthermore, been held to be the physical perpetrators of sexual violence. For example, at the age of 13, a Tutsi boy, Faustin Kayihura, was raped by a Hutu woman three times a day over the course of three days.[153] In Rwanda, sexual violence committed against men was most of the times in fact committed by women.[154] In Sierra Leone, around 10–30 per cent of all fighters were women.[155] Women in Sierra Leone have been known to be involved in gang rapes by holding down the victim (women participated in mixed gender groups in about one in four (26 per cent) of the reported incidents of gang rape), as well as rapes performed with the insertion of bottles and sticks into the body of the victim.[156]

In the former Yugoslavia, a well-known case involved a female camp commander who took female prisoners to the front lines for soldiers to rape them.[157] In another high profile international case before the ICTY, which will be discussed in more depth below, the Serbian politician, Biljana Plavšić, pleaded guilty to persecution as a crime against humanity, which included rapes and other forms of sexual violence. In Haiti, women have been reported to have committed sexual violence, including gang rape, against other women and members of enemy gangs.[158] Simone Gbagbo, a member of the inner circle

---

151 K. Johnson *et al.*, 'Association of Combatant Status and Sexual Violence with Health and Mental Health Outcomes in Postconflict Liberia' (2008) 300 *Journal of the American Medical Association* 676–690; and D. Cohen, 'Female Combatants in Armed Groups: Women and Wartime Rape in Sierra Leone Civil War' (2013) 65 *World Politics* 385.

152 A.-M. de Brouwer and E. Ruvebana, 'The Legacy of the Gacaca Courts in Rwanda: Survivors' Views' (2013) 13 *International Criminal Law Review* 949; U. Kaitesi, *Genocidal Gender and Sexual Violence*, Intersentia 2013, p. 169 ('Hutu women gave their sons, husbands, Interahamwe and social outcasts Tutsi women to sexually assault'), p. 166 ('Out of a total of 4,060 current female inmates, 2,230 are genocide indictees serving jail sentences ranging from a few years to life imprisonment and most of these women are first category offenders including those convicted of rape and sexual torture').

153 A.-M. de Brouwer and S. Ka Hon Chu, *The Men Who Killed Me: Rwandan Survivors of Sexual Violence*, Douglas & McIntyre 2009, pp. 93–94.

154 U. Kaitesi, *Genocidal Gender and Sexual Violence*, Intersentia 2013, p. 166.

155 C. Coulter, 'Female Fighters in the Sierra Leone War: Challenging the Assumptions' (2008) 88 *Feminist Review* 54.

156 Cohen, above n. 149, p. 404.

157 M. Husejnovic, 'Bosnian War's Wicked Women Get Off Lightly' *Balkan Insight*, 7 February 2011 <http://www.balkaninsight.com/en/article/bosnian-war-s-wicked-women-get-off-lightly> accessed 11.09.2016.

158 B.F. Duramy, 'From Violence against Women to Women's Violence in Haiti' (2010) 19 *Colum. J. of Gender & L.* 1052.

of Mr Gbagbo (the former President of Ivory Coast and her husband), is wanted by the ICC for crimes against humanity, including rape and other acts of sexual violence, which were allegedly committed during post-electoral violence in Ivory Coast between 16 December 2010 and 12 April 2011.[159] This international case will also be addressed below. Another well-known case involves the prisoner abuse scandal at Abu Ghraib, in which photographs of Iraqi male prisoners being sexually abused and humiliated by US female soldiers were broadcast by American media outlets. Private Lynndie England became particularly well-known for an image in which she held a naked prisoner on a leash, while in others she posed with a pyramid of naked detainees and pointed at one man's genitals while a cigarette hung from the corner of her mouth. In Darfur, Sudan, it has been held that women have played a role both in the commission of sexual violence crimes against other women and in the encouragement and celebration of men's commission of these crimes. For example, Janjaweed women "stirred up racial hatred against black civilians during attacks on villages in Darfur and celebrated the humiliation of their enemies" by singing during the commission of rapes and other atrocities.[160]

That female perpetrators of conflict-related sexual violence are not a recent phenomenon is made clear by the cases of female perpetrators that go back as far as the Armenian genocide (1915) and World War II (1933–1941). During World War II, several German women who served as prison guards in the concentration camps have been held to be involved in sexual violence crimes. Two women in particular stood out for this, namely Ilse Koch and Dorothea Binz. Koch, a guard at the Buchenwald concentration camp and wife of the concentration camp's commander, was well known for her sadism and cruelty towards prisoners. She was particularly cruel against women, whom she allegedly abused physically and sexually; this was ultimately a key factor in her receiving a life sentence at the end of the war.[161] Binz, who was a guard at Auschwitz (and allegedly at the all-female concentration camp Ravensbrueck), was similarly accused of torturing

---

159 *Prosecutor v. Simone Gbagbo*, Warrant of Arrest, Case No. ICC-02/11-01/12, 29 February 2012, para. 7. Ivory Coast refused to hand her over to the ICC and tried her in a domestic court for undermining state security. The trial started in December 2014 and she was sentenced to 20 years in prison in March 2015. See: 'Ivory Coast Trial of Simone Gbagbo Begins' *BBC News*, 26.12.2014 <http://www.bbc.com/news/world-africa-30604755> accessed 11.09.2016; 'Ivory Coast's former First Lady Simone Gbagbo jailed' *BBC News*, 10.03.2015 <http://www.bbc.com/news/world-africa-31809073> accessed 11.09.2016.

160 L. Sjoberg, *Women and the Genocidal Rape of Women: The Gender Dynamics of Gendered War Crimes* (undated and no publisher), p. 7 <www.history.vt.edu/Ewing/Sjoberg_GRISTPaper.pdf> accessed 11.09.2016.

161 ibid., p. 10 (citing A. Przyrembel, *Transfixed by an Image: Ilse Koch, the 'Kommandeuse of Buchenwald'*, German History 2001). See also, D.M. Amann, 'Women at Nuremberg: Defendants' (IntLawGrrls, 20.09.2007) <http://www.intlawgrrls.com/2007/09/women-at-nuremberg-defendants.html> accessed 11.09.2016.

and sexually abusing women prisoners.[162] During the Armenian genocide, women have been reported to have sexually violated other women and sold other women and girls into sexual slavery. According to Sjoberg, citing a study of Sansarian, 'women [in the Ottoman Empire] were described as sexually abusing and then selling Armenian women who had been brought into their households (often, ironically, by their husbands for protection) because they were jealous of their husbands' (imagined or actual) sexual relationships with these women (who were often in their early teen years)'.[163]

Collectively, these cases indicate that the involvement of women in conflict-related sexual violence is certainly not an anomaly. However, because of the absence of prevalence studies inquiring about the sex of the perpetrators of sexual violence in conflict (the DRC and Sierra Leone studies cited above being the exceptions), it remains unclear how extensive the phenomenon of females as perpetrators of sexual violence really is. What is clear, however, is that the number of female perpetrators of sexual violence is much larger than has been generally thought to date.[164] The reason why many more men have been involved in committing international crimes, including sexual violence, is likely because the main organisations (militarised units) responsible for the physical perpetration of international crimes are still male dominated.[165] The reason why only one per cent of all the people convicted by international criminal courts and tribunals are female is because these tribunals focus on those in leadership positions and the physical executioners and women are underrepresented amongst these two groups; however, this may change over time.[166] Below, we will discuss the cases before international criminal tribunals that involve(d) women as perpetrators of international crimes, including sexual violence.

What this brief overview of the scope and prevalence of sexual violence committed by women during conflict intends to show is that the absence of, or peripheral, discussions and debates about female perpetrators should not be understood as a sign of its non-existence. Rather, the relative invisibility of female perpetrators has been attributed to the gender norms that, *inter alia*, define perpetrators of sexual violence as men and women as victims. In this regard, several scholars have offered in-depth insights into the meaning of female perpetrators in relation to femininity, which shall constitute the object of study of the following section.

---

162 Sjoberg, above n. 160, p. 10 (citing *Washington Post*, by A. Christie, 'Guarding the Truth', 26.02.2006).

163 ibid., p. 12.

164 A. Smeulers, 'Female Perpetrators: Ordinary or Extra-ordinary Women?' (2015) 15 *International Criminal Law Review* 220–25, 252.

165 ibid.

166 ibid.

4.2. FEMALE PERPETRATORS OF SEXUAL VIOLENCE AND FEMININITY

Charging a woman with international crimes brings to the fore questions about gender that we rarely ask when the accused is a man. It brings to light long-held assumptions embedded in law and in society about who the usual suspects/accused of international crimes are. As put forward by Grey and Chappell:

> It undermines the usual view of men as the agents and women as the victims of crime. It challenges the dichotomy that sets up men, masculinity and violence on one side and women, femininity and passivity on the other. It upsets the archetype of women as vulnerable, 'rapeable', and incapable of wielding power.[167]

Hogg noted that in cases of female perpetrators of international crimes it has been usually deemed impossible for women (good by nature) to commit such acts and thus they were treated 'not like men, not like women, but something else, like monsters'.[168] When the perpetrator is female and the crimes committed, ordered or facilitated (also) involve sexual violence, it has been seen as even more unnatural for women to do.[169] Sjoberg, focusing on female-to-female sexual violence, states: 'If, after all, ..., rape is a cornerstone of women's oppression, women's participation in rape is a perpetration of gendered oppression – *by the oppressed*.'[170]

When women do commit international crimes, including sexual violence, they are thus often held to be exceptions to the rule. These women are framed as instances of 'femininity gone awry'.[171] However, as seen above, citing examples of female perpetrators of sexual violence in different conflicts, women committing sexual violence in conflict are certainly not exceptions. The reasons given for women to commit sexual violence in conflict have been identified by Sjoberg and Gentry as 'the mother, monster and whore narratives':

> the mother narrative has two general strands – one that portrays women perpetrators of genocide as nurturing mothers, whose role in the conflict is to take care of and provide for their men – the fact that those men happen to be participating in genocide (and therefore nurturing them is too) does not change the women's role in society or perception of their familial duty. The other strand of the mother narrative portrays

---

167 R. Grey and L. Chappell, 'Simone Gbagbo & the International Criminal Court: The Unsettling Spectre of the Female War Criminal' *IntLawGrrls*, 26.11.2012 <http://www.intlawgrrls.com/2012/11/simone-gbagbo-international-criminal.html> accessed 11.09.2016.

168 N. Hogg, 'Women's Participation in the Rwandan Genocide: Mothers or Monsters?' (2010) 92 *International Review of the Red Cross* 100.

169 Sjoberg, above n. 160, p. 5 <www.history.vt.edu/Ewing/Sjoberg_GRISTPaper.pdf> accessed 11.09.2016.

170 ibid.

171 ibid.

> women who commit genocide as vengeful mothers – avenging the deaths of their husbands, brothers, or fathers at the hand of those on the other side of the conflict. The second narrative … is the monster narrative. This story of women's motivation for involvement in genocide frames women perpetrators as severely psychologically disturbed. These stories tell women perpetrators as crazier and more monstrous than the men that they act with or alongside. Women's monstrosity, in these stories, comes from the sort of irrational anger only women could have, or feelings of personal inadequacy coming from the inability to marry or have children. The final narrative … is the whore narrative. In the whore narrative, women's participation in genocide is either defined by erotomania or erotic dysfunction. The erotomania story tells of women sexually obsessed with and therefore controlled by men – of women's sexuality gone wrong and out of control. These women are portrayed as having committed genocide because their sex drive had gone out of control, and female sexuality at its worst is violent and brutal. The story of erotic dysfunction tells a story of a woman who has turned to violence because she is either unwilling to or unable to please men. These women are portrayed as having turned to violence because they were unable to function/serve as real women, which requires getting married and having children.[172]

However, holding on to these kind of explanations, gender stereotypes, as a lens through which to view, condemn or justify atrocities is not only an unhelpful means of analysis, but one that ultimately diminishes our humanity.[173] Sperling concludes that social and cultural constructions of women as innately good, innocent and incapable of committing atrocities are in themselves dehumanising.[174] According to Durham and O'Byrne:

> A gender perspective on IHL [International Humanitarian Law] enforcement attempts to debunk this kind of mythology by traversing more dynamic understandings of the different experiences of gendered actors in differing contexts. [A female perpetrator of international crimes] should be recognised not just as a woman acting within a certain power structure, but as a human being. It is this fact, rather than her femininity or lack thereof, which compounds the monstrosity of her alleged actions.[175]

Kaitesi underlines that the classical male domination/female subordination and sisterhood/womanhood as a homogenous group discourses insufficiently explain the phenomenon of female perpetrators and states that other power dimensions that may be at stake for women must indeed be analysed also, such as ethnic and political ideologies.[176] The present authors also contend that

---

172 ibid., pp. 4–5.

173 H. Durham and K. O'Byrne, 'The Dialogue of Difference: Gender Perspectives on International Humanitarian Law' (2010) 92 *International Review of the Red Cross* 41.

174 C. Sperling, 'Mother of Atrocities: Pauline Nyiramasuhuko's Role in the Rwandan Genocide' (2006) XXXIII *Fordham Urban Law Journal* 637.

175 Durham and O'Byrne, above n. 178, p. 42.

176 U. Kaitesi, *Genocidal Gender and Sexual Violence*, Intersentia 2013, p. 168.

gender stereotyping is unhelpful in analysing conflict-related sexual violence perpetrated by women; rather, each instance should be merited on the facts of the case.

5. GENDER AND THE INTERNATIONAL PROSECUTION OF SEXUAL VIOLENCE COMMITTED BY WOMEN IN CONFLICT SITUATIONS

As mentioned before, studies on female perpetrators of international crimes reveal that women have played a much larger role as perpetrators of international crimes than has generally been assumed and that women, just like men, are capable of committing terrible atrocities, including sexual violence. Although women are generally far less involved than men in mass atrocities and are often acting in a supporting capacity, many women have displayed a more active role as leaders and instigators or even as the physical perpetrators of the crimes. In this section the cases before international criminal tribunals in which women were charged and/or prosecuted for sexual violence crimes are discussed. In chronological order (by finalisation of the case), these cases involve Biljana Plavšić, Ieng Thirith, Pauline Nyiramasuhuku and Simone Gbagbo.[177] It will be demonstrated that the existence of female perpetrators of sexual violence in conflict is at odds with ideals of femininity and that females accused of such crimes tend to make use of those conceived ideals, i.e. denying their ability – as women – to commit sexual violence.

5.1. ICTY

The first and only woman prosecuted before the ICTY for international crimes, including sexual violence, was Biljana Plavšić. On 27 February 2003, Plavšić (1930) – as the co-President of Bosnia and Herzegovina at the time of the conflict in the former Yugoslavia and a former scholar (biologist) – was sentenced to 11 years' imprisonment on the basis of a guilty plea.[178] The Trial Chamber found Plavšić guilty of persecution as a crime against humanity of Bosnian Muslims, Bosnian Croats and other non-Serbs in Bosnia and Herzegovina through various acts, including rapes and sexual violence.[179] By pleading guilty, Plavšić

---

177 The cases of Biljana Pavšić and Pauline Nyiramasuhuko are also discussed in detail by Sheri Labenski in this volume.

178 *Prosecutor v. Biljana Plavšić*, Sentencing Judgment, Case No. IT-00-39&40/1-S, 27 February 2003, para. 134.

179 During a hearing on 2 October 2002, Plavšić pleaded guilty to count 3, namely persecutions as a crime against humanity. The Trial Chamber, being satisfied that the plea was voluntary,

accepted responsibility under Article 7(1) for acting individually and in concert with others in a joint criminal enterprise that planned, instigated, ordered, and aided and abetted persecutions of the Bosnian Muslim, Bosnian Croat and other non-Serb populations of 37 municipalities in Bosnia and Herzegovina between 1 July 1991 and 30 December 1992. The Trial Chamber held that Plavšić embraced and supported the objective and contributed to achieving it, but she did not participate in its conception and planning and had a lesser role in its execution than others.

Nevertheless, it should be noted that, as Plavšić entered a guilty plea to persecution as a crime against humanity only, other charges, including sexual violence charges, were withdrawn as part of the guilty plea negotiation.[180] As a consequence, Plavšić was found not guilty by the Trial Chamber of causing serious bodily or mental harm as genocide and deliberately inflicting conditions of life calculated to bring about physical destruction as genocide and complicity in genocide under Articles 7(1) and 7(3) for subjecting Bosnian Muslim and Bosnian Croat detainees at various detention facilities to sexual violence.

The Trial Chamber, in reaching a sentence of 11 years' imprisonment on the then 72-year-old former President, stated that 'these crimes did not happen to a nameless group but to individual men, women and children who were mistreated, raped, tortured and killed'.[181] The Trial Chamber had to balance, on the one hand, Plavšić's participation, as a senior leader, in a crime of the utmost gravity; on the other hand, it called for very significant mitigating circumstances, in particular her guilty plea and post-conflict conduct.[182] Nonetheless, the Trial Chamber remarked that 'undue leniency would be misplaced'.[183] The 11 years' imprisonment sentence was a lower penalty than had been advised by

informed and unequivocal, and that there was a sufficient factual basis for the crime and the accused's participation in it, then entered a finding of guilt under Rule 62bis of the Rules of Procedure and Evidence of the ICTY. Plavšić's plea was entered pursuant to a Plea Agreement made between the parties dated 30 September 2002. See: *The Prosecutor v. Momcilo Krajinik and Biljana Plavšić*, Plea Agreement, Case No. IT-00-39&40-PT, 30 September 2002; and *The Prosecutor v. Momcilo Krajinik and Biljana Plavšić*, Factual Basis for Plea of Guilt, Case No. IT-00-39&40-PT, 30 September 2002.

180 In the amended consolidated indictment of 7 March 2002, Momcilo Krajisnik and Biljana Plavšić were charged with genocide, complicity in genocide, crimes against humanity (persecutions, extermination, murder, deportation, inhumane acts (forced transfer)) and violations of the laws and customs of war (murder) under both Articles 7(1) and 7(3) of the ICTY Statute. See: *The Prosecutor v. Momcilo Krajinik and Biljana Plavšić*, Amended Consolidated Indictment, Case No. IT-00-39&40-PT, 7 March 2002.

181 *Prosecutor v. Biljana Plavšić*, Sentencing Judgment, Case No. IT-00-39&40/1-S, 27 February 2003, para. 126.

182 ibid., paras. 94, 126–132 (i.e. Plavšić was found to be instrumental in ensuring that the Dayton Agreement was accepted and implemented in Republika Srpska by which she made a considerable contribution to peace in the region).

183 ibid., para. 132.

the Prosecution to the ICTY Judges; the Prosecution had argued for a sentence of 15–25 years to be appropriate in the current circumstances.[184]

In her guilty plea statement, Plavšić

> states that by 'accepting responsibility and expressing her remorse fully and unconditionally, [she] hopes to offer some consolation to the innocent victims – Muslim, Croat and Serb – of the war in Bosnia and Herzegovina'. She 'invites others, especially leaders … to examine themselves and their own conduct'. And, as a leader and later an accused, she learned a great deal about the gravity and nature of the crimes committed by the forces which she led and inspired during the war; and she recognises her obligation to accept responsibility for acts committed by others.[185]

Although Plavšić, as a former senior leader, thus acknowledged the crimes, accepted responsibility and expressed remorse, it has been held that 'for the victims, any initial relief at her remorse was drowned in the disappointment at her lenient sentence, as well as the very general and strangely detached tone of the apology', 'without any direct apologies to the victims or specific recounting of the crimes committed'.[186]

Traits associated exclusively with femininity come to the surface when explaining Plavšić's role in and conviction of the sexual violence that had taken place in the former Yugoslavia under her reign. Firstly, Plavšić's good looks and specifically her gender have been offered as an explanation for why the ICTY treated her with more leniency than other accused charged with similar crimes.[187] Witnesses used her womanhood to point out her humanity and argued for mitigating circumstances and a lighter sentence.[188] In reports, Plavšić is often portrayed as an innocuous and naïve woman, caught up in a 'man's game', i.e. in politics.[189] Often the centrality of her role in the overall implementation of the Dayton Agreement is emphasised, which highlights Plavšić's femininity by portraying her as a pacifist who genuinely wanted to end the conflict in the Balkans.[190] Very interestingly, Plavšić, in her memoirs, described herself as a lady scholar who did not belong with her male colleagues, who were primitive

---

184 ibid., para. 128.

185 ibid., para. 19.

186 J. Subotić, 'The Cruelty of False Remorse: Biljana Plavšić at The Hague' (2012) 36 *Southeastern Europe* 46, 48.

187 ibid., p. 42.

188 L. Sjoberg, 'Women and the Genocidal Rape of Women: The Gender Dynamics of Gendered War Crimes' (2009), p. 8 <www.history.vt.edu/Ewing/Sjoberg_GRISTPaper.pdf> accessed 11.09.2016.

189 S. Gilani, 'Transforming the "Perpetrator" into "Victim"': The Effect of Gendering Violence on the Legal and Practical Responses to Women's Political Violence', para. 4.2. <https://genderandlaw.murdoch.edu.au/index.php/sisterinlaw/article/view/23/62> accessed 11.09.2016.

190 ibid.

Bosnian men.[191] Plavšić herself thus appealed to her womanhood as if she – as a woman – had not had any agency in the crimes that had been taking place at all.

Second, accounts of Plavšić's participation in the genocide have consistently featured sexualised stories, including allegations that she had sexual relationships with several Serbian warlords. One such incident concerns a situation where Plavšić steps, after having witnessed the slaughter of civilians, over the body of a killed Bosniac civilian to kiss a certain Arkan, a well-known brutal Serbian warlord. It has been held that such narratives insinuate that 'Plavšić's attraction to the murderous warlord hinged on an errant sexuality that somehow found brutality attractive'.[192] Plavšić's alleged leading role in the genocidal rape in the Republica Srpska is therefore often associated with her oedipal attraction to warlords in the conflict.[193]

Third, her violent character has also been attributed to her maternal instinct to challenge men into masculinity, inciting men to commit rape and other crimes.[194] Fourth, Plavšić's involvement in conflict-related sexual violence was also blamed on her (apparent) madness; she was labelled a 'female Mengele' by Slobodan Milošević.[195] Throughout her academic and political careers, Plavšić had given many speeches advocating ethnic cleansing, sometimes even inferring that rape was an appropriate method to achieve political goals.[196] She 'used her knowledge of biology to convince people to share her ethnic hatred' and argued that 'Bosnian Muslims were "genetically deformed Serbs"'.[197]

5.2. ECCC

On 9 October 1975, at a meeting of the Khmer Rouge Standing Committee, Ieng Thirith (1932) was appointed Minister of Social Affairs in Democratic Kampuchea responsible for, *inter alia*, gender equality policies. She remained with the Khmer Rouge until her husband Ieng Sary (who was a co-accused in this case) was granted a Royal amnesty and pardon in 1996. Thereafter, they lived together in Phnom Penh until being placed in pre-trial detention by the Extraordinary Chambers in the Courts of Cambodia (ECCC) in November 2007.

Ieng Thirith was charged, together with three other accused, in the so-called Nuon Chea *et al.* case, also referred to as Case 002. The other co-accused in this

---

191 Subotić, above n. 184.
192 Gilani, above n. 198.
193 Sjoberg, above n. 165.
194 ibid., p. 8.
195 ibid.
196 ibid.
197 ibid., P. Fitzpatrick, 'It Isn't Easy Being Biljana' (2000) 22(2) *Central Europe Review* <http://www.ce-review.org/00/22/fitzpatrick22.html> accessed 11.09.2016.

case concern: (1) Nuon Chea, former Chairman of the Democratic Kampuchea National Assembly and Deputy Secretary of the Communist Party of Kampuchea; (2) Khieu Samphan, former Head of State of Democratic Kampuchea; and, as mentioned, (3) Ieng Sary, the former Foreign Minister of the Khmer Rouge, and her husband. Ieng Thirith and Ieng Sary were the first husband and wife to face charges of genocide, crimes against humanity and war crimes before an international criminal tribunal.

Thirith was charged, in the closing order (indictment) of 15 September 2010, with rape as a crime against humanity, which included forced marriage, and other inhumane acts as a crime against humanity, which similarly covered forced marriage as well as sexual violence.[198] According to the indictment the unions 'were part of the attack against the civilian population, in particular the imposition of sexual relations aimed at enforced procreation'.[199] The purpose of the regime's forced marriage policy, with both female and male victims, was to breed a new population able to contribute to the agrarian work of the country.[200] Both charges were brought under committing (via a joint criminal enterprise), planning, instigating, ordering, or aiding and abetting, or by virtue of superior responsibility punishable under Article 29 (new) of the ECCC Law. However, the accused appealed the closing order, stating that during the relevant time (1975–1979), rape was not yet applicable as an enumerated crime under crimes against humanity. The Pre-Trial Chamber agreed that during that time period rape was not a crime in its own, but ruled that the facts described as rape could be subsumed as 'other inhumane acts'.[201] Accordingly, on 13 January 2011, the Pre-Trial Chamber struck rape as a crime against humanity from the indictment.[202]

On 22 September 2011, the Trial Chamber severed Case 002 in two trials. The first trial of Case 002 was limited to forced transfers of the population. The second trial of Case 002 included forced marriage and rape (nationwide) as crimes against humanity. Trial hearings in Case 002/02 commenced on 17 October 2014 and the presentation of evidence started on 8 January 2015. However, Thirith was already found unfit to stand trial in 2011 due to dementia, and the Trial Chamber stayed the proceedings against her. She was released from provisional detention on 16 September 2012. The Supreme Court Chamber

198 *Case against Nuon Chea et al.*, 002/19-09-2007-ECCC/OCIJ, D427, 15 September 2010.

199 ibid., para. 1445.

200 See, e.g., S. Studzinsky, above n. 61, pp. 180–81 for further explanation on the concept of forced marriage during the Khmer Rouge period.

201 *Case against Nuon Chea et al.*, 002/19-09-2007-ECCC/PTC, D427/1/30, 11 April 2011, paras. 366–72.

202 See, e.g., Pre-Trial Chamber Decision on Ieng Thirith's and Nuon Chea's Appeals against the Closing Order, 002/19-09-2007-ECCC/OCIJ (PTC145&146), D427/2/12, 13 January 2011, para. 11(2).

subsequently imposed a regime of judicial supervision. She died on 22 August 2015, with no judgment rendered against her. The proceedings against Ieng Sary had by then already been terminated, following his death on 14 March 2013.

Although Ieng Thirith died before a finding by the ECCC could be made in her specific case, some general remarks on this case, as it concerns sexual violence charges, can be made here. First, this case was a setback in international criminal law as the Chamber decided that rape was not yet recognised as a crime in itself in the relevant time period that the crimes had taken place (1975–1979), which is widely disputed.[203] Another setback was the long duration of the trial, the severance of the case (with forced marriage to be dealt with in the second trial), and the death of Thirith, which delayed or halted all together justice for victims, including victims of sexual violence.[204] Third, the indictment did not hold the accused liable for the cases of rape in security centres, even where a link up the chain of command could be made. It was, instead, held that even though the official Khmer Rouge policy did not manage to prevent rape, it could not be considered that rape was one of the crimes used by the Khmer Rouge leaders to implement the common purpose.[205]

Maybe most importantly, the ECCC will never be able to judge Thirith on her alleged 'gender equality' policies during the Khmer Rouge reign. It has been held that she, as Social Affairs Minister, 'emancipated' women by separating single women from their parents and mothers from their (husband and) children soon after birth, conscripting women to do the same heavy labour as men, and having them executed if they resisted.[206] Instead of allowing the women raise their children, the children were sent to collective childcare centres while the mothers went to work in other places (e.g. building dams, irrigation channels). Productivity was the main concern of the Khmer Rouge regime, and everything else, including family ties, was not important. One Khmer Rouge four-year plan said 'mothers must not get too entangled with their children; there should

203 See, e.g., Studzinsky, above n. 61, p. 182 (see Studzinsky for further discussion on the challenges related to sexual violence charges before the ECCC); and Amicus Curiae Human Rights Center, University of California, Berkeley, School of Law, and International Experts on Sexual Violence Under International Criminal Law, *Rape and Other Forms of Sexual Violence as Crimes against Humanity, War Crimes, and Torture under Customary International Law* (A filing before the Extraordinary African Chambers Seated at the Court of Appeals, Dakar, Senegal, 8 December 2015).

204 F. So, 'Remembering Ieng Thirith's Radical Gender Policy' *The Phnom Pen Post*, 25.08.2015 <http://www.phnompenhpost.com/analysis-and-op-ed/remembering-ieng-thiriths-radical-gender-policy> accessed 11.09.2016 ('Thirith's many victims, mainly female victims, have died without receiving any justice').

205 *Case against Nuon Chea et al.*, 002/19-09-2007-ECCC/OCIJ, D427, 15 September 2010, paras. 1426–29.

206 J. Cox and T. Sokhavuth, 'A Mother Remembers Ieng Thirith's Brutal Gender Policy' *Khmer Times*, 30.08.2015 <http://www.khmertimeskh.com/news/15130/a-mother-remembers-ieng-thirith---s-brutal-gender-policy/> accessed 11.09.2016.

be time to go and work'.[207] Maternity leave was furthermore very limited: the longest period for maternity leave was up to one month and the lowest was as short as one week to two weeks.[208] Pregnant women received little medical care and nutrition and were still expected to carry out a considerable amount of work during their pregnancy or after delivery.[209] Disguised as efforts to end gender discrimination, Thirith's policies were actually aimed at conscripting more women into the labour force. As one person explained: 'Gender equality [policy] attempted to eradicate the traditional family life, … It did not emancipate women. Rather, it destroyed their relationships without raising their [women's] status.'[210] Thirith has always denied her involvement in any of the charges against her. She rather claimed: 'I don't know why a good person is accused of such crimes and I have suffered a great deal, and I cannot really be patient because I have been wrongly accused.'[211]

Thirith's case shows similarities with the next to be discussed case of Pauline Nyiramasuhuko, as both women were in high government positions mandated to advance women's rights and both defended themselves for their involvement in the crimes on the basis of their kind character.

5.3. ICTR

Pauline Nyiramasuhuko (1946) was the Minister of Family and Women's Development during the genocide of 1994 in Rwanda. She was jointly accused with five others in the so-called 'Nyiramasuhuko *et al.* case', also known as the 'Butare case', as it dealt with six accused who held senior positions in the region of Butare, south Rwanda, which also included Nyiramasuhuko's son, Arsène Shalom Ntahobali, an infamous militia-leader who, like his mother, was convicted of sexual violence. Nyiramasuhuko was the first and only woman indicted by the ICTR, the longest trial in the history of international criminal justice, and charged with genocide, crimes against humanity and war crimes.[212]

Nyiramasuhuko was found guilty by the Trial Chamber on 24 June 2011 of several sexual violence charges, i.e. rape as a crime against humanity and outrages upon personal dignity as a violation of Article 3 common to the Geneva Conventions and of Additional Protocol II as a war crime under Article 6(3)

207 ibid.
208 So, above n. 213.
209 ibid.
210 ibid.
211 ibid.
212 *The Prosecutor v. Pauline Nyiramasuhuko and Shalom Ntahobali*, Amended Indictment, Case No. ICTR-97-21-I, 1 March 2001.

(command responsibility) for ordering Interahamwe under her effective control to rape Tutsi women at the Butare prefecture office.[213] Nyiramasuhuko was, however, found not guilty by the Trial Chamber of sexual violence as genocide, persecution as a crime against humanity, and violence to life, health and physical or mental well-being as a violation of Article 3 common to the Geneva Conventions and of Additional Protocol II as a war crime, and other inhumane acts as crimes against humanity under Articles 6(1) (direct responsibility) and 6(3) (command responsibility) due to insufficient notice of the Prosecutor's intention to pursue these sexual violence crimes.[214] She was similarly found not guilty for other inhumane acts as crimes against humanity under Articles 6(1) (direct responsibility) and 6(3) (command responsibility). The reasons being insufficient notice of the Prosecutor's intention to pursue these sexual violence crimes and that insufficient evidence had been adduced to prove that Nyiramasuhuko forced her victims to undress completely before forcing them into vehicles and taking them to their deaths.[215] Nyiramasuhuko received a sentence of life imprisonment for these and other charges she was convicted of. On 14 December 2015, the Appeals Chamber upheld the findings in respect of the sexual violence conviction.[216] Her sentence was reduced to 47 years' imprisonment, in particular due to a violation of the accused's right to be tried without undue delay.

Much has been written about Pauline Nyiramasuhuko who, as a woman, was accused of sexual violence and who euphemistically was the Minister of Family and Women's Development at the time of the genocide in Rwanda.[217] Her gender, rather than her high profile position, has often been the focus of much of the media attention.[218] Several things are noticeable in this case. First of all, the failure of the Prosecution to charge rape and sexual violence as genocide. On this issue, the Trial Chamber expressed disappointment with the Prosecution as the evidence in the case against Nyiramasuhuku made clear that rape was used as a form of genocide. In the Trial Chamber's legal findings it became clear that

---

213 *The Prosecutor v. Pauline Nyiramasuhuko, Arsène Shalom Ntahobali, Sylvain Nsabimana, Alphonse Nteziryayo, Joseph Kanyabashi, Élie Ndayambaje*, Judgment and Sentence, Case No. ICTR-98-42-T, 24 June 2011, paras. 6183, 6186.

214 ibid., paras. 5831–32.

215 ibid., paras. 6133–37.

216 *The Prosecutor v. Pauline Nyiramasuhuko, Arsène Shalom Ntahobali, Sylvain Nsabimana, Alphonse Nteziryayo, Joseph Kanyabashi, Élie Ndayambaje*, Judgment, Case No. ICTR-98-42-A, 14 December 2015, para. 3539.

217 One of the first writings on her and other women involved in the Rwandan genocide comes from: African Rights, Rwanda Not So Innocent: Women as Killers (London: African Rights, 1995).

218 E.g. Sperling, above n. 179, pp. 637–64; and S.K. Wood, 'A Woman Scorned for the "Least Condemned" War Crime: Precedent and Problems with Prosecuting Rape as a Serious War Crime in the International Criminal Tribunal for Rwanda' (2004) 13 *Columbia Journal of Gender and the Law* 287.

had the Prosecution not erred in its charges or had it managed to rectify the defect in time, Nyiramasuhuko would have been held accountable for the sexual violence she had instigated.[219] Kaitesi attributes the failure of the Prosecution to both a lack of understanding and a failure to appreciate the facts and the need to charge as such, i.e. rape and sexual violence as genocide.[220] Although the Prosecution had been given the opportunity to amend the indictment twice, it failed to link sexual violence and genocide (as in most other cases), whereas such a link was more easily made in cases of murder as genocide. The second point, flowing from the first point, is the impact of the failure to charge sexual violence as genocide on its victims. Witness TA, who was a rape victim and who testified in this case told Kaitesi:

> [I] wonder[ed] why the Tribunal and the prosecuting lawyers could not understand that genocide for them was committed through rape and sexual violence which is far worse than an immediate physical death, as it entails death from the pain of the assault, life thereafter and even the justice process itself.[221]

According to Kaitesi, 'the Tribunal left a legacy that is incomplete and controversial for genocide in Rwanda generally and particularly for the victims of genocidal gender and sexual violence'.[222] The extent of genocidal sexual violence has therefore not been brought to light.

A third point of interest is Nyiramasuhuko's line of defence, which directly goes to the gender debate. Nyiramasuhuko claimed that, as a mother/woman/nurturer, she was incapable of committing violent crimes. An argument that finds inspiration from the essentialist feminist school that claims that men are inherently more warlike than women.[223] Even before she was charged, she claimed in a BBC interview: 'I cannot even kill a chicken. If there is a person who says that a woman – a mother – killed, then I'll confront that person.'[224] During her defence in court, Nyiramasuhuko claimed that she could not have been responsible for crimes against women as charged, because such charges are contrary to her character and the fact that she had worked for many years to promote Rwandan women.[225] Her Defence team painted a very different picture

---

219 On this, see further: U. Kaitesi, *Genocidal Gender and Sexual Violence*, Intersentia 2013, pp. 161–63.

220 ibid., p. 181. See also: A.-M. de Brouwer and U. Kaitesi, 'Sexual Violence' in A.M. de Brouwer and A. Smeulers (eds.), *The Companion to the International Criminal Tribunal for Rwanda*, Edward Elgar Publishing 2016.

221 ibid., p. 174.

222 ibid., p. 184.

223 ibid., p. 169.

224 P. Landesman, 'A Woman's Work' *The New York Times*, 15.09.2002.

225 *The Prosecutor v. Pauline Nyiramasuhuko, Arsène Shalom Ntahobali, Sylvain Nsabimana, Alphonse Nteziryayo, Joseph Kanyabashi, Élie Ndayambaje*, Judgment and Sentence, Case No. ICTR-98-42-T, 24 June 2011, para. 2153.

of her, describing their client as 'very nice, a mother hen'.[226] Furthermore, the Nyiramasuhuko Defence submitted that the Prosecution witnesses were not credible and suggested they fabricated evidence of her involvement in rapes.[227] This was all put forward, while Nyiramasuhuko was held to have had the highest leadership role of all six accused in the Butare case, in control of genocidal sexual violence and killings. In addition, Nyiramasuhuko held that she was powerless in a male-dominated government and could thus not have stopped the genocide.[228] Thus, Nyiramasuhuko played the 'double-sided coin of using power to commit violence and denying its presence when faced with accountability'.[229] As mentioned above, Kaitesi underlines that the classical male domination/female subordination and sisterhood/womanhood as a homogenous group discourses insufficiently explain the phenomenon of female perpetrators, and states that other power dimensions that may be at stake for women must also be analysed, such as ethnic and political ideologies.[230]

5.4. ICC

Before the ICC there is currently one case involving a woman who (also) faces charges of sexual violence, namely Simone Gbagbo. Simone Gbagbo (1949) is the wife of Laurent Gbagbo, the former President of Ivory Coast, who is likewise charged with international crimes, including sexual violence, before the ICC. In the warrant of arrest, Simone Gbagbo is charged with four counts of crimes against humanity. Of these, one count involves rape and other forms of sexual violence as committed during the post-election crisis from 28 November 2010 onwards by the Ivorian Defense and Security Forces, which were reinforced by youth militias and mercenaries loyal to President Gbagbo.[231] For this, she is held to bear individual criminal responsibility as an indirect co-perpetrator under Article 25(3)(a) of the ICC's Rome Statute. Simone Gbagbo has been said to be ideologically and professionally very close to her husband. Although not elected, Simone Gbagbo acted as an alter ego for her husband, exercising the power to make state decisions. She was also close to other members of Laurent Gbagbo's inner circle who were involved in the implementation of the so-called 'Common Plan'.

---

226 Hogg, above n. 166, p. 93.

227 ibid.

228 Hirondelle News Agency, 'ICTR/Butare – Nyiramasuhuko Denies She Was a Powerful Woman' *Hirondelle News Agency*, 21.09.2005 <http://www.hirondellenews.com/content/view/2904/26/> accessed 11.09.2016; See also: Hogg, above n. 166, p. 93.

229 U. Kaitesi, *Genocidal Gender and Sexual Violence*, Intersentia 2013, p. 170.

230 ibid., p.168.

231 Situation in the Republic of Cote D'Ivoire in the Case of the Prosecutor v. Simone Gbagbo, Warrant of Arrest for Simone Gbagbo, Case No. ICC-02/11-01/12, 29 February 2012 (unsealed on 22 November 2012).

Simone Gbagbo is, unlike her husband, however, not in the custody of the ICC. She was nevertheless prosecuted in Ivory Coast and was sentenced to 20 years' imprisonment on 10 March 2015 for undermining state security, disturbing public order and organising armed gangs in the aftermath of the country's election.[232] Despite this conviction, the ICC ruled that she is still wanted by the ICC. According to the Appeals Chamber of the ICC, the domestic authorities of Ivory Coast have, *inter alia*, not taken tangible, concrete and progressive steps aimed at ascertaining whether Simone Gbagbo is criminally responsible for the same conduct that is alleged in the case before the Court.[233] The Appeals Chamber concluded that it was not unreasonable for the Pre-Trial Chamber, who dealt with this matter before, to find the conduct being investigated domestically (i.e. economic crimes and crimes against the state) to be of a different nature to Simone Gbagbo's conduct, as alleged before the ICC (which includes rape and sexual violence). The arrest warrant against Simone Gbagbo thus remains pending.

Then, on 17 March 2016, it was announced by Africa News that Simone Gbagbo was going to be tried for war crimes and crimes against humanity by a court in Ivory Coast on 25 April 2016.[234] Apparently Ivory Coast was no longer willing to send those accused of international crimes to the ICC and claimed that it had now an operational judicial system, so that those accused of international crimes, like Simone Gbagbo, could be tried at home, complying therefore with the ICC's complementarity principle.[235] No official ICC response to these new charges and trial were at the time given, but for the ICC's acceptance of this trial, it seemed that much would depend on the exact crimes that would be charged as crimes against humanity and war crimes and whether the trial was not going to be a sham trial, actually trying to protect the accused from sincere prosecution. Then, one year later, in March 2017, Simone Gbagbo was in fact acquitted of war crimes and crimes against humanity by a unanimous jury of the Ivory Coast court, which caused great disappointment among victims.[236]

---

232 K. Moodley, 'Simone Gbagbo, Former Ivory Coast First Lady, Sentenced to 20 years in Prison' *Independent*, 10.03.2015 <http://www.independent.co.uk/news/world/africa/simone-gbagbo-former-ivory-coast-first-lady-sentenced-to-20-years-in-prison-10097881.html> accessed 11.09.2016.

233 *Situation in the Republic of Côte D'Ivoire in the Case of the Prosecutor v. Simone Gbagbo*, Judgment on the Appeal of Côte d'Ivoire against the Decision of Pre-Trial Chamber I of 11 December 2014 entitled 'Decision on Côte d'Ivoire's Challenge to the Admissibility of the Case against Simone Gbagbo', Case No. ICC-02/11-01/12 OA, 27 May 2015.

234 'Simone Gbagbo to Face Trial in Ivory Coast for Crimes against Humanity' *Africa News*, 17.03.2016 <http://www.africanews.com/2016/03/17/simone-gbagbo-s-to-face-trial-in-ivory-coast-for-crimes-against-humanity/> accessed 11.09.2016.

235 ibid.

236 'Ivory Coast Ex-First Lady Simone Gbagbo Acquitted for Crimes Against Humanity' *France 24*, 29.03.2017 <http://www.france24.com/en/20170328-ivory-coast-ex-first-lady-simone-gbagbo-acquitted-crimes-against-humanity-trial> accessed 16.07.2018.

Her conviction for offences against the state, for which she had received a sentence of 20 years in prison March 2015, was, however, upheld on appeal in the same month (March 2017).[237] Surprisingly, in August 2018, Simone Gbagbo - and 800 other people - was granted amnesty by the President of Ivory Coast in a move to foster reconciliation.[238] Some observations can be made. First of all, what is noticeable is how Simone Gbagbo is called for by the ICC itself, namely, in the arrest warrant, as 'Ms. Gbagbo' or 'the alter-ego of her husband'.[239] According to Burke-White

> That claim, of course, is a gendered one in and of itself. The fact that Simone Gbagbo was married to Laurent Gbagbo should be legally irrelevant. No one should be criminally responsible for his or her marital choices - even very, very bad ones. The ICC's indictment might better have been written to say that she was the 'alter ego of the president,' regardless of whether she was married to him.[240]

Referencing to Simone Gbagbo as 'the wife of' could be used to reinforce gender stereotypes; Simone Gbagbo and her defence team could use her relationship as the wife of a powerful man to cast her as a faithful delegate, rather than as an independent actor.[241] However, hopefully, this case - if ever tried before the ICC - goes to book as the case that marked a shift in international criminal justice beyond focus on formal authority and towards a more subtle understanding of political influence and responsibility.[242] Simone Gbagbo's influence cannot be traced back in formal authority, like the people who usually appear before international criminal tribunals (e.g. senior government and military officials). The indictment of Simone Gbagbo, however, recognises that those most responsible for international crimes may rather (also) be civilians with extraordinary influence. Therefore, from that perspective, Simone Gbagbo's case may become known far beyond being the first case of a woman indicted before the ICC for international crimes, including sexual violence. It is to be seen if her case will now still come before the ICC. Some have argued that her acquittal was

---

237 'Ivory Coast's Former First Lady Simone Gbagbo Acquiteed of War Crimes' *The Guardian*, 28.03.2018 <https://www.theguardian.com/world/2017/mar/28/ivory-coast-simone-gbagbo-acquitted-war-crimes-humanity> accessed 16.07.2018.

238 'Ivory Coast ex-first lady Simone Gbagbo granted amnesty', *BBC*, 07.08.2018 <https://www.bbc.com/news/world-africa-45095830> accessed 16.07.2018.

239 This language has also been used in the introduction of this subsection.

240 W. Burke-White, 'A Wife Accused of War Crimes: The Unprecedented Case of Simone Gbagbo' *The Atlantic*, 03.12.2012 <http://www.theatlantic.com/international/archive/2012/12/a-wife-accused-of-war-crimes-the-unprecedented-case-of-simone-gbagbo/265828/> accessed 11.09.2016.

241 Grey and Chappell, above n. 165.

242 Burke-White, above n. 240.

'based on a process marred by fair trial concerns and a critical lack of evidence shows the importance of the International Criminal Court's case against her'.[243]

6. CONCLUSION

Just like gender has been shown to be a pivotal element in the understanding of the prosecution of male perpetrators of sexual violence against women, gender appears to be crucial when it comes to the prosecution of sexual violence committed against men and perpetrated by women. Gender is so pervasive in the work of international jurisdictions in relation to these two categories of actors that, on one hand, male sexual victimisation has been, more often than not, prosecuted under categories of crimes in line with the traditional understanding of men's experiences of conflict and, on the other hand, the prosecution of female perpetrators of sexual violence has been married with ideas of femininity as incompatible with committing atrocities.

In both cases, the result is injustice. The legal characterisation of a crime should only depend on the acts committed. The sentence handed down to a perpetrator should only depend on the crimes committed. Neither should depend on the sex/gender of the victim or perpetrator. The ICC currently finds itself in the position to learn from the experiences of the ICTY, ICTR, ECCC and SCSL. So far, its practice has been ambivalent in this regard. More understanding, cooperation and training on gender, male sexual violence and female perpetrators of sexual violence on all levels within the Court is therefore recommended.

243 Human Rights Watch, *Côte d'Ivoire: Simone Gbagbo Acquitted After Flawed War Crimes Trial: First Lady's Acquittal Highlights ICC Process As Critical Path for Victims*, 29 March 2017.

PROSECUTING SEXUAL AND GENDER-BASED CRIMES IN THE INTERNATIONAL CRIMINAL COURT

Inching Towards Gender Justice

Rosemary GREY and Louise CHAPPELL*

1. INTRODUCTION

Sexual and gender-based crimes are crimes that reflect and reinforce socially constructed gender norms. The rape of women and girls in conflict situations, for example, draws on deeply ingrained ideas of women as the 'booty' of war,[1] while sexual violence against men is often used to humiliate, 'emasculate', or 'homosexualise' the victim.[2] Similarly, the deliberate targeting of school girls by fundamentalist groups expresses a contempt for female education, to give an example of a 'non-sexualised' gender-based crime.[3] Due to their serious physical

* Rosemary Grey acknowledges the financial support of the University of Sydney Postdoctoral Fellowship scheme. Louise Chappell acknowledges the financial support of the Australian Research Council (DP 1410102274) in the writing of this chapter.

1 R. COPELON, 'Gender Crimes as War Crimes: Integrating Criminal Law' (2000) 46 *McGill Law Journal* 217, p.223.

2 S. SIVAKUMARAN, 'Sexual Violence Against Men in Armed Conflict' (2007) 18(2) *European Journal of International Law* 253.

3 E.g. ICC, *Situation in Afghanistan, Public redacted version of "Request for authorisation of an investigation pursuant to article 15"*, ICC-02/17-7-Red, 20 November 2017, [116].

and psychological effects, as well as their social and cultural significance, sexual and gender-based crimes are among the most devastating consequences of war. Despite that, these crimes have historically been overlooked in international criminal tribunals and trivialised in conventions on the laws of war. This is in part because sexual and gender-based crimes are committed primarily against women and girls, a population whose voices 'have been thoroughly obscured by and within the international legal order'.[4] Other key reasons include a failure to recognise the gravity of sexual and gender-based crimes, and a tendency to view them as 'private' matters rather than crimes of the most serious concern to the international community as a whole.[5]

The hard-won gender justice provisions of the Rome Statute, the treaty establishing the International Criminal Court (ICC),[6] provide a means to change this historical path. The Statute gives the ICC power to prosecute a broad range of sexual and gender-based crimes in situations of war, conflict and genocide. By prosecuting these crimes, the ICC can challenge a long-standing pattern of impunity, recognise the harm suffered by the victims, and send a strong message that sexual and gender-based crimes are among the most serious crimes of concern to the international community as a whole. As the ICC approaches its twentieth anniversary, it is timely to ask how effective the Court has been in achieving these goals. Against that backdrop, this chapter examines the ICC's track record in prosecuting sexual and gender-based crimes from 1 July 2002, when the Rome Statute entered into force, until 1 July 2017.

The chapter begins with a brief background on the prosecution of sexual and gender-based crimes under international law, including in the Rome Statute. It then considers how those provisions of the Rome Statute have been applied in the ICC to date, taking into account both quantitative factors (such as how often sexual and gender-based crimes have been charged, and how many of these charges have been proved compared with other crimes) and qualitative factors (such as whether the charges capture a diverse range of sexual and gender-based crimes against men, women and children).

The chapter shows that although the ICC has been slow to convict any individuals for sexual and gender-based crimes – a fact that remains true in 2018 following the reversal of Court's first and only conviction for rape[7] – it is

4 H. Charlesworth and C. Chinkin, *The Boundaries of International Law: A Feminist Analysis*, Manchester University Press 2000), p. 1.

5 Copelon, above n. 1; K. Askin, 'Prosecuting Wartime Rape and Other Gender Related Crimes: Extraordinary Advances, Enduring Obstacles' (2003) 21(2) *Berkeley Journal of International Law* 28; B. Bedont and K. Hall-Martinez, 'Ending Impunity for Gender Crimes Under the International Criminal Court' (1999) 6(1) *Brown Journal of World Affairs* 65.

6 Rome Statute of the International Criminal Court, 2187 UNTS 90, adopted 17 July 1998, entered into force 1 July 2002.

7 ICC, *Bemba*, Judgment on the appeal of Mr Jean-Pierre Bemba Gombo against Trial Chamber III's "Judgment pursuant to Article 74 of the Statute", ICC-01/05-01/08-3636-Red, 8 June 2018.

beginning to make progress on that front. The Office of the Prosecutor, the unit charged with investigating and prosecuting crimes within the jurisdiction of the Court, has committed to paying particular attention to sexual and gender-based crimes and integrating a 'gender perspective' into all its work.[8] Reflecting this commitment, the Office is increasingly including charges for sexual and gender-based crimes in cases, and explaining the cultural and political significance of these crimes. As the ICC Prosecutor noted in November 2015, 'To date, my Office has charged 19 individuals with gender related crimes in the context of 14 cases. Excluding [administration of justice] offences, specific sexual violence charges were proffered in 70 per cent of the Court's cases and with respect to 59 per cent of the suspects'.[9] Building on these efforts, in March 2016, the Court confirmed numerous charges for gender-based crimes in the case against Ugandan rebel commander Dominic Ongwen, including charges for forced marriage and forced pregnancy, neither of which have previously been prosecuted in the ICC.[10]

These recent successes show that despite some significant losses, the ICC is developing a stronger track record in prosecuting sexual and gender-based crimes. However, the journey to this point has not been smooth, and there have been disappointments along the way. Evidence of sexual and gender-based crimes has at times been too weak to support the charges, or has been introduced too late in the proceedings. Judges have at times seemed to underestimate the gravity of sexual and gender-based crimes such forced nudity,[11] and have appeared less willing to hold perpetrators responsible for these crimes compared with other common wartime crimes such as murder and pillage.[12] There has also been a great deal of debate about the meaning of the new crime of 'sexual violence',[13] while the crime of 'gender persecution' remained, until after the period under analysis, unexplored in cases before the Court.[14]

---

8 ICC Office of the Prosecutor, *Strategic Goal 2, Strategic plan 2016–2018*, The Hague 2015, Strategic Goal 2; ICC Office of the Prosecutor, *Policy Paper on Sexual and Gender-Based Crimes*, The Hague 2014.

9 Prosecutor Bensouda, Keynote Address, Launch of Louise Chappell's *The Politics of Gender Justice at the International Criminal Court: Legacies and Legitimacy* (Oxford University Press), 25.11.2015, Australian Embassy, The Hague.

10 ICC, *Ongwen*, Decision on the confirmation of charges against Dominic Ongwen, ICC-02/04-01/15-422-Red, 23 March 2016.

11 L. Chappell, *The Politics of Gender Justice at the International Criminal Court: Legacies and Legitimacy*, Oxford University Press 2016, pp. 117–18; R. Grey, 'Conflicting Interpretations of "Sexual Violence" in the International Criminal Court' (2014) 21(89) *Australian Feminist Studies* 273 at 277; N. Hayes, 'Sisyphus Wept: Prosecuting Sexual Violence at the International Criminal Court' in W.A. Schabas, Y. McDermott and N. Hayes (eds.), *The Ashgate Research Companion to International Criminal Law*, Ashgate, Surrey 2013, pp. 7, 39.

12 C. Stahn, 'Justice Delivered or Justice Denied? The Legacy of the Katanga Judgment' (2014) 12 *Journal of International Criminal Justice* 809.

13 Rome Statute, article 7(1)(g); 8(2)(b)(xxii); 8(2)(e)(vi).

14 Rome Statute, article 7(1)(h). Note: In March 2018, the ICC issued a warrant of arrest against Mr Al Hassan, a member of Ansar Dine, one of the fundamentalist groups present

These mixed outcomes reflect the challenges of investigating sexual and gender-based crimes in conflict-affected countries, and the difficulties of meeting the strict evidentiary standard at trial. In addition, this chapter argues, these mixed outcomes indicate that in the ICC, as in many most new institutions, old ideas and habits continue to shape outcomes alongside the new formal rules.[15] Thus, despite the visibility of sexual and gender-based crimes in the Rome Statute, and despite the efforts of internal and external actors to ensure that these crimes are investigated and prosecuted effectively, sexual and gender-based crimes remain at risk of being overlooked, trivialised or seen as incidental to armed conflict, as has historically been the pattern in international criminal law.

2. SEXUAL AND GENDER-BASED CRIMES IN INTERNATIONAL CRIMINAL LAW IN HISTORICAL PERSPECTIVE

As noted above, sexual and gender-based crimes have historically been overlooked in treaties on the laws of war, and in tribunals enforcing those laws. In recent years, details of prosecutions for conflict-related sexual violence crimes in national jurisdictions in the post-World War II period have begun to emerge.[16] However, in the more widely-publicised international criminal tribunals by the allied victors of the war, these crimes were not properly addressed. For example, sexual and gender-based crimes were not expressly recognised in the Charter of the Nuremberg Tribunal, established in 1945. Echoing this silence, the Tribunal's judgment makes no reference to these crimes,[17] although it

in northern Mali in 2012–2013. This warrant includes a charge of persecution on gender grounds, indicating that a subsequent prosecution of this crime might be on the horizon. See: R. Grey, 'International Criminal Court poised to interpret the crime of "gender-based persecution" for the first time', *Int Law Grrls*, 12.04.2018 <https://ilg2.org/2018/04/12/international-criminal-court-poised-to-interpret-the-crime-of-gender-based-persecution-for-the-first-time/> accessed 14.07.2018.

15 L. Chappell, 'Nested Newness and Institutional Innovation: Expanding Gender Justice in the International Criminal Court' in M.L. Krook and F. Mackay (eds.), *Gender, Politics and Institutions: Towards a Feminist Institutionalism*, Palgrave Macmillan 2011; L. Chappell, 'Conflicting Institutions and the Search for Gender Justice at the International Criminal Court' (2014) 16(1) *Political Research Quarterly* 183; F. Mackay, M. Kenny and L. Chappell, 'New Institutionalism through a Gender Lens: Towards a Feminist Institutionalism?' (2010) 31(5) *International Political Science Review* 578; F. Mackay, 'Nested Newness, Institutional Innovation, and the Gendered Limits of Change' (2014) 10(4) *Politics & Gender* 549; R. Grey, 'Prosecuting Sexual and Gender Violence Crimes at the International Criminal Court: New Opportunities and Historical Legacies' (PhD Thesis University of New South Wales 2015).

16 See, e.g., D. Plesch, *Human Rights after Hitler. The Lost History of Prosecuting Axis War Crimes*, Georgetown University Press 2017, Chapter 1.

17 International Military Tribunal, 'Judgment and Sentence' (1947) 41(1) *American Journal of International Law* 172–333.

heard evidence of sexual violence crimes against women throughout Europe,[18] as well as the persecution of homosexual men under Nazi rule.[19] The Tokyo Tribunal, established in 1946, also largely failed to address sexual and gender-based crimes. While it recognised the widespread rape of women during the invasion of Nanking, it made no reference to the rape and enslavement of an estimated 80,000 to 200,000 women in 'comfort stations' run by the Japanese military.[20]

The lack of attention to sexual and gender-based crimes in the post war tribunals indicate that:

> Before the 1990s, sexual violence in war was, with rare exception, largely invisible. If not invisible, it was trivialized; if not trivialized, it was considered a private matter or justified as an inevitable by-product of war, the necessary reward for the fighting men.[21]

The 1949 Geneva Conventions, the key treaties on the laws of war adopted after World War II, also failed to recognise the seriousness of sexual and gender-based crimes. Unlike violations such as wilful killing or torture, sexual and gender-based crimes are not expressly classified as 'grave breaches' of the Conventions – a class of breaches for which individuals can be prosecuted under international criminal law.[22] This apparent gap in the Conventions reinforced the perception that sexual and gender-based crimes are less serious than other attacks on civilian life or property, and fails to recognise that sexual and gender-based crimes can destroy individuals and communities, and can be used a tool of persecution, an instrument of genocide and a weapon of war.

In the 1990s, sexual and gender-based crimes started to become more visible in international criminal law, beginning with a series of landmark prosecutions for sexual and gender-based crimes in the United Nations *ad hoc* tribunals for

---

18 See International Military Tribunal, *Trial of the major war criminals before the International Military Tribunal, Nuremberg, 14 November 1945–1 October 1946* (Vol. 7), pp. 456–57; C. Niarchos, 'Women, War, and Rape: Challenges Facing the International Tribunal for the Former Yugoslavia' (1995) 17(4) *Human Rights Quarterly* 629, pp. 664–65.

19 International Military Tribunal, *Trial of the major war criminals before the International Military Tribunal*, Nuremberg, 14 November 1945–1 October 1946 (Vol. 4), 507; International Military Tribunal, *Trial of the major war criminals before the International Military Tribunal*, Nuremberg, 14 November 1945–1 October 1946 (Vol. 5), 176; International Military Tribunal, 1947, *Trial of the major war criminals before the International Military Tribunal*, Nuremberg, 14 November 1945–1 October 1946 (Vol. 6), 310.

20 Copelon, above n. 1, pp. 221–23; Niarchos, above n. 18, pp. 663–66.

21 Copelon, above n. 1, p. 220.

22 Bedont and Hall-Martinez, above n. 5, pp. 70–71; L. Chappell, 'Women, Gender and International Institutions: Exploring New Opportunities at the International Criminal Court' (2003) 22(1) *Policy Organisation and Society* 3, 7; Charlesworth and Chinkin, above n. 4, pp. 314–16; Copelon, above n. 1, p. 221.

the former Yugoslavia and Rwanda.[23] The Rome Statute, which was adopted in 1998 and entered into force in 2002, built on this progress. Due to strong lobbying from the Women's Caucus for Gender Justice and like-minded states,[24] the Statute includes a wide range of sexual and gender-based crimes as war crimes and crimes against humanity, including a new offence of persecution on the grounds of gender.[25] It also highlights the need for sensitive interactions with victims of these crimes,[26] calls for 'a fair representation of male and female judges',[27] and requires the ICC Prosecutor to appoint a special advisor with expertise on sexual and gender-based violence.[28]

These provisions fall under the rubric of 'gender justice' as they focus on the need to empower women and potentially, through reparations rulings, challenge structural inequalities that contribute to sexual and gender-based violence.[29] They fit neatly within various definitions of gender justice including addressing 'gender bias', meaning the 'leakage of gender norms into seemingly impartial laws and policy'.[30] They also cover the three core aspects of social theorist Nancy Fraser's model for gender justice: recognition, redistribution and representation, which refer to the cultural, economic and political sides of gender justice, respectively.[31]

This chapter is most interested in the ICC's potential to advance gender justice by *recognising* – that is, investigating, prosecuting, and properly describing – sexual and gender-based crimes. By realising its full potential in this regard, the Court can send a powerful message about the international community's commitment to gender equality and its respect for the rights of women and girls, in line with the goal of 'recognition'.[32] This power to express global norms is

---

23 Askin, above n. 5, pp. 317–46; H. Brady, 'The Power of Precedents: Using the Case Law of the Ad Hoc International Criminal Tribunals and Hybrid Courts in Adjudicating Sexual and Gender-Based Crimes at the ICC' (2012) 18(2) *Australian Journal of Human Rights* 75; S. Brammertz and M. Jarvis, 'Lessons Learned in Prosecuting Gender Crimes Under International Law: Experiences from the ICTY' in C. Eboe-Osuji (ed.), *Protecting Humanity: Essays in International Law and Policy in Honour of Navanethem Pillay*, Martinus Nijhoff Publishers 2010.

24 See Chappell, above n. 11, pp. 88–129; M. Glasius, *The International Criminal Court: A Global Civil Society Achievement*, Routledge 2006, pp. 77–93.

25 Rome Statute, arts. 7(1)(g); 7(1)(h); 8(2)(b)(xxii); 8(2)(e)(vi).

26 Rome Statute, arts. 54(1)(b); 68(1); 68(2).

27 Rome Statutes, art. 36(8)(a)(iii).

28 Rome Statute, art. 42(9).

29 Chappell, above n. 11, pp. 5–8.

30 A.M. Goetz and R. Jenkins, *Reinventing Accountability: Making Democracy Work for Human Development* Palgrave Macmillan 2005, p. 163.

31 N. Fraser, *Justice Interruptus: Critical Reflections on the Postsocialist Condition*, Routledge 1997; N. Fraser, *Scales of Justice: Reimaging Political Space in a Globalizing World*, Colombia University Press 2009. See also: Chappell, above n. 11, pp. 5–8; A. Durbach and L. Chappell, '"Leaving Behind the Age of Impunity": Victims of Gender Violence and the Promise of Reparations' (2014) 16(4) *International Feminist Journal of Politics* 543.

32 Chappell, above n. 11, pp. 88–129.

arguably the ICC's greatest strength.[33] For that reason, it is imperative that sexual and gender-based crimes are not invisible in the ICC, as they were too often in international criminal tribunals in the past.[34] Prosecuting these crimes also enables the Court to recognise the victims' experiences and provide them with reparations following a conviction, in line with restorative justice principles.[35]

3. ACCOUNTABILITY FOR SEXUAL AND GENDER-BASED CRIMES

In the initial cases before the Court, the ICC Office of the Prosecutor did not consistently include charges for sexual and gender-based crimes. Over time, however, drawing learning lessons from these initial cases, especially the first trial of Democratic Republic of the Congo (DRC) militia leader Thomas Lubanga (discussed below), the Office has become increasingly vigilant about investigating and prosecuting sexual and gender-based crimes. The leadership of Prosecutor Fatou Bensouda, who has strongly emphasised her commitment to addressing such crimes, has also been critical to institutionalising this ethos in the Office.

The first case to be opened, in May 2005, focused on Ugandan rebel leader Joseph Kony and other members of his militia. In the arrest warrant application, the (then) ICC Prosecutor, Luis Moreno Ocampo, charged Kony with a wide range of crimes, including rape and sexual slavery.[36] The Prosecutor is yet to seek confirmation of these charges, as Kony has not yet been arrested and brought before the Court. However, Kony's co-accused Dominic Ongwen has come before the ICC and, as noted in section 1, has been charged with a wide range of sexual and gender-based crimes.

The next two cases, initiated in January 2006, did not include charges for sexual and gender-based crimes. These two cases concerned Thomas Lubanga Dyilo and Bosco Ntaganda, leaders of a militant armed group in the DRC. Despite reports that this group was responsible for widespread sexual violence crimes against civilian men, women and children, there were no charges for sexual or gender-based crimes in either case. Instead, the charges were limited

---

33 M. DeGuzman, 'An Expressive Rationale for the Thematic Prosecution of Sex Crimes' in M. Bergsmo (ed.), *Thematic Prosecution of International Sex Crimes*, Torkal Opsahl Academic EPublisher 2012.

34 Chappell, above n. 11, pp. 36–37; Copelon, above n. 1; Bedont and Hall-Martinez, above n. 5.

35 Chappell, above n. 11, pp. 130–59; B. Schiff, *Building the International Criminal Court*, Cambridge University Press 2008, pp. 33–34.

36 ICC, *Situation in Uganda*, Warrant of arrest for Joseph Kony issued on 8 July as amended on 27 September 2005, ICC-02/04-01/05-53, 27 September 2005, [5].

to conscripting and enlisting children under the age of 15 and using them to participate actively in hostilities. This was, in part, a result of time pressures: in the arrest warrant application, the Prosecutor noted that Lubanga had been in detention in the DRC since March 2005, and was expected to be released 'in the near future, possibly within three to four weeks'.[37] The Prosecutor urged the Pre-Trial Chamber to issue the warrant before Lubanga was released from detention because once released, he would be in a position to flee.[38] However, it was also a result of priorities: the Prosecutor could have prioritised accountability for sexual and gender-based crimes over expediency, despite pressures to quickly build up the ICC's case load, but comments by ex-ICC investigators indicating that the Prosecutor instead de-prioritised the investigation of sexual and gender-based crimes in order to bring a simpler, and quicker, case.[39]

In March 2006, when the arrest warrant against Lubanga was made public, organisations including Avocats Sans Frontières, Center for Justice and Reconciliation, Coalition Nationale pour la Cour Pénale Internationale, Fédération Internationale des Ligues des Droits de l'Homme, Human Rights Watch, International Center for Transitional Justice, Redress, and Women's Initiatives for Gender Justice were dismayed by the apparent gaps in the charges. They urged Prosecutor Moreno Ocampo to charge Lubanga with a broader range of crimes, warning that a failure to do so could damage the ICC's credibility in the DRC and limit victims' participation in proceedings.[40] The Prosecutor claimed that it was not feasible to investigate a broader range of charges due to the aforementioned time pressures surrounding Lubanga's arrest.[41]

Women's Initiatives for Gender Justice, one of the lead organisations involved in this campaign, sent the Prosecutor a dossier of evidence of systematic sexual violence crimes committed by Lubanga's group.[42] However, the Prosecutor

---

37 ICC, *Situation in the 0044emocratic Republic of Congo*, Decision on the Prosecutor's Application for Warrants of Arrest, Article 58, ICC-01/04-02/06-20-Anx2, 10 February 2006, [33]; see also [112].

38 ibid., [112].

39 K. Glassborrow, 'ICC Investigative Strategy Under Fire' (2008) *Institute for War and Peace Reporting* 27.10.2008 <https://iwpr.net/global-voices/icc-investigative-strategy-under-fire> accessed 14.07.2018.

40 Human Rights Watch, 'DR Congo: ICC Charges Raise Concern' (2006) *Human Rights Watch* 31.07.2006 <http://www.hrw.org/news/2006/07/31/dr-congo-icc-charges-raise-concern> accessed 23.10.2015.

41 P. Yates, *The Reckoning: The Battle for the International Criminal Court*, Skylight Pictures 2009. See also: Chappell, above n. 9, p. 111.

42 Women's Initiatives for Gender Justice, 'Public redacted version of confidential letter to ICC Prosecutor' (2006) August *Women's Initiatives for Gender Justice* <http://www.iccwomen.org/news/docs/Prosecutor_Letter_August_2006_Redacted.pdf> accessed 14.07.2018; Women's Initiatives for Gender Justice, 'Special Issue 1: Legal Eye on the ICC' (2012) May *Women's Initiatives for Gender Justice* <http://www.iccwomen.org/news/docs/WI-LegalEye5-12-FULL/LegalEye5-12.html> accessed 14.07.2018; Chappell, above n. 11, pp. 111–12.

did not expand the charges against Lubanga at the pre-trial stage, as was his prerogative under the Rome Statute. This decision was to provoke ongoing criticism throughout the trial. As one critic, K'Shaani O. Smith argued: 'excluding serious sexually-based crimes from the indictment against Lubanga was not only a tactical misstep on the Prosecutor's part, but also a colossal failure in adhering to his duty to do justice for the women and girls of the DRC'.[43]

When the trial began in January 2009, after being widely criticised for not charging Lubanga with sexual violence crimes, the Prosecutor changed his approach. In his opening address, he told the Trial Chamber that girl soldiers in Lubanga's group were raped daily by their commanders, and that boy soldiers were instructed to rape civilians in the context of attacks.[44] As the trial progressed, the Prosecution called several former girl soldiers to testify about their experiences of sexual violence in Lubanga's group. The issue of sexual violence against boy soldiers, by contrast, received less attention in the Prosecution's case.[45]

The Prosecution's increased attention to the experiences of girl soldiers went some way towards recognising sexual and gender-based crimes, but it did not address the gap in the charges. Five months into the trial, the victims' counsel asked the Trial Chamber to add charges for sexual slavery and cruel or inhumane treatment, by using a regulation which permits the Trial Chamber to 'modify the legal characterisation of the facts'. While the Defence and Prosecution opposed this motion, the majority of the Trial Chamber found it had the power to grant the victims' request. However, the Appeals Chamber overturned that decision, finding that because the Prosecutor had not led evidence of sexual violence at the pre-trial stage, it would be a breach of the regulations and a violation of Lubanga's fair trial rights to add charges for sexual violence once the trial was underway.[46] The Appeals Chamber's decision sent a clear message: if the Prosecutor wanted to bring charges for sexual and gender-based crimes, he needed to include evidence of these crimes at the *beginning* of the case.

In January 2010, the UN Special Representative on Children and Armed Conflict, an expert witness in the *Lubanga* case, urged the Trial Chamber to interpret the war crime of 'using' children in hostilities to include using them for sexual purposes – an interpretation which, if adopted, would allow the Trial Chamber to convict Lubanga for the sexual exploitation of child soldiers within

43 K.O. Smith, 'Prosecutor v. Lubanga: How the International Criminal Court Failed the Women and Girls of the Congo' (2011) 54(2) *Howard Law Journal* 467, 474. See also Hayes, above n. 11.

44 ICC, *Lubanga*, Transcript, ICC-01/04-01/06-T-107-ENG, 26 January 2009, 11.

45 Grey, above n. 15, pp. 120–24.

46 ICC, *Lubanga*, Judgment on the appeals of Mr Lubanga Dyilo and the Prosecutor against the Decision of Trial Chamber I of 14 July 2009 entitled 'Decision giving notice to the parties and participants that the legal characterisation of the facts may be subject to change in accordance with Regulation 55(2) of the Regulations of the Court', ICC-01/04-01/06-2205, 8 December 2009.

his militia, although he had not been charged with any sexual violence crimes.[47] The Prosecution echoed this argument in its closing brief,[48] prompting Judge Odio Benito, the only female judge on the Bench and one with a history of 'asking difficult gender questions',[49] to asked the Prosecution how it expected the Bench to adjudicate the allegations of sexual violence when these allegations were not formally part of the charges.[50] The Prosecutor's reply suggested that in his view, these acts of sexual violence were part of the crimes for which Lubanga had been charged. He explained:

> What we believe in this case is a different way to present the gender crimes. It presents the gender crimes not specific as rapes. Gender crimes were committed as part of the conscription of girls in – in the militias ... That is why the Prosecutor decided to confine the charges – to present the suffering and the sexual abuse and the gender crime suffered by the girls in the camps just as conscription, showing this gender aspect of the crime ... We believe when a commander ordered to abduct girls to use them as sexual slaves or rape them, this order is using the children in hostility.[51]

Not all commentators were convinced by this evolution in the Prosecution's case. Niamh Hayes for example, argued that the Office of the Prosecutor's belated attempt 'to retrospectively justify a clearly inept and insufficient range of charges' was 'unbecoming and reeked slightly of panic'.[52]

In March 2012, six years after the case began, the Trial Chamber delivered its judgment in the *Lubanga* case. The majority of the Chamber convicted Lubanga for conscripting, enlisting and using child soldiers, but made no finding regarding his guilt for the alleged acts of sexual violence. It also reprimanded the Prosecutor for asking that these acts be taken into account the sentencing stage, despite having declined to include any charges for sexual violence crimes at the appropriate time.[53] Kai Ambos was one of many academic commentators who agreed with the majority, criticising the Prosecutor for trying to 'squeeze the sex crimes' into the child soldier crimes at trial, rather than seeking to add charges for sexual violence at an earlier stage of proceedings.[54]

---

47 ICC, *Lubanga*, Transcript, ICC-01/04-01/06-T-223-ENG, 7 January 2010, 14–16.

48 ICC, *Lubanga*, Prosecution's closing brief, ICC-01/04-01/06-2748-Red, 21 July 2011, [139]–[143].

49 L. Chappell, A. Durbach and Judge E.O. Benito, 'Judge Odio Benito: A View of Gender Justice from the Bench' (2014) 16(4) *International Feminist Journal of Politics* 648, 648.

50 ICC, *Lubanga*, Transcript, ICC-01/04-01/06-T-356-ENG, 25 August 2011, 53–54.

51 ICC, *Lubanga*, Transcript, ICC-01/04-01/06-T-356-ENG, 25 August 2011, 54–55.

52 Hayes, above n. 11, p. 14.

53 ICC, *Lubanga*, Judgment pursuant to Article 74 of the Statute, ICC-01/04-01/06-2842, 14 March 2012, [629]–[630]; ICC, *Lubanga*, Decision on Sentence pursuant to Article 76 of the Statute, ICC-01/04-01/06-2901, 10 July 2012, [60].

54 K. Ambos, 'The First Judgment of the International Criminal Court (Prosecutor v. Lubanga): A Comprehensive Analysis of the Legal Issue' (2012) 12 *International Criminal Law Review* 115 at footnote 156.

Judge Odio Benito took a different approach. Rather than treating the allegations of sexual violence as external to the charges, her Honour determined that sexual violence is an 'intrinsic element' of the war crime of using children to participate actively in hostilities. Her Honour reasoned: '[i]t is *discriminatory* to exclude sexual violence which shows a clear gender differential impact from being a bodyguard or porter which is mainly a task given to young boys'.[55] In reaching her conclusions, Judge Odio Benito sought to interpret and apply the Rome Statute without discriminating on the grounds of gender, as directed by article 21(3).[56] As she has explained:

> The Rome Statute created, at least in writing, an inclusive gender-sensitive system whose goals, among others, are to put an end to impunity for the most serious crimes (which sexual violence crimes are), to recognise the rights of victims to participate and to receive reparations. It is impossible to do so without a precise gender perspective. A careful reading of the Preamble spells out these principles and, as a judge, I followed them and also upheld article 21 of the Statute.[57]

Yet while Judge Odio Benito's dissenting opinion highlighted important gender issues, it did not change the outcome of the case: Lubanga was not convicted or sentenced for sexual violence crimes, and as a consequence, was not liable to pay reparations for these crimes.[58] This first trial before the ICC highlights the influence of gender legacies of international law: a failure to recognise sexual and gender-based crimes as grievous acts, and inadequate evidence-gathering procedures.[59] It demonstrated that the formal recognition of a wide range of sexual and gender-based crimes in the Rome Statute does not guarantee that these crimes would be investigated and prosecuted in practice. Rather, faced with time pressures, and seeking to build the caseload of the newly-created Court, the former Prosecutor prioritised the timely arrest of Lubanga and the investigation of a limited range of 'child soldier' offences over accountability for sexual and gender-based crimes. This decision was not surprising, given the long history of sexual and gender-based crimes being overlooked in international criminal tribunals. It was, however, deeply disappointing to human rights activists and academic commentators who viewed sexual and gender-based crimes as among

---

55 ICC, *Lubanga*, Judgment pursuant to Article 74 of the Statute, Separate Opinion of Judge Odio Benito, ICC-01/04-01/06-2842, 14 March 2012, [21] (emphasis added).

56 See Chappell, above n. 11, pp. 114–17; S. Mouthaan, 'Barefoot, Pregnant, and in the Kitchen: Am I a Child Soldier Too?' (2015) 51 *Women's Studies International Forum* 91, p. 98.

57 Chappell *et al.*, above n. 49, p. 650.

58 L. Chappell, 'The Gender Injustice Cascade: 'Transformative' Reparations for Victims of Sexual and Gender-Based Crimes in the Lubanga Case at the International Criminal Court' (2017) 21(9) *International Journal of Human Rights* 1223–42. For a detailed discussion of the reparations regime at the ICC, see Jurasz, in this volume.

59 Chappell, above n. 11, pp. 110–17; Grey, above n. 15, pp. 256–60.

the most serious crimes of concern to the international community as a whole, and expected that these crimes would be thoroughly investigated and prosecuted in the ICC.[60]

The *Lubanga* case also demonstrated the efforts of gender justice actors inside and outside the Court to address the gaps around sexual violence in the charges. These efforts sometimes met resistance, including sharp critiques of Judge Odio Benito's judgment,[61] but also some important lesson drawing and revision. For example, Prosecutor Fatou Bensouda has stated that in the *Lubanga* case, her Office 'explained the gender dimension of the crime of enlisting and conscripting children under the age of 15. It took note, however, of the reactions of civil society's preference for these aspects to be explicitly charged'.[62] Reflecting that lesson, the Office of the Prosecutor became more consistent in including charges for sexual and gender-based crimes in subsequent cases. For example, in 2006, approximately one-third of cases that had been brought before the Court included charges for sexual and gender-based crimes, whereas by 2016, that figure had climbed to approximately 70 per cent.

One key area where the Office of the Prosecutor has developed its strategy is the prosecution of sexual violence crimes against child soldiers by other soldiers within the same military force. Rather than seeking to address this conduct through the war crimes of 'conscripting', 'enlisting' or 'using' child soldiers as the Prosecution tried to do in the *Lubanga* case, the Prosecution has instead sought to prosecute this conduct using the war crimes of rape and sexual slavery. This new strategy was introduced for the first time in 2014 in the *Ntaganda* case, under the leadership of Prosecutor Bensouda.[63] It is a bold approach, as it challenges traditional conceptions of war crimes as crimes committed against those on the 'other side' of the conflict.[64] The endorsement of this interpretation of Statute by the Appeals Chamber in 2017[65] reflected well on the Prosecution's

---

60 See, e.g., Women's Initiatives for Gender Justice (2012) *Gender Report Card on the International Criminal Court* 158–59; Smith, above n. 43; Hayes, above n. 11.

61 For examples, see Chappell, above n. 11, pp. 115–16.

62 F. Bensouda, 'Gender Justice and the ICC' (2014) 16(4) *International Feminist Journal of Politics* 538, 540.

63 See Chappell, above n. 11, p. 116.

64 R. Grey, 'Prosecuting Sexual Violence against Child Soldiers: The Ntaganda Case at the International Criminal Court' (2014) 16(4) *International Feminist Journal of Politics* 601; R. Grey, 'Protecting Child Soldiers from Sexual Violence by Members of the Same Military Force: A Re-Conceptualisation of International Humanitarian Law?' (2015) April *International Crimes Database* <http://www.internationalcrimesdatabase.org/upload/documents/20150423T113341-Grey%20ICD%20Brief_AB_FINAL.pdf> accessed 23.10.2015.

65 ICC, *Ntaganda*, Judgment on the appeal of Mr Ntaganda against the 'Second decision on the Defence's challenge to the jurisdiction of the Court in respect of Counts 6 and 9', ICC-01/04-02/06-1962, 15 June 2017.

efforts to respond to the lessons learned in the *Lubanga* case and change its charging practices in this respect.

These case studies discussed above indicate that the ICC Office of the Prosecutor is indeed committed to addressing impunity for sexual and gender-based crimes and to learning lessons from the early cases before the Court. While it may take some time before these lessons translate into conviction rates which accurately reflect the prevalence of sexual and gender-based crimes in contemporary armed conflicts, it is clear that the increasing number of sexual and gender-based crimes at the ICC puts the Court in a stronger position to hold the perpetrators to account and deliver justice to the victims.

Of course, including charges for sexual and gender-based charges does not on its own guarantee accountability: the Prosecution must also bring sufficient evidence to prove that these crimes happened, and that the person on trial is criminally responsible. To date, the ICC Office of the Prosecutor has been largely unsuccessful in holding perpetrators in this respect.

By 1 July 2017, the Court had issued final judgments in four cases, the first three concerning conflicts in the DRC in 2002–2003, a conflict where conflict-related sexual violence was endemic, and the fourth in relation to the destruction of cultural property in Mali in 2012. A conviction on the grounds of rape, murder and pillage had also been issued in the *Bemba* case, concerning the conflict in the Central African Republic (CAR) in 2002–2003. However, as noted in the introduction to this chapter, that conviction was reserved.[66]

A close analysis of Court documents, as well as secondary sources such as reports published by Women's Initiatives for Gender Justice, shows that charges for sexual and gender-based crimes have in general been less successful than charges for other crimes at every stage of the proceedings.[67] The fall-off in charges is not uncommon across all categories of crimes, given that the burden of proof increases at each stage of criminal proceedings. However, at the ICC, charges for sexual and gender-based crimes have been particularly vulnerable compared to other crimes.

The reasons for this drop-off in charges for sexual and gender-based crimes are complex, but a close reading of the cases highlights three recurring problems: insufficient evidence advanced by the Prosecutor to support the charges; a failure by the Prosecution to address of all of the elements of the crimes; and a narrow and sometimes confusing interpretation of the charges by the Chambers.[68] In terms of evidentiary weaknesses, the most significant problems have been in the Prosecution's evidence linking the accused to the crimes. While the Prosecution has generally succeeded in proving that sexual

---

66 See above n. 7.

67 Grey, above n. 15, 229–230; Chappell, above n. 11, Chapter Four.

68 Grey, above n. 11, pp. 230–36.

and gender-based crimes were committed, it has often failed to establish that the accused person was liable for those crimes.[69]

Importantly, proving liability has not only been difficult in relation to sexual and gender-based crimes; this problem has arisen in relation to a broad spectrum of charges before the Court. However, in certain cases, including the *Katanga* case, the issue arose specifically in relation to sexual and gender violence crimes. This case focused on an attack on a village in Ituri, DRC, during an ethnic conflict in 2003. The Prosecution alleged that the village was attacked by militias aligned with the Lendu and Ngiti ethnic groups, while the civilian inhabitants of the village, and the soldiers camped there, were aligned with the Hema ethnic group. Katanga, the alleged leader of one of militias that attacked the village, was charged for a broad range of war crimes and crimes against humanity, including rape and sexual slavery.

The Trial Chamber unanimously found that Katanga was not responsible for any of the crimes as indirect co-perpetrator, as the Prosecution alleged. The majority of the Chamber then re-characterised the facts, in order to consider whether Katanga could be convicted for contributing to the commission of the crimes.[70] It found that Katanga was responsible under that mode of liability for murder, directing attacks against a civilian population, destruction of property and pillage. However, it found that Katanga was *not* responsible under that mode of liability for rape and sexual slavery as those crimes were not part of the 'common purpose' of the group – which the Chamber defined as to 'wipe out' the Hema civilians and soldiers in the village.[71]

Outside the Court, the judgment was widely criticised. For example, Brigid Inder, (then) Executive Director of Women's Initiatives for Gender Justice and Gender Advisor to the ICC Prosecutor, stated 'what we see in this judgment, emblematic of so many cases, is a perhaps subconscious but clear bias requiring sexual violence to be a more explicit component of a common plan, than is expected for any other category of crimes'.[72] Kelly Askin, Senior Legal Officer for Open Society, observed that:

> While most judges [in international criminal tribunals] seem to accept that leaders and others can be convicted of crimes such as killings, torture and pillage even when they are far from the crime scenes, there is great reluctance to hold individuals accountable

---

69 Women's Initiatives for Gender Justice, *Modes of Liability: A Review of the International Criminal Court's Current Jurisprudence and Practice – Expert Paper November 2013*, The Hague 2013.

70 Rome Statute, art 25(3)(d).

71 ICC, 'Summary of Trial Chamber II's Judgment of 7 March 2014, pursuant to article 74 of the Statute in the case of The Prosecutor v. Germain Katanga', [75]–[76].

72 B. Inder, 'Prosecuting Sexual Violence in Conflict – Challenges and Lessons Learned: A critique of the Katanga Judgment' (2014) June 11 Global Summit to End Sexual Violence in Conflict <http://iccwomen.org/documents/Global-Summit-Speech.pdf> accessed 14.08.2018.

> for sex crimes unless they are the physical perpetrators, they were present when crimes were committed, or they can be linked to evidence encouraging the crimes. It's an appalling double standard, and perpetuates the view that rape is a by-product of war, instead of an instrument of warfare. (It can [be] and usually is both, not just the former).[73]

Professor Carsten Stahn also noted the seeming gender injustice of this decision. As he pointed out in relation to this case, the judges' reasoning 'implies that physical destruction (e.g. pillaging) carried greater weight in the purpose than the destruction of community structures through acts of sexual or gender-based violence. This distinction raises doubts whether sexual or gender-based crimes were held to a separate and unjustifiably higher standard'.[74] While Prosecutor Bensouda lodged an appeal against Katanga's acquittals for rape and sexual slavery, she later withdrew this appeal after the Defence withdrew its appeal against the conviction and affirmed that it would not appeal the sentence either, and Katanga expressed his regret for his conduct.[75] The Prosecutor's decision sparked criticism from Women's Initiatives and victims' groups.[76] In the view of Women's Initiatives, by not pursuing the appeal, the Prosecution was contributing to 'a step backwards in the body of jurisprudence on sexual violence'.[77]

As the critiques of the judgment highlight, the Trial Chamber's reasoning in *Katanga* echoed an old narrative of sexual violence crimes as opportunistic crimes, which are incidental to the 'main' face of the conflict. At times, allusions to this narrative could also be seen in the Prosecution's case. For example, in his opening statements, Prosecutor Moreno Ocampo stated that Katanga's troops raped the women of Bogoro *after* the attack had 'achieved its goal' – suggesting that the sexual violence crimes were incidental to, rather than closely linked to, the aims of the attack.[78] The idea that sexual and gender-based crimes are necessarily opportunistic crimes committed by unruly soldiers, rather than crimes committed as part of an attack, has a long history. As SáCouto and Cleary

---

73 K. Askin, 'Katanga Judgment Underlines Need for Stronger ICC Focus on Sexual Violence' *Open Society Foundations*, 11.03.2014 <https://www.opensocietyfoundations.org/voices/katanga-judgment-underlines-need-stronger-icc-focus-sexual-violence> accessed 20.03.2014.

74 Stahn, above n. 13, p. 821.

75 ICC, *Katanga*, Notice of Discontinuance of the Prosecution's Appeal against the Article 74 Judgment of Conviction of Trial Chamber I dated 7 March 2014 in relation to Germain Katanga, ICC-01/04-01/07-3498, 25 June 2014.

76 Women's Initiatives for Gender Justice, 'Statement of the Women's Initiatives for Gender Justice: Appeals Withdrawn by Prosecution and Defence in The Prosecutor vs. Germain Katanga', 26 June 2014, *Women's Initiatives for Gender Justice* <http://www.iccwomen.org/documents/Katanga-Appeals-Statement.pdf> accessed14.07.2018; J. Easterday, 'Lack of appeal in Katanga is unjust, Victims lawyers Say' *International Justice Monitor*, 14.07.2014 <http://www.ijmonitor.org/2014/07/lack-of-appeal-in-katanga-is-unjust-victims-lawyers-say/> accessed 30.07.2014.

77 Women's Initiatives for Gender Justice, above n. 76.

78 ICC, *Katanga and Ngudjolo*, Transcript, ICC-01/04-01/07-T-80-ENG, 24 November 2009, 25.

have argued, this idea found expression in several cases in the *ad hoc* tribunals for the former Yugoslavia and Rwanda, creating impunity gaps for sexual and gender-based crimes.[79]

In addition to struggling to prove liability for sexual and gender-based crimes in several cases, the Prosecution also at times failed to bring sufficient evidence of the crimes themselves. For example, in the *Mbarushimana* case, concerning the conflict in the DRC, the Prosecution relied exclusively on hearsay evidence to substantiate several allegations of rape. Hearsay evidence refers to evidence related by someone who did not personally witness the alleged facts, but heard those facts from another person. Decisions of the ICC and other international criminal tribunals consistently indicate that the weight of hearsay evidence is generally considered to be low.[80] Despite those decisions, in *Mbarushimana*, one of the Prosecution's allegations of rape was based solely on hearsay evidence contained in a Human Rights Watch report and another was based solely on the statement of a witness who claimed to have heard soldiers bragging about raping women during a previous attack. The Pre-Trial Chamber held that this evidence was not sufficiently strong to confirm the charges.[81] Thus, due to evidentiary problems, compounded by historically determined ideas about the nature of sexual and gender-based crimes, charges for sexual and gender-based crimes have tended to be more vulnerable than other charges in ICC proceedings.

Recently, however, this pattern has begun to shift. In 2014, for the first time in the ICC's history, the Pre-Trial Chamber confirmed all charges of sexual and gender-based crimes alleged by the Office of the Prosecutor. There were 10 charges of sexual and gender violence crimes in total: six in the *Ntaganda* case; two in the *Laurent Gbagbo* case; and two in the *Blé Goudé* case.[82] More recently, in March 2016, the Pre-Trial Chamber confirmed 70 charges against Dominic Ongwen, an alleged LRA militia leader from Uganda, including, rape, torture, sexual slavery, enslavement, forced marriage (as an inhumane act)

---

79 S. SÁCouto and K. Cleary, 'The Importance of Effective Investigation of Sexual Violence and Gender Based Crimes at the International Criminal Court' (2009) 17(2) *American University Journal of Gender, Social Policy & the Law* 337, 352–56. See also P.V. Sellers, 'Gender Strategy is Not Luxury for International Courts' (2009) 17(2) *American University Journal of Gender, Social Policy & the Law* 301, p. 316.

80 R. Cryer et al., *An Introduction to International Criminal Law and Procedure*, 3rd edition, Cambridge University Press 2014, 469; ICC, *Lubanga*, Decision on the confirmation of charges, ICC-01/04-01/06-803-tEN, 29 January 2007, [106]; ICC, *Bemba*, Decision Pursuant to Article 61(7)(a) and (b) of the Rome Statute on the Charges of the Prosecutor Against Jean-Pierre Bemba Gombo, ICC-01/05-01/08-424, 15 June 2009, [47]–[51]; *Katanga and Ngudjolo*, Decision on the confirmation of charges, ICC-01/04-01/07-717, 30 September 2008, [117]–[120]; [137].

81 ICC, *Mbarushimana*, Decision on the confirmation of charges, ICC-01/04-01/10-465-Red, 16 December 2011, [194], [220]–[221].

82 R. Grey, 'The ICC's First 'Forced Pregnancy' Case in Historical Perspective' (2017) 15(5) *Journal of International Criminal Justice* 905–30.

and forced pregnancy – a crime which has never before been prosecuted by an international court.[83]

These more recent positive outcomes demonstrate that both the Office of the Prosecutor and judges are learning some valuable lessons from past experiences and are developing the skills to successfully investigate, prosecute and adjudicate sexual and gender violence crimes. Having said that, the path of progress has not been smooth. A major backward step was the 2018 decision of the Appeal Chamber reversing the conviction of Jean-Pierre Bemba Gombo. At trial, an all-female Bench found Bemba guilty of two crimes against humanity (murder and rape) and three war crimes (murder, rape and pillage), thus marking the first conviction of sexual violence crimes at the ICC. Bemba was convicted not as a direct perpetrator of these crimes, but for *failing* to use his powers prevent and repress the crimes, pursuant to the doctrine of 'command responsibility'. As the analysis of former International Criminal Tribunal for the Former Yugoslavia (ICTY) Prosecutor Michelle Jarvis and the Women's Initiatives for Gender Justice have demonstrated, recognition of command responsibility for sexual crimes has been a major challenge to successful prosecution of sexual and gender violence crimes not only at the ICC but also other international criminal tribunals.[84] The *Bemba* appeal judgment, which focused primarily on the Trial Chamber's application of that mode of liability, shows that this continues to a challenge in the ICC.

Importantly, these quantitative metrics (such as the number of charges for sexual and gender-based crimes that have been brought, and the number that have been established) are only one way to measure the ICC's progress; it is also relevant to consider qualitative issues, such as *whose* experiences of sexual and gender-based crimes have been recognised and *how* these crimes have been understood in cases before the Court. The ICC's performance on these qualitative issues has been improving, as detailed below.

4. CAPTURING DIVERSE EXPERIENCES OF SEXUAL AND GENDER-BASED CRIMES

The charges of sexual and gender-based violence before the ICC reflect the diverse forms of sexual violence experienced in conflict situations, including

83 ICC, *Ongwen*, Decision on the confirmation of charges against Dominic Ongwen, ICC-02/04-01/15-422-Red, 23 March 2016.

84 M. Jarvis and E. Martin Salgado 'Future Challenges to Prosecuting Sexual Violence under International Law: Insights from ICTY Practice' in A.-M. de Brouwer, C. Ku, R. Romkens and L. van den Herik (eds.), *Sexual Violence as an International Crime: Interdisciplinary Approaches*, Intersentia 2013, pp. 101–22; Women's Initiatives for Gender Justice, *Modes of Liability: A Review of the International Criminal Court's Current Jurisprudence and Practice – Expert Paper November 2013*, The Hague 2013.

rape, sexual slavery, cutting or mutilating breasts and genitals, forcing victims to watch or participate in the rape of family members, and cutting open the bellies of pregnant women. This ensures that as sexual and gender-based crimes have become more visible at the ICC, a more nuanced picture of sexual and gender-based crimes has emerged.

Importantly, this picture has increasingly included sexual and gender-based crimes against men and boys, which have historically been largely left unrecognised in international criminal tribunals.[85] Initially, male experiences of sexual and gender-based crimes were not so obvious in cases before the ICC. In the *Lubanga* case, the Prosecution made some references to boy soldiers being forced to rape civilians and bring girls to the camps for the commanders to use as sexual slaves. However, this gender-specific treatment of boy soldiers received relatively little attention in the Prosecution's submissions compared to the gender-specific treatment of girl soldiers, and is not mentioned once in the trial judgment or appeal judgment.[86]

Male experiences of sexual and gender-based crimes against men and boys were also largely invisible in the *Katanga & Ngudjolo* case, which concerned an attack on a village in Ituri, DRC. The Prosecution charged Katanga and Ngudjolo for the rape and sexual and enslavement of women and girls during and after this attack, but did not bring any charges of sexual violence against men. This became noticable later in the trial, when one of the Prosecution witnesses referred to sexual violence crimes against both men and women in Bogoro, including the amputation of male sexual organs. However, the Prosecution did not probe the witness about other sexual violence crimes against men, and it did not refer to the mutilation of men's sexual organs in its closing statements.[87]

Gradually, sexual and gender-based crimes against men and boys have become more visible at the ICC. For example in *Mbarushimana* and *Ntaganda* cases, both from the situation in the DRC, the Prosecution brought charges for the rape of men, the mutilation of men's genitals, and forced sexual acts between male and female victims. In the *Bemba* case, from the situation in the Central African Republic, the Prosecution brought charges for men being raped, forced to undress in public, and being forced to watch the rape of family members. In the *Ahmad Harun & Ali Kushayb* and *Hussein* cases, the Prosecution brought charges for the massacre of men from the Fur ethnic group in Darfur. In *Kenyatta* case, the Prosecution brought charges to capture men's experiences of genital mutilation and forced circumcision during the post-election violence in Kenya. All of these cases also included charges for sexual and gender-based crimes

85 Sivakumaran, above n. 2; D.A. Lewis, 'Unrecognized Victims: Sexual Violence Against Men in Conflict Settings Under International Law' (2009) 27(1) *Wisconsin International Law Journal* 1.

86 See Grey, above n. 15, pp. 123–25.

87 See ibid., p. 141.

against women and girls.[88] By addressing a wide range of sexual and gender-based crimes against men and women, the ICC can better recognise the diverse experiences of victims. This recognition of the victims' experiences is integral to the ICC's truth-telling function, and is critical to ensuring that the Court realises its full potential as a tool of holding to account perpetrators of gender injustices.

In addition to asking whether sexual and gender-based crimes have been charged, and whose experiences have been recognised, it is important to ask how sexual and gender-based crimes have been 'understood and represented' in the ICC.[89] For example, do trial records recognise the fact that these crimes may be committed opportunistically, while also being used as a weapon of war? What other explanations are offered for sexual and gender-based crimes? Answering this question requires an analysis of how the crimes have been charged, or legally characterised, by the ICC Prosecutor.

One of the interesting features of the ICC's charging history has been the use of what can be called a 'blended' charging strategy. This is in line with the goals of the Women's Caucus involved in the Rome Statute negotiations, who intended that that sexual and gender violence crimes are seen as offences against victims in their own right, while also recognising that these crimes may be committed to persecute, punish and destroy whole communities.[90] As leading Women's Caucus advocate Rhonda Copelon explained:

> One [aim of the Women's Caucus] was to codify explicitly a range of serious sexual violence crimes in order to ensure that they are always on the checklist and always understood as crimes in themselves. The second [aim] was to incorporate, as a principle, what had developed in the customary law and jurisprudence of the tribunals, that sexual violence must be seen as part of, and encompassed by, other recognised egregious forms of violence, such as torture, enslavement, genocide, and inhumane treatment.[91]

In the early years of ICC practice, in most cases, the Prosecution has followed this blended approach in its charging strategy. It has used evidence of sexual violence to support charges of rape and sexual slavery, while also using this evidence to support charges such as persecution, torture, mutilation, outrages on personal dignity, cruel or inhumane treatment and genocide. This is critically important to recognising the multiple uses of sexual and gender-based violence in conflict situations.

Significantly, in terms of recognition, the crime against humanity of persecution on the grounds of gender remains largely invisible in cases before

88 See ibid., pp. 220–21.

89 D. Buss, 'The Curious Visibility of Wartime Rape: Gender and Ethnicity in International Criminal Law' (2007) 25 *Windsor Yearbook of Access to Justice* 3, 22.

90 Chappell, above n. 11, pp. 94–95, 101; Grey, above n. 15, pp. 92–93, 222–26.

91 Copelon, above n. 1, p. 234.

the Court. This crime, which was not included in previous statutes or charters of international criminal tribunals, was one of the most significant gender justice provisions built into the Rome Statute.[92] In 2010, the Prosecution included a charge of gender persecution in its application for the arrest of Callixte Mbarushimana, the Executive Secretary of a militia in the DRC.[93] However, the Prosecution subsequently changed this to persecution on political grounds.[94] Since then, no charges for persecution on the grounds of gender have been confirmed (although as noted above, this may change with the *Al Hassan* case). Rather, where persecution has been charged, it has been on political, ethnic, national or religious grounds.

The absence of charges for persecution on gender grounds may simply reflect evidentiary challenges, such as a lack of statements, records or other evidence indicating that the victims were targeted because of their gender, or a preference for focusing on those traits that are common to the victims (such as their ethnicity or their perceived political affiliation) rather than distinctions within the targeted group. However, when considering the absence of charges for 'gender persecution' to date, it may also be relevant that this crime was a hotly contested issue during Rome Statute negotiations. While a majority of State delegations supported the inclusion of this crime, the Vatican and several Arab League States were strongly opposed. Their chief concern was that persecution on the grounds of 'gender' could include persecution on the grounds of sexual orientation. There was also some debate about whether the term 'gender' could be translated into some languages.[95] According to Cate Steains, a member of the Australian delegation at Rome Statute negotiations, the fact that gender persecution was not recognised in the statutes of the *ad hoc* tribunals for the former Yugoslavia and Rwanda fuelled the perception that 'the international community continue[s] to regard gender-based persecution as less prevalent – or less important – than persecution on other grounds'.[96] While it is difficult to determine emphatically, the legacy of these negotiation debates may have

---

92 V. Oosterveld, 'Prosecuting Gender-Based Persecution as an International Crime' in A.-M. de Brouwer *et al.* (eds.), *Sexual Violence as an International Crime: Interdisciplinary Approaches*, Intersentia 2013, p. 57.

93 ICC, *Situation in the Democratic Republic of Congo*, Prosecution's Application under Article 58, ICC-01/04-01/10-11-Red2, 20 August 2010, Count 11, [7], [11], [97].

94 ICC, *Mbarushimana*, Prosecution's document containing the charges, ICC-01/04-01/10-330-AnxA-Red, 3 August 2011, Count 13.

95 V. Oosterveld, 'The Definition of Gender in the Rome Statute of the International Criminal Court: A Step Forward or Back for International Criminal Justice' (2005) 18 *Harvard Human Rights Journal* 55, 63; Oosterveld, above n. 92, p. 66; V. Oosterveld, 'Constructive Ambiguity and the Meaning of 'Gender' for the International Criminal Court' (2014) 16(4) *International Feminist Journal of Politics* 563, p. 566.

96 C. Steains, 'Gender Issues' in R.S. Lee (ed.), *The International Criminal Court: The Making of the Rome Statute*, Kluwer Law International 1999, p. 370.

contributed to a sense within the Office of the Prosecutor that persecution on the grounds of gender is a 'risky' charge to pursue and so to be avoided in a charging strategy.

Another possible explanation for the lack of gender persecution charges is the 'newness' of this crime.[97] The fact that this crime did not exist in any instruments of international criminal law prior to the Rome Statute means there is no jurisprudence to guide the ICC's interpretation of this crime, making it more difficult for the Office of the Prosecutor to use this provision. However, there are signs that the Office may be ready to take on this challenge. In its 2014 Policy Paper on Sexual and Gender-Based Crimes (the 'Gender Policy'), the Office of the Prosecutor signalled a commitment to using the crime of gender persecution 'to the fullest extent possible'.[98] This is positive news for those looking to the Court to advance gender justice.

In analysing how sexual and gender-based crimes have been understood in the ICC, it is also important to consider how these crimes have been explained in court records. In previous tribunals, there has been almost no understanding of the way that sexual and gender-based crimes take place in a social and political context and are linked to gender hierarchies and gender norms.[99] By contrast, the ICC Office of the Prosecutor has demonstrated an awareness of these contextual factors when prosecuting sexual and gender-based crimes. For example, in the aforementioned *Bemba* case, which concerned crimes allegedly committed during the 2003 armed conflict in the CAR, the Prosecution described sexual violence crimes as 'gender crimes', explaining that '[w]omen were raped systematically to assert dominance and to shatter their resistance. Men were raped in public to destroy their capacity to lead and protect'.[100] In the *Kenyatta* case, which focused on the 2007–2008 post-election violence in Kenya, the Prosecution explained that '[w]omen who were gang-raped were violated, humiliated, desecrated so as to lower their status and deprive them of their dignity and equality as human beings and, for some of them, to reduce their value as wives or potential wives'.[101]

---

97 On newness and the ICC, see L. Chappell, "New,' 'Old,' and 'Nested' Institutions and Gender Justice Outcomes: A View from the International Criminal Court' (2014) 10(4) *Politics & Gender* 572.

98 ICC Office of the Prosecutor 2014, above n. 8, [67].

99 R. Copelon, 'Surfacing Gender: Re-engraving Crimes Against Women in Humanitarian Law' (1994) 5 *Hastings Women's Law Journal* 243; Buss, above n. 89; D. Buss, 'Sexual Violence, Ethnicity, and Intersectionality in International Criminal Law' in E. Grabham *et al.* (eds.), *Intersectionality and Beyond: Law, Power and the Politics of Location*, Routledge 2009; C.S. Mibenge, *Sex and International Tribunal: The Erasure of Gender from the War Narrative*, University of Pennsylvania Press 2013.

100 ICC, *Bemba*, Transcript, ICC-01/05-01/08-T-364-ENG, 12 November 2014, 21–22.

101 *The Prosecutor v. Francis Kirimi Muthaura, Uhuru Muigai Kenyatta and Mohammed Hussein Ali*, Transcript, ICC-01/09-02/11-T-5-Red-ENG, Pre-Trial Chamber II, 22 September 2011, 84.

Such explanations have helped to make visible the connection between sexual and gender-based violence in conflict situations and gender norms in everyday life – a connection which many feminist scholars argue should be made explicit.[102] It can be expected that this contextualised approach will continue in line with the Office of the Prosecutor's 2014 Gender Policy, which states that the Office 'will apply a gender analysis to all of the crimes within its jurisdiction',[103] meaning it will consider 'whether, and in what ways, crimes, including sexual and gender-based crimes, are related to gender norms and inequalities'.[104]

Whereas the Prosecution has demonstrated a growing awareness of the gender aspects of crimes, and has taken steps to embed this in practice in its 2014 Gender Policy, the same cannot be said of all members of the judiciary. ICC judges have at times struggled to understand the gravity and the nature of sexual and gender-based crimes. This has been most apparent in relation to the crime against humanity of 'sexual violence', which was codified for the first time in the Rome Statute. The relevant provision refers to 'rape, sexual slavery, enforced prostitution, forced pregnancy, enforced sterilization, or *any other form or sexual violence of a comparable gravity*' as crimes against humanity.

Confusion over the meaning of this crime first arose in the *Bemba* case, where Prosecution brought charges for a wide range of sexual and gender-based crimes, including a charge of 'sexual violence' as a crime against humanity. The charge was based on evidence that soldiers under the command of the accused forced civilian men and women to undress in public, in order to humiliate them.[105] While the Chamber was satisfied that the conduct took place, it reasoned that forcing people to undress in public was not sufficiently grave to constitute 'sexual violence' as a crime against humanity under the Rome Statute.[106] This interpretation of the Statute was at odds with the intention of the drafters, who had anticipated that the crime of 'any other form of sexual violence' would include forced nudity.[107] It also sat uncomfortably with existing jurisprudence on forced nudity such as the 1998 *Akayesu* case, in which the International Criminal Tribunal for Rwanda held that sexual violence, including rape and

102 See, e.g., Copelon, above n. 99; K. Grewal, 'Rape in Conflict, Rape in Peace: Questioning the Revolutionary Potential of International Criminal Justice for Women's Human Rights' (2010) 33 *The Australian Feminist Law Journal* 57; C. MacKinnon, 'Creating International Law: Gender as Leading Edge' (2013) 36(1) *Harvard Journal of Law & Gender* 105.

103 ICC Office of the Prosecutor 2014, above n. 8, [20].

104 ibid., p. 3.

105 ICC, *Bemba*, Prosecutor's Submission on Further Information and Materials, ICC-01/05-01/08-29-Red, 27 May 2008, [69(c)(v)]; Amnesty International, *Central African Republic: Five months of war against women*, London 2004, pp. 5, 9.

106 ICC, *Bemba*, Decision on the Prosecutor's Application for a Warrant of Arrest against Jean-Pierre Bemba Gombo, ICC-01/05-01/08-14-tENG, 10 June 2008, [40].

107 V. Oosterveld, 'Gender-Sensitive Justice and the International Criminal Tribunal for Rwanda: Lessons Learned for the International Criminal Court' (2005) 12(1) *New England Journal of International and Comparative Law* 119, 124.

forced nudity, could constitute crimes of genocide, crimes against humanity and war crimes under the tribunal's statute.[108]

The greatest confusion around the new crime of 'sexual violence' came in the *Kenyatta* case, which concerns crimes allegedly committed during the 2007–2008 post-election violence in Kenya. The Prosecution brought a charge of 'sexual violence' based on evidence that supporters of one political party had targeted men from an ethnic group aligned with the opposing political party, and subjected them to genital mutilation. For example, one witness recalled that the attackers 'grabbed one man, about 30 years old, and told him to remove his pants ... they forcibly removed his pants. One person was holding his penis, and another one was cutting his foreskin with a piece of a broken Fanta bottle'.[109] The Pre-Trial Chamber held that these acts were not sexual in nature, and should instead be charged as 'inhumane acts'.[110] Women's Initiatives described the Pre-Trial Chamber's refusal to recognise the sexual nature of these acts as a 'worrying move', and criticised the Prosecution for 'merely stating that the acts were of a sexual nature, without elaborating on this point'.[111]

At the confirmation of charges stage, the Prosecution provided a fuller explanation of the charges. It argued that the attacks on the men's genitals 'weren't just attacks on men's sexual organs as such but were intended as attacks on men's identities as men within their society and were designed to destroy their masculinity', and continued that 'men who were castrated were deprived of their manhood and debased in front of their families'.[112] This explanation, which focused on the victims' 'identities as men within their society', echoed the definition of 'gender' in article 7(3) of the Rome Statute, which states that '"gender" refers to the two sexes, male and female, *within the context of society*' (emphasis added). However, while the Prosecution explained how the acts related to 'gender', it did not satisfy the Pre-Trial Chamber that the acts were 'sexual' as such. The Chamber ruled:

> [N]ot every act of violence which targets parts of the body commonly associated with sexuality should be considered an act of sexual violence ... the determination of whether an act is of a sexual nature is inherently a question of fact. The Chamber finds that the evidence placed before it does not establish the sexual nature of the acts of forcible circumcision and penile amputation visited upon Luo men. Instead, it appears

---

108 ICTR, *Akayesu*, Trial judgment, ICTR-96-4-T, 2 September 1998, [10A], [688]. See also Chappell, above n. 11, p. 117; Grey, above n. 11, p. 277.

109 ICC, *Muthaura et al*, Transcript, ICC-01/09-02/11-T-5-Red-ENG, Pre-Trial Chamber II, 22 September 2011, 88–89.

110 ICC, *Muthaura et al*, Decision on the Prosecutor's Application for Summonses to Appear for Francis Kirimi Muthaura, Uhuru Muigai Kenyatta and Mohammed Hussein Ali, ICC- 01/09-02/11-01, 8 March 2010, [27].

111 Women's Initiatives for Gender Justice, 'Legal Eye on the ICC: July 2011' (2011) <http://www.iccwomen.org/news/docs/LegalEye7-11/LegalEye7-11.html> accessed 14.08.2018.

112 ICC, *Muthaura et al*, Transcript, ICC-01/09-02/11-T-5-Red-ENG, 22 September 2011, 84.

> from the evidence that the acts were motivated by ethnic prejudice and intended to demonstrate cultural superiority of one tribe over the other.[113]

This decision represented a step backwards in terms of understanding sexual and gender-based crimes. In particular, the Pre-Trial Chamber's suggestion that these particular acts were 'motivated by ethnic prejudice' *instead of* constituting sexual violence seemed to be at odds with previous decisions of the ICC and other international criminal tribunals, where sexual violence, much like other crimes such as murder and torture, was regarded as a tool of ethnic persecution. The Prosecution re-opened the debate about the definition of 'sexual violence' after the case came before the Trial Chamber, by which time Fatou Bensouda has been sworn in as Prosecutor. In July 2012, Prosecutor Bensouda proposed that the Trial Chamber re-characterise the acts of genital mutilation as 'sexual violence'. In support of this proposal, the Prosecutor highlighted multiple cases and academic publications where acts of genital mutilation were described as 'sexual violence' and argued:

> The harm caused by the amputation or disfigurement of one's sexual organs is not merely physical; it also attacks the victim's sexuality. This is particularly true in patriarchal societies, where an assault on a man's sexual organs also constitutes an assault on his masculinity and identity within society. It is simply impossible to divorce the physical harm caused by forcible circumcision and penile amputation from the harm caused to the victim's sexuality. It is this latter form of harm – to the victim's sexuality – that is inherently 'of a sexual nature'.[114]

The victims' counsel agreed that the acts of genital mutilation should be characterised as 'sexual violence' and argued that in refusing to recognise the sexual nature of these acts, the Pre-Trial Chamber had 'relied on an outdated conceptualization of sexual violence; namely, that such are purely about sex and not about the complex power dynamics at play'.[115] The victims' counsel further explained that the acts had effected the victims 'physically and psychologically, including on their ability to have sexual intercourse' and their 'sense of manhood'.[116] In a disappointing outcome, the definition of 'sexual violence'

---

113 ICC, *Muthaura et al*, Decision on the Confirmation of Charges Pursuant to Article 61(7)(a) and (b) of the Rome Statute, ICC-01/09-02/11-382-Red, 23 January 2012, [265]–[266].

114 ICC, *Muthaura and Kenyatta*, Prosecution's application for notice to be given under Regulation 55(2) with respect to certain crimes charged, ICC-01/09-02/11-445, 3 July 2012, [19].

115 ICC, *Muthaura and Kenyatta*, Victims' Observations on the "Prosecution's application for notice to be given under Regulation 55(2) with respect to certain crimes charged", ICC-01/09-02/11-458, 24 July 2012, [12].

116 ICC, *Muthaura and Kenyatta*, Victims' Observations on the "Prosecution's application for notice to be given under Regulation 55(2) with respect to certain crimes charged", ICC-01/09-02/11-458, 24 July 2012, [14].

did not continue to be litigated, as the Prosecutor subsequently withdrew the charges after several key witnesses recanted their testimony or were found to have accepted bribes, and Kenya refused to provide evidence necessary to the Prosecution case.[117]

In both the *Bemba* and the *Kenyatta* case, the alleged acts of 'sexual violence' were committed primarily, if not exclusively, against men. The Chamber's refusal to recognise the gravity and the sexual nature of these acts demonstrates that, as with other international criminal tribunals, there is a still a long way to go to recognise the complexities of sexual and gender-based violence and undo stereotypes about the gender of the victims and perpetrators of these crimes.[118] As the above indicates, the Office of the Prosecutor is taking steps to recognise a diverse range of sexual and gender-based crimes and ensure that these crimes are properly understood in cases before the Court. It is hoped that the setback in the *Bemba* case will only make the Office more determined to ensure that sexual and gender-based crimes are meticulously investigated and charged based on clear and consistent case theory – especially in terms of modes of liability – in future. The judicial arm of the Court, by contrast, has been slow to present a nuanced and consistent understanding of these crimes.

5. CONCLUSION

In the initial period of ICC operations, recognition of gender justice has been partial and incomplete. Looking at the prosecution record of the Court, there is evidence to demonstrate that the Office of the Prosecutor and the judiciary have often struggled to challenge existing gender-biased norms of international criminal law, with negative outcomes in terms of gender justice. Ongoing problems of a lack of adequate evidence, difficulties establishing liability for sexual and gender-based crimes and a confusion around the definition of new gender justice provisions has left the Court with the unenviable record of having no convictions for sexual or gender-based crimes as of July 2018.

There is some reason to hope that as the ICC moves into its next phase, it will learn lessons from its early failures and produce more favourable outcomes. The trend towards more gender-sensitive charging strategy, and an increased understanding of the types of evidence required to make these charges 'stick', at least at the pre-trial stage, are significant developments.

---

117 ICC Office of the Prosecutor, *Statement of the Prosecutor of the International Criminal Court, Fatou Bensouda, on the withdrawal of charges against Mr. Uhuru Muigai Kenyatta, 5 December 2014*, The Hague 2014.

118 See Sivakumaran, above n. 2; Lewis, above n. 85; R. Grey and L. Shepherd, "Stop Rape Now?' Masculinity, Responsibility, and Conflict-related Sexual Violence' (2013) 16 *Men and Masculinities* 115.

The willingness of the Office of the Prosecutor to reflect critically on its performance in the first decade and to develop a wide ranging and tightly focused gender policy is a particularly promising development. To ensure that the ICC is better able to advance gender justice, the challenge now rests with the Office to ensure that this policy is implemented. The judiciary must also continue to reflect on its position in order to secure in practice the promise of the gender justice provisions of the Rome Statute.

REPARATIONS FOR GENDERED HARMS AT THE INTERNATIONAL CRIMINAL COURT

Towards Transformative and Gender-Just Reparations?

Olga JURASZ

1. INTRODUCTION

Reparations for harms suffered by individuals in armed conflict are an essential part of the process of transition from conflict to peace and securing post-conflict justice. Gender-sensitive reparations for women who are victims of international crimes and gross violations of human rights are an integral part of these processes and a critical element in addressing the long-term impact of armed conflict on women. Although the right to reparations is recognised in international law, the gender dimension of reparations for conflict-related harms has only fairly recently emerged as a topic of inquiry in international law.[1] For instance, the issue of reparations for victims of sexual and gender-based violence (SGBV) suffered during World War II was not addressed at the International Military Tribunals at Nuremberg or in Tokyo.[2]

In the past two decades, international law's efforts to address the long-term impact of armed conflict on women focused predominantly on attempting to close the impunity gap for conflict-related sexual violence (CRSV) through the jurisprudence of international criminal courts and tribunals. However, international criminal prosecutions of gender-based crimes have provided an important but somewhat limited avenue of redress for the victims. While international criminal tribunals such as the International Criminal Tribunal for the Former Yugoslavia (ICTY) and the International Criminal Tribunal for Rwanda (ICTR) delivered symbolic justice in many cases by holding the key perpetrators of gender-based crimes to account, they did not have the powers or jurisdiction to award reparations for the victims.[3] The jurisdictional and functional distinction between civil and criminal courts meant that in order to obtain further redress for harm suffered, the victims needed to resort to national courts to claim compensation.[4] This process brought inherent challenges, illustrated by the shortcomings in domestic legislation, different rules on the recognition of victims under domestic laws, and substantive delays in adjudication of such claims.[5] In the meantime, women living in post-conflict societies had to face the challenges of day-to-day life with the consequences of physical, psychological and economic harms suffered as a result of international crimes and gross violations of human rights.

Introduction of the reparations regime under the Rome Statute of the International Criminal Court (ICC) marked an unprecedented shift in the approach to reparations in international criminal justice, making it possible for the victims to access redress in cases which are successfully prosecuted

[1] R. Rubio-Marín (ed.), *What Happened to the Women? Gender and Reparations for Human Rights Violations*, New York: Social Sciences Research Council 2006; R. Rubio-Marín (ed.), *The Gender of Reparations. Unsettling Sexual Hierarchies While Redressing Human Rights Violations*, Cambridge University Press 2009; L. Ford, 'Sexual violence in war: women must get reparations, says head of UN Women' *The Guardian*, 11.06.2014 <http://www.theguardian.com/global-development/2014/jun/11/ending-sexual-violence-conflict-summit-reparations-un-women-mlambo-ngcuka> accessed 17.07.2016; UN Office of High Commissioner on Human Rights, 'A Guidance Note of the Secretary General: Reparations for Conflict-Related Sexual Violence' (June 2014) <http://www.unwomen.org/en/docs/2014/6/reparations-for-conflict-related-sexual-violence> accessed 17.07.2016.

[2] Y. Totani, 'Legal Responses to World War II Sexual Violence: The Japanese Experience' in E.D. Heineman (ed.), *Sexual Violence in the Conflict Zones. From the Ancient World to the Era of Human Rights*, University of Pennsylvania Press 2011, pp. 223–26.

[3] With the exception of restitution of property: Rule 105 ICTY RPE, Rule 105 ICTR RPE.

[4] Rule 106 ICTY RPE, Rule 106 ICTR RPE.

[5] For an in-depth discussion, see Gopalan, in this volume.

before the Court. This chapter analyses the right to reparation in international law through a gender lens and explores the idea of redressing conflict-related gendered harms. Analysing the ICC's decisions on reparations in *Prosecutor v. Lubanga* and in *Prosecutor v. Katanga*, the chapter explores the concept of gender-sensitive and transformative reparations in the context of the ICC. It demonstrates the importance of providing transformative reparations for victims of gendered harms with a view of subverting the existing gender inequalities and unequal power relations which are root causes of violence against women and girls both in conflict and the period of transition from conflict to sustainable peace.

2. GENDERED HARMS IN INTERNATIONAL LAW

The term 'gendered harm' relates to a harm which is inflicted upon an individual due to their gender. However, the term encompasses harms which can be experienced only by women, such as forced pregnancy or harms associated with the female reproductive system.[6] Second, while some gendered harms may not be limited to women in a biological sense, they are more likely to be experienced by women than men or may affect women disproportionately. In addition, it ought to be noted that a particular violation may be differently experienced by a woman than by a man and involve different types of harm.[7]

Feminist legal scholars have long recognised that law, both at domestic and at international level, has demonstrated a limited engagement with fully addressing the needs and experiences of women.[8] The shortcomings in legal responses to female experiences of harm are common, with domestic violence, SGBV and regulation of property ownership being only a few examples illustrating this detrimental dynamic. International law is generally perceived to be universal and impartial, yet its creation and development was informed mainly by male experiences and male assumptions, which largely marginalised the experiences of women and effectively excluded them from shaping the international legal framework.[9]

---

6 J. Conaghan, 'Gendered Harms and the Law of Tort: Remedying (Sexual) Harassment' (1996) 16(3) *Oxford Journal of Legal Studies* 407, 407–08.

7 R. Rubio-Marín, 'The Gender of Reparations in Transitional Societies' in R. Rubio-Marín (ed.), *The Gender of Reparations. Unsettling Sexual Hierarchies While Redressing Human Rights Violations*, Cambridge University Press 2009, pp. 97–99.

8 J. Conaghan, 'Law, Harm and Redress: A Feminist Perspective' (2002) 22(3) *Legal Studies* 319; F. Ní Aoláin, 'Exploring a Feminist Theory of Harm in the Context of Conflicted and Post-Conflict Societies' (2009–2010) 35 *Queen's Law Journal* 219, 220–21; C. Chinkin and H. Charlesworth, *The Boundaries of International Law. A Feminist Analysis*, Manchester University Press 2000, pp. 4–14.

9 Chinkin and Charlesworth, above n. 8, pp. 14–18.

Over the past three decades, international law has started to recognise the wide spectrum of the impact of armed conflict on women, as well as the urgent need to address this matter. Generally, efforts to address this problem focused predominantly on strengthening protection from SGBV and, to a large extent, prosecution of gender-based crimes. However, the issue of remedying gender-specific violations through reparations has remained marginalised. Despite some notable advances in fighting impunity for wartime SGBV, international law only relatively recently started to engage with the notion of gendered harms sustained during armed conflict, doing so predominantly through the lens of international criminal law. Nonetheless, the understanding of gendered harms which arises from the jurisprudence of international criminal courts and tribunals demonstrates a somewhat narrow conceptualisation of such harms sustained by women during armed conflict, often reliant on essentialist notions of female victimhood.[10] The treatment of forced marriage as a sex-only crime, to the exclusion of its non-sexual aspect, or the flawed approach towards prosecution of crimes committed against girl soldiers are illustrative in that respect.

Provision of gender-sensitive and adequate reparations for women in the aftermath of conflict relies heavily on a gender-inclusive understanding of the nature and wide spectrum of gendered harms. Therefore, a greater understanding of gendered harms is required in order to provide a basis for developing a comprehensive approach towards gender-sensitive reparations at an international level.[11]

2.1. THE TYPES OF GENDERED HARMS

Gendered harms occur as a result of social and power relations. Therefore, they need to be assessed and understood in the broader social context and with a broad understanding of the possible types of harms.[12] Such an approach to gendered harms may avoid the risk of producing an essentialist picture of a female victim who suffers only sexual harms, leaving out a range of other egregious violations to which women are subjected during conflict.[13] Gendered harms are inherently interlinked with the gender-specific impact of armed conflict on women, which often involves, but is certainly not limited to, sexual violence. Acts of SGBV

---

10 Several authors criticise the essentialist approach in international law: Chinkin and Charlesworth, above n. 8, pp. 52–56; M.A. Drumbl, '"She makes me ashamed to be a woman": The Genocide Conviction of Pauline Nyiramasuhuko' (2012–2013) 34 *Michigan Journal of International Law* 559, 581–90.

11 F. Ní Aoláin, 'Exploring a Feminist Theory of Harm in the Context of Conflicted and Post-Conflict Societies' (2009–2010) 35 *Queen's Law Journal* 219, 222–26 (noting the need for development of feminist theory of harm).

12 J. Conaghan, above n. 8, p. 322.

13 Rubio-Marín, above n. 7, p. 80; F. Ní Aoláin, above n. 11, pp. 233–34.

have profound long-term impacts on women's post-conflict lives as well as their physical and mental health. Although the severe impact of CRSV is generally recognised in international law, particularly through international humanitarian law and international criminal law, violations of women's reproductive rights (e.g. loss of reproductive capacity) are not typically included or conceptualised as distinct violations in these two bodies of law.[14] Instead, reparation programmes tend to focus on remedying harms arising from violation of the right to life, such as executions or disappearances, therefore creating a gender-biased hierarchy of harms.

While international law focuses largely on sexual violence, women's experiences of conflict include harms of a non-sexual nature, such as post-traumatic stress disorder (PTSD), forced labour, loss of housing, forced displacement and violations of economic, social and cultural rights. Sankey further emphasises a range of socio economic forms of violence experienced by women, which deprive them of the basic subsistence resulting in subsistence harms.[15] Despite their grave impact, subsistence harms, in the form of forced displacement and attacks on homes, livelihoods and basic resources, have been largely marginalised in international law. The treatment of such harms in international law has been reduced to viewing them through the lens of their material impact, without focusing on the physical, psychological, social as well as the gendered aspect of the harms. Although some subsistence harms have been recognised by the ICTY and the Special Court for Sierra Leone (SCSL), these courts focused exclusively on the material aspects of such harms.[16] While the impact on the victims was to an extent acknowledged, the courts did so in general terms, without deepening the understanding of the specific and varied aspects of the impact of subsistence harms, especially its gendered character. Reparations for gendered harm should therefore employ an understanding of harms including those of a non-sexual nature. Otherwise, the full spectrum of the impact of the violations of human rights sustained by women during armed conflict remains curtailed, which is likely to lead to incomplete and inadequate reparation awards for the victims.

2.2. A GENDER PERSPECTIVE ON THE RIGHT TO REPARATION IN INTERNATIONAL LAW

The key purpose of reparations, albeit often practically impossible, is to restore the order which was disturbed by the violation, to 'undo' the wrong and to

---

14 Rubio-Marín, above n. 7, p. 81.

15 D. Sankey, 'Gendered Experiences of Subsistence Harms: A Possible Contribution to Feminist Discourse on Gendered Harm?' (2015) 24(1) *Social & Legal Studies* 25–45.

16 *Prosecutor v. Kupreškić*, Trial Judgment, IT-95-16-T, 14 January 2000, para. 631; *Prosecutor v. Brima, Kamara, and Kanu*, Trial Judgment, SCSL-04-16-T, 20 June 2007, para. 670; *Prosecutor v. Stakić*, Appeal Judgment, IT-97-24-A, 22 March 2006, para. 277.

remedy the breach. The right to reparation for sustained harms and wrongs has been long established in international law. In the 17th century, Hugo Grotius famously declared in *De Jure Belli Ac Pacis* the underlying principle that 'every fault creates the obligation to make good the loss'.[17] The Permanent Court of International Justice (PCIJ) confirmed in the *Chorzów Factory Case* that "[i]t is a principle of international law that the breach of an engagement involves an obligation to make reparation in an adequate form. Reparation therefore is the indispensable complement of a failure to apply a convention and there is no necessity for this to be stated in the convention itself".[18] The Court also noted that:

> reparation must, as far as possible, wipe out all the consequences of the illegal act and reestablish the situation which would, in all probability, have existed if that act had not been committed. Restitution in kind, or, if this is not possible, payment of a sum corresponding to the value which a restitution in kind would bear ...[19]

Nonetheless, there has been a gradual shift towards including natural and legal persons as direct beneficiaries of reparations. This shift was particularly due to the rise in recognition of the importance of human rights and its impact on the evolution of other branches of international law, especially with regard to recognition of rights of individuals in international law.[20] The official commentary to Article 33 of the International Law Commission (ILC) Draft Articles views individuals as direct beneficiaries of reparations. It acknowledges that

> ... a State's responsibility for the breach of an obligation under a treaty concerning the protection of human rights may exist towards all the other parties to the treaty, but the individuals concerned should be regarded as the ultimate beneficiaries and in that sense as the holders of the relevant rights. Individual rights under international law may also arise outside the framework of human rights.[21]

---

17 H. Grotius, edited by S.C. Neff, *Hugo Grotius on the Law of War and Peace*, Cambridge University Press 2012, p. 252.

18 *Case Concerning the Factory at Chorzów (Germany v. Poland)*, Jurisdiction, (1927) PCIJ Series A No. 9, 21.

19 *Case Concerning the Factory at Chorzów (Germany v. Poland)*, Merits, (1928) PCIJ Series A No. 17, 47.

20 For an overview of the evolution of the status of individuals under international law see: K. Parlett, *The Individual in the International Legal System. Continuity and Change in International Law*, Cambridge University Press 2011.

21 International Law Commission, Draft Articles on Responsibility of States for Internationally Wrongful Acts. General Commentary, *Yearbook of the International Law Commission* (2001) vol. II, Part Two, 91 (Article 33, para. 3) ('ILC Draft Articles, General Commentary').

As evidenced by the decisions of the International Court of Justice as well as other sources of international law, the types of reparations in general international law focus primarily on re-establishing the *status quo ante* through mechanisms of restitution and compensation. These two categories are also reflected in the 1985 General Assembly Declaration of the Basic Principles of Justice for Victims of Crime and Abuse of Power and in the ILC Draft Articles which additionally include satisfaction (Article 37) amongst the types of reparations for international wrongs.[22] However, these two types of reparations have a limited effect in cases involving armed conflict, especially where gender-based crimes are concerned. The irreversible nature of gendered harms (particularly their reproductive aspect) as well as the level of both physical and mental pain and suffering experienced by the victims make it impossible to effectively apply the concept of *restitution in integrum* in such cases.[23]

The principles of state responsibility to make reparations for breaches of international law developed without taking into account the gendered nature of certain violations or the need to incorporate gender-sensitive reparations into the existing legal framework. Some progress in this regard has been made at the UN level by the adoption of UNSCR 1888 and UNSCR 2106, which form a part of the UN Women, Peace and Security (WPS) Agenda. Both resolutions articulate the responsibility of states to make reparations for conflict-related gender-based violence: UNSCR 1888 emphasises the need to address sexual violence in the context of justice and reparations; UNSCR 2106 stresses the importance of 'supporting survivors in accessing justice and reparations'.[24] UNSCR 2122 further recalls the right to reparations for violations of individual harms, especially in relation to international crimes committed against women and girls.[25] While the above resolutions were not adopted under Chapter VII of the UN Charter, they can be seen as important developments from the standard-setting perspective. The WPS resolutions brought the topic of reparations for gender-based violence into the realm of the UN Security Council and framed it in the context of international peace and security. As such, it not only emphasised the importance of full and effective reparations for CRSV as an essential component of a durable peace, but also paved the way for other developments at the UN level, such as

22 UNGA Resolution 40/34, Declaration of the Basic Principles of Justice for Victims of Crime and Abuse of Power, UN Doc. A/RES/40/34, 29 November 1985, Annex, paras. 8–13; Article 34 (restitution) and Article 36 (compensation) ILC Draft Articles.

23 It is further argued in this chapter that restoring the system existing before the violations took place is an inadequate form of reparation for gender-based harms sustained in armed conflict as it likely to reinforce the system of inequality and structural discrimination existing before the conflict.

24 UNSCR 1888, S/RES/1888, 30 September 2009, Preamble; UNSCR 2106, S/RES/2106, 24 June 2013, para. 21.

25 UNSCR 2122, S/RES/2122, 18 October 2013, para. 13.

the UN Secretary-General's Guidance Note on Reparations for Conflict-Related Sexual Violence (June 2014).[26]

The key modern developments in relation to reparations in international law have been advanced through international human rights law (IHRL), both in hard law (e.g. notable jurisprudence of the Inter-American Court of Human Rights) and soft law form. In 2005, the UN General Assembly adopted the most comprehensive set of guidelines on reparations to date.[27] The Basic Principles and Guidelines on the Right to a Remedy and Reparation for Victims of Gross Violations of International Human Rights Law and Serious Violations of International Humanitarian Law ('The Basic Principles') do not create legally binding international obligations but, rather, set out international standards, although themselves not legally binding, in relation to reparations for violations of international humanitarian law (IHL) and IHRL. They do so by 'identifying mechanisms, modalities, procedures and methods for the implementation of existing legal obligations under international human rights law and international humanitarian law which are complementary though different as to their norm'.[28] According to the Basic Principles, victims, defined as 'persons who individually or collectively suffered harm, including physical or mental injury, emotional suffering, economic loss or substantial impairment of their fundamental rights, through acts or omissions that constitute gross violations of international human rights law, or serious violations of international humanitarian law', are entitled to five key types of reparation: compensation, restitution, rehabilitation, satisfaction and guarantees of non-repetition.[29] However, none of the principles take particular account of the gendered harms nor engage with the concept of gender-just and transformative reparations.

Two years later, the Nairobi Declaration on Women's and Girls' Rights to a Remedy and Reparation was developed by a coalition of civil society organisations in an attempt to promote a more gender-sensitive approach to reparations and to the 2005 Basic Principles.[30] The Nairobi Declaration called

---

26 UN Office of High Commissioner on Human Rights, 'A Guidance Note of the Secretary General: Reparations for Conflict-Related Sexual Violence' (June 2014) <http://www.unwomen.org/en/docs/2014/6/reparations-for-conflict-related-sexual-violence> accessed 17.07.2016 (UNSG, Guidance Note).

27 UN Basic Principles and Guidelines on the Right to a Remedy and Reparation for Victims of Gross Violations of International Human Rights Law and Serious Violations of International Humanitarian Law, UN Doc. A/RES/60/147, adopted by the General Assembly on 16 December 2005 ('2005 Basic Principles').

28 2005 Basic Principles, Preamble.

29 ibid., Article 8.

30 Nairobi Declaration on Women's and Girls' Rights to a Remedy and Reparation ('the Nairobi Declaration') <https://www.fidh.org/IMG/pdf/NAIROBI_DECLARATIONeng.pdf> accessed 17.07.2016.

for a greater recognition of particular experiences of women and girls in the context of designing, awarding and delivering reparations. It also advanced a concept of inclusive, gender-sensitive and transformative reparations, which was further developed by the CEDAW (Convention on the Elimination of all forms of Discrimination Against Women) Committee in its General Recommendation No. 30 on women in conflict prevention, conflict and post-conflict situations.[31] The Committee commented on the right of women to prompt, adequate and effective reparations for violations of rights under the CEDAW suffered during armed conflict.[32] Importantly, the Committee stressed the obligation of parties to CEDAW not only to provide reparations which are gender-sensitive and responsive to women's needs but also emphasised the need for transformative reparation measures which would 'seek to transform the structural inequalities which led to violations of women's rights'.[33]

By emphasising the applicability of state obligations under Article 5(a) CEDAW to post-conflict reparations, the Committee broke new ground in relation to promoting gender-sensitive reparations at an international level. First, it confirmed the applicability of state obligations under CEDAW in conflict and post-conflict situations. To that end, it also emphasised the importance that states should fulfil obligations under Article 5(a) with a view to providing gender-sensitive and adequate reparations.[34] Second, the CEDAW Committee sought to remedy the existing pattern of looking at reparations through the lens of restitution, which in the case of violence against women merely reinstates the system of inequalities that enabled the gender-based violations in the first place. Furthermore, the Committee emphasised the need for reparations to be made with respect to not only gender-based violence but also violations of women's economic, social and cultural rights.[35] Finally, the Committee noted that women's active participation is crucial to the process of designing gender-sensitive reparations, which indirectly echoes the principles underpinning the UN WPS Agenda.[36]

---

31 CEDAW, General Recommendation No.30 on women in conflict prevention, conflict and post-conflict situations, UN Doc. CEDAW/C/GC/30, 18 October 2013.

32 ibid., paras. 74–79.

33 ibid., para. 79.

34 CEDAW Committee also confirmed that states are required to make 'changes to relevant laws and practices' as a part of an obligation to provide an appropriate remedy under Article 2(b) of CEDAW. CEDAW, General Recommendation No. 28 on the Core Obligations of States Parties under Article 2 of the Convention on the Elimination of All Forms of Discrimination against Women, UN Doc. CEDAW/C/GR/28, 16 December 2010, para. 32.

35 CEDAW, General Recommendation No. 30, supra 77, para. 81(g).

36 ibid., para. 81(e).

3. REPARATIONS AT THE INTERNATIONAL CRIMINAL COURT

The ICC Statute established a unique mechanism which allows the victims of international crimes subject to ICC jurisdiction to submit claims to the Court for reparations.[37] The ICC is the first international criminal court to provide such a system, as the international criminal courts and tribunals preceding it lacked jurisdiction with regard to reparations for harms arising as a consequence of the commission of international crimes.[38] The Court has jurisdiction only in relation to individuals who have allegedly committed international crimes – not states. Accordingly, the ICC reparations system does not take account of state responsibility for international crimes or gross violations of human rights and humanitarian law, even in situations where crimes are perpetrated by the Head of State and state agents and/or institutions. However, state parties to the ICC Statute are required to assist the Court with implementation of the orders for reparations, including assistance in tracing the defendant's assets as well as facilitation of searches and forfeiture proceedings.[39]

The ICC reparations regime is laid out in Article 75 and Article 79 of the ICC Statute and further explained in Rules 94 to 99 of the ICC RPE. When ordering reparations, the ICC is required to carry out an assessment into the scope and extent of the damage, loss or injury suffered by the victim.[40] On the basis of this assessment, the Court can then award individual and/or collective reparations.[41] Articles 75(1) and 75(2) allow the Court to award reparations, including restitution, compensation and rehabilitation, to victims

37 For the overview of the system of reparations at the ICC see: C. Ferstman, 'The Reparation Regime of the International Criminal Court: Practical Considerations' (2002) 15(3) *Leiden Journal of International Law* 667–86; C. McCarthy, *Reparations and Victim Support in the International Criminal Court*, Cambridge University Press 2012.

38 However, the Statutes and Rules of Procedure of the ICTY and the ICTR provided for the restitution of property or the proceeds thereof to victims. The Extraordinary Chambers in the Courts of Cambodia allow victims to take part in the proceedings and to claim reparations. Although there exist no direct provisions regarding the right to reparations in the Statute of the ECCC, the Internal Rules of the ECCC (which are based on the Cambodian Criminal Code) provide for reparations for victims: Rules 23, 100(2), 110(3), 113(1) of the Internal Rules of Extraordinary Chambers for in the Courts of Cambodia (Rev.3), as revised on 6 March 2009.

39 Articles 75(5), Article 93(1)(h) and (k), Article 109 ICC Statute; Rules 217, 218(3) and 219 ICC RPE. On the topic of domestic implementation of the provisions of the ICC Statute and the ICC orders with regard to reparations see C. Ferstman, 'The Reparation Regime of the International Criminal Court: Practical Considerations' (2002), 15(3) *Leiden Journal of International Law* 679–84; E. Kristjándóttir, 'Who is the most able and willing? Complementarity and victim reparations at the International Criminal Court' in C.M. Baillett, *Non-State Actors, Soft Law and Protective Regimes. From the Margins* (Cambridge University Press 2012) 78–82.

40 Article 75(a) ICC Statute; Rule 97 ICC RPE.

41 Rule 97(1) ICC RPE.

of international crimes.[42] Although the provisions refer to three types of reparations, the Court may award other remedies, as per Rule 91(1)(f) of the ICC RPE. The Court can order reparations either directly against the convicted person (Article 75(2)) or through the Trust Fund for Victims (TFV) (Article 79(2)). The TFV was established by the Assembly of the Parties for the benefit of the victims of international crimes and their families. The TFV, which is sponsored through voluntary donations from states, plays a dual role.

First, the TFV is responsible for disbursement of the Court-awarded reparations. As a part of this mandate, the TFV acts as a depository of assets seized through fines and forfeitures which form the basis for victims' reparations, especially where at the time of the reparations order it is impossible or impracticable to make individual awards directly to each victim.[43] Furthermore, where large numbers of victims are concerned and a collective reparations award is made, the TFV is tasked with implementation of the Court order.[44] Second, the TVF plays a humanitarian role as an agency providing physical, psychological and material support to the victims, their families and communities through assistance programmes. However, unlike with reparations, the 'assistance mandate' of the TFV is not linked to the conviction of the accused and should be viewed as separate from the TFV's role in assisting the Court with the implementation of the reparation orders.[45]

3.1. *PROSECUTOR v. LUBANGA* (REPARATIONS)

On 3 March 2015, the ICC Appeals Chamber, in its first judgment to award reparations, laid down certain principles regarding their award in *Prosecutor v. Lubanga*. The judgment, which gives effect to the Court's obligation under Article 75(1) of the ICC Statute, reversed the earlier decision of the ICC Trial Chamber with regard to reparations and clarified several crucial concepts.

The Appeals Chamber emphasised that the obligation to repair is directly linked to individual criminal responsibility under the ICC Statute and, as such, lies with the convicted person.[46] In this context, destitution of the accused was rendered irrelevant and more emphasis was placed on the notion of the attribution

42 Article 75(1) and 75(2) ICC Statute.

43 Rule 98(2) ICC RPE.

44 Rule 98(3) ICC RPE.

45 This was confirmed by the ICC Appeals Chamber in *Situation in the Democratic Republic of the Congo: Prosecutor v. Thomas Lubanga Dyilo* (Judgment on the appeals against the 'Decision establishing principles and procedures to be applied to reparations' of 7 August 2012 with AMENDED order for reparations (Annex A) and public annexes 1 and 2), ICC-01/04-01/06-3129 (3 March 2015), para. 182 ('*Lubanga* Reparations Judgment' (3 March 2015)).

46 *Lubanga* Reparations Judgment (3 March 2015), para. 99.

of guilt and responsibility (both for the criminal acts and consequences of them) to the convicted person.[47] This approach reversed the position of the Trial Chamber which failed to make awards of reparations directly against Lubanga, based on his indigence. The Appeals Chamber reasoned that indigence is not an obstacle to award of reparations against the convicted person and that, based on the principle of accountability, the ICC needs to make a reparations order against the convicted person even if reparations are ordered through a TFV.[48] However, while the presented reasoning is correct in principle, its practical aspect is highly questionable. The alleged indigence of the individual will inherently have an impact on reparations for individuals who suffered harms as a result of international crimes committed by the convicted person. While the TFV can supply some funds for reparations, the assets of the convicted person contribute towards the overall value of the reparation funds awarded by the ICC.

However, the award of reparations is subject to different tests than those pertinent to the determination of individual criminal responsibility under international criminal law (ICL). The 'liability to remedy harm' requires the establishment of a causal link between the criminal act and the harm based on 'but for' test and the 'proximate cause' standard.[49] Furthermore, in contrast to criminal proceedings, the causality does not have to be proven beyond reasonable doubt. Instead, a 'sufficient causal link' between the crime and the sustained harm needs to be established.[50]

Nonetheless, the Appeals Judgment also raises some concerns regarding the ICC's approach towards reparations. Stahn notes that the Order for Reparations issued in the *Lubanga* case appears to prioritise accountability over other societal concerns, such as security, well-being or deterrence measures preventing the violations from recurring in the future.[51] While this approach is reflective of the general priorities of any criminal court, it raises the issue of suitability of such an approach in the post-conflict context, as well as the prospects of transformative reparations. Arguably, the exclusive focus on criminal accountability of the high-level convicted person as a key determinative factor for award of reparations moves away from remedying other effects of armed conflict which must be addressed in the process of transition from conflict to peace. In particular, it may lead to prioritisation of victims of prosecuted and convicted crimes to the detriment (if not exclusion) of victimhood of other persons who have suffered

---

47 ibid. paras. 102–05.

48 ibid., paras. 69–70.

49 ibid., paras. 125–29.

50 *Situation in the Democratic Republic of the Congo: Prosecutor v. Thomas Lubanga Dyilo* (Order for Reparations), ICC-01/04-01/06-3129-AnxA (3 March 2015), para. 22.

51 C. Stahn, 'Reparative Justice after the Lubanga Appeals Judgment on Principles and Procedures of Reparations' *EJIL: Talk!*, 07.04.2015 <http://www.ejiltalk.org/reparative-justice-after-the-lubanga-appeals-judgment-on-principles-and-procedures-of-reparation/> accessed 01.08.2015.

harms resulting from international crimes which may have not been prosecuted at the ICC or, if prosecuted, no conviction was secured. For instance, victims of SGBV and victims of crimes committed by child soldiers illustrate groups of victims who were excluded from the award of reparations in *Lubanga*.

Furthermore, the focus of the Court on remedying harms sustained by a select group of victims may lead to further societal divisions in a society recently emerging from conflict, and creation of a 'reparation gap'.[52] The ICC acknowledged the danger of such an approach, noting that the focus of the Reparations Order on victims from the Hema community may 'give rise to a risk of resentment on the part of other victims and the re-stigmatisation of former child soldiers within their communities'.[53] However, this shortcoming is also attributed to flaws in the earlier stages of the case, principally the type and number of charges in the indictment linking back to the weaknesses in prosecutorial strategy and investigations. Accordingly, the limited scope of charges brought against Lubanga automatically narrowed the number of eligible victims, including victims of SGBV, hence limiting the opportunity to award reparations to other victims.

A similar difficulty arose in relation to reparations for victims of SGBV in *Lubanga*. Although the first decision on reparations included provision of reparation for such victims, the Appeals Chamber reversed that finding. It was held that harms arising from SGBV suffered by the victims were not linked to the crimes of which Lubanga was convicted (i.e. the enlistment, conscription and use of child soldiers under Article 8(2)(e)(vi) and (vii) of the ICC Statute). Therefore, in the Appeals Chamber's view, Lubanga could not be held liable for reparations in respect of these harms. The decision further illustrates the importance of adequate and detailed charging of sexual and gender-based crimes at the pre-trial stage, as well as their diligent prosecution during the trial. These two elements not only influence the future award of reparations to victims of SGBV, but also have a real and practical impact on victims' lives in post-conflict reality.

The negative impact of the questionable finding of the Trial Chamber in *Lubanga* establishing that acts of SGBV are not a part of the crime of enlistment, conscription and use of child soldiers to participate actively in hostilities is particularly demonstrable in this context. This interpretation effectively led to exclusion of victims, predominantly girls, who suffered harms resulting from sexual violence committed in the context, or as a result, of recruitment and/or use of child soldiers from benefitting from reparations ordered against Lubanga.

---

52 L. Moffett, 'Reparative complementarity: ensuring an effective remedy for victims in the reparation regime of the International Criminal Court' (2013) 17(3) *The International Journal of Human Rights* 368, 375.

53 *Situation in the Democratic Republic of the Congo: Prosecutor v. Thomas Lubanga Dyilo* (Order for Reparations), ICC-01/04-01/06-3129-AnxA (3 March 2015), footnote 44.

Judge Odio-Benito also emphasised the discriminatory aspect of the decision in her dissenting opinion, stating that:

> Invisibility of sexual violence in the legal concept leads to discrimination against the victims of enlistment, conscription and use who systematically suffer from this crime as an intrinsic part of the involvement with the armed group.[54]

Such a result is particularly worrying given the commitment of the ICC to the principle of equality and non-discrimination, as well as the promise of special attention to the needs of child victims and victims of SGBV.[55]

Furthermore, while the ICC Appeals Chamber acknowledged the appropriateness and the positive effects of transformative and preventative modalities of reparations, further commitment to applying these types of reparations in *Lubanga* is not demonstrated.[56] The Amended Order for Reparations makes it clear that the TFV has discretion to direct its assistance activities towards victims of SGBV and that 'programmes that have transformative objectives, however limited, can help prevent future victimisation'.[57] Nonetheless, the TFV plan for collective reparations in *Lubanga*, which was approved by the ICC in October 2016, does not include details regarding how the transformative aspect of collective reparations will be realised, particularly in cases where victims of SGBV are concerned.[58] Although the TFV plan commits to fair and equal gender representation of women and girls in planning and implementation of reparations, it offers little reassurance that transformative reparations will be delivered and in what form. Arguably, collective reparations aimed at transforming power relations and addressing the structural inequalities could go a long way in subverting the root causes of violence against women and, as such, violations suffered by women and girls during the conflict in the Democratic Republic of the Congo (DRC). In addition, the human rights obligations of the state (here, the DRC) to provide reparations should include particular consideration of the needs of victims of SGBV and ought to be focused on the transformative aspect. In this context, guarantees of non-repetition from the state can include positive steps to facilitate the progressive realisation of women's rights and to address the existing gender inequalities through legal and institutional reforms.

---

54 *Situation in the Democratic Republic of the Congo: Prosecutor v. Thomas Lubanga Dyilo* (Judgment), ICC-01/04-01/06-2842 (14 March 2012), Dissenting Opinion of Judge Odio-Benito, para. 16.

55 Article 21(3) and Article 68 ICC Statute; Rule 86 ICC RPE.

56 *Situation in the Democratic Republic of the Congo: Prosecutor v. Thomas Lubanga Dyilo* (Order for Reparations), ICC-01/04-01/06-3129-AnxA (3 March 2015), paras. 34, 67.

57 ibid., para. 67(v).

58 *Situation in the Democratic Republic of the Congo: Prosecutor v. Thomas Lubanga Dyilo* (Public Redacted version of Filing regarding symbolic collective reparations projects) ICC-01/04-01/06-3223-Red (19 September 2016), paras. 18, 36.

3.2. *PROSECUTOR v. KATANGA* (REPARATIONS)

Prosecutor v. Katanga is the second case in which the ICC considered reparations.[59] On 7 March 2012, Katanga was convicted by the ICC on a count of murder as a crime against humanity and on four counts of war crimes (murder, attacking a civilian population, destruction of property and pillaging) and subsequently sentenced to 12 years' imprisonment.[60] Disappointingly, the case illustrates another example of a failed prosecution by the ICC of gender-based crimes committed in the DRC conflict and is demonstrative of many 'blind spots' in delivering gender justice at the ICC. Although the charges of SGBV were confirmed and proceeded to trial, Katanga was acquitted of counts of rape and sexual slavery as crimes against humanity and war crimes. In reaching that conclusion, Trial Chamber II did not view acts of rape and sexual slavery as constituting a part of the 'common purpose' of the attack on civilian population in Bogoro in the eastern DRC.[61] Given the ethnic background of the conflict, it is even more astounding that the Trial Chamber failed to make a connection with the large body of jurisprudence from ad hoc tribunals, which emphasises the role of sexual violence in inter-ethnic conflict. Furthermore, this finding stands in sharp contrast with the approach demonstrated towards property-oriented crimes (destruction of property, pillage) and murder, which were held to constitute a part of the 'common purpose', therefore forming a ground for the conviction of Katanga.[62] It was considered that transporting, storing and distributing weapons and ammunition demonstrated planning, intent and preparation for the attack and proved Katanga's contribution to the common purpose.[63] Nonetheless the judges failed to make the connection between the act of amassing large volumes of arms and the subsequent occurrence of sexual violence.

On 24 March 2017, Trial Chamber II issued the decision on reparations in *Katanga*, assessing the total amount monetary value of physical and psychological harms suffered by the victims at $3,752,700. Based on the principle of proportionality, the Trial Chamber held Katanga personally liable for $1 million while finding him indigent for the purposes of reparations.[64] However, the gender blindness of the Trial Chamber II decision had a significant impact on the recognition of the victims of SGBV committed during the attack on Bogoro,

---

59 *Situation en République Démocratique du Congo: Le Procureur c. Germain Katanga* (Ordonnance de réparation en vertu de l'article 75 du Statut), ICC-01/04-01/07 (24 March 2017) ('*Katanga* (Reparations Judgment)').

60 *Situation in the Democratic Republic of the Congo: Prosecutor v. Germain Katanga* (Judgment pursuant to article 74 of the Statute), Trial Chamber II, ICC-01/04-01/7-3436, 7 March 2014.

61 ibid., paras. 1663–64.

62 ibid., paras. 1657–62.

63 ibid., paras. 1671–73.

64 This decision was upheld by the ICC Appeals Chamber on 8 March 2018.

the visibility of the gender impact of these crimes in the ICC jurisprudence, as well as avenues for redress available to the victims. Due to the earlier acquittal on the charges of rape and sexual slavery, no reparations have been awarded to the victims of these crimes. However, Trial Chamber II invited the Board of Directors of the TFV to consider using its assistance mandate to respond to harms resulting from SGBV crimes committed during the Bogoro attack.[65] The need for reparations for victims of SGBV were also highlighted by the UN in the Joint Submission on Reparations submitted to the ICC. The UN emphasised that the gendered nature of harms suffered by the victims needs to be understood and, accordingly, the needs of such victims need to be addressed through participatory, gender-sensitive and transformative reparations.[66] The submission also noted the option of TFV using is discretion to facilitate reparations for SGBV victims through 'other resources' available to the TFV under its assistance mandate – an avenue which was raised by the TFV itself in its observations on reparations procedure in *Katanga*.[67] While the opportunity to use the flexibility enshrined in the TFV assistance mandate offers an opportunity to address the 'gender gap' in *Katanga* reparations, such option suffers from several potential pitfalls. In practical terms, the viability of providing support to the SGBV victims through this route is largely dependent on the already limited resources of the TFV. However, it is unrealistic to assume that TFV can be a sustainable solution to reparation gaps, especially those resulting from flawed prosecutions and procedural inadequacies occurring prior to the case reaching reparations stage. In addition, large numbers of victims in cases currently before the ICC, as well as a growing number of cases being brought before the Court, place additional burdens on the TFV and both its practical and financial capability to address the needs of victims involved in these cases.

Although the reparations decision in *Katanga* resembles some of the pitfalls of *Lubanga* reparations, it is significant in two aspects. First, it is the first time that the ICC ordered both individual and collective reparations. Out of 341 victims who applied for reparations, 297 were held by the Court to be eligible. Trial Chamber II decided that in addition to collective reparations, each of the victims should receive a symbolic compensation of $250, therefore combining the individual and collective methods of redress. Second, it is the first decision of the ICC where the Court elaborated on the monetary aspect of specific harms. In quantifying the monetary value of material, physical and psychological harms suffered by the victims of the Bogoro attack, the ICC examined the

65 *Katanga* (Reparations Judgment), paras. 153–54.

66 *Situation in the Democratic Republic of the Congo: Prosecutor v. Germain Katanga* (United Nations Joint Submission on Reparations) ICC-01/04-01/07-3550, 14 May 2015, paras. 9, 30, 60–69.

67 ibid., paras. 66–69; *Situation in the Democratic Republic of the Congo: Prosecutor v. Germain Katanga* (Observations on reparations procedure) ICC-01/04-01/07-3548, 13 May 2015, para. 130.

jurisprudence of the Inter-American Court of Human Rights with regard to reparations, as well as the practice of French and Belgian courts, the UN Compensation Commission and the military courts in the DRC.[68] Although none of the harms considered in *Katanga* were of gendered nature, the ICC's approach offered some insight as to how reparations for harms arising from crimes involving SGBV may be treated in the future. With the decision on reparations for rape in *Bemba* still to come, it is also encouraging to see the Court's engagement with the jurisprudence of the Inter-American Court of Human Rights, which can be seen as progressive in approach to reparations, particularly transformative reparations in cases involving SGBV.

3.3. CRITIQUE OF THE ICC REPARATIONS SYSTEM

The system of reparations established in the ICC Statute is quite novel in modern ICL. It was aimed at reaching beyond the punitive function of the ICC, and ICL in general, to provide effective remedies for the victims while promoting a more inclusive and participatory approach.[69] Nonetheless, the practice of the ICC to date with regard to reparations raises questions regarding the appropriateness and effectiveness of the established regime. Several commentators have also raised doubts regarding the actual substantive and procedural expertise of the ICC as a criminal court regarding adjudication of what essentially amounts to a civil claim.[70]

The complementary nature of the ICC jurisdiction means that only selected cases will ever reach it. These are likely to involve high-level perpetrators, especially where there exists a lack of genuine domestic investigation and/or proceedings by the state with jurisdiction over the alleged crimes. In practice, this means that only a narrow group of victims is likely to be eligible for reparations, assuming that the alleged perpetrator is convicted by the ICC. Even then, the victims may receive reparations only in relation to harms sustained as a result of crimes successfully prosecuted by the Court. In addition, as de Brouwer and Heikkilä point out, the lack of awareness amongst the victims of the possibility of seeking reparations, as well as the lack of understanding of practical details (such as the need to fill in the claim form), effectively prevents many victims from receiving reparations.[71]

---

68 *Katanga* (Reparations Judgment), para. 230.

69 *Situation in the Democratic Republic of the Congo: Prosecutor v. Thomas Lubanga Dyilo* (Decision establishing principles and procedures to be applied to reparations), ICC-01/04-01/06-2904 (7 August 2012), para. 177.

70 Stahn, above n. 51; L. Zegveld, '"Victims" Reparation Claims and International Criminal Courts. Incompatible Values?' (2013) 8 *Journal of International Criminal Justice* 79, 100.

71 A.-M. de Brouwer and M. Heikkilä, 'Victim Issues: Participation, Protection, Reparations, and Assistance' in G. Sluiter, H. Friman, S. Linton, S. Vasiliev and S. Zappalà (eds.), *International Criminal Procedure: Principles and Rules*, Oxford University Press 2013, p. 1371.

Despite these limitations, the ICC faces potentially large numbers of victims seeking reparations.[72] This immediately raises a question about the effectiveness of such an approach. If the overarching aim of the post-conflict reparations is to remedy the harms suffered by individuals in armed conflict and to assist in the process of transformation from conflict to peace, then the ICC regime provides a rather limited scope for achieving these objectives. A large number of claimants raises questions about the financial aspects of awarding reparations. Thus far, the ICC has had to rely on the funds of the TFV to finance reparations for victims of crimes perpetrated in the DRC as both Lubanga and Katanga were found to be destitute, thereby precluding the TFV from seizing any assets. Furthermore, as Moffett notes, even where the defendant's assets are seized (as in *Bemba*), the final award to the victims is likely to be far less than reparations ordered by regional human rights courts, including rehabilitations and measures of satisfaction.[73] The strong reliance of the ICC reparations mechanism on the TFV is also questionable. Given that the TFV relies on voluntary donations from wealthier countries, it hardly offers a sustainable source of finance for future reparations. Schabas also doubts the utility of providing funds for the humanitarian activities of the TFV, which essentially amount to 'expensive overseas development assistance' and are already carried out by specialised agencies such as Oxfam or the UN Development Programme.[74]

Finally, the ICC practice with respect to gender-inclusive and transformative reparations is yet to be observed. In principle, the ICC reparations system recognises the need for gender-sensitive reparations, which applies equally to cases involving gender-based crimes and those that do not. The transformative aspect of reparations has also been acknowledged, both in *Lubanga* and in *Katanga*. The reparations system is additionally supported by the general principles enshrined in the ICC Statute which prohibit gender discrimination and envisage special attention to the needs of victims of SGBV.[75] However, flaws in the earlier procedural stages of a case may lead to gender-based crimes not being included in the conviction, therefore significantly limiting the eligibility of victims to claim reparations, as illustrated by the two cases discussed in this chapter. Also, there is no clarification on what gender-inclusivity actually means when it comes to implementation of reparation orders. The Order for

72 For instance, in the *Bemba* case, there are 4452 victims. *Prosecutor v. Bemba* (Public redacted version of the 'Decision on the Tenth and Seventeenth Transmissions of Applications by Victims to Participate in the Proceedings') ICC-01/05-01/08-2247-Red (19 July 2012).

73 The value of defendant's assets seized by the ICC in *Bemba* case is estimated at €5.2 million. Given the number of victims (4452 in 2012), each victim would only receive €1168. Moffett, above n. 52, p. 377.

74 W.A. Schabas, 'The International Criminal Court at Ten' (2001) 22 *Criminal Law Forum* 493, 501.

75 Article 21(3), Article 68 ICC Statute; Rule 86 ICC RPE.

Reparations in *Lubanga* merely states that a 'gender-inclusive approach should guide the design of the principles and procedures to be applied to reparations' with a view to attaining gender parity in reparations, but does not elaborate further on practical means through which these goals are to be achieved.[76] Given the early practice of the ICC with regard to gender-inclusive reparations, the court has an opportunity to clarify this matter in its future decisions, especially in *Bemba*. Given the first successful prosecution of rape as a war crime and a crime against humanity in *Bemba*, the case creates an opportunity for the ICC to conceptualise in greater detail the principles of gender-sensitive, inclusive and transformative reparations for harms arising from acts of SGBV.

4. REPARATIONS FOR CONFLICT-RELATED GENDERED HARMS: ESSENTIAL FEATURES

Although the right to reparations is established in international law, the flaws in many reparations programmes, or even the lack of such programmes in the aftermath of violent conflicts, effectively prevent women who have suffered violations of their rights during armed conflict from enforcing these rights and obtaining material reparations. This evident gap in relation to provision of effective remedies for women is illustrative of, as Ní Aoláin notes, 'a consistent pattern of disjunctive responses by law to women's needs'.[77]

While each type of reparations has its own form and method of delivery, some overarching principles and issues, which are relevant to reparations for gendered harms in general, can be identified. Such principles are not restricted to reparations awarded by human rights courts or international criminal courts; rather, they aim to point towards characteristics of reparations which can provide meaningful change for women who suffered gendered harms in conflicts.

4.1. INDIVIDUAL AND COLLECTIVE REPARATIONS

Many of the debates about post-conflict reparations raise the distinction between individual and collective reparations, as well as the appropriateness of these modes of reparations in relation to gendered harms arising from gross violations of IHRL and/or IHL. While there is no fixed definition of collective reparations in international law, they can be understood with reference to reparations provided

76 *Situation in the Democratic Republic of the Congo: Prosecutor v. Thomas Lubanga Dyilo* (Order for Reparations), ICC-01/04-01/06-3129-AnxA (3 March 2015), para. 18.

77 F. Ní Aoláin, C. O'Rourke and A. Swaine, 'Transforming Reparations for Conflict-Related Sexual Violence: Principles and Practice' (2015) 28 *Harvard Human Rights Journal* 97, 102.

to a group of victims who suffered violations of IHRL/IHL or to the community where victims were from or where they reside.[78] Gendered harms are suffered by primary victims but also have a detrimental impact on their families and communities. In that context, collective reparations, which aim at supporting not exclusively the primary victim but also the broader community, may appear as an appropriate mode of reparations. Arguably, the collective nature of these reparations makes them better tailored to remedy the social effects of gendered harms, for instance by supporting community programmes, ensuring provision of education and/or vocational courses or reintegration of the former child soldiers into their native communities. According to the UN Secretary-General collective reparations may work better in cases of sexual violence as they allow victims to benefit from reparation without the need for naming individual victims and the types of violations suffered by them.[79] However, while avoidance of stigmatisation and revictimisation is an important element in the design and distribution of reparations, it remains equally significant to ensure that individual victims directly benefit from reparations and that any such reparations are adequately tailored to redress gendered harms suffered by the individual.

While collective reparations certainly further the aims of repairing some of the harms suffered, they are not designed to address the individual needs of the victim; nor do they constitute full and adequate reparation. In support of that view, the UN Human Rights Committee ruled that 'symbolic' or less than full reparations are inadequate and ineffective as a remedy, while the UN OHCHR study on reparations in the DRC revealed that victims of CRSV expressed a clear preference for the tangible benefits of individual reparations which address the more concrete needs of the victims, rather than symbolic reparations.[80] Furthermore, addressing the remedies for gendered harms only through a collective reparations system carries a potential danger of viewing the female victim of gendered harms only through the lens of the impact of these violations on the broader community, rather than viewing her as an independent individual whose human rights have been violated by the state.

---

78 International Center for Transitional Justice, 'The Rabat Report: Concept and Challenges of Collective Reparations' (1 February 2009), p. 10 <https://www.ictj.org/publication/rabat-report-concept-and-challenges-collective-reparations> accessed 01.10.2015.

79 UNSG Guidance Note, 7.

80 *Albert Wilson v. The Philippines*, Communication No. 868/1999, UN Doc. CCPR/C/79/D/868/1999 (2003), para. 5.14.; UN Office of High Commissioner for Human Rights, 'Report of the Panel on Remedies and Reparations for Victims of Sexual Violence in the Democratic Republic of Congo to the High Commissioner for Human Rights', March 2011, para. 150 <http://www.ohchr.org/Documents/Countries/CD/DRC_Reparations_Report_en.pdf> accessed 01.10.2015.

That said, individual and collective reparations are not mutually exclusive and should not be approached as substitutive for one another.[81] Arguably, only the combination of the two perspectives shows the complete picture of victimhood arising in relation to gendered harms. Such an approach enables treatment of the female victim as an equal rights-holder but also emphasises the extent to which gendered harms affect the broader community, creating what Ní Aoláin refers to as 'communities of harm'. Accordingly, a mixed approach, combining individual and collective reparations, is recommended as the best way to achieve comprehensive reparations for conflict-related gendered harms. This approach is evidenced in the decision of the ICC in *Katanga*, where victims received individual symbolic compensation of $250 in addition to collective reparations. Although Katanga's acquittal on charges of SGBV prevented victims of such harms from receiving direct compensation in *Katanga*, it is hoped that the forthcoming decision on reparations in *Bemba* will make meaningful advances in this regard.

4.2. TRANSFORMATIVE REPARATIONS

Another key issue relates to the manner in which reparations and reparation programmes for gendered harms are designed and implemented. When considering the harmful effect of gendered harms arising from violations of IHRL and/or IHL, it is essential to take account of the wide-ranging impact and diverse nature of these harms but also their root causes, including structural discrimination and gender inequality. In cases involving CRSV in particular, it remains crucial that, as a part of reparations, the existing taboos surrounding victims of sexual harms are challenged. Collective reparations have the potential to address such stereotypes with a view to transforming attitudes towards victims of sexual harms, e.g. through community reintegration programmes, as well as gender equality education. Similarly, the awards of individual reparations ought to take account of the situation of the victim, with particular attention to how gender and the system of structural discrimination may have positioned her within social and economic structures.

Transformative reparations are therefore an important aspect of redressing conflict-related gendered harms in that they offer an opportunity to take account of gender inequalities and structural discrimination and attempt to disrupt these patterns.[82] As such, emphasis on the transformative aspect of reparations

[81] UN Committee Against Torture, General Comment No. 3: Implementation of article 14 by State parties, UN Doc. CAT/C/GC/3, 19 November 2012, para. 32 ('Culturally sensitive collective reparation measures … do not exclude the individual right to redress').

[82] Article 3 Nairobi Declaration. For an example of the desired transformative effect, see Gopalan, in this volume.

allows to address underlying causes of violence against women and girls but also facilitates progressive realisation of women's socio-economic, as well as civil and political rights. Transformative reparations can include a wide range of measures, from land restitution and redistribution, access to credit, to providing income-generating skills and guarantees of non-repetition. Manjoo notes that the latter 'offer the greatest potential for transforming gender relations. In promising to ensure non-recurrence, such guarantees trigger a discussion about the underlying structural causes of the violence and their gendered manifestations and a discussion about the broader institutional or legal reforms that might be called for to ensure non-repetition'.[83] Guarantees of non-repetition highlight the importance of the role of the state in reparations processes, especially with regard to implantation of the state's human rights obligations, including the obligations to take practical steps to address gender inequalities and structural discrimination. The necessity of transformative reparations in cases involving violence against women was emphasised by the Inter-American Court of Human Rights in the *Cotton Field Case*, where the Court held that

> bearing in mind the context of structural discrimination in which the facts of this case occurred, which was acknowledged by the State …, the reparations must be designed to change this situation, so that their effect is not only of restitution, but also of rectification. In this regard, re-establishment of the same structural context of violence and discrimination is not acceptable".[84]

Furthermore, it is important to ensure that reparations are accessible and inclusive and that they actually reach the intended beneficiary. To that end, practical obstacles faced by many female victims of gendered harms (such as the lack of a personal bank account or mobility) should be addressed.

4.3. PARTICIPATORY AND INCLUSIVE REPARATIONS

The link between peace agreements and reparations for gendered harms needs to be strengthened. Reparation programmes for victims of gendered harms, including CRSV, should be meaningfully incorporated into the peace processes and into peace agreements. For instance, the Lomé Peace Accord, where women or women's groups took no part in the peace negotiations process, established a blanket amnesty for crimes committed during the civil war, including crimes

---

83 UN Human Rights Council, Report of the Special Rapporteur on Violence Against women, its causes and consequences, Rashida Manjoo, UN Doc. A/HRC/14/22, 23 April 2010, para. 62.

84 *González et al. ("Cotton Field") v. Mexico*, IACtHR, Judgment (Preliminary Objection, Merits, Reparations and Costs), 16 November 2009, Ser. C, No. 205, para. 450.

involving sexual violence or reproductive harms.[85] Active participation of women in the design of reparation programmes should form an integral part of women's participation in the peace processes and peace agreements, which are the goals of the WPS Agenda and UNSCR 1325.[86] Ultimately, the full participation of women in the design of reparation programmes is also a way of implementing the principle of equal participation of women and men in public and political life enshrined in IHRL in Article 7 of the CEDAW and Article 25 of the International Covenant on Civil and Political Rights.

5. CONCLUSION

Reparations for gendered harms arising from violations of ICL, IHRL and IHL form an integral part of transitional justice processes in which international law plays a significant role. However, the key responsibility for providing reparations in international law rests on states as the key actors in international legal system and holders of human rights obligations. In this context, the reparations regime at the ICC offers a complimentary, albeit not flawless, avenue of redressing gendered harms suffered as a result of international crimes. Thus far, the ICC committed to providing gender-sensitive reparations and acknowledged the importance of gender parity and inclusion of women in the processes of designing, awarding and delivering reparations. At the same time, the decisions in *Lubanga* and *Katanga* remain illustrative of the shortcomings in the process of delivering gender justice at the ICC and highlighted the importance of prosecutions of sexual and gender-based crimes and their impact on the realisation of reparative justice goals.

Nonetheless, reparations awarded by the ICC are complimentary to the efforts of states who bear the primary responsibility for redressing gendered harms arising from violations of human rights law and international humanitarian law which occur in conflict. While the ICC and the TFV play an important role in redressing such violations, they are not designed to provide a remedy to all victims of such harms. Therefore, it is crucial that the award and implementation of the ICC reparations is seen as complimentary rather than absolving the states of their responsibility under international law to award reparations to victims.

In order for reparations to be meaningful, the decision-making process leading to the design and award of reparations needs to incorporate a thorough

85 Peace Agreement Between the Government of Sierra Leone and the Revolutionary United Front of Sierra Leone, para. 9 <http://www.sierra-leone.org/lomeaccord.html> accessed 07.10.2016.

86 UNSCR 1325, S/RES/1325, 31 October 2000; CEDAW, General Recommendation No.30 on women in conflict prevention, conflict and post-conflict situations, UN Doc. CEDAW/C/GC/30, 18 October 2013.

understanding of women's experiences of armed conflicts and take into account the multifaceted short-, medium- and long-term consequences of gendered harms suffered by them.[87] The meaningful involvement of women in the design of reparations should form an integral part of that process. Furthermore, gender-sensitive reparations must address structural inequalities and take into account the particular ways in which women and girls experience harm. The transformative nature of reparations, especially those that are collective in nature, should promote the weakening of the system of structural inequality and discrimination, which enabled the violations in first place. The forthcoming decision on reparations in *Bemba* creates an ample opportunity for the ICC to give practical effect to its existing commitment to gender-sensitive reparations and to provide transformative justice for the victims of gendered harms.

87 Ní Aoláin, O'Rourke and Swaine, above n. 77, p. 99.

PART IV

GENDERED EXPERIENCES OF TRANSITIONAL JUSTICE

CHILDREN IN TRANSITIONAL JUSTICE PROCESSES

Still Sidelined?

Alison Bisset

1. INTRODUCTION

Children[1] are among those most negatively affected by conflict and political repression. Some are direct victims of physical violence. Some witness the killing of family and friends. Many more suffer displacement, lose their homes and access to schooling and are deprived of food and health care. Internal instability, the breakdown of the rule of law, separation of families and fragmentation of communities make children additionally vulnerable to abduction, trafficking, sexual violence and recruitment as child soldiers.[2] Longer term, children who have experienced conflict-related trauma often develop anxiety and depression.[3]

---

1 Children are defined as those under 18 years in accordance with the United Nations Convention on the Rights of the Child 1989, General Assembly Resolution 44/25, Art. 1.

2 UNICEF, *Machel Study 10 Year Strategic Review, Children and Conflict in a Changing World*, UNICEF 2009, Ch. 3.

3 K. Kostelny and M. Wessels, 'Children and Youth in Conflict and Post-Conflict Societies: From Plights of War to Paths of Peacebuilding' in A. Schnabel and A. Tanyshalieva (eds.), *Escaping Victimhood: Children, Youth and Post-Conflict Peacebuilding*, United Nations University Press 2013, p. 74.

Exposure to violence affects their values, political beliefs and ability to function as future leaders and decision-makers.[4] The absence of effective state institutions typically suffered by transitional states also disproportionately impacts children, hampering their short-term development as well as their future prospects.

Children ought, therefore, to be a central focus of transitional justice. In many post-conflict countries skewed age pyramids mean that children and youth[5] make up over half the population.[6] Along with adult members of society, they have suffered the violence of the past, but, as the next generation, they will inherit and must progress the results of post-conflict agreements and initiatives. They occupy a pivotal position in the reconstruction, reconciliation and long-term stability of transitional states. It is perhaps surprising then that children have typically been underrepresented in transitional justice schemes. The purpose of this chapter is to explore the reasons for the continued marginalisation of children within this context, despite the importance of transitional justice for children and the significant role that children can play within its processes.

In recent years, international institutions and organisations have devoted considerable attention to the formulation of guidelines and policies aimed at facilitating the participation of children within transitional justice processes.[7] International legal regimes lay down obligations requiring states to respect and ensure children's rights and provide remedy and redress for violations.[8] Yet despite some positive results in the inclusion of violations against children within truth-seeking mandates and the prosecution of crimes against children in hybrid and international courts, these efforts have yielded little in the way of tangible improvements. This chapter will consider the international legal frameworks that ensure the rights of children within transitional contexts before moving to analyse recent transitional justice practice in order to ascertain the extent of children's participation and how their rights and interests are being represented across transitional justice processes. This chapter will demonstrate that children, their varied experiences, potential and capabilities, continue to be overlooked, both to the detriment of transitional justice and in contravention of children's rights to be consulted and heard in matters affecting them. The chapter will argue that the adoption of a rights-based approach is necessary for mainstreaming the participation of children within transitional initiatives;

---

4 No Peace Without Justice and UNICEF Innocenti Research Centre, *International Criminal Justice and Children*, No Peace Without Justice and UNICEF Innocenti Research Centre 2002, pp. 31–32.

5 The UN defines 'youth' as persons aged between 15 and 24. See United Nations Department of Economic and Social Affairs, *Definition of Youth Factsheet* <https://undesadspd.org/Youth.aspx> accessed 16.05.2015.

6 UN DESA, *World Population Prospects: The 2012 Revision*, Population Division of the Department of Economic and Social Affairs of the United Nations Secretariat 2013.

7 *Machel Study*, above n. 2, Chs. 8 and 9.

8 See Section 3 below.

as without the inclusion of children and reflection of their needs and interests, transitional justice objectives will be difficult to realise.

2. CHILDREN AND TRANSITIONAL JUSTICE

Transitional justice is concerned with the strategies employed to deal with past human rights abuses in countries moving from conflict or repressive regime to democratic rule in order to ensure accountability, serve justice and achieve reconciliation.[9] Advocates of transitional justice argue that dealing with the past is essential to long-term peace and stability, as failure to pursue accountability undermines the rule of law,[10] the rights and needs of victims,[11] and perpetuates cycles of violence.[12] The transitional justice framework utilises prosecutions, truth commissions, reparations and reforms, among other measures,[13] to meet the diverse needs of transitional states, contribute to a sustainable peace and bring about healing and repair.[14] It is believed that through prosecution, truth recovery and the formulation of reform recommendations, transitional processes can expose and address past grievances, promote institutional and security sector reform and inform reparation programmes. These initiatives, in turn, contribute to the consolidation of democracy, inculcation of a rule of law culture and national reconciliation,[15] and lay the foundations for long-term stability. The forward focus of transitional justice makes it particularly important for children.

The need to create inclusive transitional justice programmes that take account of the needs and voices of children and youth is widely acknowledged.[16] Children are recognised as a key stakeholder group in transitional settings, with their own unique perspectives on the past. Without the inclusion and consultation of children in transitional programmes, an incomplete account of the nature and impact of the violations they have suffered and how best to

9 UN Security Council, *The Rule of Law and Transitional Justice in Conflict and Post-Conflict Societies*, S/2004/616 2004, para. 8.

10 L. Huyse, 'Amnesty, Truth or Prosecution' in L. Reychler and T. Paffenholz (eds.), *Peace-Building, A Field Guide*, Lynne Rienner 2001, p. 325.

11 P.B. Hayner, *Unspeakable Truths: Confronting State Terror and Atrocity*, Routledge 2001, p. 28.

12 UN Security Council, above n. 9, para. 2.

13 ibid., para. 8.

14 C. Villa-Vicencio and E. Doxtader, *Pieces of the Puzzle: Keywords on Reconciliation and Transitional Justice*, Institute for Justice and Reconciliation 2004, p. 72.

15 P. van Zyl, 'Promoting Transitional Justice in Post-Conflict Societies' in A. Bryden and H. Hänggi (eds.), *Security Governance in Post-Conflict Peacebuilding*, Geneva Centre for the Democratic Control of Armed Forces 2005, pp. 209–233.

16 S. Parmar, M.J. Roseman, S. Siegrist and T. Sowa (eds.), *Children and Transitional Justice: Truth Telling, Accountability and Reconciliation*, Harvard University Press 2010; Schnabel and Tanyshalieva, above n. 3.

address them will be recorded.[17] As children are in their formative years and therefore more impressionable, exposure to violence and conflict may result in a loss of sense of what constitutes acceptable behaviour at individual and societal levels, and a consideration that resort to violence is an appropriate means of dispute resolution. In order to halt cyclical, cross-generational violence, it is crucial to include children within transitional programmes aimed at reforming social arrangements.[18] Involving children, particularly adolescents, gives them the opportunity to express themselves and contribute their voice, opinions and ideas to the social dialogue. It builds self-esteem, helping them to find a role for themselves in their communities.[19]

Failure to include children wastes their potential and capacity to further the cause of reconciliation and peacebuilding.[20] Studies stress the contribution that children can make to their families, communities and societies in post-conflict processes through their creativity, energy and resourcefulness.[21] Recent innovations have seen children contribute to peace talks, shape HIV/AIDS policy and act as peer educators and therapists.[22] This has prompted the UN Committee on the Rights of the Child (the Committee) to recommend that children affected by conflict and other emergencies should be encouraged and enabled to participate in analysing their situation and future prospects.[23] Indeed, there is an emerging consensus that failure to address the concerns of children can undermine the long-term recovery of post-conflict societies and that children must be involved in developing an understanding of the past if they are to play a constructive role in building the future.[24]

3. CHILDREN'S RIGHTS IN TRANSITIONAL JUSTICE

It is not only sensible to include children in transitional processes from a peace and stability perspective, it is also necessary because children have rights under

---

17 A. Smith, 'Basic Assumptions of Transitional Justice and Children' in S. Parmar, M.J. Roseman, S. Siegrist and T. Sowa (eds.), above n. 16, p. 31.

18 C. Aptel and V. Ladisch, *Through a New Lens: A Child Sensitive Approach to Transitional Justice*, International Center for Transitional Justice 2011, p. 6.

19 UNICEF, *Adolescent Programming Experiences During Conflict and Post-Conflict*, 2004 <http://www.unicef.org/adolescent_conflict(1).pdf> accessed 03.06.2016.

20 UN General Assembly, *Impact of Armed Conflict on Children: Report of the Expert of the Secretary General, Ms Graca Machel*, UN Doc. A/51/306 1996, Foreword, pp. x–xi.

21 For example, see UNICEF, *The Participation of Children and Young People in Emergencies. A Guide for Relief Agencies Based Largely on the Experiences in the Asian Tsunami Response*, Bangkok 2007.

22 See case studies in UNICEF, above n. 19.

23 Committee on the Rights of the Child, *The Right of the Child to be Heard*, CRC/C/GC/12, General Comment No. 12, 2009, para. 125.

24 Aptel and Ladisch, above n. 18, p. 4.

international law to have the violations committed against them addressed, to participate in the mechanisms created to provide redress and to have their needs and interests accounted for in transitional initiatives. In the aftermath of serious violations of human rights, international human rights law, in conjunction with international humanitarian law[25] and international criminal law,[26] stipulates that victims, including child victims, have rights to justice, truth, reparation and non-recurrence, and places corresponding obligations upon states.[27] These rights and obligations correspond to the mechanisms of transitional justice. Trials enable states to fulfil their obligation to investigate and punish perpetrators and provide victims with their right to justice and an effective remedy. Fact-finding investigations are a means by which states implement their duty to investigate and identify perpetrators, thereby providing victims, their families and wider society with the right to know or the right to truth. Through reparations, states fulfil their obligation to provide restitution and compensation to victims and provide them with their right to reparation. Finally, justice reforms allow a state

---

25 On the protection of children under international humanitarian law (IHL), see the Fourth Geneva Convention Relative to the Protection of Civilian Persons in Time of War, 12.08.1949, Arts. 14, 17, 23–26, 50 and 82; Additional Protocol I to the Geneva Conventions Relating to the Protection of Victims of International Armed Conflicts, 08.06.1977, (API), Arts. 74–78; and Additional Protocol II to the Geneva Conventions Relating to Victims of Non-International Armed Conflicts, 08.06.1977, Arts. 4 and 6. On the shortcomings of IHL from a children's rights perspective, see V. Popovski, 'Protection and Participation of Children in Post-Conflict Peacebuilding: International Law and Evolving Practice' in Schnabel and Tanyshalieva (eds.), above n. 3, pp. 116–118.

26 Under international criminal law, many violations of children's rights constitute offences and attract individual criminal responsibility. Forcibly transferring children of the group to another group or undertaking measures designed to prevent births, carried out with the intent to destroy, in whole or in part, a national, ethnical, racial or religious group as such amounts to the crime of genocide, see Convention on the Prevention and Punishment of the Crime of Genocide, 09.12.1948, Art. 2; *Rome Statute of the International Criminal Court* (Rome Statute), A/Conf.183/9, 17.07.1998, entered into force 01.07.2002, Art. 6. When widespread and systematic and committed against civilian, including child, populations pursuant to an organisational policy, murder, extermination, enslavement, torture, persecution, deportation or forcible transfer of a population, enforced disappearance, apartheid and crimes of sexual violence constitute crimes against humanity under the Rome Statute, Art. 7. Enslavement is understood to encompass trafficking, particularly of women and children, see International Criminal Court, *Elements of Crimes*, UN Doc. PCNICC/2000/1/Add.2 2000, Art. 7(1)(c), fn. 11. Intentional attacks on schools, crimes of sexual violence, using starvation as a method of warfare (in international armed conflict) and using children under 15 as soldiers amount to war crimes when committed in the context of an armed conflict, see Rome Statute, Art. 8.

27 See General Assembly Resolution, *Basic Principles and Guidelines on the Right to a Remedy and Reparation for Victims of Violations of International Human Rights and Humanitarian Law*, A/C.3/60/L.24 2006 (Bassiouni Principles). See also L. Joinet, *Set of Principles for the Protection and Promotion of Human Rights Through Action to Combat Impunity*, UN Doc. E/CN.4/Sub.2/1997/20/Rev.1 1997 (Joinet Principles), updated by D. Orentlicher, *Updated Set of Principles for the Protection and Promotion of Human Rights Through Action to Combat Impunity*, UN Doc. E/CN.4/2005/102.Add.1 2005 (Updated Principles).

to implement its duty to take effective measures aimed at preventing future violations and thereby guarantee the right of non-repetition.[28]

In involving children within these processes, the Convention on the Rights of the Child (CRC) provides a normative framework for the protection and promotion of children's rights. The CRC enjoys near universal ratification[29] and obligates states parties to respect and ensure, to all children within their jurisdiction,[30] a full range of civil, political, economic, social and cultural rights. It is underpinned by four guiding principles: non-discrimination;[31] the best interests of the child;[32] the right to life, survival and development;[33] and the right to be heard.[34] The CRC contains no general derogation clause, meaning that the rights of children are to be respected at all times, including during public emergencies and armed conflict.

States parties are under obligations to protect and care for all children affected by armed conflict.[35] For children who have taken an active part in hostilities, states parties to the Optional Protocol on the Involvement of Children in Armed Conflict[36] must ensure that they are demobilised and receive such assistance as is necessary for their recovery, rehabilitation and reintegration.[37] In addition, states parties to the CRC must take all appropriate measures to promote the physical and psychological recovery and social reintegration of children who have been the victims of exploitation, abuse, torture or any other form of cruel, inhuman or degrading treatment or punishment,[38] whether during periods of conflict or authoritarianism.

With regard to economic, social and cultural rights, states parties are required to take measures to the maximum extent of their available resources.[39] UN bodies have consistently stressed that progressive realisation of economic, social and cultural rights should not be misinterpreted to deprive the obligation of meaningful content but should be moved towards with deliberate, concrete and targeted steps.[40] States parties are required to be proactive and to take all

28 ibid.

29 Only the USA is a non-state party.

30 CRC, Art. 2.

31 ibid.

32 ibid., Art. 3.

33 ibid., Art. 6.

34 ibid., Art. 12. Committee on the Rights of the Child, *General Measures of Implementation of the Convention on the Rights of the Child General Comment No. 5*, CRC/GC/2003/5 2003, paras. 6, 12.

35 ibid. CRC, Art. 38.

36 UN General Assembly, *Optional Protocol to the Convention on the Rights of the Child on the Involvement of Children in Armed Conflict*, A/Res/54/263 2000.

37 CRC, above n.30, Arts. 6(3) and 7.

38 ibid., Art. 39.

39 ibid., Art. 4.

40 Committee on Economic, Social and Cultural Rights, *General Comment No. 3 on the Nature of States Parties' Obligations (Art. 2, para. 1, of the Covenant)*, 1990, para. 2; Committee on

possible measures[41] in providing children with the following rights: the right to education;[42] the right to the highest attainable standard of health, freedom from disease and malnutrition and access to clean drinking water;[43] the right to social security;[44] the right to a standard of living adequate for physical, mental, spiritual, moral and social development;[45] and the right to rest, play and leisure.[46] The equal importance given to economic, social and cultural rights is important within transitional contexts, where many children continue to be exposed to poverty, hunger and a lack of access to health care and education.[47] It is increasingly considered that for transitional justice processes to make a positive contribution to long-term stability, particularly for the next generation, they must engage with socio-economic violations,[48] use their reform mandate to promote social justice and lobby for economic and social policy that ensures investment in schools and housing, access to health care and availability of jobs.[49]

Importantly, Article 12 of the CRC stipulates that the child who is capable of forming his or her own views has the right to express those views freely in all matters affecting him or her, with views being given due weight in accordance with age and maturity.[50] To that end, children are to be given the opportunity to be heard in judicial or administrative proceedings affecting them, either directly or through a representative.[51] As discussed above, Article 12 is one of the CRC's four general principles,[52] connected to all other articles of the Convention, which cannot be fully implemented if the child is not respected as a subject with his or her own views.[53]

---

the Rights of the Child, *General Comment No. 15 on the Right of the Child to the Enjoyment of the Highest Attainable Standard of Health (Art. 24)*, CRC/C/GC/15 2013, para. 7.

41 Committee on the Rights of the Child, above n. 34, paras. 5–8.

42 CRC, above n. 30, Arts. 28 and 29.

43 ibid., Art. 24.

44 ibid., Art. 26.

45 ibid., Art. 27.

46 ibid., Art. 31.

47 S. Siegrist, 'Child Rights and Transitional Justice' in S. Parmar, M.J. Roseman, S. Siegrist and T. Sowa (eds.), above no. 3, p. 7.

48 R. Duthie, 'Towards a Development Sensitive Approach to Transitional Justice' (2008) 2 *International Journal of Transitional Justice* 292.

49 L.J. Laplante, 'Transitional Justice and Peacebuilding: Diagnosing and Addressing the Socioeconomic Roots of Violence through a Human Rights Framework' (2008) 2 *International Journal of Transitional Justice* 331, 334–338; W. Lambourne, 'Transitional Justice and Peacebuilding After Mass Violence' (2009) 3 *International Journal of Transitional Justice* 28.

50 CRC, above n. 30, Art. 12(1).

51 ibid., art 12(2).

52 Committee on the Rights of the Child, above n. 23, para. 2.

53 ibid., para. 68.

The Committee views Article 12 as both an individual and collective right[54] and has emphasised that states parties ought to view children as a group with relevant perspectives and experiences that should be considered in decision-making, policy-making and the preparation of laws and other measures.[55] Children are a group with a right to be heard, not only momentarily, but in 'intense exchanges with adults' in all relevant contexts of their lives.[56] The Committee has held that states parties cannot fulfil their obligation of acting in a child's best interests without first meeting the requirements of Article 12.[57] Furthermore, Article 12 rights do not cease in situations of crisis or in their aftermath.[58] Indeed, the Committee has stressed that in post-conflict contexts, 'children's participation helps them to regain control over their lives, contributes to rehabilitation, develops organizational skills and strengthens a sense of identity.'[59] States parties are therefore encouraged to 'support mechanisms which enable children … to play an active role in … post-conflict resolution processes.'[60] In accordance with the non-discrimination principle, this means that all children, including girls and children from vulnerable or marginalised groups, must be enabled to participate on an equal basis.[61]

These binding international legal rights and obligations are bolstered by numerous soft law sources, which aim to facilitate the realisation of CRC standards for children in transitional justice practice. The Cape Town and Paris Principles, primarily concerned with children associated with armed groups and armed forces (CAAFAG), constitute globally accepted norms on the immediate, medium and long-term standards of best practice in relation to affected children.[62] The Millennium Declaration includes an international commitment to assist and protect children affected by armed conflict.[63] This was further emphasised at the Millennium Summit, which reaffirmed the need to promote and protect the rights of children in armed conflict, to ensure their receipt of timely and effective humanitarian assistance and to provide for their education,

54 ibid., para. 9.
55 ibid., para. 12.
56 ibid., para. 13.
57 Committee on the Rights of the Child, *General Comment No. 14 (2013) on the Right of the Child to Have his or her Best Interests Taken as a Primary Consideration (Art. 3, para. 1)*, CRC/C/GC/14 2013, para. 43.
58 ibid., para. 125.
59 ibid.
60 ibid., para. 126.
61 ibid., paras. 75–79.
62 J-C. Legrand, *Cape Town Principles and Best Practices on the Prevention of the Recruitment of Children into the Armed Forces and on the Demobilization and Reintegration of Child Soldiers in Africa*, UNICEF 1997; The Paris Principles, *Principles and Guidelines on Children Associated with Armed Forces or Armed Groups*, February 2007.
63 UN General Assembly, *United Nations Millennium Declaration*, A/Res/55/2/ 2000, para. 26.

rehabilitation and reintegration into society.[64] Indeed, the UN has created a complex framework around children in armed conflict, establishing the Office of the Special Representative of the Secretary General for Children and Armed Conflict to strengthen protection, raise awareness and foster international cooperation on the issue.[65] The UN Security Council has identified six categories of violations and established a monitoring and reporting mechanism to monitor, document and report upon them and name parties to conflicts that recruit, kill or maim children, commit sexual violence, abduct children and attack schools and hospitals.[66] Parties to conflicts listed in the Secretary-General's annual report on children and armed conflict are then requested by the Security Council to develop action plans to address grave violations against children.[67] The UN Security Council,[68] General Assembly[69] and Economic and Social Council[70] have repeatedly adopted resolutions and issued reports calling for the safeguarding of children's rights, both during and after conflict, recognising the protection of children as a key aspect of humanitarian assistance, conflict resolution and development.

International institutions and organisations have undertaken extensive analyses of legal frameworks and their implementation with respect to children in conflict situations and transitional justice operations. These efforts have led to the identification of standards of best practice and the development of guidelines,[71] which are intended to inform efforts to involve children across the breadth of transitional justice processes. Yet despite the wealth of legal provisions, policies and guidelines, many transitional processes remain woefully inadequate in their inclusion and consideration of the needs, rights and interests of children. The remaining sections of this chapter explore this issue and the factors behind it.

---

64 UN General Assembly, *2005 World Summit Outcome*, A/Res/60/1 2005, para. 117.

65 See <www.childrenandarmedconflict.un.org> accessed 25.05.2016.

66 See UNSC Res 1612 (26.07.2005) UN Doc S/RES/1612; UNSC Res 1882 (04.08.2009) UN Doc S/RES./1882; Office of the Special Representative of the Secretary-General for Children in Armed Conflict, *The Six Grave Violations against Children in Armed Conflict: The Legal Foundation*, Working Paper No. 1, October 2009 (updated November 2013).

67 For details of the action plans signed to date see <https://childrenandarmedconflict.un.org/our-work/action-plans/> accessed 26.05.2016.

68 UNSC Res 1261 (30.08.1999) UN Doc S/RES/1261; UNSC Res 1314 (11.08.2000) UN Doc S/RES/1314; UNSC Res 1379 (20.11.2001) UN Doc S/RES/1379; UNSC Res 1460 (30.01.2003) UN Doc S/RES/1460; UNSC Res 1539 (22.04.2004) UN Doc S/RES/1539; UNSC Res 1612 (26.07.2005) UN Doc S/RES/1612; UNSC Res 1882 (04.08.2009) UN Doc S/RES/1882; UNSC Res 1998 (12.07.2011) UN Doc S/RES/1998 and UNSC Res 2068 (19.09.2012) UN Doc S/RES/2068.

69 UN General Assembly Declaration, *A World Fit For Children*, appended to A/Res/S-27/2 2002; UN General Assembly Resolution, *Rights of the Child*, A/Res/62/141 2008; UN General Assembly, *Right of the Child*, A/Res/63/241 2009.

70 UN General Assembly, *Report of the Economic and Social Council for 1999*, A/54/3/Rev.1, Part VI Humanitarian Affairs, paras. 21–22.

71 For an extensive list see UNICEF, above n. 2, p. 93.

4. CHILDREN IN TRANSITIONAL JUSTICE PRACTICE

Facilitating the participation of children within transitional justice mechanisms is undoubtedly challenging. It requires outreach and careful planning of how to enable children to participate through appropriate channels, while ensuring that the necessary systems, services and safeguards are in place to protect their vulnerability and provide them with adequate support. International principles recognise the need for the state to safeguard the psychological well-being, as well as the physical security, of all those who participate in transitional justice initiatives, including children.[72] However, in many transitional states, child welfare and psychological support services are lacking,[73] making outside assistance essential if transitional initiatives are to effectively include children. There are, additionally, resource implications associated with including children in contexts where resources are typically constrained.

Yet, the failure to include children by recognising their right to participate, representing their needs and interests and acknowledging the contribution they can make, often seems not to stem from either technical or resource hurdles, at least not exclusively. Instead, it emanates from a general political indifference and inertia as pertains to children's issues.[74] Too frequently, children have been viewed as objects of charity, passive and in need of protection. These inaccurate conceptualisations of children mean that their agency goes unrecognised and unexercised.[75] By categorising children as vulnerable, it becomes easier to mute their voices and downplay their needs and interests,[76] which are often considered to be the responsibility of family rather than government.[77] Moreover, as children are an under-enfranchised group, governments are not directly accountable to them, making it difficult for them to exert influence on the policy making process.[78] When children are included, they are very often treated as a homogenous group. The variations in experience between boys and girls, younger and older children and those from particular social, ethnic, religious and other groups are seldom recognised. Yet sociological studies demonstrate that children do not have identical interests and opinions.[79] A host

---

72 Joinet Principles, above n. 27, Principle 9; Updated Principles, above n. 27, Principle 10.

73 Truth and Reconciliation Commission, *Truth and Reconciliation Commission of South Africa Report* (hereinafter TRC Report), 2002, Vol. 1, Ch. 10, p. 289; Truth and Reconciliation Commission, *Final Report of the Truth and Reconciliation Commission for Liberia*, 2009, p. 84.

74 A. Nolan, *Children's Socio-Economic Rights, Democracy and the Courts*, Hart Publishing 2011, p. xxvii.

75 ibid., p. 11.

76 Schnabel and Tanyshalieva, above n. 3, pp. 12 and 17.

77 Nolan, above n. 74, p. 8.

78 ibid., p. 44.

79 B. Mayall, 'The sociology of childhood in relation to children's rights' (2000) 8 *The International Journal of Children's Rights* 243–259.

of factors, both practical and ideological, converge to make the participation of children and the representation of their needs and interests within transitional processes difficult. This chapter now moves to analyse the participation of children across the four key mechanisms of transitional justice: criminal trials, truth commissions, reparations and reforms.

4.1. CRIMINAL TRIALS

Prosecution remains a key response to the commission of serious human rights violations. Criminal justice is considered essential to provide redress, assist with healing and halt the impunity that threatens sustainable peace.[80] This is as important for children as it is for adult populations. Yet, despite their frequently widespread and egregious nature, violations of children's rights have historically seen relatively little acknowledgement within international courts and tribunals. Crimes against children attracted some condemnation at the Nuremberg and Tokyo trials,[81] and were treated as aggravating factors in sentencing by the *ad hoc* tribunals.[82] In 2002, the Special Court for Sierra Leone became the first internationalised court to prosecute and convict[83] for the crime of conscripting or enlisting children under 15 into armed forces or groups or using them to participate actively in hostilities.[84] Sexual crimes committed against girls forcibly taken as 'bush wives' were also prosecuted under the category of 'other inhumane acts'[85] constituting crimes against humanity.[86] While the Court made significant advances in bringing accountability for crimes against children, it has also been suggested that it missed opportunities to advance the cause of many child victims.[87] The focus on the recruitment and use of child soldiers and sexual violence meant that more generic crimes committed against children, such as killing, maiming, persecution and deprivation of access to basic services,

---

80 No Peace Without Justice and UNICEF Innocenti Research Centre, above n. 4, pp. 31–32.

81 C. Aptel, 'International Criminal Justice and Child Protection' in S. Parmar, M.J. Roseman, S. Siegrist and T. Sowa (eds.), above n. 3, pp. 67–113, 88–9.

82 *Prosecutor v Kunarac, Kovac and Vukovic*, Judgement, IT-96-23-T and IT-96-23-T/1, 22 February 2001, Part VI; *Prosecutor v Kristic*, Judgment, Case No. IT-98-33-T, 2 August 2001; *Prosecutor v Akayesu*, Case No. ICTR-96-4-T, Judgment, 2 September 1998.

83 *Prosecutor v Fofana and Kondewa*, Judgment, SCSL-01-14-T, 2 August 2007; *Prosecutor v Brima, Kamara and Kanu*, Judgment, SCSL-04-16-T, 20 June 2007; *Prosecutor v Taylor*, Judgment, SCSL-03-01-T- 1283, 26 April 2012.

84 Statute of the Special Court for Sierra Leone, Art. 4(c).

85 ibid., Art. 2(i).

86 *Prosecutor v Brima, Kamara and Kanu*, Appeals Judgment, SCSL-2004-16-A, 22 February 2008. See also A.S.J. Park, '"Other Inhumane Acts": Forced Marriage, Girl Soldiers and the Special Court for Sierra Leone' (2006) 15 *Social and Legal Studies* 315.

87 C. Aptel, 'Unpunished Crimes: The Special Court for Sierra Leone and Children' in C.C. Jalloh (ed.), *The Sierra Leone Special Court and its Legacy: The Impact for Africa and International Criminal Law*, Cambridge University Press 2015, p. 359.

which reflect the widespread suffering and, sometimes, victimisation of large numbers of children, were not prosecuted.[88] The Court's recognition of 'forced marriage' as a crime against humanity, although lauded by some,[89] has also been criticised. It has been argued that the term 'marriage', which implies a consensual agreement, does not reflect the reality of the abduction behind the practice.[90] Nor did the Court take the opportunity to challenge the peacetime practice of forced marriage of young girls, which remains prevalent in Sierra Leone.[91] Finally, it has been noted that the Court's focus on forced marriage and sexual crimes risks portraying girls as powerless victims and undermining their agency. This is reinforced by the use as witnesses of boys as former combatants and girls as victims of sexual violence, representing a typical gender division in understandings of the experiences of boys and girls during conflict.[92]

The trend of focusing on child soldiers has continued at the International Criminal Court (ICC), where the Court's first trial concerned the war crime of using child soldiers in the Democratic Republic of Congo (DRC).[93] The ICC has spent considerable energy on crimes related to child soldiers during its early years, listing them in seven of the first twelve indictments.[94] Sexual offences against girls have also been charged.[95] However, studies in Ituri, DRC, reveal dissatisfaction with this emphasis, with many expressing concern that children who were killed, orphaned and deprived of food, shelter and medical care during the conflict receive no attention.[96]

At the national level, even less has been achieved. Many states do not possess the requisite domestic legal frameworks criminalising child recruitment and use as soldiers and, even where they do, weak judicial systems mean that, despite ample evidence to initiate investigations and prosecutions, action is not forthcoming.[97]

---

88 ibid.

89 On forced marriage as a crime against humanity, see M. Scharf, 'Forced Marriage as a Separate Crime Against Humanity' in C.C. Jalloh (ed.), above n. 87, p. 193.

90 Aptel, above n. 87, p. 357.

91 ibid.

92 A. Michels, 'As if it was Happening Again: Supporting Especially Vulnerable Witnesses, particularly Women and Children at the Special Court for Sierra Leone' in K. Arts and V. Popovski (eds.), *International Criminal Accountability and the Rights of Children*, Springer 2006, p. 135.

93 *Prosecutor v. Thomas Lubanga Dyilo*, Judgment pursuant to Article 74 of the Statute, ICC-01/04-01/06, 14 March 2012.

94 See the indictments of Joseph Kony, Vincent Otti, Okot Odhiambo, Bosco Ntaganda, Germain Katanga and Matthieu Ngudjolo Chui, ICC-02/04, July 2004 <http://www.icc-cpi.int> accessed 04.07.2015.

95 See for example, Warrant of Arrest for Ahmad Harun, ICC-02/05-01/07-2, 27 April 2007; Warrant of Arrest for Ali Kushayb, ICC-02/05-01/07-3, 27 April 2007.

96 Aptel and Ladisch, above n. 18, p. 22.

97 Child Soldiers International, *Louder than Words: An Agenda for Action to End State Use of Child Soldiers*, Child Soldiers International 2012, pp. 64–68. United Nations Secretary-General,

While the issue of child soldiering is undoubtedly serious, it represents only a fraction of the violations suffered by children during conflict. It might be argued that there is currently something of a disproportionate focus on children who are soldiers,[98] with the result that, as shown in the contexts of Sierra Leone and the DRC, only a small percentage of children experience criminal justice for the crimes committed against them. Commentators have called for more systematic investigation of the extent to which children are victimised by serious international crimes and prosecution of the full extent of the crimes committed against them.[99] The idea that crimes against children should be treated simply as an aggravation upon sentencing has been rejected and argument advanced that, in light of specific obligations 'to protect children [under international humanitarian law], their particular vulnerability and the disproportionate impact of crimes on them, crimes committed against children should ... receive greater attention' by international courts and tribunals.[100]

At the same time, attention has been drawn to the need for criminal justice systems to take active measures to be more accessible to children.[101] Studies show that children and parents often lack confidence in courts and avoid them due to security concerns or in order to avoid public scandal, particularly in cases of sexual violence,[102] if indeed they are even aware of their existence as a means of redress.[103] Where children are involved in criminal proceedings as victims or witnesses, child friendly procedures, such as anonymous testimony and identity protection, must be adopted in order to ensure the right to participation while minimising distress and preventing re-traumatisation.[104] The ICC, although considered 'pioneering' and 'innovative' in its provisions for the participation and protection of victims and witnesses,[105] has faced significant challenges in realising these standards in relation to children. In the *Lubanga* case, child witnesses were interviewed multiple times and subjected to rigorous

---

Implementation of the World Programme of Action for Youth: Progress and Constraints with Respect to the Well-Being of Youth and Their Role in Civil Society, UN Doc. A/64/61-E/2009/3 2008, p. 12.

98 On this point in the DRC, see P. Clark, 'In the Shadow of the Volcano: Democracy and Justice in Congo', Dissent Magazine 2007 (Winter), pp. 29, 34.

99 Aptel, above n. 81, p. 96.

100 ibid., pp. 87–88.

101 On outreach, see S. Darehshori, 'Lessons Learned for Outreach from the ad hoc Tribunals, the Special Court for Sierra Leone and the ICC' (2008) 14 *New England Journal of International and Comparative Law* 299.

102 Aptel and Ladisch, above n. 18, p. 21.

103 Committee on the Rights of the Child, above n. 32, para. 25.

104 UN Office on Drug and Crime, *UN Guidelines on Justice in Matters Involving Child Victims and Witnesses of Crime*, ECOSOC Res. 2005/20 2005, Art. 30(a); S. Beresford, 'Child Witnesses and the International Criminal Justice System: Does the International Criminal Court Protect the Most Vulnerable?' (2005) 3 *Journal of International Criminal Justice* 721.

105 C. Chamberlain, *Children and the International Criminal Court*, Intersentia 2015, p. 1.

cross-examination in court.[106] The first witness to testify initially recanted due to feelings of intimidation in the presence of the accused[107] and, ultimately, the Court found that all child witnesses in the case, bar one, were unreliable due to their contradictory testimonies and likely manipulation by intermediaries[108] and removed their participatory status.[109]

The events surrounding child witnesses in the *Lubanga* trial have been strongly criticised and accusations made that ICC practice falls short of the standards set in the ICC Statute, which requires the Court to protect the safety, physical and psychological well-being, dignity and privacy of victims and witnesses.[110] It has been argued that a children's rights approach is required, informed by the CRC, which takes into account the specific needs of child witnesses,[111] rather than adopting a general, all-purpose approach to all victims and witnesses.[112] Warnings have also been sounded regarding the portrayal of all child soldiers as coerced victims, lacking the capacity to make decisions and broken by their experiences.[113] This may be an effective prosecutorial strategy in trying the crimes of conscripting, enlisting and using children in hostilities, as was deployed by Moreno-Ocampo in the *Lubanga* trial. However, this typification paints an overly simplistic, singular model of the child soldier,[114] risks damaging their credibility as witnesses and casts doubt on their recollections should they testify against others or claim reparations.[115]

Thus, the scope and modalities of prosecuting crimes against children[116] must be strengthened if a wider group of children are to experience a sense of justice and are to be enabled to participate effectively as victims and witnesses in legal proceedings. This requires the prosecution of a wider range of crimes committed against children in order to capture and record the full extent of the suffering experienced by them during periods of conflict. Crimes of killing, displacement, persecution and denial of access to services impact far greater numbers of children than those of recruiting and using child soldiers and sexual violence, though these remain significant. Judicial authorities must be aware of the impediments children face in accessing justice, whether those relate to a lack of awareness of the possibility of criminal redress or the reluctance of parents to

---

106 ibid., p. 3.
107 Aptel, above n. 81. p. 76.
108 *The Prosecutor v Thomas Lubanga Dyilo* (14 March 2012) ICC-01/04-01/06-2842, paras. 479–480.
109 ibid., para. 484.
110 CRC, above n. 30. Art. 68(1); Chamberlain, above n. 105, p. 4.
111 See CRC, Art. 21 and R86 ICC RPE.
112 Chamberlain, above n. 105, p. 5.
113 M. Drumbl, *Reimagining Child Soldiers in International Law and Policy*, Oxford University Press 2012, p. 154.
114 ibid.
115 ibid.
116 On potential improvements at the ICC, see Chamberlain, above n. 105, pp. 145–215.

become involved in judicial proceedings due to security or social concerns. The formulation of policies and programmes aimed at outreach and alleviation of such concerns should therefore be a priority.[117] Where children do participate, protections that accord with international standards[118] should be in place to protect them during proceedings and provide them with support during and after criminal trials.

4.2. TRUTH SEEKING

Truth seeking, typically undertaken by truth commissions,[119] is also considered an important element of transitional justice. Its primary purpose is to compile a historical record, but the focus on victims and the generation of public discussion on accountability and social reform can build capacity for active citizenship and democratic process. The historical record is used to inform the development of recommendations for reform, thereby making a valuable contribution to strengthening the rule of law.[120] As well as possessing a right to be considered and to express their views in these processes, studies show that the perspectives and experiences of children can be a valuable resource in documenting the past and informing the way forward.[121]

Historically, truth commissions, like criminal trials, neither focused on the crimes committed against children nor included children within their processes, instead discussing them largely in connection with violations committed against their parents. Gradually, commissions have become more child-focused. The South African[122] and Guatemalan[123] commissions of the 1990s worked to ensure that the impact of past violence upon child populations was documented.

---

117 Aptel and Ladisch, above n. 18, p. 21.

118 Office of the High Commissioner for Human Rights, UN Guidelines for Action on Children in the Criminal Justice System, 1997; UN Standard Minimum Rules for the Administration of Juvenile Justice, Adopted by General Assembly Resolution 40/33 of 29 November 1985, Rule 8.

119 For definitions, see: E. Wiebelhaus-Brahm, *Truth Commissions and Transitional Societies: The Impact on Human Rights and Democracy*, Routledge 2010, pp. 3–4; P.B. Hayner, *Unspeakable Truths: Transitional Justice and the Challenge of Truth Commissions*, (2nd edn.) Routledge 2010, p. 11.

120 P. De Greiff, 'Truth Telling and the Rule of Law' in T.A. Borer (ed.), *Telling the Truths: Truth Telling and Peace Building in Post-Conflict Societies*, University of Notre Dame Press 2006, p. 188.

121 UNICEF Innocenti Research Centre and International Center for Transitional Justice, *Children and Truth Commissions*, UNICEF 2010.

122 See P. Pigou, 'Children and the South African Truth and Reconciliation Commission' in S. Parmar, M.J. Roseman, S. Siegrist and T. Sowa (eds.), above n. 3, pp. 155–159.

123 See S. Totten, 'The Plight and Fate of Children vis-à-vis the Guatemalan Genocide' in S. Totten (ed.), *The Plight and Fate of Children During and Following Genocide*, Transaction Publishers 2014, Ch. 6.

However, neither commission allowed children to directly testify or participate in hearings, instead taking statements from adult representatives. In 2002, the Sierra Leone Truth and Reconciliation Commission (TRC) became the first commission with a specific mandate to address violations against children. Children participated in truth seeking through closed and thematic hearings and, with the help of child protection agencies, made an official submission to the TRC, producing the first child friendly version of a truth commission report. The 2005 Commission for Liberia included children systematically within all of its activities and created a task force to develop strategies and procedures to effectively include and protect children within statement taking.[124] Likewise, the Kenyan Commission for Truth, Justice and Reconciliation of 2008 treated children as a special group of victims and as participants within truth seeking processes.[125]

The inclusion of children within truth seeking operations has led not only to the documentation of the nature, extent and consequences of violations against children,[126] but also to the identification of the structural causes of abuse and the formulation of recommendations on how systems can be strengthened and recurrence avoided.[127] Notably, many commissions have called for educational reform and curriculum revision, viewing it as a means of addressing the legacies of conflict and inculcating a human rights culture.[128] However, although there is definite progress in the work of truth commissions, their final reports often fail to recognise the full range of violations suffered by children and contain little analysis or reflection on the gendered dimensions of past harms.[129] For example, other than the TRC for Sierra Leone and, to a lesser extent, Liberia, none of the truth commission reports considered the ways in which boys and girls experienced past violations due to their gender. While some commissions have provided statistical data on crimes committed against children and youth,

---

124 See T. Sowa, 'Children and the Liberian Truth and Reconciliation Commission' in S. Parmar, M.J. Roseman, S. Siegrist and T. Sowa (eds.), above n. 3, pp. 193–231.

125 C.G. Ndungú, *Lessons to be Learned: An Analysis of the Final Report of Kenya's Truth, Justice and Reconciliation Commission*, International Center for Transitional Justice 2014, pp. 7–8.

126 See for example Truth and Reconciliation Commission, *TRC Report*, above n. 73, Vol. 4, Ch. 9; Commission for Reception, Truth and Reconciliation in East Timor, *Chega!, Report of the Commission for Reception, Truth and Reconciliation for East Timor*, 2006, Chs. 7 and 8.

127 See for example ibid., *TRC Report*, Vol 5, Ch. 6.

128 J. Paulson, 'Truth Commissions and National Curricula: The Case of *Recordándonos* in Peru' in S. Parmar, M.J. Roseman, S. Siegrist and T. Sowa (eds.), above n. 3, p. 327. See also E.A. Cole, 'Transitional Justice and the Reform of History Education' (2007) 1 *International Journal of Transitional Justice* 115; J. Paulson, *(Re)Creating Education in Post-Conflict Contexts: Transitional Justice, Education and Human Development*, International Center for Transitional Justice 2009.

129 D. Mazurana and K. Carlson, *Children and Reparation: Past Lessons and New Directions*, UNICEF Innocenti Research Centre 2010, p. 9.

that data is not disaggregated by gender.[130] Thus, 'the gendered aspect of [children's] experiences – the different ways in which boys and girls were affected by the violence and in the aftermath of violence – has been poorly addressed and largely neglected'[131] by most commissions. This has resulted in calls for a gendered analysis that can inform 'the commission, state institutions, citizens, groups and children's own families, communities and societies to determine how best to address the realities of the children's experiences and help recover their rights.'[132]

Concerningly, there has been a recent decline in the inclusion and consultation of children and youth in truth seeking.[133] In Côte d'Ivoire, where transitional processes have suffered from a host of shortcomings,[134] children and youth consider that their experiences of the conflict have neither been sought nor recorded by the established truth commission. As a result, a coalition of young activists[135] has collected testimonies and compiled a series of broadcasts to explain the impact of the conflict and its long-term consequences for children.[136] While these efforts demonstrate the capabilities of children and youth, they also highlight the failure to engage, include and represent these groups within truth seeking at a national level. In Nepal, despite children being consulted on the draft Truth and Reconciliation Commission Bill in 2009,[137] there are few references to children in the enacted legislation. Where they are included, they are mentioned alongside 'senior citizens, differently able people and victims of sexual violence,'[138] demonstrating an 'all purpose' approach to vulnerable groups. In Tunisia's enacting legislation children are identified as a group for special consideration in various aspects of the commission's work,[139] but they represent

---

130 ibid., p. 10.

131 ibid.

132 ibid.

133 See for example, 'Ivorian Youth Find New Ways to be Heard on Truth, Justice and the Future of their Country', International Center for Transitional Justice 2014; and Aptel and Ladisch, above n. 18, pp. 13–14, on the failure to acknowledge children in the Nepalese legislation.

134 Anonymous, 'Côte d'Ivoire Truth Panel Seen Faltering', *IRIN News*, Abidjan, 13.01.2014; C. Koffi, 'Côte d'Ivoire Reconciliation at "Dead End"', *Mail and Guardian Africa*, 24.07.2013.

135 The activist group is known as Le Réseau Action Justice et Paix.

136 R. Goodman and V. Ladisch, 'Youth Working for Justice: Key Agents of Change', International Center for Transitional Justice, 12.08.2015 <https://www.ictj.org/news/youth-justice-key-agents-change> accessed 03.06.2016.

137 UNICEF, 'Children Participate in Consultation on Draft Truth and Reconciliation Commission Bill', UNICEF Kathmandu, 24.11.2009.

138 Commission on Investigation of Disappeared Persons, Truth and Reconciliation 2071 (2014), ss. 13(7) and 17(6).

139 Organic Law on Establishing and Organising Transitional Justice, Law No. 53, 2013, Arts. 4, 11, 12, 43(2) and 53. See also, 'To Protect Victims' Rights, Tunisian Civil Society Looks Ahead to Engaging with Truth Commission', International Center for Transitional Justice 2013.

only one group in a list of those designated as vulnerable. External pressure led to the inclusion of a 'Women's Committee' within the Commission's structure, but there is no committee dedicated to the consideration of children.[140] This is perhaps symptomatic of a general deterioration of truth seeking standards in recent years,[141] rather than a deliberate strategy to exclude children from truth seeking processes. Yet to overlook children is to hamper the potential of truth recovery mechanisms to deliver transitional justice objectives. Exclusion of the experiences of children and youth results in the construction of a narrower, less representative truth and limits the possibilities for truth commissions to make a meaningful contribution to reform.

4.3. REPARATIONS

Reparations also play a role in addressing the violations of the past and charting a way forward to a peaceful future. Under international law, victims of gross violations, including child victims, have a right to reparation.[142] Reparations acknowledge the violations committed against victims, seek to establish their equal citizenship within society and aim to rebuild trust among citizens and between citizens and public institutions.[143] They do so by demonstrating that the government is committed to making a contribution to the survivors' quality of life.[144] In relation to children, they serve an important function in signalling that past modes of governance will not be tolerated and help children to understand their place in a society based on rights, rather than violence.[145]

Recent times have seen some progress in court proceedings on reparations for child victims. While the process has been slow, the ICC Appeals Chamber

---

140 R. El Gantri, *Tunisia in Transition: One Year After the Creation of the Truth and Dignity Commission*, International Center for Transitional Justice 2015, p. 5.

141 See A. Bisset, 'The Role of Truth Commissions in Adjudicating Human Rights Violations' in J.A. Green and C.P.M. Waters (eds.), *Adjudicating International Human Rights*, Brill: Nijhoff 2014, pp. 192–211.

142 See generally, International Covenant on Civil and Political Rights, General Assembly Resolution 2200A (XXI) 1966, Art. 2(3); Bassiouni Principles, above n 27; Nairobi Declaration on Women's and Girls' Right to a Remedy and Reparation 2007. On child victims specifically, see UN Guidelines on Justice in Matters Involving Child Victims and Witnesses, above n. 92; CRC, above n. 30, Art. 39.

143 L. Magarrell, *Reparations in Theory and Practice*, International Center for Transitional Justice 2007.

144 D. Mazurana and K. Carlson, 'Reparations as a Means for Recognizing and Addressing Crimes and Grave Rights Violations against Girls and Boys during Situations of Armed Conflict and under Authoritarian and Dictatorial Regimes' in R.R. Marin (ed.), *The Gender of Reparations: Unsettling Sexual Hierarchies while Redressing Human Rights Violations*, Cambridge University Press 2009, pp. 162–214.

145 Aptel and Ladisch, above n. 18, pp. 26–27.

ordered collective reparations in the *Lubanga* case in March 2015,[146] and the Trust Fund for Victims is expected to submit its implementation plan for these later this year.[147] In 2011, Colombian courts ordered that reparations be paid to those unlawfully recruited as minors into paramilitary groups. The rulings also required the provision of medical and psychological treatment for trauma suffered by recruited youth and their families.[148] Colombia has additionally established an administrative reparations programme in which children are recognised as primary victims of the violations suffered through their recruitment as minors.[149]

Yet, on the whole, a litany of problems has been encountered in delivering reparations generally and for children especially. Studies show that reparations programmes have typically focused on crimes committed against parents, which indirectly impact children,[150] as well as on a narrow range of particular crimes. The result is that the majority of crimes committed against children have not qualified them for reparations because the crime was not recognised or was not seen as being sufficiently grave to trigger reparations.[151] This may stem, at least in part, from the failure to consult child survivors or children's rights organisations in determining the scope of reparations programmes.[152] Interestingly, this reinforces the argument that truth commissions should be given mandates to investigate and report the full extent and nature of violations against children as commissions' findings are very often used to inform reparations packages.[153]

Even in instances where they are eligible, limiting provisions often prevent children from receiving reparations. For example, in South Africa and Peru, age and time limits operated to prevent children gaining all the benefits they qualified for. In Sierra Leone and Timor Leste, children whose mothers were victims of sexual violence were eligible for benefits only while their mothers

146 *The Prosecutor* v. *Thomas Lubanga Dyilo*, Judgment on the Appeals against the Decision Establishing the Principles and Procedures to be Applied to Reparations of 7 August 2012, with amended order for reparations, Case No. ICC-01/04-1/06 A A 2 A 3, 3 March 2015.

147 The Trust Fund for Victims, *Assistance and Reparations: Achievements, Lessons Learned and Transitioning, Programme Progress Report*, The Trust Fund for Victims 2015, p. 6.

148 J. Sochor, *Colombia's Landmark Ruling Orders Reparations for Former Child Soldiers*, International Center for Transitional Justice 2012.

149 Aptel and Ladisch, above n. 18, p. 28.

150 In Nepal, children are entitled to receive benefits only to the extent that their parents were victimised. Government of Nepal, 'Measures for Financial Support and Relief for Conflict Victims' (under the Cabinet decision on 25 April 2008); Government of Nepal, 'Guidelines for Providing Relief to Beneficiary of Deceased Person' (under the Cabinet decision on 05 October 2008); Government of Nepal, 'Guidelines for Providing Relief to the Beneficiary of Disappeared Person' (under the Cabinet decision on 12 January 2009).

151 Mazurana and Carlson, above n. 129, p. 11.

152 ibid., p. 9.

153 ibid., p. 15.

remained single.[154] In addition, a shortage of information, inadequate outreach campaigns, lack of full legal autonomy required to present claims and access documentation can make it difficult for children to realise their right to reparations.[155]

The type of reparation also needs careful consideration. Reparations might be material and include financial compensation and service packages. They may also be symbolic and focus on the provision of public apologies, the erection of memorials and monuments or the creation of learning centres and museums.[156] In order to be most effective, it is believed that reparations should have both symbolic and material elements.[157] The simple payment of cash lump sums seen in Colombia and Nepal is problematic.[158] Children typically lack bank accounts and financial literacy. They may come under pressure to use the money to the benefit of wider family and, in some cases, the money may end up under the control of parents who use it for themselves.[159] As noted by Nolan, the presumption that family relationships are underpinned by social justice is not accurate; instead, they are pervaded by the same attitudes and practices of society, which are often adultist and gendered.[160] It is therefore essential that the child's right to resources be viewed as independent of the parent or caregiver.[161] It has been suggested that payments be made in small amounts to combat such problems.[162] However, whether this presents a complete solution to the issues discussed above is questionable.

In addition, the discourse on reparations evinces a consensus on the need for reparations programmes to be gender and culturally sensitive and mindful of the need to avoid further stigmatisation or marginalisation.[163] However, the reality remains that in the majority of transitional states reparations are not forthcoming, least of all for children, despite their potential to make a positive long-term impact and equip children with the resources and support needed to move forward to a productive life.

---

154 ibid., p. 16.
155 ibid.
156 UNICEF Innocenti Research Centre and International Center for Transitional Justice, above n. 121, pp. 51–57.
157 Magarrell, above n. 143, p. 5.
158 Aptel and Ladisch, above n. 18, pp. 29–30.
159 ibid., p. 30.
160 Nolan, above n. 74, p. 9.
161 ibid., p. 10.
162 Aptel and Ladisch, above n. 18, p. 30.
163 S.M. Miano, 'Towards a Child Oriented Approach to Reparations: Reflecting on the Rights and Needs of Child Victims of Armed Conflict' (2013) XXVIII *Praxis The Fletcher Journal of Human Security* 28, 34–37; Mazurana and Carlson, above n. 129, p. 200.

4.4. REFORM

The final component of transitional justice is institutional reform, which involves reviewing and restructuring state institutions so that they are accountable, operate in accordance with and preserve the rule of law and respect human rights. From a children's rights perspective, institutional reform should build a protective environment for children, preventing their abuse and exploitation, and ensure that health and education systems, social welfare institutions and the judiciary, police and security sectors promote children's rights.[164] Reform should also include the creation of institutionalised structures that facilitate the participation of children in the formulation of local and national policy making.[165]

Disarmament, demobilisation and reintegration (DDR) schemes are an important element of institutional reform for CAAFAG.[166] These are important not only because frustrated or marginalised youth can destabilise a fragile peace, but also as a means of providing former child soldiers with the possibility of playing a constructive role in society.[167] Despite this, studies show that many former child combatants do not go through any sort of DDR scheme and where they do, the focus is typically on demobilisation and disarmament, with inadequate provision for reintegration.[168] Girl soldiers are frequently marginalised because they are viewed as less of a security threat than male combatants. They are also more likely to self-demobilise in order to avoid social stigma when they return to their communities or to avoid sexual violence in male dominated demobilisation camps.[169]

Dealing with CAAFAG is only one component of institutional reform. Legislative reform can serve as an important means of mainstreaming children's rights. A number of transitional states have taken the opportunity to ratify

---

164 ibid., p. 59.

165 UN Committee on the Rights of the Child, *Tenth Anniversary of the Convention on the Rights of the Child Commemorative Meeting: Achievements and Challenges*, UN Doc. CRC/C/87, Annex IV, 22nd Session (30 September-1 October 1999), 7 December 1999, para. 91(w) and (x). See also A. Parkes, *Children and International Human Rights Law: The Right of the Child to be Heard*, Routledge 2013, p. 182.

166 L. Waldorf, 'Just Peace? Integrating DDR and Transitional Justice' in L. Sriram et al. (eds.), *Transitional Justice and Peacebuilding on the Ground*, Routledge 2013, p. 63.

167 R. Duthie and I. Specht, 'DDR, Transitional Justice and the Reintegration of Child Combatants' in A. Cutter, P. De Greiff and L. Waldorf (eds.), *Disarming the Past: Transitional Justice and Ex-Combatants*, Social Sciences Research Council 2010, p. 194.

168 ibid., p. 196; M. Wessels, *Child Soldiers: From Violence to Protection*, Harvard University Press 2006, p. 155.

169 B. Verhey, *Reaching the Girls: Study on Girls Associated with Armed Forces and Armed Groups in the Democratic Republic of Congo*, Save the Children UK and the NGO Group CARE, IFESH and IRC 2004.

the CRC,[170] implement national laws consistent with CRC principles and promote a focus on children in domestic legal processes.[171] However, in order for these legislative frameworks to have meaningful impact, they must be accompanied by international and domestic political commitments to allocate the funding needed to create the supporting infrastructure necessary to implement mechanisms aimed at ensuring children's access to these rights. Key demographic indicators paint a depressing picture of children's rights, particularly economic and social rights, in transitional states.[172]

Educational reform can also be an important transitional initiative.[173] Training teachers to deliver new curricula based on the lessons of the past and which introduce civic and human rights education, conflict resolution and gender studies can play an effective role in social reconstruction, reconciliation and building peace and democracy.[174] Yet, despite the convincing discourse on the need for educational reform in post-conflict contexts, a lack of political will and, sometimes, divergent social opinions, has hampered the development and implementation of new curricula.[175] For example, in Rwanda, twenty years after the genocide, history is still not being taught in schools. Like the rest of the country, the education system was severely damaged by the genocide and surviving teachers lacked the materials to teach such a complicated and painful history.[176] At the same time, teaching Rwanda's recent history is made more difficult by national laws that prohibit discussion of ethnicity. Laws against 'divisionism' are justified on the grounds that they aim to prevent a repeat of the 1994 tragedy.[177] However, for children, the result is an inability to engage in debate and analysis with peers of an event that has and will continue to shape and influence community, societal and national development. Such an approach arguably falls short of the standards of Article 13 CRC, which gives children the right to seek and receive information and ideas of all kinds. While

---

170 For example: Bosnia and Herzegovina ratified following conflict in 1993; South Africa ratified in 1995 post-apartheid and Timor Leste ratified following independence in 2003.

171 See generally, Government of the Republic of Sierra Leone, Ministry of Social Welfare, Gender and Children's Affairs <http://mswgca.gov.sl> accessed 28.07.2015; B. Al-Dhayi, *Children's Law Offers Promise and Protection to Liberia's Children*, UNICEF Liberia 2012.

172 UNICEF Data, *Monitoring the Situation of Children and Women* <http://data.unicef.org/countries/ZAF.html> accessed 20.10.2015.

173 Aptel and Ladisch, above n. 18, p. 34.

174 E.A. Cole and K. Murphy, 'History Education Reform, Transitional Justice and Transformation of Identities' in P. Arthur (ed.), *Identities in Transition: Challenges for Transitional Justice in Divided Societies*, Cambridge University Press 2011, pp. 335–336.

175 For an overview see UNICEF Innocenti Research Centre and International Center for Transitional Justice, above n. 121, pp. 61–63.

176 G. Duruz, *Speaking History in Present Rwanda: Constrained History Enunciation and Management of Conflicting Narratives in Secondary School Students in Rwanda* [Masters Dissertation], National University of Rwanda 2012.

177 J. Melvin, 'Correcting History: Mandatory Education in Rwanda' 2013 (2) *Journal of Human Rights in the Commonwealth* 14.

the Convention recognises the possibility of lawful restrictions to this right,[178] many view the Rwandan laws against divisionism as serving a political agenda that favours the purposes of the ruling Rwandan Patriotic Front government.[179]

5. CONCLUSION

This chapter set out to ascertain the extent to which children are represented within transitional justice processes. The chapter has identified positive steps across all four key mechanisms. Crimes committed against children have been prosecuted before international courts and investigated and reported upon by truth commissions. Children have appeared and been represented in both trial and truth seeking proceedings. While progress on delivering reparations for children remains slow, recognition of children as a group deserving of reparations is in itself a step forward. Likewise, the reform agenda in a number of transitional states has included children's issues.

Nevertheless, much work remains to be done. International preoccupation with child soldiers has resulted in prosecutions of those who conscript, enlist and use children in armed hostilities, the creation of DDR programmes designed to facilitate the return of CAAFAG to their communities and the payment of reparations to former child soldiers. Although important, this focus on CAAFAG has diverted attention from the significant and varied impact that armed conflict has on other groups of children, particularly the economic and social rights implications of periods of violence and the long-term consequences of their denial. Beyond child soldiers, there remains something of a one-size-fits-all approach to children within transitional justice practice, which treats them as a homogenous group and fails to recognise the discrete experiences created by gender, disability and membership of minority groups. Moreover, outdated approaches that fail to view children as rights bearers and link their experiences, voices and opportunities for redress to those of adults remain all too common. A sea change in how children are viewed is required. Only when the agency, potential and capabilities of children are recognised and harnessed under a rights-based approach, and they are systematically consulted and included across all processes, will transitional justice mechanisms maximise their capacity to deliver long-term peace, stability and reconciliation to transitional states.

---

[178] CRC, above n. 30, Art. 13(2).

[179] Human Rights Watch, *Law and Reality. Progress in Judicial Reform in Rwanda*, Human Rights Watch 2008, pp. 34–43.

CONFLICT-RELATED SEXUAL VIOLENCE IN KOSOVO

Gendering Justice Through Transformative Reparations

Priya Gopalan*

1. INTRODUCTION

Conflict-related sexual violence (CRSV) has been historically perceived as a lesser crime that is incidental, opportunistic or divorced from other war-time atrocities.[1] Conceptualising sexual violence in this manner rendered these

* The views expressed in this chapter are solely those of the author. The author wishes to thank Siobhan Hobbs, Preetha Gopalan and Michelle Jarvis for their valuable feedback on this chapter, and UN Women Kosovo for the information and support provided.

1 CRSV refers to incidents or patterns of sexual violence against women, men, girls or boys occurring in conflict or post-conflict settings that have direct or indirect links with the conflict itself or that occur in other situations of concern such as in the context of political repression. CRSV encompasses the following acts: rape, forced pregnancy, forced sterilisation, forced abortion, forced prostitution, trafficking, sexual enslavement, forced nudity, castration and any other form of sexual violence of comparable gravity. See UN Analytical and Conceptual Framing of Conflict-Related Sexual Violence (June 2011), summarised at <http://gbvaor.net/wp-content/uploads/2015/03/Analytical-and-Conceptual-Framing-of-Conflict-Related-Sexual-Violence-UN-Action-against-Sexual-Violence-in-Conflict-2011.pdf> accessed 05.07.2018.

crimes invisible in the theatre of war and consequently denied victims justice.[2] The conflicts in the former Yugoslavia in the 1990s triggered a dramatic shift that challenged the marginalisation and silencing of sexual violence. Media coverage of the courageous testimony of victims of 'rape camps' in Bosnia and Herzegovina (BiH) catapulted CRSV into the public domain. Sexual violence was recast as a 'weapon of war' that was integral to the ethnic cleansing campaigns in the former Yugoslavia.[3] These developments spearheaded calls to end impunity for sexual violence in this conflict.[4]

Sexual violence was also prevalent during the conflict in Kosovo.[5] As the former Yugoslavia disintegrated, in the late 1990s Serb forces clashed with the Kosovo Liberation Army (KLA), which sought to establish an independent Kosovo (then a province of Serbia within the former Yugoslavia).[6] Civilians experienced a raft of atrocities during the fighting: murder, beatings, deportation, property destruction and sexual violence. Serb forces used sexual violence to terrorise and expel Kosovo Albanian civilians from Kosovo during their ethnic

---

2 This is due partly to the gendered nature of international law that is addressed in a rich body of academic work. See, e.g., J. Gardam and M. Jarvis, *Women, Armed Conflict and International Law*, Kluwer Law International 2001 (arguing that international humanitarian law is inherently discriminatory because it assigns gendered roles to men and women by prioritising men as male combatants while consigning women to the status of victims or mothers); L. Chappell, *The Politics of Gender Justice at the International Criminal Court: Legacies and Legitimacy*, Oxford University Press 2016, p. 36 (describing the gender legacies of international law as the silences, formal and informal rules, norms and processes that "situate men and women differently before the law, and to produce different sex and gender (in)justice outcomes").

3 The phrase 'weapon of war' or related phrases such as 'strategic rape' served as a useful shorthand to capture international attention and to provide visibility to these crimes. As our understanding of CRSV has deepened, these conceptual frameworks have been broadened to include a more nuanced and contextual assessment of these crimes. We have learnt that even if it is not 'strategic', perpetrated in a widespread or systematic manner, pursuant to orders, or used as a weapon of war, sexual violence can be integral to a violent conflict. Determining its occurrence, considering its links with other crimes, and the broader context of the conflict enables a better assessment of the multiple functions, facets and impact of sexual violence, thus furthering accountability. For a critical analysis of this issue, see M. Eriksson Baaz and M. Stern, *Sexual Violence as a Weapon of War? Perceptions, Prescriptions, Problems in the Congo and Beyond*, Zed Books 2013.

4 This call was taken up by the ICTY that has delivered the landmark judgments on CRSV. See, e.g., *Mucić et al.*, Case No. IT-96-21-T, Trial Judgment (16 November 1998), *Prosecutor v. Furundžija*, Case No. IT-95-17/1-T, Trial Judgment (10 December 1998) (rape as a form of torture), and *Prosecutor v. Kunarac et al.*, Case Nos. IT-96-23-T & IT-96-23/1-T, Trial Judgment (22 February 2001) (sexual enslavement and rape as crimes against humanity).

5 Reference to Kosovo should be understood to be in full compliance with United Nations Security Council Resolution 1244 (1999) and without prejudice to the status of Kosovo. See UN SC Res 1244 (10 June 1999) UN Doc S/Res/1244.

6 See OSCE, 'Kosovo/Kosova: As Seen, As Told: An Analysis of the Human Rights Findings of the OSCE Kosovo Verification Mission October 1998 to June 1999', OSCE 1999, pp. 3–8.

cleansing of the province.[7] Sexual violence was omnipresent – in detention, in homes and in convoys as women fled.[8]

Has there been justice for victims of CRSV in Kosovo almost 20 years after the end of conflict?[9] Following a long and hard-fought battle, they are now entitled to receive reparations as a legal right, arising from their status as CRSV victims. This is significant. The reparations process has commenced, and women who have been recognised as CRSV victims are awaiting compensation in the form of a monthly pension. Nonetheless, in terms of domestic prosecutions of CRSV, a lack of accountability for this crime is the norm. There have been no convictions entered in respect of CRSV in domestic courts in Kosovo. However, at the international level, sexual violence has been successfully prosecuted at the International Criminal Tribunal for the Former Yugoslavia (ICTY). The Appeals Judgments of *Šainović et al.*[10] and *Đorđević*[11] are amongst the ICTY's most important appellate precedents on sexual violence, confirming the occurrence of sexual violence, and its relationship and parity with other serious conflict-related crimes.[12] Nonetheless, these legal precedents contain discrete legal and

---

7 Human Rights Watch, Women's Rights Division, 'Kosovo: Rape as a Weapon of "Ethnic Cleansing"' (1 March 2000), available at <https://www.hrw.org/report/2000/03/01/kosovo-rape-weapon-ethnic-cleansing> accessed 29.04.2018, Section I Summary. See also OSCE, 'Human Rights in Kosovo: As Seen, As Told' vol. II, 14 June to 31 October 1999, pt. 3 (documenting many allegations of rape, among other crimes); Human Rights Watch, 'Under Orders: War Crimes in Kosovo', 26.10.2001, pp. 130–33 available at <https://www.hrw.org/report/2001/10/26/under-orders-war-crimes-kosovo> accessed 29.04.2018.

8 See OSCE, above n. 6. While men and women from other communities and ethnicities (Roma, Ashkali, Egyptian and Serbian, for example) also suffered sexual violence in this conflict, their experiences were less reported and/or documented when compared to the crimes perpetrated by Serb forces against Kosovo Albanian women. As a result, the experience of Kosovo Albanian women is the focus of this chapter. Women should be understood to include women and girls, unless otherwise specifically noted.

9 For a comprehensive account of justice initiatives relating to CRSV victims in Kosovo, see Annex 1: 'A Summary of Reparative Initiatives for CRSV' in S. Hobbs, 'The Conflict Did Not Bring Us Flowers: The Need for Comprehensive Reparations for Survivors of Conflict-Related Sexual Violence in Kosovo', UN Women 2016, available at <http://www2.unwomen.org/-/media/field%20office%20eca/attachments/publications/country/kosovo/the%20conflict%20did%20not%20bring%20us%20flowers_eng.pdf?la=en&vs=2544> accessed 27.04.2018.

10 *Prosecutor v. Šainović et al.*, Case No. IT-05-87-A, Appeal Judgment (23 January 2014). *Šainović et al.* was known as *Milutinović et al.* at trial.

11 *Prosecutor v. Đorđević*, Case No. IT-05-87/1-A, Appeal Judgment (27 January 2014).

12 These cases concern the ethnic cleansing campaign unleashed against Kosovo Albanian civilians by Serb forces, leading up to NATO's 'humanitarian bombing' of Kosovo in March 1999. The accused in *Šainović et al.* and *Đorđević* were the top brass in the Serbian military, police, and political hierarchy who had responsibility over Kosovo: Nikola Šainović (Deputy Prime Minister of the Federal Republic of Yugoslavia), Sreten Lukić (Head of the Serbian Ministry of Internal Affairs (MUP) Staff for Kosovo), Vlastimir Đorđević (Assistant Minister of the MUP and Chief of the Public Security Department) and Nebojsa Pavković (Head of the Third Army), together, 'the Accused'. Aside from these two cases, ethnic cleansing in Kosovo was also prosecuted in the Kosovo component of the case of *Prosecutor v. Slobodan Milošević* (*Prosecutor v. Slobodan Milošević*, Case No. IT-02-54-T).

factual findings that do not reflect the scale and nature of CRSV in Kosovo due to the evidence presented in these cases.

Taking the promotion of gender justice in post-conflict Kosovo as its goal, this chapter recommends a cohesive transitional justice strategy that delivers both judicial and non-judicial remedies including transformative, gender-sensitive reparations.[13] Transformative reparations address not only the immediate consequences of CRSV, but seek to reform underlying gender inequalities that are embedded in social, economic and political structures, and which obstruct effective remedies for victims.[14] While pivotal, the prosecution of perpetrators is only one amongst the suite of reparative remedies that would improve the lives of victims.[15] The current reparative framework in Kosovo requires further development to ensure that these goals are met.

This chapter begins with an assessment of the successes and limitations of retributive justice delivered through domestic and international criminal prosecutions for CRSV in Kosovo.[16] It then advocates a transformative justice agenda that includes gender-sensitive reparations for CRSV as a necessary complement to the process of retributive justice. In doing so, it explores the structural gender inequalities permeating Kosovo Albanian society that provided the canvas for sexual violence, and now hinder remedies for the same. The chapter also considers the limitations of the domestic legislation

---

However, this case was not completed due to Milošević's death in 2006. The ICTY also prosecuted members of the KLA for their conduct in the Kosovo conflict in two cases: *Prosecutor v. Limaj et al.* (Fatmir Limaj, Haradin Bala and Isak Musliu, Case No. IT-03-66) and *Prosecutor v. Ramush Haradinaj et al.* (Ramush Haradinaj, Idriz Balaj and Lahi Brahimaj, Case No. IT-04-84).

13 'Gender justice refers to the protection and promotion of civil, political, economic and social rights on the basis of gender equality. It necessitates taking a gender perspective on the rights themselves, as well as the assessment of access and obstacles to the enjoyment of these rights for both women, men, girls and boys and adopting gender-sensitive strategies for protecting and promoting them.' See P. Spees, 'Gender Justice and Accountability in Peace Support Operations' (International Alert, February 2004), p. 9, available at <http://www.un.org/womenwatch/osagi/feature/postconflict/gender%20justice-international%20alert.pdf> accessed 29.04.2018.

14 '"Transformative reparations" … means land restitution, coupled with land redistribution and access to credit, skills and means to transform that land into a source of livelihood. … providing fistula surgery to survivors of rape as well as income-generating skills.' See P. Mlambo-Ngcuka, Executive Director of UN Women in R. Coomaraswamy, 'Preventing Conflict, Transforming Justice, Securing the Peace: A Global Study on the Implementation of United Nations Security Council resolution 1325', UN Women 2015 ('UN Women Global Study'), p. 115.

15 V. S. Rames, *Healing the Spirit: Reparations for Survivors of Sexual Violence Related to the Armed Conflict in Kosovo*, Prishtinë/Priština, OHCHR Stand-alone Office in Kosovo 2013, available at <http://www.ohchr.org/Documents/Issues/Women/WRGS/PeaceAndSecurity/StudyHealingTheSpirit.pdf> accessed 29.04.2018. This study examined the patterns and consequences of sexual violence committed during the Kosovo conflict (February 1998 and June 1999), pp. 57–72.

16 Within the criminal justice framework, the purpose of retributive justice is the prosecutions and punishment of perpetrators who violate the law.

establishing a reparations programme for victims of the Kosovo conflict: the Law no. 04/L-172 On Amending and Supplementing the Law no. 04/L-054 on the Status and the Rights of the Martyrs, Invalids, Veterans, Members of Kosovo Liberation Army, Sexual Violence Victims of the War, Civilian Victims and their Families (the '2014 Law').[17] It concludes with strategies to improve the 2014 Law and strengthen Kosovo's transitional justice framework in order to deliver transformative gender-sensitive reparations to CRSV victims.

2. RETRIBUTIVE JUSTICE – PROSECUTING PERPETRATORS

Transitional justice comprises the full range of judicial and non-judicial processes and mechanisms that seek to address mass violations that as a result of their severity and scale, are beyond the wherewithal of the normal domestic processes.[18] Comprising four pillars – criminal prosecutions, legal and institutional reform, truth seeking and reparations – transitional justice seeks to ensure accountability, reconciliation and collective healing in societies emerging from conflict and repression.[19] In Kosovo, the transitional justice process for CRSV victims has concentrated on criminal prosecutions and reparations delivered through the 2014 Law.[20] This section discusses the successes and limitations of criminal prosecutions in delivering justice to CRSV victims in Kosovo. While there is no official or authoritative data on the number of women who experienced sexual violence during the Kosovo conflict,[21] the consensus is that sexual violence was widespread. Considering the scale of these crimes,

---

17 See the 2014 Law, available at <http://www.kuvendikosoves.org/common/docs/ligjet/04-L-172%20a.pdf> accessed 29.04.2018.

18 OHCHR, 'Analytical Study Focusing on Gender-based and Sexual Violence in Relation to Transitional Justice' A/HRC/27/21 (30 June 2014) para. 6 (internal citations omitted).

19 See the International Centre for Transitional Justice, an international non-profit organisation specialising in the field of transitional justice, available at <https://www.ictj.org/about/transitional-justice> accessed 29.04.2018.

20 Accordingly, this chapter will focus on criminal prosecutions in contrast to reparations. Institutional reforms will be dealt with to the extent they fall within reparative measures. Truth commissions and other truth-seeking initiatives can have a reparative function as well. In February 2017, based on the proposal of Hashim Thaci, the President of Kosovo, consultations on a Truth and Reconciliation Commission were launched. See D. Morina and D. Baliu, 'Kosovo's Thaci Announces Post-War Reconciliation Commission' Balkan Transitional Justice, 13.02.2017, available at <http://www.balkaninsight.com/en/article/kosovo-s-president-with-an-initiative-of-reconciliation-02-13-2017> accessed 29.04.2018; K. Rexhepi, 'Kosovo "Trapped by the Past": Thaci' Balkan Transitional Justice, 1 March 2017, available at <http://www.balkaninsight.com/en/article/kosovo-trapped-by-the-past-thaci-03-01-2017> accessed 29.04.2018.

21 Rames, above n. 15, pp. 7, 39 noting that the data on the incidence of sexual violence during the conflict in Kosovo is inaccurate and incomplete.

the cases prosecuted thus far – both at the national and international levels – do not capture the scope, nature and multiple facets of sexual violence in the Kosovo conflict.

In accordance with the principle of complementarity espoused by the International Criminal Court (ICC), domestic courts are best placed to undertake the prosecutions of CRSV.[22] In Kosovo, there have been three prosecutions for CRSV.[23] The first prosecution was undertaken by the UN Interim Administration Mission in Kosovo (UNMIK) in the Gjilan/Gnjilane District Court, and was completed in 2002.[24] In 2008, UNMIK's justice competencies were superseded by EULEX, the European Union's rule-of-law mission. EULEX completed two further cases before the Basic Court in Mitrovice/Mitrovica in 2013 and 2016.[25] In 2017, it initiated the first-ever investigations into cases in which sexual violence was classified as war crimes.[26] EULEX had three cases under investigation and three cases under preliminary investigation, having completed two investigations and dismissed two investigations.[27] Despite these efforts, there have been no convictions for CRSV in Kosovo at the time of writing.[28] In contrast, in BiH, 134 defendants have been convicted of CRSV, in over a quarter of the 400 completed war crimes cases in domestic courts.[29]

---

22 'The Long Road: Accountability for Sexual Violence in Conflict and Post-Conflict Settings', Human Rights Center UC Berkeley School of Law 2015, p. 1, available at <https://www.law.berkeley.edu/wp-content/uploads/2015/04/The-Long-Road-Executive-Summary-August-2015.pdf> accessed 29.04.2018. See also CEDAW General Recommendation No. 33 on women's access to justice (CEDAW/C/GC/33, 23 July 2015) highlighting the importance of effective domestic remedies.

23 Serbia has also conducted prosecutions for CRSV in Kosovo. Serbia's Special War Crimes Chamber in Belgrade prosecuted the 'Gnjilane Group', who were KLA members, for rape, inhumane treatment, violation of the bodily integrity of Kosovo Serbian and other non-Albanian women in Gnjilane. All 16 defendants were eventually acquitted ('Gnjilane Group' case, Court of Appeals in Belgrade, case no. Kž1 Po2 2/13, Judgment, 13 November 2013). Another case, also against the KLA resulted, in a conviction. Amnesty International, '"Wounds that Burn our Souls": Compensation for Kosovo's Wartime Rape Survivors, but Still No Justice', 13 December 2017, pp. 7, 29, available at <https://www.amnesty.org/en/documents/eur70/7558/2017/en/> accessed 25.04.2018.

24 Rames, above n. 15, p. 70.

25 See P. No. 13/2013 (PPS 89/2012) enacting clause available at <http://www.eulex-kosovo.eu/eul/repository/docs/2013-17-04_BC_Mitro_-_D__B_-_Engl.pdf> accessed 29.04.2018 and P. No. 62/2016 (PPS 23/2013) enacting clause available at <http://www.eulex-kosovo.eu/eul/repository/docs/20161111-enacting-clause_Haxha_redacted.pdf> accessed 29.04.2018. For all EULEX judgments see <http://www.eulex-kosovo.eu/en/judgments/> accessed 29.04.2018.

26 B. Borchardt, EULEX Head of Mission, 'EULEX and War Crimes', available at <http://www.eulex-kosovo.eu/en/news/000427.php> accessed 17.03.2017.

27 Email correspondence between the author and EULEX (02.02.2017).

28 30 April 2018. These cases ended with acquittals upon appeal as the courts found that there was insufficient evidence to identify the perpetrators. Amnesty International, 'Wounds that Burn our Souls', above n. 23, p. 7.

29 Amnesty International, '"We Need Support, Not Pity": Last Chance for Justice for Bosnia's Wartime Rape Survivors', September 2017, Index: EUR 63/6679/2017 available at

The limited and slow pace of CRSV prosecutions is symptomatic of the broader difficulties of prosecuting war crimes in Kosovo. In February 2017, the Council of Europe Commissioner for Human Rights, Nils Muiznieks, stated that the prosecutions for war-time violence have been ineffective, with war victims in Kosovo being ignored.[30] Confirming this view, the Humanitarian Law Centre Kosovo reported that in 2016, Kosovo conducted the fewest war crimes trials in any year since the war.[31] There are several reasons for this. First, investigations into alleged perpetrators are limited to the jurisdiction of Kosovo, whereas most suspects in relation to crimes committed against Kosovo Albanians during the war are Kosovo Serbs or Serbian nationals who are no longer in Kosovo. Arrest warrants cannot be executed outside Kosovo's borders and domestic law does not permit trials *in absentia*.[32] Second, the lack of witness protection is a grave threat to the integrity of the judicial process. Third, practical hurdles relating to court management and the professional capacity of judicial actors are further impediments. These challenges are compounded in cases of sexual violence by the reluctance of victims to come forward, oftentimes due to stigma. The absence of victim-sensitive arrangements can also discourage victims from testifying.

The prospects for domestic accountability for CRSV in Kosovo remain dismal. As EULEX's mandate ends, the Special Prosecution Office of the Republic of Kosovo (SPRK) will inherit EULEX's investigative and prosecutorial responsibilities. EULEX intends to transfer 1000 case files to the SPRK which may include CRSV cases. However, with only two war crimes prosecutors in the SPRK, the mammoth task of investigating and prosecuting these crimes would appear to be insurmountable, without a significant increase in resources.[33]

Turning to international prosecutions of CRSV in Kosovo, these have been undertaken by the ICTY. The cases of *Šainović et al.* and *Đorđević* litigated crimes perpetrated during an ethnic cleansing campaign in Kosovo. These cases delivered progressive international legal precedents on crimes of sexual violence that built on earlier jurisprudence.[34] Sexual violence can and does play

<http://www.amnesty.ie/wp-content/uploads/2017/09/BiH-report-final-for-print.pdf> accessed 09.07.2018, pp. 11, 22. Trials for CRSV in BiH have also been completed at the ICTY and in Serbia.

30 'Council of Europe Says Kosovo War Victims "Ignored"' Balkan Transitional Justice, 09.02.2017, available at <http://www.balkaninsight.com/en/article/council-of-europe-says-kosovo-war-victims-ignored--02-09-2017> accessed 29.04.2018.

31 D. Morina, 'Kosovo "Holding Fewer War Crimes Trials Than Ever"' Balkan Transitional Justice, 30.03.2017, available at <http://www.balkaninsight.com/en/article/kosovo-scores-decrease-in-the-number-of-war-crimes-trials-03-30-2017> accessed 29.04.2018.

32 Borchardt, above n. 26; D. Morina, 'Kosovo Confirms Arrest Warrant for 57 Serbians' Balkan Transitional Justice, 15.02.2017, available at <http://www.balkaninsight.com/en/article/warrants-follow-the-arrest-of-former-kosovo-pm-02-15-2017> accessed 29.04.2018.

33 Amnesty International, 'Wounds that Burn our Souls', above n. 23, pp. 7, 24–25.

34 See, e.g., *Prosecutor v. Stakić*, Case No. IT-97-24-T, Trial Judgment (31 July 2003), *Prosecutor v. Krstić*, Case No. IT-98-33-T, Trial Judgment (2 August 2001).

an integral role in conflict, as it did in Kosovo. Significantly, the Appeals Chamber in *Đorđević* emphasised that crimes of sexual violence 'must not be treated differently from other violent acts simply because of their sexual component'.[35] By recognising crimes of sexual violence as international crimes of a gravity comparable to other war crimes, the Appeals Chamber promoted accountability and advanced the equal treatment of victims of sexual violence under the law.

Despite these advances, the legal victories in *Šainović et al.* and *Đorđević* appear pyrrhic because they did not result in convictions in *Šainović et al.* nor in more punitive sentences for the accused in *Đorđević*. The Appeals Chamber in *Šainović et al.* declined by a majority to enter convictions, despite finding the accused responsible for the sexual assaults.[36] The Appeals Chamber did not give reasons for this inconsonance between legal culpability and commensurate sanction, but merely referred to its discretion to affirm, reverse or revise Trial Chamber decisions.[37] In *Đorđević*, the Appeals Chamber entered convictions, but ultimately reduced the Accused's sentence.[38] The Appeals Chamber noted that this reduction in sentence did not imply that the crimes for which Đorđević was convicted on appeal were not grave. Notwithstanding this disclaimer, the Appeals Chamber's sentencing approach harks back to the traditional hierarchical approach, which subordinates sexual violence to other conflict-related crimes that are perceived to be more serious.

In addition, based on the limited evidence presented, the cases of *Đorđević* and *Šainović et al.* contain restricted findings on discrete incidents of sexual violence. These cases do not capture the prevalence and extent of these crimes against Kosovo Albanian women or the experiences of men as victims. Nor do they reflect the crimes of sexual violence perpetrated against victims from other ethnicities and communities.[39] The narrow scope of sexual violence evidence presented in these cases, despite the mass scale of these crimes as documented by other reliable sources, can be explained by several factors. First, uncovering evidence of sexual violence and encouraging victims to testify can be challenging, not least due to the actual and perceived effects of shame and stigma.[40] Creating an enabling environment for CRSV victims to testify can require additional time and resources. While securing the evidence of other types of witnesses can also

---

35 *Đorđević*, above n. 11, para. 887.

36 *Šainović*, above n. 10, para. 1604; Dissenting Opinion of Judge Ramaroson.

37 Referring to Article 25(2) of the ICTY Statute and jurisprudence that permits such discretion. *Šainović*, above n. 10, para. 1604, fn 5269.

38 It found that convictions overturned on appeal for other crimes (deportation, forcible transfer and murder) outweighed the new convictions entered on appeal for sexual assaults due to the number of victims of sexual assault and Đorđević's level of responsibility, thus reducing the length of the overall sentence. *Đorđević*, above n. 11, paras 976–80, fn 2879.

39 Rames, above n. 15, highlighting this lack of information as a lacuna at pp. 7, 39.

40 See section 4.

entail additional effort, investigators and other judicial actors may be less inclined to make this investment for sexual violence due to the misconception that it is a lesser offence.[41] It is noteworthy that partly due to investigative difficulties and the prioritisation of other crimes, the first draft of the ICTY indictment relating to the conflict in Kosovo did not contain sexual violence charges.[42]

Second, even when evidence of sexual violence is obtained, the adversarial nature of ICTY prosecutions and an emphasis on securing criminal convictions may result in the winnowing out of evidence that is deemed less critical to the case. This could result in the prioritisation of other conflict-related crimes such as murders that are perceived to be more serious or critical to the litigation strategy, especially when faced with limited resources and the widespread criminality of conflict. When sexual violence is marginalised in this way, it is difficult to properly situate it within the landscape of the conflict, thus entrenching the invisibility of and impunity for these crimes.

Further, as international prosecutions focus on those 'most responsible', the majority of direct perpetrators remain unscathed by any judicial process, resulting in an impunity gap that undermines the rule of law, long-term stability and post-conflict reconciliation.[43] From the victims' perspective, limited prosecutions can signal society's failure to regard their violations worthy of legal sanction. By contrast, successful criminal prosecutions serve to publicly condemn the crime and the perpetrator, while providing moral recognition of the harm suffered by victims and contributing to a sense of justice and closure for many of them.[44] The paucity of both domestic and international prosecutions for CRSV coupled with the limited findings on sexual violence call for greater efforts in prosecuting CRSV in Kosovo and promoting accountability for this crime.[45]

---

41 M. Jarvis and K. Vigneswaran, 'Challenges to Successful Outcomes in Sexual Violence Cases' in S. Brammertz and M. Jarvis (eds.), *Prosecuting Conflict-Related Sexual Violence at the ICTY*, Oxford University Press 2016, pp. 36–37.

42 ibid., p. 56. Only when NGOs put forward allegations of sexual violence following the arrest of *Slobodan Milošević* in 2001, were further investigations conducted, and the indictment amended to include charges of sexual violence.

43 See, e.g., UNSC Res 1820 (19 June 2008) UN Doc S/RES/1820, UNSC Res 1325 (31 October 2000) UN Doc S/RES/1325 and UNSC Res 2122 (18 October 2013) UN Doc S/RES/2122.

44 Khadidja Zidane, a witness who provided sexual violence testimony that was critical to the conviction of former Chadian dictator, Hissène Habré expressed this sentiment eloquently: 'But at least I was able to face him. If I die today, I'll die in peace. I had the opportunity to tell the whole world what he did to me …'. See R. Maclean, '"I told my story face to face with Habré": courageous rape survivors make history' *The Guardian*, N'Djamena, 18.09.2016 available at <https://www.theguardian.com/global-development/2016/sep/18/hissene-habre-chad-dictator-couragous-rape-survivors-make-history> accessed 29.04.2018.

45 For successful cases of domestic CRSV prosecutions that ended decades-long impunity, see D. Kravetz, 'Promoting Domestic Accountability for Conflict-Related Sexual Violence: the cases of Guatemala, Peru, and Colombia' (2017) 32(3) *American University International Law Review* 707.

3. REPARATIVE JUSTICE – REPAIRING HARMS THROUGH REPARATIONS

Criminal prosecutions, by ending impunity for CRSV, are an integral part of a comprehensive transitional justice strategy that embraces truth, justice, reconciliation and peace.[46] However, formal legal justice is only a part of the repertoire of measures that afford justice to victims. Victims of CRSV in Kosovo have articulated the importance of combining judicial measures with non-judicial measures that are better able to meet their day-to-day needs: medical and psychological care; financial compensation; monetary support for their children's education; and 'satisfaction'.[47]

Within the transitional justice toolbox, reparations have the greatest potential to directly impact victims.[48] Reparations consist of concrete measures to address the suffering of victims and to help rebuild their lives. These measures include legislative and administrative acts, financial compensation, restitution, rehabilitation, apologies and memorialisation. The traditional forms of reparations comprise restitution, compensation, satisfaction, rehabilitation and guarantees of non-repetition.[49] Reparations are unique because they can provide comprehensive redress to CRSV victims – an attribute that is significant due to the far-reaching physical and psychological toll of these crimes.[50] Beyond the individual, the scale and often targeted nature of sexual violence against a particular group can cause 'communal scars' that harm families and communities.[51]

In order to fully address this plethora of harms, reparations must go above and beyond the immediate reasons and consequences of violations by

---

46 See e.g., UNSC Res 1820, above n. 43, Operative Paragraph 4.

47 Rames, above n. 15, pp. 57–72. 'Satisfaction' includes truth-seeking and disclosure measures such as public apologies, official declarations, commemorations or tributes to victims and, judicial and administrative sanctions. See UN General Assembly, *Basic Principles and Guidelines on the Right to a Remedy and Reparation for Victims of Gross Violations of International Human Rights Law and Serious Violations of International Humanitarian Law* (UN Doc A/RES/60/147, 21 March 2006) ('UNGA Basic Principles'), Principle 22. See also UNSC Resolution 2106 (24 June 2013) (highlighting the importance of a comprehensive approach to transitional justice in armed conflict and post-conflict situations, encompassing the full range of judicial and non-judicial measures).

48 See UN Human Rights Council, *Report of the Special Rapporteur on Violence Against Women, its Causes and Consequences*, R. Manjoo, UN Doc. A/HRC/14/22, 23.04.2010 available at <http://www2.ohchr.org/english/bodies/hrcouncil/docs/14session/A.HRC.14.22.pdf> accessed 29.04.2018.

49 See UNGA *Basic Principles*, above n. 47, Principles 18–23.

50 'ICC Policy Paper on Sexual and Gender-Based Crimes' (International Criminal Court, June 2014), para. 45.

51 K.T. Seelinger, H. Silverberg and R. Mejia, 'The Investigation and Prosecution of Sexual Violence' (A Working Paper of the Sexual Violence and Accountability Project, Human Rights Center, University of California Berkeley, May 2011), p. 8, available at <http://www.usip.org/sites/default/files/missing-peace/seelinger-the-investigation.pdf> accessed 27.04.2018.

addressing structural inequalities – whether political, social or economic – which shape the lives of women and girls.[52] Transformative, gender-sensitive reparations are premised on a comprehensive understanding of the nature and consequences of the harm.[53] Accordingly, they necessitate a rebuttal of the erroneous presumption 'that remedies are a neutral legal space, unfettered by the complexities of gender and other intersectional identities'.[54] The foundational basis for gender-sensitive reparations is transformative justice which 'address[es] not just the consequences of violations committed during conflict but the social relationships that enabled these violations in the first place, and this includes the correction of unequal gender power relations in society.'[55]

Although lauded as a fulsome remedy for gender-based violence, transformative reparations have been criticised for overreaching, both politically and practically, and in doing so, 'displac[ing] reparative justice as a distinct and distinctly victim-centred imperative'.[56] The nub of this criticism is that transformative reparations are inconsistent with a core feature of reparations – a victim-centred remedy that values their agency and autonomy, and responds to their immediate needs. It is argued that in seeking to address deeper social structural inequalities, transformative reparations move away from supporting individual victims.[57] In an environment where victims lack the most rudimentary forms of redress, it is said that the ambitious nature of transformative reparations renders justice for victims even more elusive.[58]

How can this critique of transformative reparations inform the transitional justice agenda for CRSV victims in Kosovo? An integrated approach can mitigate the criticism that transformative reparations overlook victims' immediate needs. A unique strength of reparations is its repertoire of remedies that

---

52 See the Nairobi Declaration on Women's and Girls' Right to a Remedy and Reparation, available at <https://www.fidh.org/IMG/pdf/NAIROBI_DECLARATIONeng.pdf> accessed 29.04.2018; United Nations Secretary-General, 'Guidance Note of the Secretary-General: Reparations for Conflict-Related Sexual Violence' (June 2014) (UNSG Guidance Note), p. 8 fn 21, citing to Manjoo, above n. 48, para. 31; *González et al. v. Mexico* (Preliminary Objection, Merits, Reparations, and Costs) IAC Series C No 205 (16 November 2009) (*Cotton Fields Case*), para. 450.

53 UNSG Guidance Note, above n. 52, p. 5.

54 F. Ní Aoláin, C. O'Rourke and A. Swaine, 'Transforming Reparations for Conflict-Related Sexual Violence: Principles and Practice' (2015) 28 *Harvard Human Rights Journal* 97, 103.

55 N. Valji, *A Window of Opportunity: Making Transitional Justice Work for Women*, UN Women 2012, p. 3, available at <http://www.unwomen.org/~/media/Headquarters/Attachments/Sections/Library/Publications/2012/10/06B-Making-Transitional-Justice-Work-for-Women.pdf> accessed 08.07.2018.

56 M.U. Walker, 'Transformative Reparations? A Critical Look at a Current Trend in Thinking about Gender-Just Reparations' (2016) 10(1) *International Journal of Transitional Justice* 108, 108.

57 ibid., p. 110.

58 ibid.

include restitution, compensation, satisfaction, rehabilitation and guarantees of non-repetition. These different forms of reparations can be transformative to varying degrees – impacting individuals directly and also engaging with and transforming their surrounding circumstances. Thus, reparations that are transformative in design, implementation and impact can be sufficiently supple to provide meaningful short and long-term redress to sexual violence victims.[59] Reparations designed in this way can be material or symbolic and delivered collectively or individually. Drawing on this array of remedies, a well-conceived, context-specific reparations programme can meet the varied demands of victims. With this in mind, the following sections provide recommendations for a transformative justice agenda for CRSV victims in Kosovo.

4. CONFRONTING GENDER INEQUALITY IN KOSOVO

Exploring the nature and extent of gender inequality in Kosovo provides important context for the development of gender-sensitive reparations for CRSV victims within a transformative justice framework. Kosovo Albanian women, like other women around the world, face gender inequality that is rooted in the patriarchal structure of society. It is thus essential that reparative measures address this patriarchal hierarchy, and in this context, stigma as a barrier to justice for CRSV victims in Kosovo.

Women in Kosovo endure high levels of gender discrimination that manifest in their low political, economic and social status. As in many parts of the world, domestic violence is one of the most prevalent forms of violence against women in Kosovo.[60] For many women, escaping domestic violence is inconceivable because it means leaving their family, which provides the nucleus for all their social interactions. They are thus faced with a devastating trade-off between family life and individual justice. As elaborated below, this calculation can also influence their willingness to seek justice for CRSV. Understanding the causes of violence against women, both in peace and in conflict, improves the reach of transformative justice.[61] Violence against women reflects the underlying power

---

59 See UNSG Guidance Note, above n. 52, p. 8.

60 See R. Wareham, 'No Safe Place: An Assessment on Violence Against Women in Kosovo', UNIFEM 2000, p. 15, available at <http://iknowpolitics.org/sites/default/files/nosafeplace_kosovo.pdf>, accessed 29.04.2018; A. Qosaj-Mustafa and N. Farnsworth, 'More than "Words on Paper"? The Response of Justice Providers to Domestic Violence in Kosovo' UNDP, Prishtinë/Priština, October 2009, available at <http://www.womensnetwork.org/documents/20130120165443203.pdf> accessed 29.04.2018.

61 This distinction between peace and conflict in categorising sexual violence has been criticised. See, e.g., K. Grewal, 'Rape in Conflict, Rape in Peace: Questioning the Revolutionary Potential of International Criminal Justice for Women's Human Rights' (2010) 33(1) *Australian Feminist Law Journal* 57 (arguing that instead of helping to dismantle the traditional public/private binary, international criminal law has created a new binary between the

relations embedded in unequal social structures and is better understood when situated within this broader structure of gender hierarchy.[62]

Gender discriminatory norms embedded in patriarchy propagate the traditional view that a man's honour is linked to the sexual purity and physical safety of the women in his family. When women are sexually assaulted, male family members are considered to have been emasculated for failing to protect them and defend their family honour. Portraying sexual violence as an attack against the honour of the family renders it the 'least visible' of crimes,[63] complicating efforts to document, investigate and prosecute it.[64] In its seminal report, *Kosovo: Rape as a Weapon of Ethnic Cleansing* (March 2000), Human Rights Watch documented only a fraction of the incidents of sexual violence because women faced formidable personal, familial and customary barriers to speaking about their experience.[65] The stigma attached to sexual violence has been described as one of the biggest barriers to holding perpetrators accountable through prosecutions.[66]

The stigma and shame underpinning sexual violence fuel a cycle of neglect that impedes accountability for this crime.[67] Several women in Kosovo have been murdered under the guise of 'honour' (honour killings) or have killed themselves due to perceived or actual communal attitudes towards sexual violence.[68]

---

experience of sexual violence in peace and in war). Another division is between sexual violence and other forms of gendered violence in conflict. For a discussion of the need for the current discourse and legal responses to include a wider range of violence that women may experience during conflict, see A. Swaine, 'Beyond Strategic Rape and Between the Public and Private: Violence Against Women in Armed Conflict' (2015) 37(3) *Human Rights Quarterly* 755.

62 Manjoo, above n. 48, para. 31.

63 O. Lubrani, UN Development Coordinator in Kosovo cited in OHCHR, 'Seeking Justice for the Victims of Sexual Violence from the Armed Conflict in Kosovo', 19.06.2013, available at <http://www.ohchr.org/EN/NewsEvents/Pages/KosovoSexualViolence.aspx> accessed 29.04.2018.

64 For a discussion on the impact of characterising sexual violence as a crime against honour or dignity on furthering accountability, see Jarvis and Vigneswaran, above n. 41, pp. 35–36.

65 Human Rights Watch, above n. 7, Section I Summary.

66 Research Report, World Vision, 'No Shame in Justice: Addressing Stigma Against Survivors to End Sexual Violence in Conflict Zones' (December 2015), available at <http://9bb63f6dda0f744fa444-9471a7fca5768cc513a2e3c4a260910b.r43.cf3.rackcdn.com/files/1614/4888/7012/WVUK_No_Shame_in_Justice_low_res.pdf> accessed 29.04.2018.

67 While conflict and patriarchy pose further obstacles, the process of achieving accountability for sexual violence remains ridden with pitfalls even when it is prosecuted as a domestic crime in less patriarchal societies. Sexual violence can be difficult to prove for a myriad of reasons including under-reporting, negative gender stereotypes and gender insensitive laws, procedures and practices. Even when reported and prosecuted, the conviction rates are paltry. See, e.g., N. Hayes, 'The Impact of Prosecutorial Strategy on the Investigation and Prosecution of Sexual Violence at International Criminal Tribunals' in M. Bergsmo (ed.), *Thematic Prosecution of International Sex Crimes*, Torkel Opsahl Academic EPublisher 2012, p. 410 (noting a 2003 study on rape convictions rates: England and Wales (8 per cent), Sweden (7 per cent) and Ireland (1 per cent) (internal citations omitted)).

68 Hobbs, above n. 9, p. 7.

In this climate, most victims of sexual violence in Kosovo are unknown and either unwilling or unable to even acknowledge their violation.[69] Consequently, they have not been able to avail themselves of the formal justice process and thus remain bereft of any remedy. As stated by the former President of Kosovo Atifete Jahjaga in 2014, '[f]ifteen years after the war, the topic of victims of sexual violence remains a taboo topic to be addressed'.[70]

Kosovo has been described as a 'legal black hole' for women's rights.[71] In general, when compared to men, women in Kosovo tend to have less access to justice and are less likely to realise legal remedies.[72] Many CRSV victims, fearing abandonment or abuse from their husbands, have concealed the fact that they were sexually violated.[73] Women who are rejected by their family are likely to become destitute. This risk is acute in gender-stratified Kosovo Albanian society, where women's economic independence is curtailed severely by their lack of education or economic opportunities.[74] Women in Kosovo face high levels of poverty and have limited access to employment opportunities.[75] Many are left in precarious positions as caregivers to dependents in circumstances where they themselves lack economic security.[76]

The stigmatisation of victims of sexual violence sends the implicit message that they are less worthy of legal protection.[77] In Kosovo, the legislative process

---

69 A. Zejneli, 'How Long Can You Keep a Secret? For Kosovo's Wartime Rape Victims, The Answer Is: Maybe Forever' Radio Free Europe / Radio Liberty, Prishtinë/Priština, 29.05.2014, available at <https://www.rferl.org/a/kosovo-wartime-rape-victims-kept-secret/25403115.html> accessed 29.04.2018.

70 'President Creates Council for Sexual Violence Survivors' *Kosovar Women's Voice Newsletter*, March 2014, available at <http://www.womensnetwork.org/documents/20140401172101439.pdf> accessed 29.04.2018.

71 S. Gjocaj, 'Vicious Cycle: Kosovo's Battered Women Syndrome', Balkan Insight, 08.11.2017, available at <http://www.balkaninsight.com/en/article/vicious-cycle-kosovo-s-battered-women-syndrome-11-03-2017-2> accessed 29.04.2018.

72 U. Färnsveden, A. Qosaj-Mustafa and N. Farnsworth, 'Country Gender Profile: An Analysis of the Gender Differences at All Levels in Kosovo' (Orgut Consulting, 2014), p. 1, available at <http://www.womensnetwork.org/documents/20140513160130237.pdf> accessed 09.07.2018.

73 See Zejneli, above n. 69. Victims' silence can be a pernicious feature of sexual violence: 'We have women who may be living among us and who are victims of (wartime) rape. But if you're not recognised and feel like a victim again, it is easier for you to stay quiet. So everyone stays silent about it. And that is the most distressing side of it, when everyone is silent' (Stanojka Tešić, Forum žena Bratunac, interviewed by Amnesty International in April 2012) (Amnesty International, 'When Everyone is Silent: Reparation for Survivors of Wartime Rape in Republika Srpska in Bosnia and Herzegovina' 31.10.2012, p. 3, available at <https://www.amnesty.org/en/documents/EUR63/012/2012/en/> accessed 29.04.2018).

74 United Nations Secretary-General, above n. 52, p. 5.

75 Färnsveden, Qosaj-Mustafa and Farnsworth, above n. 72, p. 2.

76 See Manjoo, above n. 48, para. 43.

77 C. Duggan and R. Jacobson, 'Reparation of Sexual and Reproductive Violence: Moving from Codification to Implementation' in R. Rubio-Marín (ed.), *The Gender of Reparations: Unsettling Sexual Hierarchies While Redressing Human Rights Violations*, Cambridge University Press 2009, p. 160.

establishing the reparations programme for war victims vividly illustrated this perception. The precursor to the 2014 Law, the Law No. 04/L.054 On the Status and Rights of the Martyrs, Invalids, Veterans, Members of the Kosovo Liberation Army, Civilian Victims of War and their Families (the '2011 Law')[78] neither recognised sexual violence victims as war victims, nor mentioned this category of victims.[79] Consequently, they were excluded from benefits to which other categories of war victims were entitled under the law, such as access to healthcare, financial assistance and a family pension.[80] Under the 2011 Law, victims of sexual violence were entitled to compensation only in their capacity as family members of other categories of individuals who fell within the law (civilian invalid or civilian victim of war).[81]

Efforts to amend the law to recognise victims of sexual violence as victims of war faced staunch opposition in Kosovo. In March 2013, Nazlie Bala, a human rights activist, appeared on Radio Television Kosova advocating the inclusion of victims of sexual violence in the category of victims of war. It was reported that following this appearance, she received an anonymous death threat, slipped under her front door ('Please do not protect the shame. Otherwise, we'll kill you'). The intimidation culminated in a physical attack at the entrance of her home.[82] The reference to 'shame' in the threat is instructive, spotlighting its pervasive effects in obstructing women's access to justice and in their continued victimisation - this time by their communities. Nonetheless, advocacy efforts prevailed. Despite vehement resistance from some of its members, the Kosovo Parliament approved the 2014 Law that recognises victims of sexual violence as war victims.[83]

---

78 See the 2011 Law, available at <http://www.kuvendikosoves.org/common/docs/ligjet/Law%20on%20the%20status%20of%20the%20martyrs%20of%20war.pdf> accessed 29.04.2018.

79 Duggan and Jacobson, above n. 77, pp. 133–34 note that sexual violence was similarly initially excluded from the *gacaca*, community justice tribunals created after the Rwandan genocide. Parliamentarians did not originally intend to include sexual violence as an international crime or as part of the genocide on the basis that domestic legislation was sufficient to address it. This was the case despite the view expressed by the then Human Rights Commission's Special Rapporteur for Rwanda, Rene Degni-Segui, that during the genocide, '[r]ape was the rule, and its absence the exception'. See also H. Rombouts, 'Women and Reparations in Rwanda: A Long Path to Travel' in R. Rubio-Marín (ed.), *What Happened to the Women? Gender and Reparations for Human Rights Violations*, Social Science Research Council 2006, pp. 201–03, for a comprehensive summary of reparations mechanisms in Rwanda.

80 Rames, above n. 15, p. 28.

81 ibid.

82 'KWN Condemns Attack on Activist Nazlie Bala' Kosovo Women's Network, 05.04.2013, available at <http://www.womensnetwork.org/?FaqeID=1&n=66> accessed 29.04.2018.

83 See 'President Jahjaga Welcomes the Approval of the Amendments of the Law on the Status and Rights of the Martyrs, Invalids, Veterans, KLA Members and of the Civilian Victims of War and their Family Members' (20 March 2014), available at <http://www.president-ksgov.net/?page=2,6,3302#.VozzyfkrK00> accessed 29.04.2018.

5. THE 2014 LAW – FROM RHETORIC TO RECOGNITION AND REDRESS?

The failure to provide reparations to CRSV victims has been described as one of the least visible but most keenly felt injustices.[84] Following their struggle for recognition spanning almost two decades, the 2014 Law finally places CRSV victims on an equal footing with other war victims. Accordingly, they are entitled to the range of legal remedies that flow from this official status: a monthly payment (pension), health services abroad, priority in employment, property tax breaks and social housing.[85] Regulation no. 22/2015 On Defining the Procedures for Recognition and Verification of the Status of Sexual Violence Victims During the Kosovo Liberation War (the Regulation) which entered into force in February 2016 triggered the implementation of the 2014 Law.[86]

Although the 2014 Law represents a significant stride forward, there are challenges obstructing the delivery of remedies to CRSV victims. At the outset, an issue that requires prompt resolution is the amendment of the current legal framework to rectify translation differences between the Albanian, Serbian and English versions of the law which significantly affect victims' access to benefits.[87] A second issue is the temporal limitation imposed by the 2014 Law which affects victims' eligibility to apply for reparative measures. Eligibility is limited to a 'person who survived sexual abuse and rape within the period from 27.02.1998 until 20.6.1999'.[88] While this end date represents the official cessation of hostilities,[89] CRSV did not abruptly cease on this date. On the contrary, it is widely known that in the aftermath of the war, power outages and poor lighting facilitated further sexual violence. While some Kosovo Albanian women

84 Amnesty International, above n. 73, p. 3. Amnesty International has published a number of reports highlighting Bosnia and Herzegovina's failure to provide victims with reparations. See, e.g., Amnesty International, 'Whose Justice? The Women of Bosnia and Herzegovina Are Still Waiting' (September 2009); Amnesty International, 'Old Crimes, Same Suffering: No Justice for Survivors of Wartime Rape in North-East Bosnia and Herzegovina' (March 2012).

85 Art. 5 (1.2.3) of the 2014 Law and applicable sections of Art. 6 of the 2011 Law.

86 See the Regulation, available at <http://kryeministri-ks.net/repository/docs/Rregullore_(QRK)_nr__222015__per_percaktimin_e_procedurave_per_njohjen_dhe_verifikimin_e_statusit_te__viktimave_te_dhunes_seksuale_gjate_luftes_.pdf> accessed 29.04.2018. See also 'Reparations Soon for Conflict-related Sexual Violence Survivors in Kosovo' UN Women, 17.03.2016, available at <http://www.unwomen.org/en/news/stories/2016/3/reparations-soon-for-conflict-related-sexual-violence-survivors-in-kosovo> accessed 01.04.2018.

87 For details of these translation difficulties and other legal amendments to properly operationalise the law, see Hobbs, above n. 9, p. 32.

88 Art. 4 of the 2014 Law which defines victims of sexual violence of the war.

89 In June 1999, NATO concluded a Military Technical Agreement with the governments of the Republic of Serbia and FRY, and an agreement on the end of hostilities with the KLA, available at <https://www.nato.int/kosovo/docu/a990609a.htm> accessed 09.07.2018.

continued to experience CRSV, those affected after this date belong primarily to the Kosovo Serbs, Roma, Ashkali and Egyptian minority communities.[90]

In this way, the 2014 Law discriminates indirectly on an ethnic basis by denying redress to women from other communities who also suffered CRSV. This contravenes the basic principle that reparations must be delivered without any discrimination.[91] The 2014 Law thus fails to address the multi-ethnic dimension of CRSV in Kosovo and the full spectrum of victimhood, thereby potentially fuelling inter-ethnic grievances and obstructing post-conflict reconciliation. This temporal limitation that indirectly excludes CRSV victims from minority communities must be removed. The 2014 Law should be amended to enable victims who experienced sexual violence in the immediate aftermath of the conflict to claim their rightful reparations.

The next critical step in the implementation of the 2014 Law was establishing the process of identifying victims of sexual violence. Pursuant to the Regulation, the Government Commission on the Recognition and Verification of the Status of Sexual Violence Victims during the Kosovo Liberation War (Verification Commission) is mandated to undertake responsibility for providing reparations to CRSV victims, having verified their status as victims. The Verification Commission's secretariat was established in June 2016, and after some delays, operationalised in 2018.[92] From 5 February 2018, CRSV victims have been able to submit their applications to the Verification Commission in order to be certified as victims of sexual violence and access their entitlements under the 2014 Law. In its first two months of operation, the Verification Commission received more than 300 applicants; 50 applicants have been granted the status of CRSV victim and are entitled to reparations in the form of a monthly payment (pension) from the Ministry of Labour and Social Welfare.[93]

Ensuring that victims' interests and needs guide the verification process is an ongoing challenge that permeates all aspects of the Verification Commission's work. The Verification Commission is alert to this challenge: its envisaged operational procedure is governed by a victim-centred approach that aims to

---

90 Hobbs, above n. 9, p. 28 (internal citations omitted).

91 UNGA *Basic Principles*, above n. 47, Art. 25.

92 E. Peci, 'Kosovo War Rape Verifications Hit by Delays' Balkan Transitional Justice, 30.06.2016, available at <http://www.balkaninsight.com/en/article/kosovo-war-rape-verifications-hit-by-delays-06-30-2016> accessed 29.04.2018; P. Collaku, 'Kosovo Plans Benefits for War Rape Victims' Balkan Transitional Justice, 22.06.2015, available at <http://www.balkaninsight.com/en/article/verification-commission-on-sexual-violence-to-create-during-this-year> accessed 29.04.2018; email correspondence between the author and UN Women Kosovo (05.02.2018).

93 Email correspondence between author and UN Women Kosovo (06.02.2018, 27.04.2018); 'First Applications in for Long-awaited Compensation for Conflict-related Sexual Violence Survivors in Kosovo' UN Women, 20.02.2018, available at <http://eca.unwomen.org/en/news/stories/2018/02/first-applications-in-for-compensation-for-conflict-related-sexual-violence-survivors-in-kosovo> accessed 29.04.2018.

protect the dignity of victims and to prevent re-traumatisation.[94] In order to achieve this aim, the application process does not require victims to testify before the Commissioners. Instead, they can apply by letter or online, in seven governmental regional centres or through four non-governmental organisations (NGOs) that have been working with CRSV victims. Before being able to serve on the Verification Commission, commissioners underwent mandatory training on methodology, data protection and confidentiality. They also received training on best practices in interacting with victims of sexual violence, and the importance of a victim-centred approach.[95] The training addressed the critical issue of creating an enabling environment for victims: recognising the unfortunate reality of shame and stigma, while avoiding reinforcing these during the claims process.[96]

A fourth challenge was balancing victims' confidentiality and privacy needs with their ability to access entitlements under the 2014 Law. For instance, women who have been financially dependent on their families may need to explain their additional income, which is problematic if their rape(s) have been kept secret. While the current legislative framework offers victims priority in employment, training and professional rehabilitation,[97] such prioritisation may inadvertently reveal that they are rape victims. Similarly, opening a bank account or visiting a government office to collect their payments might also compromise confidentiality. In Kosovo, four authorised NGOs specialised in working with CRSV victims are supporting and guiding applicants through this process.[98] This cooperation with organisations trusted by victims has served to assist victims in navigating state services to access their entitlements.

A further challenge was the determination of an appropriate sum for payments to CRSV victims under the 2014 Law: an amount that is sufficiently substantial to encourage victims to come forward notwithstanding fears of jeopardising their privacy.[99] If the risk outweighs the reward, fewer victims would be inclined

94 For a discussion on the importance of a victim-centred approach, see P. Gopalan, D. Kravetz and A. Menon, 'Proving Crimes of Sexual Violence' in Brammertz and Jarvis, above n. 41.

95 K. Chick, 'Ending the Shame of Kosovo's Rape Victims' *Foreign Policy*, Drenas, 22.02.2016, available at <http://foreignpolicy.com/2016/02/22/the-rape-victims-of-kosovo-bosnia-commission/> accessed 29.04.2018.

96 The author delivered to the commissioners this part of the mandatory training that was organised by UN Women and the Kosovo Institute for Public Administration: 'Legal Obligations and Methods to Verify Survivors of Conflict-Related Sexual Violence'; 'Culture of Shame Slowly Lifts for Conflict-related Sexual Violence Survivors in Kosovo' UN Women, 06.09.2017, available at <http://eca.unwomen.org/en/news/stories/2017/09/news-kosovo-culture-of-shame-slowly-lifts-for-conflict-related-sexual-violence-survivors> accessed 23.04.2018.

97 Article 6 (1.8) of the 2011 Law; Hobbs, above n. 9, p. 31.

98 Email correspondence between the author and UN Women Kosovo (05.02.2018).

99 '... Many are afraid their husbands would divorce and leave them. They say it's been 17 years and we've gotten nothing, so why register now? The risk is too big.' (quoted in Chick, above n. 95).

to apply.[100] There is also a symbolic dimension to a reasonable payment – the recognition it grants victims may provide psychological support.[101] While it could be argued that a small sum may appear to trivialise the suffering of victims, in reality any payment has the potential to alleviate some victims' indigence or absolute financial dependence on their families.

In November 2017, the Ministry of Finance announced that those certified as CRSV victims would receive a payment of 230 Euros per month as reparations.[102] At almost 90 per cent of the average salary for women in Kosovo, this sum is deemed a just and appropriate amount.[103] This leads to another issue, which is whether the Government of Kosovo can muster the budgetary and political commitments to make reparative payments. In 2016, payments due under the 2014 Law faced a funding shortfall, with war veterans' claims alone exceeding the budget.[104] Nonetheless, in October 2017, CRSV victims were granted a separate allocation, with the Ministry of Finance announcing that one million Euros would be set aside to fund the verification process and payment of compensation to CRSV victims.[105] With the verification process having commenced in February 2018, and 50 individuals certified as CRSV victims, the stage appears set for the delivery of reparations to more CRSV victims in Kosovo. It is hoped that these victims receive their reparations without undue delay. Justice delayed eviscerates the notions of empowerment and dignity that underscore reparations.

6. TRANSFORMING TRANSITIONAL JUSTICE FOR CRSV VICTIMS

Aside from the practical implementation challenges discussed above, the 2014 Law lacks a comprehensive and transformative gender perspective that is responsive to the specific needs of CRSV victims. Remedies such as guarantees of non-repetition and satisfaction are absent from the legislation. Against this backdrop, this section considers strategies and mechanisms that could enhance the 2014 Law and strengthen the delivery of transformative justice to CRSV victims.

---

100 ibid.

101 ibid. ('Every day we think about it. When we get support, we heal little by little. Maybe the shame will touch us forever, but we know we are not guilty').

102 UN Women, above n. 93.

103 Amnesty International, 'Wounds that Burn our Souls', above n. 23, pp. 8, 35.

104 D. Morina, 'Kosovo Faces Up to War Veterans Pension Cost' Balkan Transitional Justice, 12.12.2016, available at <http://www.balkaninsight.com/en/article/kosovo-amending-the-law-on-war-veterans-12-09-2016> accessed 29.04.2018.

105 'Kosovo Pledges 1 Million Euro for Sexual Violence Survivors' UN Women, 07.11.2017, available at <http://eca.unwomen.org/en/news/stories/2017/11/kosovo-pledges-1-million-euros-for-sexual-violence-survivors> accessed 29.04.2018.

Transformative justice is furthered by an integrated approach that deploys the full armoury of mechanisms that promote gender equality. For instance, the Convention on the Elimination of all Forms of Discrimination Against Women (CEDAW) is well-equipped to reinforce the process of delivering transformative remedies to CRSV victims.[106] CEDAW General Recommendation No. 30 notes that 'transitional justice mechanisms have the potential to secure a transformative change in women's lives'.[107] While Kosovo is not party to CEDAW, its constitution states that international human rights conventions including CEDAW, take precedent over national legislation.[108] There are thus possibilities to harness the international legal framework in order to strengthen domestic processes.

CEDAW General Recommendation No. 30 also calls on states to ensure that reparations are gender-sensitive, promote women's rights and include women in its design.[109] Women's participation in the process of designing, implementing and evaluating reparations programmes is key to assessing their needs and concerns.[110] The Government of Kosovo's consultative efforts in respect of the 2014 Law were channelled through the National Council for Sexual Violence Victims (the 'National Council'), which was created by former President Jahjaga. The National Council sought to unite government officials, victims and stakeholders in developing the 2014 Law.[111] As Rubio-Marín and de Greiff argue, victim participation in designing reparation programmes is inherently valuable, as it serves to affirm their status as valid and valued contributors to the process.[112]

Despite attempts to foster an inclusive and collaborative approach, CRSV victims in Kosovo have had limited involvement in efforts to provide redress

---

106 Convention on the Elimination of All Forms of Discrimination Against Women (18 December 1979) 1249 UNTS 13 (entered into force 3 September 1981).

107 CEDAW, General Recommendation No. 30 on women in conflict prevention, conflict and post-conflict situations, CEDAW/C/GC/30 18 October 2013 ('CEDAW General Recommendation No. 30') para. 77. '[R]eparation measures should seek to transform the structural inequalities which led to the violations of women's rights, respond to women's specific needs and prevent their re-occurrence' (para. 79).

108 Art. 22(6) Constitution of the Republic of Kosovo, available at <http://www.kryeministri-ks.net/repository/docs/Constitution1Kosovo.pdf> accessed 29.04.2018. Although this clause is rarely used, in 2013, the Constitutional Court of Kosovo referenced international human rights law in a groundbreaking domestic violence decision, illustrating the potential for synergies between domestic and international processes. See Kosovo Constitutional Court Judgment in Case No. KI 41/12 with applicants Gëzim and Makfire Kastrati against the Municipal Court in Prishtinë/Priština and the Kosovo Judicial Council, available at <http://gjk-ks.org/wp-content/uploads/vendimet/gjkk_ki_41_12_ang.pdf> accessed 16.07.2018.

109 CEDAW General Recommendation No. 30, above n. 107.

110 Manjoo, above n. 48, para. 32. See also, the Guidance Note of the Secretary-General on the United Nations Approach to Transitional Justice (March 2010), p. 9; UNSG Guidance Note, above n. 52, p. 1 (noting the importance of victim consultations).

111 Hobbs, above n. 9, pp. 12, 33.

112 See R. Rubio-Marín and P. de Greiff, 'Women and Reparations' (2007) 1(3) *International Journal of Transitional Justice*, p. 324, available at <https://ssrn.com/abstract=1405108>.

partly because their requests for confidentiality have been perceived as an unwillingness to participate in these processes. Providing victims with avenues to contribute to these processes thus remains an ongoing challenge.[113] A further issue is ensuring that the diversity of their viewpoints is captured by dispelling the presumption that victims are homogeneous, with identical interests and needs.[114] Despite its stellar contributions, the National Council was disbanded with the expiry of former President Jahjaga's term in April 2016.[115]

The international human rights architecture discussed above is fortified by the Security Council's Women, Peace and Security (WPS) agenda – the suite of resolutions adopted by the Security Council that focuses on gender equality in conflict prevention, conflict and post-conflict situations.[116] The first in this series, Resolution 1325 on Women, Peace and Security, calls on all parties to protect women and girls from gender-based violence and to put an end to impunity for such crimes. Subsequent resolutions highlight the role of reparations in the transitional justice process. For example, UNSC Resolution 2242 (2015) recommends victim-appropriate reparations.[117] In January 2017, the Government of Kosovo finally approved the Action Plan for the Implementation of UNSC Resolution 1325.[118] The implementation of this plan should be monitored and consideration given to incorporating subsequent resolutions into Kosovo's transitional justice framework.[119]

In terms of traditional reparative remedies, guarantees of non-repetition, particularly when effected through institutional reform, further the WPS agenda

---

113 Hobbs, above n. 9, p. 7.

114 ibid., pp. 14, 37.

115 ibid., p. 12.

116 CEDAW General Recommendation No. 30 underscores the value of an integrated approach by affirming CEDAW's linkages with the WPS agenda in prioritising gender equality in these situations. See UN Women, 'Guidebook on CEDAW General Recommendation No. 30 and the UN Security Council Resolutions on Women, Peace and Security' (2015), pp. 9–10. In Kosovo, gender equality is protected by the state, under Article 7.2 of the Constitution of the Republic of Kosovo, above n. 108. For further discussion, see Färnsveden, Qosaj-Mustafa and Farnsworth, above n. 72, pp. 4–7. The following resolutions have addressed CRSV against women and girls: UNSC Res 1325 (31 October 2000) UN Doc S/RES/1325 was followed by UNSC Res 1820 (19 June 2008) UN Doc S/RES/1820, UNSC Res 1888 (30 September 2009) UN Doc. S/RES/1888, UNSC Res 1889 (5 October 2009) UN Doc S/RES/1889, UNSC Res 1960 (16 December 2010) UN Doc. S/RES/1960, UNSC Res 2106 (24 June 2013) UN Doc S/RES/2016 and UN SC Res 2122 (18 October 2013) UN Doc S/RES/2122.

117 UNSC Res 2242 (13 October 2015) UN Doc S/RES/2242.

118 Amnesty International, 'Wounds that Burn our Souls', above n. 23, p. 50 fn 284.

119 See Kosovo Women's Network, 'Monitoring Implementation of United Nations Security Council Resolution 1325 in Kosovo' Prishtinë/Priština, 2007, available at <http://www.womensnetwork.org/documents/20130120165532196.pdf> accessed 29.04.2018; Kosovo Women's Network, '1325 Facts & Fables: A Collection of Stories About the Implementation of the United Nations Security Council Resolution 1325 on Women, Peace, and Security in Kosovo' Prishtinë/Priština, 2011, available at <http://www.womensnetwork.org/documents/20130120165559661.pdf> accessed 29.04.2018.

and the integrated approach recommended in this chapter. The 2014 Law does not provide for guarantees of non-repetition. Guarantees of non-repetition are embodied in measures that contribute to the prevention of future violations, and as such, are wide-ranging: promoting the observance of codes of conduct and ethics, human rights training and strengthening the independence of the judiciary.[120] Amongst the various forms of reparations, guarantees of non-repetition are well-placed to harness the transformative potential of reparations. When initiated through institutional or legal reforms that embrace gender equality, guarantees of non-repetition foster engagement with the underlying structural causes of gender-based violence.[121] Reform in Kosovo has sought to increase female participation in security and law-enforcement forces, given the link between institutional gender-sensitivity and the reporting rates of sexual and gender-based violence.[122] A greater number of female personnel in all areas of the transitional justice process can reduce the obstacles faced by women in accessing justice.[123] For example, it has been demonstrated that increasing the number of female police officers increases the reporting rate of sexual violence.[124]

In October 2013, during a meeting with former President Jahjaga, victims of CRSV identified four areas of reparations: legal recognition and access to justice; economic support and empowerment; healthcare; and awareness raising to tackle stigma and discrimination (also articulated as satisfaction).[125] On the issue of economic empowerment and restitution (which are distinct from the economic support provided by way of compensation payments), the 2014 Law is lacking. With funds provided by the European Union, UN Women has provided CRSV victims with micro-grants for their small businesses under the project 'Gender Sensitive Transitional Justice', implemented jointly with local organisations.[126] Although this partnership has thus far proven to be beneficial to participants, there is scope to widen the reach of such projects by harnessing state infrastructure and systems.

---

120 For more examples of guarantees of non-repetition, see Principle 23 of UNGA *Basic Principles*, above n. 47.

121 Manjoo, above n. 48, para. 62 ('Guarantees of non-repetition offer the greatest potential for transforming gender relations. In promising to ensure non-recurrence, such guarantees trigger a discussion about the underlying structural causes of the violence and their gendered manifestations and a discussion about the broader institutional or legal reforms that might be called for to ensure non-repetition').

122 OHCHR Analytical Study, above n. 18, para. 60 (internal citations omitted).

123 See Art. 10, UNSC Resolution 2122, above n. 116 (stressing 'the need for continued efforts to address obstacles in women's access to justice in conflict and post-conflict settings, including through gender-responsive legal, judicial and security sector reform and other mechanisms').

124 UN Women Global Study, above n. 14, p. 121.

125 Hobbs, above n. 9, p. 33.

126 A total of 177 CRSV victims have benefitted from this scheme. Email correspondence between the author and UN Women Kosovo (05.02.2018 and 01.05.2018).

This micro-credit scheme was coupled with the delivery of psychosocial support to victims. The latter addresses a further lacuna in the 2014 Law: a lack of provision for psychological and psychosocial assistance which is critical to recovery and rehabilitation, and gravely required by many victims. NGOs have been valiantly and diligently filling this gap for decades, but this is another area that must fall within the remit of government policy and action. While victims of CRSV are entitled to medical treatment abroad, they crucially require free healthcare within Kosovo, which is an entitlement afforded to other civilian victims of war in Kosovo. Rehabilitation, both physical and mental, is a core component of reparations and this remains a critical need that is not adequately met for CRSV victims in Kosovo.

The 2014 Law also does not contain measures relating to satisfaction. Symbolic measures such as public statements or apologies recognising violations play a vital role in de-stigmatising sexual violence and raising awareness.[127] The need for such public measures is particularly acute in Kosovo, given the rhetoric of shame and honour that infiltrates public discourse on sexual violence. For example, conferences on this topic that are accessible to the public serve to raise awareness, elevate victims and destigmatise the crime by situating it in the public domain.[128]

Truth commissions or other truth-seeking initiatives also fall within the ambit of satisfaction. Thus, the Commission for Truth and Reconciliation that is being established is a positive step in developing this form of reparative justice in Kosovo.[129] The Office of the President that established this body has expressed a commitment to mainstream a gender perspective throughout this process.[130] The gender composition and competence of the commissioners due to be appointed in 2018 could provide a litmus test for this commitment.

Symbolic measures promote changes in culture and behaviour in the longer term, which it is hoped will ultimately disrupt entrenched gender inequalities in society. The discussion surrounding the inception of a reparations programme lays the foundation for dismantling the deep-seated gender discrimination that

---

127 Art can also serve this purpose. In 2015, an art installation in Prishtinë/Priština paid tribute to victims of sexual violence in the Kosovo conflict. See M. Tran, 'Dresses on Washing Lines Pay Tribute to Kosovo Survivors of Sexual Violence' *The Guardian*, 11.06.2015, available at <http://www.theguardian.com/world/2015/jun/11/kosovo-sexual-violence-survivors-art-dresses> accessed 29.02.2016. See UNGA *Basic Principles*, above n. 47, principle 22 for further examples.

128 There have been such initiatives in Kosovo in 2017. For e.g. conferences such as, 'Access to Justice and Reparations for Conflict-Related Sexual Violence Survivors' that was hosted by UN Women (31.10.2017), podcasts and talk shows on public radio on topics such as how society can support CRSV survivors, and the distribution of bracelets made by victims as the official symbol of 16 Days of Activism against Gender-Based Violence in Kosovo. (Email correspondence between the author and UN Women Kosovo (27.04.2018)).

129 D. Morina and D. Baliu, above n. 20.

130 Email correspondence between the author and UN Women Kosovo (06.02.2018).

underlies the social perceptions relating to sexual violence.[131] Transferring the 'blame', shame and responsibility of sexual violence from victims to perpetrators is critical to this process of social transformation. In Kosovo, the support of former President Jahjaga and the establishment of the National Council in March 2014 (under the aegis of the President's Office) elevated the issue to a matter of national concern, paving the way for its inclusion in the 2014 Law. These developments further the goal of creating an environment that facilitates and encourages victims to access justice by providing them with accurate information, accessible processes and guarantees of confidentiality.[132]

Satisfaction can also include judicial and administrative sanctions,[133] thus highlighting the need to prosecute perpetrators as part of the transformative justice package.[134] Reparations that are delivered through the judicial system – judicial reparations – thus provide another avenue for transformative redress for CRSV victims. The Inter-American Court of Human Rights has been a trailblazer in this area, offering innovative and groundbreaking approaches.[135] Moving beyond the traditional paradigm of financial compensation as the main form of judicial reparations, the Court has ordered non-financial forms of reparations – moral or symbolic measures that combine guarantees of non-repetition and satisfaction. These include effectively investigating cases to try perpetrators and end impunity, protecting the security of victims, witnesses and justice actors, honouring victims and providing for their education and medical (physical and psychological) care.[136]

The Court has also relied extensively on orders to publicise its judgments, noting that this measure exposes the truth while promoting moral satisfaction, the recovery of victims' reputation and a culture of legality.[137] It has also sought

---

131 C. Duggan and A. Abusharaf, 'Reparation of Sexual Violence in Democratic Transitions: The Search for Gender Justice' in P. de Greiff (ed.), *The Handbook of Reparations*, Oxford University Press 2008, pp. 627–635.

132 See M.U. Walker, 'Gender and Violence in Focus: A Background for Gender Justice in Reparations' in R. Rubio-Marín (ed.), above n. 77, p. 45.

133 UNGA *Basic Principles*, above n. 47, principle 22(f).

134 See section 2.

135 E.g., in its seminal judgment in the *Cottons Fields Case*, above n. 52, the Inter-American Court of Human Rights pioneered jurisprudence on gender-sensitive and transformative reparations for victims of gender-based violence.

136 See, e.g., *Plan de Sánchez Massacre v. Guatemala* (Judgment) IAC Series C No 116 (19 November 2004); *Rochela Massacre v. Colombia* (Merits, Reparations, and Costs) IAC Series C No. 163 (11 May 2007); *Serrano-Cruz Sisters v. El Salvador* (Merits, Reparations and Costs) IAC Series C No. 131, (1 March 2005) (Serrano-Cruz Sisters); *Ituango Massacres v. Colombia* (Preliminary Objections, Merits, Reparations and Costs) IAC Series C No. 148, (1 July 2006); *Rosendo Cantù et al v. Mexico* (Preliminary Objections, Merits, Reparations and Costs) IAC Series C No. 216 (31 August 2010); *Fernández Ortega et al v. Mexico* (Preliminary Objections, Merits, Reparations and Costs) IAC Series C No. 215 (30 August 2010).

137 *Plan de Sánchez Massacre v. Guatemala* (Judgment) IAC Series C No 105 (29 April 2004).

to prevent future abuses by ordering human rights training for state actors, and by requiring states to ratify human rights instruments and rectify domestic legislation to ensure compliance with international law.[138] This rich range of reparative measures that have been tailored to address the specific violations and circumstances of victims provide invaluable precedents for domestic CRSV prosecutions.

Other international and regional precedents also indicate that judicial reparations are gaining traction as a remedy, marking a shift from a retribution-based approach to a victim-centred reparative approach. The ICC noted in its first reparations decision in *Lubanga* that reparations should be symbolic, preventative, transformative and gender-sensitive.[139] At a regional level, in June 2015, Bosnia's War Crimes Chamber issued a 'revolutionary verdict' granting a rape victim's compensation claim during criminal proceedings. The Court imprisoned two former Bosnian Serb soldiers and ordered them to pay compensation to a Croat woman whom they had repeatedly raped in 1992 during the conflict in BiH.[140]

These developments accord with the holistic approach advocated in this chapter, while also demonstrating the challenges of securing concrete outcomes for victims. In the *Lubanga* appeal, victims of sexual and gender-based violence were eventually excluded from reparations on the basis that Lubanga was not convicted of these crimes.[141] In BiH, although enforcement efforts are ongoing, none of the victims had received their Court-ordered reparations from the perpetrators at the time of writing.[142] As judicial reparations are delivered

---

138 See, e.g., *Ticona-Estrada et al. v. Bolivia* (Merits, Reparations and Costs) IAC Series C No 191 (27 November 2008); *Serrano Cruz Sisters*, above n. 136; *Myrna Mack Chang v. Guatemala* (Judgment) IAC Series C No. 101 (25 November 2003); *Ticona Estrada et al. v. Bolivia* (Interpretation of the Judgment on Merits, Reparations and Costs) IAC Series C No. 199 (1 July 2009); *Bámaca-Velásquez v. Guatemala* (Merits, Reparations and Costs) IAC Series C No. 91 (22 February 2002).

139 *Prosecutor v. Thomas Lubanga Dyilo* ICC-01/04-01/06-2904, Decision establishing the principles and procedures to be applied to reparations (7 August 2012), para. 222. The Rome Statute of the ICC took the novel step of recognising the right of victims to participate in judicial proceedings in Art. 68(3) and their right to reparations in Art. 75. See also *Prosecutor v. Germain Katanga* ICC-01/04-01/07, Order for Reparations Pursuant to Article 75 of the statute (24 March 2017) (although this case did not involve charges of sexual violence).

140 J. Borger, 'Bosnia Rape Victims May Claim Compensation for the First Time' *The Guardian*, 30.06.2015, available at <https://www.theguardian.com/world/2015/jun/30/bosnia-victims-compensation-landmark-ruling> accessed 29.04.2018.

141 Cf. *Prosecutor v. Thomas Lubanga Dyilo* ICC-01/04-01/06-3129, Judgment on the appeals against the 'Decision establishing the principles and procedures to be applied to reparations' of 7 August 2012 with amended order for reparations (Annex A) and public annexes 1 and 2 (3 March 2015) para. 198.

142 30 April 2018. 'Bosnian War Rape Victims Struggle for Compensation' Balkan Transitional Justice, 09.09.2016, available at <http://www.balkaninsight.com/en/article/bosnian-war-rape-victims-struggle-for-compensation-09-09-2016> accessed 29.04.2018. See also 'Bosnian Serb Convict Fails to Compensate Rape Victim' Balkan Transitional Justice, 09.06.2016,

through the judicial process, they can replicate the weaknesses inherent in legal proceedings. Victims may therefore experience re-victimisation, social ostracism or re-traumatisation in the process of realising this remedy.[143] These negative effects are amplified in a small country like Kosovo, exacerbating the problem of stigmatisation and entrenching victimhood.

On the other hand, judicial reparations can empower victims by furthering their active participation in the legal process. Victims perceive the combination of legal sanctions and monetary compensation as recognition of their suffering by the legal process. This newfound status as valued participants in judicial proceedings is a crucial step in restoring victims' dignity.[144] In order to achieve this end result, the high personal cost for victims who participate in the criminal justice system in Kosovo must be mitigated, not least by making available psychological support or measures to protect their identity. Such a victim-centred approach can provide recognition and justice long-denied and lay the groundwork for transforming the status of CRSV victims in Kosovo.

7. LOOKING AHEAD

The combined efforts of victims, civil society and state actors in Kosovo, as well as international organisations, have shattered the historical silence shrouding CRSV in Kosovo. The Verification Commission has been operationalised, triggering the implementation of the 2014 Law. Victims have begun receiving historic reparations. It is time to further the transformative justice agenda for CRSV victims by capitalising on this momentum. The 2014 Law must be supplemented with transformative and gender-sensitive measures. The criminal justice process must be properly situated within the spectrum of judicial and non-judicial transitional justice measures. Perpetrators of CRSV must be prosecuted in Kosovo. Upending entrenched gender discrimination is an ambitious aim that will require time and concerted multi-sectoral contributions. To this end, frameworks and mechanisms that protect women's rights and further gender equality should be leveraged. The requisite political and financial commitments must be honoured. CRSV victims in Kosovo have been awaiting justice for almost two decades. It is time to deliver justice that is transformative.

---

available at <http://www.balkaninsight.com/en/article/bosnian-serb-convict-fails-to-pay-rape-victim-06-09-2016> accessed 29.04.2018. In addition, seven other verdicts that incorporate judicial reparations have been issued in the BiH (Email correspondence between author and Adrijana Hanušić Bećirović, Senior Legal Adviser, Trial International, the advocacy group that pursued the case (09.05.2017)).

143 See Manjoo, above n. 48, paras. 34–37.

144 Email correspondence between the author and Adrijana Hanušić Bećirović, Senior Legal Adviser, Trial International, the advocacy group that pursued the case (02.03.2016).

STAYING THE COURSE

A Call for Sustained Support of Accountability for Conflict-Related Sexual Violence in Bosnia and Herzegovina

Susana SáCouto and Chanté Lasco*

* This chapter is based on research conducted before its submission in September 2016.

1. INTRODUCTION

An estimated 20,000 girls and women and an unknown number of men and boys were victims of sexual violence during the war in the former Yugoslavia.[1] This sexual violence took many forms and occurred in many different contexts: in victims' own homes when soldiers came to the door; in perpetrators' homes, with victims sometimes being held for months as sexual slaves; and in detention centres and police stations in the context of interrogations and imprisonment.[2] Since 1993, the International Criminal Tribunal for the former Yugoslavia (ICTY) has prosecuted some of these violations, along with other serious war crimes, crimes against humanity and acts of genocide. Yet only a fraction of these crimes – including the widespread sexual and gender-based violence (SGV) that occurred during the war – have been addressed by the ICTY. In light of the tribunal's mandate to complete its work within a limited timeframe,[3] since 2003, the ICTY has focused on the prosecution 'of the most senior leaders suspected of being most responsible for crimes within the ICTY's jurisdiction

1 European Council Parliamentary Assembly Resolution 1670 (2009) 6, available at <http://assembly.coe.int/nw/xml/XRef/Xref-XML2HTML-en.asp?fileid=17741&lang=en> accessed 05.04.2016.

2 See further discussion in section 2.1.

3 UNSC Res 1503 (28 August 2003) S/RES/1503 (2003), 7 ('Calls on the ICTY and the ICTR to take all possible measures to complete investigations by the end of 2004, to complete all trial activities at first instance by the end of 2008, and to complete all work in 2010 (the Completion Strategies)'); United Nations Security Resolution 1534 (March 26, 2004) S/RES/1534 (2004).

and transferr[ed] cases involving those who may not bear this level of responsibility to competent national jurisdictions',[4] meaning the vast majority of serious crimes that occurred during the war remain to be addressed by domestic criminal justice systems in the former Yugoslavia, including in Bosnia and Herzegovina (BiH). Although an internationally supported special War Crimes Section was established over a decade ago within the national judicial system of the BiH to deal with such cases, a significant backlog remains, in particular with respect to cases involving SGV.[5] This chapter explores the issues faced by justice system actors trying these cases. While some of the challenges relate to evidentiary difficulties, others stem from the withdrawal of international support of the War Crimes Section, rendering accountability efforts vulnerable to attack by domestic actors opposed to such efforts.

This chapter begins with a background section describing: (1) the incidence of sexual violence committed during the conflict in the former Yugoslavia; (2) the prosecution of serious international crimes at the ICTY as well as in Bosnian courts, including by the War Crimes Section of the State Court of Bosnia and Herzegovina (WCS-BiH or State Court) and the courts in the entities and Brčko District; and (3) the prosecution of SGV offences in particular at these tribunals. Next, the chapter explores the difficulties facing the WCS-BiH and the district and cantonal courts throughout Bosnia in the prosecution of these crimes, including issues concerning victims and witnesses, other legal challenges and political pressures on the courts. The authors then describe the limited ways in which the international community is currently supporting the continued prosecution of conflict-related SGV in Bosnia and Herzegovina, stressing the risk of backlash in the absence of such support and, thus, the critical need for continued international engagement to ensure effective access to justice for victims of these grave offences. The chapter not only makes recommendations

---

4 UNSC Res 1503 (28 August 2003) S/RES/1503 (2003).

5 OSCE Report, 'Delivering Justice in Bosnia and Herzegovina: An Overview of War Crimes Processing from 2005 to 2010', pp. 21–22 (reporting that as of April 2010, the BiH Prosecutor's Office reported the existence of approximately 1,381 war crimes case files pertaining to some 8249 suspects distributed among the 17 jurisdictions dealing with war). Presumably, the backlog has been reduced below the 1,381 figure in the interim period between 2010 and 2015. See State Court of Bosnia and Herzegovina, 'Registry Quarterly Report' (September 2012), p. 14 (forecasting 20 ongoing war crimes cases being heard in trial each month), available at <http://www.osce.org/bih/108103?download=true> accessed 29.09.2016. Special Rapporteur on violence against women, its causes and consequences, Addendum, Mission to Bosnia and Herzegovina, A/HRC/23/49/Add.3, (4 June 2013) 22 (noting the 'extremely low' number of conflict-related sexual violence cases closed by the State Court of Bosnia and Herzegovina as of the end of 2011 – 29 – given the incidence of sexual violence perpetrated during the war). But see OSCE Report, 'Processing of War Crimes at the State Level in Bosnia and Herzegovina' (16 June 2016), p. 11 (noting that the head of the Bosnian prosecution war crimes department, Gordana Tadić, stated that the department had recently raised a lot of indictments related to rape and sexual violence offences during the war, suggesting that the backlog on these cases may be decreasing), available at <http://www.osce.org/bih/247221> accessed 18.09.2016.

for improving the prosecution of these cases in Bosnia, but also highlights lessons learned from the Bosnian experience for those considering similar approaches in other post-conflict contexts. Significantly, the authors conclude that for an internationally supported mechanism of accountability to make a real and lasting contribution to justice, ongoing international engagement and support must continue until such time as substantive benchmarks, rather than arbitrary timelines, are met.

2. CONFLICT-RELATED SGV IN THE FORMER YUGOSLAVIA AND ITS PROSECUTION BEFORE INTERNATIONAL AND DOMESTIC COURTS

2.1. THE INCIDENCE OF SEXUAL VIOLENCE IN THE ARMED CONFLICT IN THE FORMER YUGOSLAVIA

In the summer of 1992, shortly after conflict erupted in the former Yugoslavia, journalists in the region began reporting widespread sexual violence being committed against civilians.[6] A UN Commission of Experts travelled to the region in 1994 and documented rapes and other forms of sexual violence occurring in several contexts: prior to active armed conflict in areas where women of one ethnic group were targeted and intimidated or attacked by members of another ethnic group; in the context of active fighting and mass transfers of civilians during 'ethnic cleansing' campaigns; and in detention centres where civilians were held.[7] Girls and women were raped in front of crowds of people or taken away from public areas and raped in hotels, apartments and empty rooms.[8] The Commission found that girls as young as five and women as old as 81 were sexually assaulted.[9] Many women reported being taken out of the rooms where they were detained every night and raped repeatedly, often by multiple perpetrators.[10] Police and other authority figures took women and girls to police stations for interrogations, during which they were raped and sexually abused.[11] Many girls and women were taken to private homes or apartments and kept there for

---

6 M. Cherif Bassiouni and M. McCormick, 'Sexual Violence: An Invisible Weapon of War in the Former Yugoslavia' Occasional Paper No. 1, International Human Rights Law Institute, DePaul University (1996), p. 1, available at <http://mcherifbassiouni.com/wp-content/uploads/Sexual-Violence-an-Invisible-Weapon-of-War.pdf> accessed 05.04.2016.

7 Final Report of the Commission of Experts Established Pursuant to Security Council Resolution 780 (1992), S/1994/674, 27 May 1994, paras. 245–48.

8 ibid., paras. 246–47.

9 ibid., para. 236.

10 ibid., paras. 230(o), 247, 250(c). See also *Prosecutor v. Boban Šimšić*, State Court of BiH Appellate Verdict (7 August 2007), paras. 51–53, 29–32, 37–39.

11 *Prosecutor v. Furundžija*, ICTY Trial Chamber Judgment (10 December 1998), paras. 263–69.

weeks or months, being raped countless times.[12] Men and boys held in detention centres were also targeted for sexual violence: soldiers frequently forced men to perform sexual acts on each other or, in at least one case, to sexually mutilate a fellow detainee.[13] The total incidence of SGV during the conflict is difficult to quantify, in large part due to reporting obstacles such as the stigma often attached to being a victim of sexual violence and the fact that many victims were attacked by members of military or paramilitary organisations who controlled local law enforcement at the time.[14] Despite these challenges, widely accepted figures estimate that 20,000 women and girls and an unknown number of men and boys were victims of sexual violence during the conflict in the former Yugoslavia.[15]

2.2. PROSECUTION AT THE ICTY

In 1993, the UN Security Council established the ICTY to try those most responsible for serious crimes committed in the context of the war in the former Yugoslavia.[16] The ICTY adopted a strategy of prosecuting the highest-level perpetrators and transferring less senior accused persons to national jurisdictions for prosecution.[17] As of August 2016, the tribunal had indicted 161 individuals,

12 Final Report, above n. 7, para. 249.

13 ibid., paras. 235, 247. See also *Prosecutor v. Tadić*, ICTY Trial Chamber Judgment (7 May 1997), paras. 194, 198, 206, 722–26.

14 M. Cherif Bassiouni and M. McCormick, 'Sexual Violence: An Invisible Weapon of War in the Former Yugoslavia' Occasional Paper No. 1, International Human Rights Law Institute, DePaul University (1996), p. 25, available at <http://mcherifbassiouni.com/wp-content/uploads/Sexual-Violence-an-Invisible-Weapon-of-War.pdf> accessed 05.04.2016. See also *Prosecutor v. Velibor Bogdanovic*, State Court of BiH Appellate Verdict (1 August 2012), paras. 73–74 (acknowledging that 'the collection of physical evidence at the time of the offence would have been entrusted to the persons belonging to the same military and police structures as the perpetrator', meaning investigations were likely subject to bias). See *Prosecutor v. Velibor Bogdanovic*, State Court of BiH Appellate Verdict (1 August 2012), paras. 68, 70 (finding that 'it is natural for rape victims to refrain from talking about their experience due to fear of retribution, embarrassment, sense of self-accusation, mistrust in the prosecution authorities, confusion and many other reasons' including 'the conservative community, lack of education, [and] a general lack of empathy'). See also *Prosecutor v. Saša Baričanin*, State Court of BiH First Instance Verdict (8 December 2011) paras. 227, 229; *Prosecutor v. Dragan Damjanović*, State Court of BiH Appellate Verdict (13 June 2007), p. 9; *Prosecutor v. Zeljko Mejakić, et al.*, State Court of BiH First Instance Verdict (30 May 2008), p. 129; *Prosecutor v. Miodrag Nikačević*, State Court of BiH Appellate Verdict (12 July 2010), para. 61.

15 European Council Parliamentary Assembly Resolution 1670 (2009), para. 6, available at <http://assembly.coe.int/nw/xml/XRef/Xref-XML2HTML-en.asp?fileid=17741&lang=en> accessed 05.04.2016.

16 UNSC Res 827, S/RES/827 (1993) 25 May 1993.

17 UNSC Res 1503 (28 August 2003). UN Doc. S/RES/1503 (2003) 1–2; United Nations Security Resolution 1534 (26 March 2004) S/RES/1534 (2004), para. 5.

of whom 83 were convicted and sentenced, 19 were acquitted, 37 had their indictments withdrawn (due to the death of the accused or another reason), and 13 were referred to national jurisdictions for prosecution.[18] Additionally, one final case is at the initial trial stage (Ratko Mladić), six individuals have their case before the Appeals Chamber, and two defendants are awaiting retrial at the Mechanism for International Criminal Tribunals (MICT).[19] Despite landmark convictions issued by the ICTY,[20] the individuals indicted and prosecuted by the tribunal represent only a fraction of people implicated in the commission of serious international crimes during the conflict in the former Yugoslavia.[21] A significant percentage of ICTY cases involved allegations of various forms of sexual violence: of the 161 individuals the ICTY has indicted, 78 were charged with a crime of sexual violence, representing 48 per cent of the accused overall.[22] Of those charged with such crimes, as at May 2016, 31 individuals had been convicted.[23]

Moreover, through its jurisprudence, the ICTY created important precedents for holding perpetrators of SGV crimes accountable, finding not only that accused could be held responsible for rape as a war crime[24] or a crime against humanity,[25] but also that rape and/or other forms of sexual violence could constitute other serious crimes, such as the war crimes of torture,[26] outrages upon

---

18 ICTY: Key Figures of Cases, available at <http://www.icty.org/en/cases/key-figures-cases> accessed 11.09.2016 (document current as of 02.09.2016).

19 ibid. Note that two additional individuals in the *Prosecutor v. Stanišić and Simatović* case are being re-tried by the United Nations Mechanism for International Criminal Tribunals.

20 See, e.g., *Prosecutor v. Tadić*, ICTY Trial Chamber Judgment (7 May 1997) paras. 558–692 (addressing several legal issues including the jurisdiction of the ICTY, the nature of the conflict in the former Yugoslavia, the customary international law status of war crimes and crimes against humanity, and modes of liability for prosecuting these offences); *Prosecutor v. Krstić*, ICTY Trial Chamber Judgment (2 August 2001) paras. 540–99 (interpreting the definition of genocide and its relationship to 'ethnic cleansing'); *Prosecutor v. Delalic et al.*, ICTY Trial Chamber Judgment (16 November 1998), paras. 344–401 (examining the issue of superior responsibility). See also landmark judgments addressing sexual and gender-based violence issues in nn. 24–33 below.

21 ICTY website, 'The Conflicts' (noting that in Bosnia and Herzegovina alone, more than 100,000 people were killed and two million were forcibly displaced), available at <http://www.icty.org/en/about/what-former-yugoslavia/conflicts> accessed 15.04.2016.

22 ICTY: In Numbers, available at <http://www.icty.org/sid/10586> accessed 15.04.2016.

23 ibid. Significantly, these included the very first case prosecuted by the ICTY, *Prosecutor v. Dusko Tadić*, which involved the sexual mutilation of a male detainee in a detention centre. *Prosecutor v. Tadić*, above n. 13, paras. 194, 198, 206, 722–726.

24 *Prosecutor v. Kunarac, et al.*, ICTY Trial Chamber Judgment (22 February 2001), paras. 408, 883, 886, 888.

25 ibid., paras. 670, 685–687, 704, 782, 798, 822, pp. 302–309. *Prosecutor v. Zelenovic*, ICTY Sentencing Judgment (4 April 2007), para. 71.

26 *Prosecutor v. Delalic et al.*, above n. 20, paras. 496, 178; *Prosecutor v. Furundžija*, above n. 11, paras. 263–269; *Prosecutor v. Kunarac et al.*, above n. 24, paras. 687, 715; *Prosecutor v. Kvocka et al.*, ICTY Trial Chamber Judgment (2 November 2001), paras. 561, 761.

personal dignity,[27] cruel treatment,[28] inhuman treatment,[29] and wilfully causing great suffering or serious injury to body or health,[30] and the crimes against humanity of torture,[31] enslavement,[32] persecution,[33] and other inhumane acts.[34] The ICTY also endorsed[35] the holding of the International Criminal Tribunal for Rwanda (ICTR) in *Prosecutor v. Akayesu*, which held for the first time that rape and sexual violence can constitute an act of genocide.[36] Nonetheless, given the widespread incidence of conflict-related SGV in the former Yugoslavia, the vast majority of mid and lower-level perpetrators have yet to be held to account.

2.3. DOMESTIC PROSECUTION OF SERIOUS INTERNATIONAL CRIMES IN BOSNIA

2.3.1. State Court of Bosnia and Herzegovina

When the United Nations Security Council (UNSC) first created the ICTY, it did not envision supporting the creation of domestic tribunals within the courts of Bosnia or other former Yugoslav countries.[37] Rather, support for domestic prosecution of serious international crimes committed during the conflict stemmed largely out of necessity: limits on the ICTY's resources and

---

27 *Furundžija*, Trial Chamber Judgment, above n. 11, paras. 272–75.

28 *Tadić*, Trial Chamber Judgment, above n. 13, paras. 722–26.

29 *Delalic et al.*, Trial Chamber Judgment, above n. 20, para. 1066.

30 ibid., paras. 1038–40.

31 *Kunarac et al.*, Trial Chamber Judgment, above n. 24, para. 687.

32 *Prosecutor v. Kunarac et al.* ICTY Appeals Chamber Judgment (12 June 2002), paras. 119–24 (affirming the Trial Chamber's judgment convicting the defendants of enslavement based on evidence that they detained several victims to use them for sexual acts).

33 *Prosecutor v. Todorovic*, ICTY Sentencing Judgment (31 July 2001) paras. 4, 37–40, 66; *Prosecutor v. Kvocka et al.*, ICTY Trial Chamber Judgment, above n. 26, paras. 197, 752, 755, 758, 761, 764. *Prosecutor v. Sainovic*, ICTY Appeals Chamber Judgment (23 January 2014), para. 599; *Prosecutor v. Stakić*, ICTY Trial Chamber Judgment (31 July 2003), paras. 881–82; *Prosecutor v. Nikolic*, ICTY Sentencing Judgment (18 December 2003), paras. 109–11, 119; *Prosecutor v. Plavsic*, ICTY Sentencing Judgment (27 February 2003), paras. 5, 27, 34, 126.

34 *Tadić*, above n. 13, para. 730.

35 See *Prosecutor v Karadžić*, Rule 98*bis* ICTY Appeal Judgment (11 July 2013), paras. 36–37; *Prosecutor v. Brđanin*, ICTY Trial Judgment (2 August 2001), paras. 690, 744, 835; *Prosecutor v. Stakić*, ICTY Trial Chamber Judgment (31 July 2003), paras. 516, 544, 546; *Prosecutor v Mladić*, ICTY Rule 98*bis* Decision, Transcript T 20939 (15 April 2014), available at <http://www.icty.org/x/cases/mladic/trans/en/140415IT.htm> accessed 15 April 2016; *Krstić*, above n. 20, para. 509.

36 *Prosecutor v. Akayesu*, ICTR Trial Chamber Judgment (2 September 1998), paras. 731–34.

37 D. Orentlicher, 'That Someone Guilty Be Punished: The Impact of the ICTY on Bosnia' (2010), p. 20, available at <https://www.ictj.org/publication/someone-guilty-be-punished-impact-icty-bosnia> accessed 19.08.2016.

mandate demanded alternative means of prosecuting outstanding conflict-related crimes.[38] In 2003, the UNSC adopted Resolution 1503 – known as the completion strategy – requiring the ICTY to limit its focus to prosecuting high-ranking accused and transferring lower-level perpetrators' cases to domestic tribunals where the crimes occurred.[39] Since many of the crimes occurred in present-day Bosnia and Herzegovina, the ICTY focused its efforts on supporting national prosecution of war crimes and other serious international crimes within this country's justice system.[40] While some courts in Bosnia and Herzegovina had heard war crimes cases during the conflict and in the years that followed, the trials produced mixed results, not always meeting minimum fair trial standards and raising concerns about the courts' ability to try such cases without actual – or perceived – ethnic bias.[41] Despite these early problems, sweeping reforms of Bosnia and Herzegovina's judicial system created an opportunity for the ICTY and the international community to support the fair and credible domestic prosecution of these crimes.[42] In an effort to ensure that domestic prosecutions would abide by international fair trial standards, the ICTY partnered with the Office of the High Representative (OHR) in Bosnia and Herzegovina to support the ongoing reforms of the Bosnian judicial system.[43] As a result of these reforms, a War Crimes Section was created within the State Court of Bosnia and Herzegovina and a Special Department

---

38 UNSC Res 1503 (28 August 2003) S/RES/1503 (2003); OSCE Report, 'Delivering Justice', above n. 5, p. 11.

39 UNSC Res 1503 [34] 1–2.

40 Letter dated 17 June 2002 from the Secretary-General addressed to the Security Council, UN Doc S/2002/678, 1; OSCE, 'Delivering Justice', above n. 5, p. 11.

41 Letter dated 17 June 2002 from the Secretary-General addressed to the Security Council, UN Doc S/2002/678, 1; OSCE, 'Delivering Justice', above n. 5, pp. 12–13. See also OSCE, 'War Crimes Courts Before the Domestic Courts of Bosnia and Herzegovina: Progress and Obstacles (March 2005) p. 4, available at <http://www.nuhanovicfoundation.org/user/file/2005_osce_report_war_crimes_trials_before_domestic_courts_in_bih.pdf_-_to_be_added%21.pdf> accessed 16.07.2018. This report details examples of local Bosnian courts violating defendants' fair trial rights, including the fact that 47 individuals were tried and convicted *in absentia*; the imposition of the death penalty in several cases (although these were later commuted to life sentences); trial delays of up to seven years; arbitrary arrests; and convictions based on insufficient evidence.

42 'Assessments and report of Judge Theodor Meron, President of the International Criminal Tribunal for the Former Yugoslavia, provided to the Security Council pursuant to paragraph 6 of Security Council resolution 1534 (2004)' Enclosure to Letter Dated May 20, 2004 to the Security Council, paras. 22–24, available at <http://www.icty.org/x/file/About/Reports%20and%20Publications/CompletionStrategy/completion_strategy_24may2004_en.pdf> accessed 15.04.2016. See also O. Martin-Ortega, 'Beyond The Hague: Prosecuting War Crimes in Bosnia and Herzegovina' in J. Gow, R. Kerr and Z. Pajić (eds.), *Prosecuting War Crimes: Lessons and Legacies of the International Criminal Tribunal for the Former Yugoslavia*, Routledge 2014, pp. 592–93.

43 ibid. 'Assessments and report of Judge Theodor Meron'.

for War Crimes within the State Prosecutor's Office (Special WC Department). Both were staffed by international and domestic personnel.[44] The Special WC Department was staffed predominantly by national prosecutors,[45] while, at least for the first several years, the three-judge panels were composed of two international judges and one national judge each.[46] In 2008 that changed, with two national judges and one international judge appointed to each panel.[47] This was consistent with the hybrid nature of the court, which was intended to be temporary, with a phase out of international personnel expected after five years of operation.[48]

Despite initial reluctance on the part of international donors to finance another tribunal to try international crimes, the WCS-BiH and the Special WC Department received significant international support, including funds, training and infrastructure.[49] The WCS-BiH was formally established on 6 January 2005, and began hearing war crimes cases later that year,[50] receiving cases from the ICTY through a referral mechanism provided by Rule 11*bis*[51] of the ICTY's Rules of Procedure and Evidence,[52] as well as cases from the Special WC Department.[53] The WCS-BiH continues to hear serious international crimes more than 10 years later, facing an immense backlog of cases and myriad challenges discussed in detail in section 3 below.

---

44 International Center for Transitional Justice (ICTJ), 'The War Crimes Chamber in Bosnia and Herzegovina: From Hybrid to Domestic Court (2008)', p. 6.

45 ibid., 7.

46 ibid.

47 ibid.

48 ibid., pp. 5–6. See also ORENTLICHER, above n. 37, p. 132. This date was later extended several times, for a total of an additional three years, until the end of 2012. ibid.

49 F. DONLON, 'Rule of Law: From the International Criminal Tribunal for the Former Yugoslavia to the War Crimes Chamber of Bosnia and Herzegovina' in D.F. HAYNES (ed.), *Deconstructing the Reconstruction: Human Rights and Rule of Law in Postwar Bosnia and Herzegovina*, Routledge 2008, p. 282.

50 OSCE, 'War Crimes Courts Before the Domestic Courts of Bosnia and Herzegovina: Progress and Obstacles' (March 2005), p. 8, available at <http://www.nuhanovicfoundation.org/user/file/2005_osce_report_war_crimes_trials_before_domestic_courts_in_bih.pdf_-_to_be_added%21.pdf> accessed 16.07.2018.

51 Rule 11*bis*(A) of the ICTY Rules of Procedure and Evidence provides that, after an indictment has been confirmed and prior to the commencement of trial, irrespective of whether or not the accused is in the custody of the Tribunal, the President may appoint a bench of three Permanent Judges selected from the Trial Chambers (hereinafter referred to as the 'Referral Bench'), which solely and exclusively shall determine whether the case should be referred to the authorities of a state: (i) in whose territory the crime was committed; or (ii) in which the accused was arrested; or (iii) having jurisdiction and being willing and adequately prepared to accept such a case, so that those authorities should forthwith refer the case to the appropriate court for trial within that state.

52 'ICTY: Status of Transferred Cases', available at <http://www.icty.org/sid/8934> accessed 15.04.2016.

53 ICTJ report, above n. 44, p. 8.

2.3.2. *Prosecutions in Courts in Entities and Brčko District*

In addition to the WCS-BiH at the state level, war crimes are prosecuted in local courts throughout Bosnia by prosecutors' offices in the cantons and districts throughout the Federation of Bosnia and Herzegovina (FBiH), Republika Sprska (RS), and Brčko District.[54] There are 10 cantonal courts in the FBiH; five district courts in the RS; and the Basic Court in Brčko District.[55] Appeals are dealt with by three different courts: the Appellate Division of the Supreme Court of FBiH, the Supreme Court of RS, and the Appellate Court of Brčko District.[56] These courts have fewer resources than the State Court, meaning many of the challenges of prosecuting serious international crimes are exacerbated, as discussed further in section 3 below.

2.3.3. *Criteria for Determining Where Cases will be Prosecuted*

Article 27(a) of the Bosnia and Herzegovina Criminal Procedure Code provides the criteria for deciding when cases can be transferred from the state level to the entity and Brčko District courts.[57] The factors for making this

---

54 The complex, decentralised judicial system reflects the power-sharing compromises reached as part of the Dayton Peace Accords, which provides for Bosnia and Herzegovina to be comprised of separate administrative divisions known as 'entities', including the Federation of Bosnia and Herzegovina (FBiH), Republika Srpska (RS). See 'Dayton Peace Agreement, The General Framework Agreement: Annex 4' (14 December 1995), available at <http://www.ohr.int/?page_id=63255&lang=en> accessed 15.04.2016. Through arbitration, Brčko district was established as a 'single administrative unit of local self-government existing under the sovereignty of Bosnia and Herzegovina'. See 'Statute of the Brčko District of Bosnia and Herzegovina' (7 December 1999), Article 1, available at <https://www.ilo.org/dyn/natlex/docs/ELECTRONIC/79577/85707/F241509038/BIH79577.htm> accessed 15.04.2016. There is no formal hierarchy between the State Court and the entity courts, meaning State Court decisions are not binding on the entity courts, leading to a fragmented system with inconsistent applications of the law. See Martin-Ortega, above n. 42, pp. 603–04, 606–07.

55 OSCE, 'Delivering Justice', above n. 5, p. 32.

56 ibid., p. 34.

57 Criminal Procedure Code of Bosnia and Herzegovina, 'Official Gazette' of Bosnia and Herzegovina, 3/G3, 32/G3, 36/G3, 26/G4, 63/G4, 13/G5, 48/G5, 46/G6, 76/G6, 29/G7, 32/G7, 53/G7, 76/G7, 15/G8, 58/G8, 12/G9, 16/G9, 93/G9. Article 27(a) of the BiH Criminal Procedure Code and provides as follows (unofficial translation): (1) If the proceedings are pending for the criminal offences referred to in Articles 171 through 183 of the Criminal Code Bosnia and Herzegovina, under its decision, the Court may transfer the proceedings to another court in whose area the criminal offence was attempted or committed, no later than by the time of scheduling the main trial, while taking into account the gravity of the criminal offence, the role of the perpetrator and other circumstances of importance in assessing the complexity of the case. (2) The Court may render the decision referred to in Paragraph 1 of this Article also upon the motion of the parties or defence counsel, while at the stage of investigation, only upon the prosecution motion. (3) The decision referred to in Paragraph 1 of this Article shall be rendered by the Panel referred to in Article 24(7) of the Code, composed of three Judges. No appeal from the decision of the Panel shall be allowed.

assessment under Article 27(a) include: the gravity of the offence, the role of the perpetrator, and 'other circumstances of importance in assessing the complexity of the case'.[58] These factors have been interpreted to include the accused's position as a police or military commander, whether acts were allegedly planned and/or ordered by the alleged perpetrator in this capacity, and the consequences of the alleged crime on the local community.[59] Of particular relevance to SGV cases is the gravity of the offence assessment, which itself requires consideration of various factors, including not only whether the alleged acts are legally characterised as genocide or crimes against humanity, but also the number of victims involved; whether the allegations involve 'severe forms of rape', such as multiple or systematic rapes, rapes committed in detention centres, or rapes committed in the context of sexual slavery; and the serious consequences experienced by the victims.[60] Additionally, the interests of victims and witnesses, including protective measures they may require, is to be taken into account.[61]

2.3.4. *History of Prosecution of SGV Cases in Bosnia and Herzegovina*

From 2005 to the end of 2013, according to the Organization for Security and Co-operation in Europe (OSCE), courts in Bosnia and Herzegovina have completed 256 war crimes cases.[62] Many of these cases involve allegations of SGV: significantly, the first two cases heard by the WCS-BiH dealt with allegations of rape and sexual slavery as crimes against humanity.[63] Courts at both the state and cantonal and district court level have had success trying conflict-related SGV cases.

---

58 ibid.

59 These criteria were developed as part of the National War Crimes Strategy, a document created by the Ministry of Justice of Bosnia and Herzegovina to help streamline the processing of war crimes. See 'National War Crimes Strategy' (December 2008), p. 3. The criteria are described in an annex to the National War Crimes Strategy, provided in OSCE, 'Combating Impunity for Conflict-Related Sexual Violence in Bosnia and Herzegovina: Progress and Challenges: An Analysis of Proceedings Before the State Court of Bosnia and Herzegovina Between 2005 and 2013', Annex 3.

60 ibid.

61 ibid., p. 41. Some measures, such as allowing a victim to testify through video-link technology or to have his or her image and/or voice distorted during testimony, require technical equipment that courts in the Brčko District and the entities historically lacked. As discussed further in section 4.1, the United Nations Development Program, the European Union, and the United States have all invested in improving technical capabilities at the entity level to provide such measures.

62 ibid., p. 8.

63 *Prosecutor of Bosnia and Herzegovina v. Samardžić*, State Court of BiH First Instance Verdict, (7 April 2006), pp. 1–3; *Prosecutor of Bosnia and Herzegovina v. Radovan Stanković*, State Court of BiH First Instance Verdict (14 November 2006), pp. 1–3.

2.3.4.1. Prosecution of SGV at the War Crimes Section of the State Court of Bosnia and Herzegovina

The OSCE reported that as of 2013, the WCS-BiH completed 36 cases involving conflict-related SGV, resulting in the conviction of 33 perpetrators and the acquittal of 12 individuals, meaning a conviction rate of 73 per cent for sexual violence charges.[64] In its monitoring of the these cases, the OSCE has observed a genuine commitment on the part of justice system actors to deliver justice to victims of conflict-related SGV, despite facing myriad challenges explored in detail in section 3 below.[65]

Beyond the conviction rate, the jurisprudence reveals that prosecutors and judges at the state level WCS-BiH have made significant substantive progress in pursuing accountability for these crimes, including convicting perpetrators of rape and other forms of sexual violence as SGV-specific war crimes,[66] crimes against humanity,[67] as well as rape and sexual violence as the crimes against humanity of torture,[68] enslavement/sexual slavery[69] and persecution.[70] Moreover, the WCS-BiH has successfully convicted defendants under various modes of liability, from superior responsibility for leaders of detention camps

64 OSCE, 'Combating Impunity: State Court', above n. 59, pp. 9, 13–14, 16–17. At the close of 2013, the State Court was handling an additional 18 cases involving sexual and gender-based violence, but there is no publicly available information on the number of cases related to sexual violence that have yet to reach the court system.

65 ibid., p. 5.

66 See, e.g., *Prosecutor v. Markovic*, State Court of BiH Appellate Division Verdict (27 September 2011), p. 3; *Prosecutor v. Bogdanovic*, State Court of BiH First Instance Verdict (29 August 2011), pp. 1–3.

67 See, e.g., *Prosecutor's Office v. Jankovic*, State Court of BiH First Instance Verdict (16 February 2007). p. 1–4; *Prosecutor v. Mejakić et al.*, State Court of BiH First Instance Verdict (30 May 2008), above n. 15, pp. 13–14; *Prosecutor v. Nikačević*, State Court of BiH Appellate Verdict, above n. 15, [46]; *Prosecutor v. Lelek*, State Court of BiH First Instance Verdict (23 May 2008), pp. 2–3, 38–39 (finding the accused guilty of 'severe sexual violence' as a crime against humanity with regard to one of the allegations against the accused).

68 *Jankovic*, above n. 67, paras. 1–4.

69 See, e.g., *Prosecutor v. Samardžić*, State Court of BiH Appellate Verdict (13 December 2006), paras. 2–4, 24 (convicting the accused of persecution as a crime against humanity 'in conjunction with' the crime against humanity of sexual slavery); *Stanković* First Instance Verdict, above n. 63, paras. 1–3, 34; *Jankovic* First Instance Verdict, above n. 68, pp. 1–4; *Baričanin*, First Instance Verdict, above n. 14, paras. 3, 241–42 (finding Baričanin guilty of enslavement for keeping witness S2 locked in an apartment for several days, repeatedly raping her, and displaying a 'proprietary relationship' with her); *Prosecutor v. Kujundzic*, First Instance Verdict (30 October 2009), para. 557 (finding the accused guilty of sexual slavery as a crime against humanity).

70 Charges involving allegations of SGV are often characterised as persecution in conjunction with other crimes against humanity including rape or other forms of sexual violence. See, e.g., *Samardžić*, Appellate Verdict, above n. 69, pp. 2–4, 24; *Prosecutor v. Šimšić*, Appellate Division Verdict (7 August 2007), paras. 1–4; *Prosecutor v. Momir Savić*, State Court of BiH First Instance Verdict (3 July 2009), paras. 3–4, 116.

who failed to prevent or punish widespread acts of sexual violence[71] to individual criminal responsibility for inciting such acts[72] or committing such acts as direct perpetrators.[73] Significantly, sexual violence against women,[74] men[75] and children[76] has been successfully prosecuted, reflecting the range of victims of these crimes.

The WCS-BiH has heard these cases in a manner largely consistent with international standards, including with respect to the elements of SGV crimes and evidentiary and procedural matters relevant to SGV. For example, as discussed in section 3.1.1 below, although the application of protective measures for SGV victim-witnesses has been uneven at times,[77] the WCS-BiH routinely applies several measures used by international tribunals, including the assignment of pseudonyms, the exclusion of the public from the courtroom during protected witnesses' testimony, and the use of screening and voice-distortion technology.[78]

---

71 See, e.g. *Mejakić et al.*, First Instance Verdict, above n. 14, paras. 1–7 (convicting two of the three defendants of sexual violence under superior responsibility and all for individual criminal responsibility, pursuant to each defendant's role in the Omarska, Trnopolje and Keraterm camps).

72 See, e.g., *Kujundzic*, First Instance Verdict, above n. 69, paras. 506–10.

73 See, e.g. *Baričanin*, First Instance Verdict, above n. 14, paras. 3–4; *Momir Savić*, First Instance Verdict, above n. 70, paras. 2–4, 94; *Mejakić et al.*, First Instance Verdict, above n. 14, paras. 1–14 (convicting two of the defendants of sexual violence under both superior responsibility and individual criminal responsibility and third for only individual criminal responsibility, depending on each defendant's role in the Omarska, Trnopolje and Keraterm camps); *Prosecutor v. Nikačević*, State Court of BiH First Instance Verdict (19 February 2009), pp. 2–3, 50; *Prosecutor v. Palija*, State Court of BiH First Instance Verdict (28 November 2007), para. 3.

74 See, e.g., *Bogdanovic*, First Instance Verdict, above n. 66, paras. 1–3; *Prosecutor v. Damjanović*, State Court of BiH First Instance Verdict (15 December 2006), paras. 1–3; *Momir Savić*, First Instance Verdict, above n. 70, paras. 1–3, 89–91.

75 See, e.g. *Prosecutor v. Zihad Kurtovic*, First Instance Verdict (24 April 2008), paras. 3, 5 (describing how two male camp detainees were forced to perform oral sex on each other).

76 *Samardžić*, First Instance Verdict, above n. 63, paras. 1–3 (convicting the accused of rape and sexual slavery as crimes against humanity for acts committed against 15-year-old 'L' and 'underage G'); *Prosecutor v. Stanković*, above n. 70, paras. 1–3 (convicting the accused of rape and sexual slavery as crimes against humanity for acts including the rape of 'underage D'); *Prosecutor v. Marko Radić et al.*, Appellate Division Verdict (9 March 2011), para. 5 (describing the rape of 15-year-old Witness X); *Prosecutor v. Jankovic*, First Instance Verdict, above n. 67, paras. 1–4 (convicting the accused of the crimes against humanity of rape and torture for the rapes of women and underage girls); *Kujundzic*, First Instance Verdict, above n. 69, para. 546 (convicting the accused of raping 'minor witness 2' who was 15 at the time of the rape).

77 See discussion in section 3.1.1.

78 See, e.g., *Kurtovic*, First Instance Verdict, above n. 75, para. 13 (noting the Court's use of pseudonyms to protect the identity of victims of SGV, Witness A and Witness B, and the exclusion of the public from the courtroom during their testimonies, acknowledging that the Court was 'particularly mindful of the nature of the offense of which Witnesses A and B were victims and the traumas which they still feel'); *Mejakić et al.*, First Instance Verdict, above n. 14, paras. 32–33 (discussing a range of protective measures offered to victim-witnesses of SGV); *Momir Savić*, First Instance Verdict, above n. 70, paras. 9–10 (describing how the Court will withhold the victim-witness's identity information for 30 years and excluded the

Moreover, consistent with the practice of international tribunals, in a number of cases, the WCS-BiH has recognised the trauma victims of SGV experience and acknowledged the effects of that trauma on victims' ability to testify, which has enabled it to accept some level of inconsistency in a victim's testimony with respect to minor issues,[79] while rejecting testimony revealing inconsistencies on more critical issues such as the identity of the perpetrator.[80] Indeed, the WCS-BiH has paid special attention to the issue of victims' credibility, admitting reports and testimony from expert witnesses explaining how the trauma and stigma SGV victims often face may prevent them from promptly reporting acts of SGV, affect their demeanour while testifying in court, and/or result in inconsistent statements.[81]

---

public from the courtroom); *Palija*, First Instance Verdict, above n. 73, para. 17 (noting that allowing the witness to testify from a separate room and closing the courtroom to the public was an 'utterly critical approach' that was 'absolutely necessary due to the severe trauma which the injured party still suffers').

79 See, e.g., *Prosecutor v. Lelek*, Criminal Division Verdict, 23 May 2008, pp. 35–36; *Prosecutor v. Nikačević*, Appellate Verdict, above n. 14, paras. 59–60 (finding that the relevant witnesses' testimony 'do not contain deviations or contradictions with respect to the key facts' and acknowledging that the witnesses' inability to recall the exact dates of the rapes that occurred is understandable given the passage of time and the circumstances of the crimes); *Prosecutor v. Jankovic*, State Court of BiH Appellate Division Verdict (23 October 2007), paras. 53–60 (noting that given the traumatic events she experienced, Witness 75's 'cannot reasonably be expected to recall the minutiae, such as the precise time of the events she described'); *Prosecutor v. Tanaskovic*, State Court of BiH Appellate Verdict (26 March 2008), p. 15.

80 See, e.g., *Prosecutor v. Darko Dolic*, Appellate Division Verdict (26 April 2011), paras. 147–51.

81 See *Bogdanovic*, above n. 14, para. 70 (finding that 'It is common knowledge that sex crime victims reluctantly decide to report these offenses, for many reasons, primarily due to the fear of retribution, embarrassment, sense of self-accusation, mistrust in the prosecution authorities, confusion and many other reasons'). *Baričanin*, First Instance Verdict, above n. 14, paras. 227, 229 (recounting the testimony of expert witness Dr Ljubović, who testified at trial that 10–20 per cent of rape victims report the rapes they experienced after a period of delay, while the majority do not report it at all, due to victims' feelings of 'shame, guilt, and helplessness'); *Damjanović*, Appellate Verdict, above n. 14, p. 9 (finding it 'easily understandable' that the victim did not talk to anyone else, including a doctor, about her experience, because of the stigma attached to rape in the patriarchal community in which she lives); *Mejakić et al.*, First Instance Verdict, above n. 14, p. 129 (finding that the fact that the victim did not report soon after her release from Omarska camp that she had been raped did not impact on her credibility because she was likely still in a 'state of shock and fear'); *Nikačević*, Appellate Verdict, above n. 14, p. 61 (observing that it was understandable for a victim of rape to remain silent out of fear in part due to the patriarchal community in which she lives). In a related example, the WCS-BiH has approached the issue of whether or not to require corroboration of SGV victims' testimony largely in conformity with international standards. While Bosnia's Criminal Procedure Code does not explicitly prohibit requiring corroboration of such testimony, the jurisprudence of the Court reflects a consistent practice of accepting the sole testimony of a witness as sufficient if it is credible and reliable. See, e.g., *Tanaskovic*, Appellate Verdict, above n. 79, pp. 14–15; *Prosecutor v. Pincic*, Appellate Verdict (15 April 2010), para. 68; *Prosecutor v. Nikačević*, First Instance Verdict, above n. 73, p. 36.

2.3.4.2. Prosecution of Conflict-Related SGV in Bosnian Courts beyond the State Court in Sarajevo

The OSCE reported in July of 2015 that from 2004 to 2014, cantonal and district courts had completed 35 cases involving allegations of conflict-related SGV against 45 defendants,[82] convicting 34 perpetrators in 27 cases, amounting to a conviction rate of approximately 75 per cent.[83] Most of the cases prosecuted at this level are focused on direct perpetrators, largely as a result of the war crimes processing strategy, which provides that less complex cases – a classification based in part on the role of the perpetrator – are to be prosecuted by local cantonal and district courts.[84] These courts have prosecuted perpetrators of sexual violence against women, men and children,[85] reflecting the fact that all were victims of such crimes during the war. Most SGV war crimes cases have involved charges of rape as a war crime against civilians, although in one case in Brčko District, an accused was convicted of torture based on evidence of rape and other forms of sexual violence.[86] Jurisprudence from cantonal and district courts – and reports from court monitors – reveal that these courts have in many cases endeavoured to prosecute SGV cases in line with international standards but have struggled in some instances to fully reflect established jurisprudence from the ICTY and other international courts on certain key issues, including the provision of protective measures for SGV victims and the definition of rape, both of which are explored in sections 3.1.1 and 3.2.1 below.[87]

---

82 The 35 cases involving allegations of conflict-related SGV were out of a total of 173 war crimes cases completed by Bosnian courts other than the State Court in Sarajevo as of the end of 2014; thus, SGV cases represented approximately 20 per cent of the war crimes cases completed by those courts within that timeframe. OSCE, 'Combating Impunity for Conflict-Related Sexual Violence in BiH: Progress and Challenges: An Analysis of Proceedings Before the Courts of the Federation of Bosnia and Herzegovina, Republika Srpska, and Brčko District BiH Between 2004 and 2014', p. 12. Since writing, the OSCE has released a more recent report regarding the prosecution of SGV in Bosnia, available at <https://www.osce.org/mission-to-bosnia-and-herzegovina/324631> accessed 16.07.2018.

83 ibid., p. 5.

84 Criminal Procedure Code of Bosnia and Herzegovina, 'Official Gazette' of Bosnia and Herzegovina, 3/G3, 32/G3, 36/G3, 26/G4, 63/G4, 13/G5, 48/G5, 46/G6, 76/G6, 29/G7, 32/G7, 53/G7, 76/G7, 15/G8, 58/G8, 12/G9, 16/G9, 93/G9, art. 27(a)(1).

85 OSCE, 'Combating Impunity: Courts of the Federation of Bosnia and Herzegovina, Republika Srpska, and Brčko District', above n. 82, p. 15.

86 ibid., pp. 25, 31. At the local level, most cases prosecuting sexual violence as a serious international crime are tried as war crimes against civilians. War crimes against civilians are prosecuted under Article 172 of the Criminal Code of the Socialist Federal Republic of Yugoslavia of 1976, which provides that 'Whoever in violation of rules of international law effective at the time of war, armed conflict or occupation, orders that the civilian population be subject to … forcible prostitution or rape … shall be punished by imprisonment for not less than five years …'. Criminal Code of the Socialist Federal Republic of Yugoslavia (28 September 1976) OG 44/6, 36/77.

87 OSCE, 'Combating Impunity: Courts of the Federation of Bosnia and Herzegovina, Republika Srpska, and Brčko District', above n. 82, pp. 25–30.

2.3.4.3. Current Status of SGV Prosecution in Bosnian Courts

Despite progress made to date on SGV cases, both by the WCS-BiH and cantonal and district courts, a tremendous backlog of war crimes cases, including SGV cases, remains: it is estimated that 1,200 to 1,300 cases representing some 8,000 or more accused have yet to be litigated.[88] Although it is unclear how many of these cases involve SGV allegations, observers, including the European Commission, have expressed concern that not enough has been done to prioritise and pursue accountability for SGV crimes in particular.[89] Yet, as discussed in the section below, both the WCS-BiH and cantonal and district courts confront a range of difficulties in effectively prosecuting such cases, including challenges related to victims and witnesses, legal hurdles and political opposition. These challenges are particularly acute in Bosnia's current post-conflict context, where decreased international support for war crimes prosecutions has coincided with increased adjudication of these cases by local courts that many view as ill-equipped to handle what are often complicated and politically sensitive cases.[90]

3. CHALLENGES FACING THE BOSNIAN COURTS IN PROSECUTING CONFLICT-RELATED SGV CRIMES

As described in the next section, prosecuting SGV cases poses unique difficulties and puts enormous pressure on victims and witnesses. These challenges have been exacerbated in the context of Bosnia, where conflict-related SGV prosecutions have occurred against a backdrop of legal challenges and political opposition, both of which reflect ongoing post-conflict legacies.

---

88 OSCE, 'Delivering Justice', above n. 5, pp. 21–22 (reporting that as of April 2010, the BiH Prosecutor's Office reported the existence of approximately 1,381 war crimes case files pertaining to some 8249 suspects distributed among the 17 jurisdictions dealing with war). Presumably, the backlog has been reduced below the 1,381 figure in the interim period between 2010 and 2015. See State Court of Bosnia and Herzegovina 'Registry Quarterly Report' (September 2012) 14 (forecasting 20 ongoing war crimes cases being heard in trial each month).

89 See European Commission, 'Bosnia and Herzegovina 2013 Progress Report Accompanying the Document Communication from the Commission to the European Parliament and the Council: Enlargement Strategy and Main Challenges 2013–2014', p. 13.

90 Martin-Ortega, above n. 42, pp. 608–09; See generally 'Combating Impunity: Courts of the Federation of Bosnia and Herzegovina, Republika Srpska, and Brčko District', above n. 82.

3.1. CHALLENGES RELATED TO VICTIMS AND WITNESSES

3.1.1. Lack of Adequate Victim Witness Support and Protection

SGV cases are often difficult to prosecute due to a lack of available evidence,[91] with physical evidence seldom documented or preserved at the times the crimes occurred,[92] and generally non-existent more than 20 years after their commission. This places a particularly heavy burden on victims of SGV whose testimony is often the only evidence in a case.[93] At the same time, SGV victims who have not revealed their victimisation to family members, friends or neighbours may be reluctant to come forward and face the stigma that is often attached to sexual violence in the region, and may also experience concern for their physical safety, especially given the fact that many victims live in close proximity to perpetrators and their families.[94] Such pressures require adequate victim support and witness protection measures.

Several verdicts from the WCS-BiH reflect an understanding of victims' reasons for not reporting their victimisation sooner, including a lack of trust

---

91 Combating Impunity: Courts of the Federation of Bosnia and Herzegovina, Republika Srpska, and Brčko District', above n. 82, p. 6.

92 This is often due to the fact that resources were often unavailable during the conflict or in the hands of the same power structures as the accused. See, e.g., *Bogdanovic*, Appellate Verdict, above n. 14, pp 73–74 (acknowledging the reasons for the lack of physical evidence to corroborate the victim's testimony and noting that 'the collection of physical evidence at the time of the offense would have been entrusted to the persons belonging to the same military and police structures as the perpetrator', thus any investigation would not have been unbiased).

93 Medica Mondiale, '"… and that it does not happen to anyone anywhere in the world": The Trouble with Rape Trials – Views of Witnesses, Prosecutors, and Judges, on Prosecuting Sexualised Violence During the War in the former Yugoslavia', pp. 70–71, available at <http://www.medicamondiale.org/fileadmin/redaktion/5_Service/Mediathek/Dokumente/English/Documentations_studies/medica_mondiale_and_that_it_does_not_happen_to_anyone_anywhere_in_the_world_english_complete_version_dec_2009.pdf> accessed 26.09.2016.

94 See *Bogdanovic*, Appellate Verdict, above n. 14, para. 70 (finding that 'it is natural for rape victims to refrain from talking about their experience due to fear of retribution, embarrassment, sense of self-accusation, mistrust in the prosecution authorities, confusion and other reasons, including the conservative community, lack of education, [and] a general lack of empathy'). See also *Baričanin*, above n. 14, paras. 227, 229 (recounting the testimony of expert witness Dr Ljubović, who testified at trial that 10–20 per cent of rape victims report the rapes they experienced after a period of delay, while the majority do not report it at all, due to victims' feelings of 'shame, guilt, and helplessness'); *Damjanović*, Appellate Verdict, above n. 14, p. 9 (finding it 'easily understandable' that the victim did not talk to anyone else, including a doctor, about her experience, because of the stigma attached to rape in the patriarchal community in which she lives). See also Amnesty International, 'Bosnia and Herzegovina: Briefing to the UN Committee on the Elimination of Discrimination against Women, 55th Session of the Committee' (8–26 July 2013), p. 10, available at <http://tbinternet.ohchr.org/Treaties/CEDAW/Shared%20Documents/BIH/INT_CEDAW_NGO_BIH_14160_E.pdf> accessed 18.05.2016.

in the authorities in power at the time the crimes occurred, embarrassment and fear of retribution.[95] However, observers have been critical of the uneven implementation of victim support and witness protection measures by the WCS-BiH and cantonal and district courts, underscoring the particular impact of the problem in cases involving SGV.[96] Indeed, while the WCS-BiH instituted a range of mechanisms to provide support and protection to victims and witnesses,[97] these measures have often been applied only partially or inconsistently. For example, soon after the WCS-BiH began operating, the OSCE reported that in some cases, although witnesses had been assigned pseudonyms in the indictment, defence lawyers or judges revealed witnesses' names in open session.[98] A recent report on the WCS-BiH noted that indictments are still routinely returned to Prosecutors because they contain the names of victims of SGV.[99] In other cases, although witnesses' names had been protected in court documents, court summonses were revealed indiscreetly or the public was permitted to observe proceedings which involved protected witnesses, being notified only that that they should not reveal what they saw or heard.[100] New laws have been put in place to protect witnesses before the WCS-BiH,[101] and the Court has taken steps to address deficiencies and provide better protection to witnesses, including developing procedures and checklists to guide judges in ordering protective measures.[102] The Court's jurisprudence demonstrates that the WCS-BiH now routinely offers critical protective measures to victims of SGV, including the use of pseudonyms, closed session hearings and other interventions.[103] Yet, cantonal and district courts continue to lag behind in

---

95 ibid.

96 OSCE, 'Witness Protection and Support in BiH Domestic War Crimes Trials: Obstacles and Recommendations a Year after the Adoption of the National Strategy for War Crimes Processing' (January 2010), p. 10.

97 M. Kreso, 'The Transplant of Customary Law and ICTY Jurisprudence to the Courts in Bosnia and Herzegovina' in R. Steinberg (ed.), 'Assessing the Legacy of the ICTY', p. 242.

98 OSCE, 'Witness Protection and Support', above n. 96, p. 15.

99 OSCE, 'Processing of War Crimes at the State Level in Bosnia and Herzegovina', above n. 5, para. 116(a).

100 OSCE, 'Witness Protection and Support', above n. 96, pp. 14–15.

101 See 'Law on Witness Protection Program in Bosnia and Herzegovina' (12 May 2014) 'Official Gazette' of Bosnia and Herzegovina, No. 36/14, available (in Bosnian) at <http://www.sudbih.gov.ba/app_dev.php/stranica/82/pregled> accessed 26.09.2016.

102 Amnesty International, 'Whose Justice? The Women of Bosnia and Herzegovina Are Still Waiting', Amnesty International 2009, p. 25.

103 See, e.g., *Kurtovic*, above n. 75, p. 13 (noting the Court's use of pseudonyms to protect the identity of victims of SGV, Witness A and Witness B, and the exclusion of the public from the courtroom during their testimonies, acknowledging that the Court was 'particularly mindful of the nature of the offense of which Witnesses A and B were victims and the traumas which they still feel'); *Mejakić et al.*, First Instance Verdict, above n. 14, pp. 32–35 (discussing a range of protective measures offered to victim-witnesses of SGV); *Momir Savić*, First Instance Verdict, above n. 71, pp. 9–10 (describing how the Court will withhold the victim-witness's identity information for 30 years and excluded the public from the courtroom); *Palija*, First Instance Verdict, above n. 73, p. 17 (noting that allowing the witness to testify from a separate

providing adequate protective measures.[104] Many of these courts lack separate entrances and waiting rooms for witnesses, the ability to testify from a separate room using video-link testimony, and victim/witness support staff.[105] Although many of the shortcomings can be attributed to a lack of resources,[106] the OSCE has noted that at times, even protective measures that do not result in monetary costs to the courts, such as assigning pseudonyms to protect witnesses' true identities, are not routinely offered.[107]

These realities highlight the need not only for investment in the infrastructure necessary to provide protective measures, such as the equipment needed to allow victim-witnesses to testify using video-link technology, but also for ongoing training necessary to ensure a comprehensive approach to witness protection and victim support from pre-trial through post-trial stages of proceedings, as discussed in our recommendations, in section 5.1 below. Importantly, this is critical not only for the victims participating in the trials, but also for encouraging other victims to come forward. If SGV victims who have not yet revealed their victimisation hear that similarly situated victims are not protected or supported in the courtroom, they are unlikely to report these crimes.[108]

---

room and closing the courtroom to the public was an 'utterly critical approach' that was 'absolutely necessary due to the severe trauma which the injured party still suffers').

104 The WCS-BiH is aware of the fact that SGV victims often require more extensive protective measures and has taken the gap between witness protection measures available at the state level and those available at the entity court into consideration when deciding which cases to transfer to entity courts. OSCE, 'Combating Impunity: State Court', above n. 59, p. 21. However, some report that entity prosecutors complain that cases are transferred from the state level to cantonal courts without adequate regard for the limited ability of cantonal courts to provide effective protection and support to victims. See M. Šoćaric, *War Victims and Gender-Sensitive Truth, Justice, Reparations and Non-Recurrence in Bosnia and Herzegovina*, Impunity Watch 2012, p. 45.

105 Authors' observations and meetings with staff during May 2014 visit to Bihać Cantonal Court. Inadequate physical infrastructure in many courthouses circumscribes their ability to provide adequate security and witness protection measures, although victim/witness personnel are resourceful in trying to support victims despite these shortcomings. As of the time of writing, a new court building is being built in Bihać.

106 See Concluding Observations of the Human Rights Committee, Bosnia and Herzegovina, U.N. Doc. CCPR/C/BIH/CO/1 (2006) ('express[ing] concern about the underfunding of district and cantonal courts dealing with war crimes cases and the unsatisfactory implementation of witness protection legislation at the Entity level' and calling on Bosnia and Herzegovina to 'allocate sufficient funds and human resources to the district and cantonal courts trying war crimes and ensure the effective application of the State and Entity Laws on Protection of Witnesses'. See also European Commission, 'Commission Staff Working Document Bosnia and Herzegovina 2012 Progress Report accompanying the document Communication from the Commission to the European Parliament and the Council: Enlargement Strategy and Main Challenges 2012–2013', available at <http://ec.europa.eu/enlargement/pdf/key_documents/2012/package/ba_rapport_2012_en.pdf> accessed 15.04.2016.

107 OSCE, 'Combating Impunity: Courts of the Federation of Bosnia and Herzegovina, Republika Srpska and Brčko District', above n. 82, p. 41; OSCE, 'Witness Protection and Support', above n. 96, pp. 15–16.

108 Amnesty International, 'Whose Justice?', above n. 102, p. 27.

3.1.2. *Inconsistent Compensation for Victims of SGV*

While determining the guilt or innocence of those accused of genocide, war crimes and crimes against humanity is the primary goal of criminal prosecutions, criminal courts in Bosnia can also order individual defendants to pay their victims compensation for crimes of sexual violence.[109] Historically, however, if victims of SGV crimes were informed at all about mechanisms to obtain such compensation, they were often advised to seek such relief through a separate civil claim following a finding of guilt in criminal proceedings,[110] an approach which is costly for victims and requires them to reveal their identities[111] and to relive yet again the violations they suffered.

In June of 2015, however, as part of a criminal prosecution for a conflict-related rape, the WCS-BiH sentenced two defendants to 10-year prison sentences and ordered them to pay 26,500 Bosnian marks (£9,655) in compensation to the victim.[112] The WCS-BiH has followed this landmark verdict with additional

109 Law on Obligations, Art. 200 ('(1) The court shall allocate a just cash compensation for suffered bodily pain, mental sufferings due to a decrease of life activity, impairment, violated reputation, honor, freedom or personal right, death of a close person as well as for fear, if it establishes that this is justified taking into account the circumstances of the case and especially the intensity of pain and fear, regardless of the fact that the compensation for material damage exists or not. (2) While deciding about the request for compensation of consequential damage, as well as about the amount of compensation, the court shall take into account the significance of the damaged goods and the purpose of the compensation, as well as ensure that the compensation does not favor the tendencies which would not be compatible with its nature and social purpose') and Art. 202 ('A person who was led into a punishable intercourse or punishable debauchery by fraud, force or abuse of a relationship of submission or dependence is entitled to a fair compensation due to suffered mental pain. The same right has a person to whom was committed some other act of crime against the personal dignity and morale'), available at <http://ruessmann.jura.uni-sb.de/BiH-Project/Data/Zakon_obliga.pdf> accessed 18.09.2016.

110 Special Rapporteur on violence against women, its causes and consequences, Addendum, Mission to Bosnia and Herzegovina, A/HRC/23/49/Add.3 (4 June 2013), para. 94; 'Freed But Not Free Yet: The Situation of Former Camp Detainees in Bosnia and Herzegovina, General Allegation to the Special Rapporteur on Torture and Other Cruel, Inhuman, or Degrading Treatment or Punishment and the Working Group on Arbitrary Detention' Report by TRIAL and Detainee Organizations (April 2012), paras. 101–06, available at <https://trial.ba/wp-content/uploads/2016/02/General_allegation_to_SR_Torture_and_WGAD_-_April_2012.pdf> accessed 16.07.2018. The ICTY has faced similar criticism for failing to obtain restitution for victims of crimes within its jurisdiction. See P. Robinson, 'The Way Forward' in R. Steinberg (ed.), *Assessing the Legacy of the ICTY*, Brill 2011, pp. 268–69.

111 TRIAL [Track Impunity Always] *et al.*, 'Follow-up Report on the Implementation by Bosnia and Herzegovina's of the Recommendations Issued by the Committee on the Elimination of Discrimination against Women in July 2013 (CEDAW/C/BIH/CO/4-5) (July 2015) paras. 39–41, available at <http://tbinternet.ohchr.org/Treaties/CEDAW/Shared%20Documents/BIH/INT_CEDAW_NGS_BIH_21073_E.pdf> accessed 01.09.2016.

112 ibid., para. 42. See also Reuters, 'Bosnian Court Grants Wartime Rape Victim Compensation in Landmark Ruling' <http://www.theguardian.com/world/2015/jun/24/bosnian-court-grants-wartime-victim-compensation-landmark-ruling> accessed 15.04.2016. See verdict at <http://www.sudbih.gov.ba/predmet/3266/show>.

decisions awarding compensation to victims of conflict-related SGV,[113] representing a potential shift in the Court's treatment of such claims. Whether this approach will be widely followed by cantonal and district courts, however, has yet to be seen, although the Bihać Cantonal Court has awarded compensation as part of plea agreements in two rape cases to date.[114]

In the absence of court-ordered compensation, SGV victims in need of resources to rebuild their lives must look to alternative sources, such as government or NGO-based programs that provide compensation or services. Some SGV victims have accessed government-funded civilian victim of war benefits, but critics have argued that the criteria to access these benefits are overly restrictive, resulting in disturbingly low compensation rates.[115] Additionally, civilian victim of war benefits are often viewed in a similar light as welfare assistance and are granted based on factors including a victim's income, rather than being framed as compensation for the violation of his or her rights.[116]

---

113 *Slavko Savić Sentenced to 8 (eight) Years in Prison*, Court of Bosnia and Herzegovina Press Release, 29 June 2015, available at <http://www.sudbih.gov.ba/vijest/slavko-savi-osuen-na-8-osam-godina-zatvora-20053> accessed 15.04.2016. Adil Vojić and Bekir Mešić each sentenced to seven years in prison, Court of Bosnia and Herzegovina Press Release, 16 March 2016, available at <http://www.sudbih.gov.ba/vijest/adil-voji-i-bekir-mei-osueni-na-po-sedam-godina-zatvora-20304> accessed 15.04.2016.

114 See 'Bosnian Ex-Fighter Jailed for Attempted Rape' (noting that as part of a plea agreement, the accused was also ordered to pay 50,000 KM in damages to the victim), available at <http://www.justice-report.com/en/articles/bosniak-ex-fighter-jailed-for-attempted-rape> accessed 18.09.2016. See also the case of 'Ćoralić Amir' on TRIAL International (noting the defendant plead guilty and agreed to pay 35,000 KM in damages to the victim), available at <https://trialinternational.org/latest-post/amir-coralic/> accessed 18 August 2016.

115 A 2010 study found that in 2009, out of 10,950 people in the Federation of Bosnia and Herzegovina receiving individual or family civilian victim of war benefits, only 612 claimed this benefit based on sexual violence victimisation. L. Popić with B. Panjeta 'Compensation, transitional justice and conditional international credit in Bosnia and Herzegovina: Attempts to reform government payments to victims and veterans of the 1992–1995 war' (June 2010) Table 3, 11. Additionally, the Human Rights Committee has expressed concern for the fact that in many places, veterans receive more compensation that victims of SGV. Human Rights Committee, 'Concluding observations on the second periodic report of Bosnia and Herzegovina, adopted by the Committee at its 106th session, 15 October to 2 November' (2012), para. 8, available at <http://docstore.ohchr.org/SelfServices/FilesHandler.ashx?enc=6QkG1d%2FPPRiCAqhKb7yhsseOnooqYJDU6whjJc%2Bd39Cr2QLMra%2Btjix35VlXk3FCAwXmYScQsNaRcocamoKXccu49QbeFfv1jSbSZz0hcDzRWWr2Fd2tvx9AupXboZW5> accessed 15.04.2016. For more information on SGV victims' views about the assistance offered to them by entity governments and NGOs, see Medica Mondiale/Medica Zenica, 'We Are Still Alive: Research on the Long-Term Consequences of War Rape and Coping Strategies of Survivors in Bosnia and Herzegovina' (June 2014), available at <http://www.medicamondiale.org/fileadmin/redaktion/5_Service/Mediathek/Dokumente/English/Documentations_studies/141128_Research_We-Are-Still-Alive_CR-Medica-Zenica_medica-mondiale.pdf> accessed 15.04. 2016.

116 Šoćaric, above n. 104, p. 50.

3.2. LEGAL CHALLENGES

The difficulties discussed above facing victims of SGV have been aggravated by a number of legal challenges affecting the prosecution of serious international crimes at both the state and local level. These include legal challenges affecting the prosecution of SGV crimes in particular – such as language in the Bosnian criminal code falling short of international standards in defining rape – as well as broader challenges, such as the application of multiple criminal codes in Bosnia, which has led to inconsistent results and given rise to a European Court of Human Rights (ECtHR)[117] case that has been improperly interpreted and used to undermine accountability efforts, with particularly grave consequences for SGV crimes.

3.2.1. Inconsistent Application of International Standards Regarding the Definition of Rape Under International Law

Article 172(g) of the 2003 Criminal Code of Bosnia and Herzegovina ('BiH Criminal Code') criminalises rape and other forms of sexual violence as crimes against humanity, providing that such crimes include:

> Coercing another by force or by threat of immediate attack upon his life or limb, or the life or limb of a person close to him, to sexual intercourse or an equivalent sexual act (rape), sexual slavery, enforced prostitution, forced pregnancy, enforced sterilisation or any other form of sexual violence of comparable gravity ...[118]

Similarly, Article 173(c) of the 2003 BiH Criminal Code prohibits two offences under the category of 'war crimes against civilians', including:

> Coercing another by force or by threat of immediate attack upon his life or limb, or the life or limb of a person close to him, to sexual intercourse or an equivalent sexual act (rape) or forcible prostitution ...[119]

Both of these definitions required coercion 'by force or by threat of immediate attack' as an element of the crime. The inclusion of this element raised concerns

117 *Maktouf and Damjanović v. Bosnia and Herzegovina*, European Court of Human Rights, Application Numbers 2312/08 and 34179/08, Judgment, July 18, 2013.

118 Criminal Code of Bosnia and Herzegovina, June 27, 2003, 'Official Gazette of Bosnia and Herzegovina' No. 3/03, 32/03, 37/03, 54/04, 61/04, 30/05, 53/06, 55/06, 32/07', art. 172(g).

119 ibid., art. 173(c). The SFRY Code, which is usually applied by the entity courts, provides for a minimum of five years of imprisonment for 'whoever in violation of rules of international law effective at the time of war, armed conflict or occupation, orders that civilian population be subject to ... forcible prostitution or rape'. Criminal Code of the Socialist Federal Republic of Yugoslavia, above n. 86, art. 142.

about whether or not Bosnia's definition of rape under these provisions was consistent with international law.[120] In a series of landmark cases, the ICTR and the ICTY defined 'coercion' broadly to include coercive circumstances, such as those present in the context of detention or during armed conflict.[121] Jurisprudence from these tribunals has endorsed defining rape by reference to an absence of consent rather than focusing only on coercion, finding that coercion can evidence a lack of consent but that force, threat of force, or coercion is not required.[122] Furthermore, the tribunals have emphasised that consent must be freely and voluntarily given.[123]

In several instances, the WCS-BiH has followed the principles distilled from this line of jurisprudence and interpreted the coercion element in the BiH Criminal Code broadly.[124] However, the application of the elements of rape has to some extent been uneven at the cantonal and district court level.[125] In *Prosecutor v. Mihajlović*, for example, the Zenica Cantonal Court acquitted the accused of one charge of rape as a war crime because the Court found that the victim did not physically resist the defendant's advances.[126] While the Court acknowledged that the defendant – a police officer – came to the victim's apartment on a curfew check during the war and brought with him a rifle, which he leaned against the couch where the alleged rape took place, the Court nonetheless held that because the victim did not physically resist, the elements of the crime were not met.[127]

120 OSCE, 'Combating Impunity: State Court', above n. 60, pp. 28–30, 42; OSCE, 'Combating Impunity: Courts of the Federation of Bosnia and Herzegovina, Republika Srpska, and Brčko District', above n. 82, pp. 22–30.

121 See, e.g., *Delalic et al.*, Trial Chamber Judgment, above n. 20, paras. 478–79; *Akayesu*, Trial Chamber Judgment, above n. 36, para. 598; *Furundžija*, Trial Chamber Judgment, above n. 11, para. 271 (finding that, for the purpose of applying the elements of rape, 'any form of captivity vitiates consent').

122 *Furundžija*, Trial Chamber Judgment, above n. 11, para. 180 (concluding after surveying several domestic jurisdictions to assess principles of common law with regard to the definition of rape that 'all jurisdictions surveyed by the Trial Chamber require an element of force, coercion, threat, *or acting without the consent of the victim*' [emphasis added]); *Kunarac*, Trial Chamber Judgment, above n. 24, para. 453. (finding that, in surveying national jurisdictions, 'In most common law systems, it is the absence of the victim's free and genuine consent to sexual penetration which is the defining characteristic of rape' and holding that 'force or threat or fear of force need not be proven').

123 *Kunarac*, Trial Chamber Judgment, above n. 24, para. 453.

124 See e.g. *Kujundzic*, First Instance Verdict, above n. 69, para. 478 (holding that to establish the crime of rape, one of the following elements must be satisfied: 'the sexual activity is accompanied by force or threat of force to the victim or a third party; the sexual activity is accompanied by force or a variety of other specified circumstances which made the victim particularly vulnerable or negated her ability to make an informed refusal; or the sexual activity occurs without the consent of the victim').

125 OSCE, 'Combating Impunity: Courts of the Federation of Bosnia and Herzegovina, Republika Srpska, and Brčko District', above n. 82, pp. 25–30.

126 *Prosecutor v. Tomo Mihajlović*, Zenica Cantonal Court Verdict (2 June 2005), p. 32.

127 ibid.

The Court interpreted the element of force or coercion narrowly, finding that 'the victim's resistance needs to be real and permanent and that the attacker's coercion has to be met with serious resistance by the attacked woman'.[128] In contrast, in another case with similar circumstances against defendants Hasanović and Pavić, the Appellate verdict in Brčko District acknowledged that the 'use of force or … threat' element could be satisfied where there is a 'specific form of coercion', such as if the act is 'carried out under the circumstances that exclude any possibility of the victim resisting her assailants'.[129] While the Brčko District Court still read into the code that resistance on the part of the victim was generally required, it recognised as 'coercive circumstances' the fact that the perpetrators were armed men in uniforms who came to the victim's home and forced her to leave the room where she stayed with her husband, thus 'exclud[ing] any possibility for voluntariness of the … sexual intercourse'.[130]

This inconsistent interpretation of the element of coercion by Bosnian courts created a significant barrier to accountability for many victims, leading groups including the UN Committee Against Torture to push for reform of the Criminal Code, arguing that continued application of a definition of rape that is inconsistent with international standards risks impunity for this crime.[131] In 2015, the BiH Criminal Code was thus amended to remove the reference to force, so that the definition of rape in the provisions addressing war crimes and crimes against humanity now prohibits, respectively, 'coercing another person to sexual intercourse or an equivalent sexual act (rape) or forcible prostitution',[132] and 'coercing another person to sexual intercourse or an equivalent sexual act (rape), sexual slavery, enforced prostitution, forced pregnancy, enforced sterilisation or any other form of sexual violence'.[133] Removing the language requiring evidence of force brings the definition more in line with international law, but

128 ibid. Note that the European Court of Human Rights rejected this interpretation of the definition of rape, finding that by failing to define rape in terms of lack of consent and by requiring force and resistance on the part of the victim, Bulgaria ran afoul of Articles 3 and 8 of the European Convention on Human Rights, which prohibit torture and inhuman and degrading treatment or punishment and protects one's right to a private life, respectively. *M.C. v. Bulgaria* App. no. 39272/98 (ECtHR 4 December 2003), paras. 181–87.

129 *Prosecutor v. Hasanović and Pavić*, Appellate Verdict, Brčko District of Bosnia and Herzegovina (11 May 2009), p. 7.

130 ibid.

131 Report of the Committee against Torture: Forty-fifth session (1–19 November 2010), Forty-sixth session (9 May–3 June 2011), General Assembly Official Records, Sixty-sixth session Supplement No. 44 (A/66/44) 12. See also OSCE, 'Combating Impunity: State Court', above n. 59, p. 6.

132 The Criminal Code of Bosnia and Herzegovina, BiH Official gazette 3/03 with amendments to the Law as published in 'Official Gazette of BiH' no. 32/03, 37/03 54/04, 61/04, 30/05, 53/06, 55/06, 32/07, 8/10, 47/14, 22/15, 40/15, art. 173(e), available (in Bosnian) at <http://www.sudbih.gov.ba/app_dev.php/stranica/82/pregled>.

133 ibid., art. 172(1)(g).

retaining the 'coercing' language without defining 'coercing' to include 'coercive circumstances' and any non-consensual sexual intercourse leaves the law open to interpretation, risking continued inconsistency with international law on this issue and potential impunity for grave acts of sexual violence. Additionally, as discussed in section 3.2.2 below, the cantonal and district courts generally do not apply the amended Criminal Code of Bosnia and Herzegovina, leading to further risk of conflicting verdicts across the country.

3.2.2. Inconsistent Application of Criminal Codes

An overarching legal challenge to the prosecution of serious international crimes in Bosnia and Herzegovina with particular implications for SGV cases is the conflict between the 1976 Socialist Federal Republic of Yugoslavia Criminal Code (SFRY Code) and the 2003 BiH Criminal Code. There are several significant differences between these two codes, particularly with regard to their provisions criminalising serious international crimes. Both codes criminalise genocide and war crimes.[134] However, only the BiH Criminal Code criminalises crimes against humanity.[135] The codes also differ with regard to modes of liability and sentencing provisions.[136] The WCS-BiH more regularly applies the BiH Code, while the entity and Brčko District courts usually rely on the SFRY Code, leading to different approaches and sometimes inconsistent results in similar cases.[137] Moreover, accused have challenged the differences in sentencing provisions, resulting in a decision by the ECtHR – *Maktouf and Damjanović v. Bosnia and Herzegovina*[138] – that has had far-reaching implications for the prosecution of all serious crimes prosecuted in Bosnia. In that case, the applicants alleged, among other arguments, that the WCS-BiH had violated Article 7 of the European Convention on Human Rights (ECHR), which prohibits both the retroactive criminalisation of acts that were not criminal at the time they were committed and the imposition of heavier penalties than what was provided

---

134 Criminal Code of the Socialist Federal Republic of Yugoslavia, above n. 86, arts. 141–53; Criminal Code of Bosnia and Herzegovina, 27 June 2003, above n. 118.

135 Criminal Code of Bosnia and Herzegovina, above n. 118, art. 172.

136 Criminal Code of the Socialist Federal Republic of Yugoslavia, above n. 86, arts. 11, 22–30 (outlining modes of responsibility), arts. 141–53 (outlining sentencing provisions for genocide and war crimes); Criminal Code of Bosnia and Herzegovina, above n. 118, arts. 29–32, 180 (outlining modes of responsibility including for serious international crimes), art. 171–84 (providing for sentences for serious international crimes).

137 OSCE, 'Moving Towards a Harmonized Application of the Law Applicable in War Crimes Cases Before Courts in Bosnia and Herzegovina' August 2008, p. 5; Human Rights Committee, 'Concluding observations on the second periodic report of Bosnia and Herzegovina, adopted by the Committee at its 106th session, 15 October to 2 November' (2012), para. 7 (noting that the Committee is 'concerned at the lack of efforts to harmonise jurisprudence on war crimes among entities' and that 'this might affect consistency in sentencing among entities').

138 *Maktouf and Damjanović*, above n. 117.

for by law at that time.[139] The applicants argued that by sentencing them under the BiH Criminal Code of 2003, the WCS-BiH violated Article 7 of the ECHR because the BiH Code, which was not in effect when the crimes were committed, provided for a heavier minimum penalty for the crimes of which they were convicted than the SFRY Code, which was in effect at the time.[140] The ECtHR agreed, holding that the Bosnian courts should have applied the SFRY Code in that case, as it allowed for a lesser penalty for the kind of minor offences of which Maktouf and Damjanović had been convicted.[141] In reaching its decision, the Court stressed that Maktouf and Damjanović had been convicted of crimes involving no loss of human life, and cautioned that the Bosnian courts should apply a case-by-case approach to determine which code provided for a lesser penalty under the particular circumstances of each case.[142] In response to this finding, Bosnia's Constitutional Court took what many have argued is an overbroad reading of the *Maktouf* decision and quashed the sentences that had been given in close to 20 of WCS-BiH's cases in which the BiH Criminal Code rather than the SFRY Code had been applied.[143] The Constitutional Court did so despite the fact that in many of these cases, the offences at issue were far more serious than those committed by Maktouf and Damjanović, subjecting the accused in those cases to higher sentencing ranges that were not always more lenient under the SFRY Code.[144] As a result, many individuals that had been convicted of genocide, as well as some convicted of war crimes, were released

139 Convention for the Protection of Human Rights and Fundamental Freedoms, (European Convention on Human Rights, as amended), art. 7 provides: '1. No one shall be held guilty of any criminal offence on account of any act or omission which did not constitute a criminal offence under national or international law at the time when it was committed. Nor shall a heavier penalty be imposed than the one that was applicable at the time the criminal offence was committed. 2. This Article shall not prejudice the trial and punishment of any person for any act or omission which, at the time when it was committed, was criminal according to the general principles of law recognised by civilised nations.'

140 *Maktouf and Damjanović*, above n. 117, paras. 54, 61.

141 ibid., paras. 70, 76.

142 ibid., paras. 65, 69.

143 M. Kapetanovic, 'The Impact of the ECtHR Ruling in the Case of Maktouf and Damjanovic v Bosnia and Herzegovina: Transitional Justice in B-H' Lancaster University Law School Blog, available at <https://lancslaw.wordpress.com/2015/03/05/transitional-justice-in-b-h/> accessed 15.04.2016; Letter to Office of the United Nations High Commissioner for Human Rights from Pablo De Greiff, Special Rapporteur on the promotion of truth, justice, reparation and guarantees of non-recurrence and Ariel Dulitzky, Chair-Rapporteur of the Working Group on Enforced or Involuntary Disappearances, 1 April 2014, available at <https://spdb.ohchr.org/hrdb/27th/public_-_OL_Bosnia_01.04.14_%282.2014%29.pdf> accessed 15.04.2016.

144 Kapetanovic, above n. 143; Letter to Office of the United Nations High Commissioner for Human Rights from Pablo De Greiff, Special Rapporteur on the promotion of truth, justice, reparation and guarantees of non-recurrence and Ariel Dulitzky, Chair-Rapporteur of the Working Group on Enforced or Involuntary Disappearances, 1 April 2014, available at <https://spdb.ohchr.org/hrdb/27th/public_-_OL_Bosnia_01.04.14_%282.2014%29.pdf> accessed 15.04.2016.

pending retrial under the SFRY Code, frustrating and intimidating victims.[145] The decisions also enabled critics of the court to undermine the credibility of the WCS-BiH by suggesting that it had run roughshod over the rights of the accused, when in fact the *Maktouf* decision had been limited to the particular facts of that case.[146] Retrials in numerous cases have resulted in drastically reduced sentences.[147] In at least one of these cases, a defendant convicted of serious crimes of sexual violence was released and then resentenced under the SFRY Code, resulting in a reduction of his nine-year sentence to six years.[148] Moreover, in at least one case, the accused fled Bosnia and absconded to Serbia after he was released and, as of this writing, had not returned to Bosnia to serve his sentence.[149]

These events not only represent a setback for the WCS-BiH in terms of arguably unwarranted reductions in sentences for those convicted of serious crimes, including SGV, but have also led to Prosecutors charging war crimes under the SFRY Code rather than crimes against humanity under the BiH Criminal Code.[150] This practice has particularly negative implications for SGV cases. As noted above, only the BiH Criminal Code criminalises crimes against humanity. This is critical because prosecuting acts of sexual violence that are committed as part of a widespread or systematic attack against a civilian population as war crimes under the SFRY Code – rather than as crimes against humanity under the BiH Criminal Code – fails to adequately reflect the nature of those crimes and to document the connections between related cases.[151] Further, the crimes against humanity provision in the BiH Criminal Code encompasses a broad range of crimes of sexual violence, including enumerated acts not criminalised anywhere under the SFRY Code, such as sexual slavery,

---

145 Report of the Working Group on Enforced or Involuntary Disappearances Addendum Follow-up report to the recommendations made by the Working Group Missions to Argentina and Bosnia and Herzegovina, 8 September 2014 (A/HRC/27/49/Add.2) p. 36, [37].

146 Kapetanovic, above n. 143.

147 ibid. See, e.g., *Prosecutor v. Milenko Trifunović, Brano Džinić, Aleksandar Radovanović, Slobodan Jakovljević and Branislav Medan*, State Court of Bosnia and Herzegovina Second Instance Verdict (23 January 2014), p. 7 [537] (resentencing the accused to 20 years of imprisonment each for genocide, the maximum penalty permitted under the SFRY, after the first instance verdict had sentenced each of the accused in the case to 40–42 years of imprisonment under the Criminal Code of BiH.)

148 OSCE, 'Combating Impunity: State Court', above n. 59, p. 32, FN 71; See Justice Report, 'Sentence against Zrinko Pincic Reduced', available at <http://www.justice-report.com/en/articles/sentence-against-zrinko-pincic-reduced> accessed 01.09.2016.

149 See 'Information on the Novak Đukić case' Press Release of 9 October 2014, of the Court of Bosnia and Herzegovina, available at <http://www.sudbih.gov.ba/vijest/informacije-o-predmetu-novak-uki-19464> accessed 01.09.2016.

150 OSCE, 'Processing of War Crimes at the State Level in Bosnia and Herzegovina', above n. 5, paras. 83–86.

151 OSCE, 'Combating Impunity: State Court', above n. 59, p. 31. See also OSCE, 'Processing of War Crimes at the State Level in Bosnia and Herzegovina', above n. 5, paras. 83–86.

forced pregnancy, enforced sterilisation and other forms 'of sexual violence of comparable gravity'.[152] Importantly, prosecuting individuals for crimes against humanity under the BiH Criminal Code has been found by the ECtHR not to violate the principle of retroactivity, as such acts were found to have triggered criminal responsibility under international law before the conflict began in the former Yugoslavia.[153] Thus, prosecutors should not avoid charging crimes against humanity when appropriate based on concerns related to retroactivity after *Maktouf*.

In addition to the limited SGV offences found in the SFRY Code, the limited modes of liability provided for under the SFRY Code presents additional challenges. The SFRY Code does not provide for superior responsibility for the acts it criminalises, creating a particular obstacle to justice for victims of SGV crimes, which were often encouraged or tolerated by military, police and other leaders who failed to prevent or punish acts of sexual violence committed by soldiers, detention centre guards or other subordinates.[154] All of these factors underscore the importance of applying the 2003 BiH Criminal Code to SGV cases to the extent permitted by the ECtHR's holding in *Maktouf*.

---

152 Criminal Code of Bosnia and Herzegovina, above n. 118, art. 172(g). In comparison, the only acts of sexual violence explicitly criminalised by the SFRY Code are the war crimes of rape and enforced prostitution. See Criminal Code of the Socialist Federal Republic of Yugoslavia, above n. 86, art. 142 (providing that 'Whoever in violation of rules of international law effective at the time of war, armed conflict or occupation, orders that civilian population be subject to ... forcible prostitution or rape shall be punished by imprisonment for not less than five years or by the death penalty'). Thus, the SFRY code cannot be utilised to prosecute alleged acts of sexual violence that fall outside these two offences. The Human Rights Committee, among others, has expressed concern about this issue. Human Rights Committee, 'Concluding observations on the second periodic report of Bosnia and Herzegovina, adopted by the Committee at its 106th session, 15 October to 2 November' (2012) [7] (noting the Committee is 'concerned at the lack of efforts to harmonise jurisprudence on war crimes among entities and that entity-level courts use the archaic criminal code of the former Socialist Federal Republic of Yugoslavia (SFRY) that does not, inter alia, define crimes against humanity, command responsibility, sexual slavery and forced pregnancy'). Despite the fact that the language requiring 'coercing ... by force or by threat' is not present in article 142, in several cases, the entity courts have read this into the definition of rape. See, e.g., *Prosecutor v. Hasanović and Pavić*, Appellate Verdict, Brčko District (11 May 2009), p. 7.

153 European Court of Human Rights, *Šimšić v. Bosnia and Herzegovina*, App. no. 51552/10 (26 August 2010), para. 25.

154 OSCE, 'Combating Impunity: State Court', above n. 59, p. 30. See, e.g., *Prosecutor v. Zeljko Mejakić et al.*, above n. 14, pp. 1–2 (convicting two of the three defendants of sexual violence under superior responsibility and all for individual criminal responsibility, pursuant to each defendant's role in the Omarska, Trnopolje, and Keraterm camps). See also OSCE, 'Processing of War Crimes at the State Level in Bosnia and Herzegovina', above n. 5, para. 116 (noting criticism of judges at the State Court of BiH that 'the majority of accused charged with sexual assault were alleged to be direct perpetrators. Rarely was the superior charged with these offences as an aider and abettor or failing to prevent or punish the crime').

3.3. POLITICAL CHALLENGES

Justice efforts for victims of conflict-related SGV crimes have also occurred against a backdrop of political opposition to accountability efforts more broadly, a reflection of unresolved political tensions in the wake of the Dayton Peace Accords.[155] Indeed, political divisions have threatened accountability efforts from the very first attempts to create a state-level court and prosecutor's unit to try war crimes and other sensitive offences such as organised crime and corruption.[156] Laws imposed by the High Representative in November of 2000 to create the State Court of Bosnia and State Prosecutor's Office were immediately challenged by representatives from the Republika Srpska National Assembly, and political and legal attacks on the Court have continued since that time, increasing in intensity since 2011.[157] The opposition to the WCS-BiH has manifested itself in several ways, from a legislative initiative to amend Bosnia's Pardon Law to allow for a presidential pardon of persons convicted of genocide, crimes against humanity, and war crimes[158] – crimes currently excluded from that law – to a more recent initiative intended to challenge the authority of the State Court over Serbs through a referendum scheduled for November 2015 but indefinitely postponed as of this writing.[159]

---

155 M. Smith Hrle, 'Building the Rule of Law: Judicial Reform in Bosnia and Herzegovina' in S. Keil and V. Perry (eds.), *State-Building and Democratization in Bosnia and Herzegovina*, Ashgate 2015, pp. 61–77.

156 ibid., pp. 64–65.

157 ibid., pp. 65, 72.

158 Bosnia and Herzegovina Ministry of Justice, Proposal of the Law on Amendments to the Pardon Law of Bosnia and Herzegovina, Number: 06-02-1-9497/13, 13 November 2013. See also letter from 'Special Rapporteur on the promotion of truth, justice, reparation and guarantees of non-recurrence and Chair-Rapporteur of the Working Group on Enforced or Involuntary Disappearances pursuant to Human Rights Council resolution 18/7 and 16/16' (1 April 2014), p. 8, available at <https://spdb.ohchr.org/hrdb/27th/public_-_OL_Bosnia_01.04.14_%282.2014%29.pdf> accessed 15.04. 2016.

159 See 'Bosnian Serb Seeks Court Referendum in Fresh Challenge to Bosnian State' Reuters, available at <http://www.reuters.com/article/2015/07/14/us-bosnia-court-referendum-idUSKCN0PO1EL20150714> accessed 15.04.2016; 'Bosnian Serbs Approve Referendum Challenging National Court', available at <http://www.rferl.org/content/bosnia-serbs-approve-referendum-challenging-national-court/27130271.html> accessed 15.04.2016; 'Bosnian Serbs Set Date for Controversial Referendum' (25 September 2015), available at <http://www.balkaninsight.com/en/article/bosnian-serbs-set-date-for-disputed-referendum-09-25-2015> accessed 15.04.2016. See also Court of Bosnia and Herzegovina Press Release (30 September 2015) 'Judges of the Court of Bosnia and Herzegovina Voice Concern about the Draft Text on the Law on the Courts of 2015', available at <http://www.sudbih.gov.ba/?id=4169&jezik=e> accessed 15.04.2016. 'Dodik: We Have Not Given Up on Referendum' Sarajevo Times (16 February 2016), available at <http://www.sarajevotimes.com/association-of-women-of-srebrenica-we-will-continue-to-fight-for-truth/> accessed 01.05.2016.

Significantly, opposition to the State Court has intensified as the role of the international community in Bosnia has contracted. When the mandate of the international judges at the WCS-BiH was set to expire at the end of 2009, supporters of the Court advocated for an extension of their mandate, which they felt was necessary to insulate national judges from accusations of ethnic bias and protect the proceedings from political interference.[160] This effort was unanimously opposed by Bosnian Serb members of the Bosnian Parliamentary Assembly, who blocked passage of the proposed law to allow international personnel to remain at the State Court beyond the original five-year period.[161] Although eventually the Office of the High Representative (OHR) extended the mandate of the international judges on the WCS-BiH for three additional years,[162] opposition to the Court has gained momentum since then.[163] Indeed, as Court observers have noted, attacks – in particular from Republika Srpska politicians and media outlets – have increased since the departure of international personnel from the Court.[164] These attacks have taken various forms, including 'interference in proceedings, attempts to undermine existing judicial and legal reforms, and denial of war crimes' despite court findings to the contrary.[165] While the State Court and State Prosecutor's Office have endured

---

160 D. Tolbert and A. Kontić, 'Final Report of the International Criminal Law Services (ICLS) Experts on the Sustainable Transition of the Registry and International Donor Support to the Court of Bosnia and Herzegovina and the Prosecutor's Office of Bosnia and Herzegovina in 2009' (15 December 2008), paras. 17, 126, 145 (finding that surveys and interviews of individuals and institutions inside and outside the State Court and State Prosecutor's Office indicated that ending the involvement of international judges at the State Court presented a substantial risk to the independence and credibility of the national judges and the ending of the role of international prosecutors also presented a grave risk, given the political climate in Bosnia and Herzegovina); Orentlicher, above n. 37, p. 132.

161 Orentlicher, above n. 37, p. 132.

162 ibid.

163 ibid. President of Republika Srpska Milorad Dodik has spearheaded various efforts to discontinue international involvement in the WCS-BiH, as well as recent efforts to end the WCS-BiH's jurisdiction over Bosnian Serbs. See also 'Bosnian Serb Seeks Court Referendum in Fresh Challenge to Bosnian State' Reuters, available at <http://www.reuters.com/article/2015/07/14/us-bosnia-court-referendum-idUSKCN0PO1EL20150714> accessed 15.04.2016. 'Bosnian Serbs Approve Referendum Challenging National Court', available at <http://www.rferl.org/content/bosnia-serbs-approve-referendum-challenging-national-court/27130271.html> accessed 15.04.2016.

164 Kapetanovic, above n. 143; Smith Hrle, above n. 155, p. 73; See also M. Ortega, above n. 42, pp. 596–97 (noting the fact that the departure of international personnel from the State Court and State Prosecutors' Office and the resulting decrease in both financial and human resources has increased the vulnerability of institutions in the face of political pressures).

165 'Bosnian Serbs Approve Referendum Challenging National Court', available at <http://www.rferl.org/content/bosnia-serbs-approve-referendum-challenging-national-court/27130271.html> accessed 15.04.2016; 'EU Foreign Ministers Condemn Bosnian Serb Referendum', available at <http://www.balkaninsight.com/en/article/european-foreign-ministers-warns-against-bosnian-serb-referendum-10-12-2015> accessed 15.04.2016; OSCE, 'Delivering Justice', above n. 5, p. 8.

despite these attacks, as the OSCE has noted, 'their occurrence raises a broader concern about the long-term sustainability and support for the vital rule of law reforms BiH has achieved in the past several years'.[166] The trust Bosnian citizens have placed in the judicial system is fragile, and observers have noted that concerted attempts to misinform the public and undermine confidence in this system present ongoing threats to the very existence of the State Court of BiH and to accountability efforts more broadly.[167]

The attempts to undermine the work of the State Court have coincided with a broader judicial reform effort known as the 'Structural Dialogue', a process initiated in 2011 to prepare Bosnia and Herzegovina for admission into the European Union.[168] Observers have expressed concern that Republika Srpska President Milorad Dodik has orchestrated undue influence on this judicial reform process, using political tools – such as a series of referenda in Republika Srpska calling into question the legality of the State Court and the State Prosecutor's Office – to stall progress.[169] Such events have raised concerns about the long-term stability of the country and the success of the peace accords.[170]

Political attacks on the State Court and the State Prosecutor's Office threaten public support for these institutions, which can make victims of conflict-related crimes reluctant to participate in the justice process,[171] especially victims of highly sensitive crimes such as SGV and, in particular, SGV victims that live in Republika Srpska.[172] Thus, attempts to limit accountability for these crimes threatens SGV victims' access to justice, denying them the opportunity to testify about what they endured, to see their perpetrators held to account and sentenced, and to pursue compensation to address the physical, psychological and economic toll of these offences.

---

166 OSCE, 'Delivering Justice', above n. 5, p. 8.

167 ibid., pp. 8–9. Smith Hrle, above n. 155, p. 72.

168 Website of the Delegation of the European Union to Bosnia and Herzegovina & European Union Special Representative in Bosnia and Herzegovina <http://europa.ba/?page_id=553> accessed 15 April 2016. See also the document on this website entitled '10 facts to know about the EU-BiH Structured Dialogue on Justice', available at <http://europa.ba/wp-content/uploads/2015/05/delegacijaEU_2012022810372059eng.pdf> accessed 15.04.2016.

169 Smith Hrle, above n. 155, pp. 72–73.

170 'Special Report of the High Representative to the Secretary General of the UN on the Implementation of the GFAP [General Framework Agreement for Peace] in BiH', para. 8 (expressing concern to the UN Security Council that Dodik's most recent call for a referendum 'represents one of the most serious violations of the [General Framework Agreement for Peace] since its signing 20 years ago and puts under serious threat peace implementation since then').

171 OSCE, 'Delivering Justice', above n. 5, pp. 85–92.

172 Special Rapporteur on violence against women, its causes and consequences, Addendum, Mission to Bosnia and Herzegovina, A/HRC/23/49/Add.3, (4 June 2013), para. 95 (expressing concern for the failure of RS to address the issue of conflict-related rape and the needs of the victims of these crimes).

4. THE NEED FOR SUSTAINED INTERNATIONAL ENGAGEMENT TO ENSURE ACCESS TO JUSTICE FOR SGV VICTIMS IN BOSNIA

As discussed below, the international community – including foreign governments, agencies within the United Nations (UN), other intergovernmental organisations and non-governmental organisations (NGOs) – is providing various forms of assistance in support of accountability for conflict-related SGV crimes in Bosnia. However, these efforts are in many cases insufficient to meet the challenges outlined above. Sustained international engagement tied to substantive progress on the ground – rather than to predetermined timelines – is critical to stemming the risk of backlash and ensuring effective access to justice for victims of these grave crimes.

4.1. LIMITED INTERNATIONAL SUPPORT FOR WCS-BiH

Following the war in the former Yugoslavia, the judicial sector in Bosnia and Herzegovina was inoperable in many parts of the country, as much of the physical infrastructure was largely destroyed and much of the population – including legal personnel – had been displaced.[173] Despite this reality, international support, particularly for the WCS-BiH, has faced serious limitations from the start.[174] Garnering financial support for the creation of the WCS-BiH was especially difficult due to the fact that the same donors called upon to provide such support had been funding the operation of the ICTY, with a biennial budget exceeding $200 million for the two years immediately preceding the creation of the WCS-BiH.[175] From the creation of the WCS-BiH to the present, the proportion of the WCS-BiH's budget funded by the international community as opposed to the Bosnian government has shifted dramatically: while in 2006, the international community funded two-thirds of the budget supporting the State Court (including not only war crimes but other crimes within the State Court's jurisdiction), the Registry and the State Prosecutor's Office,[176] by 2008, the Bosnian government's contribution exceeded that of the international community.[177] Although the move towards increased Bosnian financing of these institutions was in line with the OHR/ICTY plan to return to Bosnia the primary responsibility for administering justice, problematically, the plan was predicated

---

173 Smith Hrle, above n. 155, pp. 62–63.

174 Donlon, above n. 49, p. 276.

175 'Report of the International Tribunal for the Prosecution of Persons Responsible for Serious Violations of International Humanitarian Law Committed in the Territory of the Former Yugoslavia since 1991: September 4, 2002', A/57/379–S/2002/985, para. 315.

176 ICTJ, above n. 44, p. 23.

177 ibid.

on a pre-set timeline rather than actual achievements on the ground.[178] As indicated in section 3.3 above, the resulting decreased international presence at, and investment in, the Court has coincided with political attacks on the work of the Court, leaving justice system actors increasingly vulnerable as they tackle a heavy caseload of sensitive cases.

While it is important to note that the international community has, to some extent, continued to support accountability efforts in Bosnia beyond its support of the State Court to respond to the increased prosecution of serious international crimes in the cantonal and district courts,[179] in many cases, the provision of support at this level has been similarly time-limited, sporadic

---

178 ibid., pp. 22–24.

179 Foreign governments, NGOs, and intergovernmental organisations, including several UN agencies, have invested considerable resources in cantonal and district courts and prosecutors' offices as local courts have taken an increasing role in the prosecution of war crimes since the adoption of the National War Crimes Strategy. Many of these forms of support are particularly critical for the prosecution of SGV, including financial contributions to pay for victim/witness personnel to support victims throughout the trial process, training focused on the investigation and prosecution of SGV as serious international crimes, technical support and improvements to entity courts' physical infrastructures to facilitate witness protection measures (including separate waiting areas for victims and equipment for shielding victims' faces or distorting their voices and testifying via video-link) funded by the European Union, the United Nations Development Programme and the United States government. See OSCE, 'Combating Impunity: Courts of the Federation of Bosnia and Herzegovina, Republika Srpska and Brčko District', above n. 82, p. 41. The international community has also invested in the provision of training and technical support for justice system actors tasked with trying serious international crimes including the OSCE in partnership with the ICTY, which has also provided evidentiary databases. See OSCE Press Releases: 'OSCE/ODIHR trains judiciary handling war crimes cases in Bosnia and Herzegovina on trial skills' (20 May 2011), available at <http://www.osce.org/odihr/77892> accessed 15.04.2016; 'Training for judges and prosecutors on international humanitarian law' (November 2012), available at <http://www.osce.org/odihr/96573> accessed 15.04.2016; 'OSCE and EU support training of judges and prosecutors in BiH on use of ICTY evidence' (27 June 2013) <http://www.osce.org/bih/103159> accessed 15.04.2016. See also J. Hocking, 'Key Elements and Leading Actors in the Comprehensive Legacy Strategy of the Tribunal' in R. Steinberg (ed.), *Assessing the Legacy of the ICTY*, Brill 2011, pp. 273–74. Other types of assistance have been provided to international or local NGOs that give direct assistance to victims of SGV. See, e.g., Track Impunity Always (TRIAL), a Swiss organisation addressing impunity for international crimes in several contexts, which has been active in Bosnia and Herzegovina since 2008. TRIAL website <https://trialinternational.org/countries-post/bosnia-herzegovina> accessed 16.07.2018. Moreover, the authors are currently engaged in a program funded by the U.S. Department of State to provide tools and training to justice system actors prosecuting conflict-related SGV in Bosnia and Herzegovina in partnership with local organisations, including Medica Zenica, an NGO that provides a range of services to SGV victims such as medical, psychological and legal support. For more information, see <http://www.genderjurisprudence.org/index.php/bosnia-project> accessed 15.04.2016. See also Medica Zenica's website <https://www.medicamondiale.org/en/nc/what-we-do/news/news-details/medica-zenica-20-years-supporting-survivors-of-sexualised-wartime-violence.html> accessed 16.07.2018. Donors from the international community have also supported independent media organizations that highlight successful prosecution of SGV cases, a critical component to encouraging more victims of SGV to come forward to seek assistance and/or prosecution of the perpetrators.

and/or lacking coordination.[180] Some support involves one-time costs for infrastructure improvement – such as funding to build victim/witness support facilities in cantonal and district courts, including separate waiting areas for victims and defendants or video-conferencing technology – but programs that pay for the hiring, training and retention of victim/witness support personnel in these institutions are predicated on agreements with local authorities to absorb salary costs after a set period of time, despite the fact that financial pressures may make such transition to internal funding of these positions problematic.[181] This puts critical victim and witness support services – which are especially crucial for victims of SGV – at risk.[182] As discussed in section 5 below, ending support for such salaries should be predicated on the readiness of Bosnian agencies to incorporate the costs rather than pre-set deadlines.

Other assistance efforts have lacked constituency or coordination. For instance, several governments and UN human rights experts have spoken out against political attacks and actions that have undermined the work of WCS-BiH, including by expressing concern about the release of convicted persons following the Bosnian Constitutional Court's decision to quash first-instance verdicts against those persons after *Maktouf*,[183] and the referendum backed by the RS National Assembly to limit the WCS-BiH's authority over Bosnian

---

180 The media has played a key role in fomenting ethnic division and mistrust of justice system efforts to hold perpetrators of serious crimes accountable, underscoring the need for objective media coverage. See, e.g., J. Hocking, 'Key Elements and Leading Actors in the Comprehensive Legacy Strategy of the Tribunal' in R. Steinberg (ed.), *Assessing the Legacy of the ICTY*, Brill 2011, p. 276. At the same time, other media outlets, such as the Balkan Investigative Reporting Network (BIRN), have taken a particular interest in raising awareness about the incidence and prosecution of SGV in the war crimes cases. See 'BIRN BiH Film Uncovers Unknown Wartime Sex Crimes' 20.05.2014, available at <http://birn.eu.com/en/news-and-events/birn-bih-film-uncovers-unknown-wartime-sex-crimes> accessed 15.04.2016.

181 See, e.g., United Nations Development Programme, 'UNDP/Swiss Project Proposal for the Introduction of Victim and Witness Support Services in Mostar and Brčko, BiH, 2013–2014', pp. 8–9; and 'UNDP Project Proposal to the Government of the United States of America: Introduction to Victim and Witness Support Services in Una-Sana and Central Bosnia Cantons, Bosnia and Herzegovina, 2012–2013', p. 10.

182 See TRIAL [Track Impunity Always] *et al.*, 'Follow-up Report on the Implementation by Bosnia and Herzegovina's of the Recommendations Issued by the Committee on the Elimination of Discrimination against Women in July 2013 (CEDAW/C/BIH/CO/4-5) (July 2015), para. 33, available at <http://tbinternet.ohchr.org/Treaties/CEDAW/Shared%20 Documents/BIH/INT_CEDAW_NGS_BIH_21073_E.pdf> accessed 15.04.2016.

183 See Balkan Transitional Justice Article 'UN Justice Experts Condemn Trbic's Release' (noting concern expressed by group of UN human rights experts that Milorad Trbic – who was sentenced to 30 years for the 1995 genocide committed in Sreberenica – might flee the jurisdiction once released pursuant to the Bosnian Constitutional Court's decision to quash the first-instance verdict against him), available at <http://www.balkaninsight.com/en/article/un-concerned-due-to-trbic-s-release-to-liberty/ekspert%C3%ABt-e-drejt%C3%ABsis%C3%AB-t%C3%AB-okb-s%C3%AB-d%C3%ABnojn%C3%AB-lirimin-e-trbic> accessed 15.04.2016.

Serbs,[184] but such efforts have been sporadic. Indeed, former WCS-BiH staff have stressed the need for a more coordinated and sustained approach to international engagement in the work of the Court.[185]

4.2. THE CONTINUING NEED FOR INTERNATIONAL ENGAGEMENT

The support described in section 4.1 above is essential but given the large backlog of war crimes cases and the relatively small number of SGV cases that have been prosecuted compared to the high number of estimated acts of SGV perpetrated during the conflict,[186] continued international engagement on several fronts is critical. International engagement should not be limited to financial support but should also include technical support to address legal challenges and training programs to continue to build local capacity to try conflict-related SGV, while providing adequate support and protection to victims and witnesses and advocacy support to counter political attacks.

5. RECOMMENDATIONS

One of the clearest lessons learned from the Bosnian experience is that for an internationally supported mechanism of accountability to make a real and lasting contribution to justice, it needs strong and sustained international engagement. While several intergovernmental and non-governmental

---

184 See Press Release from U.S. Embassy in Bosnia and Herzegovina, 'Statement on the RSNA Vote to hold a referendum on the State Judiciary' (15 July 2015), available at <https://ba.usembassy.gov/statement-rsna-vote-hold-referendum-state-judiciary> accessed 16.07.2018. See also Letter to Office of the United Nations High Commissioner for Human Rights from Pablo De Greiff, Special Rapporteur on the promotion of truth, justice, reparation and guarantees of non-recurrence and Ariel Dulitzky, Chair-Rapporteur of the Working Group on Enforced or Involuntary Disappearances, 1 April 2014, available at <https://spdb.ohchr.org/hrdb/27th/public_-_OL_Bosnia_01.04.14_%282.2014%29.pdf> accessed 15.04.2016. See also Balkan Transitional Justice Article 'EU Foreign Ministers Condemn Bosnian Serb Referendum', 12 October 2015, available at <http://www.balkaninsight.com/en/article/european-foreign-ministers-warns-against-bosnian-serb-referendum-10-12-2015> accessed 15.04.2016.

185 Conversation with Patricia Whalen, former international judge at the WCS-BiH (November 2015).

186 See 'European Parliament resolution of 17 June 2010 on the situation in Bosnia and Herzegovina', para. J (noting the fact that 'those in positions of political responsibility in BiH have not adequately ensured justice and reparation for thousands of women and girls who were raped during the 1992–95 war, since the number of cases of sexual war crimes which have resulted in a prosecution remains exceptionally low'), available at <http://www.europarl.europa.eu/sides/getDoc.do?type=TA&language=EN&reference=P7-TA-2010-0238> accessed 15.04.2016.

organisations have provided support and resources to justice system actors involved in the prosecution of serious crimes throughout Bosnia, ongoing support must continue until such time as substantive benchmarks, rather than arbitrary timelines, are met.[187] This means decisions about when to decrease or end international support should be determined based on achievement-based criteria rather than predetermined timelines.[188] The nature and quality of international support should evolve to respond to conditions on the ground and should seek to encourage increased local capacity to deliver justice to victims of serious international crimes, including SGV crimes. A balance should be struck between departing too soon – leaving progress vulnerable to reversal – and prolonging externally driven institutions that undermine domestic capacity to fulfil state obligations.[189] Determining a comprehensive set of substantive benchmarks tied to international support for the prosecution of conflict-based SGV in Bosnia and Herzegovina is beyond the scope of this piece but deserves further reflection.[190] Importantly, the processing of war crimes cases and broader judicial reform are subject to a range of complex criteria intertwined with the EU pre-accession process which do not respond to all of the myriad challenges raised here. Bearing in mind this need for the development of a

187 Human Rights Watch, *Justice for Atrocity Crimes: Lessons of International Support for Trials before the State Court of Bosnia and Herzegovina*, Human Rights Watch 2012, pp. 32–34 (stating that 'the Bosnia example highlights the dangers of using a preset deadline to phase out international staff' as indicated by the failure of the Bosnian parliament to extend the presence of international personnel at the State Court and the State Prosecutor's Office in 2009 despite clear indications that these institutions were not ready for such a departure).

188 M. Peter, 'No Exit: The Decline of the International Administration in Bosnia and Herzegovina' in S. Keil and V. Perry (eds.), *State-Building and Democratization in Bosnia and Herzegovina*, Routledge 2015, p. 146 (noting that time-defined mandates for state-building efforts in BiH should be avoided as they encourage obstructionist behaviour because radical parties will 'sit the international community out,' waiting for the departure of international actors and impeding progress in the process). See also D.F. Haynes, 'The Deus ex Machina Descends: The Laws, Priorities and Players Central to the International Administration of Post-Conflict Bosnia and Herzegovina' in D.F. Haynes (ed.), *Deconstructing the Reconstruction: Human Rights and Rule of Law in Postwar Bosnia and Herzegovina*, Routledge 2008, p. 16 (noting the balance that must be struck in post-conflict reconstruction between extended international intervention motivated by self-perpetuation and premature departure based on cost and political unpopularity).

189 Peter, above n. 188, p. 131.

190 Human Rights Watch has suggested such substantive benchmarks could include 'not only the number of cases that have reached a final verdict, but also their level of complexity and the official position of the defendant' as well as '[i]nstitution building benchmarks [including] whether there is a functioning witness protection program, a prosecutorial strategy for handling cases that is being consistently implemented, and concrete efforts to standardize judicial practice in routine areas'. Human Rights Watch also suggests exit strategy criteria include an assessment of the political climate with regard to the pursuit of accountability, including 'evaluating public statements made by politicians and media reporting of trials involving atrocity crimes'. See Human Rights Watch, 'Justice for Atrocity Crimes', above n. 187, p. 34.

more coherent approach to evaluating when international support for the prosecution of conflict-based SGV in Bosnia and Herzegovina should be scaled back, in the following sections the authors offer general recommendations to address the challenges outlined above, including to better meet the needs of victims and witnesses, respond to the legal challenges, and confront political opposition.[191]

5.1. ADDRESSING THE NEEDS OF VICTIMS AND WITNESSES OF SGV

- *Assess, on an ongoing basis, the needs on the ground, both within the legal system and supporting institutions such as NGOs serving victims, to determine what needs persist and where interventions are duplicative in an effort to make international assistance responsive and effective.* For instance, regular and consistent needs assessment activities should be incorporated into international assistance projects.
- *Ensure adequate financial support for the salaries of victim/witness personnel working within the judicial system on war crimes cases until these cases are complete or until local and state-level government agencies credibly demonstrate that they can bear these costs.*[192] Avoid pre-set timelines that jeopardise adequate victim/witness support staffing, especially those working with vulnerable victims of SGV.
- *Support the application of victim protections provided for at the WCS-BiH to cantonal and district courts.* Work towards the promulgation of witness protection laws at the district and cantonal level that currently protect only victims and witnesses involved in cases at the State Court[193] to expand application to all victims of SGV or at the very least develop peer-to-peer training opportunities facilitating the sharing of best practices from WCS-BiH victim/witness staff with district and cantonal-level court personnel and prosecutors' offices.

---

191 For more on capacity building for the prosecution of war crimes in Bosnia and Herzegovina, see also D. Schwendiman, 'Capacity Building: The Institutional War Crimes Legacy of the ICTY and the International Donor Community in Bosnia and Herzegovina' in R. Steinberg (ed.), *Assessing the Legacy of the ICTY*, Brill 2011, pp. 212–30.

192 European Commission. 'Bosnia and Herzegovina: Financial Assistance Under IPA 2007–2013: Transitional Justice and Institution Building: National Programmes and Project Fiches: Justice Sub-Sector, p. 15, available at <http://ec.europa.eu/enlargement/pdf/bosnia_and_herzegovina/ipa/2013/ipa_2013_023590.01_bih_justice_sub_sector.pdf> accessed 15.04.2016.

193 OSCE, 'Processing of War Crimes at the State Level in Bosnia and Herzegovina', above n. 5, paras. 111, 115.

- *Provide ongoing financial support for local victim support organisations furnishing much-needed legal, psycho-social and other forms of support directly to victims of SGV*. While judicial system personnel are needed to ensure critical services to victims throughout the trial process, local victim support organisations are often the sole providers of post-trial assistance such as counselling, job training and help applying for civilian victim of war benefits.
- *Encourage further coordination between justice system and community-based victim/witness support efforts to ensure such support is offered pre-trial, during trial and post-trial.*[194] Facilitate the creation and sustainability of institutional networks like those created by NGO Medica Zenica[195] to provide for continuity of support beyond the courtroom by expanding collaboration between government agencies and non-government institutions that serve a wide range of victims' needs.
- *Expand funding allotted to restorative justice approaches such as legal aid programs to represent victims seeking compensation through civil claims or criminal proceedings and other individual or collective restitution schemes designed to help victims of SGV rebuild their lives*. Recent successes at the State Court of BiH obtaining court-ordered compensation for victims of SGV as part of criminal convictions have been led by a lawyer from an NGO and efforts are underway to expand this practice to cantonal and district courts, underscoring the need for additional legal support for these cases. Victims should inform efforts to determine what forms of restorative justice would best serve their needs.

5.2. RESPONDING TO LEGAL CHALLENGES

- *Create sustainable training programs for investigators, prosecutors, judges, victim/witness support staff, and others engaged in the prosecution of conflict-related SGV.* Incorporate best practices and international standards on how to interpret existing laws in the context of conflict-related SGV. Invest in train-the-trainer approaches that allow international support to phase out once local actors can provide ongoing training to personnel, including the training of new staff due to turnover. Incorporate more peer-to-peer learning opportunities for WCS-BiH judges and prosecutors to share best practices

194 Amnesty International, 'Whose Justice?', above n. 102, p. 25. See also European Commission, 'Bosnia and Herzegovina 2013 Progress Report', accompanying the document 'Communication from the Commission to the European Parliament and the Council: Enlargement Strategy and Main Challenges 2013–2014', p. 14.

195 See information about Medica Zenica's institutional networks available at <http://medicazenica.org/en/cooperation> accessed 16.07.2018.

with local court personnel. Provide training focused on SGV prosecution in particular to ensure effective and consistent approaches to these crimes.[196]

- *Fund international and national organisations that provide justice system actors in Bosnia with tools to enhance their capacity to deliver effective accountability for SGV.* Providing stakeholders with resources that will continue to assist them beyond the period of direct support from the international community ensures the benefits of capacity-building activities are long lasting. Examples include training materials, bench books and ongoing access to collections of relevant jurisprudence and best practices.
- *Support proposals to align the legal definitions of rape as a war crime and as a crime against humanity with international standards.*[197] While recent amendments to the BiH Criminal Code represent progress towards this goal, the splintered court system and the resulting continuing ambiguity in the statutory language which results in a range of interpretations underscores the need for further amendments and/or ongoing training and cross-jurisdiction communication that allows prosecutors and others to compare case law and develop consistent approaches regarding how to interpret statutory language in line with international law criminalising all forms of non-consensual intercourse.[198]
- *Link salary support for international legal officers, prosecutors, judges and staff to substantive benchmarks rather than pre-set timelines or politically motivated markers.* Arbitrarily terminating such support undermines the sustainability of war crimes prosecutions. Indeed, a cutback in resources based on pre-set expectations rather than an assessment of actual needs on the ground not only threatens the courts' capacity to address the backlog of war crimes cases, but also increases the vulnerability of the courts to corruption or other forms of influence.[199]

---

196 The OSCE has acknowledged the role of international donors in supporting training on the prosecution of SGV which has resulted in increased prioritisation of SGV war crimes cases within entity-level prosecutors' offices. OSCE, 'Combating Impunity: Courts of the Federation of Bosnia and Herzegovina, Republika Srpska and Brčko District', above n. 82, p. 12. The OSCE is now providing training components for investigators, prosecutors and judges focused on the prosecution of sexual violence.

197 In response to the inconsistent application of the law with respect to the definition of rape and other forms of conflict-related sexual violence, several organizations, including the United Nations Committee Against Torture, have called for an amendment to remove the language 'force or by threat of immediate attack', but to date, efforts to amend the law have not been realised. Report of the Committee Against Torture, Forty-fifth session (1–19 November 2010), Forty-sixth session (9 May–3 June 2011) A/66/44, para. 9.

198 Special Rapporteur on violence against women, its causes and consequences, Addendum, Mission to Bosnia and Herzegovina, A/HRC/23/49/Add.3 (4 June 2013), p. 20.

199 A. Aitchison, *Making the Transition: International Intervention, State-Building and Criminal Justice Reform in Bosnia and Herzegovina*, Intersentia 2011, pp. 121–22.

- *Ensure the 2003 BiH Criminal Code is applied to SGV cases to the extent permitted by the ECtHR's holding in Maktouf.* Include in training opportunities for prosecutors and judges information about the limitations of the SFRY Code when prosecuting SGV and address in particular misconceptions about trying cases as crimes against humanity rather than war crimes.[200] Increase awareness of the relatively narrow parameters of the *Maktouf* holding and confront the ongoing application of this case that exceeds the ECtHR's findings.

5.3. COUNTERING POLITICAL OPPOSITION

- *Track progress on the prosecution of SGV war crimes cases to ensure that prosecutors are adequately prioritising these cases in line with the prevalence of SGV committed during the war.* While the OSCE monitors and periodically reports on the prosecution of SGV at the WCS-BiH and by cantonal and district courts, without increased transparency and access to timely information that accurately represents how SGV cases are being handled, it is difficult for stakeholders both inside and outside of Bosnia and Herzegovina to counter political interference and press for greater accountability for these crimes. If victims of SGV see successful prosecution of SGV cases resulting in adequate sentencing, they are more likely to come forward and provide evidence of their own victimisation and pursue accountability for these violations.[201]
- *Support both local and international media outlets that cover war crimes prosecutions objectively and that focus on the prosecution of SGV to decrease the cultural stigma attached to SGV victimisation, encourage victims to come forward, and sustain public support for prosecutors to continue to focus on these types of cases.* The Balkans Investigative Reporting Network (BIRN)'s project on Wartime Sexual Violence provides an example of such targeted reporting efforts.
- *Fund the translation of critical documentation including SGV-related war crimes verdicts to ensure a wider audience is aware of the status of these cases.* Decreased support for court translators at the WCS-BiH and the absence of translation services in the cantonal and district courts means fewer verdicts are translated into English or other languages, limiting the ability of the international community to have a clear picture of how SGV cases are being

---

200 OSCE, 'Processing of War Crimes at the State Level in Bosnia and Herzegovina', above n. 5, para. 86.

201 ICTJ Report, above n. 44, p. 35. See Medica Mondiale, '... and that it does not happen to anyone anywhere in the world', above n. 94, pp. 52–54, available at <http://www.medicamondiale.org/fileadmin/redaktion/5_Service/Mediathek/Dokumente/English/Documentations_studies/medica_mondiale_and_that_it_does_not_happen_to_anyone_anywhere_in_the_world_english_complete_version_dec_2009.pdf> accessed 15.04.2016.

handled in the face of political pressures and to press for robust prosecution for these crimes in line with international law.

- *Maintain political support for fair accountability measures and develop a coordinated approach to counter efforts to undermine existing accountability mechanisms.*[202] Politically motivated measures seeking to limit Bosnian courts' power to effectively prosecute war crimes deny SGV victims their right to justice for the harms they suffered.[203] An effective response requires vocal opposition to anti-impunity measures by foreign governments, NGOs and intergovernmental organisations, including personnel involved in Bosnia and Herzegovina's EU Accession efforts.

6. IS THE BOSNIAN EXPERIENCE A MODEL FOR DOMESTICATING INTERNATIONAL JUSTICE EFFORTS?

Bosnia's transition from international to domestic accountability for serious international crimes is often touted as a model approach to post-conflict justice. Before the Bosnian experience is advanced as a model for domesticating international justice efforts;[204] however, its successes and failures should be assessed on multiple fronts. Two preliminary observations are worth making in advance of such an assessment. First, while a significant number of perpetrators of conflict-related SGV have been held accountable in Bosnia, overall accountability for these crimes represents a mere fraction of the total crimes committed.[205] Second, it is important to acknowledge the limits of what a criminal accountability process can achieve.[206]

---

202 Peter, above n. 188. pp. 139–40; Smith Hrle, above n. 155, p. 77.

203 Amnesty International, 'Whose Justice?', above n. 102, p. 3.

204 Human Rights Watch, 'Justice for Atrocity Crimes: Lessons of International Support for Trials before the State Court of Bosnia and Herzegovina' (2012) (assessing the successes and shortcomings of Bosnia's War Crimes Section of the State Court and identifying lessons learned for future use of international personnel in the prosecution of international crimes in domestic courts), available at <https://www.hrw.org/report/2012/03/12/justice-atrocity-crimes/lessons-international-support-trials-state-court-bosnia> accessed 08.04.2016.

205 OSCE, 'Combating Impunity: State Court', above n. 59, p. 6; OSCE, 'Combating Impunity: Courts of the Federation of Bosnia and Herzegovina, Republika Srpska, and Brčko District', above n. 82, p. 12 (finding that Bosnian courts have convicted a total of 78 perpetrators of conflict-related SGV, which as compared to an estimated 20,000 or more victims, represents a small proportion of offenders). See also R. Coomaraswamy, 'Preventing Conflict Transforming Justice Securing the Peace: A Global Study on the Implementation of United Nations Security Council resolution 1325', p. 107.

206 I. Vukušić, 'Successes and Failures of Transitional Justice in BiH: The Case of the ICTY' in S. Keil and V. Perry (eds.), *State-Building and Democratization in Bosnia and Herzegovina*, Ashgate 2015, p. 163 (acknowledging that any war crimes tribunal offers only 'imperfect justice' because there is no punishment adequate for systematic expulsion, detention, torture, and violence like that which the people of Bosnia have experienced).

Given the large number of people who experienced sexual violence during the war, it is clear that the justice system will not be able to deliver criminal accountability for every violation. It is equally clear that a narrow focus on providing only retributive justice fails to deliver critical resources to help victims rebuild their lives.[207] Victims of atrocities deserve acknowledgement of the wrongs suffered, an accounting of the crimes committed, and whatever measure of healing may come from punishing the perpetrator. Indeed, this notion of needing to acknowledge the truth of what happened applies to victims of SGV in very specific ways: in cultures in which victims of SGV are often not believed and in communities in which shame and stigma attaches to victims rather than perpetrators of SGV, establishing culpability in a legal forum can play a very real role in victims' healing process.[208] Yet, while reckoning for criminal acts is necessary, it is often not sufficient. As commentators have noted, it is hubris to believe such justice annuls the effects of the crime itself or can ever truly restore its victims to their previous positions.[209] As a result, it is important to bear in mind the real need for other forms of transitional justice assistance to victims of atrocity crimes, including non-judicial measures such as reparations and victim assistance programs.[210] A comprehensive response to the widespread perpetration of SGV during the conflict in Bosnia and Herzegovina is not a short-term project. Indeed, any and all models of justice require sufficient resources and the political will to complete the mission. Without consistent support from the international community, justice – in any form – will be incomplete for thousands of victims of conflict-related SGV throughout Bosnia and Herzegovina.

---

207 See TRIAL *et al.*, 'Follow-up Report on the Implementation by Bosnia and Herzegovina's of the Recommendations Issued by the Committee on the Elimination of Discrimination against Women in July 2013.

208 See Medica Mondiale, '... and that it does not happen to anyone anywhere in the world', above n. 93, p. 52.

209 N. Biggar, 'Making Peace or Doing Justice?' in N. Biggar (ed.), *Burying the Past: Making Peace and Doing Justice after Civil Conflict*, Georgetown University Press 2001, pp. 12–13.

210 See, e.g., Committee on the Elimination of all Forms of Discrimination Against Women, 'Concluding observations on the combined fourth and fifth periodic reports of Bosnia and Herzegovina' CEDAW/C/BIH/CO/4-5 (30 July 2012), paras. 10(c) and 10(e).

PART V

CONCLUSIONS

CONCLUSIONS

Olga Jurasz and Solange Mouthaan

1. INTRODUCTION

The perspectives represented in this volume highlight some of the most recent developments and debates concerning international and transitional justice responses to addressing gendered realities and consequences of armed conflict. These include, but are not limited to, the involvement of children, especially girls, in modern conflicts and their exclusion from transitional justice processes; pursuits of accountability for CRSV at international and domestic levels; as well as the growing (albeit slowly) recognition of the need for transformative and gender-sensitive reparations.

But first and foremost, this study is a testament to the significant changes to the ways in which we have begun to understand, conceptualise and critique the complex relationships between gender, war and peace. The academic as well as public understanding of these issues has significantly evolved over the past three decades. When the war in the Former Yugoslavia broke out in 1991, the 'new wars' fuelled by the competing ethnic, religious and national interests became the reality. Soon after, in 1994, the world woke up to the horrors of mass scale killings and violence during the Rwandan Genocide. Violations of human rights and humanitarian law taking place both in the Former Yugoslavia and in Rwanda, have also revealed the highly gendered nature of such violations, especially in the form of mass-scale sexual violence. While today we focus on critiquing how conflict-related sexual violence (CRSV) is prosecuted by international criminal courts and tribunals, at the time of these atrocities it was far from common to criminalise conflict-related rape, not to mention other forms of sexual and gender-based harms, such as forced marriage, sexual enslavement or sexualised torture. Back in the early 1990s, a significant degree of international feminist activism as well as feminist academic scholarship calling for immediate recognition of rape and other forms of CRSV as tools of warfare as well as for ending impunity for such acts contributed to the momentous shift in not only legal categorisations but also in public perception of these acts. Over the years, the discussions have also moved to consider gender in the context of 'post-conflict'[1] reality and the long-term impact of gender-based harms sustained during the conflict. Transitional justice studies have advanced the understanding of the gendered reality of transition from conflict to peace, as well as highlighted its many problematic aspects. In this volume, we focus on not only selected aspects of transitional justice: accountability for CRSV (Anne-Marie de Brouwer and Laetitia Ruiz, Rosemary Grey and Louise Chappell, Susana SaCouto and Chante Lasco), reparations for gendered harms (Olga Jurasz, Priya Gopalan), but also participation of children in transitional justice processes (Alison Bissett).

Even more crucially, this study challenges the assumptions about the role of gender in shaping the experiences of modern armed conflicts. Lauren Vogel's insightful discussion of women's involvement in modern conflicts and motivations for engaging in violence and extremism is further contextualised by Sheri Labenski, Alette Smeulers and Olivera Simić, whose contributions challenge the 'image' of female perpetrators of violence. They demonstrate that women can, in fact, be as brutal as men in deployment of violence. Valorie Vojdik and Solange Mouthaan explore the positioning of gender within modern conflicts and critically examined the ways in which gender shapes the experiences of other actors – men and children – who are involved in such atrocities. Refreshingly, these chapters subvert many of the myths and silences concerning gendered experiences of actors in modern armed conflicts, exposing the motivations behind the use of sexual violence against men, as well as stressing the different and diverse consequences of conflict on boys and girls.

2. GENDER AND POST-CONFLICT SITUATIONS: WHERE ARE WE NOW?

Whilst a lot has changed in the past 25 years in terms of fostering a greater understanding of gendered experiences of conflict and its effects, the authors in this volume voice caution over resting on laurels when it comes to celebrating such developments. As we bring this book project to an end, we inevitably reflect on the state of the world today and how much impact (or not) the last 25 years

1 We recognise that the term 'post-conflict' is problematic as gender-based violence continues and exists in times of 'peace', as well as in what may be perceived as 'the aftermath' of war. From the legal perspective, the use of the term also brings to question the temporal aspect of what 'post-conflict' means and the implications for the legal regime which applies to such situations.

of developments in international law and transitional justice have actually had. Gender-based violence and mass violations of human rights continue around the globe while the victims of the conflicts of the 1990s and early 2000s still await justice and reparations. Although we celebrate the achievements of the International Criminal Tribunal for the Former Yugoslavia (which officially closed on 31 December 2017) in bringing accountability for conflict-related sexual violence, we are also reminded by Priya Gopalan that bringing gender justice and gender-just reparations for women in the territories of the Former Yugoslavia has been too slow. The ICC, too, is slowly progressing in its commitment to gender justice. As the Court celebrates its twentieth anniversary, this lends itself to a reflection on how successful the Court has been in pursuit of accountability for gender-based crimes. Since the celebration of the first successful prosecution of rape as a war crime and crime against humanity in *Bemba* in 2016[2] (discussed in Rosemary Grey and Louise Chappell's chapter), the ICC has continued to include charges involving sexual and gender-based violence in its cases. However, as argued by Olga Jurasz, such charges do not always translate into successful convictions, which have further impact on reparations – at least those awarded by the ICC. Reparations for conflict-related gendered harms are still far too rare, despite a much celebrated decision of the Extraordinary African Chambers in 2016 to award substantive monetary reparations to victims of sexual violence in the Hissène Habré case.[3] Much work remains to be done, especially on the conceptual, legal and implementation levels, in a strive to transform the lives of victims of gendered, conflict-related harms. As Olga Jurasz argues in her chapter, although there exist some glimpses of hope, the issue of transformative remedies remains one that international law and national jurisdictions are yet to fully endorse and implement in their working practices.

The plight of children in the Syrian conflict, eloquently critiqued by Solange Mouthaan in her chapter in this volume, continues seven years after the conflict broke out. Girls in Syria are particularly exposed to specific forms of CRSV such as survival sex or early marriage – gendered harms that are not specifically included in the UN mechanisms on child protection. With the conflict in Syria still ongoing, the hopes for peace have been dealt a severe blow by the dire and prolonged humanitarian crisis which affects millions of Syrians in the region. The prospects of transitional justice in Syria appear to be remote, but nonetheless

---

2 Whilst this volume was being finalised, on 8 June 2018 the ICC Appeals Chamber acquitted Jean-Pierre Bemba from the charges of war crimes and crimes against humanity. Reversing Trial Chamber III's decision from 21 March 2016.

3 International Justice Resource Centre, 'Extraordinary African Chambers grants reparations to victims in Habré case' (8 August 2016) <http://www.ijrcenter.org/2016/08/08/extraordinary-african-chambers-grants-reparations-to-victims-in-habre-case/#gsc.tab=0> accessed 08.07.2018.

one may wonder how various gendered harms and gendered impacts of this war – not least CRSV, but also gendered aspects of forced migration and gendered impact of war on girls – will be reflected in such mechanisms? Finally, what would be the role of women in peacebuilding process in Syria? As demonstrated by the Colombian peace process, meaningful inclusion of gender and significant representation of women in peace talks are not just crucial but possible in the effort to bring together society torn apart by conflict.[4]

3. SOLUTIONS FOR THE FUTURE?

Without doubt are there still lessons that need to be learned which will shape and contribute to more meaningful future international and national prosecutions and transitional justice processes. Valerie Oosterveld usefully reminds us of the importance to understand the gendered nature of the war economy and the gendered impacts of its resulting crimes. Susana SaCouto and Chante Lasco's contribution to this volume highlights the complex nature of seeking justice for CRSV before domestic courts: is not only a matter of political will and continued international commitment and support, but also of capacity in post-conflict environments to tackle the magnitude of such violations.

However, ending impunity for CRSV is not (nor should be) the sole focus of international efforts to address gendered realities and consequences of modern conflicts. After all, the United Nations (UN) was created to 'maintain international peace and security' and international law and its institutions should act to fulfil this aim, including a gender perspective into its policies and actions. Nonetheless, this would require the rethinking of current strategies deployed by the UN and by UN member states in pursing this goal. In particular, whilst there exist mechanisms at the UN-level which could be put to use in bringing meaningful change, they are seldom used in the context of gender, peace and security. One example is the sanctions regime which can be used by the UN Security Council to prevent and to tackle CRSV. However, as argued by Solange Mouthaan in this volume, sanctions do not have to be limited to cases of CRSV: 'An important first step would be to include conflict-related violations of children's rights on the agendas of the different sanction committees'.

Another area within the work of the UNSC is the Women, Peace and Security (WPS) agenda. Whilst this volume does not address WPS specifically, the

[4] H. Salvesen and D. Nylander, 'Towards an inclusive peace: women and the gender approach in the Colombian peace process' Norwegian Centre for Conflict Resolution, July 2017, available at: <https://noref.no/Publications/Regions/Colombia/Towards-an-inclusive-peace-women-and-the-gender-approach-in-the-Colombian-peace-process> accessed 08.07.2018.

themes explored in this book speak to the very core of the conceptual framework of the WPS. WPS rests on four pillars: prevention, protection, participation, relief and recovery. However, prevention of conflicts and conflict-related violence against women and girls, as well as women's crucial participation in such processes, appears to be overshadowed by other activities (including, but not limited to, efforts to bring accountability for CRSV through international criminal courts and tribunals). Although UNSC Resolution 2242 (2015) linked the WPS to preventing and countering violent extremism, relatively little has been achieved since in terms of conflict and (gender-based) violence prevention, as well as peaceful resolution of disputes. Furthermore, Resolution 2242 brings into question the underlying premise behind the preventing and countering violence extremism agenda, which, unlike WPS, is deeply rooted in militarisation and armed forces. This not only highlights the ultimate tension between the two agendas, but also poses a critical question about the financing of gender equality, peace and security worldwide. For instance, in 2016 alone, the global military spending amounted to $1.69 trillion,[5] whereas gender equality, peace and security remains significantly underfunded. In contrast, as noted in the 2015 Global Study on WPS, there exists 'consistent, striking disparity between policy commitments to gender equality and women's empowerment, and the financial allocations to achieve them'.[6] Looking into the future, we hope that a much-needed shift in thinking about gender, peace and security will take place at an international level – not least moving the focus away from increased militarisation to addressing the root causes of conflicts and investing in prevention of violence, including all forms of gender-based violence. Such shift would need to be further reflected in pragmatic steps – such as appropriate financing – to operationalise commitments to gender equality and maintenance of international peace and security.

Finally, the importance of the national implementation cannot be underestimated. In order to address gender, peace and security in a meaningful and sustainable manner, efforts must be made at both international and domestic levels and involve women in all stages, including conflict prevention as well as peacebuilding. As this study shows, we are beginning to understand the nuanced nature of modern conflicts as well as the role that gender plays in shaping experiences of everyone affected by conflicts: women, men, girls, boys. Equally, whilst noting some successes, this volume also demonstrates areas in which international law needs to improve in order to be more responsive to gendered

---

5 SIPRI, 'Military Expenditure' (April 2017), available at <https://www.sipri.org/research/armament-and-disarmament/arms-transfers-and-military-spending/military-expenditure> accessed 08.07.2018.

6 UN Women, *A Global Study on the Implementation of United Nations Security Council resolution 1325* (2015) 372, available at <http://wps.unwomen.org/> accessed 08.07.2018.

consequences of conflicts and also capable of facilitating a transformative change in post-conflict societies. Although the current political situation calls for scepticism regarding placing gender at the forefront of international law and international politics, we remain hopeful that efforts will continue to be made in order to transform the way we think about gender and conflict and to achieve *gender equal* peace and security worldwide.

ABOUT THE EDITORS

Solange Mouthaan is Associate Professor in the School of Law at the University of Warwick. Her research implies a deep critical engagement with individuals and their experiences of armed conflict, law and legal systems. The principal focus of this engagement lies in the field of international criminal law. Her work, which is informed by an interdisciplinary theoretical framework, has examined the gendered nature of law and is motivated by a desire to give a voice to non-hegemonic narratives.

Olga Jurasz is a Senior Lecturer in Law at the Open University, specialising in international law, human rights, and legal responses to violence against women (including online violence). Her research focuses on how various mechanisms of public international law address the long-term impact of armed conflicts on women, and how women's rights are protected in the aftermath of war, during the process of transition from war to peace.

www.ingramcontent.com/pod-product-compliance
Ingram Content Group UK Ltd.
Pitfield, Milton Keynes, MK11 3LW, UK
UKHW051919100926
8556IPUK00021B/1271

9 781780 686868